Aloys Hüttermann
Unitary Patent and Unified Patent Court

Unitary Patent and Unified Patent Court

edited by

Prof. Dr. Aloys Hüttermann
Patent Attorney, Düsseldorf
Honorary Professor of the Niederrhein University of Applied Sciences

2nd Edition

Carl Heymanns Verlag 2026

Citation: Hüttermann, Unitary Patent and Unified Patent Court, 2nd ed, para 101

Bibliographic Information published by the Deutsche Nationalbibliothek
The Deutsche Nationalbibliothek lists this publication in the Deutsche Nationalbibliografie; detailed bibliographic data are available in the internet at http://dnb.d-nb.de.

ISBN 978-3-452-30662-3

www.wolterskluwer.com

Cover: Martina Busch, Grafikdesign, Homburg Kirrberg
Typesetting: Datagroup-Int SRL, Timisoara, Romania
Printed by: Sowa Sp. z o.o., Piaseczno, Polen

Printed on non-acid and aging resistant paper.

Preface 2nd Edition

By the time this second edition of the handbook is published, the Unitary Patent system will have been in place for three years. Important decisions have since been made, both in terms of procedure and substantive law, and the time has therefore come to present a completely revised new edition.

Düsseldorf, March 2026,

Aloys Hüttermann

Preface

With the creation of the Unitary Patent and the Unified Patent Court, a new era is beginning in patent law in Europe. What to do? How to adjust to the new?

The impetus for this book, which will be co-published with the 2nd German edition, was a presentation I had the privilege of giving at the 2012 Intellectual Property Owners Association (IPO) Annual Meeting in San Antonio, USA. Since 2013 until 2022, I have had the honor of being Vice Chair of the European Practice Committee of this organization. The discussions and exchange of information within the committee have been very helpful to me.

This book is aimed at the practitioner, i.e. members and heads of patent departments, patent attorneys and attorneys-at-law.

Strategic considerations are a main focus of the work. For each possible course of action, there are concrete suggestions that are strictly oriented towards practicality. The first part gives a very brief historical overview of the origin of the unitary patent system. The second part deals with the unitary patent, the third, longest, with the Unified Patent Court.

At this point I would like to thank those who contributed to the success of this book: Tilmann Büttner and Stephan Deblon, who reviewed a preliminary version and whose comments decisively improved this book; esteemed colleagues Thomas Adocker, Michaël Beck, Henrik Benriksen, Cesare Corradini, Frank Eijsvogels, Kim Finnilä, Anders Hansson, Suvi Julin, Judith Krens, and Pierre Veron, who wrote chapters on national enforcement as well as the comparison with their national jurisdictions; Young-Ki Ha, Junwei Li, Peipei Liu, Shimako Kato, John Richards, and Qinghua Zhou, who have written additional chapters comparing their jurisdictions with the UPC; Wasilis Koukounis LL. M., Dr. Stefan Luginbühl and Sarah Grunwald for their help with finalizing the 2nd German and this English edition; my co-partners and colleagues at Michalski Hüttermann & Partners, who have always supported me. The final thanks, however, go to my family.

It should be explicitly mentioned that the recommendations and strategic considerations are my personal views and are not necessarily shared by everyone who contributed to the success of this book.

Every system change brings opportunities. It is to be hoped that those who will shape the new system will seize this opportunity, because *"It is an exciting opportunity to develop a system which is better than anything that has gone before"* (*Kitchin* on the 17 Symposium of European Patent Judges, Official Journal EPO Special Supplement 5/2015, p. 46).

Düsseldorf, February 2023

Aloys Hüttermann

List of contributors

Thomas Adocker
Judge at the Central Division of the Unitary Patent Court, Vienna, Austria

Michaël Beck
Patent attorney, European Patent attorney, IPLodge, Leuven, Belgium

Henrik Bendiksen
European Patent attorney, Director Global IP at Bavarian Nordic A/S, Kvistgård, Denmark

Cesare Corradini
Patent attorney, European Patent attorney, AVERA-IP, Milan, Italy

Frank Eijsvogels
Attorney-at-law, Hoyng ROKH Monegier B.V., Amsterdam, Netherlands

Kim Finnilä
Patent attorney, European Patent attorney, Berggren Oy, Helsinki, Finland

Young-Ki Ha
Korean Patent Attorney, Samsung SDI Co. Ltd., Yongin, Südkorea

Anders Hansson
Patent attorney, European Patent attorney, EIP, Technical Judge at the UPC, Stockholm, Sweden

Aloys Hüttermann
Patent attorney, European Patent attorney, Michalski · Hüttermann Partner mbB, Düsseldorf, Deutschland

Junwei Li
Legal Assistant, Advance China IP Law Office, Guangzhou, China

Peipei Liu
Patent Attorney and Attorney-at-law, Advance China IP Law Office, Guangzhou, China

Suvi Julin
Patent attorney, Berggren Oy, Helsinki, Finland

Shimako Kato
Patent attorney, Abe, Ikubo & Katayama, Tokyo, Japan

Judith Krens
Attorney-at-law, Pinsent Masons Netherlands LLP, Amsterdam, Netherlands

John Richards
British, European and U.S. Patent attorney, (New York Bar), Ladas & Parry LLP., New York. USA

List of contributors

Pierre Véron
Honorary President EPLAW, Bormes-les-Mimosas, France

Qinghua Zhou
Patent Attorney and Attorney-at-law, Advance China IP Law Office, Guangzhou, China

Overview

Table of Contents

Bibliography

Books and Monographs

Ann/Hauck/Maute	*Auskunftsanspruch und Geheimnisschutz im Verletzungsprozess* (Confidentiality Claims and Secrecy in Infringement Proceedings) Verlag Carl Heymanns, Cologne, 2011
Bopp/Kircher	*Handbuch Europäischer Patentprozess* (Handbook of European Patent Proceedings) C.H. Beck, Munich 2025
Benkard	*EPÜ* (Commentary on the European Patent Convention) C. H. Beck, Munich 2023
Benkard	*Patentgesetz* (Commentary on the German Patent Act) C. H. Beck, Munich 2023
Busche/Meier-Beck	*Tagungsband zu den Düsseldorfer Patentrechtstagen* 2019 (Proceedings of the 2019 Düsseldorf Patent Law Conference)
Büscher/Erdmann/Fuchs/ Jänich/Loschelder/McGuire	*Festschrift für Hans-Jürgen Ahrens on the 70 Geburtstag, Carl Heymanns* (Commemorative Publication for the 79th Birthday of Hans-Jürgen Ahrens), Carl Heymanns), Cologne, 2018
Busse/Keukenschrijver	*Patentgesetz*, (Commentary on the German Patent Act) De Gruyter, Berlin, 2020
Callens/Granata	*The Unitary Patent and the Unified Patent Court*, Wolters Kluwer, Alphen aan den Rijn, 2017
Dunlop	*European Unitary Patent and Unified Patent Court*, CIPA, London, 2014
England	*A Practitioner's Guide To European Patent Law*, Hart, Oxford, 2025
Erdmann/Rojahn/Sosnitza	*Handbuch des gewerblichen Rechtsschutzes* (Handbook on Industrial Property-Right Protection) Carl Heymanns, Cologne, 2018
Geiger/Nard/Seuba	*Intellectual Property and the Judiciary*, Elgar, Cheltenham, 2018
Götting/Meyer/Vormbrock	*Gewerblicher Rechtsschutz und Urheberrecht* (Industrial Property-Right Protection and Copyright), Nomos, Baden-Baden, 2011
Keukenschrijver	*Patentnichtigkeitsverfahren*(Patent Revocation Proceedings), Verlag Carl Heymanns, Cologne, 2020
Kolonko	*Justizgrundrechte in Verfahren vor dem Einheitlichen Europäischen Patentgericht* (Basic Judicial Rights in Proceedings Before the Unified Patent Court), Hagener Juristische Beiträge, Vol. 4, readbox, Dortmund 2017
Klein	*Einheitspatent: Der Konflikt von Verletzungs- und Nichtigkeitsurteil* (The Conflict Between Infringement and Revocation Decisions for Unitary Patents) Verlag Carl Heymanns, Cologne, 2018

Krasser/Ann	*Patentrecht* (Commentary on German Patent Law), C. H. Beck, Munich, 2016
Kühnen	*Festschrift zum 80-jährigen Bestehen des Patentgerichtsstandortes Düsseldorf am 1. Oktober 2016* (Commemorative Publication for the 80th Anniversary of the Patent-Court Venue of Düsseldorf on 1 October 2016), Carl Heymanns, Cologne, 2016
Kühnen	*Handbuch der Patentverletzung* (Patent-Infringement Handbook), Verlag Carl Heymanns, Cologne, 2023
Kurz	*Weltgeschichte des Erfindungsschutzes* (A World History of Invention Protection), Verlag Carl Heymanns, Cologne, 2000
Larroyed	*Translation Accuracy and Dissemination of Disclosure of Patent Information*, Maastricht, 2019
Luginbühl/Hüttermann	*Kommentar zum Einheitspatentsystem* (Commentary on the Unitary Patent System), Verlag Carl Heymanns, Cologne, 2024
Metzger	*Methodenfragen des Patentrechts* (Methodology Issues in Patent Law), Mohr Siebeck Tübingen 2018
Sokol	*Patent Assertion Entities and Competition Policy*, Cambridge University Press, Cambridge 2017
Tilmann/Plassmann	*Einheitspatent / Einheitliches Patentgericht* (Unitary Patent / Unified Patent Court), C.H. Beck, Munich, 2024
Véron	*Saisie-Contrefaçon*, Dalloz, Paris, 2014
Zeiler/Zojer	*Resolving IP Disputes*, NWV, Vienna 2018

Part 1: Historical Survey

Chapter 1: Historical Survey

Contents | Para

A. Historical Survey up to the Emergence of the Unitary Patent System

I. The International Patent Institute

The earliest conceptual planning to create – or at least work towards – something approaching a common patent system for at least some of the European states can be traced as far back as the early 20th century. The subsequent founding of the so-called "International Patent Institute"[1] in The Hague in 1947 can be regarded as the first concrete measure to this end. The Institute did not conduct patent prosecution proceedings, however, but rather merely performed research on behalf of the Benelux States and France. 1

Two important initiatives were to follow during the 1970s. The first was the establishment of the European Patent Office on the basis of the European Patent Convention.[2] It bears noting that the buildings in The Hague which had previously housed the International Patent Institute were taken over at this time by the local branch of the European Patent Office. 2

---

1 On this and the following topics, see *Kurz, Weltgeschichte des Erfindungsschutzes*, p. 548 et seqq.

2 Convention on the Grant of European Patents (European Patent Convention) of 5 October 1973, revised on 13 December 2007.

II. The Community Patent Convention (CPC)

3 The second key initiative was the so-called "Community Patent Convention"[3] (EPC), which was supposed to eventually replace all national patents with unitary patents,[4] but which proved unsuccessful in the end. Though concluded in 1975, the Convention did not make it through the ratification process (see Para. 61). A second attempt was made in December 1989 with the "Agreement Relating to Community Patents,"[5] its aim being to ratify the Community Patent Convention, but this effort, too, came to naught. Nonetheless, the text of the Community Patent Convention would later be taught at universities and in seminars and would be discussed in scholarly commentaries on patent law.[6]

4 In the year 2000, the European Commission finally took the bull by the horns with a proposal for a "Council Regulation on the Community Patent."[7] It looked at first as if this third attempt had indeed brought a consensus solution within reach. This turned out to be a false hope, however. Here again, mutual agreement proved elusive, particularly due to the draft provisions governing the use of different languages.

III. The European Patent Litigation Agreement

5 By this time, the whole debate had shifted. Since it had become evident that the European Patent Office was successfully granting a large number of European patents every year on the basis of the European Patent Convention, many began to ask whether it might not be better to focus on creating a shared court system, while leaving the patents themselves and the patent-granting system unchanged for the time being.[8]

6 A significant player in this process was the European Patent Office itself, under whose aegis the so-called "European Patent Litigation Agreement" (EPLA) was hammered out. But this agreement, too, was to falter in the end. Although a final text[9] was drafted in 2005, no efforts were made to pursue it further.

---

3 On this topic and on the entire remaining subchapter, also see *Grabinski/Adam* in Benkard, EPÜ, Note 33 et seqq. before the Preamble; *Götting* in Götting/Meyer/Vormbrock, Note 15 et seqq. on Article 3; *Krasser/Ann*, in *Patentrecht* on Section 7 II; *Ohly* in ZGE/IPJ4, 2012, p. 419; *Götting* in ZEuP, 2014, p. 319; *Luginbühl* in GRUR Int 2013, p. 305; *Troncoso* in Marquette Intellectual Property Law Review, 2013, p. 231; *Plomer* in IIC 2015, p. 508.

4 See, inter alia, *Sédrati-Dinet*.

5 See http://eur-lex.europa.eu/LexUriServ/LexUriServ.do?uri=OJ:L:1989:401:0001:0027:-DE:PDF; with a text of the EPC as an annex.

6 E.g. also see Busse/Keukenschrijver in *Patentgesetz*, 6th Edition, 2003, e.g. Note 144 before Section 34. These comments were later removed in the 7th Edition of 2012.

7 See Official EU Journal No. C 337 E of 28/11/2000 pp. 0278–0290, for a text, see: http://eur-lex.europa.eu/LexUriServ/LexUriServ.do?uri=CELEX:52000PC0412:DE:HTML.

8 Cf. *Jaeger*, Max Planck Institute for Innovation & Competition; Competition Research Paper No. 14–08.

9 For an English version, see: https://web.archive.org/web/20070929140614/http://www.european-patent-office.org/epo/epla/pdf/agreement_draft.pdf.

B. Evolution of the Unitary Patent System

I. The European Commission's Renewed Attempt to Create a Unitary Patent System

In 2009 the European Commission launched a renewed attempt which eventually gave rise to what we know today as the "Unitary Patent System."[10] To better elucidate this new, ultimately fruitful initiative, it bears noting that the European Union had by this time become fruitfully engaged in various parallel domains of industrial property right protection.[11] It had acquired this competence by passing EU Regulations in the 1990s to create the European Union Intellectual Property Office[12] in Alicante, Spain, which proceeded to register genuine European protective patents – for trademarks at first,[13] but later also for designs.[14] 7

Evidently, the key driving factors behind this development was not just the disappointment felt over the failure of the prior initiatives, but also the positive experiences that had been made with the European Union Intellectual Property Office.[15] It is also safe to assume that the European Union was loath to allow its leadership role to be arrogated by the European Patent Office, which had an in-house EPLA initiative of its own. *Jaeger*[16] comments as follows: 8

> "EPLA posed an immediate threat to any further realization of the EU's own patent plans: The more comprehensive and complete the EPO system becomes, the less pressing and less likely a patent solution on the EU level would be. The Commission was accordingly quick to bring EPLA to fall [...]"

Moreover, the factual and legal environment which governed the European Union's sphere of activity had changed in the meantime. Thanks to the conclusion of the Lisbon Treaty,[17] it was now possible to proceed within the framework of so-called "enhanced cooperation." One of the things made possible by such enhanced cooperation, for example, was for a group of Member States to introduce mutually shared regulations in which the other Member States did not necessarily have to participate. 9

10 Note: The expression "Unitary Patent System" (*Einheitspatentsystem*) stems from *Haedicke*, GRUR Int, 2013, p. 609. In English-speaking countries, the expression "Unitary Patent Package" is frequently used as well.

11 Cf. here also *Tattay*, GRUR Int 2013, 2012.

12 So designated as of 23 March 2016 by virtue of Regulation (EU) 2015/2424 of 16 December 2015; former name: Office for Harmonization in the Internal Market.

13 Regulation (EU) 40/94 of 20 December 1993.

14 Regulation (EU) 6/2002 of 12 December 2001.

15 Formerly: Office for Harmonization.

16 *Jaeger*, Max Planck Institute for Innovation & Competition; Competition Research Paper No. 14–08; cf. also *Plomer*, European Law Journal 2019, p. 57; cf. also *Moerland*, IIC 2017, p. 760.

17 A text may be found under: http://register.consilium.europa.eu/pdf/de/08/st06/st06655.de08.pdf.

This new option apparently proved to be the key difference relative to previous efforts, one that allowed consensus to be reached in rather expedited fashion.

II. Enhanced Cooperation in the Area of Patent Protection

10 In 2011, the EU Council gave the go-ahead for such enhanced cooperation among all Member States of the European Union except Italy and Spain.[18] In December 2012, the two EU Regulations that served to create the Unitary Patent – No. 1257/2012 (relating to the Unitary Patent)[19] and No. 1260/2012 (relating to translations) – were adopted by the European Parliament. Whereas all the earlier versions had made translations mandatory,[20] this time the requirement for translations was waived for a certain transitional period (see Para. 152 et seqq.).[21]

11 This had been preceded by a good deal of debate over the Regulations' final wording. In their original version, Articles 6–8 of Regulation (EU) 1257/2012 had defined the substantive effects of the Unitary Patent in a manner which was widely interpreted to mean that, assuming the Regulation's adoption, the European Court of Justice (ECJ) would henceforth enjoy decisional competence over all matters involving general substantive patent law.[22] But this was rejected by some of the Member States, including Great Britain.[23] In the end, the Articles in question were stricken.[24] Thus, Regulation (EU) 1257/2012[25] now states that the Unitary Patent is to exert the same effect as a national patent (for more detail, see Para. 93 et seqq.).

III. The Unified Patent Litigation System

12 In 2009, parallel to the initiative to create a Unitary Patent, the European Commission also proposed a new court system, the so-called "Unified Patent Litigation System"[26]

18 Resolution of the EU Council of 10 March 2011, 2011/167/EU; also see *Grassie*, JIPLP 2013, p. 93; *Jaeger*, NJW 2013, 1998; and *Haberl/Schallmoser*, GRUR Prax, 2011, p. 7. Worth noting is that the Unitary Patent is only the second initiative where enhanced cooperation has been applied; the first was a revision of divorce law in 2010.

19 Note: These two Regulations are discussed in more detail in Chapter 3, starting in Para. 76.

20 Note: depending on the version, this applied either to the patent claims or to the entire patent text.

21 Here, see *Ullrich* in: "Harmonization of European IP Law: From European Rules to Belgian Law and Practice," M.-Chr. Janssens, G. Van Overwalle, Editors., Brussels (Bruylant) 2012.

22 Note: On the role of the ECJ, see Para. 472 et seqq.

23 Here, see e.g. *Tilmann* in GRUR 2013, p. 157; as well as in GRUR 2015 p. 527, where he compares the conduct of Great Britain with the maritime piracy practiced by English privateers under Queen Elisabeth I. Intense criticism of this section of the Regulation came from other quarters as well: see inter alia, *Stjerna*, Mitt. 2012, pp. 54–59, as well as the articles under www.stjerna.de; a critical view is also taken by *Pagenberg* in JIPLP 2013, p. 480.

24 For a critical view on this, see *Wadlow*, JIPLP 2013, p. 207.

25 See e.g. Articles 5–7 of Regulation (EU) 1257/2012.

26 Document 7927/09; for an English text, see: http://register.consilium.europa.eu/pdf/en/09/st07/st07927.en09.pdf.

(UPLS). Since the UPLS envisioned the possible participation of Non-EU states as well, the European Commission now asked the European Court of Justice (ECJ) to evaluate whether the UPLS could be reconciled with European law. In a corresponding Legal Opinion, which created something of a furor,[27] the ECJ concluded that the two were not reconcilable.[28]

IV. The Agreement on a Unified Patent Court (UPC Agreement)

Much like the EPLA before it, the presently existing Agreement on a Unified Patent Court (UPC Agreement) was structured as an international treaty, i.e. without any formal involvement on the part of the European Union. This despite the fact that only Member States of the European Union are allowed to accede to the UPC Agreement.[29] The European Parliament did issue a recommendation – during the same session in which it adopted the EU Regulations relating to the Unitary Patent – which calls upon the Member States to ratify the Agreement as soon as possible. In addition, certain clauses in the Agreement and in the EU Regulations stipulate that the Unitary Patent and Unified Patent Court can only come into force at the same time,[30] whereby the Unitary Patent can come into force only in those countries which have signed the UPC Agreement.[31] **13**

Thus, the Unitary Patent and the Unified Patent Court are closely interconnected.[32] The ultimate decision to make the Unified Patent Court a reality by means of an international treaty[33] was most likely made for several reasons: **14**

- As already noted, certain EU Member States had repeatedly expressed their intention[34] – this was particularly true of Great Britain[35] – to deny the ECJ any right of co-determination in the area of general substantive patent law, namely on the

27 ECJ Legal Opinion 1/09 of 8 March 2011, GRUR Int 2011, p. 309.

28 Here, also see *Grabinski/Adam* in Benkard, EPÜ, Notes 60–63 before the Preamble; also, *Tilmann* in GRUR Int, 2011, p. 499, and *Haberl/Schallmoser*, GRUR Prax 2011, p. 143.

29 Cf. Art. 2 of the UPC Agreement; cf. also *Jaeger*, EuZW 2013, p. 15; and *Plomer*, IIC 2020, p. 791.

30 Note: This is discussed more precisely in Para. 76 et seqq.

31 Article 18 of Regulation (EU) 1257/2012. Interestingly enough, the converse case does not apply. At least for a time, Italy's intention was to accede to the UPC Agreement but not to the EU Regulation(s).

32 For a full discussion see *Haedicke*, GRUR Int 2013, p. 609 as well as *McGuire*, Mitt. 2015, p. 537.

33 Here, also see *Dreyfuss*, IIC 2016, p. 88.

34 Cf. *Jaeger*, IIC 2013, p. 389, and *Jaeger*, Max Planck Institute for Innovation & Competition; Competition Research Paper No. 14–08.

35 In a hearing on 2 July 2014, British Prime Minister *David Cameron* stated that the Unitary Patent Court should not be "snarled up" by the ECJ; see: http://www.publications.parliament.uk/pa/cm201213/cmhansrd/cm 120702/debtext/120702-0001.htmcolumn_586. cf. e.g. *Tilmann*, GRUR 2013, p. 157; *Stjerna*, July 2014, Interview; *Lehne* in Juve 1/2013, pp. 87–93; *Tilmann*, GRUR 2015, p. 527.

grounds that the Court supposedly lacked the necessary technical expertise.[36] Now the ECJ already exerted an influence on patent law in certain technological domains – in biotech, for example, by virtue of EU Biopatent Directive 98/44/EC. But this was seen, and continues to be seen, as an unfavorable development by many observers.[37]

– Moreover, the ECJ itself may have steered the discussion in this direction with the reasoning it gave in its Legal Opinion:

> "As regards an international agreement providing for the creation of a court responsible for the interpretation of its provisions, the Court has, it is true, held that such an agreement is not, in principle, incompatible with European Union law. The competence of the European Union in the field of international relations and its capacity to conclude international agreements necessarily entail the power to submit itself to the decisions of a court which is created or designated by such agreements as regards the interpretation and application of their provisions."[38]

V. Lawsuits Challenging the Unitary Patent System

15 The EU Council had only just approved "enhanced cooperation" for purposes of elaborating the Unitary Patent Regulations, when Italy and Spain promptly tried to challenge this by bringing legal action before the European Court of Justice. The ECJ denied these lawsuits, however.[39] Italy later changed its position and acceded to the Unitary Patent System on 30 September 2015.

16 All this did not keep Spain from filing two additional lawsuits against the two EU Regulations relating to the Unitary Patent (Nos. 1257/2012 and 1260/2012) shortly after their adoption. The provisions specifically challenged by these lawsuits included those governing translations and those which empowered the European Patent Office to conduct grant and validation proceedings for Unitary Patents.[40] Both lawsuits were again denied by the ECJ.[41]

---

36 See *Metzger/Godt*, with additional references; cf. also *Pagenberg*, GRUR 2009, p. 314; see also *Pagenberg* in GRUR Int 2010, p. 195, who takes a highly critical view of the entire process surrounding the Unitary Patent System; as well as *Xenos* in SCRIPTed 2013, pp. 246–277.

37 See, for instance, *Taupitz* in GRUR 2012, p. 1; cf. also *van Overwalle*, IIC 2011, p. 1.

38 Note 74 of ECJ Legal Opinion 1/09; see also *Jaeger*, IIC 2013, p. 389 (who cannot concur with such an interpretation of Opinion 1/09); *Jaeger*, Max Planck Institute for Innovation & Competition; Competition Research Paper No. 14–08; as well as *Troncoso* in Marquette Intellectual Property Law Review, 2013, p. 231; see also the following discussion of the judgments relating to Spain.

39 ECJ, Case Nos. C-274/11 and C-295/11 of 16 April 2013.

40 ECJ, Case Nos. C-146/13 and 147/13 of 5 May 2015; see also *Eck*, GRUR Int 2014, p. 114 and *Stjerna* in *Einheitspatent und Gerichtsbarkeit – Die mündliche Verhandlung der Klagen Spaniens beim EuGH*, as well as *Tilmann* in GRUR 2015, p. 527.

41 ECJ Judgment of 5 May 2015; see also *Arnz*, EuZW 2015, p. 544 as well as *Hüttermann* in Mitt. 2015, p. 498 and *Jaeger* in EuR 2015, p. 461.

It also bears noting that the Belgian Constitutional Court found a lawsuit against Belgium's ratification law for the Unified Patent Court to be inadmissible – if only due to a failure to meet a key deadline.[42] **17**

In Hungary, on the other hand, the ratification process was broken off after the country's Constitutional Court, responding to a referral from the Hungarian Justice Minister, ruled that the Hungarian Constitution would have to be amended before ratification could take place.[43] **18**

In Germany, a constitutional complaint against the ratifying law did meet with success, at least at first (see Para. 27 et seq.) **19**

VI. The Ratification of the UPC Agreement

In order for the Agreement on a Unified Patent Court to come into force, it first had to be ratified (as per Article 89 of the UPC Agreement) by thirteen Member States, including the three Member States "*...in which the highest number of European patents had effect in the year preceding the year in which the signature of the Agreement takes place...*" At the time of the UPC Agreement's signature, these were Germany, Great Britain[44] and France. **20**

Thus, the Unified Patent Court's territorial jurisdiction would encompass not all but only some of the EU Member States once it came into force. It remains to be see whether the territory covered by the UPC Agreement will ever become coterminous with that of the EU.[45] **21**

Until early 2016, it still looked as if the final entry into force of the UPC Agreement – and thus the commencement of the Unified Patent Court's operations – would occur around the middle of 2017.[46] After all, Austria had already ratified the Agreement in August 2013, the first Contracting Member State to do so, followed by France (one of the three mandatory signatories) in March 2014, and by several additional Member States in quick succession.[47] **22**

Nonetheless, the UPC Agreement's entry into force would eventually be delayed by several years, particularly due to problems with the two other, mandatorily required signatory states: Great Britain and Germany. **23**

---

42 Belgian Constitutional Court, Judgment of 21 May 2015, 71/2015; see *Arnz*, EuZW 2015, p. 544.

43 Judgment X/1514/2017 of 28 June 2018; also see: http://patentblog.kluweriplaw.com/2018/06/29/constutional-court-hungary-rules-upca-cannot-ratified/ as well as *Lantos*, Mitt. 2020, p. 264, and *Gombos/Orban* in JIPLP 2022, p. 24.

44 Here, see *Karet*, JIPLP 2016, p. 75.

45 Cf. *Ullrich*, IIC 2015, p. 1.

46 Cf. *Tilmann* in GRUR Int 2016, p. 409.

47 The exact data can be found on the website of the Council of the European Union: https://www.consilium.europa.eu/de/documents-publications/treaties-agreements/agreement/?id=2013001.

1. The Ratification Process in Great Britain

24 On 23 June 2016, a "Referendum on the Continued Participation of the United Kingdom in the European Union" was held, with 72.2 % of the British voting population going to the polls. In the end, 51.9 % voted in favor of exiting the European Union. This has of course come to be known as "Brexit."

25 Given that Great Britain had not yet ratified the Agreement at this time, a lively debate ensued over the future of the Unitary Patent System.[48] One particularly vexed question was whether Great Britain could even remain part of the Unitary Patent System, given the Brexit decision and the fact that EU membership was defined as an express precondition for participation in the system, namely under Article 2 of the UPC Agreement and also pursuant to ECJ Legal Opinion 1/09 (see Para. 12 above).[49]

26 Both conflicts were resolved in that Great Britain ultimately ratified the Agreement on 26 April 2018,[50] only to later declare (in 2020) that it did not intend to take part in the Unitary Patent System. Britain's ratification of the UPC Agreement was then withdrawn effective as of 20 July 2020.[51]

2. The Ratification Process in Germany

a) Process

27 The delay encountered by the ratification process in Germany had an altogether different cause, namely a constitutional complaint lodged by a private individual on 30 March 2017 against the Law to Ratify the Agreement on the Unified Patent Court (Docket No: 2 BvR 739/17). In response, Germany's Federal President Frank-Walter Steinmeier announced that he would withhold his signature – the only one still missing – until a decision was handed down.[52]

---

48 See e.g. *Hüttermann*, Mitt. 2016, p. 353; *Jaeger* IIC 2017, p. 254; *Ahrens*, GRUR Int. 2016, p. 548.

49 The literature is abundant, so what follows is merely a selection. Among those taking a strong "pro" stance (assuming corresponding amendments to the UPC and the inclusion of appropriate provisions in the EU Exit Agreement): *Tilmann* in GRUR Int. 2016, p. 409 as well as in GRUR 2016, p. 753; *Gordon/Pascoe* in Advice on UPCA; also, if somewhat less forcefully, *Ohly/Streinz* in GRUR Int. 2017, p. 1, and *Leistner/Simon* in GRUR Int. 2017, p. 825. Taking a "contra" stance: *Ubertazzi* in GRUR Int. 2017, p. 301 and in GRUR Int. 2017, p. 674; especially strong is the contra view of *Ulrich/Lamping*, a reaction to which is provided by *Tilmann* in GRUR Int. 2018, p. 1094, and by *Finch*. On the Brexit's possible consequences for British patent law, cf. also *Rahmatian*, JIPLP 2017, p. 510, and *Joseph*, JIPLP 2018, p. 1; also noteworthy is *Sellens*, IIC 2018, p. 136.

50 Cf. *Köllner*, Mitt. 2017, p. 23.

51 See https://www.consilium.europa.eu/en/documents-publications/treaties-agreements/agreement/?id=2013001; cf. also *Tilmann*, GRUR 2020, p. 847.

52 Cf. *Hirse/Sakowski* in Mitt. 2017, p. 297, *Tilmann*, GRUR 2017, 1177; see also *Bross* in GRUR Int. 2017, p. 670 and *Bross/Lamping*, GRUR Int. 2018, p. 907; for an Asian perspective, see *Lee*, Korean Journal of Intellectual Property, 2018, p. 205.

In a decision issued on 16 February 2020 and published on 20 March 2020, the German Federal Constitutional Court did indeed quash the Ratifying Law, albeit on the (sole) grounds that the vote held to approve the law in the Lower House of Parliament (Bundestag) had not met the quorum which the Court deemed necessary, namely two thirds of all delegates. In all other respects, the complaints submitted were denied as inadmissible.[53] 28

Barely three months later, on 20 June 2020, the Federal Ministry of Justice and Consumer Protection (BMJV) proposed a draft law which the Bundestag duly approved on 26 November 2020 with a voting majority of 571 out of 709 delegates, or well above the required two-thirds margin. The only party to vote against the law was the right-wing populist Alternative for Germany (AfD), which had already made attempts to hold up the draft bill.[54] 29

This renewed attempt at ratification, too, was challenged, this time by two constitutional complaints in tandem.[55] Once again, the German Constitutional Court asked Federal President Steinmeier to withhold his signature for the time being. But this time the suspense lasted only about six months: On 9 July 2021,[56] the Federal Constitutional Court denied the emergency petitions that had been filed, stating that their underlying complaints were inadmissible.[57] A formal denial of the complaints was issued on 8 August 2022.[58] 30

---

53 Federal Constitutional Court, in GRUR 2020, p. 506 Case No. 2 BvR 739/17; see also *Tilmann*, GRUR 2020, p. 441. A decidedly critical view of the judgment can also be found in *Schallmoser/Haberl*, GRUR Prax 2020, p. 199.

54 During its 36th session of 20 February 2019, the Bundestag Committee for Legal Affairs and Consumer Protection had deliberated a motion by the AfD which called upon the Federal Government to promptly submit a draft bill rescinding the Law on the Agreement of 19 February 2013 on a Unified Patent Court as well as the Law to Adjust Patent-Law Regulations on the Basis of the European Patent Reform, and to communicate this in advance to the Federal Constitutional Court (cf. Bundestag Document No. 19/1180). Acting as a bloc to outvote the AfD, the parties CDU/CSU, SPD, FDP, Die Linke and Bündnis 90/Die Grünen jointly resolved to advise the Bundestag to reject the motion (cf. Bundestag Document No. 19/7961). This after similar resolutions had already been adopted by the participating Committees for Economic Affairs and Energy (30th session of 20 January 2019), for Education, Research and Technology Assessment (20th session of 20 January 2019), and for European Union Affairs (28th session of 20 January 2019). All the other political parties (CDU/CSU, SPD, FDP, Die Linke and Bündnis 90/Die Grünen) had already joined forces to outvote the AfD delegation during the 32nd session of the Committee for Legal Affairs and Consumer Protection of 30 January 2019: Here, they had rejected the AfD's motion to hold a public hearing on the proposed law (cf. Bundestag Document No. 19/7961).

55 See *Tilmann*, GRUR 2021, p. 435.

56 The date of publication of the decision handed down on 23 June 2021 in Case No. 2 BvR 2216/20 and No. 2 BvR 2217/20; see GRUR 2021, p. 1157.

57 See *Tilmann*, GRUR 2021, 1138.

58 Date of publication of the Decision handed down on 13 July 2022.

31 Germany eventually ratified both the UPC Agreement as well as its appurtenant Protocol (see Para. 42) by virtue of the "Law on the Agreement of 13 February 2013 on the Unified Patent Court," which was adopted on 7 August 2021.[59] The instrument of ratification was not yet officially filed, however, since this step was supposed to be preceded by the so-called "Protocol Phase" (see Para. 42).

b) Cancellation of the Prohibition of Double Protection

32 By virtue of an accompanying law which came into force shortly after the Ratifying Law (see Para. 31),[60] Germany to a large extent eliminated the prohibition of double protection which had applied to German and European patents until that time. Thus, the prohibition now applies only to those European Patents which:

> "...are not subject to the exclusive jurisdiction of the Unified Patent Court due to recourse having been taken to Article 83 (3) of the Agreement[61] on a Unified Patent Court."

In other words, double protection is now possible, but only for those European patents for which no effective "opt-out" (cf. Para. 299 et seqq.) has been lodged. Note that this is automatically the case for Unitary Patents, since the "opt-out" option is precluded for such patents.

33 Around this same time, a statutory provision was adopted making it possible to assert the legal defense of duplication of claim (*doppelte Inanspruchnahme*), i.e. Article II, section 18 of the *Gesetz über internationale Patentübereinkommen* (IntPatÜG, Law on International Patent Conventions). The aim here was prevent patent proprietors from "shooting their bolt twice." Thus, the provision makes it impermissible to bring a national patent-infringement action if a substantively equivalent legal action is already pending before the Unified Patent Court, provided the defendant/respondent raises the defense at the point in time defined below:

> "...during the first court date falling between arisal of the legal defense and commencement of oral hearings in the main case."

34 However, no statutory provision was adopted (since competent jurisdiction was lacking) to govern the converse situation, i.e. when an action is brought before the Unified Patent Court even though a German action is already pending. In such cases, it would be up to the Unified Patent Court to deny the action, e.g. on the basis of a Preliminary Objection lodged pursuant to Rule 19 of the Rules of Procedure (cf. Para. 827 et seqq.)

35 It bears noting that an analogous regulation was also chosen in France, meaning that there, too, double protection is possible, but only if an "opt-out" has not been expressly declared.

---

59 Federal Law Gazette (BGBl.), 2021 Issue, Part II No. 18, p. 850.

60 Exact title: *Gesetz zur Anpassung patentrechtlicher Vorschriften aufgrund der europäischen Patentreform* (Law to Adapt Patent-Law Regulations on the Basis of the European Patent Reform), dated 20 August 2021, Federal Law Gazette (BGBl.) Part I No. 59, p. 3914.

61 Note: This is the "opt-out" request.

3. Completion of the Ratification Processes

The first agreement to come into force in this context, namely on 27 October 2021, was the Protocol on the Privileges and Immunities of the Unified Patent Court,[62] which serves to ensure that the Unified Patent Court will dispose over the appropriate competences and will thus be recognized as a court by each Member State (cf. also Para. 274 et seqq. and 484 et seqq.) 36

VII. Statute, Rules of Procedure and Protocol

1. Statute and Rules of Procedure

The Statute of the Unified Patent Court were adopted concomitantly to the UPC Agreement, but not the corresponding Implementing Regulations, respectively, Rules of Procedure. These Rules of Procedure were instead elaborated from 2009 onwards by an Expert Commission of seven specialists[63] drawn from the judiciary sector and the legal profession.[64] 37

The Expert Commission already had a basis on which to proceed, however: the so-called "Second Venice Resolution," a proposal issued by a group of European patent judges in 2006.[65] 38

The 15th Version of these "Draft Rules of Procedure" was published online on 25 June 2013, so as to give members of the general public until 1 October 2013 to present their points of view and make suggestions. 39

The persons and/or organizations who took advantage of this option to offer input and suggestions were then given the opportunity to deliberate a later version – the 17th Version of 31 October – in a public hearing held on 26 November 2014 at the Academy of European Law (ERA) in Trier, Germany. The resulting 18th Version of 18 July 2015 was officially accepted by the preparatory Expert Commission in a meeting held on 19 October 2015.[66] 40

Following the Unified Patent Court's acquisition of legal personality by virtue of the Protocol's entry into force (see Para. 42 et seqq.), the Rules of Procedure were eventually adopted by the UPC Administrative Committee – with a few final changes – on 8 July 2022. These took effect on 1 September 2022, i.e. even before the coming into force of the Unitary Patent System. This was because certain rules, particularly 41

62 For the text, see: https://www.unified-patent-court.org/sites/default/files/ppi_final_ii_en_clean.pdf.

63 These experts were: *Mooney* (GB, Chairman), *Grabinski* (DE), *Hoyng* (NL), *Tilmann* (DE), *Véron* (FR), *Pezard* (FR) and *Floyd* (UK).

64 Here, also see *Grabinski*, GRUR Int 2013, p. 310, and also the Foreword to the 14th Version.

65 For a text, see: https://eplaw.org/wp-content/uploads/2015/12/Second-Venice-Resolution-dated-4-November-2006.pdf.

66 See also *Schallmoser/Grabinski*, Mitt. 2016, p. 425 and Mitt. 2017, p. 245.

those concerning the "opt-out" (see Para. 299 et seqq.), had already become applicable during the Protocol Phase (see Para. 44).

2. The Protocol to the UPC Agreement

42 The UPC Agreement stipulated that the Unified Patent Court ought to be – and indeed had to be – fully functional right from day one following the UPC Agreement's entry into force. Thus, on 1 October 2015, the so-called "Protocol to the Agreement on a Unified Patent Court,"[67] was adopted, its aim being to enable a smooth start for the Unified Patent Court's operations.[68]

43 The protocol came into force on 19 January 2022, which meant that the Unified Patent Court had now formally acquired legal personality and the process of constituting the various committees could begin (see Para. 289). Other tasks could now commence in parallel as well, such as the hiring of personnel or the work of adopting the required supplemental legal texts (e.g. the Rules of Procedure, see Para. 40).

44 As soon as Germany deposits its ratification (cf. Para. 46) it will be possible to submit opt-out requests to the Unified Patent Court (see Section 1, Para. 299 et seqq.) or to have oneself certified as a qualified European Patent Representative (see Para. 734 et seqq.). Thus, the Protocol authorized the Unified Patent Court to make the necessary preparations before the UPC Agreement's actual entry into force and to take all appropriate organizational measures to ensure that the Unified Patent Court would be fully functional right from the outset.

Entry into force of the System

45 On 17 February 2023, Germany completed the ratification process by depositing its instrument with the EU[69]. Thus, the unitary patent system finally began on 1 June 2023.

46 On 1 March, 2022, the so-called "sunrise period" began during which, among other things, anticipatory opt-outs (see Para. 299) and registration as a representative were possible.

67 For a text, see: https://www.unified-patent-court.org/sites/default/files/upc_documents/Protocol_to_the_Agreement_on_Unified_Patent_Court_on_provisional_application.pdf.

68 See also: Interview with *Ramsay* at http://www.unitarypatentpackage.com/2015/12/15/alexander-ramsay-about-the-unitary-patent-and-the-unified-patent-court/.

69 https://www.bmj.de/SharedDocs/Pressemitteilungen/DE/2023/0217_Einheitliches_Patentgericht.html.

Chapter 2: Strategic Considerations – How Should the Unitary Patent System Be Evaluated?

In a sense, the Unitary Patent System serves to close an existing gap in the European system for protecting industrial property rights. This is because European industrial property rights were previously available only for trademarks and design patents. And also because unitary utility models will probably never be introduced Europe-wide, even though there have been initiatives in this direction.[1] 47

It bears noting, however, that the approach which was ultimately selected for the Unitary Patent System is the exact opposite of the one chosen for trademarks and designs. In the latter case, a new agency was created, namely the European Union Intellectual Property Office,[2] but no new court system was introduced. Instead, the individual courts of the Member States were designated to function as patent courts having jurisdiction over European Union trademarks,[3] respectively European Community designs.[4] Thus, these national courts are now in a position to adjudicate infringements of European Union trademarks and European Community designs.[5] 48

When it came to the Unitary Patent System, on the other hand, an existing agency was retained, namely the European Patent Office (EPO). At the same time, a new court system was created, one having its own legal tradition, legal system and rules of procedure.[6] 49

The reasons for this approach seem plausible, certainly as far as retaining the EPO is concerned. After all, patents require a more thorough examination than trademarks or designs (at least in the European approach, where designs are merely registered), and this can only be performed by a staff of technically expert examiners. So it would have been a considerable waste of resources to conceive the Unitary Patent System without resorting to an existing institution that was already well equipped as 50

1 See The EU Commission's Green Paper 19 July 1995 on the "Protection of Utility Models in the Single Market," COM (1995), p. 370 (Final Version), or the proposal issued by the Max Planck Institute in Munich in 1990; see GRUR Int 1994, p. 569; see also *Königer*, JIPLP 2017, p. 75.

2 Formerly the Office for Harmonization in the Internal Market.

3 So designated on the basis of EU Regulation 2015/2424 of 16 December 2015; the old term was "Community trademarks."

4 Cf. Art. 95 et seqq. of Regulation 40/94 (relating to trademarks), respectively Art. 80 et seqq. of EU Regulation 6/2002 (relating to design patents).

5 Cf. also *Kur*, GRUR Int, 2014, p. 749.

6 This is given particular emphasis by *Hilty* et al., Max Planck Institute for Intellectual Property & Competition; Competition Law Research Paper No. 13–16; here, the rules are even treated as a possible model for national proceedings and regulations. A more critical view is taken by *Pedersen*, "Transitions in European Patent Law – Influences of the Unitary Patent Package;" cf. also *Graevenitz/Garanasvili* GRUR Int. 2019, p. 221.

a patent-examining body: the European Patent Office, universally recognized as one of the best patent agencies in the world, if not the best.[7]

51 A possible alternative would have been to assign this function to the respective national patent offices, but this would almost certainly have led to serious capacity overloads. In addition, it could well have given a predominant role to the German Patent and Trademark Office (DPMA), one that other Member States might have found hard to accept. Recall that the DPMA is Europe's largest national patent office and the only national agency of its kind among the Member States to still conduct patent examinations on a large scale.

52 The reasons for creating a Unified Patent Court are somewhat less obvious. As in the case of European Union trademarks and European Community designs, one could have simply resorted to the national courts, for example, at least as courts of first instance. To be sure, the required professional expertise and capacities were and are available in at least some of the relevant Member States – particularly Germany, of course. Proposals of this kind were certainly discussed.[8]

53 Nonetheless, every one of the initiatives meriting serious consideration called for the creation of a court with parallel jurisdiction. Hotly debated in this context was whether and to what extent this parallel jurisdiction ought to also encompass existing European Patents, rather than just the newly envisioned Unitary Patents. One frequently floated proposal was to give proprietors a free choice in this regard.[9] But it seems such elective options were never really seriously considered by the system's "architects."[10]

54 This is where the definition of a patent proposed by the author of the present text[11] comes into play. This definition holds that a patent system is a mechanism which allows a state to indirectly promote innovation in a manner which is cost-effective, low in risk, and which thus ultimately *benefits the state.* For the state outsources both the costs and the risks which it would otherwise bear if it were to promote innovation directly. More specifically:

- The state outsources the associated costs – in the form of higher product costs – to the market as well as to patent applicants, who assume the patent system's administrative costs via application fees, etc.;

7 Cf. *van Pottelsberghe*, Bruegel Working Paper, 2010/42; see also. *Ann*, GRUR Int. 2018, p. 1114.

8 See e.g. the opinion on the EPLA issued by the German Bar Association (DAV) under the auspices of *Tilmann*, which expresses support for such a solution, cf. also *Tilmann*, in GRUR 2001, p. 1079. For an opposing view, see e.g. *Steenbeck* in his lecture at the Young EPLAW Congress in July 2011.

9 See e.g. *Pagenberg*, GRUR Int 2010, p. 195; *Smits/Bull*, Maastricht European Private Law Institute Working Paper, 2012/16.

10 E.g. according to *Fröhlinger* in her post-lecture remarks at the VPP Conference in Berlin, May 2011.

11 See *Hüttermann*, Mitt. 2013, p. 181.

- The state outsources the associated risks primarily to patent applicants, since it is they who ultimately decide which of their innovations are worth promoting (i.e. worthy of a patent registration).

From a risk standpoint, the Unitary Patent as currently conceived has essentially been placed on an equal footing with existing European Patents over the long-term horizon. This is because patents initially granted by the European Patent Office will later be enforced by the Unitary Patent Court once an "opt-out" declaration is no longer possible (see Para. 299 et seqq.) **55**

The newly founded Unified Patent Court, however, comes with the risk that applicants will face a trade-off between a higher level of legal certainty as to a given decision's territorial effects and greater legal uncertainty as to the fairness and equity of the actual adjudication. **56**

This legal uncertainty will involve only one court, however: the Unified Patent Court. The past practice of bringing parallel national actions, by contrast, always entailed the risk of diverging court decisions – a risk which could never be fully eliminated despite intensive dialogue among patent judges in the various states.[12] **57**

This said, few would dispute the proposition (advanced e.g. by *Mejer/van Pottelsberghe de la Potterie*)[13] that – at least in Germany – the vast majority of industrial property-right holders were quite satisfied with the existing enforcement options based on an international comparison. **58**

> "Germany is the country with the cheapest and most renowned judicial system for patent-related litigations within Europe."

This is evidenced by the high number[14] of legal actions filed in Germany, especially by foreign plaintiffs, who are even prepared to face the hurdle of conducting proceedings in German, a language with which they usually have no experience. According to data provided by JUVE[15] for new patent-infringement actions filed e.g. in 2020, roughly 2/3 of all such legal actions were brought in Germany. **59**

So it is hardly surprising that the business and industrial sector has attempted to influence the solutions proposed thus far in a manner which ensures that costs (for translations, etc.) will be kept low, and that the possibilities of enforcement and the predictability of decisions will, at a minimum, not be made markedly worse than under the existing system. After all, it will ultimately be up to the players in business and industry – who essentially account for most patent applicants – to bear the costs **60**

---

12 See e.g. *Arnold*, JIPLP 2019, p. 657; *Walsh*, IIC 2019, p. 408; or the interview with *Sabotier/Gillet* on the JUVE Patent website; cf. also *Geiger/Nard/Seuba/O'Malley/Lynn*, p. 357 et seqq.

13 *Document de treball de l'IEB*, 2009/31.

14 See *Kühnen/Claessen*, GRUR, 2013, p. 592.

15 https://www.juve-patent.com/news-and-stories/legal-commentary/patent-cases-decline-across-europe-but-courts-report-increasing-complexity/ cf. also https://www.juve-patent.com/news-and-stories/people-and-business/case-numbers-soar-at-french-patent-courts-although-germany-remains-ahead/.

and the risks. Whereas the state – in this case, the EU and its Member States – will "only" provide the legal instruments and legal options.

61 More than a few observers[16] see the main cause of the previous initiatives' ultimate failure in the fact that the trade-off between costs and risks was simply out of balance. And they consider it wholly unacceptable that, under the European Patent Convention, the Unitary Patent did not serve as an alternative solution but was instead conceived to replace the national systems.[17] This conception was unable to find acceptance, however, either for patents or for trademarks and design patents/registered designs – the latter being another domain where serious thought had been given to abandoning national industrial property rights in favor of purely European solutions.[18] But this ultimate rejection seems entirely logical if we recall the definition of patents presented earlier.

62 In the case of European trademarks and design patents/registered designs, one can safely say that the situation for applicants has markedly improved. In a word, they now have entirely new tools and options at their disposal, whereas the existing national systems for trademarks and design patents/registered designs remain unchanged.

63 On the other hand, the new system that is in the offing now still entail a certain level of uncertainty with regard to the costs and risks involved.

64 Wholly unproblematic, by contrast, is the Unitary Patent, which merely represents an alternative solution that gives applicants an additional option, one which they can exercise or waive at their free discretion. Since Unitary Patents are issued by the European Patent Office, the question of whether to use them will eventually boil down[19] to a mere cost analysis for most applicants, given that the associated legal implications will remain essentially unchanged (see Para. 172 et seqq.)

65 When it came to the Unified Patent Court, however, it was decided that the old system of European Patents was to be subordinated to a newly created jurisdiction, i.e. not everything would stay the same in this regard. This has given rise to great uncertainty on the part of patent proprietors, if only because they have no past experience with the new court to use as a guide. As an "orientation aid," patent proprietors have been given a transitional period in which to exercise the so-called "opt-out" option (see Para. 299 et seqq.), which allows them to circumvent the Unified Patent Court and to continue taking part in the current system of purely national infringement proceedings. But this in no way alters the fact the UPC will at some point have sole jurisdiction.

---

16 E.g. *Götting*, in Götting/Meyer/Vormbrock, Note 41 to Section 3.

17 See *Keukenschrijver/Busse*, Note 21 to the Introduction, IntPatÜG; *Schäfers*, GRUR 1999, p. 820. According to *Schäfers*, getting the national agencies to gradually surrender their competencies was already the intended purpose (e.g. on the part of the German Federal Government) back when the EPO was created.

18 See e.g. *Westerholt*, GRUR Int 1976, p. 39. But it bears noting that the EU's preliminary concept for a European Trademark from 1964 was already calling for coexistence between national and European trademarks.

19 I.e. once the transitional period for an "opt-out" expires; see Para. 323 et seqq.

The last possible "escape hatch," as it were, would be Article 87 of the UPC Agreement, which stipulates that a "broad consultation" of the patent system's users is to be performed, followed by a possible revision of the Agreement, once seven years have passed or once 2,000 infringement cases have been decided, whichever comes later (see Para. 776). Although some observers have raised the prospect that this could be used to torpedo the UPC Agreement at some later time in order to return to the old national system, this would seem to be a highly unlikely scenario.[20] 66

The fact that applicants have therefore been placed in a comparatively worse position for the time being has not failed to spark protest.[21] It also remains to be seen whether applicants will make extensive of the "opt-out" option or not (see Para. 299 et seqq. and 537 et seqq.). 67

It therefore follows that applicants will be left with only two options over the long run, to wit: 68

a) To register patents at the European Patent Office and thus have recourse to the Unified Patent Court as the infringement court; or
b) To select national solutions and thus continue having recourse to national infringement courts and/or the ability to avoid revocation actions.[22]

It bears noting, however, that a significant number of the Member States signatory to the UPC Agreement have closed off the national route for international registrations, i.e. so that the protection arising from an international patent application can only come from the European Patent Office.[23] These are: Belgium, Cyprus, France, Greece, Ireland, Latvia, Lithuania, Malta, Monaco, Montenegro, the Netherlands, and Slovenia.[24] 69

So if one wishes to seek patent protection in these countries, the only way to obtain it via the national route would be to file a retroactive registration under the Paris Convention for the Protection of Intellectual Property while making use of the twelve-month priority period. This obviously limits the options open to patent applicants. 70

Depending on the national legal system involved, the two options a) and b) can be understood to apply in either a mutually exclusive manner or a cumulative manner. 71

It is possible in many Member States to pursue both national and European Patents in parallel. Both types of patents will then be legally effective once issued. This would therefore be a possible way of keeping one's enforcement options open in situations where the protectable rights in question are of exceptional importance.[25] 72

---

20 See e.g. Pagenberg, GRUR Int 2010, p. 195.
21 See e.g. *Pagenberg*, GRUR Int 2010, p. 195.
22 See e.g. *Köllner*, Mitt. 2013, p. 253; cf. also *Holzwarth-Rochford*, GRUR Prax 2013, p. 374.
23 See https://www.wipo.int/pct/en/texts/reg_des.html.
24 Effective as of 1 February 2026.
25 According to the brochure *Nationales Recht zum EPÜ* (2th Edition) and the brochure *Nationale Massnahmen zum Einheitspatent*, the Prohibition of Double Protection prevails (at least partially) in the EU Member States of Belgium, Bulgaria, Germany, Estonia, France,

73 The option to obtain double protection is not available in most of the Member States signatory to the UPC Agreement, however. Here, national patents become ineffective whenever parallel European patents exist (see Para. 142).

74 It bears nothing here that the prohibition of double protection which was previously applicable to German patents and European patents has been largely eliminated by virtue of the Accompanying Law to Ratify the Unitary Patent System (see Para. 31 et seqq.)[26] So if an "opt-out" has not been lodged for a given European patent, the respective applicant would in principle still be entitled to keep both options open and thus be able to obtain double protection.

75 In Germany, there is yet a third option, one which should not be underestimated:

c) To deviate off a utility model – in essence, to register a protective right with the European Patent Office and to bring legal action on the national level.[27] This is discussed in more detail in Para. 574 et seqq.

Greece, Ireland, Italy, Croatia, Latvia, Lithuania, Luxemburg, Malta, the Netherlands, Portugal, Romania, Slovakia, Slovenia, Czech Republic, Great Britain and Cyprus. It usually does not apply for utility models, however. Double protection is possible in Denmark, Finland, Austria, Poland, Sweden and Hungary.

26 In effect, this served to implement the main substance of the proposals that had gone before, cf. *Bardehle*, Mitt. 2011, p. 452; see also *Nieder*, GRUR Int 2014, p. 1033; as well as *Chudziak*, GRUR Int 2015, p. 839. For a legal analysis, see *McGuire* GRUR 2011, p. 767. For a British discussion (before the Brexit Referendum) also cf. http://ipkitten.blogspot.de/2016/02/the-unitary-patent-reason-to-allow.html;.

27 See e.g. *Teschemacher*, Mitt. 2013, p. 153.

Part 2: The Unitary Patent

Chapter 3: Overview of the Unitary Patent

Contents Para

A. Introduction

The Unitary Patent was created by virtue of EU Regulations Nos. 1257/2012 and 1260/2012 of 17 December 2012. Article 18 of Regulation (EU) 1257/2012 will apply as of 1 January 2014 or as of the date of entry into force of the Agreement on a Unified Patent Court, whichever is later. This means that the Unitary Patent will become available starting on the day on which the Unified Patent Court takes up its work, i.e. on 1 June 2023 (cf. Para. 46). 76

77 Although the Unitary Patent was adopted by 25 of the then 27 Member States[1] in the context of so-called "enhanced cooperation," the Unitary Patent will not automatically become applicable in all these states once the Unified Patent Court comes into being. Instead, Article 18 of Regulation (EU) 1257/2012 stipulates that the Unitary Patent will be applicable only for those states which have granted the Unified Patent Court exclusive jurisdiction over Unitary Patents, i.e. states which have also ratified the corresponding Agreement on the Unified Patent Court (UPC Agreement).

78 This effectively serves to interlink the Unitary Patent and the Unified Patent Court. It also means that the Unified Patent's reach will not yet extend to a country like Poland, for example, which has communicated its intention not to ratify the UPC Agreement for the time being.[2]

79 So at first, it was be possible to obtain Unitary Patents only for those signatory Member States that took the lead in ratifying the UPC Agreement i.e. the following countries:

> Belgium, Bulgaria, Denmark, Germany, Estonia, Finland, France, Italy, Latvia, Lithuania. Luxemburg, Malta, the Netherlands, Austria, Portugal, Sweden and Slovenia.

80 Starting 1 September 2024, Romania has joined the Unitary Patent system.

81 The following map illustrates this situation:

1 Note: In the meantime (on 1 July 2013), Croatia joined the European Union as the 28th Member State. As mentioned earlier, Italy announced on 30 September 2015 that it, too, would accede to the EU Regulations.

2 Cf. *Zawadzka*, IIC 2014, 383; for a comprehensive discussion. also see *McGuire*, Mitt. 2015, p. 537.

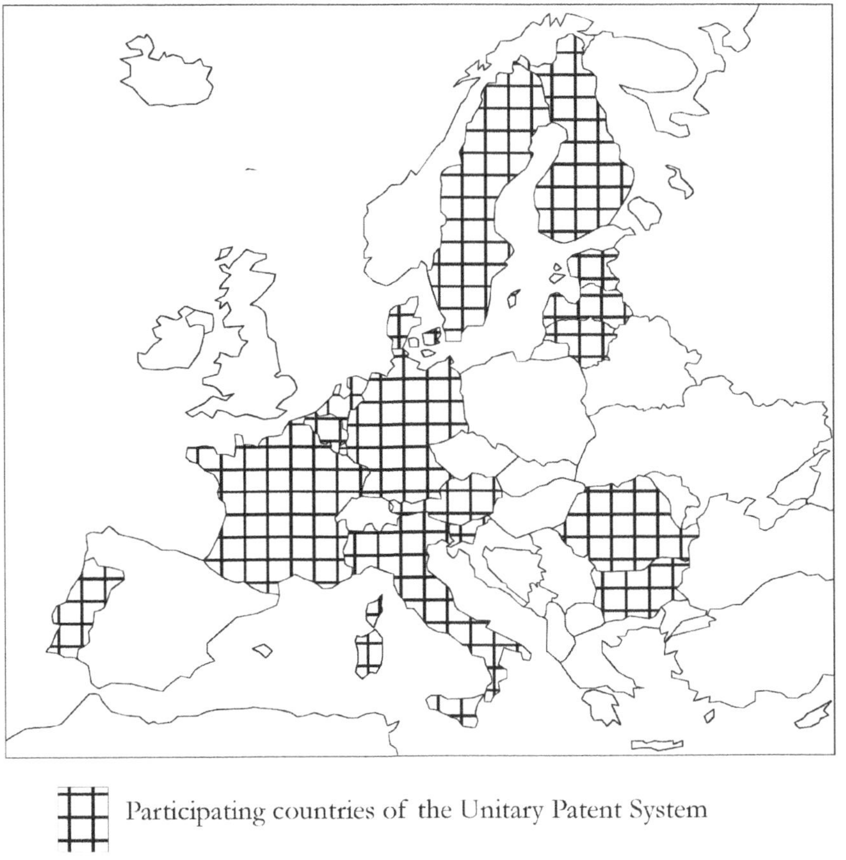

Fig. 3.1 Map: States Participating in the Unitary Patent System

Given that more additional states are likely to ratify the UPC Agreement even after its entry into force, it follows that the territorial reach of the Unitary Patent's unitary effect will gradually expand as the years go by. Ireland, however, after announcing[3] that it plans to hold the referendum required for ratification in 2023 or 2024, has meanwhile decided to defer its plans.[4] So at the moment it is unclear which country will be the 19th to join the Unitary Patent System. **82**

3 See: https://enterprise.gov.ie/en/News-And-Events/Department-News/2022/June/280620222.html.

4 See: https://enterprise.gov.ie/en/news-and-events/department-news/2024/april/20240416.html.

83 This does not apply to Unitary Patents that have already been registered, however, since it was stipulated that "*...a European patent for which unitary effect is registered... shall have unitary effect only in those participating Member States in which the Unified Patent Court has exclusive jurisdiction with regard to European patents with unitary effect at the date of registration*" (Article 18 (2) of EU Regulation 1257/2012), i.e. in states which are Member States participating in the UPC Agreement as of the patent's registration date. Thus, if new Member States ratify the UPC Agreement and join the Unitary Patent System, they will not fall under the territorial reach of already existing Unitary Patents (in contrast to European Union trademarks, for example).

▶ Example

84 The practical ramifications of this situation are illustrated:

At the time of its entry into effect on 1 June 2023, the Unitary Patent System encompassed the following states:

Belgium, Bulgaria, Denmark, Germany, Estonia, Finland, France, Italy, Latvia, Lithuania. Luxemburg, Malta, the Netherlands, Austria, Portugal, Sweden and *Slovenia*

This means that a Unitary Patent valid in all these seventeen states could be obtained for all European Patents for which the mention of grant was published on this date or later.

But for all other states which are party to the European Patent Convention, including Member States which are potential participants in the UPC Agreement, a national validation option was necessary.

On 1 September 2024 *Romania* joined the UPC Agreement (cf. Para. 80).

European patents for which a request for Unitary Patent effect was registered (see Para. 134 et seqq.) on this date or later would now automatically encompass Romania within their territorial scope. The applicant would not need to take any additional steps for this to occur.

On the other hand, Unitary Patents registered before 1 September 2024 do *not* cover Romania. Here, an applicant would have to obtain national validation in order to secure patent protection.

Assuming *Ireland* were finally to accede to the UPC Agreement effective as of 1 October 2029; in this case, only those Unitary Patents which are registered on this date or later would exert their protective effect in Ireland.

85 As seen from the standpoint of the European Patent Office, respectively the European Patent Convention (EPC), the Unitary Patent falls under Article 142 of the EPC. This provides that a special agreement may be concluded among Contracting States with the goal of ensuring that European patents acquire a unitary character throug-

hout the territories of those states.[5] Until now, this has been the case for Switzerland and Lichtenstein. Thus, the EU itself will not become a party to the EPC – contrary to what has sometimes been suggested in discussions of this topic – nor is it necessary for it to do so.

B. Preconditions for Obtaining a Unitary Patent

I. Overview

The preconditions for obtaining a Unitary Patent are as follows: 86
- A European Patent must have been granted, whereby mention of the grant must be published in the European Patent Bulletin on the day of the EU Regulation's date of application or later (Article 18 (6) of EU Regulation 1257/2012).
- The states designated in the European Patent must include all Member States which are party to the UPC Agreement.
- The European Patent must state the same claims with respect to all Member States which are party to the UPC Agreement.[6] Formulating the claims differently for non-Member States is permissible, on the other hand.

The last two preconditions are derived from the mandatory unitary character of the patent. 87

II. The "Malta Problem"

On 9 December 2014, Malta ratified the UPC Agreement. Yet Malta has been a member of the European Patent Organization only since 1 March 2007. Thus, Malta can be designated only for those European Patent applications whose application date falls on this date or on a later date. 88

Since the designation states of the European Patent must encompass all the Member States which are party to the UPC Agreement, this means that a Unitary Patent cannot be requested for any European Patent whose application date falls before 1 March 2007. This has come to be known as the "Malta Problem".[7] However, due to the time delay in coming into force of the system (cf. Para. 20 et seqq.), this will probably only affect a few applications. 89

If Croatia accedes to Unitary Patent System, then Unitary Patents will become possible only for those European Patents whose application date falls on 1 January 2008 or later, since this was the date on which Croatia joined the European Patent Organization. 90

5 For a critical view of this, see *Sédrati-Dinet*, for example.

6 Note: Formulating patent claims differently for different Contracting States is permitted under Rule 138 of the European Patent Convention in order to make allowance for so-called "national rights" (also see Para. 120 et seqq.). Also see *Nieder*, Mitt. 2017, p. 540.

7 For a case where indeed the request for an Unitary Patent was denied cf. UPC_CFI_1771/2025 (CD Paris), Decision of 30 December 2025, Papst Licensing v. EPA.

C. Supplemental Protection Certificates

91 No reference whatsoever to supplemental protection certificates for Unitary Patents is to be found in the relevant EU Regulations. This means that the requirement to apply for supplemental protection individually, i.e. country by country, will continue to apply for Unitary Patents as well. While it would be desirable for the EU to issue a Regulation on a unitary European protection certificate, such a Regulation is currently still in the planning phase at the EU.

D. Effect of the Unitary Patent

I. Equivalence with National Patent

92 The effect of a valid Unitary Patent is defined as follows:

> The European patent with unitary effect shall confer on its proprietor the right to prevent any third party from committing acts against which that patent provides protection throughout the territories of the participating Member States in which it has unitary effect, subject to applicable limitations. (Article 5 para. 1 of EU Regulation 1257/2012.)

93 As already mentioned (Para. 11), there is no definition of these "acts" as such in the EU Regulation. Instead, Unitary Patents are placed on an equal footing with a national patent:

> The acts against which the patent provides protection referred to in paragraph 1 and the applicable limitations shall be those defined by the law applied to European patents with unitary effect in the participating Member State whose national law is applicable to the European patent with unitary effect as an object of property in accordance with Article 7 (Article 5 para. 3 EU Regulation 1257/2012).

94 Thus, the effects exerted by the Unitary Patent are defined in an indirect manner by being made equivalent to the effects of a national patent (see the remarks below).

95 It should be noted that no statutory provision was made to enshrine a positive right of usage such as the one applicable under German law.[8]

II. Which Body of National Law is Applicable to Unitary Patents?

96 As already mentioned, a Unitary Patent is treated as being equivalent to a national patent not only with respect to its effect, but also with respect to its status as an object of property. In this context, the Unitary Patent will be subject to the national legal system of the relevant country (Article 7 of Regulation (EU) 1257/2012), namely:

- the country in which the applicant, according to the European Patent Register, had his residence or principal place of business (or, as the case may be, merely a place of business/establishment) at the time of filing the application for the European patent; or
- the country of the first-named applicant, insofar as there are multiple applicants.

8 Cf. Ruling of the German Federal Court of Justice (BGH) in the *Trägerplatte* case, GRUR 2009, p. 655.

This only applies, however, so long as the relevant country is one in which the Unitary Patent was valid at the time at which it was recorded in the Register (= "validation"), i.e. if it is a Member State party to the UPC Agreement. If there are multiple applicants and the country of the first-named applicant is not a Member State, then the national legal system of the second-named applicant's country will govern, provided said country is a Member State. If this country, too, is not a Member State, then the country of the third-named applicant (insofar there is one) will be used as the reference point, and so on. **97**

If none of the above applies, i.e. if none of the applicants has a residence or place of business in a Member State, then the applicable country of reference will be: **98**

> "...the state in which the European Patent Organization has its headquarters..." (Art. 7 of Regulation (EU) 1257/2012).

In other words: Germany. **99**

▶ Practical tip:

The judgment handed down by the European Court of Justice (ECJ) in the *Hummel/Nike* Case (C-617/15) probably serves to fatally undermine a conclusion that had previously been advanced in the scholarly commentaries[9] as well as in the first (German) edition of this book: Namely, that the subsidiarity of German law would cause 80% of all Unitary Patents to fall under the applicable scope of German law. While the ECJ Judgment deals mainly with EU trademark law, it is relevant in this context as well, since it makes reference to the Brussels I Directive.[10] According to ECJ Judgment C-617/15, a subsidiary or second-tier subsidiary having its seat within the EU already qualifies as an "establishment" within the EU. Moreover, such subsidiaries or second-tier subsidiaries do not necessarily have to operate in the same area as the defendant/respondent; it already suffices if they merely provide services. This means that many enterprises which seem to be foreign at first glance will, by virtue of ECJ Decision C-617/15, actually qualify as enterprises of a Member State within the meaning of Article 7. This said, the percentage of Unitary Patents that will ultimately be subject to German law will still be significant. Indeed, the corresponding percentage will probably be higher than in any other country.

Another important point is that the status of the Register for Unitary Patent Protection at the time of the patent filing will be dispositive; any later transfer of title to the patent will be irrelevant. **100**

9 See also *Müller-Stoy, Paschold*, GRUR Int 2014, p. 646; *Kunzmann*, VPP-Rundbrief 2015, p. 158; *Tochtermann*, GRUR Int 2016, p. 721, in *Busse/Keukenschrijver*, Note 56 to the section on Unified Patent Protection in Europe (*Einheitlicher Patentschutz in Europa*); *Sonntag* in *Bopp/Kircher*, Note 141 to Section 13; as well as *Tilmann* in *Tilmann/Plassmann* Note 62 to Article 7 of Regulation (EU) 1257/2012.

10 See *Hüttermann* Mitt. 2021, p. 4.

▶ Example

101 The practical ramifications of the above are illustrated in the following three hypothetical scenarios:

Scenario A:

A French enterprise and a German university jointly file an international patent application. During the international phase, however, the French enterprise acquires the application and becomes the patent's sole proprietor. A European patent is later granted for this application following the regionalization process. Said patent is validated as a Unitary Patent.

Assuming the French enterprise is the first applicant to be named in the Patent Cooperation Treaty (PCT) application, then the Unitary Patent is governed by French law. If the German university is the applicant first named in the PCT application, then the Unitary Patent will be governed by German law. The fact that the French enterprise later becomes the patent's sole proprietor is irrelevant in this case.

Scenario B:

A US enterprise and a Belgian enterprise jointly file a European patent application. The US enterprise is the first applicant named in the application filing.

During the application process, the application is sold off to a German enterprise, which successfully prosecutes the patent and eventually validates it as a Unitary Patent.

Belgian law governs for this Unitary Patent, because:
– Belgium is an EU Member State whereas the USA is not; and
– The status of the Register at the time of the application filing is dispositive.

The fact that the US enterprise is named first in the application is irrelevant here, as is the fact that a German enterprise later acquires ownership of the application.

Alternative Scenario B:

The US enterprise owns a subsidiary in the Bahamas, which in turn maintains a branch office in the Netherlands. In this case, this Unitary Patent would be governed by Dutch law, given that the branch office already qualifies as an establishment according to ECJ Judgment No. 617/15.

Scenario C:

A Japanese and a South Korean enterprise jointly file an PCT application. Pursuant to the regionalization process, a European patent is granted. This is followed by patent's validation as a Unitary Patent.

Neither Japan nor South Korea are EU Member States, so that this Unitary Patent will be governed by German law, regardless of the sequence in which the applicants are named on the application.

Alternative Scenario C:

The South Korean enterprise has a research center in Germany as well as a sales office in France. The Japanese enterprise, for its part, does not have any branch operation in the EU.

In this case, it not entirely clear which national system applies. According to ECJ Judgment No. 617/15, the South Korean enterprise has an establishment in both Germany as well as in France. Here, the relevant court of jurisdiction – in practice, usually the Unified Patent Court – would have to make an assessment and also decide whether the matter requires referral to the ECJ (see Para. 470 et seqq.).

This approach of making Unitary Patents equivalent to national patents was ostensibly based on the intended objective, already discussed above (see Para. 11), to not give the European Court of Justice any decision-making competence in this context. It also gives rise to several important consequences, however. These are discussed below, particularly in connection with those provisions of German law which have subsidiary applicability to Unitary Patents under Article 7 of Regulation (EU) 1257/2012. **102**

E. Transfer and Licensing of Unitary Patents

A Unitary Patent may be transferred only in its entirety. On the other hand, "*it may be licensed in respect of the whole or part of the territories of the participating Member States.*" (Article 3 of Regulation (EU) 1257/2012). **103**

I. Transfer of Unitary Patents

The Unitary Patent Regulation stipulates that the transfer/acquisition of a Unitary Patent may not be made dependent on any entry in a national patent register (Article 7 (4) of Regulation (EU) 1257/2012). **104**

Since the Unitary Patent is made equivalent to the corresponding national patents as an object of property, it follows that the sale, respectively, transfer of a patent will also be governed in all other respects by the relevant body of national law, which will frequently be German law. The rules applicable in such cases can sometimes vary widely. **105**

German law will govern for a significant number of Unitary Patent transfers. It bears noting that, under German law, a transfer is not dependent on the entry of acquisition of title in any register, so that German law fulfills the preconditions of the Unitary Patent Regulation in this regard. **106**

II. Actions for Vindication

107 It is expressly stipulated that the Unified Patent Court is not competent for actions to vindicate a patent (see Para. 287). This means that the vindication of Unitary Patents will also be handled in accordance with the respective national legal system, which will frequently be the German one. It bears noting, however, that vindication constitutes ground for revocation and that the Unified Patent Court may have a role to play in this connection (see Para. 658).

III. Insolvency

108 Since the UPC Agreement is silent on this topic as well, it follows that national law will be applicable here, too. In practice, German law will often be applicable vis-a-vis third parties.[11]

IV. Licenses

109 As pointed out above, the Unitary Patent may also be licensed in respect of only a portion of a participating Member State's sovereign territory.

110 In principle, the licensor and licensee will be free to select the applicable system of laws when structuring their contractual licensing agreement. The only possible implications of this will be the license's effects on third parties.[12]

111 According to German law, namely Section 15, paragraph 3 of the Patent Act (*Patentgesetz*, PatG), a transfer of rights to a patent will not affect any licenses previously granted for that patent. The German courts, however, have diverged from international practice in their case law by refusing to regard agreements that merely constitute so-called "covenants not to sue" as licenses. In consequence, they ruled that a new proprietor was not restricted by such a covenant following the transfer of rights.[13]

112 This said, the current trend seems to be a gradual convergence with the international practice of treating such "covenants not to sue" as licenses – ones which will be conveyed along with the transfer of rights to the patent.[14]

113 It bears noting, however, that a point yet to be clarified is whether German law permits joint applicants to grant licenses independently of one another when no corresponding contractual arrangement has been made.[15]

114 Also worth mentioning is that, under the established case law of the German courts, if a patent proprietor sues an alleged infringer and subsequently issues an exclusive license, then this exclusive licensor will be prevented from bringing a standalone legal

11 See *Stoy/Paschold*, GRUR Int 2014, p. 646.

12 See also *Tochtermann* GRUR Int 2016, p. 721.

13 See *Kunzmann*, VPP-Rundbrief 2015, p. 158 with additional references.

14 E.g. Judgment of the Higher District Court of Munich I of 8 January 2015, Case No. 7 O 28263/13, cited in *Kunzmann*, VPP-Rundbrief 2015.

15 See *Kunzmann*, VPP-Rundbrief 2015.

action against this same infringer so long as the first action is still pending.[16] Instead, the judgment obtained by the patent proprietor will work both for and against him.

F. Lapse of Unitary Patents

A Unitary Patent may be limited, revoked (even partially) or surrendered (Art. 3 (3) of Regulation (EU) 1257/2012) only in its entirety. 115

It is not possible to surrender a patent for individual countries only, or to uphold a patent with differing sets of claims for different countries. 116

G. Actions for Revocation of Unitary Patents/Prior Rights

Since actions for the revocation of Unitary Patents are heard before the Unified Patent Court, any resulting limitation or revocation of the patent will always exert unitary effect. 117

On the other hand, the fact that Unitary Patents are treated as equivalent to national patents will have consequences for the state of the technical art which can be adduced as grounds against the Unitary Patent. This is explained below: 118

The grounds on which a Unitary Patent may be revoked are not specified in the relevant EU Regulations or in the UPC Agreement. Instead, Article 65 of the UPC Agreement refers to the corresponding provisions in Article 138 (1) and Article 139 of the European Patent Convention (EPC). (For a detailed discussion, see Para. 658 et seqq.) 119

This reference to Article 139 EPC, as read in conjunction with the EU Unitary Patent Regulation (1257/2012), means that, depending on the applicant's place of residence, the state of the technical art will not be unitary for purposes of a Unitary Patent, specifically when it comes to post-published national patent applications ("prior rights").[17] 120

Patent applications which are filed in a Member State at a time prior to a European patent application but which are post-published, i.e. published only after the filing date, respectively priority date, of the respective European patent application (so-called "prior rights"), will not be examined by the European Patent Office.[18] According to the European Patent Convention, such an examination may occur later in the context of a national action for revocation once the European patent has been issued. According to Article 139 of the EPC, such national prior rights may then be asserted in such a proceeding. 121

16 Judgment of the German Federal Court of Justice (BGH) No. X ZR 70/12 in the *Wundverband* case.

17 See *Hüttermann*, Mitt. 2014, p. 72; this is affirmed at least in part by *Schneider* in *Busse/Keukenschrijver*, Note 58 to *Einheitlicher Patentschutz in Europa* (Unified Patent Protection in Europe), and implicitly also by *McGuire*, Mitt. 2015, p. 537; a contrary view is taken by *Diez*, Mitt. 2017, p. 481, by *Ackermann/Vissel*, GRUR 2016, p. 641, as well as by *Tilmann* in *Tilmann/Plassmann*, Note 61 to Art 3 of the EU Patent Regulation.

18 Note: The exception here is the aforementioned Rule 138 of the European Patent Convention, but in this case a prior right must be notified to the European Patent Office.

122 According to Article 139 of the European Patent Convention, however, these national prior rights will only apply for the relevant country but not for the European patent as a whole. For example, a post-published British patent could be asserted only for the British portion of a European patent, whereas a post-published French patent could be asserted only for the French portion.

123 As far as the Unitary Patent is concerned, the reference made to national law in Article 7 of Regulation (EU) 1257/2012 means that, under Article 139 of the European Patent Convention, the national prior rights of the country to whose national patents the Unitary Patent is equivalent may be adduced as grounds for a challenge.

▶ Example

124 To illustrate the consequences of this practice, we will once again use the above-described Scenario A:

A French enterprise and a German university jointly file an international patent application. During the international phase, the French enterprise acquires the filing as sole proprietor. A European patent is subsequently issued for this application filing following regionalization. This is validated as a Unitary Patent.

Assuming the French enterprise is the first to be named in the PCT application, then the Unitary Patent will be governed by French law. If the German university is the first named in the PCT application, then the Unitary Patent will be subject to German law instead. The fact that the French enterprise later became the application's sole proprietor is irrelevant in this regard.

Assuming French law governs, then only patents and patent applications that were post-published in France can be adduced as grounds to challenge the new Unitary Patent in an action for revocation. If German law governs, then only the corresponding German industrial property rights can be adduced in this fashion.

125 The number of applications filed can vary markedly from country to country, which can in turn make a substantial difference.

H. Procedural Formalities

126 When it comes to the procedural formalities involved, the EU has outsourced key procedures and tasks to the European Patent Office, i.e. almost all the formalities are organized by the EPO.[19] The European Patent Office is also responsible for maintaining the Register for Unitary Patent Protection. Critics have levelled a number of objections at this outsourcing process. Said objections have been adduced in support

19 See the guide released by the European Patent Office under: https://www.epo.org/law-practice/unitary/unitary-patent/unitary-patent-guide_de.html.

of several legal challenges, such as the second lawsuit brought by Spain before the European Court of Justice.[20]

The tasks in question specifically include: 127
- performing the registration procedures required to create a unitary protective effect, including taking receipt of the required translations;
- maintaining the register, including the registration of rights transfers and taking receipt of statements of willingness to grant a license (see Para. 164);
- organizing the compensation system for translation services (see Para. 155); as well as
- administering the annual fees.

The basic underlying regulations for this, particularly the Rules Relating to Unitary 128 Patent Protection (UPP Rules)[21] and the Rules Relating to Fees (RFeesUPP) were adopted by the so-called "Select Committee of the Administrative Council of the European Patent Organization" on 15 December 2015.

I. Applicable Requirements

When it comes to regulating the proceedings conducted by the European Patent 129 Office, Rule 20 of the UPP Rules stipulates that European Patent Office's own regulations will be co-applicable, particularly in the following areas:
- rights of due process;
- rules governing the use of languages;
- rules for the inspection of records;
- representation;
- legal services and deadlines.

An important exception applies, however, with respect to further processing and the 130 re-establishment of rights. As a rule, there will be no further processing in the proceedings which the European Patent Office conducts in connection with Unitary Patents.[22]

The re-establishment of rights, on the other hand, has been provided for. This was 131 done not by way of a reference to Art. 123 of the European Patent Convention, however, but rather through a dedicated regulation, namely Rule 22 of the UPP Rules.

II. Bringing Legal Action before the Unified Patent Court

Decisions taken by the European Patent Office in the proceedings under discussion 132 here may be contested by means of appeal proceedings before the Unified Patent Court. The means that the procedural actions of the European Patent Office will

20 ECJ Judgments C-146/13 and C-147/13; see also Para. 16 and Para. 470 et seqq. with further references.

21 These can be found here: https://www.epo.org/law-practice/legal-texts/official-journal/2022/04/a41.html; the Rules Relating to fees can be found here: https://www.epo.org/law-practice/legal-texts/official-journal/2022/04/a42.html.

22 Cf. UPC_CFI_628/2025 (CD Milan), Decision of 6 August 2025 – Bodycap./. European Patent Office.

become subject to court review for the first time.[23] The proceedings involved in this context will be discussed further on (see Para. 1202 et seqq.).

III. The Patent Register for Unitary Patents

133 Unitary Patents will be recorded in the Register for Unitary Patent Protection which forms part of the European Patent Register and the corresponding data will be kept on file there. As already mentioned, the rules governing the inspection of records are the same ones that apply at the European Patent Office, i.e. the Patent Register will also be open to online inspection.

IV. Registration of Unitary Effect/"Validation"

134 In order for a Unitary Patent to arise after a European patent application has been granted by the European Patent Office – i.e. for a Unitary Patent to become "validated within the EU" – the proprietor must first file an application with the European Patent Office. The application must request that unitary effect be registered in the Patent Register (Rule 5 and 6 of the UPP Rules). This is referred to hereinbelow as an "request for unitary effect" and is analogous to the national validation applications.

1. Request for Unitary Effect

135 The request for unitary effect must be filed with the European Patent Office by no later than one month after publication of the mention of grant of the European patent in the European Patent Bulletin.[24] This is a shorter deadline than the one for national validations, which must amount to at least three months according to Article 65 of the European Patent Convention (see also Para. 1203 et seqq.).

136 The request for unitary effect must be lodged in writing in the language of the proceedings and must contain (as per Rule 6 of the UPP Rules):

- particulars on the proprietor of the European patent making the request (the "requester");
- the number of the European patent to which unitary effect is to be attributed;
- particulars on the representative, assuming one has been appointed by the requester;
- and, during the transitional period, a translation (see the discussion starting at Para. 152 et seqq.)

137 Insofar as compensation is sought for the translation, this, too, must be applied for in the request (see Para. 155).

138 The European Patent Office allows the request to be made via epoline and has also published corresponding templates.

---

23 See *Hüttermann*, Mitt. 2014, p. 546.

24 This follows from Article 9 (g) of Regulation 1257/2012 (EU); also see Rule 6 (1) of the Rules Relating to Unitary Patent Protection.

No fee will be charged for filing the request. 139

2. Course of the Proceeding

Upon being received, the request will be examined by the European Patent Office's so-called "Unitary Patent Protection Division." 140

If the objective preconditions (i.e. same Member States, same formulation of claims) as well as the formal preconditions have been met, then the European Patent Office will register the unitary effect in the Register for Unitary Patent Protection and notify the date of the registration to the requester (Rule 7 of the UPP Rules). The date of the registration will determine the territorial extent of the Unitary Patent, whereby the date on which it is notified may have an influence on the annual fees to be paid (see Para. 163).[25] 141

If the objective preconditions have not been met or if the one-month deadline was missed, then the request will be rejected forthwith. 142

If some other deficiency is present, the requester will receive a deficiency notice giving him a one-month grace period in which to correct. If the deficiency is not corrected within this time limit, then the European Patent Office will reject the request (Rule 7(3) of the UPP Rules).[26] 143

A rejection may be contested through an appeal proceecing before the Unified Patent Court (see Para. 1202 et seqq.) 144

V. No "Double Validation"/National Patents

If patent proprietor opts for a Unitary Patent, he will not be able to revalidate the same patent nationally at some later time in a country covered by the Unitary Patent (Article 4 (2) of Regulation (EU) 1257/2012). So the patent proprietor will have to take a decision in this regard. 145

He will be fully able, however, to obtain corresponding national patents, since these are covered neither by the UPC Agreement nor by the EU Regulations. It bears noting in this context that a prohibition of double protection is in place in many countries, i.e. it is not possible to take legal action on the basis of a national patent when a parallel or overlapping European patent already exists.[27] 146

25 Note: According to *Tilmann*, however, the Unitary Patent is valid immediately, rather than upon registration, which merely serves as retroactive confirmation; see *Tilmann* in *Tilmann/Plassmann*, Note 3 to Article 4 of the EU Patent Regulation.

26 Cf. UPC_CFI_628/2025 (CD Milan), Decision of 6 August 2025 – Bodycap./. European Patent Office.

27 According to the brochure *Nationales Recht zum EPÜ* (17th Edition), a prohibition of double protection is in place in the following EU Member States: Belgium, Bulgaria, Estonia, Greece, Ireland, Italy Croatia, Latvia Lithuania, Luxemburg, Malta, the Netherlands, Portugal, Romania, Slovakia, Slovenia, Czech Republic, Great Britain and Cyprus. This prohibition does not usually apply to utility models, however. Double protection *is*

147 Germany and France have opted for a special arrangement in this context: They do allow double protection for those European patents for which an "opt-out" has not been declared (see also Para. 74 et seqq.).

VI. Regulations Relating to Translations

148 According to Regulation (EU) 1260/2012, there are generally no obligations in effect with respect to translations. This principle is subject to two important exceptions, however:

1. Translations in the Event of Legal Disputes

149 In the event of a dispute over an alleged infringement of a European patent with unitary effect, the patent proprietor must provide, at the request and the choice of an alleged infringer, a full translation of the European patent with unitary effect (Article 4 (1) of EU Regulation 1260/2012), namely:
- into an official language of either the participating Member State in which the alleged infringement took place; or
- into an official language of the Member State in which the alleged infringer is domiciled.

150 If the alleged patent infringer is not a major company but rather "*an SME, a natural person or a non-profit organization, a university or a public research organization*" (Article 4 (4) of Regulation (EU) 1260/2012), then the infringement court may take the fact that the infringer did not have a translation available into consideration when awarding damages, i.e. this can serve to reduce the damages.

151 The infringement court may also order a translation upon its own motion (Article 4 (2) of Regulation (EU) 1260/2012).

2. Translations During a Transitional Period

152 During a transitional period which is to last no longer than 12 years following the date of application of EU Regulation 1260/2012, a patent proprietor applying for a Unitary Patent must submit his request for unitary effect along with a translation of the patent's description, namely:
- in a language of the European Union,[28] where the European patent was granted in English; or
- in English, where the European patent was granted in German or French.

possible in Denmark, Finland, Austria, Poland, Sweden and Hungary and under special conditions in France and Germany.

28 Note that this language does not necessarily have to be a language of a Member State participating in the EPC Agreement; i.e. Polish or Spanish would also be possible in principle, even though both countries remain (by choice) outside the Unitary Patent System; see also *Keussen* in *Tilmann/Plassmann* Note 7 to Regulation (EU) 1260/2012.

This translation is intended to serve informational purposes only. Six years after the date of application of Regulation (EU) 1260/2012 and every two years thereafter, an independent expert committee will carry out an objective evaluation to determine whether the machine-translation software developed by the EPO is good enough to warrant dispensing with the required translations. If this is the case, the transitional period of 12 years may be terminated prematurely. 153

The respective mandatory translation must be enclosed along with the request for unitary effect (see Para. 136). If this is not done, a deficiency notice will be sent out (see Para. 143), whereupon the missing translation many still be submitted within one month's time. If this deadline is missed, the only remaining option will be to seek a re-establishment of rights. 154

3. Compensation for Translations

Under specific circumstances that occur relatively rarely in practice, compensation may be obtained for having to prepare the aforementioned translations. 155

According to Rule 8 of the UPP Rules, compensation will be granted to the patent proprietor for preparing a mandatory translation if the following conditions apply: 156
- The residence or principal place of business of the proprietor of a European Patent – or, if there are multiple proprietors, of all proprietors – is located in a Member State of the European Union;
- The respective European patent application – or the prior international patent application, if any – was not filed in one of the official languages of the European Patent Office i.e. either in German, English or French, as required under Article 14 EPC;

whereby the patent proprietor must also be one of the following:
- a small or medium-sized enterprise as defined by the EU;[29]
- a natural person; or
- a non-profit organization as defined by the EU,[30] or a university or public research organization.

The compensation in question will be limited to the fixed sum of 500 €, however (Article 4 of the Rules Relating to Fees).

The request for compensation is to be lodged as a declaration along with the request for unitary effect. The European Patent Office will then confirm that the appropriate declaration was lodged and that there are no doubts as to its veracity. The lump-sum compensation amount will then be paid out via wire transfer. Reimbursement of the compensation cannot be demanded once it has been lawfully paid out. This will hold true even if the patent is transferred or if the status of the patent proprietor changes, e.g. if the relevant enterprise experiences strong growth. 157

29 Recommendation (EC) 2003/361 of the European Commission of 6 May 2003.
30 Regulation (EU) 1290/2013.

158 But if the European Patent Office has justified reservations, then it can invite the patent proprietor to provide corresponding evidence, such as a balance sheet or a declaration on the size of his workforce (Rule 10 of the UPP Rules). If this review leads the European Patent Office to conclude that a false declaration was filed, it will invite the patent proprietor to pay an additional fee composed of the compensation amount paid plus an administrative fee of 50%, i.e. a total of 750 €. This amount will be payable along with the next annual fee to fall due (if applicable, within the grace period). If this additional fee is not paid in time, the patent will lapse.

I. Annual Fees

159 The annual fees for the Unitary Patents were approved on 15 December 2014, when the so-called "True TOP 4" Proposal made by the European Patent Office was accepted (Article 2 of the Rules Relating to Fees).

160 This proposal was based on the cumulative fees of Germany, France, Great Britain and the Netherlands.[31] Thus, the following schedule of annual fees was derived:

2nd Year: 35 €	8th Year: 815 €	15th Year: 2,830 €
3rd Year: 105 €	9th Year: 990 €	16th Year: 3,240 €
4th Year: 145 €	10th Year: 1,175 €	17th Year: 3,640 €
5th Year: 315 €	11th Year: 1,460 €	18th Year: 4,055 €
6th Year: 475 €	12th Year: 1,775 €	19th Year: 4,455 €
7th Year: 630 €	13th Year: 2,105 €	20th Year: 4,855 €
	14th Year: 2,455 €	

I. Payment of the Annual fees

161 According to Article 9 (1) (e) of the EU Unitary Patent Regulation, the annual fees are to be remitted to the European Patent Office. This is regulated in more detail under Rule 13 of the UPP Rules, which also stipulates, quite sensibly, that the payment deadlines for the annual fees for Unitary Patents will be the same as for European patent applications.

162 Accordingly, the due date will be the respectively last day of the month. Late payment may still be made within six months' time by adding a surcharge of 50%. After that, the only remaining option will be to seek a re-establishment of rights.

31 Note: These were the four Member States participating in the EPC Agreement which had the highest number of performed validations before Italy's announcement that it would accede to the Unitary Patent System. Otherwise, Italy would have ranked as the fourth state in lieu of the Netherlands. These annual fees were not changed even after the exit of Great Britain.

An interim regulation applies to patents already granted: If an annual fee would normally fall due after the mention of grant is published, but before the communication of the registration date is notified (see Para. 141), then this latter date of notification will serve as the due date. The fee may still be paid free of any surcharge within three months of this date.[32] 163

II. Statement of Willingness to Grant a License

As is the case with many national annual fees, the patent proprietor may also reduce the annual fees by submitting a statement to the European Patent Office in which he declares that he is prepared to allow any person to use the invention as a licensee in return for appropriate consideration. The statement of willingness to grant a license will then be published in the Register for Unitary Patent Protection (Rule 12 of the UPP Rules). 164

If a license is granted, the reduction in the annual fees will amount to only 15%, however, (Article 3 of the Rules Relating to Fees). When it comes to German Patents, for example, the reduction would equal 50%. 165

If the statement of willingness to grant a license is withdrawn, then said withdrawal will not take effect until the amount by which the renewal fees were reduced is paid to the European Patent Office 166

A statement of willingness to grant a license may not be issued if an exclusive license has already been registered or applied for. Conversely, an exclusive license may not be registered so long as a patent is covered by a statement of willingness to grant a license. 167

Legal actions brought for payment of license fees on the basis of a statement of willingness to grant a license will fall under the jurisdiction of the Unified Patent Court (see Para. 1256 et seqq.). 168

32 See also the thorough explanation provided in the European Patent Guide published by the European Patent Office.

Chapter 4: Strategic Considerations for the Unitary Patent

Contents Para

169 The strategic considerations discussed in this chapter will first of all focus on the question of whether European patent applications granted in the future ought to be validated as Unitary Patents or if they should continue to be validated nationally, as hitherto, in the corresponding Member States. Only after this first step will we proceed to the second step of examining the strategic considerations that appear purposeful in connection with pursuing a Unitary Patent.

170 The current validation rate of Unitary Patents is about 30%, which, for the reasons that will be discussed in the following, must be called a success.

171 It again bears noting at this point that a national validation will necessarily have to be performed in those designation states which are not covered by the Unitary Patent if one wishes to obtain protection in these countries.

A. Unitary Patent or National Validations?

172 Let us now address the first question: Should the Unitary Patent be selected or not? In making this decision, the following key points will have to be weighed:

- Cost factors and competition-related aspects;
- Legal questions, particularly ones relating to the Unified Patent Court.

I. Cost Considerations

For many applicants, the aforementioned decision of whether to opt for a Unitary Patent or for national validations will depend primarily on the costs involved. Key cost variables to be considered include: the one-time validation costs which can be saved through the Unitary Patent; the annual renewal fees which will have to be paid over the long term; the translation costs that may accrue during the transitional period. 173

1. Costs of Validation

The illustration on Page 50 shows the translation requirements applicable for the Member States potentially participating in the Unitary Patent[1] when it comes to validating national patent rights. 174

No translations are required in: *Belgium, Germany, France, Ireland, Luxemburg* and *Monaco.* 175

Translations of only the patent claims are required in: *Denmark, Finland, Croatia, Latvia, Lithuania, the Netherlands, Sweden, Slovenia* and *Hungary.* 176

However, an English translation of the patent description will usually have to submitted as well. This is the case in *Denmark, Finland, Croatia, the Netherlands, Sweden* and *Hungary.* 177

Translations of the entire patent[2] are required in *Bulgaria, Estonia, Greece, Italy, Malta, Austria, Poland, Portugal, Romania, Slovakia, Czech Republic* and *Cyprus.* 178

1 Note: This is effective as of March 2026. States which belong to the EPC but which are (by necessity) not covered by the Unitary Patent, such as Great Britain, Norway or also Switzerland, are not marked in the diagram, since national validation cannot be substituted by the Unitary Patent in these countries anyhow. Given that Poland has stated that it will not ratify the UPC Agreement for the time being, the Unitary Patent will not become applicable there either, at least for the foreseeable future. Poland was nevertheless included in the UPC Agreement, since it had signaled a willingness to ratify in principle.

2 Note: One must of course also consider that translations may be waived in Austria depending on the language used in the original application filing.

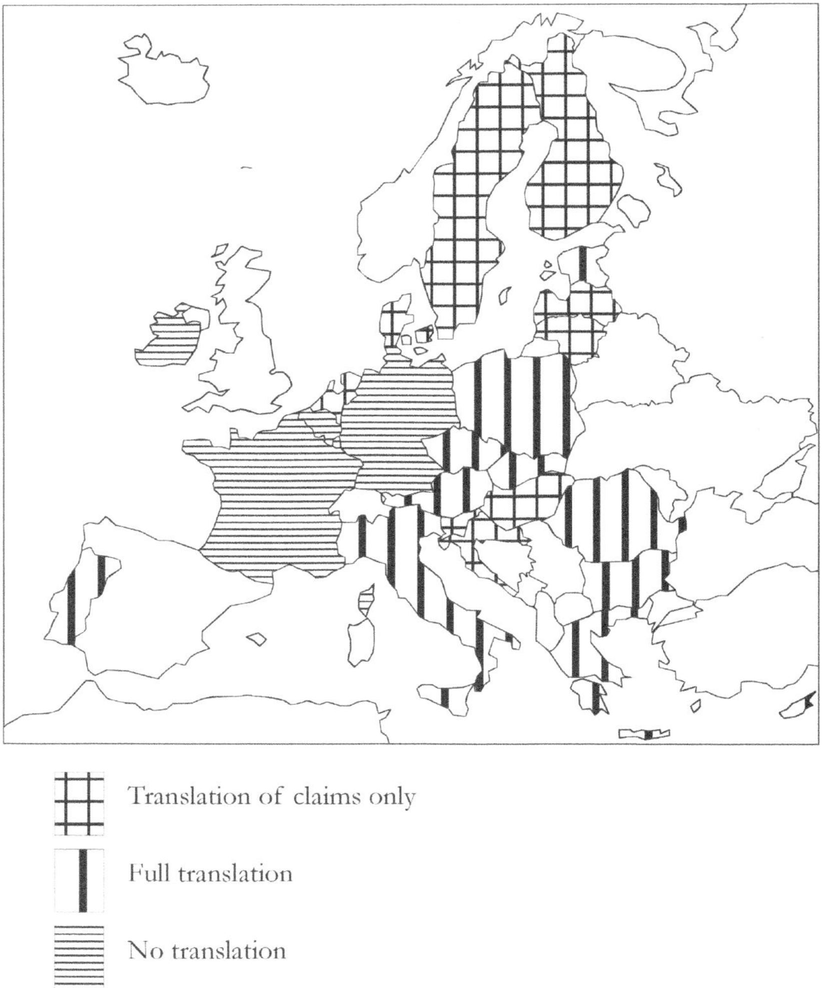

Fig. 4.1 Translation requirements for UPC countries

179 Many of the countries which demand full or partial translations also require that national representatives be appointed, which further increases the associated cost.

180 Given the requirements, the best strategy to follow will be the one which is best fit for the respective applicant and for the specific patent, given that the relevant factors may vary widely depending on the standard practices followed in each field of

technology. This can be illustrated by looking at applications and nationalizations performed under the Patent Cooperation Treaty (PCT).

In the mechanical engineering sector, for example, where applications rarely comprise more than 20 pages of text, the annual renewal fees usually constitute the main cost item in the overall cost calculation over a patent's entire life. Thus, these annual renewal fees become the decisive factor for selecting the identity and number of the countries in which to pursue the nationalization of PCT applications (this according to *Meyer*[3]). But in the biotechnology sector, where applications with 100 or more pages are not uncommon, the annual renewal fees almost always take second place to the translation costs.[4] 181

Renewal fees for applications and patents accrue annually and increase in amount year by year. Translations, by contrast, have to be prepared only once, albeit at the very outset of the granting and nationalization process. Thus, these are two completely worlds from the standpoint of patent strategy. 182

It also bears noting in conclusion that, particularly when validations are pursued in a large number of countries, increased administrative time and effort will have to be incurred, not to mention the heightened risk of losing a patent due to missed deadlines or formal errors – the latter being an area where the danger rises particularly steeply. A Unitary Patent, by contrast, merely requires a single filing, and there is also no need to coordinate with a bevy of correspondent attorneys in other countries. 183

Calculating the internal cost-savings involved will naturally be difficult, but they must be duly factored in if the cost projection is to be reliable. So they should at least be estimated. 184

2. Annual Renewal Fees

Every nationally validated patent-protection right entails the payment of annual renewal fees under the respective national legal system. These fees have to be weighed against the annual renewal fees associated with the Unitary Patent. As in the validation procedure itself (see Para. 135 et seqq.), here, too, the administrative time and expense involved, as well as a risk of forfeiting rights, will rise disproportionately as the number of validated countries increases. 185

The annual renewal fees for the Unitary Patent are derived from the fees charged in the four states with the highest number of validations: Germany, France, Great Britain and the Netherlands (i.e. before Italy's announcement that it would join the Unitary Patent System and before Great Britain's announced exit from the System). Yet the majority of European patents are actually validated in three or fewer states, 186

3 *Meyer*, lecture at the *Patente-Tagung* (Patent Conference) held on 15 March 2010.

4 Note: The upshot, of course, is that biotech patents are significantly more costly than mechanical engineering patents.

i.e. Germany, France and Great Britain at the most,[5] whereby this last country does not even participate in the Unitary Patent System.

187 The following schedule compares the cumulative annual renewal fees for Germany and France[6] with those charged for the Unitary Patent and by the European Patent Office:

Year	DE + FR	Unitary Patent	European Patent Office
2	38 €	35 €	0 €
3	108 €	105 €	690
4	108 €	145 €	845
5	138 €	315 €	1000
6	226 €	475 €	1155
7	306 €	630 €	1310
8	416 €	815 €	1465
9	530 €	990 €	1620
10	650 €	1,175 €	1775
11	800 €	1,460 €	1775
12	980 €	1,775 €	1775
13	1180 €	2,105 €	1775
14	1380 €	2,455 €	1775
15	1590 €	2,830 €	1775
16	1830 €	3,240 €	1775
17	2070 €	3,640 €	1775
18	2320 €	4,055 €	1775
19	2570 €	4,455 €	1775
20	2,830 €	4,855 €	1775

5 For a full discussion, see the strategic considerations presented in Para. 251 et seqq.

6 Note: Britain has been omitted; national validation is the sole option effective here. Data of as of 15 March 2026.

The comparative situation is further illustrated in the following diagram:

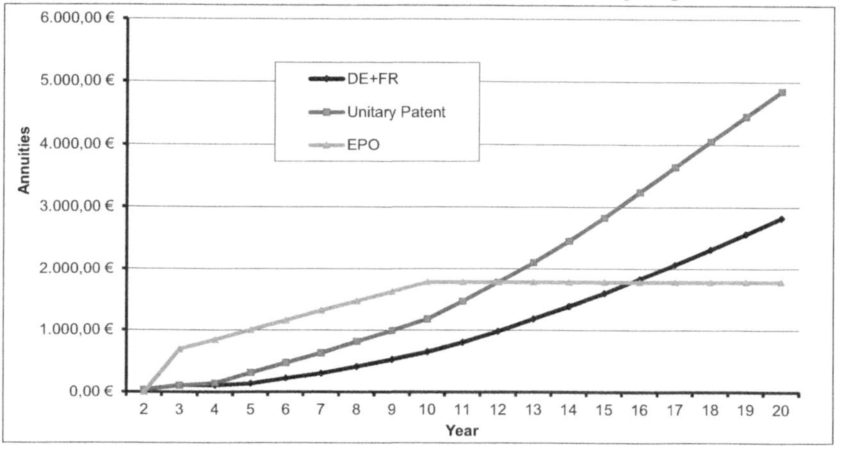

Fig. 4.2 Comparative annuities

This clearly shows that the Unitary Patent is markedly more expensive than nationalization in Germany and France alone. Thus, applicants/patent proprietors will have to decide whether the Unitary Patent's additional territorial reach is worth paying the higher annual renewal fees. 188

But there are two additional factors to be considered in connection with fees: 189

a) The "Quantum Leap" or "Marginal Cost" Effect

The Unitary Patent needs to be evaluated from the standpoint of the so-called "quantum leap" effect or "marginal cost" effect. 190

Under the current validation system, each additional country added to the validation list entails added costs. This will no longer be the case with the Unitary Patent, however, since its costs are not contingent on the number of countries involved. 191

The standard practice thus far has been to validate in, say, five or six countries simply because the marginal cost of adding one or two more did not justify the extra cost. Bu this may well change in the future thanks to the Unitary Patent. For in certain situations, the added costs that would normally have sufficed for just a single additional validation country could now bring all the countries covered by Unitary Patent within reach in one fell swoop. Thereby more than justifying the additional cost. The following graph makes this clear: 192

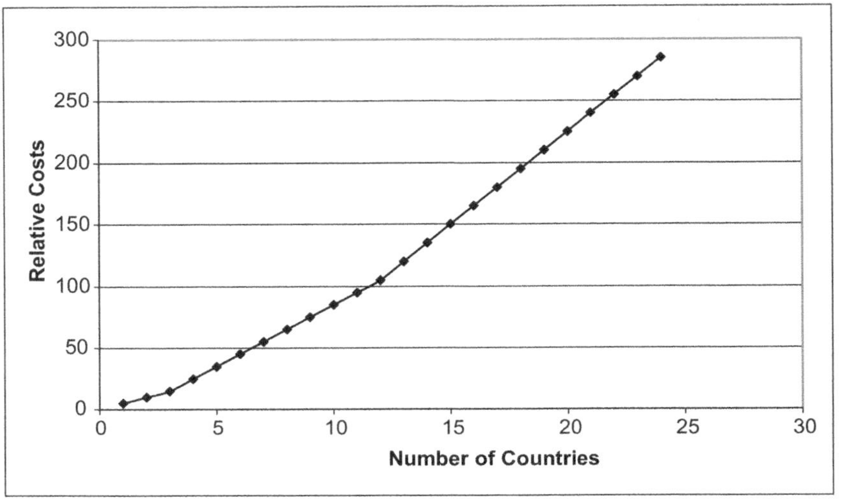

Fig. 4.3 Schematic validation costs

193 The graph provides a useful, if highly schematic, overview of the estimated marginal costs (i.e. validation costs and annual renewal fees) which accrue within the first years of a patent's date of grant depending on the number of countries involved. For the sake of simplicity, the marginal costs were assigned a value of 5 for states that do not require translations, a value of 10 for states requiring translations of patent claims only, and a value of 15 for states requiring full patent translations. This is obviously a rough approach, but it suffices for purposes of our strategic analysis. Particularly given the fact that the cost situation can differ markedly from patent to patent.

194 Now if one were to draw the same curve for the Unitary Patent, the result would be a straight line, since the Unitary Patent applies for all countries. If we assign a value of, say, 30 to the Unitary Patent's marginal costs – merely as an estimate, since precision is not crucial here – then the graph would look like this:

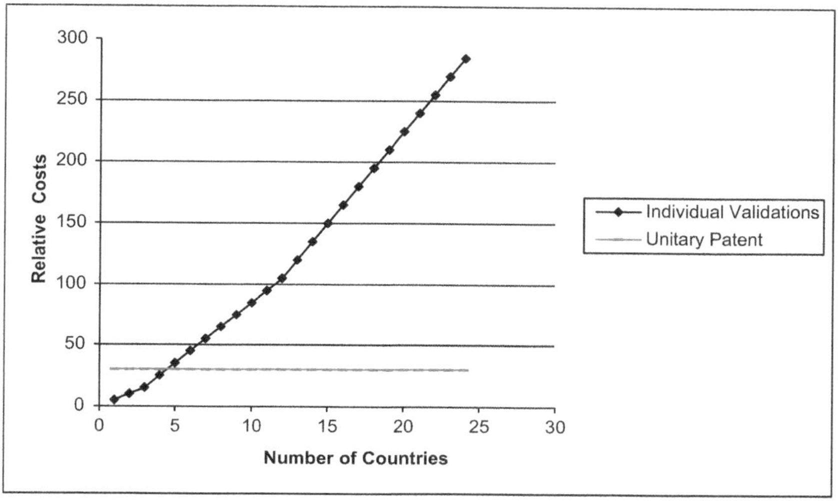

Fig. 4.4 Schematic validation costs and unitary patent

What jumps out at us from the graph is that the Unitary Patent becomes cheaper than the national validation approach once the threshold of five countries is reached. But there is another point to consider as well: 195

We also see from the graph that there is a "grey area" – starting at three or four countries or so – in which bearing the added costs for the Unitary Patent is worth considering even though the Unitary Patent is more expensive than the national validation route. The reason is simple: Under the old, individual nationalization system, the added amount otherwise spent on the Unitary Patent would only suffice to secure one or two more countries. But spending that same amount on the Unitary Patent can now serve to secure all the countries that are still missing, i.e. possibly twenty or more. 196

Thus, one can speak of a veritable "quantum leap" in that the marginal costs for additional countries are reduced to zero. So that if one switches over to the Unitary Patent, one can obtain these countries practically for free. Which in turn could encourage an applicant/patent proprietor to reevaluate some of the countries which he had perhaps dismissed as not sufficiently promising. 197

If one had to obtain individual validation in those countries while having to provide a full patent translation, one would probably decide that paying the added costs was not worthwhile. But if one were to obtain this additional patent protection for nothing, this could well change the calculus of priorities. 198

199 The Unitary Patent option becomes particularly interesting when the patent proprietor is at least potentially interested in granting licenses. Licensees[7] will be willing to pay license royalties in return for their revenues only if corresponding patent-protection rights are in place, and this wholly irrespective of whether the licensor is likely to enforce the patents or not. The disadvantages that used to prevail till now in countries like Romania – i.e. comparatively high validation costs due to the need for a full patent translation and (at least presumed) uncertainties regarding enforceability – will no longer exist with the Unitary Patent. Which in turn opens up entirely new opportunities.

200 There is a parallel mechanism in the patent universe, namely the system of designation fees for European Patent applications. Back when individual designation fees still applied, along with a maximum limit of seven designation countries, it was practically unheard of for anybody to pay the designation fees for just six or five countries. Instead, applicants preferred to pay the seven-fold fee so as to get all countries "into the bargain."[8] Even further back in time, when the maximum limit was not yet in place, the opposite trend was observed: Designating five or six countries was the norm; all countries, the exception.[9]

201 All these factors clearly speak in favor of the Unitary Patent when one is working in the "grey area" in terms of the number of intended national validations. Still, the exact point at which the "quantum leap" effect becomes relevant for a specific patent-protection right is something that will have to be determined on a case-by-case basis. For as explained earlier, the prevailing situation for each patent will depend on a slew of individual factors, not least of which being the length of the patent description.

202 All things considered, one can safely assume that benefits will begin to kick in once the number of intended validation states reaches four or five, i.e. it will then make sense to consider the Unitary Patent as a potentially preferable solution.

b) The "Dilution" Effect

203 When performing the cost calculation, one must by no means overlook the so-called "dilution" effect. This refers to the observed phenomenon that, as the duration of the intended patent protection increases, there will be a tendency to abandon individual countries in order to save costs. With the result that only a few countries will be left in the end – often only Germany, France and Great Britain, but in most cases Germany alone. This cost-saving tendency is a factor that needs to be considered on the "pro" side of individual validation.

7 Note: In certain cases, it is actually forbidden under cartel law to make royalty payments when no patent protection is in place; i.e. here one should substitute "will be willing to" with "will be permitted to."

8 See, inter alia, *Eaton* et al, "International Patenting and the European Patent Office: A Quantitative Assessment," National Bureau of Economic Research, 2003; this is available online at http://www.nber.org/CRIW/papers/eaton.pdf.

9 See the EPO's Annual Reports from 1994–1997.

The strength of the dilution effect will naturally depend on each applicant's individual patent strategy. Not to mention on whether the applicant is a major corporation handling several hundred patent grants per year or just a small to mid-sized company. Then there is also the strategy – followed by many applicants – of limiting one's filings right from the outset to those patents deemed to be the most important, and to then secure (territorially) broad and (temporally) long-lasting protection for said patents. In certain technological sectors such as pharmaceuticals, experience has shown that patents are seldom abandoned. On the contrary, supplemental protection certificates are used to further extend the duration of patent protection, if they are available. 204

This said, it can still be useful to at least approximate the cost-savings achievable through such dilution. Statistical surveys on this topic may be found in the work of *Danguy/Pottelsberghe de la Potterie.*[10] 205

According to these surveys, the initial validation rate for Germany amounts to 90 %.[11] The numbers remain high for later years as well, particularly for patents that were validated right at the outset. These are still in force in the 8th, 12th, 16th and 20th patent year at a rate of 87 %, 64 %, 39 % and 19 %, respectively. The numbers for France are somewhat lower but still on the same order of magnitude. 206

For countries like Sweden, on the other hand, the initial validation rate is only 19 %. Of these initially validated patents, only 43 %, 31 %, 17 % and 9 % are still in force in the 8th, 12th, 16th and 20th patent year, respectively. The numbers for other countries such as Denmark, Finland, Ireland and Belgium are comparable. 207

So we see that a marked dilution effect occurs. Whereby many of the relatively few patents validated in countries like Sweden and Denmark are abandoned after a rather short time. Only in Germany and France do we see roughly 15–20 % of all patents run until the very end of their term. 208

In the case of the Unitary Patent, however, no such dilution will be possible. This has to be duly factored into the cost calculation. We can see how this works from a simple case example. Let us consider a patent which is to be validated in Germany, France, the Netherlands and Sweden. 209

10 *J. Danguy/B. Pottelsberghe de la Potterie*, "Cost/Benefit Analysis of the Community Patent," Brueghel Working Paper 2009/08. Although the cost analysis performed in this book is not found in this paper, (surprisingly enough). More recent data is not publicly available, unfortunately.

11 It bears noting that the ratio of European Patents issued but never validated is estimated at 10 % by the aforementioned authors. This is based on data for 2006, however, i.e. before the London Agreement's entry into force. Even if corroborating data is still lacking, we can safely assume that the ratio has fallen markedly since then due to the more relaxed requirements that prevail in the "core countries" of Germany, France and Great Britain.

210 Assume that the annual renewal fees for the 8th, 12th, 16th and 20th patent year are as follows:[12]

Year	DE	FR	NL	SE	Total
8	240.00 €	136.00 €	280.00 €	240.00 €	896.00 €
12	620.00 €	300.00 €	600.00 €	380.00 €	1,900.00 €
16	1,230.00 €	510.00 €	1,000.00 €	540.00 €	3,280.00 €
20	1,940.00 €	790.00 €	1,400.00 €	700.00 €	4,830.00 €

211 Now we also have to allow for the fact that, e.g. in the 12th year, 64 % of all the originally validated German patents will still be in force, as compared with only 55 % of all French ones, and a mere 31 % of all Swedish ones. So that over time, the average patent will become more "German," somewhat less "French" and decidedly less "Swedish."

212 According to the available data, the retention ratio of valid patents in Germany is invariably higher than in other countries. So in order to arrive at a quantitative estimate, we should reflect this reality by applying adjusting factors. This is done below:

Year	DE	FR	"Factor"	NL	"Factor"	SE	"Factor"
8	87 %	80 %	0.92	51 %	0.59	43 %	0.49
12	64 %	55 %	0.86	37 %	0.58	31 %	0.48
16	39 %	33 %	0.85	22 %	0.56	17 %	0.44
20	19 %	17 %	0.89	11 %	0.58	9 %	0.47

213 Just to be clear: The fact that the patent-retention rate in Germany falls from 87 % in the 8th patent year to 19 % in the 20th patent year is not significant in this context. What counts is that the ratios for the other countries fall even more steeply by comparison – there would be no dilution effect if this were not so. This is why Germany's respective ratio in a given patent year was taken the benchmark and assigned a value of 1. The respective percentages for the other countries were then calculated in relation to that benchmark.

214 If we apply these factors to the above schedule of fees, we arrive at the following revised fee schedule:

Year	Germany	France	Netherlands	Sweden	Total	Variance
8	240.00 €	125.06 €	164.14 €	118.62 €	647.82 €	27.70 %

12 Effective as of 1 December 2020. Sweden's figures are converted and rounded in euros. The exactitude of the numbers is not crucial here; what counts is the approximate order of magnitude, thus these data has not been updated ever since.

Year	Germany	France	Netherlands	Sweden	Total	Variance
12	620.00 €	257.81 €	346.88 €	184.06 €	1,408.75 €	25.86 %
16	1,230.00 €	431.54 €	564.10 €	235.38 €	2,461.03 €	24.97 %
20	1,940.00 €	706.84 €	810.53 €	331.58 €	3,788.95 €	21.55 %

If we now compare the cumulated annual renewal fees to the factor-adjusted annual renewal fees, we get the following picture: 215

Year	Cumulated Annual Fees	Adjusted Annual Fees	Variance
8	896.00 €	647.82 €	27.70 %
12	1,900.00 €	1,408.75 €	25.86 %
16	3,280.00 €	2,461.03 €	24.97 %
20	4,830.00 €	2,788.95 €	21.55 %

After duly allowing for the "dilution" effect, we arrive at a variance of ca. 20–30 %, i.e. a significant value. Here we should also bear in mind that switching over to the Unitary Patent will probably not make sense for patents which are to be validated in only three states. Meaning that the "dilution effect" will generally make itself felt above the 20 % threshold rather than below it. 216

Admittedly, the above schedule is just a basic calculation model. The results could well vary depending on the national fees of the state one choses to examine. But this is not really relevant to our present discussion of strategic patent considerations. What is relevant and worthy of note is that a variance of more than negligible extent exists, i.e. one that amounts to least ca. 20 % but more frequently ranges around 30 %. 217

If we now wish to make a quantitative comparison between the annual renewal fees of the Unitary Patent and the national fees, then we will have to take this variance into account. To put it another way: The variance represents the margin by which the Unitary Patent is too expensive, given that it can be temporally extended only in its entirety, thus making dilution impossible. The upshot is that the longer the duration of patent protection, the less attractive the Unitary Patent becomes by comparison. 218

3. Translation Costs During the Transitional Period

For the first few years after the Unitary Patent becomes available, it will be mandatory to submit translations of the patent description in English or in another language of the European Union. 219

In practice, this will translate into higher costs for German-speaking applicants only when no English-language equivalent exists, such as a US patent filing for the European Patent. But since such an English equivalent usually does exist, it is likely that any added costs will generally be limited. In any case, many states signatory to the 220

London Agreement, such as the Netherlands or Denmark, already make it mandatory to submit an English translation during the validation process. Thus, the applicant must expect to pay analogous translation costs in these countries assuming they are of interest to him.

221 Those applicants who usually submit their filings in English, on the other hand, will frequently incur additional effort and expense unless they rely on machine translations. These should be used with caution, however, since there is always the risk that they could cause a patent to become unenforceable during an infringement proceeding. In other words, the infringement court could find that the text submitted – even if only intended for informational purposes – deviates so markedly from the substantive content of the original text that it can no longer be deemed a proper translation. The fact that precisely this finding was made in a number of judgments handed down by the German courts of instance in 2009 and 2010 should serve as a strong warning.[13] (Although it should also be noted that these judgments no longer involve currently applicable law and that they were ultimately overturned by the German Federal Court of Justice (BGH)).

222 The aforementioned translation costs will be incurred on top of the costs that already come with the validation of a Unitary Patent.

4. Italy as the Decisive Factor?

223 An applicant's decision on whether to opt for a Unitary Patent will frequently depend on whether or not he is interested in securing patent-protection in Italy, which is a member of the Unitary Patent System. Two key factors come into play here:

1) Italy requires a full patent translation and the appointment of national representatives; and
2) Italy represents a rather sizeable European market, one that accounts for ca. 10 % of the EU's GDP.

224 These costs for a full translation and for national representatives can be saved if the applicant opts to validate his patent as a Unitary Patent in Italy. In other words, the Unitary Patent becomes more attractive in direct proportion to Italy's commercial importance to the applicant.

225 It bears noting that if a patent validated in Italy as a Unitary Patent is infringed in Italy, this will not necessarily entail conducting a proceeding before a local Italian division of the Unified Patent Court (see Para. 383 et seqq.). On the other hand, legal proceedings before an Italian court are currently mandatory if one intends to pursue

---

13 See the Ruling of the Düsseldorf District Court (*Landgericht*), No. InstGE 11, 1, in the *Aufblasventil* case, Mitt. 2009, p. 234 as well as the Ruling of the Higher District Court (*Oberlandesgericht*) of Munich, No. 6 U 3322/06 of 28 May 2009; see also *Kühnen*, Mitt. 2009, p. 345. This case law was vacated by the Federal Court of Justice's Judgement No. Xa ZR 74/09 of 18 March 2010 in the *Nabenschaltung II* case, which overturned the prior Ruling of the Higher District Court (OLG) of Munich, GRUR 2010, p. 708.

a patent infringement case in Italy. This, too, makes the Unitary Patent interesting for an applicant seeking to obtain patent protection in Italy.

5. Cost Considerations and Overall Conclusion

Thus, a proper breakdown of costs would look as follows: 226

For **individual validations**: The costs for the validation, including translations, national representatives (if applicable), administrative costs and payment-transaction costs, plus the annual renewal fees, which should however be reduced by a "dilution factor" of between 20 % to 30 %.

For the **Unitary Patent**: The costs for the validation, plus any translations and annual renewal fees, whereby the marginal costs impact associated with the "quantum leap" effect must also be taken into account. 227

A factor that makes selecting the right patent strategy more difficult is that the added costs for the validation will accrue shortly after the patent's date of grant, while the cost-savings achieved through dilution will only become evident as the years go by. Nevertheless, the following principles can provide general guidance: 228

Individual validations will become more cost-effective the more of the following conditions prevail: 229

- Validation is intended in fewer than five states, particularly when these are just the "Big Three," i.e. Germany, France and Great Britain;
- Validation is intended only, or at least predominantly, in states which either require no translations or which only require translations of the patent claims;
- The patent text is relatively short, e.g. fewer than twenty pages long;
- The patent text is in English, i.e. a translation into another official EU language is necessary;
- The relevant patents will be upheld for an extended duration, albeit subject to a selective "dilution;"
- The validation costs are, at most, only slightly higher than the costs for the Unitary Patent; and
- The patent proprietor is not interested in granting licenses.

The **Unitary Patent** will become more cost-effective the more of the following conditions obtain: 230

- Validation is intended in four or more states;
- Validation is also intended in states which require full patent translations, particularly Italy;
- The patent text is relatively long and contains e.g. 50 pages or more, thus making full translations expensive;
- The relevant patents are to be abandoned after only a few years **or** the relevant patents are to have a long duration without any dilution;
- Licensing is a possibility, so that the "quantum leap" effect plays an especially prominent role;

– Translations in English and in one additional official EU language are already available, e.g. because the proceeding was conducted in German and a parallel US patent filing exists, or because an English version was produced in order to facilitate translations for parallel filings in Asian countries.

231 To put it even more simply, the key question in practice will often boil down to: "Is Italy of interest?" If yes, then a Unitary Patent will be the better option. If not, then individual validation will often be preferable.

II. Legal Questions

1. Pros and Cons of the Unified Patent Court

232 Leaving aside the disadvantage that a Unitary Patent can be voided through a revocation challenge (discussed in Para. 242), the pros and cons of the Unified Patent Court must also be weighed as part of the overall picture. This is because a Unitary Patent will be intrinsically be tied in with the Unified Patent Court, while patents validated in the normal fashion will come with the option to "opt out" of the UPC, at least during a transitional period (see Para. 299 et seqq.)

233 In the early days, there was naturally a certain amount of uncertainty regarding the case law of the Unified Patent Court. However, the court has since demonstrated through its excellent work that it can be trusted.

234 However, it must also be emphasized that the Unified Patent Court undoubtedly offers patent proprietors a number of advantages and new opportunities as well. These are explained below.

235 Until now, it has usually been an unattractive proposition for a patent proprietor to sue an infringer in Eastern Europe or Italy if that infringer's production activities are confined exclusively to Eastern Europe or Italy, even if corresponding national patents are in place. Although the legal action could be moved to Germany, e.g. by making test purchases, this would not change the obvious reality that infringement proceedings brought in Germany would apply only in that country. So that a further legal action would have to be brought to force the infringer to cease and desist in his own home country.

236 Thanks to the Unified Patent Court, however, it will now be possible to obtain an enforceable writ, e.g. by bringing legal action before the local chamber in Düsseldorf,[14] which will also serve to enjoin the infringing actions committed by an Italian infringer in Italy, for example, thereby obviating the need for a second legal action.[15]

237 This possibility – and the resulting prospect of a flood of actions from foreign patent proprietors against the domestic industrial sector – is one of the main reasons why a

---

14 Note: Insofar as the (relatively low) hurdles for an infringement proceeding in Germany can be overcome. This will usually be the case, however; see Para. 383 et seqq.

15 Cf. also *Romandini/Kliczník*, IIC 2013, p. 524.

country like Poland, for example, has announced its intention to withhold ratification of the UPC Agreement for the time being.[16]

This territorial coverage is one of the main advantages of the Unified Patent Court; even with broad application of CJEU C-339/22 (BSH v. Electrolux) – see the discussion in paragraph 493 – there remains an advantage over national infringement courts. 238

Going forward, this could mean that, in order to exploit these specific advantages of the Unified Patent Court, a Unitary Patent will be selected even in cases where validation was previously obtained in only three or four countries – a situation that would normally speak against a Unitary Patent. 239

On the other hand, foregoing a Unitary Patent in favor of national validations would allow one to obtain a temporary injunction on the national level during the transitional period while still reserving the right to bring the main proceedings on the merits before the Unified Patent Court, given that this is not precluded under the "Brussels I Regulation" (see Para. 486 et seqq. for a full discussion). 240

The Unitary Patent is at a disadvantage in this regard, since exclusive jurisdiction lies with the Unified Patent Court. On the other hand, the option of suing in "double-barreled fashion," as it were, would only become an advantage if the national courts turned out to be more generous in their awards than the Unified Patent Court. So it would seem illogical to reject a Unitary Patent solely on the grounds of the UPC's exclusive jurisdiction. 241

2. Disadvantages of One-Stop Revocation Actions

A disadvantage of the Unitary Patent which must be given great weight when selecting the right patent strategy is the fact that a Unitary Patent can be overturned by bringing a "one-stop" action for revocation (see Para. 1162 et seqq.). In the individualized system, by contrast, a revocation action must be brought, at least in principle, in each and every validated state. Which can become prohibitive, given the cost and effort involved. 242

Yet if we recall that revocation challenges are usually only initiated in connection with infringement proceedings, then this disadvantage loses much of its threatening character. Since infringement proceedings, too, are national in character, the standard practice is to select one country as an "anchor country" or "first-strike jurisdiction," this almost always being Germany. Both proceedings are then conducted in only this one country.[17] 243

16 See e.g. http://www.worldipreview.com/news/will-poland-join-the-unitary-patent-system; see also *Zawadzka*, IIC 2014, p. 383.

17 According to what the author was told in person by a high-ranking staffer at a major global corporation's patent department (who wishes to remain anonymous), this goes even further in actual practice: In the mobile phone sector, for example, the infringement action will usually be abandoned, or efforts to settle will be redoubled, if and when the Higher District Court (*Landgericht*) of Düsseldorf or Mannheim suspends an infringement action because a revocation action is pending before the German Federal Patent Court. Since this

Depending on the outcome, either a settlement will be reached for the other countries or one party will simply accept defeat.[18]

244 It nevertheless remains to seen whether applicants deem the risk of a one-stop revocation action to be serious enough to avoid the Unitary Patent entirely – particularly in the pharmaceutical sector, which would otherwise stand to gain the most from the Unitary Patent. That pharma companies currently do not file Unitary Patents on a regular basis, seems mainly due to the lack of an Unitary Supplementary Protection Certificate.

3. Territorial Reach of the Unitary Patent

245 It is important to keep in mind that, in the first years after its entry into force, the Unitary Patent's territorial reach does not cover all 25 of the potential Member States,[19] but at the beginning 17, at present 18, depending on how the ratification process progresses. This will naturally serve to limit the Unitary Patent's attractiveness in the beginning. What remains to be seen is whether this temporary effect will peter out about five years or less, or whether certain states will continue to drag out the required ratifications or withhold them entirely – as Poland, for example, has said it will do.[20] In the latter case, the attractiveness of the Unitary Patent could indeed suffer.

4. Increased Legal Certainty of the Unitary Patent

246 The Unitary Patent offers increased legal certainty compared with national validations because – as explained earlier – a Unitary Patent only requires a one-time "validation." And the fact that this can be performed by the patent proprietor himself means that the administrative costs of corresponding with national attorneys in other countries can be dispensed with. Which in turn lowers the risk of missing deadlines or of forfeiting rights due to formal errors.

247 The Unitary Patent does not require any additional translation of the patent claims. The only thing needed is a translation of the patent description during a transitional period, and this only for informational purposes.

248 On the other hand, many of the states which have acceded to the London Agreement continue to require a legally binding translation of patent claims, e.g. the Netherlands or many Scandinavian countries. These countries will often also require an English translation of the text of the application filing.

---

will already be seen as a defeat for the patent proprietor, awaiting the further proceedings will often be deemed pointless.

18 Note: In Germany, prior to June 2023 only 2 % of all patent infringement actions are accompanied by a parallel proceeding in another EU Member State; see the discussion in Para. 505 et seqq.

19 The original 25 states signatory to Regulation (EU) 1257/2012 (implementing enhanced cooperation) plus Italy, which joined on 30 September 2015, but minus Great Britain, which declared in 2020 that it would not join the Unitary Patent System.

20 Cf. *Zawadzka* IIC 2014, p. 383; see also *Wszolek*, IIC 2021, p. 1142.

While translations of patent claims are often a negligible cost factor, they do pose a legal risk that must not be underestimated. For when errors in translation arise, the patent claims will initially apply as translated. And as shown by commentators like *Wurzer/Grünewalt*,[21] errors in translations are hardly a rare occurrence.[22] 249

All things considered, therefore, a Unitary Patent allows patent proprietors to obtain increased legal certainty. 250

III. Overall Conclusion

Currently approximately 30% of all patents that are granted by the European Patent Office are valiated as Unitary Patents. This is indeed a success that should not be underestimated. 251

This even more so that due to the fact that in the pharmaceutical industry, the unitary patent is often not used due to the lack of a central supplementary protection certificate. 252

On the other hand, about 70% of all granted patents by the EPO will not become Unitary Patents later on. This is not surprising. Validating in only a few states tended to be the rule in industries such as consumer goods, chemicals and automobiles, as well as in the supply sectors of these industries. 253

Indeed, the steadily increasing fees of the European Patent Office have already induced some enterprises in these industries to consider dispensing with the filing of European patent applications entirely in the future, and to instead register only one or two patents in Europe on the national level. For many of these companies, the additional costs of the Unitary patent, especially in later years, are a decisive factor not to chose the Unitary Patent at all. In the end the Unitary Patent does not generate the huge cost-savings that were envisioned at the outset for most applicants. The London Agreement probably has had a greater impact in this regard. 254

Notwithstanding the above, every applicant should keep the option of selecting a Unitary Patent open as a realistic possibility. One reason is simple: The considerable territorial coverage compared to the costs is very attractive. 255

Another advantage is that the Unified Patent Court will make it possible to bring an action in, say, Düsseldorf in order to also go after infringers operating in countries such as Bulgaria or Romania for infringements committed in their home countries.[23] Under most of the validation strategies currently in use, by contrast, there would not even be any legal basis to go after such infringements, since said strategies do not call for validation to be obtained in Bulgaria or Romania. Both countries, however, are covered by an Unitary Patent. 256

---

21 *Wurzer/Grünewalt*, Mitt. 2014, p. 520.

22 On the role of translations in patent law generally, cf. *Larroyed*, "Translation Accuracy and Dissemination of Disclosure of Patent Information."

23 Note: This is assuming that the (relatively low) hurdles for an infringement proceeding in Germany can be overcome.

B. Strategic Considerations Once the Unitary Patent is Selected

257 Presented below are a number of additional factors that ought to be considered once the decision to select a Unitary Patent has been taken.

I. Organizational Matters

258 It bears noting that no further processing is possible in the context of validating a Unitary Patents or in connection with the annual renewal fees; here, only a re-establishment of rights is possible (see Para. 130).

259 It also bears noting that this point was not regulated by means of a reference to Art. 123 of the European Patent Convention, but rather by adopting an independent provision, namely Rule 22. This was ostensibly done in order to minimize the Unified Patent Court's influence on the practical operations of the European Patent Office (see also Para. 128 et seqq.). Conversely, this also means that the proprietor of European Patents will have to proceed with particular caution so long as no established legal precedent exists on this topic, since there is no assurance that the established legal precedent of the European Patent Office will apply.

260 For attorneys acting as legal representatives in connection with Unitary Patents, this specifically means that, at least at first, they will not be able to rely on the European Patent Office's Decision No. T0942/12,[24] which would otherwise be very advantageous for them. This Decision stipulates that if a legal representative has not been expressly commissioned to monitor payment of the annual renewal fees, then his duties of care as legal counsel will not include the performance of such monitoring.

II. Should Registration Be Delayed Before a further member state joins?

261 When Romania acceded, the European Patent Office made it possible to request that the Unitary Patent be registered only after Romania's accession. If the European Patent Office proceeds in the same way for future accessions, this request should definitely be made

262 A possible, yet unfavourable, alternative strategy in such a situation might be to delay the registration by submitting an application that contains formal errors. But this would naturally entail the risk of scuttling the entire process of Unitary Patent validation. So any such stratagem should be approached with caution.

III. Sequence of Applicants

263 The Unitary Patent Regulation stipulates that, when there is more than one applicant, the Unitary Patent will be governed by the national legal system of the first-named applicant on the application. Under the old system of filing European patents, the sequence of applicants was a secondary issue. It will now play a decisive role, howe-

24 Cf. Mitt. 2016, p. 91.

ver. This will already hold true for PCT applications which are to be subsequently regionalized by the European Patent Office.

One should therefore consider whether the sequence in which the applicants are named could have ramifications for applications which have multiple applicants/ proprietors. This would be the case if two of the applicants have their place of residence or business in a Member State of the UPC Agreement. As discussed earlier (see Para. 99), this is likely to the case for many applicants, even if they appear at first glance to be coming from abroad. **264**

Assuming it is determined that the sequence of applicants will indeed have an effect, thought should be given to which national legal system should apply so that the sequence can be determined accordingly.[25] **265**

IV. Translations

As mentioned earlier (Para. 152), the process of Unitary Patent validation also requires – at least during a certain transitional period – that a translation of the patent description into English or into one other official language of the European Union be submitted as part of the filing. **266**

This translation will be for informational purposes only, however. One might therefore conclude that resorting to a machine translation would be a way to save costs. But there is always the risk that a machine translation will not prove adequate. Or that the submitted translation text will contain inaccuracies so egregious that the Unified Patent Court will reject its suitability for filing purposes. Which would then cause the patent to become null and void. As mentioned earlier (Para. 221), one is well-advised to take warning from the judgments handed down by the German courts of instance in 2009 and 2010 which led to this precise outcome.[26] **267**

So thought should be given to whether submitting a translator-prepared translation might not be preferable after all, just to be on the safe side. **268**

V. Compensation for Translations

It stands to reason that compensation for translations should be requested from the European Patent Office, assuming the very strict preconditions for this are met (see Para. 155 et seqq.) This also makes sense in view of the fact that such compensation is not recoverable even if the patent proprietor's identity or status changes. Which **269**

25 Cf. *Boos/Kreutzmann*, GRUR-Prax 2015, p. 428, with additional suggestions on contractual structuring.

26 See the Ruling of the District Court (LG) of Düsseldorf, No. InstGE 11, 1 in the *Aufblasventil* case, Mitt. 2009, p. 234; as well as the Higher District Court (OLG) of Munich's Ruling No. 6 U 3322/06 of 28 May 2009; see also *Kühnen*, Mitt. 2009, p. 345. This case law was vacated by the German Federal Court of Justice's Judgement No. Xa ZR 74/09 of 18 March 2010 in the *Nabenschaltung II* case, which had previously been adjudicated by the Higher District Court (OLG) of Munich, GRUR 2010, p. 708.

in turn means that there is no need to spend money to review said status, in contrast to the situation in the USA, for example, where "small entity status" has to be formally verified.

VI. Statement of Willingness to Grant a License

270 It bears noting here that many applicants, especially major corporations, opt to issue a statement of willingness to grant a license for their patents wherever possible, thereby saving on costs.[27] Based on practical experience, the potential negative consequences of this approach – namely that a competitor will simply go ahead and request a license – are manageable. Some companies have actually never encountered such a situation in practice. If the decision is later taken to go after a competitor on the basis of a patent, the obvious first step will be to revoke the statement of willingness to grant a license and to pay down the patent's outstanding renewal fees.

271 The 15 % savings rate achievable in this context through the Unitary Patent is rather modest, however. This is in contrast to the roughly 50 % savings rate which can usually be achieved in most European countries like Germany or Great Britain. But since the annual renewal fees for the Unitary Patent are relatively high, this cost-savings should probably not be dismissed. Thus, one should not be overly hasty in ruling out a statement of willingness to grant a license.

27 See e.g. *Bauch*, lecture presented to the *VPP-Bezirksgruppe Mitte-Nord* (Mid-North District of the Association of Intellectual Property Experts) on 1 April 2014 in Hanover, Germany.

Part 3: The Unified Patent Court

Section 1: Structure and Jurisdiction

Chapter 5: Structure and Jurisdiction of the Unified Patent Court

Contents Para

A. Legal Personality and Jurisdiction of the Unified Patent Court

I. Legal Personality

272 The Unified Patent Court was established based on the Agreement on a Unified Patent Court of 19 February 2013 (UPC Agreement), which was conceived as an international treaty but which is open exclusively to Member States of the EU

(Article 2).[1] In theory, Member States of EU which do not belong to the Unitary Patent System could also accede to the UPC Agreement, since being part of the system is not a precondition (cf. Article 84 (4) of the UPC Agreement). Italy was following this approach for a certain time, but ultimately agreed to accede to the EU Regulations concerning the Unitary Patent on 30 September 2015.

Both the UPC Agreement as well as the associated EU Regulations must be regarded as something completely new, as a *sui generis* legal framework.[2] If this should turn out to have legal gaps, one cannot simply assume that they will be filled by adopting customary practices from this or that national legal system. **273**

The Unified Patent Court is described as follows in Article 4 of the UPC Agreement: **274**

> "The Court shall have legal personality in each Contracting Member State and shall enjoy the most extensive legal capacity accorded to legal persons under the national law of that State."

Based on the wording, however, this only applies to the Court as a whole; the Court's individual organs, such as its various divisions, will not possess independent legal personality.[3] The Unified Patent Court's status as a European Court and as a court within the meaning of Article 149a of the European Patent Convention (EPC) is discussed in Para. 484 et seqq. and then also in Para. 490 et seqq.

The Unified Patent Court is represented externally by the President of the Court of Appeal. He also serves as Chairman of the UPC's Presidium (see Para. 297). **275**

It bears noting that, by virtue of the Protocols on the Privileges and Immunities of the Unified Patent Court,[4] the UPC's judges enjoy the corresponding privileges and immunities in each Member State (cf. Para. 36). **276**

II. Jurisdiction

The Unified Patent Court is competent for: (Article 3) **277**

- all Unitary Patents; as well as
- all European patents, including those which were already granted by the time the UPC is established. These latter patents will be covered by the so-called "opt-out" option, however (see Para. 299 et seqq.).

1 Note: The question of whether and how Great Britain could still have remained part of the Unitary Patent System as a "former EU Member State" has already been discussed; see Para. 24 et seqq.
2 Cf. *Hilty* et al, Max Planck Institute for Intellectual Property & Research; Competition Law Research Paper Nos. 13–16; here the rules are even regarded as a possible model for national proceedings and regulations; cf. also *Hilty/Romandini*, Max Planck Institute for Innovation and Competition Research Paper Nos. 18–09; as well as *Schovsbo* et al., IIC 2015, p. 27.
3 Cf. *Tilmann* in *Tilmann/Plassmann*, Note 29 et seqq. to the introduction to the UPC Agreement.
4 Protocol on the Privileges and Immunities of the Unified Patent Court of 29 June 2016.

278 In addition, the UPC is also competent for:

- all supplementary protection certificates derived from European Patents, including ones which already exist.[5]

279 With respect to all the aforementioned patents, the Unified Patent Court is competent for (Article 32):

- patent-infringement proceedings and patent validity proceedings; as well as
- all legal actions challenging decisions made by the European Patent Office with respect to unitary effect.

280 This last area of jurisdiction means that, for the first time, decisions of the European Patent Office will be subject to review by an external court.[6]

281 The Unified Patent Court is furthermore competent for actions for compensation for licenses on the basis of a statement of willingness to grant a license for a Unitary Patent (see Para. 164 et seqq. and Para. 1256 et seqq.)

282 The UPC's territorial jurisdiction first and foremost covers the Member States. These are the same states for which a Unitary Patent can be obtained (cf. Para. 79). As of this writing, these are:

> Belgium, Bulgaria, Denmark, Germany, Estonia, Finland, France, Italy, Latvia, Lithuania. Luxemburg, Malta, the Netherlands, Austria, Portugal, Romania, Sweden and Slovenia.

5 See also *Czettritz/Schallmoser*, Mitt 2018, p. 309.
6 Cf. *Hüttermann*, Mitt. 2014, p. 546.

The current situation is illustrated by the following map: **283**

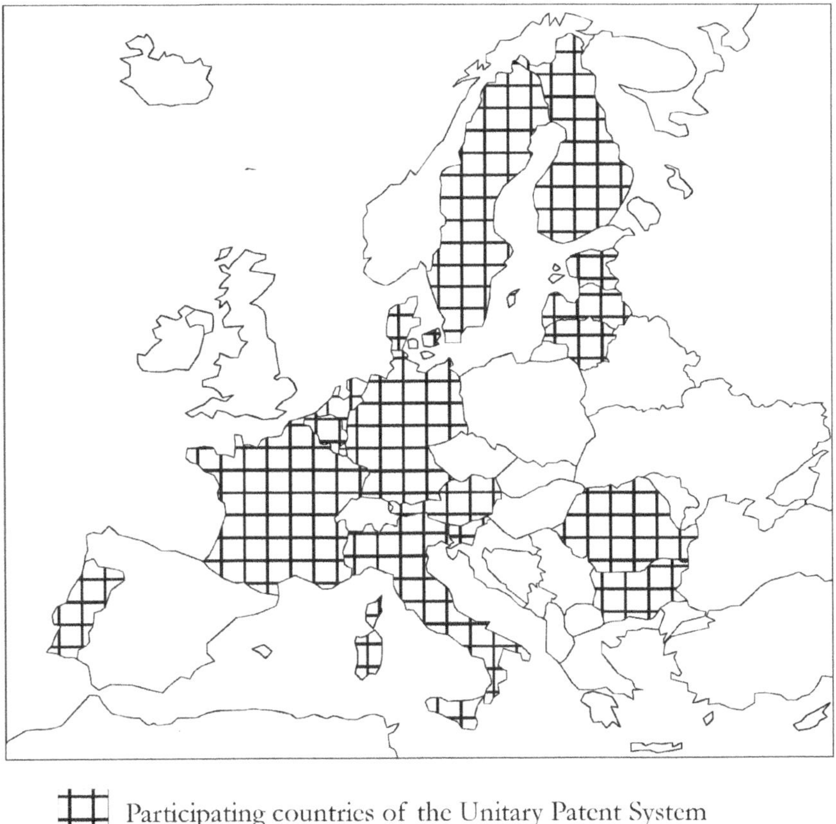

Participating countries of the Unitary Patent System

Fig. 5.1 Member States of the UPC Agreement

As regards the possible implications which rulings by the Unified Patent Court may have on other states, please see the discussion in Para. 490 et seqq. **284**

Due to the lack of any transitional provisions, the UPC is principially competent for infringing acts that occurred before 1 June 2023.[7] Similarly, the Unified Patent Court has jurisdiction over infringements that occurred when the patent in question was 'opted out' (see Para. 299 et seq. below) if this was later withdrawn ('opt-in', see Para. 332) and an infringement action was filed.[8] **285**

7 UPC_CoA_464/2024, Decision of 25 November 2025 – Edwards v. Meril.

8 UPC_CoA_156/2025, Order of 2 June 2025 – XSYS v. Esko Graphics.

286 The same applies when a new Member State joins the UPC Agreement. Since there are no interim regulations to govern such a case, e.g. like those for the Unitary Patent (see Para. 83), it is to obtain a writ of injunction for such a newly acceding Member State, even if said state is not yet part of the Unitary Patent System when the corresponding legal proceeding is opened.[9] This creates a sort of "retroactive local jurisdiction." The question of whether and to what extent this will depend on the lodging of a corresponding application will be examined in Para. 1052.

287 On the other hand, the Unified Patent Court **is not competent for:**

- actions for vindication. It will be possible, however, to bring a revocation action on the grounds of insufficient entitlement (see Para. 658 et seqq.). This results in a dual jurisdiction shared by the Unitary Patent Court and the national courts, one which will therefore remain in place even after the "opt-out" deadline expires.[10]
- actions involving claims arising from licensing agreements – subject to the aforementioned exception – and from other contractual arrangements agreed between the parties. Due consideration will have to be given to ECJ Judgment No. C-666/18,[11] however, which holds that a contractual breach does not rule out the infringement of a protected property right, which in turn will fall under the jurisdiction of the Unified Patent Court.
- compulsory license proceedings. These must be conducted on the national level and will thus apply nationally, also in the case of Unitary Patents.
- disputes involving liquidated damages,[12] unless these resulted from conciliation settlements concluded before the Unified Patent Court. These will be enforceable just like final and conclusive decisions on the merits (Para. 761).
- claims for unjustified warnings of infringement; as well as
- the criminal prosecution of patent claims.[13]

288 These types of proceedings will have to be conducted on the national level as has been the case till now. Where Unitary Patents are involved, however, special rules will come into play to determine the applicable national legal system in accordance with the prevailing situation (see Para. 92 et seqq.).

B. Institutional Structure

289 The UPC consists of a Court of First Instance, a Court of Appeal and a Registry (Article 6 of the UPC Agreement). These Courts are discussed below. The Registry essentially performs the administrative tasks of the courts (Article 10). It has its seat in Luxemburg, as well as sub-registries at all the local and regional divisions (see Para. 339 et seqq.).

9 UPC_CoA_523/2024, Order of 3 March 2025 – Syngenta v. Sumi Agro.
10 See *Hüttermann*, Mitt. 2015, p. 100.
11 ECJ Judgment No, C-666/18 in the *IT Systems SAS/Free Mobile SAS* case.
12 For the German practice, cf. *Metzger*, GRUR 2019, p. 1015.
13 See *Königer*, JIPLP 2016, p. 153.

There are two additional institutions besides the two Courts and the Registry: a Mediation & Arbitration Center and a Training Center. 290

The Mediation & Arbitration Center has two seats: one in Ljubljana, Slovenia and one in Lisbon, Portugal (Article 35 of the UPC Agreement). The purpose of the Center is to help bring about the amicable resolution of legal disputes (see Para. 748 et seqq.) 291

The Training Center (Article 19 of the UPC Agreement) is intended to provide training for judges, particularly judges coming from countries where a low number of patent-related legal disputes are handled. The Center's seat is in Budapest, Hungary. 292

The UPC also has an Administrative Committee, a Budget Committee and an Advisory Committee (Article 11 of the UPC Agreement). 293

The Administrative Committee is composed of representatives delegated by the Member States, whereby each state is entitled to send one representative (Article 12 of the UPC Agreement). This Committee is the final decision-making body on many key questions, particularly including financial matters and the process of selecting the UPC's judges. 294

As its name suggests, the Budget Committee deals with financial matters. Here, too, each of the Member States sends one representative (Article 13 of the UPC Agreement). 295

The Advisory Committee (Article 14 of the UPC Agreement) consists of patent judges and practitioners in patent law and patent litigation, i.e. either patent attorneys or attorneys at law. Put briefly, its function, is to support the work the Administrative Committee. For example, the Advisory Committee during the Protocol Phase (cf. Para. 43) preselected the judges to be appointed to the Unified Patent Court and placed their names on a list of candidates. The Administrative Committee to finally approved this list on 19 October 2022 (cf. Para. 357) 296

Besides the various Committees, the Unified Patent Court also has a Presidium (Article 15 of the Statute of the UPC) which consists of: 297

- the President of the Court of Appeal as Chairperson;
- the President of the Court of First Instance;
- two judges from the Court of Appeal selected by the judges of said Court;
- three judges from the Court of First Instance selected by the judges of said Court; as well as
- the Registrar as a non-voting member.

The Presidium is responsible for managing the UPC. Its tasks include: proposing amendments to the UPC's Rules of Procedure (see Para. 775 et seqq.) and Financial Regulations; preparing the annual budget; laying down the rules governing the Registry. 298

C. The "Opt-Out" Option/National Actions

I. The "Opt-Out" Option

299 The Unified Patent Court is competent not just for Unitary Patents but for European patents as well. Nonetheless, an option to opt out of the exclusive jurisdiction of the Unified Patent Court will apply for European Patents and their appurtenant supplementary protection certificates during a transitional period of six years and eleven months, reckoned as of the date on which the Unified Patent Court commences its work:[14]

> "Unless an action has already been brought before the Court,[15] a proprietor of or an applicant for a European patent granted or applied for prior to the end of the transitional period under paragraph 1 and, where applicable, paragraph 5, as well as a holder of a supplementary protection certificate issued for a product protected by a European patent, shall have the possibility to opt out from the exclusive competence of the Court. To this end they shall notify their opt-out to the Registry by the latest one month before expiry of the transitional period. The opt-out shall take effect upon its entry into the register." (Article 83 (3) of the UPC Agreement)

300 This course of action is generally referred to as an "opt-out."[16]

II. Consequences of an Opt-Out Application

301 The consequences of an effective opt-out have not yet been made entirely clear. Thus, the following specific issues are still in dispute:

1. Duration of the Opt-Out Application:

302 Does an opt-out apply for the entire lifetime of a patent? Since this is practically the consensus view among commentators,[17] we will adopt it as our operative premise in the discussions that follow.

2. Does an Opt-Out Apply to the Unified Patent Court as a Whole?

303 According to the wording of Article 83 (3), an opt-out merely serves to preclude the "exclusive competence" of the Unified Patent Court. So does opting out from this "exclusive competence" serve to preclude the Court's "jurisdiction" as a whole? More specifically: Does an opt-out rule out the possibility of a revocation action before

---

14 Six years and eleven months because Article 83 paragraph 3 stipulates that the application for an opt-out must be lodged at least one month before expiry of the seven-year transitional period; see Para. 323 et seqq.

15 Note: This refers to the Unified Patent Court as defined in Article 2a.

16 Cf. *England*, JIPLP 2014, p. 915, although he uses the 16th Draft Version of the Rules of Procedure as a basis.

17 See *Tilmann*, VPP-Rundbrief 2013, (2), pp. 56–60; *Tilmann*, Mitt. 2014, pp. 58–65.

the Unified Patent Court? While this is affirmed by certain commentators,[18] there are others who take a decidedly more skeptical view.[19] Thus, two alternatives would appear conceivable:

- Alternative 1: An opt-out serves to preclude merely the exclusive competence of the Unified Patent Court, but the UPC still retains jurisdiction in principle. This would mean that proceedings before the Unified Patent Court would still be possible. These would specifically include revocation actions or actions for declaration of non-infringement brought by third parties.
- Alternative 2: An opt-out serves to preclude the jurisdiction of the Unified Patent Court as a whole. Thus, third parties would be barred from bringing revocation actions or actions for declaration of non-infringement. Even the patent proprietor himself would no longer be able to seise the Unified Patent Court.

This second alternative will be the operative assumption adopted throughout this book (see Para. 545 et seqq.)

3. Applicable Law Following an Opt-Out

Once an opt-out has been declared and a national patent-infringement action brought, **304** will the body of law of the Unified Patent Court apply or will it be national law? This is discussed in Para. 617 et seqq.

4. Torpedo Actions

A "torpedo action" is defined as an action for declaration of non-infringement which **305** is brought before a national court of the EU[20] where such proceedings tend to be time-consuming, and which thus serves to thwart a patent-infringement action before a faster-acting court in a different EU country. This is fundamentally reconcilable with European law, according to the *Folien-Fischer* judgment of the ECJ.[21]

Given that the Unified Patent Court qualifies as a European Court under the Brussels Ia **306** Regulation (for a full discussion, see Para. 484 et seqq.), it follows that torpedo actions stemming from EU Member States that do not belong to the UPC Agreement, such as Spain or Poland, will be possible by virtue of the Brussels Ia Regulation, regardless of any opt-out and even after expiry of the opt-out deadline (see Para. 484 et seqq.).

This begs the question as to whether the same will hold true for EU Member States **307** which are also party to the UPC Agreement. According to the wording of Article 83

---

18 A clear affirmative stance is taken, for example, by *Tilmann*, Mitt. 2014, pp. 58–65; in this vein, also see the "Note" added by the Rule-Drafting Committee to Rule 5 in the 15th and 16th Versions of the Rules of Procedure. (This was stricken in the 17th Version, however.)

19 For example, *Nieder*, GRUR 2015, p. 718; also see *Forwood*, Letter to *Beukering*, Chairperson of the Preparatory Committee, dated 19 March 2014.

20 For a very thorough discussion, see *Kühnen*, *Handbuch der Patentverletzung*, Chapter C, Note 170 et seqq.; see also *Sack*, GRUR 2018, p. 893.

21 ECJ Judgment No. C-133/11.

of the UPC agreement, only actions for infringement and revocation can be brought in these countries on the national level in the absence of an opt-out (see Para. 561). Thus, the wording seems to preclude national actions for declaration of non-infringement, which in turn means that torpedo actions from these countries would no longer be possible once the UPC Agreement comes into effect.[22] It bears noting that there are commentators who take a contrary view.[23]

308 Given that an opt-out causes the Unified Patent Court to lose its exclusive competence, it follows that actions for declaration of non-infringement will definitely be possible following the opt-out.

309 So does an "opt-out" effectively open the way for a so-called "torpedo action"? This would mean that a patent proprietor would be placed in a worse position than before by an opt-out. Or is an opt-out not needed for this purpose? In other words, will torpedo actions continue to be possible even without an opt-out once the UPC Agreement comes into effect?

5. Clarifying the Open Questions

310 Since the opt-out option is envisioned in the UPC Agreement itself, it will probably be impossible to attain legal certainty on this point, e.g. by amending the UPC's Rules of Procedure or by obtaining a supplementary opinion from the Preparatory Committee.

311 This especially applies to the question of whether an opt-out serves to preclude a revocation action before the Unified Patent Court. So far, however, no appriopriate case has reached the court.

312 Clarification could be obtained under the following scenario for example: Despite the prior declaration of an opt-out, a revocation action is brought before the UPC's Central Division, whereupon a complaint by the patent proprietor is promptly decided (see Para. 827) and an appeal lodged with the UPC's Court of Appeal (see Para. 1095 et seqq.).

III. Ineffectiveness of an Opt-Out Application

313 An opt-out will no longer be possible if legal action has already been brought before the Unified Patent Court to defend or challenge a disputed European patent (Article 83(3)). The subsequent outcome of the action is irrelevant here, since the option to opt out will not be reactivated even if the action is later denied or withdrawn.

---

22 Note: These include Italy and Belgium, both of which have become notorious as "torpedo-states."

23 E.g. by *Tilmann*, Mitt. 2014, p. 58 = JIPLP 2014, p. 9; cf. also *Nieder*, Mitt. 2015, p. 97, as well as *Bennett*, Mitt. 2015, p. 301.

IV. Opt-Out: Procedural Aspects

1. The Applicant

The opt-out application must be lodged by the proprietor of the patent and/or of the relevant patent application (Rule 5.1 of the Rules of Procedure). This could have be donen as early as the Protocol Phase (cf. Para. 46 et seqq.). The opt-out application then became effective once the UPC Agreement entered into force (Rule 5.13). If there are multiple proprietors, then all the proprietors must lodge the opt-out application jointly (Rule 5.1a)).[24] This also applies if there are multiple proprietors for multiple national parts of a patent,[25] whereby it is irrelevant whether the corresponding countries belong to the Unitary Patent System or not.[26] In this case, too, all the proprietors must jointly lodge the application. 314

The owner recorded in the European Patent Register will be treated as the presumptive proprietor in this context. If the Register is not correct, then the true proprietor may lodge a declaration affirming his entitlement to apply along with his opt-out application (see the discussion below). 315

2. Contents of the Opt-Out Application

The application to opt-out must contain the following (Rule 5.3 of the Rules of Procedure): 316

- information on the proprietor of the relevant patent, and/or patent application, as well as on any supplementary protection certificate based thereon and on any appointed representative. This effectively serves to eliminate the provisions governing representation pursuant to Art. 48 of the UPC Agreement and Rule 8 of the Rules of Procedure. In fact, some commentators take the view that Rule 5.4. serves to generally lift all restrictions on representation, so that anyone holding a corresponding power of attorney could act as representative, although the proprietor himself could also lodge the application.
- information on the relevant patent or patent application, including the serial number as well as details on the supplementary protection certificate, if any; as well as
- a declaration of ownership, insofar one is needed; i.e. one that states that the applicant is the proprietor of the protected right and is authorized to lodge the application.

The opt-out application is free of charge and may be lodged in electronic form via the CMS of the Unified Patent Court. 317

24 Cf. UPC_CoA_79/2024, Order of 4 June 2024, APL_9578/2024 – Neo Wireless v. Toyota. For the sake of simplicity, the term "proprietor" will in the following be used in the singular.

25 UPC_CoA_79/2024, Order of 4 June 2024, APL_9578/2024 – Neo Wireless v. Toyota.

26 E.g. in the clarification/explanation for the final version of Rule 5.

3. Course of the Proceeding

318 Once the Registry receives an opt-out application, it will enter the opt-out in the Register. The opt-out will be effective as of the date of entry in the Register. Valid applications received during the "sunrise period" (Para. 46) were effective from 1 June 2023 on, the day that the Unitary Patent System started.

319 If the requirements recorded in the Register are missing or incorrect, this does not mean that the application has to be lodged all over again: a correction may be lodged with the Registry instead. The date of entry of the correction will be noted in the Register. The opt-out will be effective from the date of correction (Rule 5.5).

320 However, if an action has been commenced before the Unified Patent Court before the UPC has entered the opt-out (see Para. 313 above), then the opt-out will become ineffective. This applies, in other words, if the national proceeding was commenced after the lodging of the application but before registration (Rule 5.7).

321 Thus, the opt-out will remain ineffective even if the proceeding before the Unified Patent Court is later withdrawn or terminated.

322 An opt-out application may also be lodged for a European Patent application. In this case, however, the opt-out will become ineffective if the patent proprietor decides in favor of a Unitary Patent after the European patent has been granted. The opt-out application will then be deemed withdrawn. In such case, the patent proprietor must notify his decision to the Registry of the Unified Patent Court, which will then enter the withdrawal in the respective Register (Rule 5.9).

V. Time Limit for an Opt-Out

323 According to the UPC Agreement, the time limit for lodging an opt-out application is six years and eleven months as of the entry into force of the UPC Agreement, i.e. one month before the end of the transitional period of seven years (Article 83(3)), i.e. until 1 May 2023. During the time limit period for lodging an opt-out application, there will be no further processing and no re-establishment of rights (see Para. 723 et seqq.).

▶ To illustrate:

324 The UPC started on 1 June 2023. Under the UPC Agreement, this means that the opt-out could be declared at any time up to 1 May 2030, namely with respect to all existing European patents as well as for any newly lodged European patent applications (for which the opt-out may have to be declared right at the time of lodgment).

Under the Treaty on International Cooperation in the Field of Patents[27] (aka: "Patent Cooperation Treaty" or "PCT") international applications (PCT appli-

27 Treaty on International Cooperation in the Field of Patents of 19 June 1970.

cations) also qualify as European Patent applications (Article 11 (3) of the PCT and Article 151 of the European Patent Convention). Thus, an opt-out may also be declared for PCT applications. It follows that this would be mandatorily required for PCT applications which have been lodged by 1 May 2030 but which have not yet been regionalized.

1. Extending the Opt-Out Time Limit

Under the UPC Agreement, the time limit for an opt-out may be extended by a further seven years if the Administrative Committee of the Unified Patent Court resolves to approve such an extension after consulting with the users of the Patent System and after conducting statistical surveys. The Administrative Committee is to perform such a consultation five years after the UPC Agreement's entry into force (Article 83 (4)). 325

No further extension will be possible, however; i.e. the Unified Patent Court will acquire sole jurisdiction after fourteen years at the latest. 326

2. Opt-Out: Procedure in the Event of an Unauthorized Opt-Out

Since no verification of the right of representation is performed for an opt-out application, it could occur that a third party lodges an opt-out application for a patent in an unauthorized manner. To ensure that this can be retroactively corrected, Rule 5A was introduced. This holds that a patent proprietor may lodge an application to have an opt-out removed from the Register. 327

The supporting reasons for the application must be set out. The application will be free of charge. After receiving it, the Registry will examine the application and take a decision as soon as practicable. If appropriate, it will then delete the opt-out from the Register. 328

An application to review this decision may be lodged with the President of the Court of Appeal. The application must be lodged within one month of the decision's notification and in one of the official languages of the European Patent Office. It must set out the relevant arguments, factual circumstances and evidence. 329

Assuming the application for a review is allowed, the President will then order the opt-out to either be re-entered into the Register or, as the case may be, to be removed from the Register. 330

The wording of Rule 5A suggests that anyone is entitled to lodge the application to remove the opt-out, even if this is not expressly stated. The fact that the term "notification" is used implies that the decision issued on the application to remove the opt-out will be made public. Whether or not the application will be subject to charge is also uncertain. It is possible that the fee charged will correspond to the fee for an appeal requiring leave from the Court (see Para. 1102 et seqq.). 331

VI. Opt-In

332 The opt-out may be withdrawn once, i.e. actions before the Unified Patent Court will then become possible again. This only applies, however, if no national action has been brought up to the time of the opt-out (Rule 5.8), however that national action must have been commenced after 1 March 2023, the so-called "Sunrise-Period" (see Para. 46).[28] Here, too, it is irrelevant whether such an action is later withdrawn or terminated.

333 An opt-in cannot be withdrawn, i.e. it is not possible to opt out twice (Rule 5.10).

334 An opt-in must be requested by lodging a corresponding application before the Unified Patent Court, whereby the same requirements as for an opt-out application apply (Rule 5.7) (See Para. 314 et seqq.).

VII. National Actions Without an Opt-Out

335 It therefore follows that, even without an opt-out, national infringement actions and revocation actions can continue to be lodged for a period of seven years after commencement of the Unified Patent Court's operations (Article 83 (1)).[29] Actions which have been timely filed will not be affected by the expiry of this transitional period, i.e. they will continue to run without change (Article 83 (2)).

336 This will not apply to actions for declaration of non-infringement, however, at least based on the wording of the relevant Article 83 (see the discussion in Para. 307 above).

337 Once a national patent-infringement action is lodged, this will in any case not preclude the bringing of actions before the Unified Patent Court, i.e. a situation could arise where the patent proprietor brings an action before a national court (e.g. before the Düsseldorf District Court) but the plaintiff reacts by bringing a revocation action before the Unified Patent Court.

D. Structure of the Unified Patent Court

338 According to the UPC Agreement, proceedings before the Unified Patent Court are conducted before two instances, namely before a Court of First Instance and a Court of Appeal. Whether or not the European Court of Justice could potentially serve as a court of final review (third instance) is an open question discussed in more detail in Para. 470 et seqq.

28 UPC_CoA_489/2023, Order of 12 November 2024, APL_596007/2023 – AIM v. Supponor.

29 It should be noted that the Court of Venice has ruled differently, Case No. 10432/2024 Geoplast v. Daliform, decision of 12 November 2025.

I. Structure of the Unified Patent: Court of First Instance

1. Subsidiary Structure

The Court of First Instance consists of a number of sub-courts known as "local divisions" and "regional divisions" plus a "central division." **339**

When it comes to a patent-infringement action, all these sub-courts have the same decision-making competence.[30] But this does not apply to revocation actions and actions for declaration of non-infringement, which, with only a few exceptions, can only be brought before the central division (see Para. 1161 et seqq.) **340**

It bears noting right at the outset that, besides bringing the normal main action in a patent-infringement case, one also has the option of seeking the pretrial remedies in the form of orders for preliminary injunction, for preserving evidence and/or for inspection/*saisie-contrefaçon*. This is discussed in greater detail in Chapter 15 (Para. 1336 et seqq.) **341**

a) Local Divisions

"Local divisions" are defined as courts located in a Member State of the UPC Agreement (Article 7(3)). In principle, each Member State of the UPC Agreement is entitled to have a local division. Depending on whether the patent proceedings that are brought in the respective country before the UPC Agreement's entry into the force number a hundred, two hundred or three hundred, that country will be entitled to two, three, or up to four local divisions, respectively (Article 7(3) and 7(4)), **342**

Accordingly, Germany, France and Italy would all be entitled to more than one local division, namely three local divisions in the case of France and Italy and four local divisions for Germany. **343**

France and Italy have not taken advantage of this, however, but only set up one just a single local division in Paris and Milan, respectively. Other countries with just one local division are Belgium (local division in Brussels), Denmark (local division in Copenhagen),[31] Finland (local division in Helsinki), Austria (local division in Vienna), the Netherlands (local division in The Hague), Portugal (local division in Lisbon), and Slovenia (local division in Ljubljana). **344**

Germany, by contrast, has claimed all four of the local divisions to which it is entitled and opened up local divisions in Düsseldorf, Hamburg, Mannheim and Munich.[32] **345**

30 Note: Although the central division will not really have jurisdiction at first, it may nonetheless come into play, e.g. by way of Luxemburg; see Para. 384.

31 See e.g. http://kluwerpatentblog.com/2014/03/27/local-upc-chamber-to-be-set-up-in-denmark/.

32 See e.g. *Opfer* et al, GRUR Int 2015, p. 904.

b) Regional Divisions

346 A regional division is simply a local division which has jurisdiction for more than one Contracting Member State of the UPC Agreement (Article 7 (5)). As explained below, it will be of advantage to a Contracting Member State, both in terms of organization and human resources, to have comparatively few legal disputes brought for adjudication before its national courts before the UPC's entry into force.

347 As things currently stand, there is one regional division comprising the Baltic States and Sweden. This has its seat in Stockholm.

348 Once three regional divisions have been set up, the so-called "Unilever Rule" of Article 33(4) of the UPC Agreement will come into play (see Para. 388).

c) Countries Without a Local or Regional Division

349 Currently four Member States have neither set up a local division nor become part of a regional division. These are Bulgaria, Luxemburg, Romania and Malta. Patent infringements in any of these countries could potentially be adjudicated by the central division (see Para. 362).

d) Central Division

350 The central division has its seat in Paris with two sections in Milan and Munich (Article 7(2), amended by the decision of the Administrative Committee of 26 June 2023[33]). Here, the relevant competences have been allocated by technical field. Thus, the section in Milan is responsible for patents falling under Patent Classifications A (Human Necessities), albeit without Supplementary Protection Certificates (SPCs) while the Munich section handles patents falling under Classification C), with Supplementary Protection Certicates, F (Mechanical Engineering). Jurisdiction for the remaining primary patent classifications is retained by Paris.[34] The exact allocation will be discussed in Para. 394 et seqq.

351 The current locations of the Unified Patent Court are shown on the following map:

33 https://www.unified-patent-court.org/sites/default/files/upc_documents/decision-d_ac_03_26062023_-amendment-upca.pdf.

34 As per the Annex to the UPC Agreement, amended by the decision of the Administrative Committee of 26 June 2023, cf. https://www.unified-patent-court.org/sites/default/files/upc_documents/decision-d_ac_03_26062023_-amendment-upca.pdf.

Participating countries of the UPC

- ◦ Seat of a local division
- • Seat of a regional divison
- ⁎ Seat of a section of the central division
- x Seat of the appeal court

Fig. 5.2 Participating of the UPC

2. Personnel Structure

The judges who sit on the Unified Patent Court are divided into "legally qualified" and "technically qualified" judges (Article 15(1)). 352

a) Legally Qualified and Technically Qualified Judges

353 Legally qualified judges – who will simply be referred to as "judges" hereinbelow – must possess the qualifications required for appointment to judicial offices in a Contracting Member State (Article 15(2)).

354 However, the foregoing is not a requirement for "technically qualified judges" – abbreviated hereinbelow to "technical judges" (Article 15(2)). Instead, these must simply possess a university degree and proven expertise in a given technical field. Technical judges are either patent attorneys or work in industry or they were recruited from Offices or courts. The fact that part-time judgeship is possible with simultaneous continuation of the previous activity, especially as an attorney, has not remained without criticism[35] and is discussed in more detail from Para. 965 on.

b) Appointment and Term of Office

355 All judges are appointed by the Administrative Committee upon the recommendation of the Advisory Committee (see Para. 296). Their term of office runs for an initial period of six years, after which they may be re-appointed one or more times.

356 Only five full-time positions were envisioned for the UPC's start-up phase, so initially and currently the majority of judges works on a part-time basis. A certain number of full-time judges was required, however, particularly given that the President of the Court of Instance must be selected by these full-time judges (see Para. 359). Moreover, the technical judges work "on call", i.e. they do not have a fixed time quota and are only called in on a case-by-case basis when a lawsuit is filed.

357 In the meantime, however, a larger number of judges, especially at the German divisions, are working full-time.

c) Presidents of the Court of First Instance and of the Court of Appeal

358 The respective Presidents of the Court of First Instance and of the Court of Appeal have an especially important role to play within the Unified Patent Court.

359 The President of the Court of First Instance is elected from among those judges of the Court of First Instance who serve full-time. His or her term of office is three years, whereby he may be re-elected up to two times (Article 14 (1) of the Statute of the Unified Patent Court). The first President of the Court of First Instance must be a French national. To be exact: He or she must come from the country in which the Central Division has its seat, i.e. France (Article 14 (2) of the Statute of the UPC); as the first president Ms *Florence Butin* from the central division was elected.

35 E.G. here: https://www.juve-patent.com/news-and-stories/people-and-business/patent-attorney-dominance-among-upc-technical-judges-leads-to-conflict-debate/.

She oversees the Court's judicial activities and administration and specifically organizes the allocation of duties and the allocation of cases to the individual divisions. More importantly she is in charge of allocating technical judges to a particular case. 360

The President of the Court of Appeal (cf. also Para. 275) is elected from among all the judges of the Court of Appeal, i.e. also those who only serve part-time. Here again, the term of office is three years with the possibility of being re-elected for another two terms (Article 13 of the Statute of the Unified Patent Court). As the first President of the Court of Appeals *Klaus Grabinski* was elected. 361

The President oversees the Court's judicial activities and administration. When decisions are taken in plenary session (see Para. 1138), he serves as chairperson. 362

d) Composition of the Panels of the Court of First Instance

In principle, a panel of the Court of First Instance will consist of three judges. However, the parties to a legal dispute may agree that their case is to be adjudicated by a single judge (Article 8(7) of the UPC Agreement). 363

A panel of a **regional** or **local division** will consist of three sitting judges. However, a fourth judge, namely a technical judge, may be added to the panel upon the request of one of the parties, or upon the panel's own motion (Article 8(5) of the UPC Agreement). 364

The addition of a fourth technical judge becomes mandatory only in a patent-infringement case where a counterclaim for revocation has been brought and the panel is to adjudicate both actions together (see Para. 879 et seqq.) 365

At least two nationalities must be represented among the three judges, whereby the distribution of nationalities will depend on several factors: 366

At the **regional divisions**, two of the judges sitting on a panel must always be nationals of the Contracting Member States belonging to the respective regional division. The third judge must not be a national of any of the Contracting Member States concerned (Article 8(4) of the UPC Agreement). 367

At the **local divisions**, the makeup of the panel will depend on the number of cases which were commenced in the respective countries either before or after the UPC's entry into force. If the average number of cases is more than fifty, then two out of the three judges of a panel must be nationals of the Contracting Member State hosting the local division. If the number is lower than fifty cases, then this applies to only one of the judges (Article 8(2) and 8(3) of the UPC Agreement). 368

This means that in proceedings conducted before local divisions in *Germany*, *France*, *Italy* and *the Netherlands*, two judges come from the respective host country. 369

But this will hold true for only one of the judges in proceedings conducted before local divisions in *Belgium*, *Denmark*, *Finland*, *Austria*, *Portugal* or *Slovenia*. 370

371 It follows that Contracting Member States with only a few cases per year will find it advantageous to merge together to form a regional division, since this will always feature two local judges as opposed to only one foreign judge. So it is hardly surprising that the only regional division in existence thus far comprises countries where the number of annual cases commenced before the UPC's entry into force was small.

372 The individual divisions are always assigned permanent judges, i.e. each division has at least one judge, and in the case of the German, French, Italian and Dutch divisions two judges, who work permanently on the cases there. The only exception is the local division in Munich, where a second chamber has been opened due to the high workload.[36]

373 At the **central division**, by contrast, a panel will consist of only two judges – who must have differing nationalities – plus one technical judge (Article 8(6)).

e) Standing Judges

374 Besides the panels, each division can – and usually will – have a so-called "standing judge" in place, one who can take charge of urgent pre-trial proceedings and who will thus be in a position to take prompt decisions (see also Para. 1347 herein as well as Article 19 (3) of the Statute of the UPC).

f) Pool of Judges

375 As we have seen, at least one of the judges of a given panel will invariably not be a national of the respective country in which the case is being heard. These judges will instead be drawn from a so-called "Pool of Judges" to which all judges and technical judges automatically belong (Article 20 of the Statute of the UPC). The technical judges of the central division will be appointed from the Pool of Judges as well.

376 The appointment will be made by the President of the Court of First Instance. She is free to decide whether a local division will have foreign judges who are permanently assigned to it or whether a new judge is to be appointed for each new case. The latter is the current practice.

II. Structure of the Court of Appeal

377 The Court of Appeal has its seat exclusively in Luxemburg (Article 9(5)).

378 The Court of Appeal takes its decisions in a panel consisting of five members, these being three judges and two technical judges. The three judges must come from at least two countries, while the technical judges will be appointed from the Pool of Judges on a case-by-case basis (Article 9(1)). One of the judges will preside.

36 Cf. https://www.unified-patent-court.org/en/news/unified-patent-court-appoints-new-legally-qualified-judges.

There is only one special case in which the panel will consist of only three judges: Namely, when actions are brought against the European Patent Office in connection with a Unitary Patent (Article 9(2)). This is discussed in more detail in Para. 1202 et seqq. 379

However, the Court of Appeal has decided on its own authority to rule without technical judges, i.e. only with a three-judge panel, in some cases that are more formal in nature and in proceedings that require admissibility (see Para. 1102). This is a clear violation of the European Convention on Human Rights and must therefore be classified as highly questionable.[37] 380

In important cases, the Court of Appeal can meet in plenary session i.e. without the limitations on the number of participating judges which are applicable to panels. This is described in Para. 1138 et seqq. 381

III. Allocation of Competences Within the Court of First Instance

The jurisdiction of a division of the Court of First Instance will be determined in keeping with the nature of the action involved and on the basis of the objective circumstances that prevail. 382

1. Jurisdiction for Patent Infringement Actions

The following are competent for **patent-infringement actions**: 383
- the local or regional division in whose territory the infringement took place; and/or
- the local or regional division in whose territory the defendant (or at least one of the defendants) has his seat;

However, the action may be brought before the central division (Article 33 (1) (b) of the UPC Agreement)[38] if either of the following situations apply: 384
- The defendant has his seat outside the territory of the Contracting Member States; or
- The infringement occurred in a country which has not set up a local division and which does not belong to any regional division (Bulgaria, Malta or Luxemburg, see Para. 349).

As a practical matter, one can assume that, given the primacy of European Union law (see Para. 608), the ECJ's two judgements in the *Hummel/Nike* case (No. C-617/15) (see Para. 99) and in the *Ams Neve vs. Heritage Audio* case (No, C-172/18) will play a key role in settling the question of which local or regional division is to have competence. 385

37 Cf. *Hüttermann/Weber* GRURPatent 2024, 50.

38 Note that *Tilmann* deems this to be irreconcilable with EU law, particularly the Brussels I Regulation; see *Tilmann* in *Tilmann/Plassmann*, Note 15 et seqq. to Art. 33.

▶ Implications for real-life practice:

386 The exception which gives jurisdiction to the central division will apply only if the defendant does not have any subsidiaries or other affiliated companies whatsoever in a Contracting Member State of the UPC Agreement. This will not hold true in many concrete situations, however: In practice, even mid-sized companies – and certainly corporations and other major enterprises active in the EU – are likely to have at least a branch office in a Member State of the UPC Agreement. But this already suffices to qualify as a business location, according to ECJ Judgement No. 617/15, i.e. the subsidiary jurisdiction the central division will not be triggered in such case. ECJ Judgment No. 617/15 furthermore holds that the subsidiaries need not be active in the same field as the defendant; instead, it already suffices if they merely offer services.

But since the act of offering services can already constitute a patent infringement, this means that the plaintiff will be able to select the local division/regional division in practically all cases. This specifically follows from ECJ Judgment C-172/18, which holds that, when offers are transmitted from one Member State into another Member State, it is permissible to seise the courts of the target Member State. The prior assumption –followed by the German Federal Court of Justice[39] in the *Parfummarken* ruling, for instance – was that an overall evaluation of the elements of the infringement would be dispositive, e.g. in view of ECJ Judgement No. 24/16 in the *Nintendo/Big Ben* case. This approach is apparently no longer permissible, however.[40]

It bears noting that Luxemburg, for example, is a country which intends to neither set up a local division nor to join a regional division (see Para. 357). Since French and German are official languages in Luxemburg and since the act of offering can constitutes a patent infringement, it follows that a claim for patent infringement can in many cases be brought in Luxemburg. Indeed, it will often suffice if the offeror merely maintains a German-language or French-language website.[41] *De facto*, this means that the central division can be freely selected by the plaintiff in most cases, albeit on the grounds of patent infringement and not because the defendant lacks a seat in one of the Contracting Member States of the UPC Agreement.

39 Judgment of the German Federal Court of Justice (BGH) in the *Parfummarken* case, Mitt. 2018, p. 136.

40 This carry-over of the *Nintendo vs. Big Ben* ruling had already been criticized as impermissible by *Kur*; see *Kur*, GRUR 2018, p. 358; as regards the issues associated with the *Parfummarken* and *Nintendo vs. BigBen* cases and their implications for the UPC, see *Jestaedt*, Mitt. 2018, p. 381, as well as *Jestaedt*, Mitt. 2019, p. 540, and *Hackbarth*, GRUR 2019, p. 1269; cf. also *Kindler*, GRUR 2018, p. 1107.

41 See also the corresponding comments made by *Grabinski* at the conference held by the Chamber of German Patent Attorneys on 20 November 2013 in Munich.

In addition, certain **pretrial proceedings** may be conducted before the UPC, such as proceedings for preliminary injunction or for preserving evidence. These must be applied for from the same division which would otherwise hear the main action on the merits (see Chapter 15, Para. 1336 et seqq.). **387**

The central division can also acquire jurisdiction on the basis of the so-called "Unilever Rule."[42] Said rule is derived from Article 33 of the UPC Agreement, which stipulates that if a patent infringement action is pending before a regional division but the infringement occurs on the territory of at least three regional divisions, then the relevant regional division must refer the action to the central division upon the defendant's request.[43] **388**

However, this provision will remain ineffective for the time being, as there is currently only one regional chamber (see Para. 346) in Stockholm and there are currently no known plans to open further regional chambers. **389**

On the other hand, it is probable that, once three regional divisions exist, the preconditions for the "Unilever Rule" will be met by most of the actions brought before a regional division. Recall that the regional divisions will usually encompass the smaller countries. Thus, an infringement that occurs in a country belonging to a regional division will often not be restricted to this country alone, but will instead be observable in multiple regions, and not infrequently across the whole of Europe. This means that the defendant would have the option to move the proceedings in the majority of all cases brought before a regional division. Whether this will eventually leave the regional divisions with nothing to do remains to be seen (see also the discussion in Para. 603 et seqq.) **390**

2. Jurisdiction for Revocation Actions and Actions for Declaration of Non-Infringement

In principle, revocation actions and actions for declaration of non-infringement must be brought before the central division. Only if an infringement proceeding involving the same patent is already pending between the parties at a local or regional division of the Unified Patent Court are the aforementioned actions to be brought before the same local or regional division (Article 33 (4) of the UPC Agreement).[44] Thus, a local or regional division may also acquire jurisdiction by virtue of the parties' choice of legal venue. **391**

42 So called because it was proposed by members of the Patent Division of the Unilever Company; see the lecture given by *Hoyng* on 27 March 2013 at the IPO Conference in Brussels.

43 Note that *Tilmann* deems this to be irreconcilable with EU law, particularly the Brussels I Regulation; see *Tilmann* in *Tilmann/Plassmann*, Note 22 et seqq. to Article 33.

44 Cf. UPC_CoA_762/2024, Decision of 5 November 2025 – Seoul Viosys v. Expert Klein (see the history of the case).

392 In derogation from German law, no precedence will be given to opposition proceedings that may be pending before the European Patent Office, i.e. instead of lodging an opposition proceeding, one will be able to directly lodge a revocation action.

393 When it comes to an action for declaration of non-infringement, however, the defendant (= patent proprietor) will be able to "thwart" said action if he brings a patent action in the same matter against the plaintiff within three months' time. In this case, the action for declaration of non-infringement will be suspended and only the patent action will be continued. This ultimately means that the plaintiff would be able to move the action away from the central division to a local division of his choice (for more details, see Para. 1198).

3. Jurisdiction Within the Central Division

394 The central division has its seat in Paris, but there also two sections for daily necessities, chemistry and mechanical engineering in Milan and Munich, respectively. Which of the central division's three locations will have jurisdiction will depend on the primary International Patent Classification (IPC)[45] into which the relevant patent falls. If this is A (except Supplementary Protection Certificates), then Milan is competent; if it is C, F or Supplementary Protection Certificates then Munich. Paris will be competent for all other cases.

395 If a proceeding involves multiple patents, the majority of which feature a single primary IPC, then the choice of venue will be in keeping with said IPC.

396 An exception applies in the following cases, however:
- if the relevant patent falls under more than one primary IPC; or
- if the proceeding before the Unified Patent Court involves multiple patents whose primary IPCs are so divergent that no single IPC can cover the majority of these patents.

In such cases, the following procedure is to be used:
- if a single patent is involved, the venue will be chosen based on the first-named primary IPC;
- if multiple patents are involved, then on the basis of the first-named primary IPC of the first-named patent in the statement of claim (Rule 17.3 (c)).

397 This classification must still be verified by the presiding judge of the corresponding panel, however. If he believes that the classification is correct, he will accept it. Otherwise, he will instruct the Registry to refer the proceeding to the venue which it considers appropriate. If the presiding judge of the division receiving the referral agrees with the classification, it will be deemed accepted. If not, the presiding judge will notify the President of the Court of First Instance, who will then perform her own classification (Rule 17.3(c)).

45 Note: Although Rule 17 and Annex II of the UPC Agreement expressly refer to a patent's "classification," this can only mean the patent's primary classification.

4. Jurisdiction for Other Types of Actions

The other types of actions which can be brought before the Unified Patent Court are to be lodged with the central division (see Chapter 13, Para. 1202 et seqq.). 398

IV. Language Regulations

As a general rule, the language used for proceedings before local and regional divisions must be an official EU language that is also an official language of the respective country or countries of the local division, or of one of the countries for which the regional division is competent. The Contracting Member States may also designate other languages, particularly English, as additional or even exclusive procedural language. 399

All divisions accept English as that additional procedural language, before the regional division in Stockholm it is even the sole language. 400

For proceedings before the central division, on the other hand, the language of the disputed patent must be used. 401

1. Peculiarities of the Language Regulations

If multiple languages are permissible, then, as a general rule, the plaintiff will be free to select the procedural language, however a request for a change of language is possible (cf. Para. 409). A number of peculiarities apply in this context, however: 402

a) Choice of Languages for Local Patent-Infringement Cases

If patent actions are brought before a local or regional division against a defendant who has his seat within the territory of that division, then the plaintiff must choose the respective national language when the nature of the patent infringement is such that it could not have been prosecuted before some other division. This would be the case if the reach of the patent infringement was only minor and an activity such as offering or selling did not take place in another country (Rule 14.2(b)). 403

If the respective country has various regions with different languages, then the plaintiff must use the respective regional language of the defendant (Rule 14.2(b)).[46] 404

b) Choice of Language by the Unified Patent Court

There is also an exception applicable to the Unified Patent Court itself (Rule 14.2(c)): The judge-rapporteur of the panel of the relevant local or regional division may order that, even if the plaintiff has not submitted the legal action in the national language, the panel will nevertheless conduct oral hearings and/or issue orders and decisions 405

46 Note: The prime example here is Belgium, which is regionally divided into Flanders and Wallonia. Indeed, it is an open secret that this Rule was adopted at the request of the Belgian government, which otherwise threatened to withhold its ratification of the UPC Agreement; see also *Tilmann*, GRUR 2015, p. 527.

in the national language. Such orders/decisions must be accompanied by a certified translation.

406 This exception does not apply to the defendant, however, who will be forced to defend himself in the language chosen by the plaintiff. Furthermore, Rule 14.2(c) of the Rules of Procedure will only apply for the national language. So that if the action is submitted in the national language, the panel will not be able to conduct the proceeding in some other language, say, English.

2. Translations

407 Once a language has been chosen, all written pleadings and documents, including written items of evidence, are to be submitted in this procedural language, unless the Court or the Rules stipulate otherwise (Rule 7.1).

408 Certified or formally confirmed translations are not required in this connection, except insofar as the translation is disputed or the Unified Patent Court itself orders such a certification.

3. Change of language

409 Pursuant to Art. 49(5), the court may, at the request of a party and for reasons of fairness, order that the language of the proceedings be changed to the language in which the patent was granted. In accordance with the case law of the Unified Patent Court, the circumstances of both parties must be taken into account and, if a balancing of interests leads to a balanced result, the interests of the defendant prevail.[47]

410 In practice, this means that it is almost always possible for a defendant who is not domiciled in the country of the chamber before which the action is brought to switch to English if the patent was granted in English (see the strategic considerations from Para. 1076 onwards).

V. Issues Relating to Representation

411 The parties must have themselves represented before the UPC. The following will be entitled to act as representatives:
- Attorneys who are admitted to the bar before a court of a Member State of the UPC Agreement;
- European patent representatives, whereby these must demonstrably possess a special qualification (see Para. 732 et seqq.)

412 This means that – unlike in Germany or most other European states – European patent representatives, too, are in principle entitled to act as direct representatives.

413 Neither the UPC Agreement nor the Rules of Procedure rule out the possibility of internal, in-house representation, subject to a single exception: During inspection

47 UPC_CoA_101/2024, Order of 17 April 2024, ApL_12116/2024 – Curio v. 10xGenomics.

proceedings (see Para. 1380 et seqq.), the participation of employees of the applicant is precluded (Rule 196.5).

Thus, representation must not necessarily be performed by an external party: Attorneys or patent attorneys who are employed in-house may also be selected. 414

Presenting a power of attorney to the UPC is not required unless specifically requested by the Court (Rule 285). 415

1. Representation by Patent Attorneys ("Lawyers")

Patent attorneys, insofar as they are European patent representatives and have the corresponding qualification, are authorized to act as independent representatives before the Unified Patent Court.[48] 416

But it is also possible for patent attorneys to function in tandem with some other representative, e.g. an attorney at law (Art. 48(4) of the Agreement). In such case, the requirement for special qualification will not apply. The mandated patent attorneys will then have the right to participate in oral hearings, namely at the discretion of the Court and under the responsible supervision of the actual representative (Rule 292). 417

2. Attorney-Client Privilege

Attorney-client privilege, i.e. the privilege not to have to disclose confidential communication between client and legal counsel, will apply for any representative who has been instructed in a professional capacity by a client in a proceeding before the Unified Patent Court (Rule 287). This will also cover mandated patent attorneys as well as representatives who are internal, in-house employees (Rule 287.2). 418

This privilege will also cover communication which representatives conduct with third parties in the course of a proceeding before the Unified Patent Court in order to obtain information or evidence of whatever nature (so-called "litigation privilege," Rule 288). 419

3. Code of Conduct

According to Rule 290, the Administrative Committee has the option to impose a binding Code of Conduct upon representatives appearing before the Unified Patent Court (Rule 290.2). 420

Such a Code of Conduct has already been elaborated by the Preparatory Committee, in coordination with EPLAW, EPLIT and epi, and was published on 18 May 2016 and finally affirmed by the Administrative Committe on 8 February 2023.[49] The Code is relatively brief in terms of its content and does not really include any 421

48 Note: cf. here also the Rulings handed down by the 10th Panel for Civil Matters of the German Federal Court of Justice (BGH) on 28 April 2020 and 26 May 2020 in Case No. X ZR 60/19.

49 https://www.unified-patent-court.org/sites/default/files/upc_documents/ac_06_08022023_en_code-of-conduct-representatives.pdf.

peculiarities. One of the stated reasons for this is that the representatives appearing before the Unified Patent Court will be subject to other codes of ethics anyway by virtue of their professional backgrounds.[50]

VI. Cost Aspects

422 As under German law, the operative principle for the Unified Patent Court is that the side which loses a proceeding must assume the costs incurred by the winning side.[51] Also as under German law, these costs are calculated on a sliding scale based on the value of the action, although this does not apply to all court fees.

1. Assessing the Value of the Action

423 The fees for at least part of the court proceeding, and especially for the recoverable representation costs (see Para. 445 et seqq.), will be geared towards the value of the action (see Rule 150.2, Rule 370.3).

424 In principle, this value will be assessed by the Court, namely during the interim procedure (see Para. 886). The plaintiff must estimate the value, however (see Para. 816 et seqq.), since this will serve as a basis for the court fees he must pay. This, too, corresponds to the German practice.

425 On 26 February 2016, the Preparatory Committee published guidelines for this purpose which had been drafted by *Mooney/Tilmann*.

426 The guidelines state that the value of the action should be assessed using a licensing analogy, namely in the following manner:
- for patent infringement actions, on the basis of the turnover earned by the defendant during the life of the patent; if necessary, this should be estimated;
- for revocation actions, on the basis of the turnover earned by both parties;
- for revocation counterclaims, on the basis of the value of the patent infringement action plus a surcharge of 50 %, since the action will also affect other market participants.

427 Ideally, the licensing factor will be derived from existing licensing agreements or from licenses customary in the respective technical field. Otherwise the Court will have to estimate the factor.

428 It bears noting that the Guidelines also suggest that the damages to be awarded in a patent-infringement action before the Unified Patent Court may be assessed using just such a licensing analogy (see Para. 803 et seqq.).

50 See *Callens/Granata*, Chapter VIII, C.
51 For a critical view, see *Fishmann*, JIPLP 2015, p. 98.

2. Court Fees

a) Court fees for the Court of first instance

The fees charged by the UPC will firstly depend on the nature the action, and secondly on the value of the action. The court fee charged for the following actions will depend on the value of the action:[52] **429**

- infringement actions;
- counterclaim for infringement in a revocation proceeding;
- actions for declaration of non-infringement;
- actions for license compensation based on a statement of willingness to license a Unitary Patent;
- damage-award proceedings (as a later part of the infringements proceedings).

The court fee for the first four types of proceedings listed above will be assessed on a sliding scale:[53] **430**

Value of the Action	Court Fee
Up to and including 500,000 €	14,600 €
Up to and includi ng 750,000 €	17,900 €
Up to and including 1,000,000 €	19,900 €
Up to and including 1,500,000 €	25,200 €
Up to and including 2,000,000 €	31,800 €
Up to and including 3,000,000 €	41,100 €
Up to and including 4,000,000 €	49,000 €
Up to and including 5,000,000 €	57,000 €
Up to and including 6,000,000 €	66,200 €
Up to and including 7,000,000 €	75,500 €
Up to and including 8,000,000 €	83,400 €
Up to and including 9,000,000 €	91,400 €
Up to and including 10,000,000 €	100,700 €
Up to and including 15,000,000 €	113,900 €
Up to and including 20,000,000 €	147,000 €

52 See the following bulletin on the website of the Preparatory Committee: https://www.unified-patent-court.org/sites/default/lodges/agreed_and_final_r370_subject_to_legal_scrubbing_to_secretariat.pdf.

53 Rule 370 differentiates between a "fixed fee" and a "value-based fee." This makes no difference in practice, however, in that a fee directly dependent on the value of the action is charged. The fees were raised by the Administrative Committee on 4 November 2025, taking effect from 1 January 2026.

Value of the Action	Court Fee
Up to and including 25,000,000 €	180,100 €
Up to and including 30,000,000 €	213,200 €
Up to and including 50,000,000 €	345,600 €
Above 50,000,000 €	444,900 €

431 In a damage-award proceeding, the fees will be lower by 10,600 € in each case:

Value of the Action	Court Fee
Up to and including 500,000 €	4.000 €
Up to and including 750,000 €	8.300 €
Up to and including 1,000,000 €	9.00 €
Up to and including 1,500,000 €	14.600 €
Up to and including 2,000,000 €	21.200 €
Up to and including 3,000,000 €	30.500 €
Up to and including 4,000,000 €	38.400 €
Up to and including 5,000,000 €	46.400 €
Up to and including 6,000,000 €	55.600 €
Up to and including 7,000,000 €	64.900 €
Up to and including 8,000,000 €	72.800 €
Up to and including 9,000,000 €	80.800 €
Up to and including 10,000,000 €	90.100 €
Up to and including 15,000,000 €	103.300 €
Up to and including 20,000,000 €	136,400 €
Up to and including 25,000,000 €	169.500 €
Up to and including 30,000,000 €	202.600 €
Up to and including 50,000,000 €	335.000 €
Above 50,000,000 €	434,300 €

432 A court fee dependent of the value of the action is also imposed for a counterclaim for revocation in an infringement proceeding. This corresponds to the fee charged for infringement proceedings plus a surcharge of 50 %, whereby the total is not to exceed 26,500 €. This results in the following sliding scale:

Value of the Action (150 % of the Value of the Infringement Action)	Court Fee
Up to and including 500,000 €	14,600 €
Up to and including 750,000 €	17,900 €

Value of the Action (150 % of the Value of the Infringement Action)	Court Fee
Up to and including 1,000,000 €	19,900 €
Up to and including 1,500,000 €	25,200 €
Above 1,500,000 €	26,500 €

For all other types of proceedings, fixed court fees are imposed (this will be mentioned when these proceedings are discussed). 433

b) Court fees for the Appeals Court

Beside fixed fees, which will be part of Chapter 11, there is also a value-based court fee, which is, however, slightly higher than in first instance: 434

Value of the Action	Court Fee
Up to and including 500,000 €	14,600 €
Up to and including 750,000 €	18,200 €
Up to and including 1,000,000 €	20,400 €
Up to and including 1,500,000 €	26,300 €
Up to and including 2,000,000 €	33,500 €
Up to and including 3,000,000 €	43,800 €
Up to and including 4,000,000 €	52,400 €
Up to and including 5,000,000 €	59,200 €
Up to and including 6,000,000 €	71,400 €
Up to and including 7,000,000 €	81,600 €
Up to and including 8,000,000 €	90,300 €
Up to and including 9,000,000 €	99,100 €
Up to and including 10,000,000 €	109,300 €
Up to and including 15,000,000 €	123,800 €
Up to and including 20,000,000 €	160,200 €
Up to and including 25,000,000 €	196,700 €
Up to and including 30,000,000 €	233,100 €
Up to and including 50,000,000 €	378,600 €
Above 50,000,000 €	487,900 €

3. Abatement of Court Fees

The court fees of the UPC may be partially abated or reimbursed under two preconditions: 435

a) Abatement for Small Enterprises and in Case of Economic Need

436 According to EU Commission Recommendation No. 2003/361 of 3 May 2003,[54] the court fees for microenterprises and small enterprises will be reduced to 60 % when these to submit an application for an action, a counterclaim, or an appeal (Rule 370.8), provided this is formulated in the language of the proceedings. The application must be accompanied by a confirmation that the applicant meets the stated requirements.

437 If the application is incomplete or does not meet the requirements, a deficiency notice will be issued. Otherwise, a decision regarding the application is to be promptly taken. The Court will also be free to demand additional documentation, including records concerning the applicant's financial situation.

438 After having heard the applicant, the Court may nonetheless order, at its own discretion and at any time, that the following additional payments be rendered:

- the balance of the court fees, if the Court believes that the abatement to 60 % was unjustified and inappropriate in view of the applicant's financial situation; or
- the balance of the courts fees plus a surcharge of 50 %, if the confirmation submitted by the applicant is found to be wholly or partially incorrect.

439 This order may be contested through an appeal in accordance with the procedure for appeals requiring leave from the Court of First Instance (see Para. 1102 et seqq.). If the additional fee is not paid, a default decision will be issued (Rule 370.8).

440 If the court fees owed threaten the economic existence of a party which is not a natural person[55] and said party can adduce reasonably available and plausible evidence, then the Court may reimburse all or part of the court fees upon the affected party's request (Rule 370.10).

441 The Court is to decide the application promptly under due consideration of all aspects of the case, particularly the procedural behavior of the party involved. The Court may hear the opposing party before making its decision.

442 A party disadvantaged by the Court's decision may lodge an appeal against the decision in accordance with the procedure for appeals requiring leave from the Court of First Instance (Rule 370.10).

b) Reimbursement Upon Premature Termination of the Action

443 A reimbursement of court fees is also envisioned under the following scenarios, however (Rule 370.9):

- If the action is heard by only one judge (see Para. 363), the court fees will be reduced by 25 %;

---

54 http://eur-lex.europa.eu/legal-content/DE/TXT/?uri=URISERV:n26026.

55 Note: Natural persons will be able to request financial aid for litigation costs; see Para. 1238 et seqq.

- If the action withdrawn or amicably settled before the final ruling, then the court fees will also be reduced, namely by:
  - 60% if the action is closed before the end of the written procedure;
  - 40% if the action is closed before the end of the interim procedure; or
  - 20% if the action is closed before the end of the oral hearing.

In certain exceptional cases, these reimbursement amounts may be further increased – or reduced – by the Court at its discretion. **444**

4. Recoverable Representation Costs

In almost all[56] proceedings before the Unified Patent Court, it will be possible for the victorious party to have its representation costs fully or partially reimbursed by the opposite side. The basis for this is Article 69 of the UPC Agreement: **445**

> "Reasonable and proportionate legal costs and other expenses incurred by the successful party shall, as a general rule, be borne by the unsuccessful party, unless equity requires otherwise, up to a ceiling set in accordance with the Rules of Procedure." (Article 69 (1) of the UPC Agreement).

This said, the general recoverability of representation costs is already established in the IPR Enforcement Directive. It bears noting that, according to the ECJ's Judgment No. C-57/15 in the *United Video vs. Telenet* case,[57] the recoverable costs must be reasonable for the losing party. Also relevant is the ECJ's Judgment No. C 531/20 in the *Novatext vs. Ruprecht-Karls-Universität Heidelberg* case, which holds that the court must always be free to perform a case-by-case evaluation (see Para. 1019). **446**

A detailed bulletin on this topic was published by the Preparatory Committee on 26 February 2016, and finally adopted by the Court. This bulletin states that there is an absolute upper limit for recoverable representation costs, one which will be the same for proceedings before the Court of First Instance and those before the Court of Appeal. This upper limit only serves as a sort of "safety net," however. **447**

Exactly which costs are recoverable will be decided by the Court in its decision on costs, but only reasonable costs are to be deemed recoverable, as opposed to unnecessary costs. Before taking its decision, the Court may also ask the parties, during the oral hearings, to submit the costs which they wish to recover (Rule 118.5). If the Court's judgment gives a partial victory to one side, the Court may also decide that each party must bear its own costs or that the costs are to be shared. **448**

The sliding scale used to assess the upper limit for recoverable representation costs is somewhat different from the one used for court fees. Thus, the upper limit will be derived from the value of the action as follows: **449**

---

56 Note: Excepted herefrom are actions challenging decisions of the European Patent Office; see Para. 1202 et seqq.

57 ECJ, Judgment No. C-57/15 of 28 July 2016 in the *United Video vs. Telenet* case.

Value of the Action	Upper Limit of Recoverable Representation Costs:
Up to and including 250,000 €	38,000 €
Up to and including 500,000 €	56,000 €
Up to and including 1,000,000 €	112,000 €
Up to and including 2,000,000 €	200,000 €
Up to and including 4,000,000 €	400,000 €
Up to and including 8,000,000 €	600,000 €
Up to and including 16,000,000 €	800,000 €
Up to and including 30,000,000 €	1.200,000 €
Up to and including 50,000,000 €	1,500,000 €
Above 50,000,000 €	2,000,000 €

a) Raising the Upper Limit in Complex Proceedings

450 In certain limited situations, such as particularly complex proceedings or proceedings involving multiple languages, the Court may, upon a party's request, raise the foregoing upper limits even further, while making due allowance for the financial resources available to all the parties, so as to ensure that they enjoy fair access to due process. The increase itself will be capped as follows based upon the value of the action:

- a maximum of 50 % when the value of the action equals 1 million € or less;
- a maximum of 25 % when the value of the action is above 1 million € and under 50 million €; as well as
- a maximum of 5 million € when the value of the action surpasses 50 million €.

451 This allows us to derive the following table:

Value of the Action	Upper Limit of the Raised, Recoverable Representation Costs:
Up to and including 250,000 €	57,000 €
Up to and including 500,000 €	84,000 €
Up to and including 1,000,000 €	168,000 €
Up to and including 2,000,000 €	250,000 €
Up to and including 4,000,000 €	500,000 €
Up to and including 8,000,000 €	750,000 €
Up to and including 16,000,000 €	1,000,000 €
Up to and including 30,000,000 €	1,500,000 €
Up to and including 50,000,000 €	1.875,000 €
Above 50,000,000 €	5,000,000 €

b) Lowering the Upper Limit Due to Economic Necessity

On the other hand, the Court may also lower the foregoing upper limits upon the request of a party which has lost the proceedings and whose economic survival would be threatened by having to pay the recoverable costs. This particularly applies when the requesting party is one of the following: **452**
- a small to midsized enterprise or a micro-enterprise;
- a natural person; or
- a non-profit organization,[58] a university or a public research institution.[59]

In taking its decision, the Court must all consider all available information concerning the parties. If possible, this information should specifically include: the parties' procedural behavior during the proceedings; the applicable upper limits for recoverable costs in relation to the parties' turnover revenues; the customary commercial activities of the parties; the effect which lowering the upper limit would have upon the opposite party.

c) Application to Change the Upper Limit

An application to change – i.e. to raise or lower – the upper limit should be lodged as early as possible during the proceedings, e.g. when the Statement of Claim or Statement of Defense is first submitted. In any case, it should be done in a timely manner so as to allow the Court to take a decision on the matter before the end of the interim proceedings. The application should contain all the available supporting evidence (see Para. 446: ECJ Decision on Costs). **453**

The application will then be decided without delay once the parties have been heard – before the end of the interim proceedings at the latest. The decision may be appealed in accordance with the procedure for appeals requiring leave from the Court of First Instance. **454**

5. Other Reimbursable Costs

The regulations discussed above relate to the costs incurred for attorneys/representatives. Thus, the aforementioned upper limits only apply to costs of this nature. **455**

Of course, the Court will also be in a position to order the reimbursement of other necessary costs, insofar as the victorious party has requested these during the damage-assessment proceedings (see Para. 922 et seqq.) Such costs include: **456**
- Costs for expert reports and outside experts;
- Costs associated with witnesses;
- Translation costs.

58 According to the EU Commission's Recommendation No. 1290/2013/EU.

59 Note: This definition of eligible institutions essentially corresponds to the definition of the patent applicants who are entitled to compensation for translations of Unitary Patents; see Para. 156.

457 When it comes to outside experts, the customary costs (e.g. per diem rates) are to be considered (Rule 153).

6. Regulations for Unnecessary Costs

458 Art. 69(3) of the UPC Agreement states that:

> "A party should bear any unnecessary costs it has caused the Court or another party."

459 It remains to be seen whether this means that Section 93 of the *Zivilprozessordnung* (ZPO, German Code of Civil Procedure) is to be apply by analogy. This provision holds that, where the defendant has not given cause for an action to be brought, the plaintiff must bear the costs of the proceedings should the defendant immediately acknowledge the claim (see the discussion in Para. 945 et seqq.). Some decisions of the Court of Appeal of the UPC, however, clearly point in this direction.[60]

VII. Capacity to Bring Legal Action/Counterclaim for Revocation

460 According to the UPC Agreement:

> "Any natural or legal person, or any body equivalent to a legal person entitled to initiate proceedings in accordance with its national law, shall have the capacity to be a party to the proceedings before the Court. (Article 46 Agreement)."

461 Also of significance in this context is Article 47 (6):

> "Any other natural or legal person, or any body entitled to bring actions in accordance with its national law, who is concerned by a patent, may bring actions in accordance with the Rules of Procedure."

This topic comes with the following peculiarities and open questions:

1. Legal Capacity for Bringing Revocation Actions

462 The following questions remain to be clarified when it comes to legal capacity for revocation actions:

- Is an anonymous revocation action possible? This seems to be precluded by the above-cited Article 46 of the UPC Agreement.
- Is it possible to bring a revocation action as a "straw man"? This could well be precluded by Article 47(6), which stipulates that a party bringing legal action must be "concerned" as a precondition, the fulfillment of which would at least have to be demonstrated. But given the fact that Article 47(6) simultaneously refers to legal capacity under national law, and given that straw-man revocations are readily permissible in all Member States of the UPC Agreement, it seems safe to assume that revocation actions brought by a straw man will be permissible before the Unified Patent Court as well.[61]

---

60 UPC_CoA_2/2024, Order of 4 October 2024, APL_83/2024 – Edwards v. Meril.

61 Cf. also *Burrichter/Kirchhofer* in *Bopp/Kircher*, Note 131 to Section 14; *Callens/Granata* maintain that the intention of Article 47 (6) is to serve as a "catch-all" that will maximize

- Will a patent proprietor, too, be entitled to bring a revocation action for his own patent? This is impossible in most national proceedings or in an opposition proceeding before the European Patent Office.
- Vindication and/or a lack of legal capacity for lodging an application will qualify as grounds for revocation before the Unified Patent Court. So will only the concerned party have legal capacity to bring a revocation action, as is currently the case in countries like Germany? Or can third parties also file such an action, as is presently the case in Italy, for example?[62]
  Unproblematic is, however, when a certain company has been sued for infringement before the Unified Patent Court, a nullity action of a sister or daughter company.[63]

2. Licensees' Legal Capacity to Bring Legal Action

In patent-infringement cases, the right to bring action generally redounds not only to the patent proprietor but also to any licensees of the patent (Article 47(2) and (3)); to wit: **463**
- Exclusive licensees will have legal capacity without further preconditions, provided that the patent proprietor was notified in advance; and
- Non-exclusive licensees will have legal capacity insofar as the respective license agreement permits this and the patent proprietor was notified in advance.

The patent proprietor may accede as a party to an action brought by a licensee (Article 47(4)). This is discussed in more detail in Para. 1220 et seqq. **464**

It bears noting that if a licensee brings an action and the patent proprietor does not accede to it, the patent proprietor will nonetheless automatically become party to any counterclaim proceeding that may be brought. This is discussed in detail in Para. 835. **465**

3. Counterclaim for Revocation

Besides revocation actions and actions for declaration of non-infringement, the UPC Agreement also recognizes counterclaims for revocation in patent-infringement proceedings. Inasmuch, this differs from the German tradition, which follows the "Segregation Principle" (*Trennungsprinzip*).[64] **466**

Insofar as a licensee of the patent in dispute – or of one of the patents – in dispute has brought an action, the counterclaim will then be directed against the patent proprietor. The Court will notify the patent proprietor and treat him going forward as the defendant of the counterclaim. **467**

---

the population of those entitled to bring action, see Chapter VII, C. I.

62 See *Nieder*, GRUR 2015, 936.

63 UPC_CoA_464/2024, Decision of 25 November 2025 – Edwards v. Meril.

64 See *Meier-Beck*, GRUR 2015, p. 929; for a more precise analysis, cf. *Cremers*, ZEW Discussion Paper 14–072.

468 When the trial court is not the central division, then the Court will be free to select from among the following courses of action when a counterclaim is received:
- to accept the counterclaim and decide on the patent infringement as well as on the revocation. In this case, it will be mandatory to allocate a technical judge;
- to refer the counterclaim to the central division. In this case, the Court will be free to either suspend the infringement action until the counterclaim has been decided or continue the infringement proceeding;
- as a third possibility – albeit only if all the parties consent – to refer the entire action, i.e. including the infringement proceeding – to the central division.

469 This is discussed in more detail in Para. 873 et seqq.

VIII. The ECJ as a Possible Court of Appeal/Review?

470 It is still unclear whether or to what extent the European Court of Justice (ECJ) will play a role in the Unitary Patent System.[65]

471 There can be no doubt, however, but that the ECJ must mandatorily be seised in matters dealing with those fields in which it already has jurisdiction, either by virtue of the Lisbon Treaty or other EU Regulations and Directives. These include, inter alia:
- antitrust law, particularly when dealing with standard-essential patents (see Para. 797 et seqq.)[66]
- biotechnology, by virtue of Directive (EC) 98/44.[67]
- enforcement of intellectual property rights on the basis of Directive 2004/48/EU. The reader is also referred to Regulation 608/2013/EU (customs enforcement).
- certification proceedings under pharmaceuticals law. Particularly important here is "skinny labeling" and the ruling on clinical trials on the basis of Directive 2001/83/EC and related Directives; as well as
- supplementary protection certificates on the basis of Regulation 469/2009/EC (as well as the supplementary Regulations 2019/933/EU and 1901/2006/EC.[68]
- "The Brussels-Ia-Regime" EU 1215/2012, here also the first referral has occured.[69]

472 What is unclear is whether the fact that the Unitary Patent is based on the Unitary Patent Regulation automatically means that the European Court of Justice is, in effect, the highest court of review for the Unified Patent Court – even though the UPC Agreement says nothing further in this regard.

---

65 Cf. also *Geiger/Nard/Seuba/Luginbühl/Kandeva*, p. 207 et seqq.; as well as *Metzger*/Ulrich, p. 229 et seqq.

66 See e.g. *Heusch*, GRUR 2014, p. 745; cf. also *Malaga*, IIC 2014, p. 621; see also *Petersen* et al, "The Unified Patent Court (UPC), Compulsory Licensing and Competition Law" as well as *Müller/Henke*, Mitt. 2016, p. 62.

67 For the debates over the EPO's Opinion No. G3/19, cf. *Aertz*, GRUR Int. 2018, p. 721; as well as *Hüttermann*, Mitt. 2020, p. 255.

68 Particularly on the aspect of protection certificates for crop-protection products, see *Arunasalam/De Corte*, GRUR Int, 2016, p. 1091.

69 UPC_CoA_789/2025, Decision of 6 March 2026 – Dyson v. Dreame.

This is a topic on which opinions diverge. Whereas authors like *Tilmann*,[70] *Romandini/Klicnik*,[71] or *Jäger*[72] explicitly affirm that the ECJ can be integrated into substantive patent law, this is more or less denied by *Haedicke*,[73] while *Ohly*[74] takes an in-between position. A more negative stance is represented by *Gruber*,[75] who believes that the Unified Patent Court has absolutely no authority to refer cases: In his view, only the national courts are competent for disputes involving Unitary Patents. The author of this book[76] takes the view that the ECJ will not play any greater role going forward than under the current system of national patent jurisdiction. **473**

On 13 March 2015,[77] a declaration was published online[78] in which more than 40 professors of law went so far as to describe the structure of the Unitary Patent System as a "dangerous precedent," while warning that the European Court of Justice must not be robbed of its competence by the EU Member States. **474**

As *Jaeger*[79] correctly points out, the ECJ had the opportunity to at least indirectly state its position on its role and on the general structure of the Unitary Patent System in the context of its "Spain Judgments," i.e. Nos. C-146/13 and C-147/13. Here, the author of this book[80] sees clear indications that the ECJ does not consider the construction of the Unitary Patent Systems to be reconcilable with European law, and yet refuses to claim any greater decision-making competence than it already has under the current system. **475**

It goes without saying that a final clarification has yet to be made. Since the ECJ is currently not involved in the Unitary Patent System – at least officially – there is also the question of how the ECJ can even take any decisions unless cases are referred to it by the Unified Patent Court itself. *Jaeger* has argued that actions pursuant to Article 259 of the Lisbon Treaty may play a role in this context.[81] **476**

---

70 *Tilmann*, VPP-Rundbrief 2013, p. 56.
71 *Romandini/Klicznik*, IIC 2013, p. 524.
72 *Jäger*, IIC, 2013, p. 389.
73 *Haedicke*, GRUR Int 2013, p. 609.
74 *Ohly*, ZGE 2012, p. 419; an ultimately similar view seems to be taken by *Metzger/Ullrich*.
75 *Gruber*, GRUR Int 2015, p. 323. cf. also *Amort*, EuR 2017, p. 56.
76 *Hüttermann/Kupka*, Mitt. 2015, p. 6.
77 Note: This was after the arguments made by Counsel General *Bot* in the "Spain Judgments" Nos. C146/13 and C147/13 had been published; the declaration did cite these arguments, but the corresponding cases had not yet been decided.
78 Here, for example: https://www.contexte.com/article/article/dangerous-precedent-of-patent-package_40086.html, for a reaction thereto, see *Pors*, http://www.eplawpatentblog.com/eplaw/2015/05/eu-the-unitary-patent-package-is-consistent-with-european-union-law.html, cf. also *Tilmann*, GRUR 2015, p. 527.
79 *Jaeger*, Max Planck Institute for Innovation & Research; Competition Research Paper No. 14–08.
80 *Hüttermann*, Mitt. 2015, p. 498, see also *Tilmann*, GRUR 2021, p. 373.
81 Additional possibilities are adduced by *Jaeger*, Max Planck Institute for Innovation & Research; Competition Research Paper No. 14–08.

1. Does the ECJ Derive Interpretational Competence from the TRIPS Agreement?

477 It bears noting that general interpretational competence in patent matters on the part of the ECJ could be derived from an entirely different source of law, namely the TRIPS Agreement. In this case, ECJ Judgment No. C-414/11 in the *Daiichi* case would be of decisive importance.[82] All Member States of the UPC Agreement are parties to the TRIPS Agreement.

478 In this specific case (whose factual circumstances are of secondary importance), the question was whether or not a country's accession to the TRIPS Agreement (here, Greece) automatically entailed a grant of retroactive patent protection for pharmaceuticals. The ECJ concluded that it did not. What is highly significant, however, is that the ECJ claimed an exclusive monopoly on interpreting the TRIPS Agreement. Yet Articles 27 et seqq. of this same TRIPS Agreement contain express provisions on fundamental patentability as well on patent-related rights. This ultimately means that the ECJ is declaring itself to be the court of final interpretation and *"could end up taking over patent law by way of TRIPS Agreement."*[83]

479 Thus, the construction of the Unitary Patent System – admittedly highly fragile as it is[84] – has already been described as a "pyrrhic victory"[85] that could have turned out differently.

480 Whether such a "takeover" of patent law will really manifest itself is impossible to predict.[86] The author knows of no relevant referrals made to the ECJ other than ones in Case No. C-414/11.[87]

2. Seising of the ECJ by the Unified Patent Court

481 If a question is referred to the Unified Patent Court and the UPC concludes that said question needs to be decided by the European Court of Justice (ECJ) before the UPC can take its own decision, then it may elect to seise the ECJ for this purpose, provided the relevant proceeding is pending before the UPC's Court of First Instance. But this elective option will not exist if the proceeding is pending before the UPC's Court of Appeal. In this case, the Court of Appeal must mandatorily seise the ECJ (Rule 266). So far, one referral has occured.[88]

---

82 ECJ, Judgment of 18 March 2013, No. C414/11 in the *Daiichi Sankyo* case.

83 Quotation from *Liebenau* et al (sic!) 2014 p. 107.

84 Cf. Para. 13 et seqq.

85 The description used by *Siegmund*, GRUR Int. 2018, p. 325.

86 Additional complications are seen by *Montañá i Mora*, IIC 2017, p. 784.

87 Note that *Fähndrich* et al. construe Judgment C-414/11 to mean that questions of patentability, particularly ones of a technical nature, must be referred to the ECJ; see *Fähndrich* et al, in *Tilmann/Plassmann*, Note 74 to Art. 554.

88 UPC_CoA_789/2025, Decision of 6 March 2026 – Dyson v. Dreame.

Unless the Unified Patent Court decides otherwise, the proceeding will be deemed suspended until the moot question is clarified (Rule 265.5). If the UPC decides not to suspend, then it must withhold its own final decision until the ECJ has issued its judgment. **482**

In all other respects, the referral proceeding corresponds to the proceedings customary before the national courts. **483**

IX. The Unified Patent Court as a European Court

According to Article 71a of Regulation 1215/2012/EU (the so-called "Brussels I" and "Brussels Ia" Regulation),[89] which was amended expressly for this purpose, the Unified Patent Court qualifies as a national court of an EU Member State.[90] **484**

This means that during the transitional period defined under Article 83 – in which actions involving European patents may permissibly be brought before the Unified Patent Court as well as before national courts – the principles normally applicable before the national European courts will also apply before the Unified Patent Court. Specifically applicable before the UPC will be Article 31 of Regulation (EU) 1215/2012, which stipulates that when multiple courts are competent, the one seised first will be competent and the one seised last must declare itself not competent.[91] This also means that, even after the transitional period, so-called "torpedo actions" (see Para. 305 et seqq.) will be precluded in countries which are EU Member States but not party to the Agreement, such as Spain or Poland. **485**

Note, however, that, according to Article 35 of Regulation (EU) 1215/2012, this does not apply to so-called "provisional measures," such as protective measures for preserving evidence and preliminary injunctions. **486**

▶ Example:

Consider the following possible scenarios during the transitional period defined under Article 83, i.e. until 1 June 2030: **487**

Scenario A)

A patent proprietor discovers that his European patent has been infringed. Given his positive experience with preliminary injunctions, he obtains such a measure against the infringer, e.g. before the District Court (*Landgericht*) of Munich. But since the infringement has occurred in multiple countries, he also submits a parallel patent-infringement action to the Unified Patent Court.

89 Amended through Regulation 542/2014/EU of 15 May 2014.

90 For a more detailed discussion, see *Luginbühl/Stauder*, GRUR Int 2014, p. 885 = JIPLP 2015, p. 135.; *Tilmann*, GRUR Int 2016, p. 409, *Alio* NJW 2014, p. 2395.

91 As regards the situation with trademarks in the EU, cf. *Heinze*, GRUR 2018, p. 160.

Both proceedings will be continued from then on. If the defendant in the proceeding in Germany decides to force a main action by petitioning the court to order the bringing of proceedings pursuant to Section 926 of the German Code of Civil Procedure (ZPO), then and only then would the German court lose its competence for the main action, namely on the basis of Article 31 of Regulation 1215/2012/EU.

Scenario B)

A patent infringer brings a revocation action against a European patent before the Unified Patent Court. Because he is convinced that the patent is invalid, he concomitantly brings a patent-infringing product to market.

The patent proprietor defends himself by seeking a preliminary injunction against the product from the District Court of Düsseldorf. Although the court will observe the pending revocation action, it will not deny the application for preliminary injunction on the grounds that it lacks jurisdiction. Thus, the proceeding for preliminary injunction will go ahead.

488 It also bears noting, however, these scenarios will no longer be possible after the end of the transitional period defined in Article 83, since the Unified Patent Court will thenceforth have exclusive jurisdiction. Nor will the above scenarios be valid for Unitary Patents, since these will fall under the exclusive jurisdiction of the UPC even during the transitional period.[92]

489 The status of the Unified Patent Court as a European court will have consequences for the enforcement of the judgments and orders issued by the Unified Patent Court; see Chapter 17, Para. 1468 et seqq.[93]

1. The implications of CJEU C-399/22 – BSH v. Electrolux

490 With its decision C 339/22 – BSH Haushaltsgeräte GmbH v. Electrolux AB, the European Court of Justice replaced the previously very restrictive approach to applying for cross-border injunctions with a very liberal one in February 2025. As a result of this decision, it has since been possible, if the defendant is based in an EU country and is being sued in that court, to apply for an injunction under a European patent for other countries as well. These countries do not even have to be members of the EU; for example, an injunction is also possible for the United Kingdom.[94] If an injunction is also possible for Non-UPCA-countries for Non-UPCA-residents, if also UPCA-residents are subject of a suit, is being referred to the CJEU.[95]

92 See *e.g.* also *Nieder*, GRUR 2015, p. 728.
93 Cf. *Leistner*, GRUR 2016, p. 217.
94 Cf. e.g. the UPC_CFI_359/202 (LD Mannheim), Decision of 18 July 2025 – Fujifilm v. Kodak.
95 UPC_CoA_789/2025, Decision of 6 March 2026 – Dyson v. Dreame.

This decision also applies in principle to national proceedings, but is particularly interesting for the Unified Patent Court due to its territorial coverage. Important: The Unified Patent Court is a unified court, i.e. it is possible to apply for a cross-border injunction against a defendant who is based in France, for example, before the local chamber in Düsseldorf or The Hague. **491**

It should be noted here that the court's broader jurisdiction is limited to injunctions. The court is not authorized to declare the respective national patents invalid (at least not *erga omnes*). Furthermore, if a national action for invalidity is pending, this must of course be taken into account by the court and, if necessary, suspended. **492**

2. Actions Challenging the Unified Patent Court for Infringements of European Union Law

According to Article 22 of the UPC Agreement, it is possible to claim compensation for damages when the Court of Appeal of the Unified Patent Court has failed to properly apply European Union law. However, the corresponding action must then be directed against a specific Member State, since the Member States are jointly and severally liable for such infringements by Unified Patent Court: **493**

> "1. The Contracting Member States are jointly and severally liable for damage resulting from an infringement of Union law by the Court of Appeal, in accordance with Union law concerning non-contractual liability of Member States for damage caused by their national courts breaching Union law.
> 2. An action for such damages shall be brought against the Contracting Member State where the claimant has its residence or principal place of business or, in the absence of residence or principal place of business, place of business, before the competent authority of that Contracting Member State. Where the claimant does not have its residence, or principal place of business or, in the absence of residence or principal place of business, place of business in a Contracting Member State, the claimant may bring such an action against the Contracting Member State where the Court of Appeal has its seat, before the competent authority of that Contracting Member State. [...]"

This Article is intended to ensure that infringements of EU law by the Unified Patent Court can be sanctioned by the stakeholders affected. It was integrated into the UPC Agreement at least in part in response to ECJ Opinion G 1/09 (see Para. 12).[96] **494**

Actions in this context must be brought by the plaintiff domiciled in a Member State and must be lodged in that Member State. If and only if no primary business location in a Member State exists (whereby ECJ Judgement No. 617/15 becomes relevant; see Para. 99), then, according to Art. 22(2), the action may also be brought in Luxemburg, the seat of the Court of Appeal. Article 22(2) makes it clear that only decisions by the Court of Appeal may be challenged, i.e. an action may be brought only if an appeal was first lodged (see Chapter 11, Para. 1098 et seqq.). **495**

---

96 Cf. *Callens/Granata*, Chapter I, p. 3.

496 If the action is successful, then the Member State must first advance the damages, but will subsequently be reimbursed by the other Member States pursuant to Article 22(3).

3. The UPC as a Court Within the Meaning of Article 149a EPC

497 As seen from the vantage point of the European Patent Convention (EPC), the Unified Patent Court qualifies as a court within the meaning of Article 149a of the EPC, where we read the following:

> 1. Nothing in this Convention shall be construed as limiting the right of some or all of the Contracting States to conclude special agreements on any matters concerning European patent applications or European patents which under this Convention are subject to and governed by national law, such as, in particular,
>
> a) an agreement establishing a European patent court common to the Contracting States party to it;

This serves to ensure, among other things, that Article 64 EPC, which stipulates that an infringement of a European Patent is to be handled under national law, cannot be used to call the competence of the Unified Patent Court into question.[97]

97 For more precise discussion and on the additional implications, see *Tilmann* in *Tilmann/Plassmann*, Note 6 et seqq. to the Introduction to the UPC Agreement.

Chapter 6: Strategic Considerations: To Seise or Not to Seise the Unified Patent Court?

Contents | Para

The strategic considerations presented below will focus on the question of whether and how the Unified Patent Court should be seised. The various possible approaches that can be taken in connection with proceedings before Unified Patent Court will be discussed in the following chapters, particularly Chapter 10. 498

A. Considerations of Relevance to Both Parties

The Unified Patent Court is a wholly novel court with its very own rules and regulations. As mentioned earlier, national law is named as a potential source of law in the UPC Agreement. Yet there is no mention of which national law should be applied or given precedence. This said, the litigating parties should be careful not to assume 499 that a resulting legal gap or omission in the UPC Agreement could simply be filled by applying the national laws of, say, France or Germany – even when the relevant panel of the Unified Patent Court happens to comprise two French or two German judges!

500 The more prudent approach would be to instead assume that the panel will begin by adhering strictly to the UPC Agreement while consulting the UPC's rules of Procedures, so as to derive a solution on that basis. If the Court ultimately does decide to borrow from national law, it will probably review the legal practice of a number of Member States before doing so. As a practical matter, the Court is likely to give primary consideration to the evolutionary history of the relevant regulations. This was the approach used, for example, in several proceedings before the Enlarged Board of Appeal of the European patent Office, such as Case No. G1/08. Besides the UPC Agreement itself, the European Patent Litigation Agreement (EPLA) (see Para. 5) and the "Second Venice Resolution" (see Para. 38) could also serve as important sources of law in this context.

501 Seasoned patent-infringement attorneys may find it particularly tempting to rely excessively on the experience garnered over decades of practice. They should instead strive to re-analyze the relevant sources of law with a fresh eye as each situation arises.

502 Only time will tell whether and to what extent national regulations will exert an influence on the established case law and regulations of the Unified Patent Court. Some observers have pointed out with good reason that the converse scenario is just as likely, i.e. that national regulations or even the practices of the European Patent Office[1] will end up being influenced[2] by the regulations of the Unitary Patent System. This would be just the sort of cross-pollination which has been observed, for example, between the EPO and German law with respect to "selection inventions" in the field of chemistry.[3]

B. Strategic Considerations for Patent Proprietors

I. To Seise or Not to Seise the Unified Patent Court?

503 This question[4] can be broken down into three aspects:
- Financial/strategic considerations;
- One's level of confidence in the newly created court;
- Possible divergences between national legal environments and Unitary Patent law.

1 Some observes see the G 1/24 of the EBA of the EPO as a first case where this has happened.

2 Cf. *Hilty* et al, Max Planck Institute for Intellectual Property & Research; Competition Law Research Paper No. 13–16; also see *Dijkman/van Paddenburgh*, European Review of Private Law 1, 2018, p. 97.

3 See *Luginbühl*, GRUR Int 2010, p. 97; on the prior situation, see, e.g. *Hansen* GRUR Int 2008, p. 891; but also see Ruling No. X ZR 77/12 issued by the German Federal Court of Justice (BGH) on 18 March 2014 in the *Proteintrennung* case, Mitt. 2014, p. 322.

4 Note: For a general survey of key motivating factors for patent plaintiffs, see *Kessler* et al. Mitt. 2018, p. 16.

The specific litigation strategies which come into play in proceedings before the Unified Patent Court will be discussed in subsequent chapters. 504

1. Financial/Strategic Considerations

The Unified Patent Court makes it possible to obtain a "one-stop judgment" for all the Member States in which a European patent has been validated, insofar as these Member States are also party to the UPC Agreement. This effectively obviates the need for parallel infringement proceeding in these Contracting Member States, which will usually represent most if not all of the validation states in question. This translates into potential costs savings for plaintiffs. 505

Data on the observed extent of parallel infringement actions prior June 2023 may be found, for example, in the research conducted by *Cremers* et al.[5] into patent-infringement practices in the Netherlands, France and Germany. 506

According to this research, 15 % of all patent actions in the Netherlands also involve at least one additional patent action in a country signatory to the European Patent Convention (EPC). But the corresponding percentage for France and Germany is only 6 %, respectively 2 %. This means that French and German infringement actions only rarely entail parallel proceedings in other Member States of the EPC. 507

Given that German proceedings (cf. Para. 349) make up the lion's share of European patent actions, it follows that parallel actions have thus far remained the exception in Europe rather than the rule. According to *Cremers* et al., only 8.4 % of European patents are associated with parallel actions. 508

It bears noting that in Germany and France, the two countries with the highest number of patent-infringement actions, only 42 %, respectively 39 %, of all such actions are conducted on the basis of European patents. If this trend continues, it is safe to assume that the national courts will not become obsolete in these countries! 509

As expected, the percentage for the Netherlands is a relatively high 73 %, however, i.e. the actions brought here are mainly based on validated European patents. 510

The aforementioned frequency of parallel proceedings (8.4 % of all cases) may seem low at first, but it is hardly negligible either. And since experience has shown that parallel infringement proceedings can lead to very different outcomes in different countries, it also implies a certain level of legal uncertainty.[6] 511

Add to this the fact that parallel proceedings can be of protracted duration, even when essentially the same decisions are reached. One good example is the dispute 512

---

5 *Cremers* et al., Discussion Paper No. 13–072, "Patent Litigation in Europe," *Zentrum für Europäische Wirtschaftsforschung GmbH*. Note: Research was also done in Great Britain, but this country is not part of the Unitary Patent System and thus not germane to the strategic considerations under discussion.

6 The classics examples being the *Epilady* cases and, more recently, the *Occlutech* case; see e.g. *Grabinski*, GRUR 1998, p. 857; cf. also *Kühnen*, GRUR 2012, p. 664.

over European Patent No. EP 153114 in *Roche vs. Chiron.*[7] In this case, revocation actions were conducted in Belgium, Germany, France, Great Britain, Italy, Luxembourg, the Netherlands and Sweden (!)

513 Parallel proceedings of these sort will be a thing of the past with the Unified Patent Court. This is a clear strategic advantage of the UPC and should not be underestimated.

a) Costs of a Proceeding Before the Unified Patent Court

514 As evidenced by the corresponding fee schedules (see Para. 445 et seqq.), representation costs make up the main expense for a proceeding before the Unified Patent Court. But one should by no means assume that the stated upper limits will equal the actual costs likely to be incurred by the losing party. Moreover, the adjudicating court must always consider whether these costs can be reasonably imposed upon the opposite Party, a precept affirmed by ECJ Judgment No. C-57/15 in *United Video vs. Telenet.*[8] Also significant in this context is ECJ Judgment No. C 531/20 in *Novatext vs. Ruprecht-Karls-Universität Heidelberg*, which held that the court must always be free to perform a case-by-case evaluation (also see Para. 1019).

515 Still, it can be useful to make a rough comparison between the UPC's fees and those charged for German proceedings under the Act on the Remuneration of Lawyers (*Rechtsanwaltsvergütungsgesetz*, RVG). One should bear in mind, however, that the value of an action in a German proceeding will always be lower than the value of an action before the Unified Patent Court, simply because Germany encompasses a much smaller territorial jurisdiction. This will hold true even if the calculation methods used by both the UPC and the German courts are essentially the same (which they presumably will be). Also note that the territory to be considered by the Unified Patent Court may vary widely depending on the territorial scope of the patent in dispute.

516 Let us assume the following for purposes of illustration:

- The value of an action before the Unified Patent Court is three times as high as in Germany; and
- Representation before the German courts of instance is provided by a lawyer acting in tandem with a patent attorney.

7 See the lecture given by *Waechter* at the 8th Rhineland Biopatent Forum held on 21 May 2015 at the Düsseldorf office of the Michalski, Hüttermann & Partners law firm. The patent was ultimately revoked in all those proceedings that were seen through to the end.

8 ECJ Judgment No, C-57/15 of 28 July 2016 in *United Video vs. Telenet.*

This allows us to derive the following schedule: 517

Value of the Action in Germany	Attorneys' Fees in Germany[9]	Value of the Action Before the UPC (3 X German Value)	Recoverable Costs Before the UPC
250,000 €	13,200 €	750,000 €	112,000 €
500,000 €	18,800 €	1,500,000 €	200,000 €
1,000,000 €	27,750 €	3,000,000 €	400,000 €
2,000,000 €	45,050 €	6,000,000 €	600,000 €
3,000,000 €	62,550 €	9,000,000 €	800,000 €
5,000,000 €	97,550 €	15,000,000 €	800,000 €
10,000,000 €	185,050 €	30,000,000 €	1.200,000 €

This can be translated into the following graph: 518

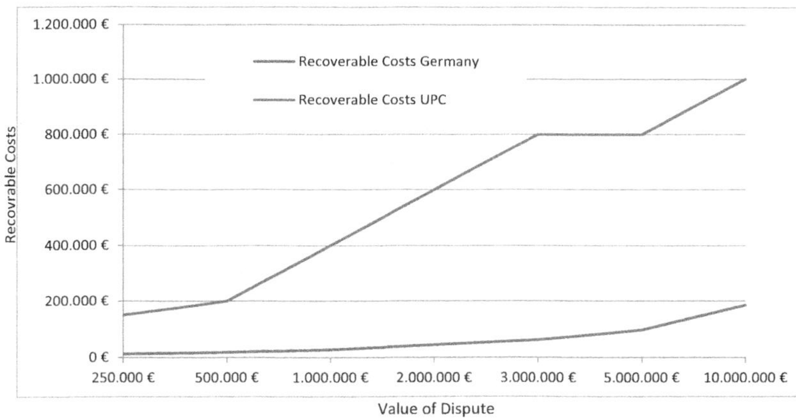

Fig. 6.1 Recoverable Costs Germany and UPC

It follows that the maximum amounts for recoverable costs before the Unified Patent Court are significantly higher than in Germany, which is naturally due to the proportionally higher value of actions before the UPC. 519

This does not mean that these calculated costs will equal the actual costs incurred, however. The costs defined under the German Act on the Remuneration of Lawyers (RVG) must always be understood as minimum costs.[10] 520

9 Note: Calculated in each case by doubling the 1.2 factor for procedural fees (RVG Fee Schedule No. 3100), the 1.3 factor for procedural fees (RVG Fee Schedule No. 3104), and the 20 € expense allowance (RVG Fee Schedule Nos. 7001 and 7002), without VTA for cases filed after 1 June 2025.

10 Note: On the question of whether the costs of foreign representatives are also recoverable, see e.g. *Gruber*, GRUR 2016, p. 1025.

521 The maximum recoverable costs before the Unified Patent Court, by contrast, merely constitute an absolute upper limit, one which is referred to as a "safety net" in Mooney/Tilmann's Guidelines on assessing the cost of an action (see Chapter 5, Para. 420). The Unified Patent Court has the right to deny costs which it deems unnecessary and excessive, and current caselaw shows that it will exploit this discretionary leeway.[11] Here, the Swiss Federal Patent Court may serve as an instructive model. In proceedings before this court, the same principles apply as before the UPC, namely the principles of applying the value of the action as a basis and of reserving discretionary leeway to the court. In Judgment No. O2013_013, for example, the Swiss Federal Patent Court readily denied the bulk of those costs which it considered excessive.[12] We have already mentioned the ECJ Judgments of relevance in this context (Para. 514), namely No. C-57/15 in *United Video vs. Telenet* and No. C 531/20 in *Novatext vs. Ruprecht-Karls-Universität Heidelberg* (also see Para. 1019).

522 The Unified Patent Court also has the right to demand that the parties estimate and specify their costs before handing down its decision, i.e. at a stage where there is still no final certainty as to the outcome of the proceedings (Rule of Procedure 118.5). This has become the standard practice before many divisions.

523 Notwithstanding the foregoing, it is safe to assume that the costs accruing in a lost proceeding before the Unified Patent Court will amount to at least double of those in a German proceeding. In most cases, they will probably be four to five times higher. The court has not yet established case law on this, however.

b) Average Costs of National Patent-Infringement Proceedings

524 The average costs for national patent-infringement proceedings are difficult to compare due to the variable nature of such proceedings. German practice tends to stand out in this context, since it provides for cost recovery as well as for a clear delineation between the questions of revocation and infringement.

525 An analysis of this topic can found in *Cremers*[13] as well as in *Mejer/Pottelsberghe de la Potterie*.[14] According to these authors, the average cost of conducting national

---

11 Cf. e.g. UPC_CFI_730/2025 LD Hamburg, Decision of 5 January 2026 – Nera v. Xiaomi et al.

12 Swiss Federal Patent Court, Judgment No. O2013_013 of 29 May 2013. There were three victorious parties in this proceeding. Of the 204,245.50 CHF in reimbursements requested by one of these parties, only 85,000 CHF were awarded, though this still exceeded what the other two parties had requested.

13 *Cremers* et al., ZEW Discussion Paper 13–072 (from September 2013) with additional references.

14 *Mejer/van Pottelsbergh de la Potterie, Documents de Treball de l'IEB 2009/31*. These authors – in contrast to *Cremers* – distinguish between 1st and 2nd instance proceedings in Germany, France and the Netherlands, so the 2nd-instance data for these three countries was taken from their work. When it comes to Great Britain, *Cremers'* data seemed more appropriate since it was more recent.

patent-infringement proceedings in the first and second instance in various countries can be broken down as follows (all numbers are in 1,000s €):

	Germany (in case of loss)	France	Netherlands	Great Britain[15]	Unified Patent Court (in case of loss)
1st Instance	50–250	50–200	60–200	2,000[16]	500
2nd Instance	90–190	40–150	40–150	2,000	500

Contrast this with the 500,000 € cost of a proceeding before the Unified Patent Court, calculated as follows (while rounding to the nearest 50,000 €): 526
- 50 % of the maximum representation costs times two (once for own counsel and once for the opposing side's counsel) for an action with an assumed value of four million €;
- court fees of 37,000 €.

This figure would seem to be a reasonable estimate in view of the arguments presented above. But one should bear in mind that, just as in a German national proceeding, very few if any of these costs will accrue before the Unified Patent Court if the proceeding is won.

c) Outcome of the Comparison

The outcome of the comparison is clear: A proceeding before the Unified Patent Court will be more expensive – at least during the initial period – than a national proceeding. Great Britain is by far the most expensive country, but it is not part of the Unitary Patent System (unless the "long-arm" jurisdiction applies, cf. Para. 487). 527

So if one were to decide on the basis of costs alone, then an action before the Unified Patent Court would appear purposeful only if an infringement occurs in all three of the other jurisdictions considered above, or if one can be relatively certain of winning the proceeding and of thus having to bear little or no expense. 528

Bringing such an action may still appear advantageous, of course, given the fact that only a single proceeding needs to be conducted and given the greater legal certainty that this provides. 529

2. Is the Unified Patent Court Worthy of Trust?

This is a subjective question of course, one which each patent proprietor/applicant will have to answer for himself. However, given the impressive number of carefully reasoned decisions, there should no longer be any fundamental doubt in this regard. In the short time since it was established and since it has been able to make import- 530

15 Though not part of the Unitary Patent System, Great Britain was included to provide a broader overview.

16 *Cremers* et al. arrive at a sum of roughly 1.5 million £ (using a conversion rate of 0.75 €/1 £).

ant decisions on substantive law, the Unified Patent Court has achieved a great deal in this area.

531 It bears noting here that the Unified Patent Court also offers other systemic advantages besides the ability to conduct one-stop infringement proceedings. Just a few of these are presented below:

532 EU Directives which limit patent protection, namely Directive 2001/82/EC (Veterinary Medicines Directive) and Directive 2001/83/EC (Human Medicines Directive) (see Para. 625), will apply before the Unified Patent Court, but they are the only ones. On the other hand, more far-reaching rights of limitation are recognized by most Member States of the UPC Agreement. Whether these furthergoing rights of limitation will have validity before the Unified Patent Court is unclear. Indeed, it seems rather improbable in view of the unambiguous formulation used in the relevant Article 27 of the UPC Agreement.

533 Also when it comes to indirect patent infringements across borders, plaintiffs will often find themselves in a better position before the Unified Patent Court than before the national courts.[17] Much the same holds true for process patents, particularly when the individual process steps described in the patent are performed in different countries.[18]

534 Also when it comes to the topic of representation, the UPC will offer broader possibilities than most national courts (see Para. 732 and the discussion in Para. 986 et seqq.).

a) Overall Conclusion

535 All in all, it is probably fair to conclude that the Unified Patent Court should always be considered a possible forum for patent-infringement actions. One should also bear in mind that, over the long run, the UPC will serve as the court of exclusive jurisdiction for actions involving European patents in the relevant Member States of the UPC Agreement.

536 Even if it is still a long way from being possible to speak of established case law of the Unified Patent Court, the following can be noted:

- When interpreting patent claims, the description and drawings (where available) are always taken into account and not only when ambiguities exist; this is clearly stated in the "10xGenomics v. Nanostring"[19] order of the Court of Appeal.
- The Munich local divisions's attempt to introduce something like an "estoppel" rule[20] has been clearly rejected[21] by the Court of Appeal, at least for the time being.

17 See *Nieder*, GRUR 2014, p. 627; as well as *Vissel*, GRUR 2015, p. 619.
18 See *Adam*, GRUR 2020, p. 1053.
19 UPC_CoA_335/2023, Order of 24 February 2024, App_576355/2023 – Nanostring v. 10x Genomics.
20 UPC_CFI_292/2023 (LD Munich), Order of 20 December 2023 – SesImagotag v. Hanshow.
21 UPC_CoA_1/2024, Order of 13 May 2024, APL_8/2024 – VusionGroup v. Hanshow.

- With regard to validity, the same standard of interpretation applies as for the infringement test[22] – in terms of validity, however, the Unified Patent Court ultimately follows the European Patent Office (even if it is sometimes referred to differently, see the discussion in Para. 662 et seqq.).

II. To Opt Out or Not to Opt Out?

Assuming that national proceedings are preferred, then two alternatives will be available, at least during the initial phase: 1) electing the "opt-out" option or 2) circumventing the UPC by resorting to national protective rights. Both alternatives are examined below. **537**

1. Should a National Action Be Brought Without an Opt-Out?

Although the possibility of bringing national actions without an opt-out is given, it does not appear purposeful from a strategic viewpoint: **538**

- This approach will not allow the patent proprietor to neutralize what is usually his opponent's most powerful weapon, namely a one-stop revocation challenge against the proprietor's patent; and
- The (presumed) infringer will not voluntarily forego this powerful weapon. Unless extraordinary circumstances prevail, he will usually respond to a national infringement action by immediately lodging a revocation action before the Unified Patent Court.

This topic will therefore not be examined further. No pending cases are known where this constellation applies. **539**

2. Timing of the opt-out

From a strategic viewpoint, the question of whether an opt-out-application should be lodged looks very different depending on whether the transitional period still has (quite) some time to go or whether its expiry is relatively imminent. So let us begin by examining the strategic variables that prevail when the transitional period is still ongoing. **540**

The question of whether an opt-out should be selected can be broken down into two subsidiary aspects: **541**

- Should an opt-out application even be lodged?

and, if so:

- When exactly should the opt-out application be lodged?

22 UPC_CoA_335/2023, Order of 24 February 2024, App_576355/2023 – Nanostring v. 10x Genomics.

a) Should an Opt-Out Application Be Lodged?

542 During the first years following the UPC's startup, the answer to this question will mainly depend[23] on one overarching consideration and three sub-variables:

543 The overarching consideration: What will the consequences of an opt-out be?

544 The three variables:
- Is one ready to place one's trust in the Unified Patent Court or does one prefer national proceedings? (See the earlier discussion.)
- How much time and effort will be required for the opt-out?
- How high will the opponent's actual expenditure of time and effort be if he is deprived of the opportunity of bringing a one-stop revocation action?

545 The first two variables have already been discussed. The overarching consideration and the last two variables will be discussed below.

b) What Will the Consequences of Opt-Out be?

546 As already explained, a number of ambiguities remain with respect to the consequences which an opt-out-application will have (see Para. 303 et seqq.)

547 If it turns out that an opt-out-application will not serve to preclude a subsequent revocation action before the Unified Patent Court, then an opt-out during the transitional period will essentially be useless.[24] This possibility does not seem very likely, however.

548 We will therefore limit our discussion to the scenario in which an opt-out does indeed preclude a later revocation action before the Unified Patent Court. Note that a necessary consequence of this scenario is that an opt-out will also preclude a later proceeding for preliminary injunctive relief before the Unified Patent Court.

c) How Much Own Effort and Expense will an Opt-Out Entail?

549 Although an opt-out application is free of charge, internal administrative effort and expense will still have to be incurred to lodge said application. It is important to estimate this as realistically as possible.

550 The opt-out application will also invariably entail a certain legal risk, given that its contents will not be subjected to any rigorous review. This risk will be particularly high when a patent's ownership is open to doubt.

551 Thus, it will be crucial to arrive at a highly precise and realistic assessment of one own's effort and expense and of the probable legal risk involved.

---

23 Six years and eleven months, to be precise – and only so long as no extension of the transitional period is made; see Para. 323 et seqq. But this would only serve to postpone the deadline; the strategic considerations would remain the same.

24 See *Nieder*, GRUR 2015, p. 718; and the letter from *Forwood* to *Beukering* of 19 March 2014.

d) How Much Effort and Expense Will the Opponent Incur?

During the seven-year transitional period, the opt-out application will essentially have only one effect: to deprive the opponent, i.e. the (presumed) patent infringer, of mounting a one-stop revocation challenge. A national infringement action, meanwhile, can also be brought without an opt-out. 552

An opt-out application will be worthwhile only if the effort and expense which the opponent actually incurs, or stands to incur, is significantly higher than in a revocation proceeding before the Unified Patent Court. 553

Not to be overlooked is the risk – also faced by the plaintiff – that a patent could be upheld in national revocation proceedings in one country but revoked in national proceedings in a different country. This uncertainly will still apply even though past experience has shown that individual rulings, e.g. by the German courts of instance, may exert a notable influence. In a one-stop revocation proceeding, by contrast, the outcome will automatically apply throughout all the patent's territories. 554

Thus, an opt-out should ideally be lodged for patents which the plaintiff himself considers to be "shaky" and unlikely to survive a revocation proceeding without serious limitation, if at all. This approach will give him the chance to retain ownership of at least a part of the relevant patent when all is said and done. The same logic will apply even if no revocation action is brought or even if the proprietor prevails in such an action (perhaps without expecting to). 555

e) When Should an Opt-Out Application Be Lodged?

This question will be relevant only with the first six years and eleven months of the Unified Patent Court's entry into force, since the deadline for an opt-out will expire on the ending date of this period. 556

Before this ending date arrives, the patent proprietor can theoretically take a wait-and-see attitude. But an opt-out-application can only be lodged so long as no action is pending before the Unified Patent Court. 557

A patent-infringement action must be lodged by the patent proprietor himself, i.e. it is up to him to select the court and, if applicable, to lodge an opt-out on short notice and to pursue a national action. Even in situations where action is brought before the UPC by licensees with the legal capacity to do so, one can assume that the patent proprietor will have been notified ahead of time. 558

The only remaining risk, therefore, is that a revocation action or action for declaration of non-infringement could be brought by a competitor. 559

So the question becomes: *How high is the risk that a revocation action or an action for declaration of non-infringement will be brought before the Unified Patent Court without being "provoked" by the patent proprietor himself?* 560

561 If this risk is (reasonably) high, then the patent proprietor should promptly lodge an opt-out application for all the patents potentially affected already during the "sunrise period" (cf paras 26 and 311). If the risk is low, then he can first wait and see.

562 It is reasonable to assume that the approach followed thus far to assess this risk will continue to prevail essentially unchanged in most technical fields. And that the same uncertainty which will confront the patent proprietor regarding the UPC's future legal precedent will also confront the plaintiff in a revocation action.

563 This said, revocation plaintiffs may have more incentive to bring revocation actions in those technical fields where parallel revocation actions in multiple countries have become the norm. A corresponding trend will probably be observed in segments of the pharmaceutical and biotech sectors. Here, a one-stop revocation challenge can save plaintiffs money. So that they will prefer to bring a preemptive revocation action before the UPC rather than waiting and potentially having to resort to parallel actions again if the patent proprietor lodges an opt-out.

564 Leaving the aforementioned technical fields aside, it therefore seems likely that revocation actions will not become more common than they have been in the past. Both past experience as well as the scholarly literature suggest that revocation actions which are in no way provoked by the patent proprietor tend to be clear exception. At most, they account for a low single-digit percentage of all actions.

f) Final Conclusion

565 Irrespective of whether or not an opt-out can serve to preclude a revocation action before the Unified Patent Court, the optimal, most cost-effective strategy for most patent proprietors will be to first wait and see without lodging a blanket opt-out. But once contact with a potential plaintiff is made, even if only through a right-to-use inquiry, then – and only then – should the question of whether to opt out rise to the fore.

3. Opting Out Shortly Before Expiry of the Transitional Period

566 The strategic picture begins to change as the expiry date of the opt-out deadline draws closer[25] (see Para. 323 et seqq.). After this date, which will presumably end 1 May 2030, an opt-out will no longer be possible. This means that an internal assessment of whether to exercise the opt-out option – and if so, to what extent – must be performed by the patent proprietor well in advance of this date. Only a duly lodged opt-out-application will make it possible to continue bringing infringement actions for European patents before the national courts.

25 Note: Insofar as this is not extended by the Administrative Committee. But even if this occurs, it would only serve to postpone the date; the strategic considerations would remain the same.

But by the time the transitional period expires, the new Unified Patent Court will have buildup an established case law (cf. Para. 536). Patent proprietors will then be able to factor this experiential information into their own strategies. If it turns out that trust in the Unified Patent Court is well-placed, for example, then an opt-out would become superfluous. But if this proves not to be case, then a blanket opt-out should definitely be considered. The current experiences with the Unified Patent Court, however, clearly speak in favour of the court. **567**

III. Is Pursuing National Patent Rights a Viable Alternative?

Besides opting out, there is also the option of leaving the European Patent Office out of the registration process entirely – at least as far as future protective rights are concerned – and registering purely national patents instead.[26] Since the Unified Patent Court is not competent for such patents, one could thus continue to bring legal action on the national level. **568**

As things currently stand, it is evident that such a strategy would only be worth considering if: **569**
- One holds such serious reservations about the Unified Patent Court that costs cease to matter;
- One is only seeking patent protection in a few countries of the EU anyway, since the administrative cost and effort incurred would otherwise outweigh the benefits of circumventing the Unified Patent Court.

Arriving at the right decision in this context can thus be boiled down to a single question: Would the option to circumvent the EPO for its own patent applications also have made sense under the old system? Only if the answer is "yes" will be it be worthwhile to register strictly on the national level going forward.[27] **570**

It bears noting, however, that many Member States have by now effectively closed off the so-called "national route," i.e. nationalization based on a registration under the Patent Cooperation Treaty (PCT) is no longer possible and the only way to obtain protection is through a European patent. This may make national patent rights less attractive of course, since one would already have to lodge the application before the end of the priority year. **571**

At present, the Member States[28] which have closed this national route are *Belgium, Cyprus, France, Greece, Ireland, Italy, Lithuania, Latvia, Malta* and *Slovenia.* **572**

---

26 See, e.g. *Köllner*, Mitt. 2013, p. 253.

27 Note: Perhaps of interest here is what the author was told by a friend, a high-ranking staffer of a major German corporation's patent department (who wishes to remain unnamed). In his opinion, individual validations before the EPO will become a thing of the past sooner or later: Either a Unitary Patent will be pursued or national patents will be selected right at the outset. The author does not entirely concur with this view.

28 Effective as of 1 February 2026, source: WIPO.

573 But if one is already lodging initial registrations in Germany on a regular basis, e.g. so as to have a research report available within the priority year, then one should consider getting these registrations granted while keeping the route to the national courts open, either by foregoing an opt-out when the European registration is granted (cf. Para. 299) or by immediately seeking a Unitary patent. Lodging an application twice in Europe – once in Germany and once on the European level – merely because the prohibition of double protection has been eliminated would seem excessive, however (see Para. 32 et seqq.).

German Utility Models

574 A potentially more attractive alternative worth mentioning is the possibility of splitting off a German utility model (= filing a German Utility model deviation) from a pending European patent application. Following such a deviation, the application date and priority date of an already existing application will then be used for purposes of the utility model (Section 5 of the Utility Models Act (*Gebrauchsmustergesetz*, GebrMG)).

575 Utility models are exclusively subject to national law. This means that legal action can be brought before German courts in this context, also in the future. Splitting off a utility model may "best of both worlds," i.e. being able to register on the European level while also bring legal action on the national level.

576 Another advantage of this alternative is that the same established procedures used in the past can be followed in the application proceeding. The applicant does not incur any effort and expense from having to change over to some other application procedure or from having to undergo a national review procedure. The only effort and expense incurred will be for the split-off itself, but this is a mere formality.

577 The deadline for a deviation ends two months after the respective European application has been decided i.e. it has either been denied or a mention of grant has been published. If an opposition is lodged, the deviation option will be deemed reactivated (Section 5 of the Utility Models Act (GebrMG)).

578 German Utility models have a maximum life of ten years (Section 23 of the Utility Models Act (GebrMG)). If the patent application is already more than ten years old, it follows that a deviation will no longer be possible.

579 It bears noting that claims for a deviated utility model do not have to be identical with those of a parallel patent application, provided they are covered by the patent description. It is also possible to perform multiple deviation filings right at the outset and thereby secure the registration of "custom-tailored" claims to various separate elements. These utility models also have the advantage of being more difficult to revoke, given that their appurtenant claims are more limited in scope. Inasmuch, a whole slew of strategic options will become available to the applicant. Although these options remain relatively unknown outside of Germany, they are gradually attracting interest from foreign applicants.[29]

29 See *Wuttke*, Mitt. 2015, p. 100.

It is not permissible to apply for a German utility models for processes[30] and applications that fall outside the medical field (Section 2 paragraph 3 of the Utility Models Act (GebrMG)).[31] But seeking double protection is definitely worth considering for any processes/applications that are eligible, since this will allow the patent proprietor to keep both avenues of legal action open until the expiry of the utility model's ten-year life. 580

IV. Before Which Division Should Action Be Brought?

If legal action before the Unified Patent Court is selected as the preferred option, then this raises the question of which division of the UPC to seise. But of course only under the proviso that one is free choose from among more than one division. This will usually be the case, however. 581

This question can be divided into two subsidiary aspects: Should action be brought before the central division or a regional/local division? And if the latter, then before which regional/local division? 582

1. Seise the Central Division or a Regional/Local Division?

This question seems relatively easy to answer, strategically speaking: The regional/local division will clearly be preferable. There are two reasons for this: 583

a) Referring a Counterclaim for Revocation Without Suspending the Action

The first reason is that an action before the central division never results in a situation where an infringement will be examined without concomitantly examining a counterclaim, given that this is not provided for under the UPC Agreement. Thus, a defendant will have an even stronger incentive to lodge a counterclaim for revocation when legal action is brought against him. 584

But when an action is brought before a local division, there is always the possibility that the Court could refer a subsequent counterclaim to the central division and continue examining the original action without any suspension. Even though this almost never happens in practice, one should not rule it out. 585

30 This has been criticized as being unconstitutional; cf. the Decision & Order of the German Federal Patent Court (BPatG) No. W (pat) 1/15 of 19 May 2016 in the *Feldmausköderstation* case, in Mitt. 2016, p. 467 with comments by *Köllner*; it has been affirmed, however, in the *Gebrauchsmuster für Verfahren* ruling of the German Federal Court of Justice (BGH), Mitt. 2018, p. 281.

31 Applications in the medical field are permissible following the BGH's judgment in the *Arzneimittelgebrauchsmuster* case, GRUR 2006, p. 135. But the Federal Patent Court (BPatG) has also held claims for applications to be admissible under certain preconditions; see the BPatG's *Verwendungsgebrauchmuster* ruling, Mitt. 2019, p. 406.

b) Composition of UPC's Divisions

586 A case before a local division, if counterclaim for revocation is filed, will be handled by four judges, before the central divison, there are only three judges.

587 This isy et another valid reason why an action should be brought before a local division.

2. Which Regional/Local Division to Choose?

588 This is of course a subjective question, i.e. the answer will depend on which division, respectively which panel of judges, inspires the greatest confidence. As the most infringement actions are before the German divisions, it is advisable to choose a German division for your case.

589 Choosing a German local division would also seem worth considering for the following reasons:

590 In principle, it would seem advisable to place one's trust in those judges who have demonstrably accumulated the most experience in the field of patent law. Since the Rules of Procedure of the Unified Patent Courts are relatively similar to German procedural rules,[32] procedural errors which could unnecessarily protract the action tend to be unlikely, i.e. one can expect a ruling to be handed down without undue delay.

591 Another characteristic of a proceeding before the Unified Patent Court is that one can lodge legal remedies against a procedural decision while the proceedings are ongoing, i.e. by having the decision reviewed by the adjudicating panel or by appealing or referring the decision to the Court of Appeal (for a full discussion, see Para. 1102 et seqq.). If the judges of a local division lack experience, these legal remedies can result in unnecessary delays.

592 The fact that around three quarters of infringement actions have so far been brought before the four German divisions speaks for itself.

V. Other Considerations

1. Choosing the Language of the Patent Application

593 According to the UPC Agreement, the language to be used before the central division must be the language of the patent which is in dispute and/or the subject of the action. This means that a revocation action must be conducted in the language of the patent at issue.

594 This creates a strong incentive for German-speaking or French-speaking applicants to lodge their European patent applications in German and French as well, since

32 Note: It again bears emphasizing that this does not necessarily mean the UPC will apply German law in the event of a legal gap, but only that it will probably have an easier time dealing with applicable law than other courts and judges. Indeed, the assumption that German law will be applied in case of doubt is an extremely risky one (see Para. 273).

this will increase the expense incurred by applicants from abroad (particularly from non-EU states). Although this approach will engender translation costs for parallel applications, e.g. in the USA, this could be outweighed by the strategic advantage of forcing third parties to use a language with which they are unfamiliar.

2. Licensees' Legal Capacity to Bring Action

According to the UPC Agreement, licensees, too, may potentially have legal capacity 595 to bring action. This holds true without further preconditions for exclusive licensees. For non-exclusive licensees, the proviso is that their legal capacity must be stipulated in the corresponding license agreement and that the patent proprietor must be notified before the licensees bring legal action.

If a licensee brings action and a counterclaim is lodged, however, then the patent 596 proprietor will automatically become party to the action, even if only as the formal defendant of the counterclaim.

Since the deadlines for lodging a statement of defense are extremely tight (cf. Chapter 9, Para. 826 et seqq.) and there is no reason to assume that they will be extended, 597 all licensing agreements should be structured with provisions that protect the patent proprietor from being caught unawares by a counterclaim. There should also be a provision requiring the licensee (i.e. the plaintiff of the infringement proceeding) and the patent proprietor to coordinate their response. Note that the interests of the licensee and patent proprietor need not be equivalent in this context. Thus, the licensee's main interest may be in seeing the defendant convicted, i.e. he would be willing to accept serious limitations on the patent so long as the defendant's infringement continues to be deemed infringing. The patent proprietor, for his part, is likely to accept limitations on his patent only to the extent they are absolutely necessary.

Thus, licensing agreements should definitely contain provisions that regulate how such 598 a situation is to be handled. Patent proprietors are also well advised to grant the licensee an independent right to bring legal action, insofar as this possible and enforceable.[33]

C. Strategic Considerations for (Potential) Patent Infringers

It stands to reason that there are fewer strategic factors for (potential) patent infringers 599 to consider than for patent proprietors, since it is the latter who will decide whether to bring a patent infringement action and where. Still, a few points are worth mentioning.

I. Prior Usage and Defensive Publications

The right of prior usage is one of the few rights whose scope continues to be restricted 600 to the individual Member States (see Para. 626). This means that prosecuted patent infringers who adduce the right of prior usage as a legal defense will be placed in a markedly worse position than patent plaintiffs even if they are successful. While a

33 Cf. also *Boos/Kreutzmann*, GRUR Prax 2015, p. 428.

patent plaintiff only needs to prove an infringement in one Member State in order to obtain an enforceable writ for all Member States, the acquirer of a right of prior usage will always be limited to adducing said right only in the country in which he took up his activities. It remains to be seen whether and how rights of usage could be extended to also cover improvements/enhancements (see Para. 788).

601 This inevitably makes prior usage a weak legal defense to adduce. The burden of having to prove such usage is yet another disadvantage. Thus, the better choice would be to lodge applications of one's own or to at least release defensive publications.[34] Such publications can be structured – at least according to current case law[35]– in a way that makes them difficult if not impossible to find, but without prejudicing their admissibility in an opposition proceeding or revocation proceeding.

II. Opposition and Revocation Proceedings

602 The Unified Patent Court opens up new ways to challenge the patents of third parties. The corresponding strategic considerations are discussed in detail in Chapter 13.

Referring an Action Before a Regional Division to the Central Division

603 As discussed earlier (Para. 388 et seqq.), it will be possible, once more than three regional divisions have been set up, to request that an action before a regional division be referred to the central division.

604 This will be subject to a further precondition: namely, that the infringement occurs within the territory covered by the three regional divisions. This will usually be the case, however, since the regional divisions usually encompass the smaller countries. What is more, an infringement occurring in a country covered by the regional division will frequently not be limited to just that country but will occur in other regions as well, sometimes even across the whole of Europe.

605 Whether a referral to the central division is a good strategy will depend on the individual case. The central division is likely to hear only a small number of infringement actions, whereas the number heard by the regional divisions ought to be somewhat higher. As already discussed, moreover, an action involving a counterclaim for revocation will be adjudicated by four judges – one of whom will be a technical judge – at a regional division, but by only three judges at the central division (see Para. 586). If nothing else, requesting a referral to the central division could be a way to play for time, so a defendant should always keep this option in mind.

34 See *Rosenich*, Mitt. 2014, p. 306.
35 For a vigorous critique of this, see *Tönnies*, Mitt. 2014, p. 309.

Section 2: Legal Foundations

Chapter 7: Legal Foundations and current jurisdiction concerning material law of the Unified Patent Court

Contents | Para

606 This chapter will focus on the legal foundations of the Unified Patent Court, in terms of both substantive law and procedural law. A short overview of the current jurisdiction of the Unified Patent Court concerning material law will be given as well.

A. Applicable Substantive Law

607 According to Article 24 of the UPC Agreement (UPCA), the Unified Patent Court is based on five sources of law:

a) European Union law, including the EU Regulations governing the Unitary Patent;
b) the UPC Agreement itself;
c) the European Patent Convention (EPC);
d) other international agreements applicable to patents and binding upon all the Contracting Member States of the UPC Agreement; as well as
e) national law.

608 According to Article 20 of the UPCA, European Union law takes primacy (see Para. 774). It has yet to be expressly codified whether a hierarchy of laws can also be derived – independently of Article 20 – from the sequence of the list set forth in Article 24 of the UPC Agreement; most commentators assume this is the case, however.[1]

1 Affirmed, for example, by *Haedicke* GRUR Int. 2013, pp. 609 and 612; *Walz* GRUR Int. 2016, pp. 513 and 516; *Tilmann*, GRUR Int. 2016, p. 409; *Tilmann* in *Tilmann/Plassmann*,

On the other hand, the UPCA contains no direct reference to generally recognized principles of procedural law, such as the one found in Article 125 of the European Patent Convention, (EPC), for example. But this does not really seem necessary, since corresponding regulations have already been codified under European Union law, under the EPC and under the respective national legal systems, and particularly since Article 42 of the UPCA expressly affirms such principles (see Para. 671 et seqq.). One major difference between the UPC and e.g. the EPO is the lack of ex officio investigations (see Para. 691 et seqq.). **609**

When it comes to the application of national law pursuant to Article 24 e) of the UPC Agreement, two separate cases must be distinguished: **610**

Article 24(2) of the UPCA defines which national legal system will be applicable in a specific case: **611**

> 2. To the extent that the Court shall base its decisions on national law, including where relevant the law of non-contracting States, the applicable law shall be determined:
> (a) by directly applicable provisions of Union law containing private international law rules, or
> (b) in the absence of directly applicable provisions of Union law or where the latter do not apply, by international instruments containing private international law rules; or
> (c) in the absence of provisions referred to in points (a) and (b), by national provisions on private international law as determined by the Court.

Article 24(2) comes into play when the specific circumstances – usually the ones prevailing between the parties – become important in an individual case.[2] The law applicable in such individual cases will be dictated by the hierarchy set forth in Article 24(2) a), i.e. stipulations under European Union law, e.g. the "Rome I Regulation" (Regulation (EC) 2008/593) will then take primacy.

▶ Practical tip:

This could apply in scenarios involving the following, for instance: **612**

- an exhaustion of rights when contract-law aspects come into play;
- a licensing objection;[3]
- a change of parties when the patent in dispute is transferred (see Para. 630);
- the capacity to be party to legal proceedings, e.g. the suspension or reactivation of such capacity;[4]
- questions to do with capacity to sue when national law (e.g. corporate law) comes into play;

Notes 1–2 to Art. 24; *Kircher* in *Bopp/Kircher*, Note 2 to Section 2, p. 13.; for a contrary view, see *Boos*, Rn. 17 et seqq. to Art. 24 in *Luginbühl/Hüttermann*, *Vissel*, GRUR 2015, p. 619.

2 See also *McGuire*, Mitt 2015, p. 537.

3 Cf. *Kircher* in *Bopp/Kircher*, Notes 21–24 to Section 2.

4 Cf. the "Zombie" Decision (No. G1/13) issued by the Enlarged Board of Appeal of the EPO, in which national law was applied as well (in this case British law).

- contractual agreements between parties (also implied agreements), or cases in which reliance in good faith plays a role;[5]
- arbitral arrangements; here the New York Convention on the Recognition and Enforcement of Foreign Arbitral Awards (NYC)[6] becomes applicable given that all Member States of the UPC Agreement have signed the NYC.

613 But national law will also serve as a potential source of law in scenarios that do not revolve primarily around the specific circumstances prevailing between the parties but rather around general questions, and in also in situations where other sources of law (such as the EPC) are not useful.

▶ Practical tip:

614 National law could be relevant in scenarios involving the following, for instance:

- an exhaustion of rights in a general sense, e.g. in demarcation from remanufacturing;[7]
- an equivalent patent infringement (see Para. 650 et seqq.);
- a specific structuring of rights of prior use, particularly for enhancements/improvements;[8]
- questions as to what constitutes a direct product-by-process, particularly in the context of data processing (e.g. in the IT sector or for 3D printing);[9]
- questions as to what "offering" should be taken to mean, particularly when a patent is about to expire, or what exactly constitutes "direct usage."[10]

I. Is the European Convention on Human Rights Applicable?

615 Not expressly included among the sources of law set forth under Article 24 of the UPC Agreement is the European Convention on Human Rights. Yet all Member States of the UPCA are also party to the Convention, which is formally known as the "Convention for the Protection of Human Rights and Fundamental Freedoms." The European Court of Justice (ECJ), moreover, in its Judgments in Case No. C-348/16 and the related Nos. C-357/19, C-379/19, C-547/19, C-811/19 and C-840/19, has made clear that there is an interlinkage between European Union Law and the Euro-

5 Somewhat analogous is the Judgment of the German Federal Court of Justice (BGH) in the *Weichvorrichtung* case, GRUR 1993, p. 886; also see *Kircher* in *Bopp/Kircher*, Note 237 to Section 13.
6 New York Convention on the Recognition and Enforcement of Foreign Arbitral Awards of 10 June 1958, cf. *Kircher* in *Bopp/Kircher*, Note 23 to Section 13.
7 Cf. BGH Judgment in the *Trommeleinheit* case, Mitt. 2018, p. 61, this decision, however, was not cited in UPC_CFI_248/2024 (LD Munich), Decision of 22 August 2025 – Brita v. Aquashield.
8 Cf. BGH Judgment in the *Schutzverkleidung* case, Mitt. 2019, p. 495.
9 For a full discussion see *Zech*, GRUR 2017, p. 475; see also *Blanke-Roeser* GRUR 2017, p. 467; more generally also cf. *Zech*, (sic!) 2018, p. 627.
10 Cf. *Kircher* in *Bopp/Kircher*, Note 154 to Section 13.

pean Convention on Human Rights. This would make the European Convention on Human Rights, even if it is not expressly mentioned, an additionally applicable source of law – and perhaps even a primarily applicable one – by virtue of Article 20 of the UPCA (see Para. 774).

The potential applicability of the European Convention on Human Rights is significant insofar as it is the (only) source of law which expressly stipulates that proceedings must be public, whereas there are no specific EU regulations on this topic.[11] (Interestingly enough, there is a whole slew of EU Directives and Regulations on the topic of protecting the public.[12]) 616

II. Applicable Law After an Opt-Out

It is not clear whether a consequence of "opting out" (see Para. 299 et seqq.) is that the national courts, which will then retain jurisdiction, will be obligated to apply the UPC Agreement or whether they will again be able to adjudicate based on purely national legal principles. While authors such as *Tilmann*[13] vigorously affirm the former possibility and strictly reject the latter one, the Preparatory Committee, for its part, takes the position that an opt-out exerts an all-encompassing effect, so that national law will apply exclusively.[14] This latter view was clearly taken by the OLG Karlsruhe.[15] 617

Yet Article 24 of the UPCA also grants the Unified Patent Court the option to apply national law where appropriate. So it is not entirely clear whether it makes a practical difference which law is applied. In the end, it will probably depend on the individual case.[16] 618

III. Rights Arising from a Patent

According to Article 25 of the UPC Agreement, a patent – as well as a supplementary protection certificate pursuant to Article 30 – confers upon its proprietor the right to prevent any third party from engaging in the following actions: 619

(a) making, offering, placing on the market or using a product which is the subject-matter of the patent, or importing or storing the product for those purposes;

---

11 Except for the EU Charter of Fundamental Rights, but this is not directly applicable before the UPC; cf. Article 47 der EU Charter of Fundamental Rights, Document No. 2010/C 83/02; see the Official Journal of the European Union C, No. 83, 30 March 2010, pp. 389–403.

12 E.g. General Data Protection Regulation (EU) 2016/679, IPR Enforcement Directive 2004/48/EC or Directive (EU) 2016/943 on the protection of trade secrets.

13 *Tilmann*, Mitt. 2014, pp. 58–65; see also *Tilmann* in *Tilmann/Plassmann*, Note 15 et seqq. to Article 83; the same general conclusion is reached by *Nieder*, GRUR 2014, p. 627.

14 Published on www.unified-patent-court.org on 29 January 2014; concurring views are taken by *Walz* GRUR Int 2016, p. 513, as well as by *Tochtermann*, GRUR 2018, p. 337; see also *Nieder*, GRUR 2014, p. 955.

15 OLG Karlsruhe, Decision of 14.2.2024 – 6 U 232/22 – Schneidmaschine.

16 See *Nieder*, GRUR 2014, p. 627, who definitely sees possible differences; cf. also *Schröer*, GRUR Int 2013, p. 1102.

(b) using a process which is the subject-matter of the patent or, where the third party knows, or should have known, that the use of the process is prohibited without the consent of the patent proprietor, offering the process for use within the territory of the Contracting Member States in which that patent has effect;
(c) offering, placing on the market, using, or importing or storing for those purposes a product obtained directly by a process which is the subject-matter of the patent.

620 These preclusive rights are identical to the ones set forth in Section 9 of the German Patent Act (*Patentgesetz*, PatG), even if Paragraph 2 of said section (infringement of processes) is formulated somewhat differently. Here, the formulation used is "*if it is obvious from the circumstances*" instead of "*where the third party knows, or should have known.*" In other words, the German Patent Act's provision places less reliance on the infringer's subjective state of cognizance.[17]

621 Also enshrined under the UPC Agreement is the principle of indirect patent infringement, namely in Article 26 (1), which reads:

> A patent shall confer on its proprietor the right to prevent any third party not having the proprietor's consent from supplying or offering to supply, within the territory of the Contracting Member States in which that patent has effect, any person other than a party entitled to exploit the patented invention, with means, relating to an essential element of that invention, for putting it into effect therein, when the third party knows, or should have known, that those means are suitable and intended for putting that invention into effect.

622 This corresponds to Section 10 of the German Patent Act (PatG), whereby here, too, "*where the third party knows, or should have known*" is replaced with the formulation "*if it is obvious from the circumstances.*"[18]

623 Just like Section 10, paragraph 2 of the German Patent Act (PatG), however, Article 26 (2) of the UPC Agreement sets limits on what constitutes an infringement, i.e. no infringement arises in the following case:

> "...when the means are staple commercial products, except where the third party induces the person supplied to perform any of the acts prohibited by Article 25."[19]

624 On the other hand, the UPC makes no provision for a positive right of use, e.g. of the type defined in Section 6 of the German Patent Act (PatG).[20]

---

17 See also e.g. *Nieder*, GRUR 2014, p. 627.
18 See *Nieder*, GRUR 2014, p. 627.
19 Note: Article 26 (3) describes indirect patent infringement in connection with the limitations set forth under Article 27, just as Section 10, paragraph 3 of the PatG does in connection with Section 11. This is of little importance in practice, however, and will not be discussed further.
20 See e.g. the Judgment of the German Federal Court of Justice (BGH) in the *Trägerplatte* case, GRUR 2009, p. 655.

1. Limitations on Patent Protection

According to Article 27 of the UPC Agreement, the effects of a patent are subject to limitations analogous to those defined under Section 11 of the German Patent Act (PatG). These are listed below (in condensed form): **625**

a) acts done privately and for non-commercial purposes;
b) acts done for experimental purposes;
c) the use of biological materials for purposes of breeding, or discovering and developing other plant varieties;
d) the clinical trials allowed pursuant to Directive 2001/82/EC (Veterinary Medicinal Products Directive) or Directive 2001/83/EC (Human Medicinal Products Directives). Note that only these two Directives serve as a legal basis; any furthergoing rights in this connection, such as those granted in most Member States, are either entirely inapplicable or applicable subject to constraints (cf. also Para. 532).[21]
e) acts which are the privilege of apothecaries;
f) uses on vessels, aircraft or other means of transport outside the Member States, by analogy to German patent law;[22]
g) acts which are the privilege of farmers pursuant to Regulation 2100/94/EC
h) Acts allowed pursuant to the Software Directive 2009/24/EC;
i) Acts allowed pursuant to the Biopatent Directive 98/44/EC.

2. Prior Use and Exhaustion of Rights

Articles 28 and 29 of the UPCA govern prior use and the exhaustion of rights. According to Article 28, prior use only applies on a purely national level,[23] i.e. also in the case of Unitary Patents (!) **626**

> Any person, who, if a national patent had been granted in respect of an invention, would have had, in a Contracting Member State, a right based on prior use of that invention or a right of personal possession of that invention, shall enjoy, in that Contracting Member State, the same rights in respect of a patent for the same invention.

Article 29, by contrast, provides for an EU-wide exhaustion of rights, as was previously the case: **627**

> The rights conferred by a European patent shall not extend to acts concerning a product covered by that patent after that product has been placed on the market in the European Union by, or with the consent of, the patent proprietor, unless there are legitimate grounds for the patent proprietor to oppose further commercialisation of the product.

---

21 See also the EU Commission's "Study on the Legal Aspects of Supplementary Protection Certificates in the EU" (authored by the Max-Planck Institute), Section 15.4.

22 Cf. District Court (LG) of Hamburg, Mitt. 2019, p. 559 – "The PatG Has No Applicability in Germany's Exclusive Economic Zone."

23 Cf. UPC_CFI_7/2023 (LD Düsseldorf), Decision of 3 Juli 2024 – Kaldewei v. Bette. This has been criticized as an unnecessary fragmentation; cf. *Machek*, MIPLC Master Thesis Series (2012/13); on the right of prior use as such, also see *Blumenröder/Bertram*, Mitt. 2014, p. 119.

628 Any other approach would probably have been irreconcilable with the established case law of the European Court of Justice (ECJ).[24]

IV. Regulations Relating to the Parties to an Action

1. Presumption of Ownership

629 The rights arising from a patent redound to the proprietor of that patent. The person shown in the Register is to be treated as the proprietor (Rule 8.4). More specifically:
- for Unitary Patents, the person recorded in the Register for Unitary Patents pursuant to the Unitary Patent Regulation (Article 2e thereof);
- for European Patents, the person recorded in the respective national register; respectively,
- the last person shown in the European Patent Register, when no entry has been made in the national patent registers.

630 If a change of proprietor occurs during a proceeding, or if the person recorded in the Register is not the actual proprietor, then a correction can be made upon application pursuant to Rule 305. As a rule, the corresponding transfer of title will be performed in keeping with the national legal system applicable in each case.[25]

631 There are no regulations in place to govern cases where a European patent has different proprietors in different Member States. This may certainly be the standard situation for certain applicants, particularly international conglomerates. In such cases, it is safe to assume that a plaintiff will naturally assert claims only for the territory in which he is also the proprietor. But in the event of a counterclaim for revocation, the second proprietor will automatically become a defendant as well (see Para. 838 et seqq.).

2. Legal Capacity to Bring Patent Infringement Actions

632 According to Article 47 of the UPC Agreement, not only patent proprietors have legal capacity to sue but also exclusive licensees and – provided this is stipulated in the licensing agreement – non-exclusive licensees as well. Besides being duly authorized in the licensing agreement, non-exclusive licensees must also notify the patent proprietor before bringing legal action. A patent proprietor is entitled to accede to a proceeding brought by a licensee. Even if he does not do so, the proprietor will still automatically become party to any counterclaim for revocation (see Para. 838).

---

24 See e.g. ECJ Judgment No. C 355/96 of 16 July 1988 in the *Silhouette* case and related decisions.

25 For a thorough discussion of the current situation under German law, see *Kühnen*, GRUR 2014, p. 137 and *Ohly*, GRUR 2016, p. 1120; cf. also *Grunwald*, GRUR 2016, p. 1126, as well as *Springorum/Knobbe-Springorum*, Mitt. 2019, p. 529.

3. Legal Capacity to Bring Revocation Actions

Legal capacity to bring revocation actions is a topic that has already been discussed, so that the reader is referred to the corresponding section (Para. 460 et seqq.) The general conclusion reached here was that straw-man actions may be possible, but not anonymous actions. 633

4. Multiple Plaintiffs/Defendants

It is possible and daily practice for multiple plaintiffs and/or multiple defendants to be party to a single proceeding. Thus, it is also possible for an action to be brought on the basis of multiple patents at the same time. No additional court fees will accrue in such case (Rule 370.7). 634

However, the UPC will have the option to separate an action lodged by multiple plaintiffs or on the basis of multiple patents into several actions. The Court will likewise have the option to bundle multiple legal actions together (Rule 302). 635

Assuming it has separated an action into several actions, the Court will have the option to impose additional court fees. This means that additional recoverable costs will accrue in such case. 636

5. Change of Party

Upon application by a party, the Court may order that a person be added as a party, that he cease to be a party, or that he be substituted for a party (Rule 305). In the process, the must Court invite other parties to the proceedings to comment on the application as soon as practicable. 637

The Court will also determine the extent to which a new party is bound by the proceedings as then constituted (Rule 306.2). 638

a) Procedure of Transferring a Patent in Dispute

If a patent in dispute is transferred in whole or in part during an ongoing proceeding, either across-the-board or only for certain Member States, then the Court may allow the new proprietor to be added as a party, while also inviting the other parties to comment on the matter (Rule 312). No prior consent from the opposing party will be required, but the opposing party will be free to demand security for costs (see Para. 742 et seqq.). 639

If the new proprietor does not accede to the proceeding, then all decisions taken by the Court will (of course) be binding upon him. 640

b) Procedure in Case of Death or Insolvency

If a party dies or ceases to exist during proceedings, then the proceedings will be stayed until such party is replaced by his successor. The Court may specify a period in this respect (Rule 310). 641

642 If there are more than two parties to the proceedings, Court may decide that the proceeding between the remaining parties be continued separately and that the stay be applied only to the proceedings regarding the party that no longer exists.

643 If the successor of the party that died or ceased to exist does not continue the proceedings, any other party may apply to have the successor added to or substituted for a party. Here, the above-described rules for a change in parties will apply.

644 If a party is declared insolvent – e.g. when a legal successor competent to make decisions, such as an insolvency administrator, is appointed – the proceedings are to be stayed for up to three months. The stay may also be imposed upon the request of an interim insolvency administrator or a comparable person.

645 The stay may continue until the competent national authority or person dealing with the insolvency has decided whether to continue the proceedings or not. Where the competent national authority or person dealing with the insolvency decides not to continue the proceedings, the Court may decide, upon a reasoned request by the other party, that the proceedings should be continued in accordance with the applicable national insolvency law. If proceedings are continued, the effect of a decision of the Court as regards the insolvent party in the action will be determined by the law applicable to the insolvency proceedings.

c) Peculiarities of Actions for Revocation (?)

646 There are differences between a national revocation action and an opposition proceeding before the European Patent Office when it comes to a change in the opposing party, respectively revocation plaintiff. Whereas effecting a change in the revocation plaintiff will usually be possible without difficulty in most national proceedings, e.g. in Germany, the status of "opponent" in a proceeding before the EPO cannot be easily transferred.[26]

647 It remains to be seen how the Unified Patent Court will rule in this context. But here are strong indications that transferability should be possible, given that the relevant rules, particularly Rule 305, are formulated in general terms and do not provide for an exception.

6. Intervention Procedure

648 It will be possible to intervene before the Unified Patent Court both actively, i.e. upon application, or passively, i.e. upon the request of the Court. This will be discussed in detail in Chapter 13, starting in Para. 1220 et seqq.

V. Interpreting the Patent

649 The UPC Agreement has nothing to say on how a patent is to be interpreted, i.e. on whether only the patent claims should be considered or whether and to what extent

26 See EPO Decision No. G 4/88 and particularly T 711/99.

the patent's description and/or grant history should play a role. Only for equivalent patent infringement, Article 69 of the European Patent Convention (EPC), along with the Protocol on the Interpretation of Article 69 of the EPC, are applicable. This is because all patents examined before the Unified Patent Court will be former European patent registrations that were covered by the European Patent Convention. Concerning the details of equivalent patent infringement, the Unified Patent Court is free to establish its own jurisdiction.

In several landmark decisions, the Unified Patent Court has established the following principles for interpreting patents: **650**
- The patent claims are the basis for determining both legal validity and infringement.
- However, the description and, if available, the drawings must always be consulted, not only in cases of uncertainty.
- Patent claims must be interpreted uniformly with regard to legal validity and infringement.[27]
- The interpretation of a patent is a legal question and the responsibility of the court.
- The patent is addressed to a person skilled in the art. This is a fictional person, equipped with 'general specialist knowledge that is customary in the relevant field of technology, as well as the average knowledge, experience, and abilities in this specialist field.'[28]

However, concerning equivalent patent infringement there is no decision of the Appeals Court oft he Unified Patent Court yet. Also there is no final decision about a "file wrapper estoppel".[29] **651**

B. Legal Consequences of a Patent Infringement

According to Article 63 et seqq. of the UPCA, the legal consequences of a conviction for patent infringement are the following: **652**
- a claim to permanent injunction (Article 63); this will also apply against "*against an intermediary whose services are being used by a third party to infringe a patent.*" (Article 63 (1)).
- a claim to having the products removed from the channels of commerce, having them deprived of their infringing property; having them definitively removed from the channels of commerce, having them destroyed (Article 64). The precise scope of the corresponding powers involved on the part of the plaintiff and/or the Court remains to be clarified, however (see the discussion starting in Para. 798)

---

27 UPC_COA 335/2023, Order of 26 February 2024 – 10xGenomics v. Nanostring.

28 UPC_CoA 768/2024, Order of 30 April 2025 – Insulet v. EOFlow.

29 An approach of the local divison Munich in which the original claims were used to interpret the claims was not followed by the Court of Appeals, UPC_CoA_1/2024, Order of 13 May 2024, APL_8/2024 – VusionGroup v. Hanshow.

- a claim to receive information on the infringing products' and processes' origins and distribution channels, quantities and prices, as well as on the identity of the third parties involved in their production, distribution or use (Article 67);
- a claim to damages (Article 68); whereby the damages may not be punitive in nature.

653 These rights can be derived from the IPR Enforcement Directive[30] (amongst other sources). Inasmuch, the European Court of Justice (ECJ) is the final court of review in this context.

I. Period of Limitation

654 According to Article 72 of the UPCA, actions relating to all forms of financial compensation may not be brought more than five years after the date on which the applicant became aware, or had reasonable grounds to become aware, of the last fact justifying the action. This provision takes primacy over national regulations, some of which may call for different time limits.[31]

II. Powers of the Court

655 However, the aforementioned legal consequences are limited – at least in theory – by the fact that the UPC Agreement invariably leaves it up to the Court to decide whether to grant the patent proprietor the corresponding rights and claims. This is in derogation from French law, for example, where permanent injunctive relief is a statutory right.[32] Articles 63 et seqq. of the UPCA clearly stipulate that the Court has **the right but not the obligation** to impose a permanent injunction on a convicted infringer. So what we have here is a judicial competence rather than an entitlement under private law.[33] However, the court will usually grant injunctive relief if it considers the patent valid and infringed (cf. the discussion starting Para. 794 et seqq.)

656 Also when it comes to the calculation of damages, the Court is essentially free to apply its discretion.[34] Admittedly, Article 68 of the UPCA states that methods and factors applied thus far, i.e. infringer's profit, damages incurred (also intangible damages) may be used.[35] But according to Article 68 3b), the Court may also apply the "licensing analogy" in order to determine a fixed sum of damages.

---

30 Directive 2004/48/EC of 29 April 2004, see particularly Articles 8, 10 and 13.
31 E.g. in Germany, see *Nieder*, Mitt. 2016, p. 1.
32 For a full discussion, see *Reetz* et al., GRUR Int 2015, p. 210 = JIPLP 2015, p. 180.
33 For a full discussion, see *Meier-Beck*, GRUR 2014, p. 144.
34 Cf. *Würtenberger* GRUR Int 2018, p. 725.
35 See *Kather*, VPP-Rundbrief 2014, p. 28.

C. Revocation of a Patent

I. Opposition Proceedings Before the EPO Have No Primacy

The UPC Agreement does not give any primacy to the European Patent Office. This is analogous to French law, for example, but diverges from German law. This means that revocation actions (see Chapter 13, Para. 1162 et seqq.) or counterclaims for revocation (see Chapter 9, Para. 835 et seqq.) may be brought even when an opposition proceeding is still pending before the EPO, or even before the nine-month deadline for lodging an opposition with the EPO has expired. **657**

II. Grounds for Revoking a Patent

The grounds for revoking a patent – be it a European Patent or a Unitary Patent – are not specified in the UPC Agreement. Instead, Article 65 of the UPCA makes reference to the corresponding Article 138 (1) and Article 139 of the European Patent Convention (EPC). This means that the practice used that far will remain unchanged, and that the following will constitute grounds for revocation: **658**

- insufficient novelty;
- insufficient inventive step;
- an impermissible alteration, including an impermissible extension of a granted patent's scope of protection in an opposition proceeding;
- insufficient feasibility; as well as
- lack of legal capacity to lodge an application. Note that this gives rise to a dual jurisdiction between the Unified Patent Court and the national courts, whereby the latter will continue to be competent for vindication actions.[36] Assuming legal capacity to lodge an application is lacking, it is also unclear whether the right to bring action will redound to any member of the public or only to the duly authorized party (cf. Para. 462).[37]

It bears noting right at the outset that whenever a patent is modified, the patent proprietor must disclose the extent to which Articles 84, 123(2) and 123(3) of the European Patent Convention (EPC) have been met, i.e. he must also state whether the claims are sufficiently clear. It remains to be seen whether the Unified Patent Court will tie into the established case law of the European Patent Office,[38] which holds that a challenge for insufficient clarity cannot be mounted when subsidiary claims have been incorporated into the primary claim (see the full discussion in Para. 1086 et seqq.). No fundamental case law exists on this topic. **659**

The effect of the reference to Article 139 of the EPC when national patents are published in the wake of a Unitary Patent has already been discussed (Para. 117 et seqq.). **660**

36 See *Hüttermann*, Mitt. 2015, p. 100.
37 On the topic of vindication, see the general remarks by *Nieder*, GRUR 2015, p. 936.
38 Decision of the EPO's Enlarged Board of the Appeal No. G 3/14 of 24 March 2015.

III. Current Juristdiction of the UPC

661 The UPC follows the case law of the European Patent Office relatively strictly, if not always in words, then at least in its findings.

1. Novelty

662 The UPC follows the EPO's line here, in particular the 'gold standard', i.e. in order for there to be no novelty, each individual feature of the respective claim must be directly and unambiguously derivable from a single document in the prior art.[39]

663 Novelty can also be implicit. Implicit disclosure refers to the clear, direct and unambiguous consequence of what is expressly mentioned in a document relating to the state of the art. Therefore, 'implicit disclosure' includes any feature that a person skilled in the art would objectively consider necessary when considering the express content of a document relating to the state of the art, e.g. with regard to general scientific laws. A claimed feature is also implicitly disclosed if the skilled person, in carrying out the teaching of a document in the prior art, would inevitably arrive at a result that falls within the scope of the claim.[40]

2. Inventive Step

664 An essential aspect in assessing inventive step is whether a person skilled in the art would have had a motivation (also known as a 'pointer'[41]) to combine two documents from the prior art or to modify the technical teaching of a document in the light of their general technical knowledge in the direction of the contested patent.[42] The mere probability of a combination of documents is not sufficient.[43]

665 The UPC moved even closer towards the EPO in a later decision[44] in which it stated that It first has to be established what the object of the invention is, i.e. the objective problem. This must be assessed from the perspective of the skilled person (m/f – hereinafter referred to as 'it'), with its common general knowledge, as at the application or priority date (also referred to as the relevant date) of the patent. This must be done by establishing what the invention adds to the state of the art, not by looking at the

39 UPC_CFI_355/2023 (LD Düsseldorf), Decision of 28 January 2025 – Fujifilm v. Kodak.

40 UPC_CFI_355/2023 (LD Düsseldorf), Decision of 28 January 2025 – Fujifilm v. Kodak.

41 Cf. UPC_CoA_523/2024, Order of 3 March 2025 – Syngenta v. Sumi Agro.

42 UPC_CoA_335/2023, Order of 26 February 2024, App_576355/2023 – Nanostring v. 10x Genomics as fundamental ruling, cf. also UPC 252/2023 (CD Munich), Decision of 17 October 2024 – Nanostring v. Harvard, UPC_CFI_255/2023 + UPC_CFI_15/2023 (CD Paris), Decision of 19 July 2024, ACT_551308/2023 – Meril v. Edwards, UPC_CFI_230/2023 (LD Paris), Decision of 4 July 2024, Dexcom v. Abbott, concerning the common general knowledge s. UPC_CFI_7/2023 (LD Düsseldorf), Decision of 3 July 2024 – Kaldewei v. Bette.

43 Cf. UPC_CoA_523/2024, Order of 3 March 2025 – Syngenta v. Sumi Agro.

44 UPC_CoA_528/2024, Decision of 25 November 2025 – Sanofi v. Amgen, identical in the result UPC_CoA_464/2024, Decision of 25 November 2025 – Edwards v. Meril.

individual features of the claim, but by comparing the claim as a whole in context of the description and the drawings, thus also considering the inventive concept underlying the invention (the technical teaching), which must be based on the technical effect(s) that the skilled person on the basis of the application understands is (are) achieved with the claimed invention.

The claimed solution is obvious when at the relevant date the skilled person, starting **666** from a realistic starting point in the state of the art in the relevant field of technology, wishing to solve the objective problem, would (and not only: could) have arrived at the claimed solution. A starting point is realistic if the teaching thereof would have been of interest to a skilled person who, at the relevant date, wishes to solve the objective problem. This may for instance be the case if the relevant piece of prior art already discloses several features similar to those relevant to the invention as claimed and/or addresses the same or a similar underlying problem as that of the claimed invention. There can be more than one realistic starting point and the claimed invention must be inventive starting from each of them.[45]

A claimed solution is obvious if the skilled person would have taken the next step in **667** expectation of finding an envisaged solution of his technical problem. This is generally the case when the results of the next step were clearly predictable, or where there was a reasonable expectation of success. The burden of proof is on the attacking party.[46]

3. Sufficiency (Art 83)

According to Article 83 EPC, the invention must be disclosed in the application and **668** thus also in the patent in a manner that is sufficiently clear and complete for a person skilled in the art to carry it out. In this regard, the application must be assessed in its entirety.

The test to be applied is whether the skilled person is able to reproduce the claimed **669** subject matter on the basis of the patent without any inventive effort and without undue burden. An invention is sufficiently disclosed if the patent specification shows the skilled person at least one way – and in case of functional features: one technical concept – of performing the claimed invention.[47]

45 UPC_CoA_528/2024, Decision of 25 November 2025 – Sanofi v. Amgen, identical in the result UPC_CoA_464/2024, Decision of 25 November 2025 – Edwards v. Meril.
46 UPC_CoA_528/2024, Decision of 25 November 2025 – Sanofi v. Amgen, cf. also UPC_CFI_146/2024 (LD Munich), Decision of 12 December 2025 – Sanofi v. Stada et al.
47 UPC_CoA_528/2024, Decision of 25 November 2025 – Sanofi v. Amgen, identical in the result UPC_CoA_464/2024, Decision of 25 November 2025 – Edwards v. Meril.

4. Amendments (Art 123)

670 With regard to Article 123(2), the Unified Patent Court follows the European Patent Office's line relatively strictly,[48] including with regard to intermediate generalisation[49] and disclosure in diovisional patents[50]. There are no noteworthy decisions regarding Article 123(3), but here too it is to be expected that the UPC will follow the EPO.

D. Procedural Law

I. Basic Principles

671 The basic principles of legal procedure to be followed before the Unified Patent Court are defined in Article 42 of the UPC Agreement (as well as elsewhere).[51] These hold that:
- The Court must conduct each proceeding in a manner in keeping with its significance and complexity; and
- The Court must ensure that the applicable regulations, procedures and decisions are applied in a fair and balanced manner which does not serve to distort competition.

672 In addition, the Preamble of the Rules of Procedure also enunciates the principles of proportionality, flexibility, fairness and equity. The Court is to apply the procedural regulations so as to ensure that decisions of the highest quality are handed down. The Court must also strive for consistency in the manner procedural regulations are interpreted and applied across all of its divisions, and also at the Court of Appeal.

673 As regards a specific time frame, the proceeding is to be conducted so that oral hearings on the questions of a patent's infringement and legal validity can be held within one year's time (cf. Para. 864 et seqq.). The parties are called upon to cooperate with the Court and to fully present their arguments in the proceeding as early as possible.

II. Case Management

674 During the written procedure and the interim procedure, the judge-rapporteur will be responsible for managing the case; after that, it will be presiding judge (Rule 331).

675 The active case-management is to encompass the following (Rule 332):
- encouraging the parties to co-operate with each other during the proceedings;

---

48 Vgl. UPC_CoA_405/2024, Order of 20 December 2024, APL_40553/2024 – Alexion v. Amgen, identical UPC_CoA_402/2024, Order of 20 December 2024, APL_40470/2024 – Alexion v. Amgen. UPC_CFI_355/2023 (LD Düsseldorf), Decison of 28 January 2025 – Fujifilm v. Kodak.

49 UPC_CFI_131/2024 (LD Den Haag), Order of 19 June 2024, Abbott v. Sibio.

50 UPC CFI 315/2023 (CD Paris), Decision of 5 November, NJOY v. Juul Labs, cf. Also UPC CFI 316/2023 (CD Paris), Decision of 17 January 2025, NJOY v. Juul Labs.

51 Also see *Kolonko, Justizgrundrechte in Verfahren vor dem Einheitlichen Europäischen Patentgericht.*

- identifying the issues at an early stage while prioritizing them in terms of order and importance;
- encouraging the parties to use the Mediation Center (see Para. 748 et seqq.) or to reach a settlement;[52]
- fixing timetables or otherwise controlling the progress of the action;
- considering whether the likely benefits of taking a particular step justifies its cost;
- making use of available technical means, so that the parties do not necessarily have to attend the action;
- giving directions to ensure that the hearing of the action proceeds quickly and efficiently;
- but also dealing with as many aspects of the action as the Court can on the same occasion;

III. Service of Documents; Time Limits

In principle, documents are to be served by and to the Court via electronic means (see Rules 270 and 271). If a representative has been appointed, then documents are to be served to him using the Court's document-management system (CMS). This ist he usual way how documents are exchanged except for the very first service of the statement of claim, as there no representative has been appointed.[53] **676**

However, the first service on the opposing party is carried out by the court in accordance with the provisions of Rule 275. This can lead to considerable delays, e.g., in the case of service to China, as it is not possible to serve on a subsidiary based in the EPG territory as a substitute and, in addition, the Hague Convention is strictly applicable.[54] **677**

When documents are served via email or the CMS, the day of dispatch will also serve as the day of receipt. In contrast to the EPO's practice, there is no provision requiring the Court to prove that a given document has been served. **678**

The time-limit calculation methods to be used are defined in Rules 300 and 301 and ultimately correspond to those used by the European Patent Office or under German law, for example. It bears noting that the only holidays recognized are the official holidays of the Member State in which the division of first instance is located, respectively in which the seat or concerned section of the central division is located, respectively in which the Court of Appeal is located (i.e. all the holidays of Luxemburg will apply).[55] **679**

---

52 On the German situation and the practice of the District Court (LG) of Munich, cf. *Brose*, GRUR 2016, p. 146.

53 Note: This does not apply even if preliminary injunction proceedings have been initiated beforehand and it can be assumed that the representatives of the opposing party in the main proceedings will be the same as in the preliminary injunction proceedings, cf. UPC_CFI_688/2025 (LD Hamburg), Order of 25 August 2025, MED-EL v. Zhejiang.

54 UPC_COA_205/2024, Order of 6 August 2024 – Nera v. Xiaomi.

55 Possibly worth mentioning is the national holiday on 23 June are well as the Luxemburg *Kirmess* (Carnival) which takes place in early September of each year.

680 It bears noting that the Court has the power to retroactively extend any of the time limits specified by the Rules or by the Court itself (Rule 9). But the Court may also abbreviate such time limits, the only exceptions being time limits for preliminary injunctions and for the lodging of appeals. The time limits defined in the UPC Agreement may not be changed by the Court, however.

681 Both the German courts of instance as well as the European Patent Office (i.e. their respective court clerks) will take charge of serving one side's pleadings/submission to the other side.[56] According to Rule 8.3 of the UPC Rules of Procedure, however, each side will be under obligation to inform the other side any communication made with the court and to provide it with a copy thereof, unless the Rules of Procedure expressly provide otherwise. Since in practice the vast majority of submissions are made via the CMS and therefore a notification is sent via the CMS, this is of lesser importance, however.

682 Such exceptions are defined mainly for pretrial proceedings, e.g. applications for preserving evidence (Rule 192.3, see Para. 1380 et seqq.), provisional measures/ preliminary injunctions (Rule 206.3, see Para. 1336 et seqq.) and protective letters (Rule 206.7, see Para. 1368 et seqq. and Para. 1412).[57]

IV. Regulations Governing Defaulted Time Limits

683 Strict regulations for defaulted time limits apply at the Unitary Patent Court. The Court may disregard any step, fact, evidence or argument which a party has not taken or submitted in a timely manner (Rule 9).[58]

684 During an appeal proceeding, Article 73 will also come into play. This stipulates that new facts and new evidence may only be introduced where the submission thereof by the party concerned could not reasonably have been expected during proceedings before the Court of First Instance. The Court of Appeal must consider the following questions, however (Rule 222):

- can the party making the new submission also justify it?
- is the new submission relevant?
- what is the opposing party's position on the new submission?

---

56 Note: While it is customary to inform the respective opposing party, particularly about submissions made just before the expiry of a deadline, this is merely a "gentlemen's arrangement." But it can also serve to make a good impression before the Court and heighten the chances of having one's arguments admitted. There is no codified obligation to serve such notice, however.

57 Cf. *Tilmann* in *Tilmann/Plassmann*, Note 9 to Rule 8.

58 For an example cf. UPC_CFI_355/2023 (LD Düsseldorf), Order of 29 November 2025, App_63445/2024 – Fujifilm v. Kodak.

V. Right to a Fair Hearing

The customary regulations governing the right to receive a fair hearing also apply before the United Patent Court. This right is codified in more detail in Rule 264: Where the Rules of Procedure provide that a party must or may be given an opportunity to be heard before the Court makes an order or takes some action, the Court must or may (as the case may be) request the parties to provide written submissions within a specified period and/or must or may invite the parties to an oral hearing on a date fixed by the Court. The Court may also order that the hearing take place by telephone or video conference. **685**

1. Form of the Decisions and Orders

Every decision of the Court must contain the following (Rule 350): **686**
- the statement that it is a decision of the Court;
- the date of its delivery;
- the names of the presiding judge, the judge-rapporteur and the other judges taking part in it;
- the names of the parties and of the parties' representatives;
- an indication of the claim, order or remedy sought by the parties along with a summary of the facts; and
- the grounds for the decision.

It should be noted that any dissenting opinions must also be attached to the Court's decision (Rule 350.3).[59] **687**

Every order of the Court must contain the following (Rule 351): **688**
- the statement that it is an order of the judge-rapporteur, of the standing judge, of the single judge, of the presiding judge, of a President of the Court or of the Court;
- the date of its adoption;
- the names of any judge taking part in its adoption;
- the names of the parties and of the parties' representatives; and
- the operative part of the order.

Generally speaking, there is no provision requiring the Court to issue instructions on the right to lodge legal remedies/appeals, whether against decisions or against orders.[60] The few exceptions hereto mainly pertain to decisions issued in connection with preliminary injunction proceedings pursuant to Rule 196 (Para. 1410) and Rule 211 (Para. 1221), submissions of evidence (see Para. 711 et seqq.), or requests for information pursuant to Rule 191 (see Para. 715). Of course, the court is free (and this would also be desirable) to include such instructions on its own initiative and this is current practice. **689**

59 So far this happened only once, UPC_CFI 1510/2025 (LD Munich), Decision of 13 January 2026, Heraeus v. Vibranz.

60 A different view is ostensibly taken by *Falck/Stoll* in *Tilmann/Plassmann*, Note 5 to Article 77.

2. Amicus Curiae Briefs

690 Neither the UPC Agreement nor the Procedural Rules of the UPC contain any clues as to whether or how *Amicus Curiae* briefs,[61] i.e. legal opinions provided by third parties, should be allowed. Such legal opinions, which are particularly common in the US legal system, are both possible and customary before the European Patent Office, but not before the German courts, for example. *Callens/Granata*[62] point out that that the originally envisioned Rule 318 was stricken during the revision of the Rules of Procedure, whereby reference was made to the regulations governing intervention (cf. Chapter 13, Para. 1220 et seqq.) But does this mean that the Court will refuse to admit such legal opinions? This remains to be seen, however, in one case[63] the Court obviously ignored such a submission.

VI. Ex Officio Investigations

691 Neither the UPC Agreement nor the UPC Rules of Procedure codify a principle of *ex officio* investigation – i.e. an examination of the facts under the Court's own motion – of the sort applicable before the European Patent Office (Article 114 of the EPC)[64] or under German Law (e.g. Section 86 of the German Code of Administrative Court Procedure (*Verwaltungsgerichtsordnung*, VwGO). As already mentioned, the proceeding must be conducted in keeping with the usual procedural principles such as fairness and the right to be heard (Para. 671), but no *ex officio* investigation as such is to be conducted by the Court.[65]

VII. Public Nature of the Proceedings

692 Proceedings before the Unified Patent Court will generally be public, but the parties – and possibly third parties outside the proceeding as well – will be entitled to have their data protected pursuant to the General Data Protection Regulation (EU) 2016/679.

1. Publication of Rulings and Decisions

693 Rule 262, which was revised in 2022, solves this conflict by stipulating that (only) rulings and decisions of the Court are to be published. To this end, an electronic case-management system will be set up at the Unified Patent Court, whereby the case file itself (but not the documents/records it contains) will be publicly accessible, i.e. third parties will be able to see that an action has been lodged, as well as by whom and against whom.

61 Cf. e.g. https://www.ecchr.eu/glossar/amicus-curiae-brief/ for a definition.
62 *Callens/Granata*, Chapter VIII, p. 5.
63 UPC_ CoA_563/2024, 11 February 2026 – Suinno v. Microsoft.
64 See e.g. *Steinbrenner/Teschemacher*, VPP-Rundbrief 4/2012, p. 190.
65 See e.g. *Nieder*, Mitt. 2018, p. 201.

2. Request for Publication of Written Submissions and Evidence

Other documents such as written submissions and evidence will only be published if a reasoned request is lodged with the Registry. Such a request can be filed by any third party, which, however, must be properly represented.[66] 694

The decision regarding publication will then be taken by the judge-rapporteur. Although not expressly stated, lodge an appeal requiring leave from the Court of First Instance (Para. 1102 et seqq.) is then possible. 695

3. Confidential Documents

Irrespective of the foregoing, a party may request that written submissions or parts thereof not be made public even if the request for publication is granted. To this end, the requesting party should provide – preferably in tandem with the request – its supporting reasons along with a duly redacted version of its submissions. The Registry will then implement confidentiality by entering the redacted submission into the Register. 696

4. Request to Lift Confidentiality

Confidentiality may be lifted by lodging a corresponding application (Rule 262.3). The application can in principle by lodged by any member of the public and will be free of charge. It must contain the following: 697

- details on the information alleged to be confidential (insofar as possible);
- the grounds upon which the applicant believes the reasons for confidentiality should not be accepted; and
- the purpose for which the information is needed.

The Court will then give the parties a chance to submit written comments before taking a decision. The application is to be allowed unless legitimate reasons given by the party concerned for the confidentiality of the information outweigh the applicant's interest in accessing such information. 698

The decision may be contested by means of an appeal proceeding requiring leave from the Court of First Instance, albeit an abbreviated version thereof (see Para. 1102 et seqq.). 699

Assuming the Court ultimately decides to grant access to the electronic case file, the Registry will take the corresponding steps (Rule 262.6). 700

5. Imposing Confidentiality On the Opposite Party

According to Rule 262A, a party can more or less block the opposite party from inspecting its submissions or parts thereof. There was an older version of this rule[67] 701

66 UPC_CoA_404/2023, Order of 8 February 2024, App_584498/2023 – Ocado vs. Autostore.

67 See *Tilmann* in *Tilmann/Plassmann*, Rule 262A for the first version of Rule 262A and a discussion; see also *Hüttermann* GRUR Int 2019, p. 1148.

which would have even made it possible to exclude the opposite party from the proceeding entirely, i.e. by means of a so-called "*in-camera*" proceeding.[68] This was later changed, however. Issues of confidentiality can obviously be of great importance, particularly in proceedings involving standard-essential patents.[69]

702 Notwithstanding the foregoing, Rule 262a also states that this level of confidentiality is to be granted only in exceptional cases. If such a case is given, then only the opposite party's attorneys, plus one natural person representing the opposite party, will be allowed to inspect the corresponding records. This is similar to German law, specifically Section 145a of the Patent Act (*Patentgesetz*, PatG), respectively Section 19 of the Law to Protect Trade Secrets (*Geschäftsgeheimnisschutzgesetz*, GeschGehG).

703 If this level of confidentiality is sought, then a corresponding, reasoned application must be lodged with the Court by no later than ten days before the date on which the documents which are to be treated confidentially are lodged with the Court.

704 The Court will then invite written comments from the opposite side, probably subject to a tight time limit, before issuing its order.

705 The order can then be challenged through an appeal proceeding requiring leave from the Court of First Instance (see Para. 1102 et seqq.) A violation against the order may be punished with a fine or a removal from the proceedings.[70]

VIII. Requirements for Means of Evidence and Offering of Evidence

1. Requirements for Means of Evidence

706 The requirements for means of evidence are defined in Rules 170 et seqq.[71] These hold that the customary regulations will continue to apply and that evidence may specifically be furnished by means of the following:
- written evidence;
- expert reports;
- "physical objects," particularly models/embodiments/exhibits;
- electronic files and audio/video recordings.

707 Evidence may be obtained by the following means:
- hearing of the parties;
- requests for information;
- production of documents;
- summoning, hearing and questioning of witnesses and experts;
- ordering inspection of a place or physical object;

68 Cf. https://www.uscourtseegov/glossary#letter for a definition.
69 Cf. *Hinojal/Mohsler*, GRUR 2019, p. 674, as well as general remarks by *Haedicke*, Mitt. 2018, p. 249.
70 UPC_CoA_755/2025, Order of 26 January 2026, Sun v. Vivo.
71 Cf. *Ahrens*, GRUR 2017, p. 323.

- conducting tests and experiments, particularly of a comparative nature, whereby this can also be ordered by the Unified Patent Court itself;[72]
- sworn statements in writing (written witness statements);
- ordering a party or third party to produce evidence; and
- ordering measures to preserve evidence.

For the last two points as well as for the ordering of inspections, a special procedure is available, the so-called "*saisie-contrefaçon.*" This is defined in Rules 190 et seqq. and is separately discussed in Chapter 15 (Para. 1380 et seqq.) 708

A party making a statement of fact that is contested or likely to be contested by the other party must indicate the means of evidence to prove it. In case of failure to indicate the means of evidence regarding a contested fact, the Court must take such failure into account when deciding the issue in question (Article 54 of the UPC Agreement and Rule 171). In case of failure to indicate the means of evidence regarding a contested fact, the Court must take such failure into account when deciding the issue in question. (Rule 171.1) (cf. Section 138 of the German Code of Civil Procedure (ZPO)). There will be no obligation on the part of the Court to perform its own *ex officio* investigation (see Para. 691). 709

Neither UPCA nor the Rules of Procedure of the UPC contain any provision governing the required standards of proof.[73] This is not unusual, however: There is also no such provision in the European Patent Convention, for instance.[74] 710

2. Offering of Evidence

The normal operative principle before the Unified Patent Court is that of "party presentation," i.e. each party must offer evidence of the factual circumstances upon which it relies (cf. the above Para. 709). 711

Exceptions to this apply when important factual evidence does not lie within the party's sphere of control. In such case, the party may then lodge a request for production of evidence pursuant to Rule 190, i.e. in addition to the application for preserving evidence which is discussed starting in Para. 1380. The preconditions for a successful request are the following: 712
- a party has presented all reasonably available and plausible evidence to support its claims; but
- certain evidence, which must be specifically indicated in the request, lies within the control of the opposite party or of a third party.

72 This is a peculiarity at odds with German Law, which does not provide for such an option; also see *Ahrens*, GRUR 2017, p. 323.

73 See *Kubis*, VPP-Rundbrief 2013, p. 1 (albeit with regard to the 14th Draft of the Rules of Procedure); as well as *Ahrens*, GRUR 2017, p. 323; for the German practice, cf. Section 286 of the German Code of Civil Procedure (ZPO) and the Ruling of the German Federal Court of Justice (BGH) in the *Anastasia* case, NJW 1970, p. 946.

74 See e.g. the Examination Guidelines of the EPO, E-III 4.3.

713 Thus, the focus here is invariably on evidence which must be specifically indicated. A catch-all "discovery" procedure will not be possible (cf. Para. 1446 et seqq.)

714 The request for production of evidence in a proceeding may be lodged during the written procedure (Para. 815 et seqq.) or the interim procedure (Para. 871). The judge-rapporteur responsible for handling these procedural phases (see Para. 824) will first grant the opposite side a hearing before issuing a corresponding decision and order. He may order, for example, that the evidence be disclosed only to individually designated persons and subject to secrecy constraints so as to protect confidential information.

715 Assuming such an order is issued, it must specifically state the following:

- under which conditions, in which form and within which time limit the evidence is to be produced; and
- any sanction which will be imposed in case of non-compliance.

If the evidence is not produced in a fashion compliant with the order, then the Court must take this failure into account when taking its final decision on the issue in question (Rule 190.7). This is somewhat comparable to the provisions governing frustration of evidence (*Beweisvereitelung*) under German Law (cf. also Section 440 of the German Code of Civil Procedure (ZPO)).

716 The order may be contested through an appeal not requiring leave from the Court of First Instance (see Para. 1098 et seqq.) An express mention of this legal remedy is to be included – by way of exception – (cf. Para. 689) in the order itself.

717 Note that, pursuant to Rule 190, a request may also be lodged to have evidence produced by third parties (cf. Para. 1384 for the separate proceeding to preserve evidence). According to Rule 190 (5), the Court must duly consider the third party's interest when issuing its order.

IX. Decision by Default

718 If one of the parties defaults on a time limit then – just as under German law – a request for a "decision by default" may be lodged pursuant to Rule 355 (for German law, cf. Section 330 et seqq. of the Code of Civil Procedure (ZPO)). While the relevant Rule 355 does not explicitly state that the request can also be made by the opposite side, this does seem logical. Note that there is also no provision on this issue in Section 330.

719 It has not been expressly codified whether a decision by default is to be issued automatically – as is mandated under German Law – or whether the Court will have the right and/or obligation to first hear one or even both parties.[75]

720 The decision by default is thus similar to a *Versäumnisurteil*, its counterpart under German law, in that it is enforceable. The Court may make such enforcement con-

75 For a full discussion of this problem, see e.g. *Kitchen*, Supplemental Publication to the Official Journal of the EPO 5/2015, p. 46.

tingent upon the provision of a security however. Likewise, the Court may grant a stay of enforcement until it has decided the application to set aside the decision by default (see below).

As in the case of a decision by default (*Versäumnisurteil*) under German law, it is possible to have a decision by default of the Unified Patent Court set aside by lodging a corresponding application within one month of service of the decision (Rule 356). There are certain requirements for the application, however: 721

- it must contain a defense pleading;
- it must be accompanied by payment of a fee of 1,000 €; and
- it must be well-founded, i.e. an explanation for the default must be included. Only if the corresponding justifying reasons are given will the decision by default be set aside.

If the decision by default is not set aside, then it can of course be contested through an appeal (see Para. 1098 et seqq.). 722

X. Further Processing and Re-Establishment of Rights

Unlike the European Patent Office, for example, the Unified Patent Court will not permit any further processing once a time limit has been missed. 723

A re-establishment of rights, on the other hand, is possible pursuant to Rule 320: 724

> "Where a party has failed to observe a time-limit set by these Rules or the Court for a cause which, despite all due care having been taken by the party, was outside his control and the non-observance of this time limit has had the direct consequence of causing the party to lose a right or means of redress, the relevant panel of the Court may upon the request of that party re-establish the right or means of redress."

Thus, a re-establishment of rights is **not** possible for those time limits which are defined in the UPC Agreement, to wit: 725

- the time limits for an appeal pursuant to Article 73, since these are not determined by the Court;
- the time limit for the "opt-out", since this is defined in Article 83(4);
- the three-month time limit within which a patent-infringement action must be lodged in response to a request for declaration of non-infringement in order to make the latter inadmissible (Article 33(6), see Para. 1198 et seqq.)
- the limitation period of five years for actions for damages pursuant to Article 72 (see Para. 654); and
- the ten-year time limit for a re-hearing/retrial.

According to Rule 320, moreover, only time limits for appeal may be reinstated. So it remains to be seen whether normal time limits will also be eligible for a re-establishment of rights, such as time limits for written pleadings. Rule 320.5 would seem to indicate that this is the case (see below).[76] 726

---

76 This is affirmed by *Plassmann/Dorn* in *Tilmann/Plassmann*, Note 6 to Rule 320.

727 An application for the re-establishment of rights must be lodged within one month after correcting the reason for missing the relevant time limit, but never later than three months after expiry of the missed time limit. The application must contain:
- the grounds and facts upon which the application is based;
- evidence in the form of sworn affidavits from the persons involved as well from those who monitor and supervise them.[77]

728 The omitted action must of course be made good and a fee of 350 € is to be paid.

729 According to Rule 320 (5), it is not possible to obtain reinstatement of the time limit for lodging the application for re-establishment of rights and for performing the omitted act once this time limit has been defaulted. This is in derogation of German law, for example. The fact that this is expressly mentioned suggests that normal time limits, such as those for written pleadings, are indeed reinstatable. Otherwise there would be no reason to place special emphasis on this point, since the time limit addressed by Rule 320 (5) would not have been reinstatable anyway.

730 The relevant panel of the Court will then decide the question of a re-establishment of rights by issuing a corresponding order, whereby the other parties must first be given an opportunity to submit their comments.

731 No appeal against this order is possible. This differs from German law, for example, which only rules out an appeal when the order grants a re-establishment of rights.

XI. Representation

732 According to Article 48 of the UPC Agreement, it is mandatory to have representation before the Unified Patent Court, i.e. the parties must be represented by lawyers who either authorized to practice before a court of a Member State of the UPC Agreement or who are qualified to function as professional European patent representatives (agents) before the European Patent Office pursuant to Article 134 of the European Patent Convention (EPC). Such qualification can consist, for example, of a certificate to conduct European patent litigation.

733 This is a new requirement for patent-infringement actions as far as most of the European countries are concerned: Until now, these countries merely required representation by a lawyer.[78]

734 The aforementioned additional requirement for special qualification was proposed by the Preparatory Committee on 3 September 2015 and, with marginal amendments, adopted[79] by the Administrative Committee of the Unified Patent Court at its first

77 More precisely: "*...from all persons involved in the nonobservance of the time-limit and the persons involved in establishing the precautionary measures of due care taken in order to avoid such cases of non-compliance.*"

78 See *Kiani/Springorum*, Mitt. 2016, p. 155.

79 Cf. here: https://www.unified-patent-court.org/sites/default/files/upc_documents/ac_06_22022022_rev_e_0.pdf.

meeting on February 22, 2022. It stipulates that a certificate to conduct European patent litigation (European Patent Litigation Certificate, or EPLC) may be obtained by completing a course lasting at least 120 hours plus a subsequent oral and written examination. Such courses may be offered by universities as well as by commercial training providers.[80]

During an interim period of one year after the UPC Agreement's entry into force, numerous pre-existing national study courses and diplomas were also recognized as equivalent to an EPLC. These included several study courses offered by the CEIPI in Strasburg, by the Queen Mary University in London, and by the Nottingham Law School. Also included is the "Law for Patent Attorneys" curriculum offered by the (Hagen Long-Distance-Learning University (*Fernuniversität Hagen*)) and by its predecessor institution in Fischbachau. **735**

Many European patent representatives have completed one or more of the additional courses of study listed by the Preparatory Committee. Indeed, the last two of the ones named above are (or were) actually prerequisites for admission to the German patent attorney examination. So it follows that a great many of the currently practicing European patent representatives will be well qualified to plead before the Unified Patent Court. **736**

A special rule applies for actions against the European Patent Office (see Para. 1210 et seqq.) In this case, the general requirement for representation is set aside by virtue of Article 48 (7) of the UPC Agreement. Thus, the patent proprietor could even represent himself. **737**

XII. Nature of the Appeal Proceeding

In principle, all decisions and orders before the Unified Patent Court – i.e. those issued during an ongoing proceeding – are subject to review by the UPC's Court of Appeal (see Chapter 11, Para. 1098 et seqq.) The aim here is to ensure that the procedural regulations are interpreted in consistent fashion across all the UPC's divisions.[81] **738**

This gives the parties far broader possibilities than in most national proceeding or in an opposition proceeding before the European Patent Office. For more details, see Para. 1098 et seqq. **739**

According to Article 74, an appeal will generally not have suspensive effect. Excepted herefrom are appeals against a decision relating to revocation actions or counterclaims for revocation, as well as appeals against decisions in connection with actions against the European Patent Office pursuant to Article 32 (1)(i). **740**

An appeal may be declared to have suspensive effective, however, either upon the request of a party or upon the Court's own motion (see Para. 1117 et seqq.) **741**

---

80 For a critical view, see *Augenstein* on the website eplawpatentblog.com.
81 Cf. the aforementioned Preamble of the Rules of Procedure (Para. 671 et seqq.).

XIII. Providing Security for Costs

1. Security to Cover the Costs of a Party

742 A reasoned request for security for costs may be lodged by any of the parties, either when the action is first brought or at any point during the proceedings. Such a request essentially asks the Court to order one or more of the parties to provide adequate security for the expected amount of recoverable costs for the proceedings (Rule 158). This provision is evidently modeled on the procedure for German patent-revocation actions, and particularly on Section 81 of the German Patent Act (PatG).

743 At the Court's discretion, this security may be lodged either by lodging a deposit with the Court or by way of a bank guarantee. (Rule 157.1).

744 The Court must hear both parties before deciding on the request. According to Rule 158.3, the decision may be contested through an appeal requiring leave from the Court of First Instance pursuant to Rule 220.2, albeit in an abbreviated form (see Para. 1102 et seqq.)

745 Rule 158.5 states that a failure to comply with the Court's decision within the relevant time limit may cause a decision by default to be issued pursuant to Rule 355. The Court will inform the party concerned accordingly (Rule 158.4).

746 Otherwise, the decision of the Court regarding the security for costs will become enforceable pursuant to Rule 354 (see Chapter 17, Para. 1468 et seqq.)

2. Providing Security for Costs of the Court

747 The Court may, upon its own discretion, also order the parties to provide security for costs incurred by the Court (Rule 159). Depending on the preference of the Court, this, too, can be provided in the form of a direct deposit or bank guarantee. When it comes to appealing and/or enforcing such an order, the procedure to be followed will be the same as one described above, i.e. for providing security for the costs of a party.

XIV. Mediation and Settlement

1. Mediation

748 The Unified Patent Court has its own Patent Mediation and Arbitration Center for patent-related disputes.[82] At any stage of the proceedings, if the Court is of the opinion that the dispute is suitable for a settlement, it may propose that the parties make use of the facilities of the Center in order to settle or to explore a settlement of the dispute (Rule 11). The possibility of using the Center will also be on the agenda of the exploratory procedure during the interim conference (see Para. 886).

82 See also *Picht*, GRUR Int 2018, p. 1.

Assuming the parties agree to mediation, then the proceeding before the Unified Patent Court will be suspended for the duration of the mediation procedure. The parties will not be prevented from continuing the proceeding – or from initiating further proceedings – once the mediation procedure comes to an end. **749**

If the mediation procedure is ended without a settlement having been reached, then the proceeding will be continued from this moment forward i.e. any suspended time limits will begin running again. **750**

2. Guidelines for Mediation

On 15 February 2016, the Preparatory Committee published a set of "Mediation Rules.", which were adopted by the Administrative Committee on 8 July 2022. These are briefly summarized below:[83] **751**

A patent may not be revoked or restricted through the mediation.[84] **752**

A request for mediation may be lodged in electronic form, either by an individual party or by the parties acting jointly. It must be reasoned and will cost a fee. If the request was lodged by only one side but the other side does not agree to the mediation, then the fee will not be reimbursed. **753**

Assuming the parties have agreed to mediation, they will be free to mutually determine many aspects of how the mediation is to proceed. If they are not able to reach agreement in this regard, the following procedure will be followed: **754**

The Center will invite the parties to agree on a mediator and will propose at least five potential candidates. The parties may also agree on some other mediator. If no agreement is reached, the Center will select the mediator. The parties may also mutually agree on the language to be used. If they are unable to reach agreement, then the langue of the patent will be used. **755**

The mediator must be a neutral, impartial and independent third person who can help the parties arrive at a settlement. He will be under obligation to invest sufficient time into the mediation procedure, and will negotiate with the parties either jointly or individually, whereby the party absent during each negotiation session must be kept informed. In the process, the attending party may designate certain facts or information as confidential. **756**

The parties may have representatives in attendance at the negotiation sessions with the mediator. **757**

83 Cf. also *Granata* in *Zeiler/Zojer*, pp. 75 et seqq., as well as *Callens/Granata*, Chapter II, F; for the practice followed at the WIPO, cf. *Schallnau/Feldges* GRUR Int 2017, p. 21 and de *Castro* et al, GRUR Int, 2018, p. 645.

84 I.e. this corresponds to German Law, cf. *Keukenschrijver*, Nichtigkeitsverfahren, Section 5.7, Note 246.

758 The mediation will be terminated either through a settlement or through a declaration, either by the mediator or by the parties, that successful mediation has proved impossible.

759 The costs of the mediation incurred by the mediator as well as by the Center will normally be shared 50/50 by the parties, but a different apportionment may also be agreed.

3. Settlement

760 It stands to reason that a proceeding may also be terminated through settlement without a mediation procedure. In such case, the parties should inform the judge-rapporteur, whereupon the Court will confirm the settlement by issuing a corresponding decision.

761 At this point, the settlement will become enforceable just like a final decision of the Court (Rule 365).

762 Upon request of the parties, the Court may order that details of settlements be kept confidential and that access to the official case files be blocked.[85]

763 As regards costs, the parties may either take their own decision or leave this up to the Court, in which case the judge-rapporteur will take a decision on costs using his own discretion (Rule 11.2 and Rule 365).

764 Save for the purpose of enforcing the terms of any such settlement agreement by any person, no opinion expressed, suggestion made, proposal put forward, concession made or document drawn up for the purposes of settlement may be relied on as evidence by the Court or the parties in proceedings before the Court or any other court unless such matter was expressed to be made on an open basis and freely disclosable to the Court or any other court (Rule 11.3).

XV. Disposal or Denial of an Action

765 The Court may dispose of an action or actions that are manifestly bound to fail or that have become irrelevant.

766 According to Rule 360, the Court may deny an action if it finds that the action has become devoid of purpose, or that the need to adjudicate is no longer given.

▶ Practical tip:

767 Such a scenario may arise, for example, if the patent in dispute in a revocation proceeding has been challenged only in part and the patent proprietor limits himself to the part that was not challenged.

Another conceivable scenario: The opposing side signs a permanent injunction declaration upon pain of sanction and all damage claims for past periods are waived.

---

85 For Example cf. UPC CFI NO. 202/2025, Order of 5 September 2025 – Edwards v. Meril or UPC_CFI_323/2025 (ZD Paris), Order of 25 September 2025 – Scantrust v. ATT.

According to Rule 361, the Court may also deny an action if it is clear that the Court has no jurisdiction over the action or certain of the claims therein, or if the action or defense is, in whole or in part, manifestly inadmissible or manifestly lacking any foundation in law. 768

According to Rule 362, the Court may at any time, on the application of a party or of its own motion, decide that an absolute bar to proceeding with an action exists. 769

In all three cases, the corresponding orders will be issued by the panel of judges concerned (e.g. the panel of first instance) following a recommendation from the judge-rapporteur. The parties must first be given a chance to submit their comments, however. The order may be contested via an appeal proceeding not requiring leave from the Court of First Instance (see Para. 1098 et seqq.) 770

XVI. Recurring Penalty Payments

In principle, rulings of the Unified Patent Court will be enforced on the national level (see Chapter 17, Para. 1468 et seqq.). This said, the Unified Patent Court will have the right to impose a recurring penalty payment for non-compliance with one of its orders (Article 82 (4) of the UPC Agreement), provided the recurring penalty payment was already indicated in the order itself (Rule 354.4) 771

▶ Practical tip:

Conceivable scenarios of this type may arise, for example: 772

- when a preliminary injunction order is violated (see Para. 1335 et seqq.);[86]
- when confidentiality requirements imposed by the Court are violated (see Para. 701 et seqq.)

To deal with such cases, the Unified Patent Court has made it customary practice to include a warning regarding a recurring penalty payment directly in the original decision.[87]

According to Rule 354.4, a recurring penalty payment must be requested by opposite party, whereby the Court must grant both parties a fair hearing before imposing the penalty. Assuming the relevant preconditions are met, the Unified Patent Court will then impose the recurring penalty payment. If the penalized party fails to make 773

86 S. UPC_CFI_177/2023 (LD Düsseldorf), APP_552740/2023, Order of 18 October 2023 – mystromer v. Revolt.

87 Note: *Tilmann* also thinks a two-step procedure might be possible, one in which a warning is first given before the recurring penalty payment is imposed, see *Tilmann/Plassmann*, Note 124 to Art. 82. But it would appear more practical to incorporate the warning directly into the decision itself. After all, the situations likely to occasion a recurring penalty payment are ones in which non-compliance would have to be treated as a grave infraction, so that first issuing a warning before imposing sanction would seem unduly lenient. It should thus be assumed that the warning pursuant to Rule 354.4 will be included in the decision.

payment as required, the Court may also enforce collection of the recurring penalty payment directly (see also Para. 1472). The Court's decision may be contested through an appeal proceeding requiring leave from the Court of First Instance (see Para. 1102).

XVII. The Role of the European Court of Justice (ECJ)

774 As mentioned earlier (see Para. 468 et seqq.), it remains unclear whether or to what extent the European Court of Justice will play a role in the Unitary Patent System. Please see the discussion in that paragraph.

E. Revisions to the UPC Agreement and to the Rules

775 Since the UPC Agreement is an international treaty among nations, revising it would not be an easy process. This said, the UPC Agreement itself spells out two ways in which it could be revised/amended:

I. Revision After Seven Years 2,000 Infringement Proceedings

776 Seven years after the UPC Agreement's entry into force, or once 2,000 infringement proceedings have been decided by the Court – whichever is later – the Administrative Committee is to conduct a consultation of the users of the Unitary Patent System (Article 87 (1)).

777 The consultation is to cover the following aspects:
- the functioning and efficiency of the Unified Patent Court;
- the cost-effectiveness of the Unified Patent Court;
- the trust and confidence of users of the patent system in the quality of the decisions of the Unified Patent Court.

778 Based on this consultation and an opinion of the Court itself, the Administrative Committee may decide to revise this Agreement with a view to improving the functioning of the Court.[88]

779 If necessary, such consultations may also be performed at regular intervals after the initial consultations.

II. Revisions Deriving from International Treaties or EU Law

780 Independently of the consultation process, the Administrative Committee may also amend the UPC Agreement to bring it into line with international treaties relating to patents or to European Union law (Article 87(2)). So far this was conducted once when the London seat of the Central Divison was transferred to Milan (Para. 350).

---

88 Note: Certain observers have actually raised the possibility of exploiting this consultation process and its resulting revisions in order to abolish the Unified Patent Court as such! (See Para. 66.)

III. Efficacy of Revisions; Objections by a Contracting Member State

781 In principle, any decisions taken to revise the UPC Agreement on the basis of one or both of the aforementioned options will be legally effective. However, decisions of the Administrative Committee taken pursuant to Article 87 (1) and (2) will not take effect if a Contracting Member State declares within twelve months of the date of the decision, on the basis of its relevant internal decision-making procedures, that it does not wish to be bound by the decision. In this case, a Review Conference of the Contracting Member States will be convened (Article 87(3)).

IV. Amending the UPC's Rules of Procedure and Statute

782 Amending the UPC's Rules of Procedure and Statute, by contrast, is a relatively simple undertaking. The Statute may be amended pursuant to Article 40 and the Rules of Procedure pursuant to Article 41, namely via a decision taken by the Administrative Committee on the basis of a proposal from the Unified Patent Court. When the amendment relates to the Statute, the Unified Patent Court must first be consulted. When the amendment relates to the Rules of Procedure, a broad prior consultation of all stakeholders must be performed and a prior opinion obtained from the European Commission. Any amendments made to the Statute may not contradict or alter the UPC Agreement. Any amendments made to the Rules of Procedure may not contradict or alter the UPC Agreement or the Statute.

Chapter 8: Strategic Considerations: What Will the Unified Patent Court's Rulings Look Like?

Contents | Para

783 The strategic considerations presented in this chapter focus on how the current jurisdiction of the Unified Patent Court concerning material patent law looks like, and on how the powers of the Unified Patent Court should be understood when it comes to injunctions orders and the award of damages. Other key strategic topics, such as whether and how the UPC should be seised and how a legal proceeding should be conducted, are discussed in other chapters (Chapter 6 and/or Chapter 10).

A. Evaluating the Overall Patent Situation/Landscape

784 In summary, it can be said that, as far as material law jurisdiction is concerned, the Unified Patent Court has not really broken new ground to date.

785 As far as legal consistency is concerned, the Unified Patent Court adheres relatively strictly to case law and also to the approach of the European Patent Office (see the discussion in paragraph 710.1). This does not, of course, mean that the court and the Boards of Appeal of the European Patent Office will come to the same conclusion.[1] On the contrary, the 'margin of error' in assessing different documents will always be greater in different courts, even if the same approach is taken, than if documents are interpreted in the same way but the approach is different.

786 As far as infringement is concerned, the Unified Patent Court has so far adhered to what is known from national proceedings, particularly in Germany. In particular, the approach that the interpretation of the patent is a legal question and that the skilled person is a fictitious person is identical.[2]

787 At present, there is also no reason to assume that the court will introduce 'file wrapper estoppel' or anything similar. The Court of Appeal did not follow an approach

1 For an example where the Munich Local Division revoked a patent, which was upheld by the Board of Appeal of the EPO see UPC_CFI_146/2024 (LD Munich), Decision of 12 December 2025 – Sanofi v. Stada et al.

2 UPC_CoA 768/2024, Order of 30 April 2025 – Insulet v. EOFlow.

taken by the Munich Local Division, which used the originally filed patent claims for interpretation.[3]

One important area where there is currently no case law from the Court of Appeal is equivalent patent infringement. Although there have already been two decisions by the District Court of The Hague in this regard,[4] the Court of Appeal has not yet had an opportunity to comment on this issue. **788**

Overall, the conclusion is therefore positive: the Unified Patent Court continues the established line of the national infringement courts - particularly the German courts - which contributes to legal certainty. **789**

There is no definitive decision concerning equivalent patent infringement issued, though. So still extreme caution is in order, particularly when examining the patent situation through "freedom-to-operate analyses" (e.g. for the approval of products, etc.), assuming one's objective is to minimize the risk of a patent infringement. Especially so long as it remains unclear how equivalent patent infringements are to be evaluated, it is better to set the external or internal benchmarks too high rather than too low if one wishes to stay on the safe side or to adequately model the risk profile. **790**

The fact that no legal provision has been made for "punitive damages" (see Para. 652 et seqq.) can and should flow into the risk analysis and the decisional process as a positive factor. Nonetheless, one should take proactive steps early on by assembling supporting materials in preparation for possible revocation actions and/or by lodging preliminary objections. **791**

When it comes to the question of the patentability and/or legal validity of patents, on the other hand, the best initial approach would be to monitor – besides of course the jurisdiction of the Unified Patent Court – the evolving case law of the European Patent Office and to deviate from it only in individual cases. **792**

B. The UPC's Powers to Order Injunctions and Award Damages

As mentioned earlier, the UPC Agreement provides rights of relief for patent infringements which are generally similar to those codified in most Member States. This is due at least in part to the EU Implementing Regulation. **793**

I. Injunctive Relief

In contrast to French law for example, which makes claims for injunctive relief a statutory entitlement of the victorious patent plaintiff,[5] the UPC Agreement leaves **794**

3 UPC_CoA_1/2024, Order of 13 May 2024, APL_8/2024 – VusionGroup v. Hanshow.

4 UPC_CFI_239/2023 (LD Den Haag), Decision of 22 November 2024 – Plant-E v. Arkyne and UPC_CFI_479/2025 (LD Den Haag), Decision of 11 September 2025 – Washtower v. Bega. Both cases are settled meanwhile.

5 For an overview of the legal situation in the most important countries of Europe, see *Reetz* et al, GRUR Int 2015, p. 210, although this picture applied before Germany's 2nd Patent Modernization Act.

the ordering such relief up to the discretionary leeway of the Court, i.e. the Court enjoys more freedom in this regard.

795 However, the court's practice is different. With two exceptions (discussed below), the court has ordered an injunction if the patent was deemed sufficiently legally valid and infringed. It should be noted, however, that in SEP/FRAND infringement actions, an injunction may of course be denied on the basis of the patent holder's conduct (see the discussion in Para. 797). However, there is no relevant case law to date.

796 The two exceptions mentioned are as follows:

- In preliminary injunction proceedings between two automotive suppliers, an injunction was issued, but parts for which the infringer had already entered into contractual obligations with an automobile manufacturer were excluded.[6]
- In proceedings concerning heart valves, certain valves for which the patent holder was unable to provide an adequate replacement were also excluded from the injunction.[7]

However, these are absolute exceptions to date. All this could not be further from current practice in the USA, for example, which was described by *Kappos*[8] as a "*compulsory licensing regime*," i.e. the sole question up for decision is not injunctive relief but the price of a compulsory license.

1. Standard-Essential Patents

797 Given the primacy of European Union law, the established case law of the European Court of Justice on standard-essential patents – particularly its Decision C-170/13 in the ZTE/Huawei case[9] – will continue to apply before the Unified Patent Court as well. There are basically no changes in this context[10] Currently before the Unified Patent Court there is no established case law and no decision from the appeals Court.

---

6 UPC_CFI_368/2024 (LD Düsseldorf), Order of 31 October 2024 – Valeo v. Magna.

7 UPC_CoA_464/2024, Decision of 25 November 2025 – Edwards v. Meril.

8 *Kappos*, Lecture at the 27th Fordham IP Conference on 24 April 2019 in New York; see also http://fordhamipinstitute.com/material/papers-and-presentations-4/ as well as *Barnett/Kappos*, "Restoring Deterrence: The Case for Enhanced Damages in a No-Injunction Patent System."

9 EJC, Ruling of 16 July 2015, No. C 170/13 in the *Huawei vs. ZTE* case; cf. Ruling of the Higher District Court (OLG) of Düsseldorf, B– I-15 U 65/15, Mitt. 2016, p. 85, discussed in *Müller/Henke*, Mitt. 2016, p. 62 as the first "post-Huawei-ZTE decision."

10 See e.g. *Petersen* et al, "The Unified Patent Court (UPC): Compulsory Licensing and Competition Law," as well as a more general discussion in *Herranz/Tapia*, "Good and Bad Practices in FRAND License Negotiations," *Zeiler/Zojer*, p. 49, and *Martinez*, GRUR Int 2019, p. 633.

Thus, it stillremains to be seen, how the Unified Patent Court will handle a number of questions that were not made in the EJC's ruling; to wit: 798

- Whether the "ZTE-Huawei Protocol," – i.e. a clear definition of the approach to be used between the two sides – is more or less compulsory, or whether it merely serves as a sort of "safe haven" and other approaches are acceptable as well.[11]
- Whether there is a fixed FRAND rate (as in the court of first instance's ruling in the Unwired Planet case), or whether a corridor exists in this context, as has been affirmed in German established legal precedent as well as in the second-instance ruling in the Unwired Planet case; and
- Which potential infringer/licensee along the chain of exploitation can be, or ought to be, sued by the patent proprietor.[12]

Another decisive practical question will be the extent to which the Unified Patent Court will require the patent proprietor/licensor to present his previously concluded licensing agreements, and whether it will be ready to grant the patent proprietor/licensor a right of confidentiality, especially against the alleged infringer/potential licensee. The latter variant seems theoretically possible to some extent (within the framework of Rule 262A, cf. Para. 701 et seqq.) and will be likely be regularly requested by the patent proprietor, at least until actual experience shows that the Unified Patent Court will deny such requests or only seldom grant them (see Para. 701, cf. Para. 1033). 799

2. Can Products Delivered Abroad Be Recalled Also?

A point that possibly remains to be clarified is the extent to which it would be conceivable to demand – as in the Federal Court of Justice's ruling in the *Abdichtsystem* case[13] – that defendants domiciled in foreign countries perform a recall for products delivered abroad, assuming they had to know that a delivery into the territorial jurisdiction of the Unified Patent Court would eventually occur. This would naturally be very advantageous for plaintiffs. Thus, whenever such a scenario is given, the plaintiff should do his utmost to obtain just such a decision, while the defendant should make effort to fend it off. It seems difficult to predict how the Unified Patent Court will rule in this connection. Still, all stakeholders should be aware of the possibility that such a case will sooner or later be heard before the Unified Patent Court. 800

11 Cf. here German Federal Court of Justice (BGH), Decision of 27 January 2026 – KZR 10/25.

12 For a full discussion of the situation in Germany, see *Kühnen*, GRUR 2019, p. 665. A corresponding referral by the District Court (LG) of Düsseldorf (Decision of 26 Nov. 2020, 4c O 17/19) to the EJC was resolved through a settlement between the parties.

13 BGH Judgment in the *Abdichtsystem* case, GRUR 2017, p. 785, but cf. the BGH, Decision of 8 June 2021 – X ZR 47/19 in the *Ultraschallwandler* case.

3. Is There a Claim to Information on Recall Letters?

801 According to the recent case law of the Higher District (*Oberlandesgericht*) of Düsseldorf,[14] a claim to product recall also entails a claim to be informed of the identity of the addressees to whom the infringer has sent out a product-recall letter. Whether this will likewise hold true before the Unified Patent Court is uncertain, but it does not appear improbable. A victorious infringer should by all means lodge a request for such information.

II. Award of Damages

802 The manner in which the UPC will handle claims for damages is obviously still more or less open as well.[15] This said, Article 68 of the UPC Agreement expressly refers to damages which are "appropriate." By its very wording, this effectively rules out like the punitive character associated with the "punitive damages" or "treble damages" that are awarded under the US legal system.[16]

1. Do the Guidelines on the Value of the Action Serve as a Benchmark (?)

803 It bears noting here that the "Guidelines" (on assessing the value of an action) published by Tilmann/Mooney (see Para. 502) also indirectly touch upon the award of damages.

804 Thus, the Guidelines hold that the value of a patent infringement action should be determined under the assumption of a license analogy and based on the turnover earned by the defendant. Section II, Para. 1) of the Guidelines expressly describes a claim for past damage as a "damage claim," i.e. the damages owed for the past would have to be determined based on a license analogy.

805 Admittedly this only applies to the calculation of the value of the action, but it is also possible that, given the "quasi-official" nature of the Guidelines, the Unified Patent Court will also apply them when awarding damages in patent-infringement cases, particularly since such an approach would be covered by the UPC Agreement and by the UPC Rules of Procedure.[17]

---

14 Higher District Court (OLG) of Düsseldorf, Ruling and Order of 20 Sept. 2021 in the *Rückrufvollstreckung I* case, I-2 W 18/21, GRUR-RS 2021, 28744, and Ruling and Order of 24 Sept. 2021 in the *Rückrufvollstreckung I* case, I-2 W 19/21, GRUR-RS 2021, 28722.

15 See inter alia *Walz*, GRUR Int. 2016, p. 513.

16 See the Ruling of the US Supreme Court in *Halo Electronics, Inc. v. Pulse Electronics, Inc.*, No. 14–1513; cf. also e.g. the CAFC decisions in *Bard Peripheral Vascular, Inc. v. W. L. Gore & Associates*, Inc., 682 F.3d, pp. 1003, 1006–08 (Fed. Cir. 2012); i4i Ltd. P'Ship. v. Microsoft Corp., 598 F.3d pp. 831 and 859–60 (Fed. Cir. 2010); *Spine Solutions, Inc. v. Medtronic Sofamor Danek* USA, Inc., 620 F.3d pp. 1305 and 1319 (Fed. Cir. 2010); In re *Seagate Technology, LLC*, 497 F.3d, p. 1360 (Fed. Cir. 2007) (en banc); *Knorr-Bremse Systeme Fuer Nutzfahrzeuge GmbH v. Dana Corp.*, 383 F.3d, pp. 1337 and 1347 (Fed. Cir. 2004) (en banc).

17 Cf. also *Kather*, VPP-Rundbrief 2014, p. 28, who argues that such an approach should also be used under German law.

It bears noting that European case law definitely allows the fact that no actual licensing agreement exists in an infringement situation to be considered when assessing the damages to be awarded. It cannot be ruled out that the Unified Patent Court will take a similar approach. Just two cases will be mentioned as examples: **806**

- The District (LG) of Düsseldorf[18] held that the fact that licensing agreements often entail an audit of the books serves to increase the license fee when applying the license analogy to assess indemnifiable damage in infringement cases.
- In a widely noted decision, the European Court of Justice held that the general approach of assessing double damages for the infringement of industrial property rights (copyright, in this case) was reconcilable with European law.[19] It should be noted, however, that this ECJ decision specifically determined that the EU Implementing Regulation does not preclude punitive damages, whereas this is expressly precluded in the UPC Agreement.

In German practice, damage-assessment proceedings are hardly ever conducted, however. Instead, the parties will normally strive for an early settlement. And this will probably prove to be the usual procedure in patent-infringement proceedings before the UPC, at least once the Court has issued a number of decisions that can serve as "signposts." **807**

2. Abatement of Damage Indemnity Due to a Missing Translation

Regulation 1257/2012/EU expressly states that the infringement court (i.e. the Unified Patent Court) is to consider the possible absence of translations when assessing damages, provided the action involves a Unitary Patent and the defendant is a small to mid-size company, a natural person, a non-profit organization, an institution of higher learning or a similar public institution devoted to research (see Para. 150). **808**

These preconditions will often not apply, but when they do, the defendant should definitely raise the missing translation as a defense. The Unified Patent Court will have to consider this point, given that the Regulation enjoys priority by virtue of Article 20 of the UPC Agreement. **809**

3. Claims to Information

It improbable that the Unified Patent Court will regularly deny claims to injunctive relief while only awarding damages. Still, a plaintiff is well-advised to present arguments well in advance, preferably when submitting the Statement of Case, which show the Court why he is entitled to all the asserted claims and why it would unfair or unreasonable to deny these or to grant the infringer a grace period for a workaround. This could be particularly applicable when a claim to information is asserted. **810**

18 Judgment of the District Court (LG) of Düsseldorf in the *Teigportioniervorrichtung* case, GRUR 2000, p. 309.

19 ECJ Judgment of 25 January 2017, C-367/15 in the *Stowarzyszenie "Oławska Telewizja Kablowa* case;" also see GRUR Int 2017, p. 1.

811 Convicted patent infringers should of course also exploit the leeway that the Court enjoys to their benefit. Namely by arguing that, in the special case scenario at hand, not all of the patent plaintiff's claims should be granted. Besides specifically targeting the patent plaintiff's claim to information,[20] for example this approach could also contest his claim to injunctive relief, although here the chances of success are likely to be poor and one will usually only be able to obtain a grace period for a workaround (cf. Para. 794 et seqq.). Both Article 67 of the UPC Agreement as well as Article 8 of the Implementing Regulation are geared towards the principle of proportionality: The patent infringer can use this an argument to fend off the patent proprietor's demand for information, or at least in part.[21]

20 Cf. *Hauck*, GRUR Int 2013, p. 713 on possible claims to information concerning the product-recall letter; see Para. 801.

21 See in particular the full discussion of German practice in *Ann/Hauck/Maute, Auskunftsanspruch and Geheimnisschutz im Verletzungsprozess.*

Section 3: 1st Instance Infringement Proceedings

Chapter 9: Course of a 1st Instance Infringement Proceeding

Contents

A. Fundamentals

This chapter describes the course of a patent infringement proceeding before a panel of first instance at the Unified Patent Court. **812**

This proceeding is characterized by a strictly specified sequence of steps, each associated with clear time limits. Like practically all proceedings before the Unified Patent Court, it essentially consists of three stages – a written procedure, an interim procedure and an oral procedure with oral hearing – after which a decision on the merits is issued.

813 The action may also encompass two additional procedures: the damage-award procedure, in which the amount of damages is determined, and the procedure for cost decision, which determines who will bear the costs of the proceedings. If we include these two stages, we arrive at the following five stages, which are also enumerated in Rule 10 of the UPC's Rules of Procedure:

1) a written procedure (Rules 12 to 36)
2) an interim procedure (Rules 37 to 41 and 101 to 110), however this is optional (cf. Para. 871)
3) an oral procedure with oral hearing and issuance of the decision on the merits (Rules 111 to 119)
4) a damage-award procedure (Rules 125 to 144)
5) a procedure for cost decision (Rules 150 to 159)

814 Until the oral procedure stage, the proceeding will be conducted by a reporting judge, also known as a "**judge-rapporteur**" (see Para. 824).

B. Written Procedure

I. Bringing the Action

815 The action – and thus also the written procedure – is initiated once a Statement of Claim is lodged. As at this stage the defendant has no representative, it will be serviced via registered mail though the court. As mentioned earlier (see Para. 676 et seqq.), all following submissions will be handled through the Court's case-management system (CMS) and sent to representatives of both sides.

816 The Statement of Claim **must** contain the following (Rule 13.1):

- details of the patent or patents concerned, as well as information on any prior, related proceedings before the Unified Patent Court (e.g. revocation actions);
- an indication of the division which is to hear the action, along with an explanation of why that division has competence;
- the claims under substantive law which are to be adjudicated by the Court (see also Para. 1048 et seqq.);
- an indication of any order the claimant will seek during the interim procedure; and
- information on the value of the action (see Para. 423 et seqq.)

It should be noted that a request may be lodged for damages to be initially awarded in principle only; the amount of the damages will then be determined in a separate damage-award procedure (Para. 922 et seqq.)

817 The Statement of Claim **must** also contain the following:

- details on the infringement as well as supporting facts and evidence which will be presented or which may be presented upon request (e.g. witness statements)

- reasons which explain why the actions described constitute a patent infringement; and
- a list of the relevant documents and, if applicable, an indication of which documents, or portions thereof, do not require translation.

The action **may** also contain: 818
- a request to assign the action to a single judge, insofar as this is desired;
- a request to raise the upper limit of recoverable costs (see Para. 450);

A court fee assessed based on the above-referenced information concerning the value 819 of the action must also be paid (Rule 15).

1. Regulations on the Use of Languages

The plaintiff will initially determine the language of the proceedings, insofar as more 820 than one language could permissibly be used before the relevant division. This has already been discussed earlier (see Para. 399 et seqq.)

2. Legal Capacity to Bring Action

On the topic of legal capacity to bring action, particularly on the part of licensees, 821 please see Para. 463 et seqq.

II. Examination of Formal Requirements and Assignment to a 1st Instance Panel

If the Statement of Claim is deficient or the fee has not been paid in full, then the 822 Registry of the Court will issue the plaintiff a deficiency notice which sets a grace period of 14 days in which to correct. If the claimant fails to correct, or to correct sufficiently (see Para. 718 et seqq.), then the Court may issue a decision by default. Before doing so, the Court may give the plaintiff another opportunity to be heard (Rule 16).

If all the preconditions have been met, on the other hand, then the Registry will record 823 the day of receipt of the Statement of Claim, open a case file, assign an action number to the file, and inform the claimant accordingly. According to Rule 17, the Statement of Claim is to be legally served upon the defendant. This is the only instance where this does not proceed via the Courts CMS system

The action will then be assigned to a panel of first instance of the respective division,[1] 824 whereupon the presiding judge of that division will designate a judge-rapporteur. This may also be the presiding judge himself.

As soon as practicable, the Registry will the proceed to notify the parties of the iden- 825 tity of the judge-rapporteur (Rule 18).

1 Note: On transfers to the central division, see Para. 394 et seqq.

III. Lodging the Statement of Defense

826 The defendant now has two options open to him:

1. Lodging a Preliminary Objection

827 Within one month of receiving legal service of the Statement of Claim, the defendant may lodge a Preliminary Objection[2] in which he contests one or more of the following (Rule 19):

- the general competence and jurisdiction of the Court, particularly on the grounds that an opt-out has been declared (see Para. 299 et seqq.), on the grounds of an arrangement between the parties (see Para. 612), or on the grounds of a national infringement action pending in Germany which has yet to be adjudicated (see Para. 34);
- the competence of the division indicated by the claimant; or
- the language of the proceedings.

The one-month time limit will also apply for the lodging of any request to have the action transferred to the central division because the so-called "Unilever Conditions" apply (see Para. 388), i.e. because the action was lodged with a regional division but the infringement occurred in the territory of at least three regional divisions (Rule 19.4).

828 Rule 19.3 stipulates that the Preliminary Objection be formulated in a language of the Court pursuant to Rule 14. But it remains unclear whether this also means that some other language than the one used in the Statement of Claim is permissible.[3] In practice this is of no particular importance.

829 The objection options under Rule 19 are exhaustive,[4] other procedural facts such as sufficient active legimitation or representation of the plaintiff may have to be asserted at a later stage.

830 When a Preliminary Objection is lodged, the plaintiff will be invited to submit his comments within 14 days' time. The judge-rapporteur will then decide whether to allow the Preliminary Objection. His decision is to contain the relevant instructions to the parties and to the Registry concerning the next step in the proceedings. The judge-rapporteur may also decide that the contents of the Preliminary Objection will not be adjudicated until the decision on the merits is issued. In this case, he will notify the parties accordingly.

---

2 Note: It is unfortunate that the term used in the official German translation of the Rules of Procedure is *Einspruch* (objection) rather than the more precise *Rüge* (complaint). Still, it is unlikely that the "objection procedure" will be confounded in practice with the "opposition proceeding" pursuant to Art 99 of the European Patent Convention (EPC) and Section 59 of the German Patent Act (PatG).

3 An affirmative view is taken by *Kircher* in *Bopp/Kircher*, Section 12, Note 94, while an essentially negative view is taken by *Plassmann/Steiniger* in *Tilmann/Plassmann*, Note 13 to Rule 19.

4 UPC_CoA_188/2024, Order of 3 September 2024, APL_21943/2024 – Aylo v. Dish.

If the judge-rapporteur allows the Preliminary Objection, then his decision may be contested before the Court of Appeal (see Para. 1098 et seqq.). If the judge denies the Preliminary Objection, then an appeal proceeding requiring leave from the Court of First Instance is possible (see Para. 1102 et seqq.). 831

If no Preliminary Objection is lodged within one months' time, then this will be taken to mean that the defendant is willing to submit to the competence and jurisdiction of the Court as such, as well as to the competence of the division selected by the claimant (Rule 19.7). Whether this will also apply to the choice of language is not clear, given that Rule 19.7 is silent on the matter.[5] 832

2. Lodging a Statement of Defense

Regardless of whether a Preliminary Objection is lodged or not (see Para. 827), the defendant will have three months after being served with the Statement of Claim in which to lodge his **Statement of Defense** (Rules 23 and 24). This must contain: 833
- the names and details of the defendant and of the defendant's representative;
- an indication of whether the defendant lodged a Preliminary Objection;
- the reasons while the infringement action should fail;
- the supporting documents and evidence to be presented, or to be presented upon request (e.g. witness statements);
- an indication of any order the defendant will seek in the interim procedure; and
- a statement whether the defendant disputes the claimant's assessment of the value of the infringement action and the grounds for such dispute.

It should be noted for clarity that the lodging of a Preliminary Objection pursuant to Rule 19 will not serve to extend the time limit for lodging a Statement of Defense. 834

IV. Counterclaim for Revocation

Together with his Statement of Defense, the defendant may also lodge a **counterclaim for revocation** (Rule 25) of the patent or patents in dispute. If he does not do so, then the legal validity of the patent will be assumed, just as in a German proceeding, i.e. the defendant will only be able to assert non-infringement as an argument in his defense.[6] On the other hand, the defendant will also be free to lodge his own separate revocation action (see Para. 1178 et seqq.)[7] 835

This counterclaim for revocation will in turn initiate a new proceeding, one in which the parties' roles will be reversed: Thus, the defendant of the infringement proceeding will become the plaintiff of the revocation counterclaim proceeding. 836

5 This is negated by *Kircher* in *Bopp/Kircher*, Section 12, Note 108, but affirmed by *Tilmann/Plassmann*, Note 15 to Rule 19.

6 Cf. UPC_CFI_33/2024 (LD Vienna), Decision of 15 January 2025, ACT_4261/2024 – Swarco v. Strabag.

7 A different view is taken by *Plassmann/Steiniger* in *Tilmann/Plassmann*, Note 4 to Rule 25 (but this is dubious in view of Art. 33(3) of the UPCA; see Para. 1162 et seqq.).

837 The defendant of the counterclaim action, for his part, will have several options open to him:

838 If the plaintiff is not also the patent proprietor, but rather a licensee, or if there are additional patent proprietors who have not yet joined the infringement action, then the licensee, respectively the additional proprietor(s), will become party to the revocation counterclaim (Rule 25.2).[8] The Court will then legally serve the counterclaim for revocation upon the newly acceding party or parties.

839 The entire proceeding will now have at least three parties, formally speaking. We will nonetheless refer to only a single "plaintiff" going forward, both for the sake of simplicity and also because we can safely assume that the licensee (plaintiff of the action) and the patent proprietor (defendant of the revocation counterclaim) will in practice act in a joint and coordinated fashion.

840 If the defendant[9] lodges a counterclaim for revocation, then the following contents are to be added to his Statement of Defense, i.e. to his response to the action (Rule 25):

- an indication of the extent to which revocation of the patent concerned is being requested;
- the grounds adduced for revocation pursuant to Article 138 of the European Patent Convention (see Para. 658 et seqq.);
- the evidence and documents relied on, and an indication of any further evidence which will be offered in support (e.g. witness statements);
- an indication of any order the defendant will seek in the interim procedure;
- an indication of the value of the action; unless contrary information is available, then, according to the Mooney/Tilmann Guidelines, this amount is to equal the value of the infringement action plus a surcharge of up to 50 %, as recommended in the Guidelines (see Para. 425 et seqq.);
- a list of the relevant documents including, if applicable, an indication of which documents do not require translation; and,
- a statement of the defendant's position with respect to the possibility of separating the proceedings and/or of transferring the case to the central division.

841 The lodging of a revocation counterclaim also entails payment of a fee contingent on the value of the action (Rule 26, see Para. 432 et seqq.) Said fee will be compu-

8 A contrary view is taken by *Nieder*, Mitt. 2017, p. 145, who holds that, when an action is brought by a licensee, a revocation counterclaim is not possible and that a revocation action must instead be brought before the central division. An affirmative view, by contrast, is taken by *Plassmann/Steiniger* in *Tilmann/Plassmann*, Note 12 to Rule 25.

9 Note: As mentioned earlier, the lodging of a counterclaim will of course turn the defendant into a plaintiff, namely of the counterclaim proceeding. For simplicity's sake, however, we will consistently refer to the parties according to the roles they play in the patent infringement proceeding, i.e. the "plaintiff" is always the plaintiff in the patent infringement proceeding, while the "defendant" is always the (alleged) patent infringer. Also these terms will be used in the singular only, whilst in practice in quite a few cases there are multiple defendants.

ted based on the value of the action (see Para. 840 as well as Para. 425 et seqq.) but subject to an upper limit of 20,000 €.

The revocation counterclaim will now be examined by the Registry for compliance with formal requirements. If formal deficiencies are found or if the fee was not properly paid, then the Registry will issue a deficiency notice giving the defendant a 14-day grace period in which to correct and/or to pay the fee (Rule 27.3). 842

If this is not done, a decision by default will be issued pursuant to Rule 355 by the judge-rapporteur, who will be free to give the defendant another hearing before issuing his decision (Rule 27.4). 843

V. Further Steps of the Written Procedure

Once the defendant's Statement of Defense has been received, the judge-rapporteur, after consulting the parties, will set a date for the interim conference in the interim procedure (insofar as one necessary) as well as for the oral hearing (Rule 28). The judge-rapporteur may also set an alternative date in each case. Thus, the timetable for the further steps of the proceedings will already be fixed at this relatively early stage. 844

1. Reply/Rejoinder in the Absence of a Counterclaim

If the defendant does not lodge a counterclaim along with his Statement of Defense, then the plaintiff will have two months from the date of being served with the Statement of Defense in which to lodge his Reply (Rule 29 b). 845

If this time limit is not met, then a decision by default will be issued, unless the time limit is extended by the judge-rapporteur, who may also do this retroactively. (We assume that this rule's applicability to all further written pleadings is understood by the reader; we will not restate it.) If the plaintiff did not have sufficient legal capacity to bring the action or is not properly represented, this will probably be the first point in time at which the defendant – assuming he does not lodge a preliminary objection (see Para. 827) – will be able to request a decision by default (Rule 355, see Para. 718). This is because missing a time limit is a precondition for a decision by default and because the bringing of an action is not subject to any deadline. It should be noted, however, that the adequacy of the plaintiff's representation must first be examined by the Registry of the Court. 846

The defendant will have one month after being served with the Reply to the Statement of Defense in which to lodge his Rejoinder, which must be limited to the matters which the plaintiff has already raised in his Reply (Rule 29 c). 847

In theory, the proceedings conducted up to this point will have lasted a total of six months. Assuming the subsequent interim procedure begins immediately and lasts three months as planned, then this will leave the parties just three months' time to prepare for the oral hearing. In this case, the twelve-month timetable envisioned for the proceedings could still be adhered to – at least up to the oral hearing stage. This is shown in the following timeline: 848

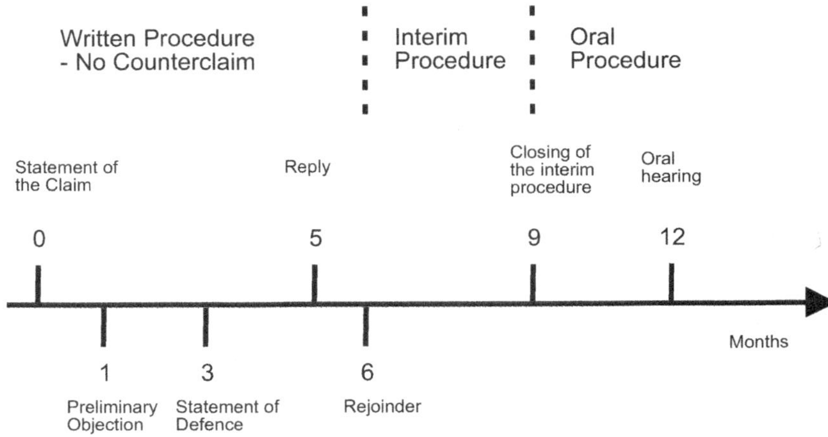

Fig. 9.1 Course of the procedure when no counterclaim is filed

849 According to the Rules of Procedure, both of the two written pleadings which each side submits must be approved by the Court. Once the Rejoinder has been received by the Court, the judge-rapporteur will notify the parties of the date on which he plans to close the written procedure and transition to the interim procedure (Rule 35 a).

850 Before this date, both sides will remain free to request permission to lodge additional written pleadings. Assuming the judge-rapporteur approves such a request – while setting a corresponding time limit – this could serve to protract the duration the written procedure's duration.

2. Defense and Reply in the Event of a Counterclaim

851 If a revocation counterclaim has been lodged along with the Statement of Defense, then the Court will have to decide the following points:

a) whether to allocate a technical judge and adjudicate both the action and the counterclaim jointly;
b) whether to transfer the revocation counterclaim to the central division and, if applicable, suspend the proceedings;
c) whether to transfer both the action and the counterclaim to the central division, subject to the consent of both parties;

852 This will generally not occur, however, until the written procedure has been closed (Rule 37) (see Para. 873), unless the panel of first instance – after granting both sides a fair hearing – takes an earlier decision. This is, however, current practice in many divisions.

853 Upon being served with a Statement of Defense containing a Revocation Counterclaim, the plaintiff will have two months in which to respond, namely with a Reply to the Defendant's Statement of Defense and with a Defense to the Defendant's

Counterclaim for Revocation. In addition, the plaintiff is to use his Defense to the Defendant's Counterclaim as an opportunity to state his own position concerning a possible splitting of the proceedings. It bears mentioning here that the Reply should also indicate which conditional claims of the patent in dispute are supposed to be patentable on their own and why (cf. Para. 1061 et seqq.).

The plaintiff's Defense to the defendant's Counterclaim for Revocation will represent the plaintiff's *only* opportunity to propose amendments to the contested patent(s), whereby he may also lodge auxiliary requests. These auxiliary requests should be limited to a reasonable number based on the circumstances of the case (Rule 30.1c). Any further amendments to the contested patent(s) may only be admitted into the proceedings with the Court's permission (Rule 30.2). **854**

If the patent proprietor lodges amended claims in this context, he will be required, pursuant to Rule 30, to include the following information: **855**

- why the amendments meet the requirements Articles 84,[10] 123(2) and 123(3) of the European Patent Convention (EPC);
- why the proposed amended claims are patentable; and
- if applicable, why they are infringed.

It bears noting that no regulation analogous to Rule 80 of the European Patent Convention (EPC) – at least in term of its wording – exists before the Unified Patent Court. Thus, the amended claims must not necessarily be occasioned by the adduced grounds for revocation.[11] This will of course hold true in practice in the vast majority of cases. **856**

Also worth noting at this juncture is that when a parallel opposition proceeding is pending before the European Patent Office, there will be no need for the patent proprietor to bring his respective applications into mutual accord.[12] **857**

The further course of the written procedure will now depend on whether or not the plaintiff amends his patent in his Defense to the defendant's Counterclaim for Revocation. **858**

a) Course of the Proceedings for a Counterclaim Without Patent Amendments

If the plaintiff does not amend his patent, then the defendant will now have two months – just like in a proceeding without a counterclaim – to lodge his Rejoinder (in the action proceeding), respectively his Reply (in the revocation counterclaim proceeding). The written procedure of the infringement proceeding will thereupon be closed. **859**

---

10 See *Hüttermann*, GRUR Int 2022, p. 633.

11 However, cf. Decision 9 W (Pat) 56/08 of the German Federal Patent Court of 17 November 2014 in the *Verdichter* case: Even though no analogous regulation exists under German law, the court nonetheless denied the amendment of claims in a revocation counterclaim proceeding because the amended claims had not been occasioned by the revocation grounds or documents adduced by the counterclaimant.

12 Cf. the corresponding demand of *Kühnen* (Section E, III, 15) as a reaction of the Ruling of the Federal Constitutional Court (BGH) in the *Maschinensatz* case, GRUR 2010, p. 904.

860 So as to allow each side to submit two written pleadings, the plaintiff will now be given the opportunity to lodge another Rejoinder within one month of receiving legal service of the Defendant's Reply. In this Rejoinder, the plaintiff must limit himself to the matters raised in the Defendant's Reply. Up this point, eight months will theoretically have passed, as shown in the following timeline:

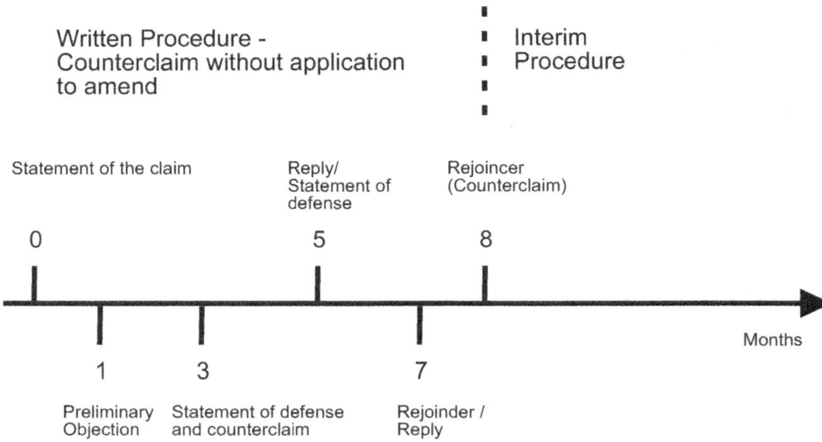

Fig. 9.2 Course of the proceedings with counterclaim but no amendment of the patent

861 Just like in a proceeding without a counterclaim, the judge-rapporteur will now notify the parties of the date on which he plans to transition to the interim procedure, during which the parties will still be able to request permission to submit additional written pleadings.

862 As shown by the above timetable, it would theoretically still be possible to adhere to the envisioned 12-month limit for the total duration of the proceedings, but only by reducing the timetable which the parties have to prepare for the following procedural stages. So it is probably more likely that the proceeding will be drawn out somewhat to make up for this. Even so, it will still be relatively expeditious.

b) Course of a Proceedings with Counterclaim and Patent Amendments

863 If the defendant lodges a counterclaim for revocation and the plaintiff amends the patent – even if only conditionally – then this will give rise to the following situation:

864 The defendant will not have two months in which to submit his Rejoinder in the Infringement proceeding and his Reply in the revocation counterclaim proceeding. The written procedure of the infringement proceeding will thereupon be closed.

865 However, both sides in the revocation counterclaim proceeding will still have one month's time in which to submit a final written submission, but this must be limited to the matters raised by the opposite side in its most recent written submission.

Thus, each side will in principle be able to make a total of three written submissions in total. By the time the final written submission is lodged, nine months will have passed, as the following timeline shows: 866

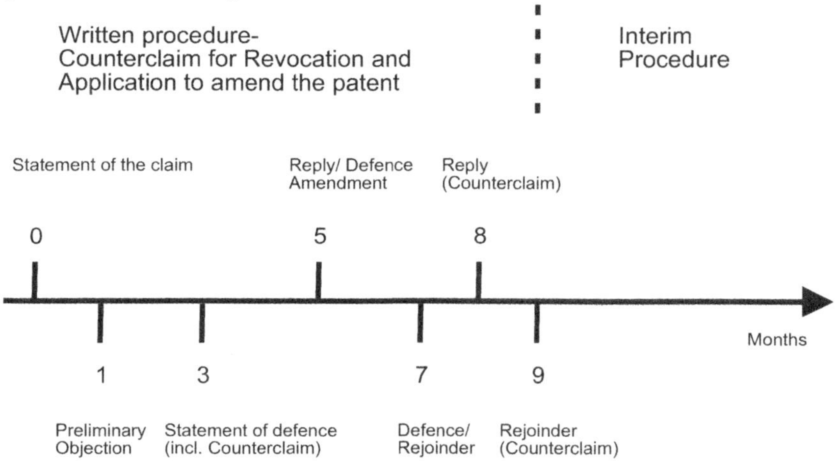

Fig. 9.3 Course of the proceedings with counterclaim and amendment

Just like in the proceedings discussed earlier, the judge-rapporteur will now notify the parties of the date on which he plans to transition to the interim procedure, during which time the parties will still be able to request permission to submit additional written pleadings. But this may not always occur, given that the proceedings will have already lasted for quite some time by this point. 867

Realistically speaking, this means that the Court will not be able to adhere to the envisioned 12-month duration of the overall proceedings, unless it were to rush through the interim procedure in a merely cursory manner. But if we assume that three months are needed for the interim procedure and another three months to prepare for the oral hearing, we arrive at a total duration of 15 months – which is still extremely expeditious! 868

VI. Allocation of a Technical Judge

Even if no counterclaim for revocation is lodged, a party may lodge an application for allocating a technical judge. This application should be lodged as early as possible in the written procedure. An application lodged after closure of the written procedure will require justification (Rule 33). 869

The judge-rapporteur will for his part also be free to have a technical judge allocated at any time without having to obtain consent from the parties, provided he has first consulted the presiding judge and the parties, even though the latter will not have any veto right in the matter (Rule 34). In practice, however, this decision will be taken 870 together with the decision not to split off the counterclaim, which is a decision that is taken by the senate.[13]

C. Interim Procedure

871 The next procedural stage will be the interim procedure, which is also conducted by the judge-rapporteur alone. It is, however, to a great extent optional and especially the Düsseldorf division tends to have no interim conference at all.[14]

872 The only necessary decision which has to be made at the latest at this stage of the proceedings is whether and how a revocation-counterclaim proceeding is to be split off.

I. Decision on Splitting Off Counterclaim Proceedings

873 The decision on whether and how a revocation-counterclaim proceeding is to be split off will be taken by the respective panel of first instance (Rule 37), subject to the following provisions:

874 The panel of first instance will first of all decide whether the revocation-counterclaim proceeding should be split off, whereby the parties will be given the opportunity to be heard (Rule 264) (see Para. 685 et seqq.). The panel is to provide a short justification for its decision.

875 In principle, there will be four alternative options in this context:
- The panel conducts both proceedings;
- The panel transfers the revocation counterclaim proceeding to the central division but continues to conduct the infringement proceeding in parallel;
- The panel transfers the revocation counterclaim proceeding to the central division and stays the infringement proceeding; or
- The panel transfers both proceedings to the central division, subject to the consent of the parties.

876 In reality, the last of these scenarios will probably occur very rarely. If this were not the case, the plaintiff could just as well bring his action before the central division in the first place.[15] Thus, this last scenario will be touched on only briefly in the discussions that follows.

877 If the revocation-counterclaim proceeding is split off, then the infringement proceeding is to be stayed only if there is a high likelihood that the relevant claims of the

13 Just to give a few examples: UPC_CFI_ 7/2023 (LD Düsseldorf), Order of 1 December 2023, ORD_581034/2023 – Kaldewei v. Bette, UPC_CFI_260/2023 (LD Düsseldorf), Order of 22 November 2023, ORD_586970/2023 – myStromer v. Revolt, UPC_CFI_499/2023 (LD Düsseldorf), ORD_59318/2024 – DexCom v. Abbott.

14 E.g. UPC_CFI_315/2024 (LD Düsseldorf), Order of 26 September 2025 – Labrador v. BioMerieux or UPC_CFI_100/2024 (LD Düsseldorf, Order of 13 October 2025 – Ona v. Google.

15 *Meier-Beck* goes even further, referring to such a case as "the division's capitulation in the face of its statutorily assigned tasks," Cf. *Meier-Beck*, GRUR 2015, p. 929.

patent will be held invalid in the revocation-counterclaim proceeding (Rule 37). This corresponds to German practice.[16] So far, however, only such counterclaims have been split off where already a nullity action was pending before the Central Division.[17]

Depending on the option selected by the panel of first instance, the following consequences will arise: 878

1. The Panel Conducts Both Proceedings

If both proceedings are to be conducted in parallel by the panel (first option), then a technical judge will be allocated, insofar as this was not already done. 879

2. The Panel Transfers the Revocation Counterclaim Proceeding to the Central Division

If the Revocation Counterclaim proceeding is split off (second and third options), then the proceeding will be transferred to a corresponding judge-rapporteur at the central division, who will set new dates for the interim conference in the interim procedure, as well as a date plus an alternative date for the oral hearing (Rule 38). 880

If the panel of first instance has not stayed the infringement proceeding, then the proceeding before the central division is to be expedited. In particular, the date of the oral hearing in the Revocation Counterclaim proceeding should be set before the date of the infringement proceeding's oral hearing if possible (Rule 40). This is intended to prevent the infringement's adjudication on the basis of a legally invalid patent claim. 881

If the language of the infringement proceeding is not the language in which the disputed patent was granted, then the judge-rapporteur of the central division may decide that the parties must have all the written pleadings and documents which they submitted in the written procedure translated within one month's time. The judge may also decide that only certain excerpts need be translated (Rule 39). 882

▶ Practical tip:

In practice, we can proceed on the premise that documents formulated in one of the three official languages of the European Patent Office will not require translation. 883

3. Both proceedings are referred to the central division

If both the infringement and counterclaim proceedings are transferred to the central division, then the dates already set for interim procedure and the oral hearing should 884

---

16 Cf. *Klepsch/Büttner*, "Zum Aussetzungsmasstab ausserhalb des Unterlassungsanspruchs", FS Düsseldorfer Patentgerichtsstand, pp. 281 et seqq.

17 For example, in the dispute between Edwards Lifescience and Meril, see UPC_CFI_255/2023 (CD Paris) ACT_551308/2023 – decision of 19 July 2024, Edwards v. Meril, the parallel infringement action had been filed before the Munich Local DIvision (UPC_CFI_15/2023).

be retained if possible (Rule 41). It remains to be seen whether this will be realistically achievable in those rare cases where both parties consent to such a transfer, or whether procedural delays will ensue at the central division.

II. Nature of the Interim Procedure

885 Based on the wording of the relevant regulations, the interim procedure seems to tie in closely with the provisions governing the "advance first hearing" under the German Code of Civil Procedure (*Zivilprozessordnung*, ZPO), particularly Section 273 et seqq. of the ZPO, even if the practice of many courts is a different one.[18] The interim procedure's function is to allow preparations to be made for the oral hearing. In derogation of the German Code of Civil Procedure (ZPO), however, the interim procedure is conducted solely by the judge-rapporteur and not by the full panel.

886 In particular, the interim procedure is intended to allow the judge-rapporteur to carry out the following tasks:

- to identify the main issues of the legal action and determine which relevant facts are in dispute;
- where appropriate, to clarify and/or specify the positions of the individual parties as regards these issues and facts;
- to establish a schedule for the further course of the proceedings;
- to explore with the parties the possibilities to settle the dispute or to make use of the facilities of the Mediation Center (see Para. 748 et seqq.);[19]
- where appropriate, to issue orders regarding production of further pleadings, documents, experts including court experts), experiments, inspections, further written evidence, the matters to be the subject of oral evidence and the scope of questions to be put to the witnesses;
- where appropriate, but only in the presence of the parties, to hold preparatory discussions with witnesses and experts with a view to properly preparing for the oral hearing;
- to set any additional dates in the oral procedure for the hearing of experts or witnesses; and
- to decide the value of the action.

III. Interim Conference

887 All the above issues can be clarified in the interim conference, which is to be conducted over the telephone or via video-conferencing or, upon the request of one the

18 Both points were confirmed to the author by *Grabinski* in a personal conversation at a conference hosted by the Chamber of German Patent Attorneys on 20 November 2013 in Munich; cf. also *Plassmann/Steininger* in *Tilmann/Plassmann*, Note 4 to Rule 28. A contrary view is taken by *Kircher* in *Bopp/Kircher*, Note 144 to Section 12, namely that "*the interim procedure is something foreign to German procedural law.*"

19 On the German situation and customary practice before the District Court *(Landgericht)* of Munich, cf. *Brose*, GRUR 2016, p. 146.

parties, in the Court (Rule 105.1). If the interim conference is conducted orally in the Court, then it will be deemed open to the public unless the judge-rapporteur decides to exclude the public.[20] It remains to be clarified whether such an exclusion of the public may also be requested by the parties. There are many indications that this will be so, however. In practice, the interim conference is usually conducted via videoconference.

As a general rule, the dates for the interim conference will already be set in the writ- 888
ten procedure (see Para. 844). Upon closure of the written procedure, the judge-rapporteur will state whether or not he deems an interim conference to be necessary and, if so, will confirm the date for the interim conference (Rule 35 b). The interim conference may also be dispensed with, however, if the judge-rapporteur does not consider it necessary (Rule 101.1). In this case, he will notify the parties accordingly upon closure of the written procedure (Rule 35 b).

The judge-rapporteur may in any case require the parties to: 889
- clarify individual points of their argumentation;
- answer specific questions;
- produce evidence; and
- submit additional documents, particularly summaries of the parties' requests/applications.

Following the interim conference, the judge-rapporteur will issue an order setting out the decisions taken (Rule 105.5).

The judge-rapporteur will also use the interim conference to explore the possibility 890
of an amicable settlement between the parties, e.g. by resorting to the Unified Patent Court's Mediation and Arbitration Center (Rule 11) (see Para. 748 et seqq.).

Insofar as the judge-rapporteur takes a decision in the interim procedure, one of the 891
parties may request, by reasoned application, that this be presented without delay to the full panel of first instance for its review (Rule 333). This review will not have any suspensive effect, however (see Para. 1102 et seqq.).

The interim procedure is to be completed within three months' time. As soon as the 892
judge-rapporteur considers that the state of preparation of the file is adequate, he will inform the presiding judge and the parties that the interim procedure is closed in view of the oral hearing (Rule 110).

D. Oral Procedure

The interim procedure is followed by the oral procedure. This is the first stage of 893
the proceedings in which all the judges of the respective panel of first instance will participate. The oral procedure will be conducted by the respective presiding judge (Rule 111) and will end with the oral hearing, which will generally be scheduled to last one day (Rule 113).

20 Cf. also *Lunze* in *Erdmann/Rojahn/Sosnitza*, Notes 955 et seqq.

894 During the oral hearing, the presiding judge will have all authority to ensure a fair, orderly and efficient oral procedure and must ensure that the action is ready for decision on the merits at the end of said hearing (Rule 111).

895 The Rules of Procedure (correctly) refer to an "oral procedure" rather than just an "oral hearing." This is because the presiding judge, just like the judge-rapporteur in the interim procedure, will be free to issue additional case-management orders in preparation for the oral hearing, e.g. orders to produce additional facts and evidence. So it is correct to speak in this context of a "procedure" forming a separate stage of the proceedings, one which will conclude with the oral hearing.

896 According to Rule 108, the judge-rapporteur summons the parties to the oral hearing, the date of which will generally have been set ahead of time in the written procedure (Para. 844). If this is not the case, then the judge-rapporteur will set the date. The summons is to be issued with least two months' advance notice before the oral hearing, unless the parties have agreed on a shorter notice period.

897 If experts or witnesses are to be questioned at the oral hearing, either party may lodge a request for simultaneous translation. This must be done at least one month before the oral hearing. The request must contain the following (Rule 109):
- an indication of the language to or from which the party requests simultaneous interpretation during the oral hearing;
- the reasons for the Request;
- the field of technology concerned; and
- any other information of relevance for the Request.

898 The judge-rapporteur will then decide whether and to what extent simultaneous translation is required and will notify the Registry accordingly. The costs for the translation qualify as recoverable costs. If the judge-rapporteur denies the request, then the parties may request that, insofar as practicable, simultaneous translations be provided at their own expense. However, a denial may also be contested by way of an appeal proceeding requiring leave from the Court of First Instance (Para. 1102 et seqq.)

899 The parties may allocate a translator at their own expense, however, provided they notify the Registry at least two weeks before the oral hearing. The judge-rapporteur, too, may order a simultaneous translation to be provided at his discretion. If so, he will notify the Registry and parties accordingly.

900 The oral hearing inasmuch corresponds to the practice of German courts and even of the European Patent Office in that the oral hearing is essentially conducted by the presiding judge, i.e. it is he who sets the agenda of issues to be discussed, and not the parties.

901 When the oral hearing commences, the presiding judge may (and in practice in most cases especially before the German divisions will) provide a preliminary introduction to the action and the presiding judge as well as the judges of the panel may put questions to the parties, to the parties' representatives and to any witness or experts (Rule 112.4). The presiding judge may set time limits for the parties' oral submissions

in advance of the oral hearing. (Rule 113.1). Oral testimony at the oral hearing or at any separate hearing will be limited to issues identified by the judge-rapporteur or the presiding judge as having to be decided on the basis of oral evidence (Rule 113.2).

In principle, the oral hearing will be public and is to be audio-recorded, unless the Court decides otherwise and declares the hearing or parts thereof to be confidential in view of the protectable interests of one or both parties or third parties, or "in the general interests of justice or public order." **902**

A party which is not represented at the oral hearing will be treated as relying only on its written case (Rule 116.3). In effect, the hearing will be conducted without that party. A decision by default (see Para. 718 et seqq.) can also be issued notwithstanding the foregoing (Rule 116.5). But the Court may also adjourn the hearing upon the reasoned request of the absent party if that party was prevented from being represented at the oral hearing by an exceptional occurrence g (Rule 116.4). **903**

If neither party is represented at the oral hearings, or if both parties have given advance notice that they do not wish to be represented at the oral hearing, then a decision will be issued on the merits based on the pleadings and evidence submitted thus far (Rule 117). **904**

In principle, the decision on the merits is to be issued after the oral hearing and deliberations are completed. In exceptional cases, the Court may, after hearing the parties' oral submissions, decide to adjourn proceedings and call for further evidence. (Rule 114). **905**

E. Decision on the Merits

The oral proceedings are followed by the judgment. However, the procedure envisaged in the rules that, as a rule, the decision in principle should follow after the oral proceedings and the statement of grounds should be submitted subsequently, as is now common practice before the European Patent Office (Rule 118.6 and 7),[21] is not usually applied. Instead, the judgment together with the statement of grounds is sent to the parties after a few weeks, usually four to six weeks. **906**

The formal requirements applicable to the decision on the merits are the same ones which apply to other decisions (see Para. 686), except that dissenting votes are to be attached to decision. In addition, the decision is to contain a summary of the requests and facts submitted by the parties and a statement of the facts and arguments on which the Court bases its decision (Rules 350.3 and 350.4, see Para. 687). In practice the decisions are usually quite lengthy and diligent. **907**

21 Note: This was still referred to as an exception in the 15th version of the Rules of Procedure. Thus, this no longer corresponded to the general German practice of issuing a decision only days or weeks after closure of the oral hearing. The revised 16th version, by contrast, reversed this practice, thereby coming closer into line with the practice of the European Patent Office. The Courts now have decided to revert to the 15th version agai.

908 Besides the fundamental decision, e.g. whether or not a patent has been infringed and/or is valid – the Court will also rule on the following issues (Rule 118.1):

- permanent injunction and award of damages (also in terms of the amount, unless the Court has been requested to make an award in principle only);
- apportionment of costs;
- claims to receive information; and
- claims to the recall, removal from the channels of commerce and/or destruction of infringing products.

If an injunction is granted, then this usually includes a claim to removal from the channels of commerce[22]

909 The Court does not have to decide all these issues at once, however, but may instead defer some of them to the subsequent costs procedure and damage-award procedure. Such a deferral will be obligatory when it comes to issues for which a decision on principle has been requested. Before taking a decision on costs, the Court may order that the parties submit a preliminary estimate of the legal costs they will seek to recover in case they prevail over the opposite party (Rule 118.5) (see Para. 448).

910 The Court may declare its decision on the merits and its associated orders enforceable in subject to the rendering of a security, this being a practice also followed in German proceedings (Rule 118.8). (On enforceability, see Chapter 17 ab Para. 1468 et seqq.) The Court also has the option to award interim damages, which must at least cover the expected costs of the procedure for the determination of damages and compensation on the part of the successful party (Rule 119).

911 If a revocation action has been split off, or if a parallel revocation action is pending before the central division or a parallel opposition proceeding is pending before the European Patent Office, then the decision on the merits may also be issued conditionally. For example, a decision that a patent has indeed been infringed may be issued subject to the condition subsequent that the validity of the patent is not held to be wholly or partially invalid in the parallel proceeding (Rule 118.2).

912 However, the Court may stay the infringement proceedings pending a decision in the revocation procedure or a decision of the European Patent Office, and must stay the infringement proceedings if it is of the view that there is a high likelihood that the relevant claims of the patent will be held to be invalid in the revocation proceedings or of the EPO where such decision of the EPO may be expected to be given rapidly (Rule 118.2 b). Otherwise a conditional decision is to be issued.

22 For an example see UPC_CFI_425/2024 (LD Munich), Decision of 28 November 2025 – JingAo v. Chint.

I. Settlement/Mediation

The proceeding may be terminated through settlement at any time (see Para. 760 et seqq.). The proceeding may also be suspended in order to conduct a mediation procedure (see Para. 748 et seqq.) 913

II. Implementation/Enforcement of the Decision on the Merits

The decision on the merits and its orders can be enforced only after the claimant has given notice to the Court which part of the orders he intends to enforce (Rule 118.8). What is more, he must have provided (where applicable), a certified translation of the orders into the official language of the Contracting Member State in which the enforcement is to take place. In addition, a certified translation of the orders and of the claimant's notice must have been served on the defendant by the Registry. 914

If it has not done so already, the Court may subsequently subject any order or measure to a security to be given by the successful party to the unsuccessful party (see Para. 1474). The enforcement process itself will then be performed on a national level in the respective countries (Rule 118.8) (see Chapters 19 to 28). 915

The decision on the merit's enforcement must not necessarily occur right after the first instance, however. The infringement plaintiff may also wait to see whether an appeal is lodged, or await the outcome of such an appeal, given that Rule 118.8 does not set a deadline for enforcement. A damage-award procedure is subject to a time limit, however: one year after legal service of the final decision in the infringement proceeding (see Para. 925 et seqq.) 916

F. Costs proceeding

The purpose of the procedure for cost decision is to apportion the costs incurred in the legal dispute, mainly court costs and attorneys' fees. It is envisioned as a separate procedure which follows the original action and which is conducted before the same judge-rapporteur who heard the action. 917

A cost decision may be sought within one month of service of the decision on the merits. Within this time limit, the party wishing to recover costs must lodge an application for a decision on costs by the Court. The application must contain the following (Rule 151): 918

- information on the applicant (analogous to the information in the Statement of Claim);
- the date of the decision and the action number of the appurtenant file;
- a statement as to whether the decision on the merits is the subject of an appeal, if known at the date of the application; and
- an indication of the costs for which compensation is requested, including those contained in the preliminary estimate of costs submitted before the decision (see Para. 909). This may include recovery of court fees and costs of representation, of witnesses, of experts, and other expenses.

919 The judge-rapporteur may request the applicant to provide written evidence of all costs requested. The judge-rapporteur must allow the opposite party an opportunity to comment in writing (Rule 156).

920 The judge-rapporteur will then issue a written decision on costs. The recoverable costs must be paid within the time limit set by the judge-rapporteur.

921 This decision may be contested through an appeal which will be conducted as a separate, abbreviated procedure (see Para. 1112 et seqq.) (Rule 157).

G. Damage-Award Procedure

922 The damage-award procedure, i.e. the procedure in which the amount of damages and compensation ordered by the Court is determined, will generally be conducted as a separate, written procedure (Rule 125) for which a separate court fee will be charged (see Para. 431). The damage-award procedure will be heard by the same panel which issued the associated decision on the merits, unless this is impossible or impracticable, in which case the President of the Court will appoint a fresh panel (Rule 135.2).

923 In principle, the damage-award procedure will consist of three parts, just like the original action proceeding, i.e. a written procedure, an interim procedure and an oral hearing. The respective judge-rapporteur may reduce the timetable, however (Rule 140.2).

▶ Practical tip:

924 This can probably be expected to be the customary practice, assuming the amount of damages to be awarded was already claimed in the infringement proceeding and the claimant did not request that damages be awarded in principle only – which will rather rarely occur.[23]

925 The damage-award procedure begins after the applicant lodges a corresponding application with the Court. This must be received by the Court within one year of service of the final decision in the infringement proceeding (Rule 126).[24] The application may already be lodged after the first instance.

▶ Practical tip:

926 This will probably be the situation in the majority of cases.

927 The application must contain the following (Rule 131):
- information on the applicant (analogous to the information in the Statement of Claim);

23 A different view is taken by *Lunze* in *Erdmann/Rojahn/Sosnitza*, Note 925.

24 I.e. after the appeal proceeding has been closed, assuming an appeal was lodged, or after the patent's infringement and legal validity have been decided, assuming a Revocation Counterclaim was lodged.

- the date of the decision on the merits and the action number of the appurtenant file;
- if require, a request to lay open the books, along with the information required for this purpose (see Para. 933).

928 If no application to open the books is lodged, then the applicant must state the following:
- the redress (damages, license fees, profits) and the interest thereon requested by him;
- an indication of the facts and evidence relied on, particularly calculations concerning lost profits or profits made by the unsuccessful party;
- assuming a final decision has not been issued: a statement as to whether the decision on the merits is the subject of an appeal.

929 The associated court fee must be paid when the application is lodged (see Para. 431) (Rule 132).

930 If the application is deficient, the Registry of the Court will issue a deficiency notice giving a grace period for correction. If the deficiencies remain uncorrected or are insufficiently corrected, a decision by default will be issued, much as in the action proceeding.

931 Otherwise the Registry will enter the application in the Register. It will notify the applicant as well as the panel and the opposite side concerning the application and its date of receipt (Rule 135).

932 The further course of the proceeding is described below (Para. 941 et seqq.)

I. Request to Lay Open the Books

933 In principle, we can probably assume that the damage-award procedure will consist of two stages. The first stage will be a request to lay open the books, in which an order forcing the infringer to release certain information will be sought. Only once this stage is completed, will the actual damage-award procedure begin.

934 The request to lay open the books is to contain the following[25] (Rule 141):
- details of any information ordered by the Court and given by the other party;
- a description of the information held by the unsuccessful party to which the applicant requests access,
- in particular, documents relating to turnover and profits generated by the infringing products or regarding the extent of use of the infringing process as well as accounts and bank documents, and any related document concerning the infringement;
- the reasons why the applicant needs access to this information; and
- the facts and evidence offered in support.

25 See also *Hauck*, GRUR Int 2013, p. 713, although he bases his arguments on the 14th draft version of the Rules of Procedure.

935 If the opposing side accepts the request to lay open the books, then it must notify the Registry accordingly, whereupon the judge-rapporteur will allow the request and issue a corresponding order.

936 If the opposing side objects to the request to lay open the books, then it must lodge a Defense within two months of service of the request. The applicant will then have 14 days to lodge a Reply to the Defense, which must be limited to matters raised in the Statement of Defense. The opposing side will for its part have 14 days to lodge a Rejoinder to the Reply, which must be limited to matters raised in the Reply. This process can be illustrated using the timeline below:

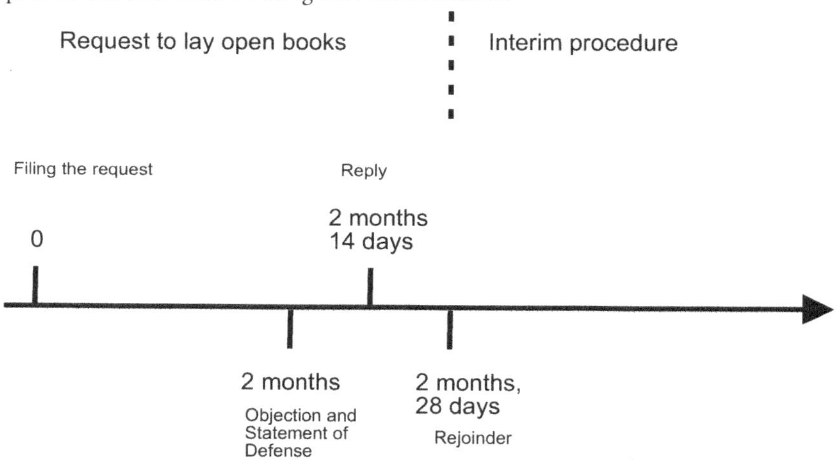

Fig. 9.4 Course of the proceedings to lay open books

937 As a final step, the Court will decide whether and to what extent the books are to be laid open (Rule 144). At the same time, it will inform the applicant and specify a time period within which the damage-award procedure is to be continued.

938 The decision on the request to lay open the books may be contested with an appeal proceeding requiring leave from the Court of First Instance (see Para. 1102 et seqq.)

939 It bears noting that, according to Rule 191, it is possible to lodge an application for an order to communicate information in a manner analogous to an application for order to produce evidence pursuant to Rule 190 (see Para. 711 et seqq.) This also makes it possible to obtain information from third parties, whereby – by analogy to Rule 190.5 – the interests of the third party must be duly considered by the Court.

940 As in an order to produce evidence (see Para. 711 et seqq.), the Court's order to communicate information may stipulate that certain items of evidence be disclosed only to individual, specifically designated persons and subject to confidentiality constraints so as to ensure that confidential information is protected. By the same token, the order to communicate information may also be contested through an appeal proceeding

not requiring leave from the Court of First Instance (see Para. 1098 et seqq.). Instructions on the availability of this legal remedy must be included in the order itself.[26]

II. Award of Damages

Once the procedure to obtain information/lay open the books, is closed, the actual process of determining the damages to be awarded will begin. As already described above, the following information must be provided: **941**

- the redress (damages, license fees, profits) and the interest thereon requested by him;
- an indication of the facts and evidence relied on, particularly calculations concerning lost profits or profits made by the unsuccessful party;
- assuming a final decision has not been issued: a statement as to whether the decision on the merits is the subject of an appeal;

If an appeal on the merits is pending, the Court may stay the application for determination of damages upon the reasoned request of the opposite party, whereby the applicant must first be heard. Alternatively, the Court also has the option to continue the proceedings subject to the rendering of a security (Rule 136). **942**

III. Course of the Procedure

As with the procedure to obtain information, the opposing side may accept the claim to damages, whereupon the judge-rapporteur will allow the application and issue a corresponding order (Rule 137). **943**

If the opposing side contests the claim, then it must lodge a Defense containing the following (Rule 138): **944**

- information on the unsuccessful party and on that party's representative as well as on the proceeding;
- the reasons why the application for the award of damages is contested; and
- the facts and evidence relied on by the opposing side.

As in the case of the procedure to obtain information/lay open the books, this will be followed by the exchange of a Defense, Reply and Rejoinder. The time limits involved in this context will be longer, however. Thus, the opposing side has two months to lodge its Defense, while the Reply and Rejoinder must each be lodged within one month's time (Rule 139). This is shown on the timeline below: **945**

26 Note: This is an exception to the usual practice, where it is not obligatory to provide any instructions on legal remedies; see Para. 901.

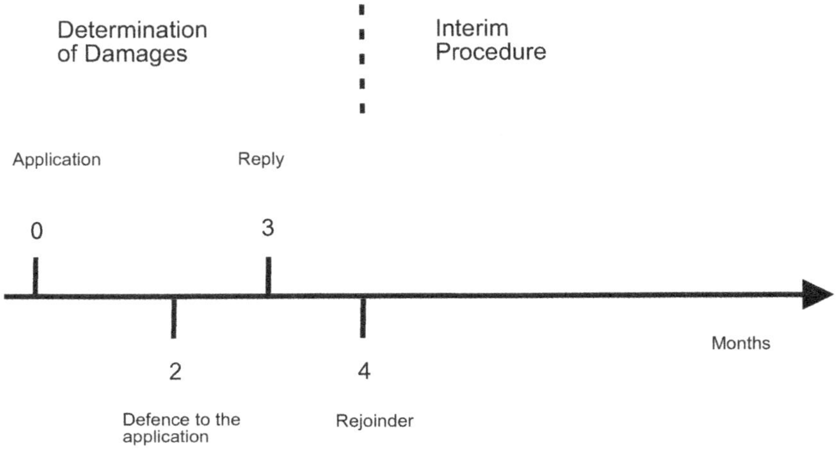

Fig. 9.5 Course of the damages determination proceedings

946 This will be followed by an interim procedure and an oral hearing, whereby the judge-rapporteur may reduce the timetable involved. As a final step, the Court will issue its decision, which may be contested through an appeal.

947 The costs for the damage-award procedure are recoverable just like the costs for the action proceeding. Here, too, the Court will issue a decision that can subsequently be appealed.

Chapter 10: Strategic Considerations: How Should an Infringement Proceeding Be Conducted?

Contents | Para

The focus of this chapter will be on the ideal strategies to conduct a patent infringement proceeding before the Unified Patent Court. For a discussion of the ques- 948 tion of whether or not the UPC should be seised in the first place, see Chapter 6, Para. 502 et seqq.

A. Strategic Considerations Relevant for Both Parties

I. Pretrial Matters and Amicable Settlements

949 If we examine how a proceeding before the Unified Patent Court unfolds, we notice right away that there are none of the incentives for a pretrial settlement that are normally found in, say, a German proceeding. The only relevant provision in this regard is Article 69(3) of the UPC Agreement, which stipulates that unnecessary costs are to be borne by the party that caused them (see Para. 458). There is case law[1] that clearly points in this direction.

950 But there is no provision analogous to Section 93 of the German Code of Civil Procedure (*Zivilprozessordnung*, ZPO) which makes it possible for the defendant to impose litigation costs on the plaintiff if the defendant gave no cause for the legal action to be brought and immediately acknowledges the claim. After all, one of the specific purposes of issuance of issuing a warning as a pretrial instrument in Germany is to deprive the opposing side of this option. A provision analogous to Section 93 of the ZPO could of course be introduced through case law, since this is not precluded by the Rules of Procedure (see Para. 1026 et seqq.)

951 On the other hand, the instrument of preliminary injunction does exist in proceedings before the Unified Patent Court (see Chapter 15, Para. 1336 et seqq.), i.e., the same possibilities of putting the opposing side under pressure with aggressive tactics that exist in the German proceedings will be available before the UPC.

952 If the instrument of preliminary injunction is not used, then it would seem advisable for the parties to attempt to settle their patent dispute right at the start, even if this is not further facilitated by the UPC's Rules of Procedure.

953 Then there is the UPC's Mediation and Arbitration Center, a feature which does not exist in most national judicial systems, or least not in institutionalized form.[2] We can assume that many divisions of the Unified Patent Court would welcome the parties' readiness to at least attempt mediation. Thus, both parties should signal their willingness – at least externally – to take part in such a procedure.[3]

954 Reaching an amicable settlement has a key advantage over national proceedings in many countries in that the settlement as such can be kept confidential, whereby any preparatory materials, such as draft proposals or offers, etc., cannot be used by the opposing side in other proceedings or before other courts (see Para. 764) Whether

1 UPC_CoA 2/2024, Order of 4 October 2024, APL_83/2024 – Edwards v. Meril.
2 Cf. *Brose*, GRUR 2016, p. 146; *Picht*, GRUR Int. 2018, p. 1.
3 Cf. *Granata* in *Zeiler/Zojer*, p. 75 et seqq.

this principle would be upheld in a discovery procedure in the USA remains to be seen, but there are plenty of indications that it would.

Thus, settlement negotiations between parties should always be conducted in parallel to the proceedings wherever possible. 955

Both practical experience and scholarly research[4] suggest that mediation negotiations tend to have the best chance of success when new facts arise in a case, i.e. when a new state of the technical art is adduced in a revocation counterclaim, or when the parties obtain a first indication of how the Unified Patent Court sees their case during the interim procedure. An experienced and capable judge-rapporteur will surely know how to exploit this to good advantage. 956

II. Organizational Matters

It is readily apparent that the organizational structure of proceedings before the Unified Patent Court is highly streamlined and that the parties have only a very limited number of opportunities to submit arguments and to lodge requests/applications. 957

It will probably be impossible to always adhere to the twelve-month timeframe envisioned in the Preamble to the Rules of Procedure for the proceeding up to the oral hearing. But the fact that such a timeframe is specified lets us conclude that the Court will be interested in seeing the proceeding conducted in an expeditious manner. This is also indicated by the Rules governing case-management. All told, a normal proceeding with revocation counterclaim and amended patent claims (see Para. 863 et seqq.) will probably take 15 months to adjudicate – an exceptionally short time! 958

But given that the entire proceeding is supposed to be concluded within 12 months, both parties should be aware that they will probably not be allowed to lodge any additional written pleadings other than the ones stipulated in the Rules of Procedure. This will apply all the more if a counterclaim for revocation is lodged. The practice of the courts to date clearly points in this direction;[5] even pleadings that were nevertheless submitted were not taken note of by the court.[6] 959

The various applicable time limits have also been given rather short durations, however time extension are almost never granted. 960

Since the Court has no obligation in principle to conduct its own *ex officio* investigations, and given the rigid rules regarding defaulted time limits, it follows that the Court will have only limited discretion to permit additional requests/applications or 961

4 E.g. the work of *Cremers/Schiessler*, European Journal of Law and Economics 2015, p. 185.

5 Just exemplarily: UPC_CFI_355/2023 (LD Düsseldorf), Order of 30 October 2024, App_54506/2024 Fujifilm v. Kodak or UPC_CFI_16/2024 (LD Düsseldorf), Order of 30 October 2024, App_59050/2024, Ortovox v. Mammut.

6 As done in: UPC_CFI_355/2023 (LD Düsseldorf), Order of 29 November 2024, App_63445/2024 – Fujifilm v. Kodak.

supplemental factual pleadings; in practice additional submissions are almost never allowed.

962 A point which bears noting and which will be discussed further in Chapter 12 (Para. 1156 et seqq.) is that the rules governing defaulted time limits also apply in the appeal proceeding, although these rules do stipulate that additional criteria such as relevance must be considered as well. Inasmuch, this seems to correspond to the practice followed in years past by the Boards of Appeal of the European Patent Office,[7] and to the current practice in Germany under the revised procedure for appealing revocations.[8]

Technical Judges

963 In the Unified Patent Court, the special feature is that technical judges can participate in patent infringement proceedings, or even have to in the case of an invalidity counterclaim. Two questions arise here:

aa) Should a technical judge be requested?

964 Even if no invalidity action is filed, it is advisable to request a technical judge in order to strengthen the technical expertise of the Senate. Many judges say that they will request a technical judge themselves if the parties do not do so. Decisions on the merits without involvement of a technical judge are at present a rare exception.[9]

bb) Motions for partiality?

965 In the course of the appointment of the judges (cf. Para. 355), the concern arose that due to the fact that the technical judges will mostly work part-time, possible conflicts of interest could arise.[10]

966 The question now arises for the parties as to whether, if necessary, they should file a request against the technical judge who has been called in because of suspected partiality (Art 7 of the Statute). However, it can be assumed that the court itself is aware of the danger that possible conflicts of interest will affect its reputation and therefore has a great interest of its own in ensuring that such conflicts of interest do not occur. On the contrary, it has been the case that – also due to the fact that not only the judge in question himself, but also his law firm must be free of conflicts – technical judges will *de facto* only be able to exercise their original profession to a

7 For the more formalized practice followed since the 2010s, see e.g. *Anetsberger* et al. epi-information 2015, p. 63; for a highly critical view, see e.g. *Wallinger*, VPP-Rundbrief 2015, p. 18; for a statistical survey of the appeal proceeding, see *Nollen*, epi information 2015, p. 17.

8 See e.g. *Meier-Beck*, VPP-Rundbrief 2013, p. 99.

9 For one example: UPC_CFI_373/2023 (LD Düsseldorf), Decision of 31 October 2024, Soda Stream v. Aarke.

10 Vgl. https://www.juve-patent.com/news-and-stories/people-and-business/patent-attorney-dominance-among-upc-technical-judges-leads-to-conflict-debate/ sehr deutlich http://techrights.org/2022/10/24/upc-has-conflict-of-interest-blunder/.

limited extent and will (have to) leave their law firms, for example, and continue to work as individual lawyers.

Thus, requests against judges because of suspected partiality should be handled with caution, but should by no means be ruled out. **967**

1. Decision by Default and Re-Establishment of Rights

A decision by default is not absolutely mandated when a time limit is defaulted; the Court will have discretionary leeway in this regard.[11] The parties should not be overly reliant on this discretion, however, especially since an order vacating a decision by default is also not issuable automatically – unlike in a German proceeding – but only on the basis of well-founded reasoning. **968**

It remains to be seen whether the relevant hurdles will be set anywhere near as high as for, say, a re-establishment of rights. But we can in any case posit that the strategy of "taking refuge in default," as observed under the German legal system, for example, is one that should be approached with extreme caution when dealing with the UPC. On the contrary, the parties would be better advised to meet all applicable time limits, particularly since it is uncertain whether these limits will even be reinstatable at a later time, and since there is no way of knowing how the Unified Patent Court will decide on a possible re-establishment of rights. **969**

Given that a decision on the re-establishment of rights is not appealable, it bears noting that this is one of the few areas in which the Court's individual divisions will be able to decide freely. It remains to be seen whether the individual divisions will establish mutually divergent legal traditions in this context or not. **970**

2. Judge-Rapporteur/Interim Procedure

In many cases, the judge-rapporteur will *de facto* serve as the central figure in a patent infringement proceeding, since he will be the one to conduct the proceeding up to the oral hearing stage. **971**

The current practice is that not only the judge-rapporteur deals substantially with the case in the written proceedings, but also (at least more than cursorily) the entire senate. Nevertheless, the interlocutory proceedings are of increased importance, as this is the first time that something like a discussion between the court and the parties takes place. The parties are therefore well advised not to treat this stage of the proceedings as a mere precursor to the oral hearing. Instead, they should give it their full attention and strive to ensure that decisions can be made quickly and that orders issued by the judge-rapporteur are implemented in a timely manner. **972**

The parallels between the interim procedure and Sections 273 et seqq. of the German Code of Civil Procedure (ZPO) have already been mentioned (Para. 885). However, the **973**

---

11 Cf. *Kitchin*, Special Issue of the EPO Official Journal (17th Symposium of European Patent Judges) 5/2015, p. 46.

practice followed by the German District Courts (*Landgerichte*), such as in Düsseldorf or Mannheim, is to conduct the initial advance hearing in a merely cursory manner. This is not the case with the so-called "New Munich Proceeding" (*neues Münchner Verfahren*),[12] where the initial advance hearing is conducted as a true court hearing.

974 But the key difference between the New Munich Proceeding and the interim procedure is that the former gives both parties a further opportunity to submit pleadings after the advance initial hearing, an opportunity not envisioned in the interim procedure. It would certainly desirable for the local divisions to also establish, if the case is appropriate, such an added opportunity to submit pleadings (see Para. 1061 et seqq.)

3. Oral Hearing

975 The oral hearing – as mentioned earlier – is structured in keeping with procedural practice before the European Patent Office or the German courts, i.e. with a presiding judge who conducts the hearing and only raises those points which are of interest to the Court. It will usually not possible to present a sort of "general pleading" on the case itself during the hearing. The practice before the divisions, including the German ones, is however so that parties have enough time to present their case.

976 However, it will almost never be possible to lodge additional applications/requests, unlike in opposition proceedings before the European Patent Office or in revocation counterclaim proceedings before the German Federal Patent Court (BPatG). Parties are therefore well advise to check their request during earlier stages of the proceedings, the interim conference at the latest, as in the Oral hearing they will be stuck to them.

977 All things considered, the oral hearing does generally not play the decisive role. In most cases, the proceeding are essentially decided earlier, namely during the written procedure or interim procedure.

4. Summary Overview

978 Given the above, it is evident that being well organized will be a key success factor in a proceeding. This will naturally pose less of a problem for the plaintiff, since he is the one who initiates the proceeding and is thus less likely to be caught by surprise and unprepared. But he, too, will have to adhere to narrow time limits. Particularly if the defendant brings a counterclaim for revocation, since this will leave the plaintiff with only two months to lodge a Defense and submit any requests/applications, including auxiliary requests.

979 But whether one lodges a legal action or is its target, one must always give the matter the highest internal priority, allocate all the appropriate personal resources and avoid any unnecessary delays. If one decides to hire external representation, one should be careful to select people with whom one can collaborate effectively and smoothly (see Para. 986 et seqq.).

12 See *Werner/Wuttke* GRUR Prax, 2020.1; *Bausch/Pfaff*, Mitt. 2012, p. 97.

III. Public Nature of the Proceedings

980 It once again bears noting here that the Unified Patent Court, after a request being filed by any interested party allows completely open electronic access to the case file of a proceeding. The only exception is if the parties have requested that their written submissions be kept confidential, either in whole or in part (cf. Para. 692 et seqq.).

981 The should be kept in mind when lodging written submissions with the Unified Patent Court. After all, a party will almost always wish to keep at least of the information contained in a written submission from becoming public knowledge. For obvious reasons, this particularly applies to procedures for cost decisions and damage-award procedures. Here, the parties should essentially get in the habit of preparing two versions of their written submissions: a complete version and a duly redacted version. They should then lodge a request that only the redacted version be made public.

982 In such situations, use should also be made of the option provided for under Rule 262a (cf. Para. 701), namely by requesting that the relevant information be kept confidential from the opposing side as well.

IV. Splitting the Proceedings Following a Revocation Counterclaim

983 One can proceed on the premise that, when a revocation counterclaim is lodged, the panel of first instance will usually conduct both proceedings together (also see Para. 584). This will not apply, however, if a separate revocation claim has already been lodged with the central division at a prior point in time (see Para. 1178).

984 While a decision on splitting the proceedings may be issued as early as the written procedure, this will probably tend to be exception. In practice, the Court is more likely to wait to receive the written pleadings which are mandatorily required from both parties before taking its decision.

985 The parties are therefore well advised to prepare accordingly. But this does not mean that one should not try to bring such a splitting about if it would be strategically advantageous. For this same reason, seising the central division will probably not be a good choice for the plaintiff (see Para. 584 et seqq. below).

V. Representation

986 It seems purposeful to examine the topic of representation from two angles:[13]

- How many participants should/will participate in a proceeding on behalf of each party?
- What are the available options in regard to representation?

13 It bears noting that the author himself is a patent attorney. But since the question of representation is a key strategic aspect that should not be overlooked, he has attempted to handle this topic as objectively as possible and from the vantage point of the litigating parties.

1. How Many Participants per Party?

987 Let us first ask how many participants per side appear necessary and purposeful. Depending on the legal environment, the answer can be just a handful of persons, as in Germany, or an entire patent-infringement team, as often seen in the USA.

988 This said, proceedings before the Unified Patent Court feature a certain similarity to German proceedings and to opposition proceedings before the European Patent Office, where it is customary for only a handful of people to participate on each side.

989 In Germany, so-called "dual representation" is the common practice, i.e. each side will have a maximum of three persons handling the patent-infringement case: an attorney, a patent attorney and an authorized agent or in-house person of the plaintiff with the power to take and/or coordinate any required decisions.

990 In the event of a revocation counterclaim, it is even typical to do without regular attorneys entirely; i.e. only two persons will participate per side in such case: a patent attorney and an authorized agent.

991 Much the same applies at the European Patent Office. Here, too, only two or three persons per side will normally participate in an opposition proceeding. Not infrequently, opposition proceedings are conducted by a company representative; in this case, only one person participates.

992 Of course these numbers are just statistical averages or derived from experience. Larger teams are definitely viable when a case is particularly complex, but the majority of cases will be conducted by a modest number of persons.

993 Although the importance of a proceeding before the Unified Patent Court will naturally be greater than that of a proceeding before a German Court – alone on account on the larger territory involved – we see no compelling reasons for bringing in large patent-infringement teams like those in the USA. Also given the fact that there will probably not be a "discovery" procedure before the Unified Patent Court analogous to the one customary in the USA (see Para. 1446 et seqq.).

994 On the contrary, being able to act and respond rapidly and effectively is likely to serve as a decisive co-factor (see Para. 978 et seqq.) and is clearly easier for modestly sized teams than for large groups. The average ideal size of a team will thus be perhaps twice as large as it has been in, for example, German patent infringement cases, but not much larger.

2. What Are the Available Representation Options?

995 Bearing the foregoing considerations in mind, one can essentially choose from among four different options when it comes to representation:

1) representation through an in-house patent attorney[14] or in-house attorney;

14 Note: It was decided to use the singular for ease of reading. It stands to reason that additional lawyers could also be involved in individual cases.

2) representation through an external attorney only;
3) representation through an external patent attorney only;
4) dual representation through both an attorney and a patent attorney.

Each of these four options has its pros and cons. 996

a) Representation by an In-House Attorney

The advantage of resorting to **solely internal** representation through an in-house patent attorney or in-house attorney is that one will not incur any external attorneys' fees if one loses the proceeding. Of course one must also consider the hours that an in-house attorney will have to invest in the case and which he will not be able to devote to other matters. 997

Such in-house counsel will obviously have to have the proper qualification to be authorized to plead before the Unified Patent Court i.e. he or she must be either an attorney admitted to the bar or a qualified patent attorney. But this will almost always be the case, at least in companies with sizeable patent departments. 998

The obvious disadvantage of not resorting to external representatives is that one will be unable to take advantage of their expertise. Thus, an in-house counsellor should have sufficient infringement cases under his belt to have acquired his own, comparable expertise. Another frequent consideration is that, before a patent-infringement action is brought, or when an action by a patent proprietor threatens, an external opinion will usually be sought from a patent attorney or attorney. If and when the proceedings begin, this external representative is likely to so well-acquainted with the matter at hand that it will make sense to assign him to the proceeding as well. 999

Another disadvantage is that, in case of victory, it will be difficult to impose the costs for in-house counsel upon the losing side, given that no invoices or other supporting records will exist. It seems rather doubtful, moreover, that the Unified Patent Court will accept internally billed hourly rates or suchlike as genuine expenditures. 1000

It follows that internal representation will only be an acceptable option if it is already the company's current practice to conduct patent-infringement proceedings mainly on its own, and to use the services of external attorneys only where needed, i.e. mainly to handle formalities. 1001

b) Representation Through an External Attorney

There are a number of arguments in favor of being represented **exclusively** by an **attorney**. One of these is that the Court will be staffed primarily by jurists/legal specialists. As *Augenstein* explains: 1002

> "The task of these attorneys is [...] in particular, to elaborate the technical facts of the case such that they become comprehensible to jurists."[15]

15 *Augenstein*, Preu-Bohlig, Newsletter June 2014, p. 7; although the question addressed here is whether the fees of patent attorneys pleading before the UPC should be recoverable.

1003 Another reason is that attorneys are certainly required to undergo long and intensive training in procedural law (albeit under the own national legal system!), and this to a greater extent than patent attorneys, for example.

1004 On the other hand, many infringement judges can also bring impressive technical expertise to bear. The author was able to experience this first-hand during his training as a German patent attorney, namely at the Higher District Court (*Oberlandesgericht*) of Düsseldorf, where he completed a two-month clerkship in accordance with Section 19a of the Ordinance on the Training and Examination of Patent Attorneys (*Patentanwaltsausbildungsverordnung*, PatAnwAPrV).[16]

1005 The panels of first instance of the respective divisions will also have the option to allocate technical judges and thereby further supplement the division's expertise as needed. When infringement and revocation counterclaim proceedings are conducted together – which we can assume will almost always occur – the allocation of a technical judge actually becomes mandatory.

1006 The fact that the Unified Patent Court has not adopted the procedural laws of any Member State but has drafted its own procedural rules effectively creates a "whole new ballgame": All participants in the new system will have to acquire the necessary expertise from the ground up. This holds true for regular attorneys as well as patent attorneys.

1007 On the other hand, regular attorneys do not normally have the technical expertise they would need to conduct a revocation counterclaim proceeding – where technical arguments are paramount– all on their own. But we can safely assume that the target of a patent-infringement action will typically defend himself by lodging a revocation counterclaim, and that both proceedings will then be conducted together.

1008 During the oral hearing, a technical judge must mandatorily be allocated to the panel of first instance. If the discussions conducted here focus on technical facts, this can be a good thing: Past experience with revocation proceedings before the German Federal Patent Court (BPatG) shows that the discussions in oral hearings often take place between the technical judges and the patent attorneys, even though the presiding judge oversees the proceedings and is a jurist.

1009 In such case, it may become necessary to bring in an in-house specialist employed by the plaintiff or a patent attorney commissioned by the plaintiff pursuant to Article 48(4) of the UPC Agreement (see Para. 416 et seqq.). This could lead to delays, given the coordination that will become necessary among the individual participants. This stage of the proceeding will be conducted under particularly heavy time pressure, however. One possible solution could be to have a patent attorney or an in-house patent expert participate in the proceeding right from the outset.

16 Note: This was in the early 2000s, but experience has shown that, if anything, the technical expertise of judges has grown since then.

Then there is also the latent risk that, at least until the Unified Patent Court establishes its own track record and legal precedent, attorneys will fall back on their own prior experiences and way of doing things under their respective national legal system, especially where it evinces similarities to the UPC's procedures. 1010

Such similarities cannot always be assumed, however. Consider the example of a judge who adjudicates on Tuesdays at the Düsseldorf District Court (*Landgericht*) and on Wednesdays as a judge-rapporteur on a panel of the UPC's local Düsseldorf division: It could well happen that this same judge will arrive at a different verdict in two cases having exactly the same factual constellation. This is because the procedural rules respectively applicable before the two courts are ultimately *not* the same. So it will be part of the due diligence of a patent attorney, especially an experienced one, to draw very careful distinctions in this regard. But we can safely assume that the vast majority of these practitioners will be up to the task. 1011

c) Representation Through a Patent Attorney

A decided advantage of being represented **exclusively** by a **patent attorney** is surely the latter's technical expertise.[17] This can make an overwhelming difference, particularly in an oral hearing where infringement and revocation are both discussed concomitantly. 1012

After all, the challenge – and frequently the art – of mastering such proceedings consists in finding a claim formulation which is patentable and relevant to the contested form of infringement, also in view of the current state of technology. And to argue in a manner which prevents the other side from exploiting the grounds adduced to prove infringement for the purpose of revoking the patent, as well as vice versa. For the defendant's side, this obviously applies exactly the other way around, i.e. a knowledgeable patent attorney working for the defendant will not allow inaccuracies or "intentional sloppiness" in the plaintiff's argumentation to go unchallenged. 1013

One disadvantage is that patent attorneys in most European countries will have no previous experience conducting infringement proceedings all on their own as sole representatives. This despite the fact that they are likely to have handled opposition proceedings and national revocation proceedings on their own, insofar as this is permitted by the respective national regulations. 1014

This said, the fact remains that the Unified Patent Court will be uncharted territory for all involved, be they regular attorneys, patent attorneys or the internal patent departments of companies. Whether this will prove to be a disadvantage cannot be conclusively determined at this early stage. 1015

So a key factor in this context will be the degree of confidence one places in patent attorneys in general – and specifically in the patent attorney who stands to receive the mandate. 1016

17 Cf. also *de Rassenfosse* et al, "Getting Patents: Does the Quality of Patent Attorneys Matter?" as well as *Andriosopoulos* et al., "Do Lawyers Matter? Evidence from Patents."

d) *Dual Representation*

1017 **Dual representation** through an external patent attorney plus a regular, external attorney is currently standard practice in Germany and has often been regarded as the ideal solution.[18] It certainly has the advantage of allowing the patent attorney to concentrate on the technical issues while the attorney takes care of the formal legalities. Currently this type of representation can be seen (for both sides) in most cases before the court.

1018 The downside of this solution is that, unlike in Germany, the recoverable costs do not increase accordingly when dual representation is selected, i.e. one would have to absorb any added costs even if one wins the case. And if one loses, the costs incurred will probably be higher than for a single representative.

1019 Another potential pitfall is the European Court of Justice's Judgment No. C 531/20 in *Novatext vs. Ruprecht-Karls-Universität Heidelberg*, which holds that there must always be a case-by-case assessment. This could be interpreted to mean that regular attorneys may not always be needed before the Unified Patent Court, since duly qualified patent attorneys are authorized to act as representatives and have greater technical expertise but comparable expertise in procedural law – a field in which neither type of attorney is required to have special training. This is in turn would imply that the costs of a regular attorney may not always be recoverable. If the European Patent Litigation Certificate (see Para. 732 et seqq.) becomes the benchmark standard in the coming years, then one can assume that the patent attorneys will be better qualified when it comes to the procedural law applicable before the Unified Patent Court.

1020 So the parties will have to decide whether and how they are willing to shoulder such potential added costs. Smooth teamwork between the patent attorney(s) and the regular attorney(s) to prevent duplications of effort will certainly be helpful in this regard. This said, if the Court were to follow the logic of the European Court of Justice's Judgement No. C 531/20 in *Novatext vs. Ruprecht-Karls-Universität Heidelberg* and hold dual representation to be unnecessary, then one would invariably have to consider whether the added costs are worthwhile.

VI. Witnesses and External Experts

1021 As expected, witnesses and external experts play a minor role before the Unified Patent Court. Expert statements during the Oral hearing are the absolute exception.[19]

1022 It stands to reason that situations can and will arise where the role of witnesses will be decisive. Thus, witnesses and their testimony will be indispensable in cases where evident prior usage is asserted in a revocation counterclaim. Analogous and similar

18 E.g. according to oral remarks made by *Grabinski* at the conference of the German Chamber of Patent Attorneys on 20 November 2013 in Munich.

19 One exception is UPC_CFI_146/2024 (LD Munich), Decision of 12 December 2025 – Sanofi v. Stada et al.

scenarios are familiar to every legal practitioner, so there is no need for us to dwell on them further here.

However, it is important point to keep in mind is that the Unified Patent Court has technical judges at its disposal who can either participate in the entire proceeding or who can be allocated as needed. This means that testimony from witnesses or external experts of a merely general technical nature can often be dispensed with. **1023**

If the technical-know of external experts is to be introduced into the proceedings at all,[20] then this should be donein the form of written expert reports submitted during the written procedure. Whether the court then makes use of that remains to be seen. On the other hand, there is no evident reason why one could not offer such external experts as witnesses for the interim procedure or the oral hearing, assuming they are willing to appear. Indeed, such a move would seem highly advisable. **1024**

VII. Costs

As far as costs go, we will have to wait and see how the Unified Patent Court handles the issue of cost recovery, as discussed in Chapter 6 (Para. 514 et seqq.) Two additional points do seem worth making, however: **1025**

1. Unprovoked Legal Action

As mentioned earlier (see Para. 950), the Unified Patent Court does not have any regulation analogous to Section 93 of the German Code of Civil Procedure (ZPO). This provision stipulates that a defendant may impose his costs upon the plaintiff if he becomes the target of unprovoked legal action (*Klageüberfall*) and if the defendant immediately acknowledges the claim – although this will effectively mean that he has lost the case. So it remains to be seen whether a nuanced system of right-to-use enquiries and infringement warnings of the sort customary under German law will also become established practice before the Unified Patent Court. **1026**

But even if the cost implications of becoming a target of an unprovoked legal action are not expressly codified in the Rules of Procedure, they could of course be clarified by the Unified Patent Court's own case law, i.e. once the Court establishes its own legal precedent on the matter. One should consider adducing such legal precedent where possible and appropriate. It will surely also be in the interest of the Unified Patent Court for the parties to reach an amicable settlement before the Court is actually seised, rather than afterward. A possible legal basis for this could be Article 69 (3) of the UPC Agreement. The current caselaw[21] clearly points in this direction. **1027**

20 Cf. Higher District Court (OLG) of Düsseldorf: Preliminary Injunction After Interim Decision in the *Cinacalcet II* case, GRUR-RR 2021, p. 249; here, the court took a very negative stance towards privately obtained expert opinions.

21 UPC_CoA 2/2024, Order of 4 October 2024, APL_83/2024 – Edwards v. Meril.

2. Cost Apportionment Following a Decision by Default

1028 According to German law, the party against whom a decision by default is issued must bear the costs of this proceedings up this point. This applies even if the party in default was otherwise successful thus far after having lodged a preliminary objection.

1029 On this topic as well, the Rules of Procedure are silent. But here, too, one should consider raising the aforementioned principle in a procedure for cost decisions, whereby Article 69(3) of the UPC Agreement could again be cited in support (cf. Para. 458). There is no caselaw yet, however.

VIII. Standard-Essential Patents

1030 The principles established by the European Court of Justice in *Huawei vs. ZTE* (see Para. 797) also apply before the Unified Patent Court. This follows from (inter alia) the primacy given to European Union law under Article 20 of the UPC Agreement.

1031 What will really count in practice, however, will be a) the varied ways in which the aforementioned ECJ ruling may be interpreted and, particularly for the patent proprietor, b) the options for requesting the imposition of confidentiality, also vis-a-vis the opposing side (cf. Para. 798). However, there is currently no established case law.

1032 So as far as the infringement/injunction situation is concerned, one should continue to base one arguments on whichever case law is most supportive to one's position, at least until such time as the Unified Patent Court's own legal precedent has begun to take shape. Since Great Britain will not be part of the Unitary Patent System, it would seem advisable to proceed on the premise that German practices will frequently be adopted.

1033 As regards confidentiality, patent proprietors should not hesitate to lodge the applications pursuant to Rule 262A (see Para. 701 et seqq.).

B. Strategic Considerations for the Patent Proprietor

I. Which Division Should be Selected?

1034 When a patent-infringement action falls under the applicable scope of the UPC Agreement, it will almost always be possible to choose from among several local or regional divisions, or also the central division. This is due to the fact that offering a good or service can suffice to constitute a patent infringement. Test purchases by straw men can be another way to more or less force the selection of a specific court.

1035 The question of which division to seise can of course not be decided solely on the basis of fixed, objective criteria. The answer will depend on the individual case and naturally also on the degree of confidence which the patent proprietor feels he can place in the Court.

1036 All in all, it still seems advisable to try to ensure that, at last in the initial phase, the panel of first instance consists of experienced judges including, if at all possible, the judge-rapporteur, since he will be the one to conduct the proceeding until the oral hearing.

A quick side comment is in order here: Having an action conducted by a single judge would not seem to be a particularly good option, even if it might allow one to economize on court fees. This is borne out by the trend observed in proceedings on the national level, where single judges are practically never selected insofar as a choice is possible. We will therefore not dwell further on this topic. 1037

It follows from the foregoing that the recommendation to lodge an action before a German local division which we made earlier in Chapter 6 (Para. 588 et seqq.) continues to be valid. In this case it is ensured that the panel comprises two German judges. 1038

Additionally it should be considered to file the case in German, even if the plaintiff is not a German company or does not speak German at all. 1039

And one would also be able to safely assume that the judge-rapporteur is either a native German speaker – and thus boasts solid experience in patent disputes – or that he is an exceptionally capable jurist, since acquiring the proficiency to conduct legal proceedings in German is an impressive achievement for any non-native speaker. If a case is filed in English before any German division then there is a realistic chance that the "third" non-German judge will be allocated as judge rapporteur. 1040

The fact that it will often be possible for the plaintiff to change the language of proceedings into English (see Para. 409) does not change these strategic considerations. The judge-rapporteur is selected right at the beginning and if such a request is filed then he or she will not be replaced. 1041

II. Lodging the Statement of Claim

As mentioned earlier, action proceedings before the Unified Patent Court are highly streamlined and their outcome will most likely be decided in the written procedure or in the directly following interim procedure. 1042

Thus, all the "can" or "should" provisions the Rules should instead interpreted as an absolute "must" rather than an elective option. As a practical matter, a plaintiff is well advised to submit the gamut of his argumentation and evidence right at the outset, as has been standard practice in Germany till now. For afterwards there will be few opportunities to introduce new requests/applications, documents and evidence into the proceedings without the express permission of the Court. 1043

The lodging of the Statement of Claim should be preceded by thorough preparation, whereby great care should be taken to ensure that the subject matter of the action as well as the infringement have been explained in a careful, comprehensible and comprehensive manner. 1044

Another point that may be worth addressing in the context of the Statement of Claim is the possible arisal of claims to obtain information. But since this will be the subject of a separate damage-award procedure – which may even be conducted by a different 1045 panel than the one which heard the action proceeding – one could also wait until the later procedure to raise the matter. But briefly mentioning it right at the outset would be a good idea in any case.

1. Choice of Languages

1046 The plaintiff will be free to choose the language of the proceedings, assuming the division he has selected allows him to choose from among more than one language. The advantages of bringing an action before a German local division in the German language have already been emphasized (see Para. 1039).

1047 However, due to the case law of the court (see Para. 409), a change of the language of the action is almost always possible, so that filing an action in a language other than the language of the patent always entails the risk that the proceedings will ultimately be held in English.

2. Determining the Subject Matter of the Action

1048 Though not defined in the Rules of Procedure, determining the subject matter of the action is a key issue in any action.

1049 Must the action focus on the infringement as such or can the action be extended to also cover the patent claims as granted?

1050 This will have important consequences. If the action focuses on the infringement question and a conviction is obtained, it may then be possible to simply make use of a writ already issued pursuant to the decision if the defendant brings an adapted product to market. But if the action also covers the granted patent claim, then this will obviously not be so easy.[22]

1051 It is, however, accepted by the court to request an injunction for the patent claim as such and list the infringing product as "especially" etc. It is even allowed to later introduce further products into the claim.[23]

3. Determining the Territorial Reach

1052 As explained earlier (Para. 283) due to the lack of corresponding interim regulations a writ of injunction may also cover Member States which were not yet part of the Unitary Patent System at the time the action was brought, but which acceded to the System at a later time.

1053 But this will only be possible if the corresponding Member States are covered by the patent in dispute, i.e. if the patent was nationally validated in those countries. This

22 A survey of German and Swiss law can be found in *Henneberger-Sudjana*, GRUR Int 2016, p. 209; for a comparison of German and British law, see e.g. *Leister*, GRUR 2016, p. 217.

23 UPC_CoA_789/2025, Decision of 6 March 2026 – Dyson v. Dreame.

is because a unitary patent's coverage specifically excludes newly acceding countries (see Para. 83 et seqq.).

Reference (cf. Para. 490 et seqq.) has already been made to the possibility opened up by the 'BSH-Elektrolux' decision to apply for an injunction, provided that the relevant conditions are met, even for non-EPG countries covered by the same EP patent. This should definitely be considered. **1054**

The proposel inter ala by *Kircher*[24] that the territorial reach of writs of injunction be derived from that of the UPC Agreement as of the time of the oral hearing, was not accepted by the Court.[25] Instead, the countries covered by the injunction must be specified when the application is filed and then corresponding requests must be made when the UPC territory is extended. **1055**

This can also be done during the appeal process; there is no reformatio in peius, i.e. even if the first instance was won and the opposing party has lodged an appeal, an application for extension can still be made.[26] However, this application must be made at the earliest opportunity, otherwise it will be considered late.[27] **1056**

4. Naming the Defendant

Another point to consider carefully is whom to designate as the defendant. If a legal entity is to be sued, then one must also specifically decide whether its representatives, e.g. its managing directors, should be sued as well. The court has permitted this in principle, but in a landmark decision has drastically reduced the liability of managing directors.[28] Nevertheless, it should be considered. **1057**

5. "Point at the mulberry tree while cursing the locust tree"?

This is the title of the 26th stratagem in the famous Chinese 36 Stratagems.[29] The original meaning is that criticism should only be levelled indirectly and officially at lower-ranking individuals. In the context of the Unified Patent Court, however, this can be an effective strategic option, as the court has drastically reduced the options available to interveners (see Para. 1228). **1058**

Specifically, if a larger company is actually aimed at, it would not be sued, but rather a (preferrably smaller) dealer who offers this company's products in the UPC territory. Very likely, the latter will now announce the dispute to the actual opponent. However, if the lawsuit does not proceed as desired, a settlement would be reached with the actual defendant, i.e. the smaller dealer, preferably in such a way that each party **1059**

24 *Kircher*, in *Bopp/Kircher*, Note 50 to Section 13.
25 U.a. UPC_CFI_15/2023 (LD Munich), Decision of 15 November 2024 – Edwards v. Meril.
26 UPC_CoA_523/2024, Order of 3 March 2025 – Syngenta v. Sumi Agro.
27 UPC_CoA_464/2024, Decision of 25 November 2025 – Edwards v. Meril.
28 UPC_CoA_534/2024, Decision of 3 October 2025 – Philips v. Belkin.
29 https://en.wikipedia.org/wiki/Thirty-Six_Stratagems.

bears its own costs (which will be manageable for the dealer). The actual opponent would then be left out and would not even be able to claim its costs.

▶ Practical Tip:

1060 Thus, a demand for injunctive relief could be formulated as follows:

It is hereby requested that [the defendant(s) = company + legal representatives such as managing directors or, alternatively, only the company] be ordered to cease and desist from offering, selling or using, or from possessing or importing for the aforementioned purposes, a Trans-Europa-Express train having the following characteristics:

[insert Claim 1 of the disputed patent],

specifically the product bearing the designation "*Europe, Endless*,"

[insert description of the product]

in [insert list of Countries, also possibly non-UPC-countries, for which injunction is sought][30] [....]

III. Auxiliary Requests in Revocation Counterclaim Proceedings

1061 If the defendant lodges a counterclaim for revocation – which can be expected to almost always occur – the plaintiff will have only one opportunity to amend his patent claims, also on an alternative basis.

1062 In order to keep the entire scope of coverage of the disputed patent open in the appeal proceeding, it would seem advisable not to amend the patent as such, but rather to lodge numerous auxiliary requests. This is because lodging requests later on will not be possible except with the express permission of the Court. But one cannot assume that the Court will necessarily grant such permission.

1063 This need to lodge the request "into the blue," as it were, without knowing which of the challenges asserted by the defendant will actually influence the Court's court decision, is regrettable and constitutes one of the few structural deficiencies of the Rules of Procedure. In this regard, the Rules constitute a sort of reversion to the way German revocation counterclaim proceedings were conducted before the reform of 2009.[31]

1064 An approach worth considering in this context would be to contact the judge-rapporteur and ask him to allow additional auxiliary requests at the end of interim conference, since by that time it will have become clearer which aspects the Court considers relevant for its decision. It might also be helpful to let the judge know that one intends

30 For a detailed discussion it is referred to Luginbühl/Hüttermann/Jestaedt, Kommentar Einheitspatentsytem, Rule 13.

31 See *Hüttermann*, Mitt. 2016, p. 212.

to make only sparing use of auxiliary requests until the interim procedure draws to a close. Such a practice would surely serve to markedly increase popular acceptance of the Unified Patent Court as a whole as well as of the division concerned. It would also be covered by the Rules of Procedure, particularly Rule 332.

Otherwise, it would seem advisable to submit a large number of auxiliary requests so as to prepare for any eventuality. If the Unified Patent Court were to adopt the practice of allowing auxiliary requests only ahead of time and, pursuant to Rule 30.1 (c), in only a generally limited number, then this would be cause to consider the possibility of an "opt-out" (see Para. 299 et seqq.) 1065

If a parallel opposition proceeding is pending, the patent proprietor should align his requests in the opposition proceeding with those in the revocation counterclaim proceeding, even if this is not a requirement. Otherwise, the issuance of a conditional decision or a suspension of the infringements proceeding will probably become inevitable (cf. Para. 914). 1066

IV. Should Enforcement of the 1st Instance Decision be Requested?

This question should probably be answered with a clear "yes" if the Unified Patent Court has granted an injunction in the operative part of its decision. It remains to seen how high the security to be lodged will be. But this should not scare off the patent proprietor, since the security will not necessarily have to be liquidated even if he loses the appeal. The advantages of driving the opposing side off the market clearly outweigh here, particularly since asserting potentially higher damage claims for the opposing side's market activities during the appeal proceeding will usually not be worth the trouble, given that damages awarded by the Unified Patent Court will not be punitive in nature (see Para. 802 et seqq.) 1067

But even if the Court only awards damages, one should still not rule out a proceeding to determine the amount of such damages. Although one can probably expect the opposing side to enter into negotiations at this point, thereby making it possible to avoid such a proceeding. 1068

V. Damage-Award Proceedings; Claim to Damages and Information

As mentioned earlier, arguments in favor of a claim to information can theoretically be raised as soon as the action is first brought. In any case, the plaintiff should not simply assert the claim to information but also explain why he is entitled to such claim. Here it would definitely be helpful to go into detail concerning the prevailing commercial situation, namely by indicating the following: 1069

- Whether the defendant sells to end consumers or to commercial customers;
- From where does the defendant source his merchandise? Is he merely a re-seller? Does the actual manufacturer have his seat outside the Member States? Can it be assumed that there are additional sellers of the patent-infringing items besides the defendant?

- The extent to which it would be reasonable for the defendant to make full disclosures of the information. This will likely depend at least in part on whether the defendant committed the patent infringement more or less unintentionally, e.g. because the patent (only) covers a portion of a highly complex product for which multiple patents have been granted. The situation will probably look rather different if the patent infringement was committed out of a willful disregard of possible infringement and the defendant is a mere re-seller who generally pays little heed to patent rights.[32]

1070 Such considerations should be raised by no later than the date of the application for determination of damages.

1071 It remains to be seen how the Unified Patent Court deals with the option of referring the damage-award procedure to some other panel, i.e. whether panels specialized exclusively in such procedures will be formed within the Court's divisions, or possibly only in those divisions with high caseloads. Due to the low number of cases at present there is no tendency towards either direction.

C. Strategic Considerations for the Defendant

1072 Given that the Plaintiff is free to decide the division to be seised and the language to be used in a given proceeding, it naturally follows that the options open to the defendant will be fewer in number. This said, the following considerations seem worthy of mention:

I. "Service-Deal"

1073 As is well known, the three-month deadline for filing a response and a counterclaim for invalidity is quite short. However, in the following scenarios, defendants have managed[33] to extend this deadline by up to six weeks:

- Multiple defendants are sued simultaneously; however, they are so closely connected that they will choose the same legal representatives (e.g., parent and subsidiary companies)
- One or more of the defendants are located in a country where service of process may take longer (e.g., China, but in some cases also the U.S. or Korea). In most cases, this is the parent company, while subsidiaries located within the UPC territory have also been sued.

1074 In this case, after service has been effected on the subsidiary, the representatives wait several weeks and then offer to act as authorized representatives for the defendants located outside the UC jurisdiction as well, provided that the court recalculates the deadline for the subsidiaries.

---

32 Cf. e.g. *Ann*, VPP-Rundbrief 2014, p. 93.

33 See further UPC_CFI_119/202 (LD Munich), Order of 22 April 2025 – Jingko v. Long or UPC_CFI_492/2025 (LD Munich), Order of 28 July 2025 – Papst v. Beijing Roboroc.

This "service agreement" has become standard practice, but caution is advised: the court may simply split the proceedings.[34] Nevertheless, it should be utilized whenever possible. 1075

II. Should a request to change the language of proceedings be lodged?

This question can probably be answered with a clear yes if this is helpful and possible. In view of the clear case law of the court (see Para. 409), such a request is almost always successful and should be made as early as possible. 1076

III. Should a Preliminary Objection Pursuant to Rule 19 Be Lodged?

This question should probably be answered with a clear "yes" if the grounds on which to base a successful preliminary objection are given. 1077

But if no such preliminary objection is lodged within the corresponding time limit then, pursuant to Rule 19, it will no longer be possible to contest formal aspects of action, such as the jurisdiction of the Unified Patent Court itself or of the relevant division. 1078

IV. Should a Preliminary Objection Be Lodged in Actions Before the Central Division?

It bears noting that *Tilmann*, for one, considers patent infringement actions before the central division to be irreconcilable with European Union law. In particular, he objects to a) the regulation which states that a patent infringement action may be brought before the central division when the defendant has his residential seat outside the EU;[35] and b) to the "Unilever Rule;"[36] as well as c) to the practice of allocating the central division when there is no local division.[37] As a logical consequence, *Tilmann* recommends that the defendant lodge a preliminary objection.[38] 1079

A preliminary objection also seems to be correct legal remedy in the event a pending parallel German patent-infringement action exists which was lodged at a prior point in time (see Para. 32). 1080

V. Should a Revocation Counterclaim Be Lodged?

In those patent infringements proceedings for which the principle of splitting does not exist, such as national proceedings in France, it is customary to argue a lack of patentability. This also turns out to be the decisive issue of the proceedings in many cases.[39] 1081

34 UPC_CFI_319/2025 (LD Munich), Order of 19 August 2025 – Solvay v. Zhejiang Fluorine.
35 Cf. *Tilmann* GRUR Int 2016, p. 409.
36 See *Tilmann* in *Tilmann/Plassmann*, Notes 15–23 to Article 33.
37 See *Tilmann* in *Tilmann/Plassmann*, Notes 15–23 to Article 33; Cf. also *Büttner* in *Tilmann/Plassmann*, Note 5 to Article 7.
38 See *Tilmann* in *Tilmann/Plassmann* Note 4/5 to Rule 19.
39 Note: This particularly applies to French patent infringement proceedings. Although French national patents do not undergo a review procedure, well over 50 % of all French

1082 In Germany, by contrast, a parallel counterclaim for revocation is lodged in only 50 % of cases.[40]

1083 In this regard, a proceeding before the Unified Patent Court is more similar to a French proceeding. This means that a counterclaim for revocation should be lodged whenever possible, if only to place the opposing side under time pressure and work pressure.

1084 The maximum limit imposed on court fees (see Para. 432) is worth mentioning here. But, as is the case with most other proceedings, these maximum court fees will probably be more than offset by the foreseeable attorneys' fees.

VI. How Should the Argumentation Be Structured?

1085 As regards the argumentation, it stands to reason that the principles applicable will be the same as those for national infringement proceedings. In particular, one should not allow the patent proprietor to "dodge and weave," i.e. to adjust his reasoning as to the interpretation of a given characteristic depending on whether the patent's infringement or the patent's validity is under discussion.

1086 One peculiarity does bear noting: Rule 30, as well as Rule 50 (Para. 1171) expressly state that the patent proprietor, when submitting patent amendments or auxiliary requests – whereby the latter will probably always occur – must explain why the criteria of Article 84 of the European Patent Convention (EPC) have been met. In other words, this Article of the European Patent Convention is expressly cited here, rather than being only indirectly alluded to as in Article 101 of the EPC.

1087 This naturally opens the door to objections regarding clarity and may even lead to a revival of the European Patent Office's Decision No. T472/88, which holds that every amendment of patent claims must be examined for clarity.[41] This would ultimately mean that objections regarding clarity would be possible on a broader basis before the Unified Patent Court than before the European Patent Office, where they now occur only rarely following EPO Decision No. G3/14.

1088 As mentioned, there is no principle of ex officio examination before the Unified Patent Court. This can be a significant problem, particularly in the context of counterclaims for invalidity, as it may result in the court failing to consider all grounds for invalidity and instead requiring the parties to prioritize them and limit their arguments to the most significant grounds.[42]

---

infringements actions are brought on the basis of national patents.

40 *Cremers* et al. arrive at a figure of 44.3 % for the period 2000 to 2008; cf. *Cremers* et al., "Invalid but Infringed? An Analysis of Germany's Bifurcated Patent Litigation System," ZEW Working Paper 14–072. Newer numbers are not known.

41 See *Hüttermann*, Mitt. 2016, p. 212, cf. also *Hüttermann*, GRUR Int, 2022, 633.

42 UPC_CFI_425/2024 (LD Munich), Decision of 28 November 2025 – JingAo v. Chint, cf. UPC_CFI_497/2024 (CD Milan), Decision of 23 October 2025 – BioMerieux v. Labrador.

Furthermore, it is virtually impossible to introduce additional documents in the reply;[43] in some cases, it is even prohibited to rephrase atttacks out of documents already filed[44] or even to refer to parts of documents that were not previously cited.[45] For stand-alone nullity actions, this means that they are at a massive disadvantage compared to European oppositions (see the discussion starting at Para. 1307 et seqq.). One should be aware of all this when drafting the counterclaim for revocation. **1089**

VII. Argumentation Regarding Injunction and Damages

The judges of the Unified Patent Court have a wider discretionary leeway when it comes to granting claims to injunctive relief and damages than the national courts, which are often subject to a statutory obligation to grant claims to injunctive relief. **1090**

This should be exploited by the defendant. If he finds himself unable to defend against a claim for injunctive relief, then he should at least try to obtain a transitional grace period. **1091**

In the case of standard-essential patents, the *Huawei vs. ZTE* decision of the European Court of Justice should obviously be brought into play. No peculiarities apply in this connection, however.[46] **1092**

When it comes to the award of damages, the defendant should likewise argue – assuming he cannot reach a settlement with the plaintiff, which is more likely than not – that the damages must not have a punitive character. And that the damages should therefore be no more than what a license analogy would dictate (see a. Para. 802 et seqq.) **1093**

Here it bears repeating once again that Regulation 1260/2012 (EU) expressly provides that the infringement court (i.e. the Unified Patent Court) must consider the possible absence of translations when awarding damages in cases where the action is based on a unitary patent and where the defendant is a small to midsized enterprise, a natural person, a non-profit organization, a university or a public research organization (see Para. 150). This is a point which the defendant should by all means raise, assuming the preconditions are given. This EU Regulation enjoys primacy by virtue of Article 20 of the UPC Agreement and must therefore be duly considered by Unified Patent Court. **1094**

---

43 UPC_CFI_278/2023 (LD Hamburg), Decision of 30 April 2025 – Agfa v. Gucci.
44 UPC_CFI_11/2024 (LD Düsseldorf), Decision of 8 May 2025 – Grundfos v. Hefei Xinhu and UPC_CFI_461/2024 (LD Hamburg), Decision of 5 November 2025 (along with other decisions cited therein).
45 UPC_CFI_26/2024 (LD Düsseldorf), Decision of 30 July 2025 – Headwater v. Samsung.
46 See *Petersen* et al., "The Unified Patent Court (UPC), Compulsory Licensing and Competition Law."

Section 4: Appeal Proceedings

Chapter 11: Overview of the Appeal Proceeding

Contents | Para

The essential feature of the second instance proceeding before the Unified Patent Court is that practically all decisions and orders of the first instance panel will be subject to review by the Court of Appeal (for the few exceptions that apply, see Para. 1116). The distinction drawn in German law between a "complaint" (*Beschwerde*) and an "appeal" (*Berufung*) does not exist here; both are subsumed under the term "appeal."[1] Thus, the term "appeal" is used exclusively in this book. **1095**

On the other hand, the UPC's Rules of Procedure do distinguish between appeals which require leave from the Court of First Instance (i.e. what would be regarded as bona fide "appeals" under the German practice) and appeals not requiring such leave (which would usually be regarded as "complaints" in Germany). **1096**

In contrast to the practice established by the European Patent Convention – but similarly to German practice, for example – the respondent in any appeal proceeding will still have time to lodge a non-independent cross-appeal even after the normal time limit for an appeal has expired. If the Appeal is withdrawn, then the Cross-Appeal will be deemed withdrawn also (see Para. 1129 et seqq.). **1097**

1 See *Meier-Beck*, GRUR 2014, pp. 144–148, cf. also the critique expressed by *Tilmann* in *Tilmann/Plassmann* Note 73 et seqq. to the Introduction to the UPC Agreement.

A. Appeals Not Requiring Leave

1098 The following may always be contested through an appeal (Rule 220):

- final decisions of the Court of First Instance, also in preliminary injunction procedure.
- orders to change the language of the proceedings without the parties' consent to the language in which the patent was granted;
- orders in legal actions against the European Patent Office about unitary patents;
- orders to produce to preserve evidence (see Para. 711 et seqq.);
- orders in the procedure to preserve evidence (see Para. 1380 et seqq.); and
- orders relating to preliminary injunction proceedings (see Para. 1336 et seqq.)

1099 Appeals not requiring leave from the Court of First Instance are subject to the same rules as complaint procedures under the European Patent Convention, i.e. the appeal must be lodged within two months of the date of service of the final decision of the Court of First Instance, while the Statement of Grounds of Appeal must be lodged within four months of said date.

1100 The Court of Appeal may hear appeals against separate decisions on the merits in infringement proceedings and in validity proceedings together (Rule 220.5).

1101 A fee is to be paid when lodging the appeal. The fee for the appeal will correspond to the court fee for the first instance proceeding.

B. Appeals Requiring Leave

1102 In principle, almost every decision (!) of the Court of First Instance may be reviewed by the Court of Second Instance during an ongoing proceeding by lodging an appeal requiring leave from the Court of First Instance.[2] Alternatively, this may also be done without leave from the Court as part of the appeal against the final decision on the merits.

I. Decision of the Panel of First Instance

1103 An appeal is only possible against a decision of the first instance panel, however. Thus, if a case-management order of the judge-rapporteur is to be contested,[3] an application for review of the order must first be submitted to the first instance panel (Rule 333). The time limit for this is within 15 days of the date of service of the order. The application must set out the grounds for review and the evidence, if any, in support of the grounds. A fee of 1,300 € will also be payable. The other party will be given the opportunity to be heard.

---

2 Note: This regulation is regarded as a violation of the UPC Agreement by *Tochtermann*; cf. *Tilmann/Plassmann*, Note 40–72 to Art 73.

3 Note: This also applies when the intention is to wait to contest the decision until the appeal against the final decision is lodged.

1104 The first instance panel will as soon as practicable decide the application for review and make any necessary revised case management order (Rule 333.4). This order (i.e. first submission to the entire Senate, only then appeal) must be strictly adhered to, skipping is not possible.[4]

1105 This decision in turn – assuming it allows the application pursuant to Rule 333 – may be contested by the opposite party, either through an appeal requiring leave from the Court of First Instance or as an appeal not requiring leave as part of the appeal against the final decision on the merits.

II. Appeal Requiring Leave During an Ongoing Proceeding

1106 If the approach select it to lodge an appeal requiring leave during the ongoing proceeding, then the next step will depend on whether or not the first instance panel decides to grant leave to the appeal.

1. Case A): The First Instance Panel Grants Leave to the Appeal

1107 If the first instance panel grants leave to the appeal, then the Statement of Appeal must be lodged within 15 days after the corresponding decision is served, whereby the Statement of Grounds of Appeal must also be lodged within the same time limit. A fee of 4,00 € must be paid for the appeal.

2. Case B) The First Instance Panel Refuses Leave for the Appeal

1108 In the event of a refusal of the Court of First Instance to grant leave within 15 days of the order of one of its panels, a request for a discretionary review to the Court of Appeal may be made within 15 calendar days from the end of that period (Rule 220.3). A fee of 1,300 € will also be payable. If the Court of First Instance does not respond within the 15-day period, then this, too, will be regarded as a refusal to grant leave. In this case, the time limit will begin from the end of that period.

If the first instance panel does issue a decision within 15 days of its order, then this, too, will constitute a denial of leave for the appeal. In this case, the time limit for lodging the request for discretionary review will commence as soon as this 15-day period expires.

1109 The request for discretionary review will be assigned to the standing judge of the Court of Appeal, who may deny the request without giving reasons (Rule 220.4). If the standing judge allows the request after having heard the other party, he will order what further steps, if any, the parties are to take. Furthermore, the fee of 4,000 € is to be paid, whereby the fee of 1,300 € for the discretionary review is credited.

4 Cf. UPC_CoA_586/2024, Order of 9 October 2024, APL_54732/2024 – Suinno Mobile & AI v. Microsoft, UPC_CoA_486/2023, Order of 11 January 2024, App_595643/2023 – Netgear v. Huawei, UPC_CoA_454/2024, Order of 21 August 2024, APL_44552/2024 – Microsoft v. Suinno Mobile & AI.

1110 The President of the Court of Appeal will assign the review to a panel of the Court of Appeal for a decision. The Court of Appeal may consult the presiding judge or the judge-rapporteur of the panel of the Court of First Instance which has refused the leave order (Rule 220.4).

1111 The following diagram provides an overview of the entire process:

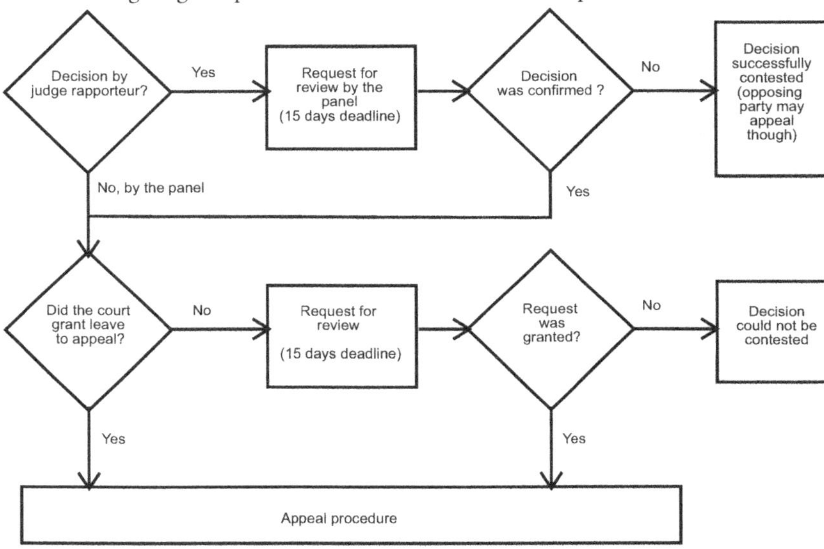

Fig. 11.1 Overview of the possibilities to loge an appeal

C. Appeals Against Cost Decisions

1112 When it comes to cost decisions, the appeal procedure is structured somewhat differently:

1113 As in the case of appeals requiring leave, an appeal against a cost decision may only be lodged if the first instance panel first grants leave. The application for leave to appeal to the Court of Appeal must be lodged within 15 days' time of the relevant cost decision's date of service (Rule 221). This time the fee will amount to 1,500 €, however.

1114 This application must contain the following (Rule 221.2):
- the reasons why the appeal should be heard; and
- where necessary, the facts, evidence and arguments relied upon by the applicant.

1115 The application for leave to appeal will then be assigned to the standing judge who will decide on granting leave to appeal; if leave to appeal a cost decision is granted, the standing judge will also decide the appeal. (Rule 221.3 and 4). The procedure described in Para. 1121 et seqq. will apply here as well.

D. Non-Appealable Decisions

Only very few decisions cannot be contested through an appeal. These include: 1116
- an order refusing an application to intervene (Rule 317); and
- orders relating to a re-establishment of rights (Rule 320), i.e. not only when a re-establishment of rights is granted but also – in derogation German law – when a re-establishment of rights is refused.

E. Application for Suspensive Effect

An appeal will generally not have a suspensive effect. A party may lodge an application for suspensive effect (Rule 223.1), however, and thereby potentially set aside the provisional enforceability of the final decision on the merits issued by the Court of First Instance. This is not possible for appeals requiring leave however, since these never have suspensive effect (Rule 223.5). These will be subject to much shorter time limits, however (see Para. 1121 et seqq.) 1117

The application is to contain the following (Rule 223.2): 1118
- the reasons why the lodging of the appeal should have suspensive effect; and
- the facts, evidence and arguments relied on.

The Court of Appeal will decide the application without undue delay (Rule 223.3) 1119

In cases of extreme urgency, the applicant may apply at any time, without formality for an order for suspensive effect, to the standing judge, who will have all the powers of the Court of Appeal and will decide the procedure to follow on the application (Rule 223.4). 1120

F. Course of the Proceeding

In principle, the stages of an appeal proceeding will be the same as in a first instance proceeding, i.e. there will be a written procedure, an interim procedure and an oral hearing. On the other hand, the appeal proceeding will be significantly more streamlined than in the first instance, particularly when it comes to the written procedure. 1121

I. Written Procedure

The appeal proceeding begins with the lodging of the appeal, whereby a distinction is made between the Statement of Appeal itself and the Statement of Grounds of Appeal. The language used for the Statement of Appeal and Statement of Grounds of Appeal will be the language of the first instance proceeding (Article 50(1) and Rule 227.1), unless the parties agree to use the language of the patent (Article 50(2)) or unless the Court of Appeal decides that, in an exceptional case, the language of a Member State will be used for the appeal proceeding (Article 50(3)). This will require the consent of the parties, however. 1122

1. Contents of the Formal Appeal

1123 The Statement of Appeal is to contain the following (Rule 225):
- the names of the appellant and of the appellant's representative, as well as the names of the respondent and of the respondent's representative;
- the date of the decision or order appealed against and the action number attributed to the file in proceedings before the Court of First Instance; and
- the order or remedy sought by the appellant, including any order for expedition of the appeal pursuant and the reasons justifying such order for expedition.

2. Statement of Grounds of Appeal

1124 The Statement of Grounds of Appeal must contain the following (Rule 226):
- an indication of which parts of the decision or order are contested;
- the reasons for setting aside the contested decision or order; and
- an indication of the facts and evidence on which the appeal is based.

1125 Default regulations for missed time limits apply for any and all facts and evidence which are not introduced until the appeal proceeding (see Para. 683 et seqq.)

3. Examination as to Formal Requirements

1126 The appeal will then be examined for any formal deficiencies. If any are found, a deficiency notice giving a 14-day grace period to correct will be issued; this is analogous to the notice issued in the first instance for payment of the court fee. If the appeal is formally correct, then an appeal file will be recorded in the Register and an action number assigned. The panel will as soon as practicable decide whether to grant any order for expedition, after having given the parties an opportunity to be heard.

1127 The case will then be assigned to a judge-rapporteur, whereby the same rules will apply as for the first instance proceeding. The judge-rapporteur will examine whether the Statement of Grounds of Appeal satisfies the minimum requirements of Rule 226 and, if applicable, will give the appellant leave to amend the Statement of Grounds of Appeal. Otherwise, the judge-rapporteur may reject the appeal as inadmissible, but must give the appellant an opportunity to be heard beforehand (Rule 233).

1128 The appellant may challenge a decision to reject the appeal as inadmissible within one month of service of the decision, without providing new grounds of appeal (Rule 234). Grounds of appeal which are not raised within the period specified for the Statement of grounds of appeal will not be admissible. (Rule 233).

4. Respondent's Statement of Response

1129 If the appeal has made it past this first hurdle – which can normally be assumed – then the respondent of the appeal will have the option to lodge a Statement of Response. He may also bring a cross-appeal (Rule 237.1).

The time limit for lodging the Statement of Response is three months for appeals not requiring leave and 15 days for appeals requiring leave, assuming leave for the appeal has been granted by the Court[5] (Rule 235.1). 1130

If no cross-appeal is lodged, then this completes the written procedure of the appeal procedure. 1131

5. Course of the Proceeding When a Cross-Appeal is Lodged

If a cross-appeal is lodged, the same fee as for the opposing side's appeal will be payable (Rule 237.4). 1132

The Statement of Cross-Appeal should not only include the reasons, facts and evidence for the cross-appeal, but also the names and address of the respondents and of persons authorized to perform legal service, as well as the action number of the appeal file (Rule 237.2, which makes reference to Rules 225 and 226). 1133

The appellant will now have a one-time opportunity to lodge a Reply to the Statement of Cross-Appeal, namely within a time limit of either two months in the case of an appeal not requiring leave, or 15 days in the case of an appeal requiring leave. 1134

This resulting timeline for appeals not requiring leave from the Court of First Instance (pursuant to Rule 220.1) is shown below. The timeline begins on the date on which the Statement of Appeal is served upon the opposing party: 1135

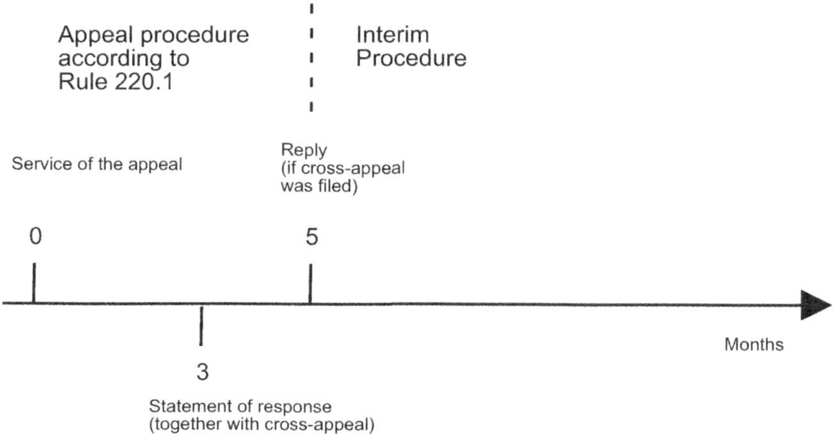

Fig. 11.2 Timeline for the appeal procedure pursuant to Rule 220.1

For an appeal requiring leave (pursuant to Rule 220.2), the timeline looks as follows: 1136

5 Note: Either by the first instance panel directly or by the Court of Appeal which accepted the appeal and which overruled the first instance panel.

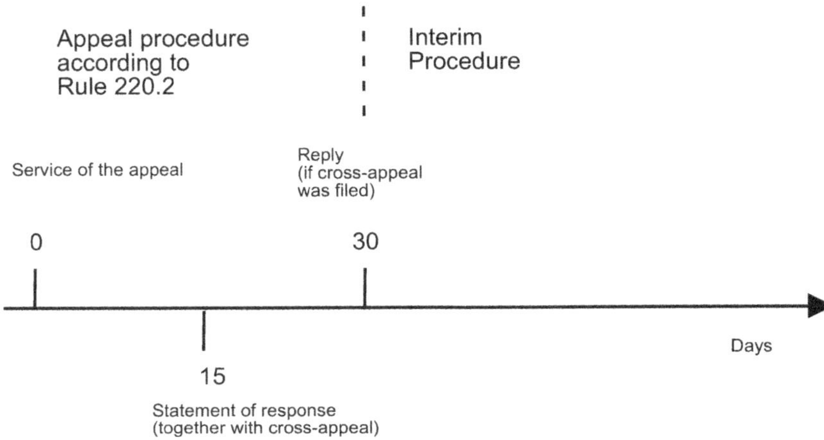

Fig. 11.3 Timeline for the appeal procedure pursuant to Rule 220.2

6. Further Course of the Proceeding

1137 Just like in the written procedure during the first instance proceeding (see Para. 844), the judge-rapporteur will set a date and time for the interim conference as well as a date and alternative date for the oral hearing. A notice period of at least two months must be given in the summons for an appeal not requiring leave from the Court of First Instance (Para. 1141).

II. Referrals to the Full Court

1138 When a proceeding is of exceptional importance and the decision taken on appeal in the proceeding could affect the consistency and unity of the case law of the Court, the relevant first instance panel, upon the proposal of its presiding judge, may refer the matter to the Full Court (Article 21 of the Statute of the Unified Patent Court, as well as Rule 238A). This is analogous to the practice under German law and US law, where a case may be referred, respectively, to the Grand Panel of the German Federal Court of Justice (BGH)[6] or to the US Court of Appeals for the Federal Circuit (CAFC).[7]

1139 This "Full Court" must comprise the President of the Court of Appeal and no fewer than ten judges of the Court of Appeal to represent the initial two panels of the Court

6 Cf. Section 132 of the German Courts Constitution Act (GVG). Note however that the Grand Panel of the BGH will only decide points of law, while the UPC's Full Court will take a decision on the merits.

7 This is an *en banc* proceeding where all judges take part in the decision; this differs from the UPC's Court of Appeals, where not all judges take part; see the discussion below.

of Appeal. In the event that the Court of Appeal has more than two panels, the Full Court will increase by five judges for each additional panel. Decisions will be taken by no less than a three-quarters majority of the judges of the Full Court.

If the Full Court becomes involved, then it will take the place of the concerned panel of first instance. The oral hearing, for example, would thus be conducted by the presiding judge of the Full Court and not by the presiding judge of the panel of first instance. 1140

III. Interim Procedure and Oral Hearing

The interim procedure and oral hearing of the appeal proceeding will essentially correspond to their counterparts in the first instance proceeding (see Para. 871 et seqq.). The following peculiarities bear noting, however (Rule 239 and Rule 240): 1141

- Insofar as the appeal proceeding is not being expedited, the summons to an oral hearing for an appeal not requiring leave must give a notice period of at least two months;
- Appeal proceedings against cost decisions will be conducted by the standing judge rather than by the presiding judge.

G. Decisions of the Court of Appeals

Decisions of the Court of Appeals are final and conclusive – except in those rare cases where they are changed by virtue of a re-trial proceeding (see Para. 1261 et seqq.) The Court of Appeal will enjoy wide discretionary leeway. In particular, it may fully adjudicate the action or refer all or part of the action back to the Court of First Instance, but only in exceptional circumstances (Rule 242). So far a referral back occured when the Court of First Instance had declared itself not competent and thus the case had not really started yet[8] or has decided in a wrong composition of the panel.[9] Otherwise it has decided fully on the case.[10] 1142

If the action is referred back to the Court of First Instance, then the Court of Appeal may decide whether the same first instance panel or some other panel is to deal further with the action. It goes without saying that the first instance panel will be bound by the decision and *ratio decidendi* of the Court of Appeals (Rule 243). 1143

Besides issuing a decision on the merits, the Court of Appeal will also take a decision on costs (Rule 242.1). 1144

8 Cf. UPC_CFI_559935/2023 (LD Hamburg), Order of 17 November 2023 – Fives v. Reel, overturned by UPC_CoA_30/2024, Order of 16 January 2025 – Fives v. Reel or UPC_CFI_214/2023 (LD Helsinki), Decision of 20 October 2023 – AIM v. Supponor, overturned by UPC_CoA_489/2023, Decision of 12 November 2024 – AIM v. Supponor.

9 UPC_CoA_233/2025, Order of 4 June 2025 – Hybridgenerator v. HGSystem.

10 UPC_CoA_302/2025, Decision of 17 February – Rematic v. Europe Forestry.

Chapter 12: Strategic Considerations for Appeals

Contents

1145 When examining the strategic considerations relevant to appeals, we should first distinguish between two separate scenarios: appeals during an ongoing proceeding and appeals against final decisions.

A. Appeals During Ongoing Proceedings?

1146 In contrast to most proceedings in Europe, proceedings before the Unified Patent Court feature the option to lodge one or more appeals even while the proceeding is still ongoing. In principle, such appeals can be used to contest practically any decision. The author, for his part, knows of no legal system in which the litigating parties enjoy such freedom of appeal.

1147 In actual practice, however, most decisions in an ongoing proceeding before the Unified Patent Court will be made by the judge-rapporteur. It follows that these decisions will first have to be referred to the relevant first instance panel. Only if the panel upholds the decision of the judge-rapporteur will the way to the Court of Appeal be open, if only through an application for discretionary review.

1148 The instrument of appeal should certainly be used during an ongoing proceeding, particularly in the first years of the Unified Patent Court's existence. While this may not exactly be welcomed in many cases, it is unlikely to be seen in an overly negative light by the first instance panel, given that the appeal process can facilitate its decision-making and help prevent uncertainties. It fits into this picture that at least initially the panels allowed an appeal in almost all cases.

1149 What also bears noting here is that even after the increase in fees exceptionally low amount of the 1,300 € application fee which must be paid to have the first instance panel review a decision of the judge-rapporteur and of the 1,300 € fee for "an appeal against refusal of leave to appeal." Although an appeal for which leave has been granted by the Court of First Instance does cost 4,000 €, even this is a decidedly modest amount.

1150 All these factors are arguments in favor of exploiting the available appeal instruments during an ongoing proceeding – particularly in connection with preliminary injunction proceedings, since this can help harmonize the procedures used by the divisions (see Para. 1421).

B. Appeals Against Final Decisions?

The other question to examine, of course, is whether a final decision by the Court of First Instance should be appealed. After all, a salient feature of any established and smoothly functioning patent system is that its appeals ratio will tend to be low, since a party which loses a case will have to proceed on the premise that the court of next instance is unlikely to change the lower court's verdict. Take the Higher District Court (*Oberlandesgericht*) of Düsseldorf, for example; The percentage of final decisions by the District Court (*Landgericht*) which end up being examined on appeal here only ranges in the low double digits. **1151**

It is both desirable and probable that the Unified Patent Court will establish its own stable and consistent body of case law relatively soon. But this is not certain and cannot be expected to happen right away. Thus, the litigating parties will be well advised to lodge appeals against adverse final decisions so long as they see even a slim chance of success. **1152**

C. Strategies for the Appeal Proceeding

I. Should a Cross-Claim Be Brought?

This would seem to be the logical step to take, since the Court would otherwise only adjudicate the applications/requests of the opposing side. **1153**

II. Should Suspensive Effect of the Appeal Be Applied For?

Here, too, the answer is an unqualified "yes," particularly in patent-infringement cases where the infringer has been convicted in the first instance. The application for suspensive effect should also contain an express request that the preliminary enforceability of the first-instance decision be set aside. It must be noted, however, that chances of success in appeals where the appeal must be allowed (Para. 1045 et seqq.) or in preliminary injunction proceedings are moderate at best.[1] **1154**

We should also recall the observations of *Meier-Beck*[2] regarding a split-off of the revocation counterclaim proceeding from the infringement proceeding without suspensive effect: **1155**

> "Even the best-case scenario for a plaintiff in a first-instance proceeding – i.e. having his action heard without an examination of patentability and without any suspension – will not necessarily work to his benefit. Namely if the action is not deemed to be provisionally enforceable, or if its provisional enforceability pursuant to Article 74 is set aside by the Court of Appeal – an objective which is most definitely worth pursuing. In an appeal, the issues of patentability and infringement will invariably be examined together in a single proceeding. If it should come to that, then this would mean that splitting the two actions

---

1 Cf. UPC_CoA_301/2024, Order of 19 June 2024, APL_33746/2024 – ICPillar v. ARM or UPC_CoA_542/2025, Order of 26 June 2025 – Easee v. Visibly.

2 *Meier-Beck*, GRUR 2014, pp. 144–148.

would ultimately work to the detriment of the plaintiff as well, given the time delay involved."

III. Organizational Aspects

1156 As already mentioned earlier (see Para. 683 et seqq.), the Court of Appeals will be able to refuse the introduction of new factual pleadings into an appeal proceeding if it deems them to come too late, although the Court must also consider the new pleading's relevance, amongst other things.

1157 Here, the wording of the Rules of Procedure more or less reflects the practice followed in years past by the Boards of Appeal of the European Patent Office[3] as well as the current German practice following the revision of the appeal procedures in revocation actions.[4]

1158 Notwithstanding the foregoing, the parties will be advised to introduce all of their applications/requests, facts and evidence into the proceedings as early as they can – and already before the Court of First Instance, if at all possible.

1159 The written procedure in an appeal proceeding will be even shorter than in the first instance proceeding. According to the Rules, each side will only be allowed one submission. This means that the appellant will essentially be able to submit nothing more than his Statement of Grounds of Appeal, unless the opposing side lodges a cross-appeal. Thus, submitting fully elaborated argumentation will be even more important than in the first instance. But even if the other side does lodge a cross-appeal, the appellant will be expected to limit his Reply exclusively to the arguments raised in the cross-appeal, i.e. he will not be able to use the Reply to shore up his own appeal, much less extend it.

1160 The Court of Appeal has, as discussed earlier (Para. 1142), the option to refer a case back to the first instance. However, so far a referral back occured only when the Court of First Instance had declared itself not competent and thus the case had not really started yet[5] or has decided in a wrong composition of the panel.[6] Otherwise it has decided fully on the case.[7]

---

3 For the more formal practice followed recently, see e.g. *Anetsberger* et al., epi-information 2015, p. 63; for a highly critical view, see e.g. *Wallinger*, VPP-Rundbrief 2015, p. 18; a statistical survey of the complaint proceedings may be found in *Nollen*, epi information 2015, p. 17.

4 See e.g. *Meier-Beck*, VPP-Rundbrief 2013, p. 99; also cf. *Bacher*, GRUR 2021, p. 134.

5 See UPC_CFI_559935/2023 (LD Hamburg), Order of 17 November 2023 – Fives v. Reel, overturned by UPC_CoA_30/2024, Order of 16 January 2025 – Fives v. Reel or UPC_CFI_214/2023 (LD Helsinki), Decision of 20 October 2023 – AIM v. Supponor, overturned by UPC_CoA_489/2023,Decision of 12 November 2024 – AIM v. Supponor.

6 UPC_CoA_233/2025, Order of 4 June 2025 – Hybridgenerator v. HGSystem.

7 UPC_CoA_302/2025, Decision of 17 February – Rematic v. Europe Forestry.

Section 5: Other Types of Proceedings

Chapter 13: Description of Other Types of Proceedings

Contents Para

This chapter will discuss the other types of proceedings that can be conducted before the Unified Patent Court. These proceedings will be examined in detail only to the extent that they differ from an infringement proceeding. In all other respects, the Rules of Procedure applicable to infringement proceedings, as described in Chapter 9, will apply here as well. This approach is also in line with the Rules of Procedure, since many of the Rules applicable to the types of proceedings covered in this chapter consist entirely of references. 1161

A. Revocation Actions

Besides a counterclaim for revocation (see Para. 835 et seqq.), one also has the possibility of bringing a revocation action before the Unified Patent Court. In principle, this proceeding will be conducted before the central division, but there are two exceptions: 1162

- If the parties have agreed in advance to resort to a different jurisdiction, as provided for under Article 33(7) of the UPC Agreement, then the action could of course also be brought before a local division. But since this will probably not apply in the vast majority of cases, this last option will not be discussed further.

– If a revocation action is brought during an ongoing infringement proceeding – i.e. against the patent in dispute by the defendant of the infringement action – then it is to be lodged with the respective division which is handling the infringement action (Art. 33 (4) of the UPC Agreement).[1]

1163 As also applies under German law, the revocation action is to be directed not against the patent itself but rather against the patent's proprietor(s).[2] The proprietor(s) in turn will able to mount a defense by lodging a counterclaim for infringement. But since the original action is already directed against the proprietor(s), there can never be three parties in a revocation action, unlike in an infringement proceeding (see Para. 838 et seqq.).

I. Lodging the Statement for Revocation

1164 The written procedure is governed by Rules 44 et seqq. The requirements for lodging the Statement of Revocation correspond *mutatis mutandis* to those for the Statement of Claim in an infringement action (see Para. 815 et seqq.). Thus, the revocation action must contain, inter alia:

– the names and postal/electronic addresses of the parties and their representatives;
– an indication of the extent to which revocation of the patent is requested;
– one or more grounds for revocation;
– an indication of the facts relied on;
– the evidence relied on (where available), and an indication of any further evidence which will be offered in support;
– an indication of any order the claimant will seek during the interim procedure; and
– a list of the documents, including any witness statements, referred to in the Statement for Revocation, together with any request that all or part of any such document need not be translated.

1165 The court fee for a revocation action will amount to 26,500 € regardless of the value of the action.

1. Entitlement to Bring the Action; Language Used

1166 The action is to be lodged in the language of the patent (Rule 45). The question of entitlement to bring legal action has already been discussed (see Para. 646 et seqq.).

2. Partial Challenge to the Disputed Patent

1167 It is also possible to challenge only a part of a patent with a revocation action. What bears noting here: The principle of *ex officio* investigations by the court does not apply

1 Vgl. UPC_CFI_238/2024 (LD Paris), Order of 24 January 2025 – Photon Wave v. Seoul Viosus.

2 Note: For the sake of clarity, the term "proprietor" will be used in the singular only throughout the rest of this chapter.

before the UPC. Thus, when a patent is only partially challenged in a revocation action, it follows that the revocation action will be automatically terminated if the patent proprietor limits himself to just the non-challenged portion of the patent during the proceeding (see Para. 765 et seqq.) In this case, the Court could dispose of the action for lack of a need to adjudicate pursuant to Rule 360. What still remains unclear is whether – by analogy to the established legal precedent of the German High Court (BGH)[3] – it would then become impermissible to include the non-challenged part of the patent (even only as alternatives) in a newly submitted set of claims.

Furthermore it is also possible to limit a nullity action to one or more member states.[4] 1168

II. Course of the Proceeding

As the defendant, the patent proprietor will now have one month to lodge a Preliminary Objection (Rule 48). 1169

In addition, he will have two months' time – just like in a revocation counterclaim in infringement proceedings (see Para. 853) – to lodge a Defense to Revocation in which he may amend the patent (also on an alternative basis), whereby the regulations governing the revocation counterclaim will apply *mutatis mutandis*. Any additional amendments will require the permission from the Court. As already mentioned earlier (Para. 1167), it remains unclear whether – by analogy to the established legal precedent of the German High Court (BGH)[5] – it would then become impermissible to include a non-challenged portion of the patent (even simply as an alternative) in a newly submitted set of claims. 1170

Just as in a counterclaim in an infringement proceeding (see Para. 854 et seqq.), a patent proprietor wishing to submit amended claims must provide an explanation as to why these fulfill the requirements of Articles 84, 123(2) and 123(3) of the European Patent Convention (Rule 50). 1171

The patent proprietor may also lodge a counterclaim for infringement along with his Defense to Revocation. He will have to pay a court fee contingent on the value of the action for this purpose (Rule 50.3). Both proceedings will then be adjudicated by the central division. 1172

The revocation plaintiff will at this point have two months to lodge his Reply to the Defense to Revocation, both for the revocation action as well as for a possible infringement counterclaim (Rule 51). 1173

The patent proprietor will now have one month to submit his Rejoinder to the Reply to the Defense to Revocation. Just as in the infringement proceeding, he will be 1174

3 See e.g. Ruling of the German Federal Court of Justice (BGH) No. X ZR 10/15 in the *Ankopplungssystem* case, Mitt. 2017, p. 262.

4 UPC CFI 198/2024 (CD Paris), Decision of 28 May 2025 – Aylo v. Dish.

5 See e.g. Ruling of the German Federal Court of Justice (BGH) No. X ZR 10/15 in the *Ankopplungssystem* case, Mitt. 2017, p. 262.

obligated to limit himself to the matters raised in the Reply. If the patent proprietor neither amends his patent nor lodges an infringement counterclaim, then the written procedure will end here (Rules 52 and 56).

1175 Assuming the patent proprietor either amends the patent and/or lodges an infringement counterclaim – whereby the first of the two will almost always occur – the revocation plaintiff (who would also be the defendant in any infringement counterclaim proceeding) would then have one month to lodge his final Rejoinder, just as in an infringement proceeding. Here again, he would have to limit himself to the matters raised in the patent proprietor's Rejoinder (Rules 52 and 56).

1176 The resulting timeline is shown below:

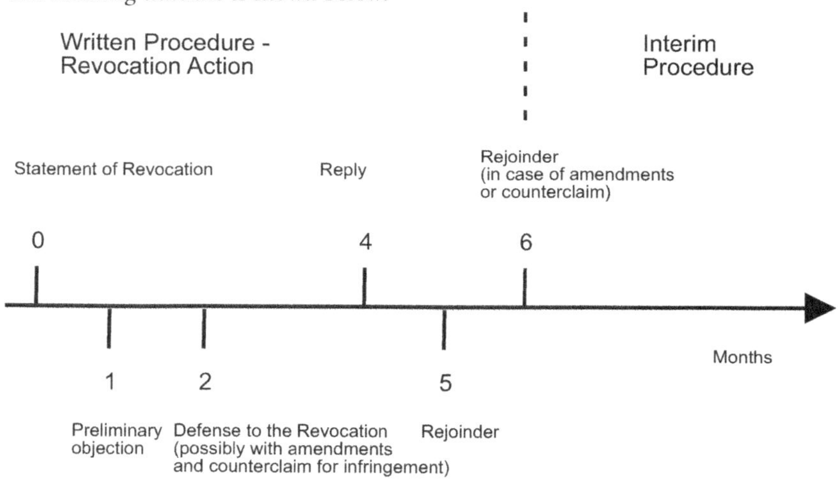

Fig. 13.1 Timeline of a Revocation Action

1177 The written procedure will be followed by the interim procedure and the oral hearing, just as in an infringement proceeding (see Chapter 9, Para. 871 et seqq.). the allocation of a technical judge is possible in this context, but not mandatory (Rule 57) – however, it is common practice.

III. Revocation Actions in Parallel with Infringement Proceedings

1178 A patent proprietor will of course be free to lodge a "normal" infringement action before a local division instead of bringing a counterclaim for infringement.[6] In such case, the defendant in the infringement proceeding, i.e. the plaintiff in the revoca-

6 Note: This is the exact reverse of the situation where a revocation action is lodged during an ongoing infringement proceeding.

tion action, would have the option of lodging a counterclaim for revocation, i.e. the patent would be challenged twice.

In order to avoid such duplicate proceedings, Rule 75 was adopted. Thus, unless the parties have agreed on some other arrangement, the first instance panel of the central division competent for the revocation action is to stay the case pending before central division if the following conditions are met: 1179
- a revocation action was lodged before the central division;
- the patent proprietor then proceeded to lodge an infringement action before a local division against the revocation plaintiff; and
- the revocation plaintiff, for his part, proceeded to lodge a counterclaim for revocation; and
- the first instance panel of the local division decided not to transfer the case to the central division.

It remains to be seen whether the above will become the customary practice, or whether it will be more usual for the local division to split the proceedings. The latter would certainly be a logical option for the local division, since the central division will already have acquired a familiarity with the patent that it would not have in a normal infringement action. So it is no surprise that this has happened in analagous scenarios already.[7] 1180

If the defendant of the infringement proceeding (i.e. the plaintiff of the revocation action) decides not to lodge a revocation counterclaim, then the local division will have the option to either issue conditional final decisions in the matter or to await the outcome of the revocation action. 1181

IV. Revocation Actions and Parallel Opposition or Limitation Proceedings

In principle, an opposition proceeding before the European Patent Office will not take any priority before a revocation action before the Unified Patent Court – unlike in Germany, for example.[8] 1182

If an opposition proceeding is brought before the European Patent Office against a European patent while a parallel revocation action is brought before the Unified Patent Court, this will not automatically serve to suspend or invalidate either one of these proceedings. 1183

7 For example, in the dispute between Edwards Lifescience and Meril, see UPC_CFI_255/2023 (CD Paris) ACT_551308/2023 – decision of July 19, 2024, Edwards v. Meril, the parallel infringement action had been filed before the Munich Local Division (UPC_CFI_15/2023).

8 Note: The fact that opposition proceedings before the EPO enjoy prior rank under German law is regarded by *Marsnik* as a reason for the relatively high number of opposition proceedings launched from Germany; see *Marsnik*, "Will the 'America Invents Act' Post-Grant Review Improve the Quality of Patents? A Comparison with the European Patent Office Opposition."

1184 The Unified Patent Court may ask the European Patent office to expedite the opposition proceeding, however (Rule 298). Whether it does so or not, it may also suspend its own proceeding until a decision is reached (Rules 298 and 295), however this is not common practice currently.

1185 There is no provision to regulate a situation where a revocation action before the UPC runs in parallel with a limitation proceeding before the European Patent Office. It is obvious, however, that such a limitation proceeding will not necessary entail any amendment of claim.

1186 The Unified Patent Court will likewise be able to terminate the proceeding pursuant to Rule 360 if the patent has been challenged only in part and the patent proprietor has limited himself to that part of the patent which was not covered by the action.

B. Actions for Declaration of Non-Infringement

1187 Besides lodging a revocation action against a patent, is it also possible to bring an action for declaration of non-infringement (action for declaration of non-infringement) before the central division.[9] An action for declaration of non-infringement may also be lodged together with a revocation action (Rule 77).

1188 Bringing an action for negative declaratory judgement is only possible if the patent proprietor has given cause for the action. According to Rule 61, this specifically means that:

- the patent proprietor or a licensee entitled to bring infringement action pursuant to Article 47 of the UPC Agreement has asserted vis-à-vis the plaintiff that a certain act constitutes an infringement (e.g. the sale or offering of a product); or
- the plaintiff has explained the act in all its particulars to the patent proprietor or to the licensee entitled to bring infringement action and has asked for a written acknowledgement of non-infringement, but the patent proprietor or licensee has failed or refused to issue such acknowledgement within one month's time.

1189 What has not yet been clearly regulated is whether an entitlement enquiry – i.e. a simple communication referring to the patent and asking why the addressee feels entitled to ignore it – will suffice for purposes of lodging an action for declaration of non-infringement in the first of the two aforementioned cases. Or whether a formal cease-and-desist letter will be required instead, i.e. one which sets a deadline, demands that the infringement be discontinued, and warns of legal action in the event of non-compliance. This said, the use of the word "assert" in Rule 61 suggests that an entitlement enquiry will not be sufficient. Consider that under the legal precedent of courts in Germany, for example, such an enquiry merely serves to launch a discussion.[10]

9 As in a revocation action, here, too, the parties may agree on a jurisdiction pursuant to Article 33(7) of the UPCA. This is unlikely to play a significant role in practice, however, and will thus not be discussed further.

10 Cf. Higher DistrictCourt (OLG) of Munich, Mitt. 1998, p. 117.

Another point that remains unregulated is whether a patent infringement must be asserted directly against the plaintiff in the first of the two aforementioned cases. Or whether representations made vis-à-vis third parties (such as customers) might also be deemed sufficient (even though this would contravene the Rule's actual wording). If not, then a plaintiff who has observed that the patent proprietor had merely written to his customers would have to directly contact the patent proprietor or the licensee entitled to bring action in order to seek an acknowledgement of non-infringement, as stipulated in the second alternative of Rule 61. 1190

I. Lodging the Statement for a Declaration of Non-Infringement

The written procedure for the proceeding is governed by Rules 62 et seqq. The requirements for the Statement for a Declaration of Non-Infringement correspond, *mutatis mutandis*, to those applicable for revocation actions or infringement actions. Thus, the Statement for a Declaration of Non-Infringement must contain the following, inter alia: 1191
- the names and postal/electronic addresses of the parties and their representatives, the court of jurisdiction involved, as well as an indication of whether the action is to be heard by a single judge;
- an indication that entitlement to bring the action (see above) is given;
- the declaration which the claimant is seeking;
- the factual circumstances of the matter, as well as the reasons why an actual or intended action of the plaintiff would not constitute an infringement of the disputed patent(s);
- the evidence, where available, or an indication of the supporting evidence that will be offered;
- an indication of any order the claimant will seek during the interim conference; and
- a list of the documents, including any witness statements, referred to in the Statement for Declaration of Non-Infringement, together with any request that all or part of any such document need not be translated.
- an indication of the value of the action.

In addition, a court fee contingent on the value of the action will fall due (see Para. 429 et seqq.) 1192

II. Written Procedure

The further course of the written procedure in an action for negative declaratory judgement will be same as for the other types of proceedings discussed thus far, i.e. each side will be allowed to submit two written pleadings. But the time limits for this will be even shorter (than in the infringement proceeding, for example). 1193

The defendant will have two months' time to make his Reply to the Statement for a Declaration of Non-Infringement (Rule 67), whereby he may of course also lodge a Preliminary Objection within one month's time. 1194

1195 After that, the plaintiff will have one month to submit a Reply (Rule 69), whereupon the defendant will have one month to issue a final rejoinder. The defendant's final rejoinder must be limited to the matters raised in the Reply of the plaintiff.

1196 This sequence is shown on the timeline below:

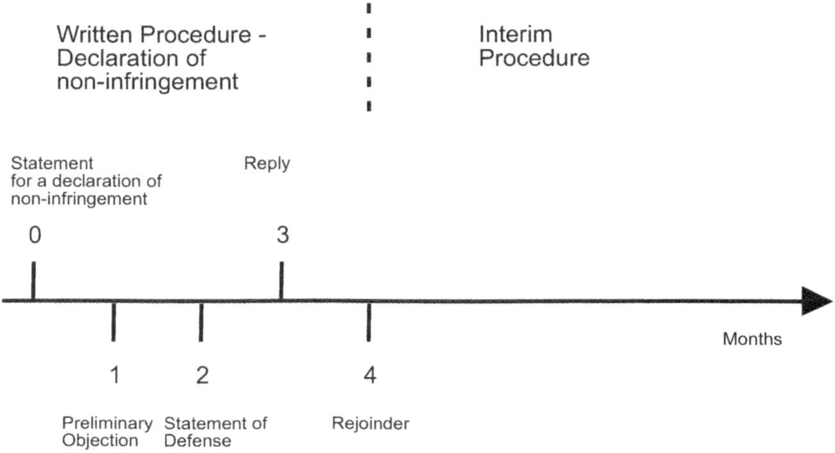

Fig. 13.2 Timeline of a declaration of non-infringement action

1197 The written procedure will then be followed by the interim procedure and oral hearing, just like in an infringement proceeding (see Chapter 9, Para. 871 et seqq.)

III. Retroactively Lodged Infringements Actions

1198 According to Article 33(6) of the UPC Agreement, an action for declaration of non-infringement is to be suspended if the defendant of the action lodges a patent infringement action against the plaintiff for the same subject matter as the action for declaration of non-infringement (i.e. the patent and its infringement) within three months after the action for declaration of non-infringement was lodged.

▶ Example:

1199 On 10 January 2029, an action for declaration of non-infringement is brought before the central division. On 23 March 2029, the defendant brings a patent infringement action against the plaintiff before the local division in Düsseldorf based on the same patent and the same legal dispute. As a result, the action for declaration of non-infringement will be suspended and only the patent infringement action will be continued.

1200 According to Rule 76, fulfillment of the preconditions will be verified by the Registry. If all is in order, the Registry will inform the president of the Court of First Instance, as well as the presiding judges of the two divisions concerned, that the action for declaration of non-infringement is to be suspended (Rules 70 and 71).

If the patent infringement action is brought more than three months after the lodging date of the action for declaration of non-infringement, then the latter will not be automatically suspended. Instead, the presiding judges of the two divisions concerned are to consult and reach agreement on suspending one of the two proceedings (Rule 76.3). **1201**

C. Actions Against Decisions of the European Patent Office

As mentioned earlier (Chapter 3, Para. 132), it is possible to bring action against decisions taken by the European Patent Office in connection with Unitary Patents, or to apply to have such decisions annulled. It bears noting right at the outset that each side in such a proceeding must bear its own costs (Rule 98), and that the obligation to be represented pursuant to Article 48 of the UPC Agreement will not apply (Article 48 (7) (see Para. 737). The corresponding proceeding will take place before the central division (Article 33 (9)). **1202**

I. Application to Annul an EPO Decision to Refuse Unitary Effect

An Application for Annulment may be lodged against a decision by the European Patent Office to refuse to validate a patent as a unitary patent or, to be more exact, to refuse the request for unitary effect (see Para. 134 et seqq.) A narrow time frame was provided for this so that if the Application for Annulment is refused, the patent proprietor will still have time to pursue any additional national validations he may deem necessary. **1203**

▶ Practical Tip:

The time limit for lodging an Application for Annulment is one month after publication of the decision refusing validation of the Unitary Patent. The time limit for national validation, on the other hand, is three months (see Para. 135). This is intended to ensure that, if the request for a unitary patent is refused, the Unified Patent Court will perform its review of the Application for Annulment of the decision quickly enough to still give the patent proprietor time to validate on the national level as an emergency workaround.[11] A "precautionary double validation" is not possible, on the other hand. Inasmuch, the patent proprietor should probably consider breaking off the proceedings and validating directly on the national level if he comes under time pressure. **1204**

The Application for Annulment (Rule 97) of an EPO decision refusing unitary effect must be lodged with the Registry within three weeks of service of the EPO's decision **1205**

11 Cf. the editorial comments in the previous versions of the Rules of Procedure, e.g. in the 16th and 17th versions.

in the language of the patent. It must contain the following (Rule 97.2 as read in conjunction with Rule 88):
- the names/postal/electronic addresses of the applicant and his representative;
- the decision of the European Patent Office which is to be annulled;
- an indication of whether a single judge is to adjudicate the matter;[12] and
- the factual circumstances and the evidence and the arguments relied on.

1206 A fee of 1,300 € will also be payable.

1207 The Registry will then assign the Application for Annulment to the standing judge of the central division. He may ask the President of the European Patent Office to issue an opinion, but should in any case decide the application within three of weeks of its receipt.

1208 The decision taken on the Application for Annulment may be appealed by the applicant or by the President of the European Patent Office within three weeks of the decision's date of service. The Statement of Appeal should contain the same information for the original application listed above plus an explanation of the reasons why the decision in the first instance should be set aside.

1209 Assuming the formal requirements have been met, the Registry will assign the matter to the standing judge of the Court of Appeal, who may invite the opposing side to submit its comments. In any case, he should decide the matter within three weeks' time.

II. Actions Against the European Patent Office

1210 It is also possible to bring an action to annul or alter a decision of the European Patent Office on the following grounds (Rule 87):
- infringement of Regulation (EU) No 1257/2012 or of Regulation (EU) No 1260/2012 or of any rule of law relating to their application;
- infringement of an essential procedural requirement;
- misuse of power.

1211 A corresponding Application to Alter or Annul a Decision of the Office is to be lodged in the language of the patent within two months of the date of service of the decision. The application must contain the same information as the above-discussed Application for Annulment of a Decision to Refuse Unitary Effect (Para. 1203 et seqq.), i.e.
- the name and addresses of the claimant and his representative(s); the obligation to have a representative pursuant to Article 48 will be set aside in this case (Para. 737);
- an indication of the decision of the European Patent Office being contested;
- an indication of whether a single judge should adjudicate the matter;
- the factual circumstances, and the evidence and arguments relied upon;

12 This is a reference Rule 88.2(f). But given that the standing judge decides the application, could this be an editorial error?

It must also contain the following supplemental information:

- if the plaintiff is not the proprietor of the patent, declarations and evidence showing that he is adversely affected by the European Patent Office's decision and that he is entitled to bring legal action;
- if applicable, information on any earlier or still ongoing proceedings over the patent concerned before the Court, the European Patent Office or other courts or authorities;
- the order or legal remedy requested by the claimant;
- one or more grounds for annulling or altering the contested decision; as well as
- a list of all documents, including witness statements, referred to in the Application, together with any request that all or part of any such document need not be translated.

A fee in the amount of 1,300 € will also be payable. **1212**

The Registry will then examine the Application to Annul or Alter a Decision of the Office as to the formal requirements. If deficiencies are found, it will issue a deficiency notice giving a grace period of 14 days in which to correct (Rule 89). In case of a failure to correct or to duly pay the court fee, the Registry will inform the President of the Court of First Instance, who may reject the action as inadmissible through a decision by default pursuant to Rule 355. He may give the claimant an opportunity to be heard beforehand. **1213**

If the action meets all the requirements, then the Registry will record a file in the Register and assign an action number to the file. The Registry will then inform both the applicant and European Patent Office accordingly. (Rule 90). **1214**

The European Patent Office will now have two months' time following receipt of the Application in which to rectify its decision (interlocutory revision) (Rule 91). If this is done, the Unified Patent Court will also have the option of ordering reimbursement of the fee paid for the action. **1215**

If no rectification of the decision occurs, then the matter will be referred to a first instance panel of the central division or the standing judge, who will than act as judge-rapporteur (Rule 92). **1216**

While examining the matter, the judge-rapporteur may invite the claimant to submit additional comments or written pleadings within a specific time limit (Rule 93). He may also invite the President of the European Patent Office to contribute comments in writing (Rule 94). **1217**

An oral hearing is not mandatory, unlike in other proceedings. But the judge-rapporteur may order an oral hearing upon his own motion or invite the plaintiff to state whether he wishes to have an oral hearing (Rule 95). If no oral hearing takes place, then the decision will be taken on the merits of the pleadings and evidence submitted up to that point (Rule 96). **1218**

The decision may be contested through an appeal for which the normal procedural rules will apply (see Chapter 11, Para. 1098 et seqq.). **1219**

D. Intervention Proceedings

1220 It is possible to intervene before the Unified Patent Court, both actively, i.e. based on an application, or passively, i.e. upon the invitation of the Court. Although this is not really an action proceeding as such, it still seems purposeful to discuss it in this chapter.

I. Intervention Upon Application

1221 A third person not party to a proceeding before the Unified Patent Court may nonetheless apply to join the proceedings as intervenor on the basis of an application if it has a legal interest in the outcome (Rule 313) – for example, because the third person is the proprietor of a patent on whose basis a licensee has brought legal action or because he is the supplier or customer of one of the litigating parties.

1222 To be admissible, an application to intervene must:
- be made in support, in whole or in part, of a claim, order or remedy sought by one of the parties;
- be lodged before closure of the written procedure.

1223 The Unified Patent Court will be free to admit the application upon its own discretion even if the above preconditions have not been met. (Rule 313.2).

1224 The intervenor must be represented just like a normal litigating party. The application must contain the following (Rule 313):
- a reference to the action number of the file recorded for the proceeding before the Court;
- the names/postal/electronic addresses of the intervenor and his representative;
- the claim, order or remedy in support of which intervention is sought by the intervener; and
- a statement of the facts establishing the right to intervene.

1225 The judge-rapporteur will give the parties an opportunity to be heard and will then issue a decision by way of an order (Rule 314). An order to refuse the intervention is not appealable (Rule 317).

1226 If the intervention is admitted, the parties will be informed and the intervenor will be given a time limit in which to lodge a Statement in Intervention. The Registry of the Unified Patent Court will furthermore provide the intervenor with all the written pleadings submitted in the proceedings, whereby the Court may order that all or part of a specific written pleading be disclosed only to certain persons and under appropriate terms of confidentiality.

1227 The Statement in Intervention must contain the following (Rule 315):
- a statement as to the issues involving the intervener and one or more of the parties, and their connection to the matters in dispute;
- the arguments of law, facts and evidence relied on.

1228 The intervenor will thenceforth be treated as a party to the proceeding unless otherwise ordered by the Court (Rule 315.4). However, the intervenor is bound to the parties insofar as when the parties settle or the action is withdrawn then – unlike in Germany – the intervenor cannot continue on his own motion or file an appeal separately.[13](Of course then he is not bound by the outcome of the case)

II. Intervention Upon Invitation by the Court

It is also possible for the Unified Patent Court to invite a third person who is not party to the proceeding to accede as intervenor. This may occur upon the judge-rapporteur's own discretion, whereby he must first give the parties a hearing, or upon the reasoned request of a party. 1229

The intervention may also be forced, i.e. the Court may issue a compulsory third-party notice. In this case, a party to the proceeding must provide a reasoned explanation of why the third person should be bound by the decision taken in the action even if he refuses to intervene. 1230

Course of the Forced Intervention Proceeding

As a first step, the judge-rapporteur will invite the third person to intervene in the proceeding within one month of being served with the compulsory third-party notice. If the forced intervention has been requested by one of the parties, then the invitation to intervene should include the reasons relied upon, as well as a statement to the effect that the third person will be bound by the decision taken in the action even if he does not intervene. 1231

If the third person agrees to intervene, he must present his application to intervene within one month of service of the invitation, and must submit his Statement in Intervention within a further time period to be specified by the judge-rapporteur or the presiding judge, whereby the aforementioned provisions will apply (Rule 316). He will then become an intervenor and will be bound to the decision taken in the action. 1232

If the third person does not agree to intervene, he may contend that he should not be bound by the decision taken in the action. He must then lodge a statement to that effect within one month of receiving the invitation to intervene. 1233

If the third person does not lodge such a statement, then he will be bound by the decision in the action and will not be able to argue that the decision taken in the action was wrong or that the party requesting the intervention did not properly conduct the proceeding leading up to the decision. 1234

But if the statement is received within the time limit, then the Court will decide the issue after hearing the parties as well as the third person. If the Court decides that the third person who was invited to intervene is to be bound by the decision notwithstanding his statement to the contrary, then that third person will have one month's time following service of the Court's decision in which to present an application to intervene. 1235

13 UPC_CoA_70/2025, Decision of 27 November 2025 – Strabag v. Swarco.

1236 The resulting sequence of steps is shown in the flowchart below:

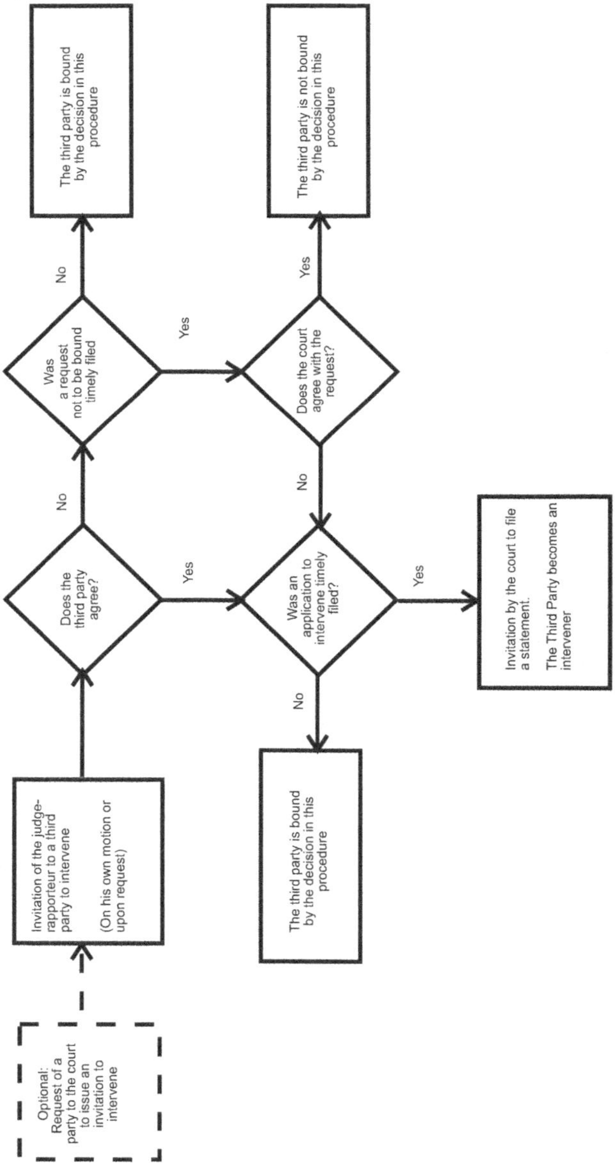

Fig. 13.3 Flowdiagram of initiating an intervention

Recovery of Costs

In principle, an intervenor is eligible to recovery of costs, same as the parties. However, if the parties settle and agree that every side takes its own costs then the recovery claim runs moot.[14] **1237**

E. Legal Aid

It is possible to apply for legal aid before the Unified Patent Court. Just like the intervention proceeding, this proceeding is also not an action proceeding. It nevertheless makes sense to discuss it in this chapter. **1238**

In principle, legal aid may be obtained in any proceeding of the Unified Patent Court (Rule 375.2) and may be used to fully or partially cover the following costs (Rule 376): **1239**
- court fees;
- costs of legal assistance and representation regarding:
- pre-litigation advice with a view to reaching a settlement prior to commencing legal proceedings;
- commencing and maintaining proceedings before the Court;
- all costs relating to proceedings including the application for legal aid; and
- enforcement of decisions;
- other necessary costs related to the proceedings to be borne by a party, including costs of witnesses, experts, interpreters and translators and necessary travel, accommodation and subsistence costs of the applicant and his representative.

In theory, this could even cover the recoverable costs that would be awarded to the opposing side if it emerges victorious in the proceeding. **1240**

Legal aid can only be granted to natural persons. These do not have to be residents of a Contracting Member State, so that just about anyone is eligible. Companies and other legal entities are not eligible to receive legal aid (Article 71(1)), but do have the option of requesting an abatement of the court fees and of the costs they must reimburse in case they lose the proceeding (Para. 436). **1241**

The Administrative Committee has the option to define thresholds in this connection: **1242**
- the maximum amount of legal aid for legal assistance, which may lie below but not above the maximum thresholds for recoverable costs in a proceeding (Rule 376A); and
- the financial thresholds above which it can be assumed that an applicant is not in need of legal aid since he has the means to finance the proceeding himself. But this does not preclude the possibility that an applicant may be granted legal aid anyway if he can show that the high cost of living in the Contracting Members State in which he resides or has his regular place of sojourn prevents him from shouldering the costs of the proceeding.

14 UPC_CoA_70/2025, Decision of 27 November 2025 – Strabag v. Swarco.

I. Application for Legal Aid and Course of the Proceeding

1243 Any natural person may apply for legal aid if the following conditions are met:
- the natural person is unable to shoulder all or some of the costs of a proceeding before the Unified Patent Court due to his financial situation; and
- the action for which legal is being requested has prospects for success.

1244 The initial application for legal aid will be valid for the first-instance proceeding only. In the event of an appeal, a new application will have to be lodged (Rule 378.4).

1245 The application must be formulated in a language of a Contracting Member State and must contain the following (Rule 378):
- the name and postal/electronic addresses of the applicant and, if applicable, the person authorized to accept service;
- the name of the opposing party and the postal/electronic addresses for service on the other party insofar as available;
- the action number of the action in respect of which the application is made or, where the application is lodged before the action has been brought, a brief description of the action;
- an indication of the value of the action and the costs to be covered by legal aid;
- an indication of the applicant's financial resources; and
- where appropriate, a reasoned request for suspension of a time limit which would otherwise need to be observed until the date of notification of the order deciding on legal aid.

1246 To be provided in addition: evidence of the applicant's family situation and, where the application is lodged before the action has been brought, an indication of the evidence in support of the action.

1247 The Registry will examine the formal admissibility of the application for legal aid. If deficiencies are found, it will issue a deficiency notice giving a grace period of 14 days in which to correct. The application will then be decided by the judge-rapporteur of the action proceeding or, if the application is lodged before the action, by the relevant judge of the division concerned.

1248 Before the decision is taken, the opposing side must be invited to submit written observations, unless this can be waived because the application is manifestly ill-founded (Rule 379.4).

1249 If the application is refused, the reasons must be given (Rule 379.5).

1250 If the Court grants the application, the order of grant may provide for any of the following:
- a partial or total exemption from the court fees;
- an interim amount to be paid to enable the applicant and/or the representative of the applicant to meet any request of the judge-rapporteur or standing judge prior to making a final order;
- an amount to be paid to the representative of the applicant or a limit which the representative's disbursements and fees may not exceed;

– a contribution to be made by the applicant to the other costs incurred (see the listing presented earlier, Para. 1239)

If the Court has ordered another party to pay the costs of the applicant for legal aid, that other party will be required to refund to the Court any sums advanced by way of legal aid. In the event of a shortfall between the costs so ordered and the sums advanced by way of legal aid, the applicant may be required to meet such shortfall from any damages or compensation awarded by the Court, or from any sum received by way of settlement (Rule 382). 1251

II. Withdrawal of Legal Aid

The applicant must promptly inform the Patent Court about any alteration in his economic situation (Rule 379A). In the event of such an alternation during the proceedings, the Court may at any time, of his own motion or on a reasoned request by the other party, withdraw all or part of the legal aid, but only after having heard the applicant (Rule 380). 1252

The legal aid can also be fully or partially withdrawn in the following cases (Rule 380): 1253
- the applicant, by inaccurately representing the circumstances of the case, has misrepresented his prospects of success, which were determinative for the approval of assistance with Court costs; or
- the applicant has grossly negligently made false statements as to his personal or economic circumstances, or has not immediately informed the Court of a considerable improvement to his financial circumstances;
- the applicant has been in arrears for longer than three months with the payment of a monthly instalment or with the payment of any other amount.

The order to withdraw legal aid must contain the supporting reasoning. The order may also place the applicant under obligation to reimburse the Court for any amounts that were advanced to him. 1254

III. Appeals in Matters Involving Legal Aid

A decision to refuse or withdraw legal aid, either in whole or in part, may be contested by lodging an appeal within one month of the decision's date of service. It is also permissible to apply for legal aid for purposes of the appeal. 1255

F. Actions for Payment of License Fees When a Willingness to License is Given

According to Article 8 of Regulation 1257/2012 (EU), the Unified Patent Court is competent to hear actions for compensation for licenses when a willingness to license a Unitary Patent is given. 1256

This proceeding is regulated in only a single Rule of Procedure (!), namely Rule 80, which essentially refers to the damage-award proceeding, i.e. the action is to be conducted as a damage-award proceeding. 1257

1258 This said, the requirements for the Application for Appropriate Compensation correspond *mutatis mutandis* to those for a Statement of Claim in an infringement action. Thus, the Application for Appropriate Compensation must contain, inter alia:

- particulars on the parties involved; and
- information on the filing of a Statement of Willingness to License pursuant to Article 8 (1) of Regulation 1257/2012 (EU), as well as on the currently valid license agreement pursuant to Article 8 (2).

1259 A court fee contingent on the value of the action will fall due.

1260 For the further course of the proceeding, the reader is referred to the discussion of the damage-award proceeding (see Chapter 9, Para. 922 et seqq.)

G. Rehearing Proceedings

1261 Article 81 of the UPC Agreement provides for the possibility of rehearing proceedings before the Unified Patent Court. Thus, the Article states that such a proceeding is possible under two conditions:

- upon discovery of a decisively important fact which was unknown to the party requesting the rehearing (as a result of an act conclusively held to be a criminal offence by a national court); or
- in the event of a fundamental procedural defect, particularly when a party was not served with an important document.

1262 An application for a rehearing must be lodged within two months of the date of discovery of the fundamental procedural error, or within two months of the date on which the criminal offence was conclusively established by the national court through a ruling or through service of a final decision (whichever is later). The application must in any case be lodged within ten years' time at the latest (Article 81 of the UPCA and Rule 245).

1263 A fundamental procedural error could consist of the following, for example:

- a judge of the Court took part in a decision in breach of Article 17 of the UPC Agreement or Article 7 of the UPC Statute (Judicial Independence and Impartiality);
- a person not appointed as a judge of the Court sat on the panel which took the final decision;
- the decision was made without deciding on a request relevant to that decision; or
- a breach of Article 6 of the Convention for the Protection of Human Rights and Fundamental Freedoms occurred.

1264 One of two further preconditions must be met before an application for a rehearing may be lodged on the grounds of a fundamental procedural error:

- an objection regarding the fundamental procedural error was already raised before the Unified Patent Court but was dismissed by the Court; or

- it was not possible to raise the relevant objection before the Unified Patent Court (Rule 248).[15]

A rehearing will not be possible if the party concerned could have brought an appeal over the fundamental procedural defect but failed to do so. **1265**

The Application for Rehearing must contain the following (Rule 246): **1266**
- names and postal/electronic addresses for the petitioner, his representative and the persons authorized to accept service for the petitioner;
- an indication of the decision to be reviewed; and
- the reasons for setting aside the final decision, as well as the facts and evidence on which the Application is based.

The fee for the application will amount to 2,500 €. Lodging the application will not have suspensive effect unless the Court of Appeal decides otherwise (Rule 252). **1267**

After the lodging of the Application for Rehearing, the Registry will examine whether the formal requirements have been met and, if applicable, will set a 14-day grace period in which to correct any deficiency (Rule 253). Failure to correct or to duly pay the fee may cause the standing judge to refuse the application as inadmissible, provided he has first given the petitioner a hearing. Once the examination as to formal requirements is completed, the application will be recorded in the Register and will be served on all the other parties concerned. The President of the Court of Appeal will be informed that a Request for Rehearing has been lodged (Rule 254). **1268**

The Application for Rehearing will then be assigned to a panel consisting of three judges, whereby the President of the Court of Appeal may order that none of the judges who participated in taking the original decision to be reviewed may sit on the panel (Rule 254). **1269**

After hearing the parties, the panel will make one of the following possible decisions (Rule 255): **1270**
- a decision to reject the Application for Rehearing as not allowable, whereby this will require a majority vote of the judges on the panel; or
- a decision to allow the Application for Rehearing; such a decision will set aside or suspend the decision under review, either in whole or in part, and re-open the proceedings for a new hearing and decisions. If proceedings are re-opened, the panel will give directions for the future proceedings.

Since this decision will be taken by the Court of Appeal, it will be non-appealable and therefore final and conclusive. **1271**

15 Note: This largely corresponds to the regulations of Article. 112a of the European Patent Convention (EPC); see *Hüttermann* et al., GRUR 2014, p. 448.

Chapter 14: Strategic Considerations for Actions for Revocation or for Declaration of Non-Infringement

Contents Para

1272 This chapter will focus on the strategic considerations relevant to revocation actions and actions for declaration of non-infringement.

1273 Many of the other types of proceedings presented in Chapter 13 will arise only rarely in practice, so we will not include them in our discussion of strategic aspects. The one possible exception might be applications to intervene, but these are subject to essentially the same considerations as interventions in national proceedings, except that the intervenor is bound to the parties (Para. 1228, however cf. Para. 1058 et seqq.).

A. Strategic Considerations for Revocation Actions

I. Strategic Considerations for Both Parties

1274 If we examine the way in which revocation actions and actions for declaration of non-infringement are structured in the Rules of Procedure, we notice that the "reaction times" applicable for both are significantly shorter than in an infringement proceeding (also see the considerations for patent-infringement proceedings, Para. 957 et seqq.).

1275 In a patent-infringement action, the defendant has three months after the Statement of Claim's date of service in which to lodge his Statement of Defense. (This is if we leave out the preliminary objection proceeding, which will be a realistic option in only the rarest of cases.) In a revocation action, by contrast, the defendant has only two months to lodge a Defense. Similarly, the plaintiff has two months to lodge his Reply to the Defense in an infringement proceeding, but only one month in a revocation action. This means that the organizational challenges involved are even tougher, which is something the litigating parties should definitely keep in mind.

II. Strategic Considerations for the Plaintiff

1. Should a Revocation Action Be Brought Before the UPC?

At least during the initial period following the UPC Agreement's entry into force, there will be four possible ways to challenge a European Patent: 1276
- an opposition proceeding before the European Patent Office;
- a national revocation action;
- a revocation action before the Unified Patent Court; or
- a counterclaim for revocation, assuming an infringement action is brought before the UPC.

The first of these options will lapse once the time limit for lodging an opposition before the European Patent Office has expired. The second will lapse if the patent to be challenged is a Unitary Patent. The pros and cons of these two options are discussed below. 1277

2. Pros and Cons of Opposition Proceedings Before the EPO

An opposition proceeding before the European Patent Office has the **advantage** of being the only type of proceeding which allows one to invalidate a European Patent *in toto*. In a national revocation action, on the other hand, only a national portion of the patent can be invalidated. And in a revocation action before the Unified Patent Court, one can seek to invalidate only the Unitary Patent, respectively the portions of the patent which have been validated in Member States of the UPC Agreement. Which means that patent validations already in place in countries like Spain, Switzerland or Great Britain will not be affected. 1278

Furthermore, an opposition proceeding before the EPO is a well-established legal procedure with predictable steps and a track record of decisional precedent. 1279

The legal principle of *ex officio* investigation, which does not apply before the UPC, does apply before the European Patent Office.[1] This principle is also followed in many national proceedings. 1280

Another advantage of an EPO opposition proceeding – but which can also become a disadvantage – is its relatively protracted duration, at least as things currently stand. According to official statistics,[2] the average duration of an opposition proceeding in the first instance is 34 months, or almost three years (from the expiry date of the time limit for lodging an opposition until the date of oral hearing). Complaint proceedings before the EPO, meanwhile, last 42 months[3] on average. Effective as of 1 July 2016, 1281

1 See *Nieder*, Mitt. 2018, p. 201.
2 EPO Annual Report for 2011; this is the most current data available, since later annual reports do not specify the lengths of the proceedings.
3 Remarks made by President *Josefsson* at the Judicial Symposium on Intellectual Property hosted by the Tokyo High Court on 1 November 2018; also see the interview with *Josefsson* published on the JUVE Patent website on 26 July 2019.

the European Patent Office introduced changes to make the opposition proceeding more expeditious.[4] While these have indeed made the proceeding faster, litigation before the Boards of Appeal still takes too long, as the European Patent Office itself admits.[5] Contrast this with a revocation action before the Unified Patent Court, which should theoretically take only 12 months – a time frame which will probably be achievable in practice. Appeals before the UPC will probably be even quicker, at least in the vast majority of cases.

1282 These long time frames for proceedings before the European Patent Office can work to the advantage of a (supposed) patent infringer when there is a parallel infringement proceeding and the infringement court, be it a national court or the UPC, suspends the proceeding until a decision is issued. In most EU countries, the advantage of being present on the market will usually outweigh the disadvantage of having to pay damages, given that damage-awards will usually be kept within reasonable limits and there will no "punitive damages" of the sort seen in the USA. Such punitive payments are actually expressly precluded for the Unified Patent Court, (see Para. 656 et seqq.). However, at present, the Unified Patent Court absolutely rarely will stay proceedings.

1283 But this advantage can become a detriment if the infringement court decides not to stay the proceedings and proceeds to issue an injunction. The damages one will be able to claim damages if the patent is later invalidated will tend to be rather low in most countries. Sometimes it will no longer even be possible to vacate the infringement decision, since this will require an action for restitution, for example, one that will be subject to specific time limits.[6]

1284 In proceedings before the European Patent Office, each side bears its own costs and the official fees are relatively low. This serves to reduce the cost risk, although there is no prospect of recovering costs in the event of victory.

1285 An obvious **disadvantage** of the opposition proceeding is that the opponent effectively puts the patent proprietor on notice that he is interested in the patent and that he has already brought a potentially infringing product to market or plans to do so. A solution to the problem might be to lodge a straw-man opposition, but this also entails procedural disadvantages.[7]

1286 A further disadvantage for the patent challenger, particularly when compared to a proceeding before the Unified Patent Court, is that after the EPO's Opposition Division has issued its preliminary opinion, the patent proprietor will still be entitled to

4 Official Journal of the EPO No. 5/2016.

5 See the interview with President *Josefsson*, published on the JUVE Patent website on 26 July 2019.

6 See, for example, the Ruling of the Higher District Court (OLG) of Düsseldorf, of 12 May 2011, Docket No. I-2 U 129/10; see also OLG Düsseldorf, Restitution Action Following Patent Nullification in the *Messsensoren II* case, GRUR-RR 2020, p. 414.

7 Cf. *de Baere/Storz*, epi Information 2015, p. 109.

lodge new requests/applications, specifically including new sets of claims (see also Para. 1061 et seqq.)

1287 But in a proceeding before the UPC – be it an action for revocation or for declaration of non-infringement – the patent challenger will be obliged – at least based on the current version of the Rules of Procedure – to lodge his claims as part of his first Defense. After that, he will not be able to submit any new sets of claims without the Court's express permission.[8] This can and probably will motivate the patent proprietor to lodge a large number of auxiliary requests just to be on the safe side. Whether these will all be granted is questionable, however (see also Para. 963 et seqq.)[9]

1288 But a situation may also result where a factor of key importance for the Unified Patent Court's decision has been overlooked in all of the patent proprietor's requests and applications, so that all these requests/applications ultimately lead to the patent's invalidation. If the proceeding had been conducted before the EPO in this same situation, the patent proprietor might have been able to save his patent, since he would have been aware of the Opposition Division's preliminary opinion and could have reacted accordingly.

1289 This opportunity to react, e.g. by submitting additional documents, can obviously also work to the benefit of a plaintiff in a revocation action. This said, the author's personal experience is that the patent proprietor will usually be in the more favorable position when the party lodging the opposition has done careful and thorough research beforehand, since the resulting information will make it easier for the patent proprietor to lodge auxiliary requests.

1290 Another evidently disadvantageous aspect of opposition proceedings before the EPO is that they are subject to time limits. This makes it more difficult to reach a settlement with the patent proprietor, e.g. by agreeing on a free or inexpensive license, since the settlement would have to be concluded before expiry of the time limit for lodging an opposition (assuming the alternative of a revocation action is not selected instead).

3. Advantages and Disadvantages of National Revocation Actions

1291 The only country with a significant number of national revocation actions is Germany. One reason is that Germany is the country where the majority of all European patent-infringement actions are brought. Another reason is that patents obtain their legal validity in most countries in the wake of a revocation counterclaim or some analogous action associated with a patent-infringement proceeding. The following

8 See *Hüttermann*, Mitt. 2016, p. 212.

9 Thus, commentators like *Mooney* assume that only a handful of auxiliary requests, usually only two or three, will be approved. This according to a personal conversation with the author at the Annual Conference on the Unitary Patent hosted by the Academy of European Law (ERA) on 22 January 2016 in Brussels.

discussion will therefore concentrate on German proceedings. Note that the situations prevailing in other countries may be quite different.[10]

1292 German revocation actions have the **advantage** that they, too, are conducted in accordance with a well-established legal procedure for which a large body of legal precedent exists.

1293 Another advantage, one which comes into play when proceedings are suspended,[11] is that proceedings tend to be rather protracted before the German courts as well – a state of affairs which unfortunately has not been much improved by the revised revocation proceeding introduced in 2009. But if proceedings are not suspended, this can course also become a disadvantage.

1294 Revocation actions are not subject to time limits. This makes it possible to negotiate in advance and without time pressure with the patent proprietor over a free license, or one that is at least inexpensive. And to thereby avoid having to invalidate the patent, which would open the floodgates for third parties.

1295 The court fees payable to the German Federal Patent Court (BPatG) are higher – sometimes markedly so – than those charged by the European Patent Office and even by the Unified Patent Court. These fees are potentially recoverable, however. The threat of such high expenditures can of course be exploited to convince the patent proprietor to settle right at the outset.

1296 German revocation actions have the **disadvantage** of alerting the patent proprietor to the plaintiff's interest in nullifying the patent. Unless of course a straw man is used to lodge the revocation action.

1297 They also have a further disadvantage in that they can only serve to nullify the German part of a European patent. On the other hand, this could "send a signal" with regard to potential proceedings in other countries, the need for which will then frequently disappear (see Para. 242 et seqq.)

1298 Similarly to opposition proceedings before the European Patent Office, which were copied as the model, the reformed German revocation proceeding also gives the patent proprietor the option to lodge further applications/requests after he has learned the preliminary opinion of the court.[12] This is a significant advantage for the patent proprietor, as already discussed (Para. 1286).

10 On revocation actions in general, see *Manu*, IIC 2017, p. 813; for a comparison between the German and French revocation proceedings, see *Chai*, GRUR Int. 2018, p. 197.

11 A perhaps extreme example is the Ruling of the German Federal Court of Justice (BGH) of 5 June 2018, No. X ZR 58/16, in which a stay was issued even though opposition proceedings before the EPO had already been successfully closed.

12 See *Gutermuth*, Mitt. 2015, p. 529; see also *Hüttermann* Mitt 2017, p. 193.

4. Pros and Cons of Revocation Actions Before the Unified Patent Court

Compared to national proceedings, a revocation action before the Unified Patent Court has the huge advantage of being able to nullify a challenged patent in all the Member States signatory to the UPC Agreement. This will often encompass all the states – excepting Great Britain – in which the European patent was actually validated. Thus, one can speak of a true "revocation action" in such cases. 1299

Revocation actions before the Unified Patent Court have the additional advantage that, just like national revocation actions, they are not subject to time limits. This gives the parties time to try to reach a settlement in advance of any litigation (see also the above Para. 1294). 1300

The fees charged by the Unified Patent Court are comparatively moderate and there is an entitlement to cost recovery (cf. Para. 445 et seqq.). However, these low court fees are likely to be outweighed in most cases by the higher attorneys' fees that will be incurred. 1301

Another structural benefit of revocation actions before the UPC is that the patent proprietor will be obliged to lodge the sets of claims with which he intends to defend his patent at a very early stage of the proceeding. Besides placing the patent proprietor at a procedural disadvantage in most cases (see Para. 1286 et seqq.), this also gives the plaintiff, as the supposed patent infringer, time to react accordingly and plan for possible workaround solutions. 1302

An obvious **disadvantage**, on the other hand, is that – as in the other two types of proceedings discussed above – the patent proprietor will now be placed on alert (unless a straw man was used to lodge the revocation action). 1303

Revocation actions before the Unified Patent Court will tend to be of very short duration, moreover. The benefit of this is that it will minimize – and sometimes totally vitiate – the effects of suspending a patent-infringement action. Conversely, it will also allow the parties to attain legal certainty in expedited fashion. 1304

The most serious shortcoming of actions for nullity (and counterclaims for nullity) before the Unified Patent Court, as has now become clear in case law, is the absence of a principle of ex officio investigation. This may result in the court failing to consider all grounds for invalidity and instead requiring the parties to prioritize them and limit their arguments to the most significant grounds.[13] 1305

Furthermore, it is virtually impossible to introduce additional documents in the reply;[14] in some cases, it is even prohibited to rephrase atttacks out of documents 1306

13 UPC_CFI_425/2024 (LD Munich), Decision of 28 November 2025 – JingAo v. Chint, cf. UPC_CFI_497/2024 (CD Milan), Decision of 23 October 2025 – BioMerieux v. Labrador.
14 UPC_CFI_278/2023 (LD Hamburg), Decision of 30 April 2025 – Agfa v. Gucci.

already filed[15] or even to refer to parts of documents that were not previously cited.[16] Although this case law primarily concerns counterclaims for revocation, it is equally applicable to isolated nullity actions.

1307 While the absence of a rule requiring the court to raise issues on its own initiative affects both parties in principle—meaning that the patent holder may also find that submitted alternative claims cannot be introduced into the proceedings[17] —the court's practice to date has been exceptionally lenient, and in most cases a large number of alternative claims can be introduced.

1308 As a result, the disadvantage for potential nullity plaintiffs is so significant that filing a standalone nullity action before the Unified Patent Court—as long as EP oppositions (and national nullity actions) remain possible—should actually be discouraged.

5. Pros and Cons of Revocation Counterclaims Before the Unified Patent Court

1309 A counterclaim for revocation before the Unified Patent Court is **advantageous** for the plaintiff – who is concomitantly the defendant of the corresponding infringement action – in that it does not alert the opposing side to the plaintiff's interest in the patent. This is because the defendant in the infringement action is the one to initiate the counterclaim.

1310 A revocation counterclaim also has another advantage: The plaintiff will be obliged to bring the question of the patent's infringement and the question of its validity's "under one roof." This means that the arguments which the patent plaintiff must adduce to prove infringement may actually be used against him when it comes to the patent's validity, e.g. the fact that the plaintiff interprets a patent characteristic in a certain way may cause an item of evidence documenting the latest state of the technical art to become particularly relevant.

1311 In a "pure" revocation action, this question will not arise at first, although the defendant will of course be advised as to the patent proprietor's position in any subsequent, parallel infringement proceeding.

1312 A fixed court fee will be charged for revocation counterclaims and it will be possible to claim recovery of costs.

1313 A **disadvantage** of revocation counterclaims is that they require swift action. In particular, they require expedited research into the current state of the technical art, since they must be lodged and supported with reasoning within three months of the date

15 UPC_CFI_11/2024 (LD Düsseldorf) Decision of 8 May 2025 – Grundfos v. Hefei and UPC_CFI_461/2024 (LD Hamburg), Decision of 5 November 2025 (along with other decisions cited therein).

16 UPC_CFI_26/2024 (LD Düsseldorf), Decision of 30 July 2025 – Headwater v. Samsung.

17 See UPC_CFI_433/2024 (CD Paris), Decision of 7 January 2026 – Microsoft v. Suinno.

of service of the infringement action. Once this time limit has expired, the Rules of Procedure will make it very difficult to submit additional documentation.

Another potential pitfall is that the subject matter of a revocation action, particularly of the documentation submitted, will become public knowledge. This, as well as the time pressure involved, will make it difficult to reach a settlement for a free or inexpensive license. 1314

Such a settlement will not necessarily be impossible, however, particularly when a final decision has yet to be issued. But a certain risk for third parties will remain even if a settlement which upholds the patent is reached: e.g. if the documents submitted are not prejudicial to novelty. In such case, it will be difficult to second-guess whether the Unified Patent Court would have nullified the patent or not if it had examined the matter. 1315

Opting to lodge a counterclaim for revocation only, i.e. acting in a merely reactive manner, always entails the risk that the patent proprietor could request a preliminary injunction, thereby creating "facts on the ground" and imposing pressure. Particularly before the Unified Patent Court, requests for injunctive relief will be a very effective weapon (see Para. 1425 et seqq.). Of course one could resort to protective briefs in this context. But practical experience has shown that the German courts will normally give less weight to a validity challenge which is adduced in a protective brief only than to a direct revocation action or opposition proceeding. So this is certainly a key downside of adopting a purely reactive strategy. 1316

However, the most serious shortcoming has already been discussed—the absence of a principle of ex officio examination has particularly severe consequences for potential patent infringers and defendants in invalidity proceedings (see the discussion above starting at Para. 1307). 1317

6. Overall Conclusions

All things considered, we can arrive at the following conclusions: 1318

- A significant novelty that the Unified Patent Court will bring is the option to request a preliminary injunction which simultaneously encompasses several – and perhaps all – of the countries covered by a European Patent (see Para. 1425 et seqq.). This should be borne in mind when selecting one's patent strategy. On the other hand, there would be little reason to change one's current patent strategy simply because an added revocation action will now be possible before the UPC.
- If it was part of one's patent strategy thus far to lodge opposition proceedings before the EPO, then one should continue doing so. This could certainly serve to mitigate – and perhaps even avert – the threat of a preliminary injunction before the Unified Patent Court. This is because the patent proprietor himself must alert the UPC to the existence of the opposition proceeding when requesting a preliminary injunction, at least insofar as the request is to be decided without hearing the opposing side (see Para. 1342).

- Nullity actions before the Unified Patent Court have the serious disadvantage that, due to the absence of a principle of ex officio investigation (see Para. 1307), the plaintiff is clearly at a disadvantage in this context. Where oppositions or, alternatively, national invalidity proceedings are available, these should be pursued.
- If one's prior practice has been to wait for a patent-infringement action to be lodged before responding, i.e. instead of proactively lodging a revocation action, then one should change track only if requesting a preliminary injunction is customary practice in the relevant technical field. If not, one should proceed just as before.

III. Strategic Considerations for the Defendant

1319 The strategic considerations for the defendant are essentially comparable to the ones applicable to a revocation counterclaim in an infringement proceeding. The reader is therefore invited to consult the relevant discussion (Para. 1061 et seqq.).

1320 The defendant should take one of two courses of action. He should either: a) take steps well in advance to ensure that he will still be able to lodge requests/applications during the interim procedure, particularly alternative sets of claims, or b) leave the patent unchanged in his first written pleading (in order to keep all options for an appeal open) but lodge a large number of auxiliary requests.

1321 The answer to this question be will "yes" if the defendant is in a position to shoulder the excess time and expense this will entail. It also bears noting that the resulting proceeding, in which nullification and infringement will be examined in tandem, will be even shorter in duration than a regular infringement proceeding. This translates into added time pressure.

1322 This time pressure can of course be exploited to discomfit the revocation plaintiff and perhaps smooth the way for a favorable settlement.

B. Strategic Considerations for Actions for Declaration of Non-infringement

I. Fundamentals

1323 A precondition for being able to lodge an action for declaration of non-infringement is that the patent proprietor must have either issued a warning or have refused to "greenlight" the actions of the plaintiff. The second of these requirements essentially corresponds to the British practice thus far.

1324 Although the Unified Patent Court has, via case law, introduced the legal concept of "unprovoked legal action" (*Klageüberfall*), and thus, it will not be necessary to issue a prior warning in order to avert court costs, this can be done with a very short deadline, usually too less to properly prepare your case.[18] A simple entitlement enquiry,

18 UPC_CoA_2/2024, Order of 4 October 2024, APL_83/2024 – Edwards v. Meril.

on the other hand, will probably not provide sufficient legitimation for an action for declaration of non-infringement.

Thus, we can assume that the majority of the action proceedings admitted by the Court will involve the second of these two possible courses of action, i.e. the plaintiff will be the one to approach the patent proprietor upon his own initiative. 1325

II. Patent-Strategy Considerations for the Plaintiff

The strategic considerations applicable here can probably be reduced to a single question: 1326

The answer is likely to be "yes" if one has customarily lodged such actions in the past – albeit as "normal" actions rather than "torpedo" actions. New possibilities will arise in this context, given the plaintiff's ability to acquire legal capacity upon his own initiative by contacting the patent proprietor in writing. This contrasts with current practice in Germany, for example, where action on the part of the patent proprietor has always been a precondition for such legal capacity. 1327

When it comes to selecting the best way to conduct the action as such, the reader is invited to consult the corresponding discussion relating to infringement and revocation actions (Para. 1072 et seqq. and 1274 et seqq.). 1328

III. Patent-Strategy Considerations for the Defendant

The strategic considerations applicable here can probably be boiled down to one question: 1329

The answer is probably an unqualified "yes" if one has little confidence in the legal precedent established by the UPC's central division and instead prefers to entrust the case to a local or regional division of one's choice. 1330

This aside, it probably remains to be seen how frequently such infringement actions will actually be brought in practice. Particularly since it has yet to be clarified whether the prevailing party will be able to claim recovery of costs for each proceeding – or face a potential doubling of litigation costs. 1331

It also bears noting that the time limit for lodging an infringement action falls after the time limit for the first Defense in an action for Declaration of Non-Infringement (!) Thus, the patent proprietor can play for time by "fleeing to an infringement action" if he comes under time pressure. 1332

The final answer to this question will depend primarily on the legal precedent established by the central division. It in any case remains an effective threat which the patent proprietor can exploit. 1333

As regards the best way to approach the action as such, the reader is invited to consult the corresponding discussion of infringement and revocation actions (Para. 1034 et seqq., respectively Para. 1274 et seqq.). 1334

Section 6: Pretrial Proceedings

Chapter 15: Introduction to Pretrial Proceedings

Contents Para

The following chapter will discuss the pretrial proceedings which may be conducted before the Unified Patent Court. These can essentially be broken down into two groups: proceedings for provisional measures and proceedings for preserving evidence. Analogously to the practice followed by the German courts, these are structured as pretrial proceedings, e.g. the party who loses a proceeding for provisional measures will still have the opportunity to conclusively clarify the matter in dispute in court in the context of a regular infringement proceeding. Indeed, regulating this topic differently would hardly have been reconcilable with the rule-of-law guarantees found in the national constitutions of many Member States. **1335**

A. Proceedings for Provisional Measures

Besides a normal patent-infringement proceeding, the Unified Patent Court also offers **1336** a proceeding for provisional measures in which one can enforce claims for injunctive relief, potentially even without the Court's having given the alleged patent infringer a hearing. Similarly to the German practice, the UPC's Rules of Procedure envision the use of protective letters as a defensive tool in this context. The course of the proceeding for provisional measures also displays significant parallels to its German counterpart.

1337 Unlike a main proceeding on the merits of a case, a proceeding for provisional measures consists merely of a written procedure and an oral hearing, i.e. there is no interim procedure (Rule 205). Upon a party's application, the Court may order provisional measures even without giving the opposing side a hearing. In this case, the proceeding would be conducted strictly in writing.

1338 In a proceeding for provisional measures, the following provisional measures are available (Rule 211):

- injunctions against a defendant, particularly against the alleged patent infringer;
- the seizure or delivery up of the goods suspected of infringing a patent right so as to prevent their entry into or movement within the channels of commerce;
- if an applicant demonstrates circumstances likely to endanger the recovery of damages, a precautionary seizure of the movable and immovable property of the defendant, including the blocking of his bank accounts and other assets; and
- an interim award of costs.

1339 Thus, the powers available to the UPC in this context are relatively far-reaching and largely correspond to those exercisable by a court in a German proceeding.

I. Course of the Proceeding for Provisional Measures

1340 An application for provisional measures must be lodged with the division of the Unified Patent Court which would also be competent for a main proceeding on the merits in the same matter.

1. Application for Provisional Measures

1341 The application for provisional measures must contain the following (Rule 206):

- particulars on the plaintiff and on the matter at hand, just as in regular main proceeding on the merits (see Rule 206.2, which refers to Rule 13 a) to i));
- an indication of the provisional measures which are being requested;
- the reasons why provisional measures are necessary to prevent a threatened infringement, to forbid the continuation of an alleged infringement or to make such continuation subject to the lodging of guarantees;
- the facts and evidence relied on in support of the application, including evidence to support the claim that provisional measures are necessary; including evidence to support the claim that provisional measures are necessary and the matters referred to in Rule 211.2 and.3;
- a concise description of the action which will be started before the Court, including an indication of the facts and evidence which will be relied on in support of the main proceedings on the merits of the case.

If the applicant requests that provisional measures be ordered without hearing the other party (hereinafter the "defendant"), the application for provisional measures must in addition contain: 1342

- the reasons for not hearing the defendant, e.g. because any delay would likely cause irreparable damage to the applicant, or because there is the danger that evidence could be destroyed or could otherwise cease to be available (Rule 197, which refers to Rule 206.3); and
- information about any prior correspondence between the parties concerning the alleged infringement.

The applicant will be under obligation to disclose any material fact known to him which might influence the Court in deciding whether to make an order without hearing the defendant, including information on any pending proceedings and/or any unsuccessful attempt in the past to obtain provisional measures in respect of the patent. (Rule 206.4). 1343

A court of fee of 14,600 € will be payable for the application. 1344

It must be noted that at least the Local Division Munich does not allow to bring forward the patent in restricted form (i.e. in form of an auxiliary request or otherwise).[1] The Local Division Düsseldorf, however, allows auxiliary request in principle.[2] 1345

2. Course of the Proceeding for Provisional Measures

The application for provisional measures will then be examined as to formal requirements by the Registry, which will also verify whether any protective letter relevant to the application has already been recorded in the Register (see below, Para. 1368 et seqq.) 1346

If a main proceeding on the merits is not yet pending, then the matter will be assigned to a first instance panel, just as in an infringement proceeding. In urgent cases, the presiding judge may decide that he or an experienced judge of the panel, acting as single judge, may decide on the application with a reduced time-table. In principle, however, the decision may also be made by the standing judge, as provided under Rule 209, respectively Rule 345. 1347

Where main proceedings on the merits of the case have already been started before the Court, the application for provisional measures will immediately be forwarded to the panel to which the action has been assigned or to the relevant single judge. In urgent cases (where the action has not been assigned to a single judge), the presiding judge may decide that he or the judge-rapporteur, acting as single judge, may decide on the application in accordance with Rules 209 to 213 with a reduced time-table (Rule 208.3). 1348

The further course of the proceeding will depend on whether the applicant has applied to have the provisional measure issued without hearing the defendant and on whether the Court grants the application. 1349

1 UPC_CFI_693/2025 (LD Munich), Order of 17 October 2025 – ONWARD v. Niche.
2 UPC_CFI_723/2025 (LD Düsseldorf), Order of 12 February 2026 – Align v. Angelalign.

a) Course of the Proceedings When the Applicant Requests Provisional Measures Without Hearing the Defendant

1350 Assuming an application for provisional measures without hearing the defendant has been lodged, the Court will decide whether to grant the requested measures without having first heard the opposing side. If yes, then the Court may immediately order the corresponding measures (Rule 212). The Court must also order the applicant to provide adequate security to cover appropriate compensation for any damage likely to be caused to the defendant which the applicant may bear in the event that the Court revokes the order. Note that this is mandatory whenever provisional measures are ordered without the defendant having first been heard, unless there are special reasons for not doing so. The Court will decide whether it is appropriate to order the security by deposit or bank guarantee. The order will be effective only after the security has been provided to the defendant in accordance with the Court's decision (Rule 211.5).

1351 However, the Court may also summon an oral hearing with or without the defendant's attendance (Rule 210).

1352 According to Rule 209.2, the Court must specifically take the following into account when exercising its discretion in this context:

- the legal validity of the relevant patent; in particular, whether the patent has been upheld in an opposition procedure before the European Patent Office or has been the subject of proceedings in any other court;
- the urgency of the action;
- whether the applicant has requested provisional measures without hearing the defendant and whether the reasons for not hearing the defendant appear well-founded; and
- any protective letter filed by the defendant; the Court must in particular consider summoning parties to an oral hearing if a relevant protective letter has been filed by the defendant.

According to Rule 211, the Court must also do the following when exercising its discretion:

- weigh up the interests of the parties and, in particular, take into account the potential harm for either of the parties resulting from the granting or the refusal of the injunction; and
- any unreasonable delay in applying for provisional measures.

1353 The hurdle, especially concerning the validity of patent, are, however, lower than in the German proceedings, concerning validity it is only necessary that the patent is more likely valid than not.[3]

1354 If the application is successful, the defendant is to be given notice of the provisional measures without delay and, at the latest, immediately at the time of execution of the measures.

3 UPC_CoA_335/2023, Order of 24 February 2024, App_576355/2023 – Nanostring v. 10x Genomics.

The defendant will then have the option of lodging an appeal not requiring leave from the Court of First Instance (Rule 211.6 as read in conjunction with Rule 220.1, see Para. 1098 et seqq.) A procedural peculiarity in this context is that a notice on the right of appeal must be included in the Court's order on provisional measures. The defendant will also have the option to lodge a request for a review of the order, namely within a time limit of 30 days after execution of the measures (Rule 212 as read in conjunction with Rule 197). This request must contain the following: 1355
- the reasons why the measures ordered should be revoked or at least modified; and
- the facts and evidence upon which the application relies.

The Court will then order an oral hearing in order to examine the application without delay. Here, the same rules applicable to a main proceeding on the merits will apply (see Para. 893 et seqq.) However, the court must refuse the application if the applicant is absent from the oral hearing without a reasonable excuse. Usually at this stage of the proceedings or earlier a technical judge will be allocated to the panel. 1356

The decision of the Court on the application is to be given in writing as soon as possible after the closure of the oral hearing. If the Court deems appropriate, the decision may be given orally to the parties at the end of the oral hearing, but is to be given in writing as soon as practicable thereafter (Rule 195). Here, too, the Court may take steps to ensure that a security to cover costs is lodged. 1357

This decision may be contested through an appeal not requiring leave from the Court of First Instance. 1358

If the Court is not willing to grant the requested measures without additional information and/or evidence, then it may order the applicant to provide such additional information and/or evidence (Rule 210.2), specifically including: 1359
- an indication of whether the applicant is duly entitled to conduct the proceeding;
- an indication of whether the relevant patent is legally valid; and
- an indication of whether his rights are being infringed or are threatened with infringement.

The Court may also decide whether to issue summons to an oral hearing which is not to be attended by the defendant (Rule 210.1 c). 1360

If the applicant has applied for provisional measures without hearing the defendant and the Court decides not to grant provisional measures without hearing the defendant, then the applicant may withdraw the application and may request that the Court order that the application and the contents of the application remain confidential. (Rule 209). 1361

Otherwise, the Court may either inform the defendant or reject the provisional measures. 1362

A rejection may be contested through an appeal not requiring leave from the Court (Para. 1098 et seqq.) 1363

The resulting flowchart looks as follows: 1364

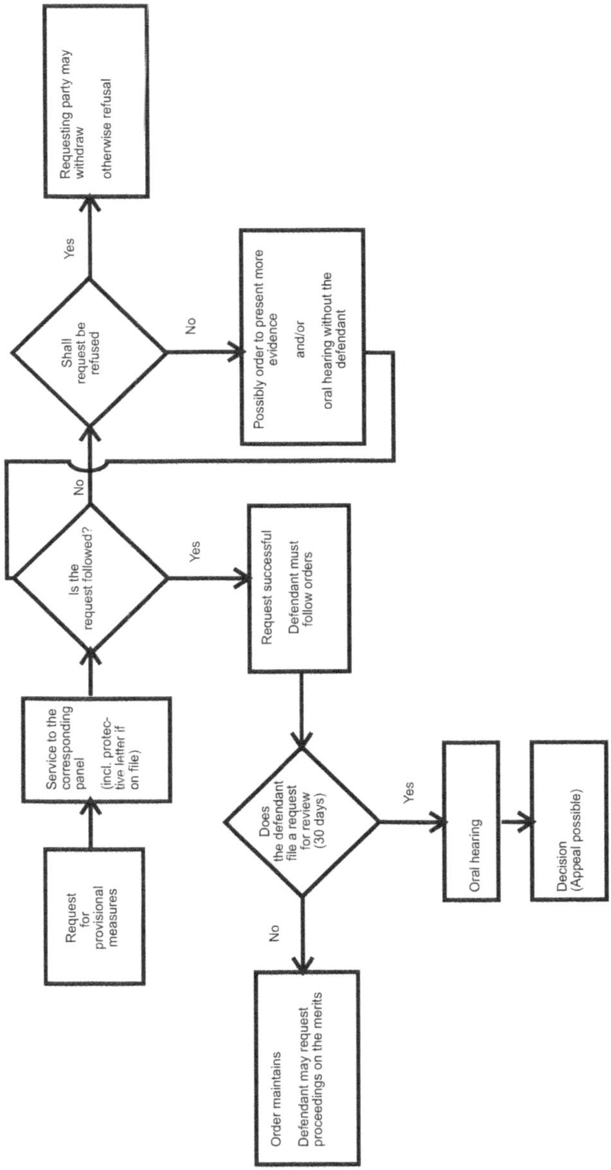

Fig. 15.1 Flow diagram preliminary proceedings

b) Course of the Proceeding Without Application Not to Hear the Defendant

On the other hand, if no application has been lodged for the Court to make its decision without hearing the other side, then the Court will be able order the following upon its free discretion: 1365
- to inform the defendant while giving him a time limit in which to lodge a defense; or
- to summon an oral hearing, whereby this may also be held without the defendant's participation.

From the oral hearing onward, the course of the proceeding will correspond to that of 1366
the review procedure discussed earlier i.e. the rules of the main proceedings will apply here as well and usually a technical judge is allocated. However, the court will have the right to refuse the application if the applicant remains absent from the hearing.

The decision of the Court on the Application for provisional measures is to be given 1367
in writing as soon as possible after closure of the oral hearing. If the Court deems appropriate, its decision may be given orally to the parties at the end of the oral hearing, prior to providing its decision in writing (Rule 210).

II. Protective Letters

The threat of a provisional measure on the part of the Unified Patent Court may be 1368
countered with a protective letter. This is analogous to legal practice in Germany, where protective letters have been in use for over a century now. Thus the concept of a protective letter is derived from the legal precedent established by the German courts, but it is specifically envisioned in the regulations governing the Unified Patent Court. This will serve to strengthen the hand of a potential defendant in proceedings for provisional measures.

According to Rule 207, a protective letter may be filed by any person entitled to start 1369
proceedings under Article 47 of the UPC Agreement if that person considers it likely that an application for provisional measures may be lodged against him as a defendant before the Unified Patent Court in the near future. We can probably assume that this is intended to mean not just proprietors but also, pursuant to Article 47 (6), any natural or legal person or other body concerned by a patent, insofar as they are entitled to bring legal action under their respective national laws. Inasmuch, this limitation will have little if any practical significance.

The protective letter is to be lodged with the Registry in the language of the patent 1370
concerned and must contain the following:
- the particulars of the defendant or defendants[4] filing the protective letter and of the defendant's representative, i.e. their names and the postal/electronic addresses for legal service;

4 Note: This is the formulation used in Rule 207. What is meant here is the "defendant" of an expected application for provisional measures, i.e. the filer of the protective letter.

- the particulars of the presumed applicant for provisional measures, i.e. his name and the postal/electronic addresses for legal service;
- where available, the number of the patent concerned and, where applicable, information about any prior or pending proceedings referred to in Rule 13.1(h); and 13; and
- the statement that the letter is a protective letter.

1371 The protective letter may also contain the following:
- an indication of the facts relied on, which may include a challenge to the facts expected to be relied on by the presumed applicant and/or, where applicable, any assertion that the patent is invalid and the grounds for such assertion;
- any available written evidence relied on;
- the arguments of law, including the reasons why any application for provisional measures should be rejected.

1372 A fee of 300 € will be payable for a protective letter.

1373 A protective letter will be valid for an initial period of six months so long as no application for provisional measures has been lodged. This time limit may be extended by a further six months by paying a fee of 130 €.

1374 Upon receiving the protective letter, the Registry will as soon as practicable examine whether all requirements have been met. If not, a deficiency notice will be issued which grants a 14-day grace period in which to correct the respective deficiency and/or render payment of the fee.

1375 If the protective letter is formally correct, it will be retained by the Registry. If an application for provisional measures is subsequently lodged, the Registrar will forward a copy of the protective letter to the first instance panel or judge appointed under Rule 208 together with the application for provisional measures and will forward a copy to the applicant as soon as practicable (Rule 207.8).

1376 In principle, a protective letter will not be available for public inspection in the Register unless and until an application is lodged and the protective letter has been forwarded to the applicant. In this case, it will also be recorded in the Register (Rule 207.7).

III. Right to Request a Main Proceeding on the Merits

1377 Since a proceeding for provisional measures is a pretrial proceeding, the losing party will have the right to request that the case be adjudicated on the merits in a main proceeding before the Unified Patent Court.

1378 According to Rule 213.1, the losing party may request that the Unified Patent Court order the (successful) applicant to start a proceeding on the merits of the case. If no corresponding proceeding is started within a time limit of 31 calendar days or 20 working days as the date of the Court's order, whichever is the longer, the provisional measures ordered will then be automatically revoked or otherwise cease to have effect. This application is usually filed together with the first reply, so that in practice, if the applicant is successful, preliminary injunction proceedings are a kind of "prelude" to regular infringement proceedings and the cases run parallel, too.

IV. Compensation of Damage

Just as under German law, an applicant whose provisional measures are later revoked as insufficiently justified will be obliged to render compensation for damage. The Court may also order the applicant to compensate damage upon the request of the opposing side (Rule 213.2). This may also occur if the application lapses due to an act or omission of the applicant (cf. the discussion starting in Para. 1436). 1379

B. Applications for Preserving Evidence and for Inspection

Apart from an application for provisional measures in infringement disputes, the Unified Patent Court also permits the lodging of an application for preserving evidence and an application for inspection, whereby both of these will be referred below to as an "application for preserving evidence" for the sake of simplicity. 1380

An application for preserving evidence can be used to obtain the following measures (Rule 196): 1381
- preserving evidence by detailed description, with or without the taking of samples;
- physical seizure of allegedly infringing goods; physical seizure of the materials and implements used in the production and/or distribution of these goods and any related document;
- the preservation and disclosure of digital media and data and the disclosure of any passwords necessary to access them;
- an inspection of products, devices, methods, premises or local situations *in situ*.[5]

The associated regulations contain a number of provisions which protect the party being inspected: 1382
- unless otherwise ordered by the Court, the outcome of the measures to preserve evidence may only be used in the proceedings on the merits of the case. (Rule 196.2);
- the preservation of evidence must be performed by independent and impartial persons and the Court must ensure that they are pledged to maintain confidentiality (see Para. 1391).

I. Course of the Proceeding

The procedural steps of the application for preserving evidence is largely identical to that of the application for provisional measures. 1383

5 Note: This is regulated in Rule 199, which is structured as a separate section, strictly speaking. The proceeding is identical to that of an application for preserving evidence, however, so that only a concise overview is presented here.

1. Application for Preserving Evidence

1384 An application for preserving evidence must be lodged with the same division of the Court at the division where the applicant has commenced infringement proceedings on the merits. If the application is lodged before proceedings on the merits have been started, then it must be lodged at the division where the applicant intends to start proceedings on the merits. (Rule 192.1). The application must contain the following (Rule 192.2):

- particulars on the applicant and the matter at hand, just as in a regular proceeding (see Rule 192.2 (a), which refers to Rule 13 a)–i) and also see Para. 816 et seqq.).
- a clear indication of the measures requested [Rule 196.1], including the exact location of the evidence to be preserved where it is known or suspected to be with good reason. (Important: The location to be inspected does not necessarily have to be on the premises of the alleged infringer; it can also be on the premises of a third party);
- the reasons why the proposed measures are needed to preserve relevant evidence; and
- the facts and evidence relied on in support of the application.
- and, if applicable, a proposed, independent and impartial person who is to perform the inspection.

1385 If main proceedings on the merits of the case have not yet been started before the Court, the application must in addition contain a concise description of the action which will be started before the Court, including an indication of the facts and evidence which may be relied on in support.

1386 If the applicant requests that measures to preserve evidence be ordered without hearing the other party, the application for preserving evidence must in addition set out the reasons for not hearing the defendant. The applicant will be under a duty to disclose any material fact known to him which might influence the Court in deciding whether to make an order without hearing the defendant.

1387 A fee of 5,000 € must be paid for the application.

2. Examination of the Application

1388 The application for preserving evidence will then by examined by the Registry. If a main proceeding on the merits is not yet pending, then the matter will be assigned to first instance panel in accordance with the procedure for an infringement action. The panel's presiding judge may decide that he or the judge-rapporteur or other single judge or the standing judge will decide the application. But the decision may in principle also be taken by the standing judge in accordance with Rule 194, respectively Rule 345.

1389 If a main proceeding on the merits is already pending, then the application will be immediately assigned to the respective first-instance panel or single judge handling the matter. Here again, the presiding judge may decide that either he or the judge-rapporteur or other single judge or the standing judge will decide the application (Rule 194.3).

According to Rule 194.2, the Court must specifically take the following into account when making its decision: 1390
- the urgency of the action;
- whether the reasons for not hearing the defendant – assuming a corresponding application has been lodged – appear to be well-founded;
- the probability that evidence may be destroyed or otherwise cease to be available.

If the Court orders measures to preserve evidence, then the order must also specify an independent, impartial person who will implement said measures. This person must be a professional person or expert, who guarantees expertise, independence and impartiality. Where appropriate and allowed under applicable national law, the person may be a bailiff or assisted by a bailiff. (Rules 196.4 and 196.5). 1391

Under no circumstances may an employee or director of the applicant be present at the execution of the measures. On the other hand, it is possible for the applicant to be represented when the measures to preserve evidence are carried out. Whether and how this is to occur may be specified by the Court (Rule 196.3). An in-house attorney of the applicant could not permissibly act as representative, for instance, since he would be an employee of the applicant. 1392

The next steps to be followed will depend on whether or not the application for preservation of evidence included the request that the defendant not be heard beforehand. 1393

3. Course of Proceedings When the Applicant Requests Preservation of Evidence Without Hearing the Defendant

If an application for preserving evidence without hearing the defendant has been lodged, the Court will decide whether to order the requested measures without hearing the opposing side. 1394

If yes, then the Court may order the measures immediately (Rule 197). In the process, the Court must demand that a security be lodged that can be used to compensate the defendant for any damage suffered if the measures to preserve evidence should later prove to be unjustified. Note that this is mandatory if the measures are ordered without first hearing the defendant (Rule 196.6). In such case, the order will not take effect until the security has been duly lodged, whereby the Court will decide whether it should take the form of a deposit or bank guarantee. 1395

The Court will have the additional option of summoning an oral hearing, also without the defendant's attendance (Rule 197.2 and Rule 195). 1396

a) Implementing the Preservation of Evidence

Once the Unified Patent Court has granted all or some of the requested measures, the preservation of evidence can be carried out, i.e. the person designated for this purpose by the Court will commence his activities. 1397

What remains unspecified in this context is the extent to which the opposing side will have a duty to cooperate. And whether a refusal to lend such cooperation could 1398 give the Court grounds to find that frustration of evidence has occurred, as is possible under the so-called "Düsseldorf Proceeding," for example.[6] This could potentially mean that the defendant would in effect bear the burden of proving that he is not infringing the patent concerned.

1399 It bears noting that measures for preserving evidence will not necessarily be limited to the defendant, but may also involve third parties. This would have to done in compliance with the relevant national legal system, however, (Rule 195.3). But it seems conceivable in principle that measures to preserve evidence could be taken at the premises of certain regulatory authorities, for example, as is done regularly during the *saisie-contrefaçon* procedures conducted in France.[7]

b) Defendant's Options for an Appeal

1400 If the application is successful, the defendant will be given notice immediately, but in any case by no later than at the time of execution of the measures to preserve evidence. The defendant will then be able to request a review within 30 days of the date of execution of the order to preserve evidence (Rule 197). This request for review must contain the following:
- the reasons why the order to preserve evidence should be revoked or at least modified; and
- the facts and evidence upon which the application relies.

1401 The Court will thereupon summon an oral hearing in order to examine the request for review without undue delay. The rules applicable to the main proceedings will apply at the hearing, but the Court must refuse the request for review if the party making the request is absent from the hearing without a reasonable excuse (Rule 195).

1402 The decision of the Court on the application for preserving evidence is to be given in writing as soon as possible after the closure of the oral hearing. If the Court deems appropriate, the decision may be given orally to the parties at the end of the oral hearing but shall as soon as practicable thereafter be given in writing. (Rule 195). In case the order is modified or revoked, the Court must oblige the persons to whom confidential information has been disclosed to keep this information confidential (Rule 197.4).

1403 This decision may be contested through an appeal not requiring leave from the Court.

1404 While there is no regulation which expressly stipulates that the Court may order the submission of additional evidence before taking its decision – as in a proceeding for provisional measures for example (Rule 210.2) – this at least seems conceivable.

1405 If the application is unsuccessful on its merits, the Court will give the applicant the opportunity to withdraw the application and to request that the Court treat the

6 Cf. *Kühnen*, GRUR 2005, p. 185.

7 See the lecture given by *Nargolwalla* auf der European Conference of the IPO on 12 May 2016 in Frankfurt.

application and its contents as confidential. Otherwise the Court may either inform the defendant or refuse the application.

The refusal may be contested through an appeal not requiring leave from the Court. 1406

This results in the following flowchart: 1407

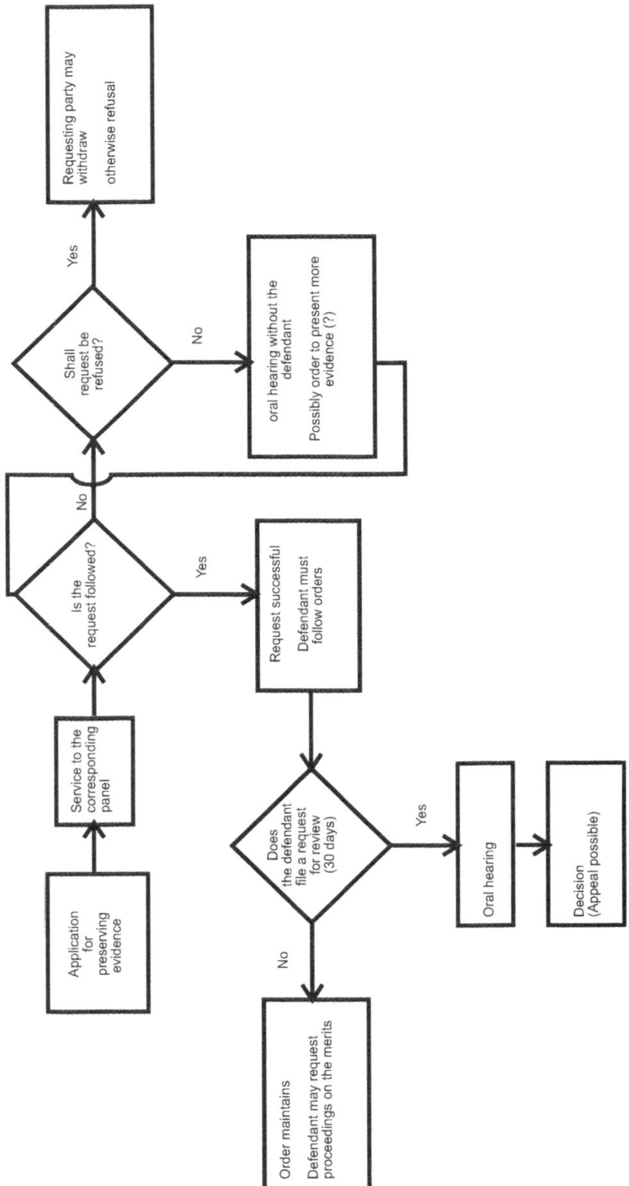

Fig. 15.2 Flow Diagramm: Preserving Evidence

4. Course of the Proceeding When the Applicant Requests Preservation of Evidence, But Not Without Hearing the Defendant

On the other hand, if the application lodged does not request that the decision on preserving evidence be taken without hearing the defendant beforehand, then the Court may decide the following upon its free discretion: 1408
- whether to inform the defendant and give a time limit for lodging a defense; or
- whether to summon an oral hearing, either with or without the participation of the defendant.

The steps to be followed from the oral hearing hearings onwards correspond to the above-described procedure for a request for review, i.e. here, too, the rules applicable to the main proceedings on the merits will hold sway. But if the applicant is absent from the hearing without a reasonable excuse, the court must refuse the application for preserving evidence. 1409

The decision on the application for preserving evidence will be issued in writing soon as practicable after closure of the oral hearing, whereby it may first be issued orally as well (Rule 210). 1410

The further course of the proceeding will be same as the one described above (ab Para. 1397 et seqq.). 1411

II. Protective Letters

It bears noting that, according to the Rules of Procedure, protective letters cannot be used in proceedings for preserving evidence. Whether they will nonetheless be accepted by the Court remains to be seen. Two interesting questions worth asking here is whether affected third parties will also be able to use a protective letter to defend themselves against measures for preserving evidence, and whether an alleged patent infringer will be able to lodge such a protective letter on behalf of a third party (e.g. a regulatory authority). 1412

III. Main Proceedings on the Merits

According to Rule 198, the Court must ensure that, upon the defendant's request, the measures for preserving evidence which have been ordered will be revoked or will cease to have effect if the (successful) applicant fails to commence main proceedings on the merits of the case within a certain time limit. 1413

Thus, the Unified Patent Court will issue a corresponding order upon the defendant's request, whereupon the applicant will be obligated to commence main proceedings on the merits of the case within 31 calendar days or 20 workdays of the date of the order, whichever is the longer. In the process, the Court must take due account of the date on which the obligatory expert report on the measures to preserve evidence was issued (Rule 198.1). 1414

IV. Compensation for Damage

1415 Where the measures to preserve evidence are revoked, or where they lapse due to any act or omission by the applicant, or where it is subsequently found that there has been no infringement or threat of infringement of the patent, the Court may order the applicant, upon request of the defendant, to provide the defendant appropriate compensation for any injury caused by those measures (Rule 198.2).

C. Order to Freeze Assets

1416 Besides ordering the preservation of evidence, the Unified Patent Court may also order the freezing of assets (Article 61 of the UPC Agreement and Rule 200).

1417 Where a party has presented reasonably available and plausible evidence in support of its claim that a patent has been or is about to be infringed, the Court may, whether before or after proceedings have been commenced, order a freezing of assets, i.e. it may order:

- that a party not remove from its jurisdiction any assets or particular assets located therein; e.g. certain products or production materials, etc.; or
- that a party not deal in any assets, whether located within its jurisdiction or not, e.g. the sale of certain properties may be prohibited or certain accounts may be frozen.

1418 Such an order may be issued regardless of whether an infringement action has been brought or not.

1419 The rules applicable to the freezing of assets are the same as those for a proceeding to preserve evidence (see Para. 1383 et seqq.) The only difference is that the fee payable, namely 1,000 €, is somewhat higher in this case.

Chapter 16: Strategic Considerations for Pretrial Proceedings

Contents Para

This chapter will present the strategic considerations relevant to proceedings for provisional measures and to proceedings for preserving evidence. **1420**

A. Strategic Considerations for Provisional Measures

I. Strategic Considerations for Both Parties

A proceeding for provisional measures before the Unified Patent Court may be similar to the same type of proceeding in Germany, but it has one decisive advantage: Whereas the German courts are partially free to create their own case law[1], the practice of **1421**

1 To mention just a few examples: The legal precedent established by the Düsseldorf courts in the *Harnkatheterset* decision and various follow-up decisions; see e.g. Higher District Court (OLG) of Düsseldorf in the *Harnkatheterset* case, InstGE 12, p. 114; see also *Böhler*,

the UPC will be more amenable to becoming progressively standardized through the lodging of appeals, even during ongoing proceedings, as well as through the influence exerted by the Court of Appeals.

1422 This ability to appeal should be exploited in order to prevent "insular" decisions from being issued.

1. Sideline: Is There Such a Thing as a Declaration of Closure in the Proceeding for Provisional Measures?

1423 In a Germany, it is customary practice to end a proceeding for provisional measures by means of a "declaration of closure" (*Abschlusserklärung*) or "letter of closure," (*Abschlussschreiben*) when the application has been (mostly) successful. In this declaration, the opposing party states that the dispute is now over and that it will forego starting a main proceeding on the merits of the case (cf. Para. 1377 et seqq.)

1424 However, this actually sensible measure is *de facto* impossible before the Unified Patent Court because the defendant usually requests in his first reply that an action on the merits must be filed (Rule 213, see Para. 1377 et seq.). This means that the appeal proceedings in the interim injunction and the main proceedings run in parallel – which makes a final declaration obsolete.

II. Strategic Considerations for the Patent Proprietor

1. Should One Apply to the UPC for Provisional Measures?

1425 Obtaining an order for provisional measures from the Unified Patent Court, if done without the Court's having heard the opposing side, is probably the most effective weapon available in the litigation toolbox. This is because the order would then apply to all the states in which the patent concerned has been validated. In a best case, these would be all the Member States of the UPC Agreement.

1426 Thus, a patent proprietor should always keep the option of seeking provisional measures in mind, but should also remember that such a step will usually be taken as an "all-out declaration of war" by the other side. Recall that one the opening shots of what came to be known as the "Smartphone Patent War"[2] between Apple and Sam-

---

GRUR 2011, p. 965, as well as the Ruling of the Higher District Court of Düsseldorf of 30 September 2010, No. I-2 U 47/10, in the *Gleitsattelscheibenbremse II* case, or the legal precedent established by the Mannheim District Court and Karlsruhe Higher District Court in the *Pralinenform II* case; see District Court of Mannheim, GRUR-RR 2011, p. 83. The "Düsseldorf Proceeding" for inspections also emerged from the case law of the courts; cf. *Kühnen*, GRUR 2005, p. 185 and *Kühnen*, Mitt. 2009, p. 211.

2 This name has even made it into Wikipedia, cf. https://en.wikipedia.org/wiki/Smartphone_patent_wars.

sung was Apple's applying for provisional measures to the District Court (*Landgericht*) of Düsseldorf.[3]

When choosing the divison, the same division should generally be called upon as in main proceedings, but the following points should be taken into account: 1427
- While most divison currently still consider two months to be urgent, the Düsseldorf chamber is considered to be stricter and to only allow one month.[4]
- On the other hand, apart from an isolated decision by the Milan Chamber, which was, however, handed down by permanent judge Sam Granata, the Düsseldorf division is so far the only one to have issued ex parte injunctions.
- The Munich division does not allow any changes to the patent during preliminary injunction proceedings or the filing of auxiliary requests; in the opinion of the divison, doing so indicates that the patent holder considers the patent as granted to be vulnerable.[5] The Local Division Düsseldorf, however, allows auxiliary request in principle.[6]

2. Or Should Provisional Measures Be Sought on the National Level While the Main Proceedings are Brought Before the UPC?

According to the Brussels I Regulation, this is a permissible alternative in Europe when the legal dispute involves a European patent (for a full discussion, see Para. 484 et seqq.) It will of course be less effective than seeking provisional measures before the Unified Patent Court, given that any provisional measure obtained will only apply nationally. Indeed, proceedings for provisional measures are hardly conducted at all in some countries, since they are not considered worthwhile for the applicant. 1428

Seeking provisional measures on the national level can be advantageous to the patent proprietor in that the proceedings involved are essentially well-established and known to all. Applying for provisional measures nationally will become particularly viable if it turns out that the Unified Patent Court makes its proceeding for provisional measure unattractive by demanding extremely substantial securities (which, however, is not current practice), or if it almost never orders provisional measures without hearing the other side, in contrast to what is frequently seen in Germany (also see Para. 1434, however), which is the current practice. 1429

3 Note, however, that this involved a design and was intended to contest a Samsung tablet computer; for a full discussion, see District Court (LG) of Düsseldorf, GRUR-RR 2011, p. 361 and Higher District Court (OLG) Düsseldorf, GRUR-RR 2012, p. 352.

4 According to the Munich divison, UPC_CFI_201/2024 (LD Munich), order of 27 August 2024 – Syngenta v. Sumi Agro, which states: 'In view of the diverging case law on temporal urgency, which grants the applicant only one month, e.g. in UPC_CFI_452/2023 (Local Division Düsseldorf), order of 9 April 2024, GRUR-RS 2024, 7207, Rz. 128, the Local Division Munich adheres to its case law granting two months.' However, in a personal conversation, Presiding Judge Thomas denied that the Düsseldorf division had such a policy.

5 UPC_CFI_693/2025 (LD Munich), Order of 17 October 2025 – ONWARD v. Niche.

6 UPC_CFI_723/2025 (LD Düsseldorf), Order of 12 February 2026 – Align v. Angelalign.

3. What is the Best Line of Argumentation to Take?

1430 In principle, it would seem advisable to model one's arguments in support of provisional measures on the current German practice in this area:[7]

- fulfillment of the formal preconditions (ownership; current legal validity of the infringed patent, etc.) should be clearly and precisely demonstrated;
- the case for the infringement action should be clearly and convincingly presented;
- the urgency and necessity of ordering the provisional measure should be indicated and supported;[8]
- reference should also be made of any prior opposition proceeding or revocation action concerning the patent. However, the hurdle is considerably lower than currently in Germany (see Para. 1353)

1431 What will require skill and finesse is formulating the application in a way that makes it logically comprehensible but without going into so much detail that the judge concerned will regard the matter as too complex for provisional measures to be ordered.

1432 According to the Rules of Procedure, the applicant for provisional measures is subject to more far-reaching duties to communicate information than in a regular legal action. This is hardly surprising and certainly justified. So that if the applicant wishes to succeed, he will be well advised to make his argumentation even more thorough and comprehensive than in a main proceeding.

1433 The Unified Patent Court is very reluctant to issue interim injunctions without hearing the opposing party. This must be taken into account when filing a corresponding application; it will usually only be possible to be successful without hearing the opposing party in trade fair cases.[9]

1434 As a result, interim injunctions usually take several months before the court makes a decision.

1435 If one is proceeding on the assumption that the opposing side has lodged a protective letter, then one should take the position – insofar as possible – that the Court ought to ignore any arguments regarding insufficient patent validity when neither a revocation action nor an opposition proceeding has been lodged. This could of course also be interpreted as an indirect admission that the defendant in the application proceeding does not fully trust his own arguments.

---

7 For a thorough discussion, see *Kühnen*, "Handbuch der Patentverletzung," Chapter G; Note 32 et seqq.

8 Cf. also *Mohr*, GRUR 2018, p. 1115.

9 One example is UPC_CFI_177/2023, Order of 22 June 2023, APL 525740/2023 – mystromer v. Revolt.

a) Argumentation Regarding Damage Compensation in the Application for Provisional Measures

The Rules of Procedure stipulate that, when the order for provisional measures is issued without hearing the opposing party, the Unified Patent Court must demand a security to cover the costs of any potential compensation of damage (Para. 1350). It may well be that the Court's practice will be to demand a security of such high amount as to make the proceeding for provisional measures unattractive. The applicant could certainly address this issue in the application, and specifically explain why the amount of the security should be kept low. As currently the court almost never issues preliminary injunctions without hearing the other party, this matter, however, is of less importance. **1436**

The applicant could argue, for example, that a high security amount would not be appropriate for trade fairs, the venue for which most provisional measures are traditionally sought in Germany. After all, it cannot be taken as a given that the defendant would actually have closed any sales had he been allowed to display his patent-infringing products. The applicant could also argue that, if the compensation for damage claimable by the patent proprietor is not supposed to be punitive in nature (see Para. 802 et seqq.), then this should also hold true for the compensation claimable by a wrongly accused patent infringer. **1437**

b) Argumentation Regarding Damage Compensation When Provisional Measures Are Revoked

As already explained, if an applicant's provisional measures are revoked, or if they lapse due to any act or omission by the applicant, or if it is subsequently found that there was no infringement or threat of infringement of the patent, then the Court may order the applicant, upon request of the defendant, to provide the defendant with appropriate compensation for any damage caused by those measures (Rule 213.2). **1438**

It bears noting, however, that this may not jibe with the logic of the judgment handed down by the European Court of Justice in the *Bayer-Richter* case.[10] Here, the ECJ upheld a provision of Hungarian law which precludes any claim to compensation when a provisional measure subsequently becomes invalid (e.g. because the patent itself has become invalid). But what the ECJ failed to clarify in the process is whether such a claim for compensation would violate the Enforcement Directive (2004/48/EC) – even if some observers interpret the judgment to mean that it would indeed constitute a violation.[11] Based on the primacy of European Union Law, such an interpretation of the judgement would serve to set aside Rule 213.2. This line of argument should be used. As an alternative, a referral to the ECJ should be requested. **1439**

10 ECJ Judgment of 12 September 2019, Docket No. C-688/17.
11 See *Tilmann* GRUR 2021, p. 997 with additional references.

c) Temporally Limited Provisional Measures?

1440 A final point to bear in mind: When provisional measures are being sought for a trade fair, for example, one should consider requesting measures of limited duration (at least as an alternative) – ones that last until the trade fair is over, for instance. Such an option has been proposed for German purposes by *Köllner* et al.[12] (albeit in a somewhat different context), but it would also seem entirely viable in proceedings for provisional measures before the UPC, given the greater flexibility provided by Article 63 et seqq. of the UPC Agreement. (see Para. 655). Indeed, this could be an effective way to convince the Court to order provisional measures.

III. Strategic Considerations for the Alleged Patent Infringer/Defendant of the Application for Provisional Measures

1. Should Protective Letters Be Lodged?

1441 In the German proceeding for provisional measures, which serves as a model for the analogous proceeding before the Unified Patent Court, protective letters are the only means of defense against a threatened – or at least anticipated – order for provisional measures.

1442 The provisional measures ordered by the Unified Patent Court will usually have an even graver impact on the defendant than those ordered in a German proceeding, given the UPC's wider territorial jurisdiction. This makes lodging protective letters before the UPC all the more advisable.

1443 This especially holds true in view of the fact that protective letters will now be legally codified instead of being derived from case law – as was the situation in Germany, for example, before the adoption in 2016 of Section 945a of the Code of Civil Procedure (ZPO). This will serve to further improve the legal position of an opposing party targeted by a provisional measure. A detail worth noting here is that the fees charged for lodging and extending protective letters are exceptionally low.

2. Which Line of Argumentation to Use in a Protective Letter?

1444 In principle, it seems advisable to use the same arguments in a protective letter as in the current German practice.[13] In other words, to provide detailed explanations of the following points:

- why no infringement has occurred;

12 *Köllner* et al, Mitt. 2020, p. 293.

13 For a full discussion, see *Kühnen*, "Handbuch der Patentverletzung," Chapter G, Notes 221–231.

- why the proceeding is not urgent, e.g. because proceedings are already ongoing or because the applicant[14] has already been aware of the infringing product for some time;
- why the patent is not legally valid. Here it is important that the hurdle is significantly lower than in current German proceedings (cf. Para. 1353) thus good arguments are needed.
- why the applicant will not suffer any detriment from a main proceeding before the Unified Patent Court;
- if none of the above points apply, or if they cannot be raised in a manner that makes them convincing on their face, then at least arguments to show why assessing a patent infringement is so complex that it cannot be properly done in a proceeding for provisional measures, but must instead be handled in a main proceeding on the merits.

The protective letter should contain an explanation of why a very substantial security should be demanded in the event the requested provisional measures are granted. Indeed, the Rules of Procedure make this a mandatory precondition for granting provisional measures without hearing the opposing party. Here, one could argue that the Court must act proceed very carefully and ensure that the defendant – whose business activities will be seriously impaired by the provisional measures – can be duly compensated if the measures later prove to have been unjustified. However, unfortunately, the court at present does only rarely issue security orders. **1445**

B. Strategic Considerations for Proceedings for Preserving Evidence

I. Is There Such a Thing as a "Discovery" Proceeding Before the Unified Patent Court?

There are various means of obtaining evidence in proceedings before the Unified Patent Court, including a request that the Court order the opposing side to produce evidence. But all the items of evidence involved must be specifically identifiable, i.e. it is not possible to venture a "shot in the dark." **1446**

It therefore follows that a "discovery" proceeding modeled on US law will probably not be possible before the Unified Patent Court. By the same token, it will be difficult to base a patent-infringement action on items of evidence which are not available when the Statement of Claim is lodged but which are merely presumed to be situated on the premises of the defendant or of a third party. A proceeding to preserve evidence may first have to be brought in such a situation, but this, too, will not be easy. **1447**

Moreover, a "discovery" along the lines of US legal practice would probably also not jibe with the Enforcement Directive (2004/48/EC), which stipulates that confiden- **1448**

14 What is meant here is the applicant of the anticipated proceeding for provisional measures (see Rule 207). The party which lodges the protective letter will thus be referred to as the "defendant" hereinbelow.

tial information must be safeguarded even in the course of proceedings for preserving evidence.[15]

1449 As a result, it is likely that already small attorney teams will suffice to manage patent-infringement proceedings before the Unified Patent Court, rather than the sizeable litigation teams commonly seen in the USA (see Para. 987 et seqq.)

II. Strategic Considerations for Patent Proprietors

1. Should an Application for Preserving Evidence Be Lodged With the Unified Patent Court?

1450 This question should probably be answered with a definite "yes." But one should be sure to request that the proceeding be conducted without the opposing party's being heard. That way, if the Unified Patent Court decides to refuse the application, one will be able to break off the proceeding and, if appropriate, pursue national proceedings instead – without any of this becoming known to the opposing party.

1451 In any case, the broader territorial jurisdiction of the Unified Patent Courts dictates that – at least as long as the Court has yet to reveal its actual practice – one should always lodge an application for preserving evidence with the Unified Patent Court first and pursue analogous proceedings on the national level only as a secondary resort.

1452 Last but not least, one should consider that the fee for the proceeding is a rather modest 5,000 €.

2. How to Argue in a Proceeding for Preserving Evidence?

1453 The fact that an order for preserving evidence before the Unified Patent Court is referred to in the Rules of Procedure as a *saisie*[16] is a clear reference to the analogous French proceeding. On the other hand, the actual procedural steps are closer to the so-called "Düsseldorf Proceeding" used in Germany.[17] This is due to the following factors:

- The Unified Patent Court is free to refuse the application for preserving evidence. This is not possible in France, where the court can at most limit the application so as to make it unattractive for the applicant. An outright refusal is not possible, however;[18]
- The person who conducts the inspection may be an expert selected by the applicant. In France, this is invariably the bailiff assigned to the respective district;
- Said expert will initially forward his report only to the Court. In France, by contrast, the applicant automatically receives a copy of the expert's report.

---

15 See the Enforcement Directive (2004/48/EC), Section 6 (1).

16 On the *saisie* proceeding in France, see *Véron*, "Saisie-Contrefaçon."

17 For a thorough discussion, see *Kühnen*, "Handbuch der Patentverletzung," Chapter B, Note 10 et seqq.

18 See the lecture by *Nargolwalla* at the IPO European Conference on 12 May 2016 in Frankfurt am Main.

It therefore follows that one should begin by using the same line of argumentation as in a proceeding for preserving evidence before the Düsseldorf District Court, i.e. by explaining the following points: 1454

- that the formal requirements with regard to the patent's legal validity and ownership etc. have been met;
- the specific technology which the patent protects;
- why it is suspected that a patent infringement occurred and how this was conclusion was reached. This could be done, for example, by presenting an advertising brochure from the opposing side which touts the special characteristics of a product. In a proceeding involving chemistry or biotechnology, this could also be accomplished by pointing out the presence (or absence!) of specific auxiliary products which characterize the inventive step;
- why the inspection is reasonable for the opposing party;
- why the applicant should be given unrestricted access to the expert report; and
- why a representative of the applicant should definitely be present at the inspection.

In bears noting hear that the District Court of Düsseldorf also regularly receives applications for inspections at trade fairs. Here, the applicant's specific intention is to obtain "court-proof" confirmation that the opposing side is exhibiting certain items at the fair. Assuming one applies for such an inspection, one should argue that it is perfectly reasonable for the opposing side – which is present at the trade fair anyway, i.e. at a "semi-public" location – to tolerate having its devices or exhibits evaluated by an expert. 1455

The application for preserving evidence should also specify which activities the opposing side has carried out thus far, e.g. whether major advertising campaigns or active marketing efforts have been observed or whether the opposing side has not yet entered the market. For it stands to reason that the more active the defendant has been on the market, the more he has stood to profit from his unauthorized usage of the patent. And thus the more reasonable it should be for him to accept an inspection. 1456

The applicant should also fully explain how the preservation of evidence is supposed to unfold, i.e. the intended means of preserving evidence should be specified as precisely as possible (visual inspection, especially at trade fairs, filming and photography, but also sampling, taking screenshots of a machine's control panel, etc.). This will give the Unified Patent Court a clear picture of what is planned and whether this can be deemed reasonable for the other side. 1457

The selection of the expert plays a key role in both the Düsseldorf Proceeding as well as in a proceeding before the Unified Patent Court. Here, the applicant should take care to ensure that a truly neutral expert is chosen. This could by a university professor or technical specialist, for example. 1458

But it is also relatively common practice before the Düsseldorf courts to propose that a patent attorney from a law firm not involved with the case be brought in as an expert. The advantage of this is that the attorney will be versed in patent law and will thus be likely to focus on the truly important aspects rather than getting lost in side 1459 issues. So this, too, could be a viable option, particularly for patents whose claims are formulated in a comparatively complex and challenging manner.

1460 Two final points bear noting: Unlike in a main proceeding on the merits (see the discussion in Para. 411), a proceeding for preserving evidence is characterized is by the explicit preclusion, under the Rules of Procedure, of representation by an in-house attorney. An external representative will therefore have to be selected.

1461 The second point is that although the Court will assess the urgency of the action associated with the application for inspection – insofar as there is such an action – the Rules of Procedure do not call for any assessment of the urgency of the application itself. This is in keeping with German practice.[19]

3. Applying for the Production of Evidence as an Alternative

1462 It bears noting that the Rules of Procedure of the Unified Patent Court also allow an application for production of evidence to be lodged during an ongoing proceeding (see Para. 711 et seqq.). This should always be considered as a possible alternative to the more involved proceeding for preserving evidence. Whether the Court's actual approach will as restrictive as the one mandated under German law – specifically by the provisions governing production of documents under Section 142 of the Code of Civil Procedure (ZPO) – remains to be seen.[20] But given the relative simplicity and zero cost of the proceeding, it will definitely be worthwhile to lodge such applications – at least until such time as the guiding principles followed by the Court become manifest. The current practice is, however, that not many requests are filed.

III. Strategic Considerations for Affected Parties

1. Should a Protective Letter Be Lodged?

1463 It is still unclear whether protective letters can be filed against threatened proceedings for preserving evidence. But one should at least make the attempt, since the Rules of Procedure do not expressly forbid it.

2. Should One Cooperate in the Preservation of Evidence?

1464 It has yet to be determined whether inadequate cooperation by a party targeted by an inspection may lead the Court to find that frustration of evidence has occurred and that the burden of proof must therefore be reversed to that party's detriment. In any case, this will probably not be possible when the measure to preserve evidence is carried out on the premises of a third party, e.g. a supplier or a public authority.

1465 If the alleged patent infringer himself is affected by a proceeding for preserving evidence, then cooperating would seem the most prudent approach to take. It may also

19 E.g. before the Higher District Court (OLG) of Düsseldorf, GRUR-RR 2011, p. 289.
20 See *Weber*, Mitt. 2021, p. 104.

be possible to keep the expert from interfering significantly in ongoing business operations by providing him in writing with all the documents and records he requires.

3. Handover of the Expert's Report to the Applicant

The Rules of Procedure do not specify what is to be done with the report prepared by the expert once he has forwarded it to the Court. **1466**

Here, the alleged patent infringer[21] should by all means lodge an application with the Unified Patent Court to request that the applicant not be given unfettered access to the expert's report. The alleged infringer should request instead that he or his representatives – and any third party on whose premises the preservation of evidence takes place – be allowed to inspect the report in advance and to at least black out certain passages. In the ideal case, the expert's report will not be provided to the applicant at all. **1467**

21 Note: Such an application should always be lodged by the patent infringer even if he is not the first one to be directly affected by the preservation of evidence, e.g. because the inspection is performed on the premises of a third party.

Section 7: Enforcement

Chapter 17: Enforcement of Decisions and Orders

Contents Para

The decisions and orders of the Unified Patent Court will be enforceable in all Members States of the UPC Agreement. The enforcement process itself will essentially follow the respectively applicable national laws. No additional writ of enforcement from the national courts will be required, i.e. a decision of the Unified Patent Court does not need to be "transposed" into national law. The regulations of the Unified Patent Court will take precedence, however. In other words, insofar as they relate to enforcement, they will have primacy over the respective national laws.[1] 1468

In those states which are not Member States of the UPC Agreement but which are signatory to either the "Brussels I Regulation" (1215/2012/EU) or the Lugano Convention, the decisions and orders issued by the Unified Patent Court will be enforceable pursuant to the provisions of said Regulation, respectively Convention. In all other respects, the corresponding national laws will apply. 1469

The enforcement of decisions and orders will almost always require the involvement of national bodies and courts of instance. For this reason, the following Chapters 19 to 28 will present an overview of the individual enforcement regulations in force in the most important Member States of the UPC Agreement. 1470

Only in certain individual cases will this not be necessary. Examples include the ones discussed in Para. 1482 as well as the blocking of accounts by the Unified Patent Court. 1471

As explained in Chapter 15 (Para. 1416 et seqq.), the Unified Patent Court has the option of blocking the bank accounts of an alleged patent infringer by issuing an order to freeze assets. In this case, the order may be served directly upon the relevant bank without having to go through any intermediary national bodies. 1472

The Unified Patent Court also has the option to impose recurring penalty payments. This was already discussed earlier (Para. 771). 1473

A. Damage Due to Enforcement and the Lodging of Securities

In cases where an enforceable decision is later varied or revoked after having been enforced against the losing party, the Court may award that party appropriate com- 1474

1 See *Leistner*, GRUR 2016, p. 217; also cf. *Augenstein/Kather*, GRUR 2021, p. 127.

pensation for the damage caused by the enforcement (Rule 354). A special case will arise, however, when a patent-infringement has been finally and conclusively affirmed but the patent in question is later declared invalid, or invalidated at least to the extent that it no longer covers the originally intended subject matter. This will be discussed further later on (Para. 1480).

1475 The Court also has the option to make an enforcement order contingent upon the lodgment of a security or bank guarantee in favor of the opposite party. Upon request, the Court may also order an exemption from such a lodgment obligation. The purpose of the security is to give the losing party assurance that it will receive compensation for any damage caused by enforcement of the decision in the event the order is later varied or revoked.

B. Timing of the Enforcement

1476 According to Rule 354, decisions and orders of the Unified Patent Court are in principle enforceable as of their date of service.

1477 This does not apply to decisions in infringement proceedings, however. Here, Rule 118.8 stipulates that the victorious infringement plaintiff must first notify the Court which part of the order he wishes to enforce and that the corresponding notice must first be served upon the defendant by the Court's Registry. A further precondition is that, where applicable and necessary, the plaintiff must also provide a certified translation of the order into the official language of the Contracting Member State in which the compulsory enforcement is to take place; this translation must then be served upon the defendant by the Registry. Here, too, the Court will naturally have the option to demand that a security be lodged. Upon application, the Court of Appeal may revoke the preliminary enforceability of a decision in the first instance, namely by declaring the appeal to have suspensive effect (see Para. 1117 et seqq.)

1478 The infringement plaintiff may also opt to wait and see whether an appeal will be lodged or not, or to await the outcome of such an appeal, given that Rule 118.8 does not set any time limit in this regard. The damage-award proceeding will be subject to a time limit, however, namely one year after the date of service of the final decision in the infringement proceeding (see Para. 925 et seqq.)

C. Suspension of Enforcement

1479 In principle, suspension of the enforcement process will be governed by national law, particularly once a decision issued by the Unified Patent Courts has become final and conclusive.

1480 An exception, applies, however, if patent infringement has been finally and conclusively affirmed but the patent in question is later declared invalid, or at least to the extent that it no longer covers the originally intended subject matter.

1481 In such case, the party which has lost the infringement proceeding may lodge an application with the Unified Patent Court requesting that the infringement decision be declared no longer enforceable. This will not serve to change the original patent-infringement decision, however, so that the applicant will not be able to claim appropriate compensation for any past damage. Any damage-compensation already paid will also not be reimbursable.[2]

D. Penalty Payments

1482 Recurring penalty payments may be imposed by the Unified Patent Court not just in the situations discussed in Para. 771 et seqq., but also in the event of non-compliance with an enforcement order (Article 82(4) of the UPC Agreement and Rule 354.4). No regulatory provision has been made for the imposition of administrative fines, on the other hand.

1483 Recurring penalty payments may be imposed in the following cases (inter alia):
- if the losing part in the infringement proceeding fails to desist from the infringement, even though it was ordered to do so after having been convicted of the infringement;
- if that same party fails to fulfills its duties to communicate information or lay open the books;
- if that party fails to render the damage-compensation awarded by the Court.

1484 In any of these cases, the Court may, either upon its own discretion or upon the request of the opposite party, issue a corresponding order after hearing both sides. The order may then be contested through an appeal requiring leave from the Court of First Instance.

1485 Finally, the Unified Patent Court will take charge of enforcing collection for recurring penalty payments, just as in a proceeding to freeze assets (see Para. 1416 et seqq.)

2 For a full discussion see *Klein*, "Einheitspatent: Der Konflikt von Verletzungs- und Nichtigkeitsurteil."

Chapter 18: Strategic Considerations for Enforcement

Contents Para

1486 Given the fact the decision on the merits will already have been issued by the time the enforcement stage is reached, it follows that the strategic considerations for enforcement play a less important role in the overall picture. Still, a few of these considerations will be briefly addressed in this chapter.

A. Conditional Decision

1487 Recall that there will be no compensation of past damage or any reimbursement of compensation already paid when a patent-infringement has been finally and conclusively affirmed but the patent in question is later invalidated, or at least invalidated to the extent that it no longer covers the originally intended subject matter. The conclusion to be drawn from this is that the defendant must by all means insist on a conditional decision (see also Para. 911).[1]

B. Seek Penalty Payments or Bring a New Infringement Action?

1488 It remains to be seen how the Unified Patent Case decides to approach a situation where the losing party, although having ceased to offer or distribute a patent-infringing product, nonetheless brings a similar product to market in modified form: Must a new infringement action or a new application for provisional measures be lodged, or can an order for a recurring penalty payment be issued directly?

1489 The Court may decide the question of a recurring penalty payment either upon its own motion or upon the request of the opposing side. Once both sides have been heard, the relevant first-instance panel of the Court will take the decision. This can be contested through an appeal not requiring leave from the Court of First Instance.

1490 The proceeding for penalty payments is inasmuch a relatively simple one. So that in the aforementioned case where the losing party brings a modified product to market, it would make sense to first apply for coercive enforcement in the form of a recurring penalty before potentially following up with an infringement action or an application for provisional measures (injunction, etc.).

1491 It should be reminded that it is possible in the course of an ongoing litigation to have products included which newly appeared on the market (cf. para 1064 et seqq). Such requests should be made whenever possible.

---

1 Note.: The provision was adopted with precisely this aim in mind according to *Klein*, "Einheitspatent: Der Konflikt von Verletzungs- und Nichtigkeitsurteil;" also cf. *Nieder*, GRUR 2017, p. 38; On the special cases which obtain for standard-essential patents, see *Altmeyer/ Weber*, GRUR 2017, p. 1182.

Chapter 19: Enforcement in Belgium

Contents Para

As Belgium is a Contracting Member State of the Agreement on a Unified Patent Court, the recognition and enforceability of decisions of the UPC follows from the Agreement itself, and the provisions of EU Regulation 1215/2012/EU (the Brussels I Regulation) and the Belgian Code of Private International Law (Act of 16 July 2004) do not apply. **1492**

A. Procedural aspects

I. Language issues

As Belgium has three official languages (Dutch, French, and German) and strict legislation about the use of these languages in judicial matters, the requirement to provide a certified translation into "the official language of a Contracting Member State" requires some further clarification. Although the use of languages in proceedings before the UPC is governed by the UPC Agreement, which takes precedence over national legislation within its scope of application, the enforcement stage is governed exclusively by national law (art. 82(3) UPC) and hence the provisions of the Act of 15 June 1935 on the use of languages in judicial matters should be strictly followed. If these provisions are applied, together with the rules on jurisdiction laid down in art. 633 of the Judicial Code, it becomes clear that the order must be served or translated in the language of the region where the goods against which the enforcement is to be carried out, are situated. If said goods are in the Flemish region, the order shall be served in Dutch; if they are in the Walloon region (except the district of Eupen), the order shall be served in French; if they are in the district of Eupen, the order shall be served in German; if they are in the district of Brussels, the order may be served in Dutch or in French at the option of the Claimant. **1493**

II. Course of an enforcement procedure

1. Role of the Bailiffs

In Belgium the competent enforcement authorities are the bailiffs[1] These are independent, legally qualified professionals, who have a legal monopoly to perform a variety of acts on behalf of parties involved in legal proceedings. **1494**

1 Dutch: "gerechtsdeurwaarder"; French: "huissier de justice"; German: "Gerichtsvollzieher".

2. Course of the procedure

1495 Every judicial decision must be served on the affected party, before it can be enforced in Belgium (art. 1495 of the Judicial Code). This service starts the period for lodging an appeal or an opposition (in the case of a decision by default) against the decision. Typically, the Claimant will allow the period for lodging an appeal or opposition (where applicable) to expire, before starting the enforcement stage. However, this is not necessary if the decision is not subject to appeal or opposition, or if it is enforceable notwithstanding appeal or opposition.

1496 Under the UPC Agreement, the period for lodging an appeal against a decision of the Court of First Instance runs from the notification of the decision.[2] The notification requirement is further detailed in the Rules of Procedure, which require that any order or decision of the Court shall be served on each of the parties at the initiative of the Registry in accordance with the provisions of Sections 1, 2 or 3 of the Chapter "Service", as the case may be.[3] When the party to be served resides in Belgium, Section 1 applies, and service must be performed by electronic means, by fax, or exceptionally in accordance by other means permitted by Regulation (EC) No 1393/2007, which may involve registered mail or the intervention of a bailiff. For the purpose of enforcement in Belgium, the service according to Rule 276.1 would take the place of the service required under art. 1495 of the Judicial Code.

1497 Subject to the rendering of a security, when required by the Court, decisions and orders of the UPC shall be directly enforceable from their date of service in each Contracting Member State (Rule 354.1). However, if an order for damages under art. 31.1(f) or art. 68 is to be enforced, the Claimant must notify the Court of his intent to do so, and this notification will also be served on the defendant by the Registry (Rule 118.8) along with, where applicable, a certified translation into the official language of a Contracting Member State in which the enforcement shall take place of the orders to be enforced, which translation has to be provided by the Claimant.

1498 After the service of the decision to be enforced and the notification under Rule 118.8 by the Registry, the first step of the enforcement proceedings is the service of a demand to comply with the decision.[4] The demand is served by a bailiff at the initiative of the interested party, i.e. the Claimant. The formal requirements of the demand and the period granted to the debtor for complying with it differ depending on whether the subsequent enforcement is to be effected against movable goods,[5] immovable goods,[6] agricultural produce,[7] or ships.[8] No demand is necessary if the enforcement is to be effected against claims held by the debtor against a third party; in that case, service

2 Art 73(1).
3 Rule 276.1.
4 Dutch: "bevel"; French: "commandement"; German: "Zahlungsbefehl".
5 Art. 1499 of the Judicial Code.
6 Art. 1564 of the Judicial Code.
7 Art. 1529 of the Judicial Code.
8 Art. 1546 of the Judicial Code.

of the notice of seizure on the third-party debtor is the first step in the enforcement proceedings, and the primary debtor is only informed afterwards.

3. Seizure

1499 If the debtor fails to comply with the demand within the applicable period for compliance, the order may be enforced against the class of goods of the defendant targeted by the demand, by means of a seizure[9]. The seizure is a collective procedure, which does not grant the Claimant who initiated it any precedence over other creditors. If any prior demands or seizures have been served on the debtor by other creditors, or if other creditors intervene in the pending seizure proceedings, they will share in the proceeds of the seized goods in proportion to their respective claims. The public auction of the seized goods and the distribution of the proceeds will be supervised by a bailiff, with further involvement of a notary public if immovable goods are concerned.

4. Temporaty Protection from creditors

1500 It must be noted that a merchant or commercial legal entity whose continued existence is threatened by the enforcement of claims against it, may attempt to use the provisions of the Act of 31 January 2009 to obtain temporary protection from its creditors. If such protection is granted by the commercial court, all pending enforcement actions (i.e., seizures) are automatically suspended and no new actions can be started. The public is notified of the commencement of proceedings under the Act of 31 January 2009 by a publication in the official gazette.[10] It is therefore important for creditors to monitor the status of their debtor, and to follow up any proceedings that could thwart the creditor's attempts to recover on his claims.

9 Dutch: "beslag"; French: "saisie"; German: "Pfändung".
10 Belgisch Staatsblad – Moniteur belge.

Chapter 20: Enforcement in Denmark

Contents

A. General Provisions

1501 On 29 April 2014 the Danish Parliament approved the bill (Lov nr 551 af 02/06/2014) relating to the implemention of the UPC into Danish legislation. Essentially, the enforcement procedure will be the procedure which currently exist for the courts of Denmark. Thus, Danish authorities enforce UPC decisions under the same conditions as they enforce decisions by the national courts, i.e. the conditions laid down in The Danish Consolidated Administrative Act (see above). In accordance with § 2 of the law a request for settlement, a decision or an order covered by the UPC Agreement should be submitted in writing to the court.

1502 The main source of substantive law relating to patents and patent litigation is the Danish Consolidated Patent Act No 108 of 24 January 2012 (Patentloven). The Danish Consolidated Administrative Act No 1308 of 9 December 2014 (Retspleje-loven) regulates proceedings before the Danish courts.

1503 Generally, a patent proprietor has two options when seeking to enforce his patent rights in Denmark. The patent proprietor can file an application for a preliminary injunction and/or initiate patent infringement proceedings.

I. Preliminary injunctions

1504 Preliminary injunction is a fast and effective way of stopping an assumed infringer. A preliminary injunction will be issued if the patent proprietor can prove that the requested injunction related to acts covered by its patent and it is probable that infringement is taking place. If a preliminary injunction is issued, the Bailiff's Court can assist the patent proprietor (see below) to enforce the injunction by, for example, seizing goods suspected of being used for infringing acts. However, once a preliminary injunction has been obtained, it must be followed up by the main proceedings, usually before The Maritime and Commercial Court. The Maritime and Commercial Court may order a permanent injunction, as well as payment of damages.

1505 The claim for an injunction requires presumptive evidence of infringement of the claimant's rights. A preliminary injunction does not require the same level of proof as applicable in ordinary proceedings. The level of proof for a defendant to avoid a preliminary injunction on the grounds that the patent may be invalid is very high.

If the claimant cannot submit very clear evidence of the infringement, the court will 1506 normally require security (such as a bank guarantee) as a condition for issuing the preliminary injunction. The amounts of security requested in patent proceedings are often considerable, such as several million of Danish kroner. The security will be used to compensate the defendant if the main action is eventually lost.

Directive 2004/48/EC on the enforcement of intellectual property rights has been 1507 incorporated into the Danish legislation. Therefore, damages are awarded taking into consideration the patent proprietor's lost profits and the infringer's unjustified profits.

The patent proprietor is entitled to reasonable compensation for having used a paten- 1508 ted invention, as well as compensation for additional damages. The patent proprietor may also request the confiscation or destruction of infringing products or machines or production equipment, or the surrender of the infringing product. Penalties for wilful infringement in the form of fines or even imprisonment are foreseen under Danish law, but rarely implemented (see above).

Reasonable compensation for having used a patented invention, as well as reason- 1509 able damages and reimbursement of any losses that the patent proprietor has suffered because of the infringing act, must be rewarded irrespectively of whether the infringing act took place in good or bad faith. To determine the amount of damages, issues such as lost revenue and the profits of the infringer are taken into account, as well as market disturbance, including estimated future loss of sales and loss of goodwill. The damages may also be cumulative, taking more issues into account. Compensation for having used the patented invention may be based on the license fee that the patent proprietor could reasonable have charged on the market. Punitive damages are not available in Denmark.

II. Criminal Proceedings

Criminal proceedings are available against an infringer of patent rights if the infrin- 1510 gement was committed intentionally or with gross negligence. The sanction for gross negligence is a fine. However, the sanction for an infringement committed intentionally or if there are aggravating circumstances, is a fine or up to one and a half year's imprisonment. In practice, criminal proceedings are only initiated in exceptional cases.

III. Other Proceedings

1. Border measures

Border measures are available for a patent proprietor who suspects that infringing pro- 1511 ducts are being imported, exported or re-exported to or from Denmark. These measures are regulated by EU Regulation (EC) 608/2013 concerning customs enforcement of intellectual property rights and repealing Council Regulation (EC) no 1383/2003.

2. Securing of evidence

1512 The patent proprietor can also apply to secure evidence. The premises of the alleged infringer, including the infringer's IT systems, are searched by representatives of the competent court and any evidence of infringement is seized by the court.

B. Procedural aspects

1513 Enforcement (tvangsfuldbyrdelse) enables a creditor to take coercive measures to ensure that a debtor honours a claim established by a court or in some other way. Enforcement cases are dealt with by the bailiff's court (fogedretten) which is a division within the district court (byretten)), in accordance with the rules laid down in the Administration of Justice Act. Most enforcement cases relate to demands for payment.

1514 A demand for money is usually enforced by the bailiff's court seizing the debtor's assets. Seizure involves the creditor being given a right of lien over the asset concerned, so that he can sell it by force, thus covering his claim wholly or in part from the proceeds of a public sale. If enforcement relates to a demand to vacate a building, enforcement involves eviction by the bailiff's court, possibly with the help of the police.

I. Course of the procedure

1515 For enforcement to take place, there must be grounds or a basis for enforcement, e.g. judgments and decisions handed down by courts or other authorities whose decisions can be legally enforced, demands for payment endorsed by the bailiff's court, and decisions on the costs of legal actions taken by these authorities.

1516 Enforcement is carried out by the bailiff's court. This means that a claimant whose claim is well-founded can submit an application for enforcement to the bailiff's court. The application is usually submitted in the jurisdiction where the debtor lives.

1517 The bailiff's court then carries out an initial examination of the case. If it is deemed to be well-founded the parties involved are summoned to a meeting which usually takes place in the office of the bailiff's court. It can, however, also be held on other premises, such as the debtor's place of residence or business.

1518 The claimant is, in principle, obliged to attend the meeting, and the case is rejected if he does not appear. The debtor can be obliged to attend the meeting; if a summons is served on him but he fails to appear, he can be brought before the court by the police.

1519 In the course of the meeting the debtor is asked to make payment and he is obliged to provide whatever financial information about himself and his household may be required by the bailiff's court. Failure to provide proper information is a punishable offence. The purpose of questioning the debtor is to find out whether he owns assets that can be seized.

1520 In certain cases the bailiff's court can decide not to grant the claimant's request for enforcement. If the debtor raises objections to the grounds for enforcement, and if in the light of the evidence which may be placed before it the court judges that it would be inadvisable to proceed, then the court must refuse to proceed further.

The bailiff's court cannot take a decision on all objections to validity raised against 1521
the grounds for enforcement. It cannot, for example, take a decision on objections concerning the correctness of judgments and decisions; and it can refuse to hear which, given its scope or nature, or for some other particular reason, should be given in ordinary proceedings.

II. Countermeasures of the debtor

The debtor has some scope for pursuing a counterclaim during enforcement. The 1522
counterclaim can then be offset – assuming that the general conditions required for this are met – in the course of the enforcement action, provided it is enforceable, or is recognized by the party that has applied for seizure, or is accepted as being justified on some other ground.

In principle, anything belonging to the debtor which has an economic value can 1523
be seized. Both immovable and movable property can be seized. Movable property includes not only physical assets (such as cars, ships or aircraft), but also legal claims, for example.

Once the debtor's assets have been seized, he no longer has the full right of disposal 1524
of the seized assets. The debtor is not entitled to dispose of the seized assets in any way that could be detrimental to the creditor with rights over the seized property; for instance, he cannot sell or transfer the assets to a third party. As a general rule, movable property which has been seized remains in the debtor‘s possession until such time as a public sale is held, unless the bailiff's court decides that the debtor is to be deprived of the right to dispose of his property.

If the debtor disposes of seized assets unlawfully, a penalty may be imposed. 1525

Debtors are obliged to provide such information as is required by the bailiff's court 1526
in order to be able to carry out enforcement. Should a debtor fail to meet his obligation to provide information, the bailiff's court can decide that he is to be given a custodial sentence of up to six months until such time as he fulfils his duty to supply information.

It is, as a general principle, possible to lodge an appeal before the High Court (lands- 1527
retten) against decisions taken by the bailiff's court. The appeal must be lodged within four weeks of the decisions being issued by the bailiff's court. However, appeals against decisions to seize assets with an economic value of a maximum of DKK 10 000 can be lodged only with the permission of the Leave of Appeal Commission (Procesbevillingsnævnet), if there are particular grounds for such an appeal.

Moreover, cases on which the bailiff's court has ruled can be revised, that is to say 1528
subjected to a fresh examination by the bailiff's court. They can be revised if the parties to the case so agree or if the bailiff's court deems revision necessary. Revision may be necessary, for instance, if the debtor or a third party provides evidence that

the ruling infringes the rights of a third party or if the debtor was not present during the enforcement action and is now invoking the rules on the debt enforcement code enshrined in the Administration of Justice Act.

Chapter 21: Enforcement in Germany

Contents Para

A. Prerequisites for enforcement

In Germany, judgments of the Unified Patent Court are enforced by an enforcement court. However, according to the Accompagning Act[1] (see Para. 32), this requires a document either in German or translated into German (§ 19. Para. 2). Translation costs shall be borne by the judgment creditor. **1529**

B. Competent enforcement court

The local court which has jurisdiction over the unsuccessful party, who is called "debtor" in the law and thus in the following, is to be assigned as the enforcement court. This is the district court in whose district the debtor has his place of residence or business. If the debtor does not have a place of residence or registered office in Germany, the district court of the district is competent in which **1530**

- in the case of claims for money or property, the property or the object is located; and
- in the case of the surrender of patent-infringing objects, these objects are located.

However, the enforcement court shall only take action at the request of the winning party, who is referred to in the law and thus in the following as the "creditor". **1531**

C. Course of the execution

Depending on the claim, the actual execution proceeds differently: **1532**

I. Enforcement in the case of movable property and objects.

In the case of movable property and objects, enforcement is carried out by a bailiff based at the enforcement court (Section 808 of the Code of Civil Procedure). The bailiff acts at the request of the creditor and, for example, seizes the infringing objects. **1533**

---

1 Exact title: "Gesetz zur Anpassung patentrechtlicher Vorschriften aufgrund der europäischen Patentreform" of 20 August 2021, Bundesgesetzblatt Teil I Nr. 59, S. 3914.

II. Enforcement of rights and claims

1534 In the case of monetary claims, if the debtor does not pay, the bailiff may also seize items in the debtor's possession. These can then be turned into money by public auction (Section 814 of the German Code of Civil Procedure) (known as liquidation). However – which will probably be of minor importance in commercial legal protection – there is protection against attachment of objects of daily use in relation to debtors who are private individuals. These items are unseizable.

1535 In the case of rights and claims (in particular monetary claims of the debtor against third parties, the so-called "third-party debtors"), enforcement shall be carried out by the enforcement court itself (Section 825 et seq. German Code of Covil Procedure).

III. Real Estate

1536 In the case of real estate, enforcement is carried out by the enforcement court and the respective land registry office. At the request of the creditor, the land registry registers a mortgage (§ 867 Code of Civil Procedure). However, this is initially only a pledge and provides the creditor with security that the debtor cannot sell the property without further ado. The actual collection of the claim then takes place through compulsory auction. This is carried out by the enforcement court at the request of the creditor.

D. Legal Remedies

1537 In the course of compulsory enforcement, the following legal remedies are possible, among others, whereby the trial court pursuant to Section 19, Paragraph 3 of the Accompanying Act (cf. Para. 1533) is in each case the regional court in whose district the debtor is domiciled, or if this is not available in Germany, the regional court in whose district the compulsory enforcement is to take place or has taken place.

I. Reminder

1538 The debtor may lodge a **reminder** ("Erinnerung" Section 766 of the German Code of Civil Procedure) against the compulsory enforcement and thus object to the manner in which the compulsory enforcement is being carried out. This reminder is possible, for example, if the debtor wants to defend himself against the fact that the bailiff has seized an unseizable item.

1539 The reminder could be of practical importance in the field of industrial property rights for the creditor, as he can file a reminder against the bailiff if the latter refuses to enforce the claim, e.g. because he mistakenly does not recognize orders of the Unified Patent Court.

1540 The reminder is not subject to a time limit and is free of charge. The enforcement court shall decide on it.

1541 An immediate appeal against a decision of the enforcement court is possible to the district court within two weeks from service of the decision. If the appeal is unsuccessful, court costs are incurred.

II. Enforcement defense action

The debtor can also file an action to defend himself against enforcement ("Vollstreckungsabwehrklage") and claim that the claim against him no longer exists, e.g. because he has paid in the meantime, the creditor has waived the claim or he has counterclaims that can be offset. 1542

III. Third-party actions

Third parties may, if they are affected by an enforcement action, file a third-party action ("Drittwiderspruchsklage") before the enforcement court (section 771 of the German Code of Civil Procedure). This may be the case, for example, if the creditor has an item (such as a machine tool, etc.) seized from the debtor, but the item does not belong to the debtor at all, but to the bank or a lessor, for example. 1543

Chapter 22: Enforcement in France

Contents Para

1544 Because the decisions handed down by the Unified Patent Court can be enforced in France almost like a French decision, this chapter first explains how the French judicial decisions in patent matters can be enforced[1], and then how the UPC decisions can be enforced.

A. Enforcing a French judicial decision in France

1545 As patent matters generally involve large or mid-size companies, a vast majority of the defendants based in France do comply with the decisions of the French courts without the need of coercion. In some cases, however, compelling compliance is needed.

1546 This section presents the legal framework and the players of such enforcement, then the enforcement measures provided by French law, and finally the provisional measures (before any decision is given on the merits of the case), which may be useful in some cases.

I. The legal framework and the players of the enforcement

1547 The winning party which has to compel the losing party to abide by a court decision must follow the provisions of two French codes: the Civil Procedure Code ("code de procédure civile", CPC) and the Civil Enforcement Procedure Code ("code des procédures civiles d'exécution", CEPC).

1548 There is nothing in French law like the common law concept of contempt of court: not abiding by a court order does not expose to any criminal sanction or to any financial sanction to be paid to the court or to the State.

1549 The task of enforcing decisions under these codes is reserved to judicial officers ("commissaires de justice")[2], who are private practitioners appointed by the government,

1 Articles of the Unified Patent Court Agreement of 19 February 2013 will be referred to as "*Article […] UPCA*". Rules of the 18th draft of the Rules of Procedure of the UPC will be referred to as "*Rule […]*". Articles of the French Civil Procedure Code will be referred to as "*Article […] FR CPC*". Articles of the French Intellectual Property Code will be referred to as "*Article […] FR IPC*".

2 As a result of a government order dated 2 June 2016, the professions of bailiff ("*huissier de justice*") and public auctioneer ("*commissaire-priseur*") were merged as of 1 July 2022 in a new profession named "*commissaire de justice*" (better tranlated as "*judicial officer*").

entrusted with part of the public authority and holding a monopoly on forced execution and protective measures.

They act under the supervision of a specific judge known as the "enforcement judge" ("Juge de l'exécution", often shortened to "JEX"), who is a judge of the French ordinary court of first instance, that is, the tribunal judiciaire. 1550

Disputes in respect of enforcement – like requests for a payment extension ("délai de paiement") or debt staggering ("échelonnement de la dette")[3] –, are brought exclusively before the enforcement judge. 1551

This judge also rules on matters of abuse of enforcement process, which constitutes a tort liability under Article 1240 of the French Civil Code and Article L. 121–2 CEPC. Such abuse is characterised by a lack of proportionality between the debt owed and the enforcement measure sought. 1552

The territorial competence for both the judicial officers[4] and the enforcement judge will depend on the nature of the enforcement sought: the location of the assets to be seized, the place of performance of the obligation underlying the claim, the place of residence of the defendant. 1553

II. Enforcement measures

The recourse to compelling enforcement measures requires an official copy of the decision of the French court issued by the court clerk with a specific enforcement order ("copie exécutoire" or "grosse") to be served ("signifiée") on the unsuccessful party[5]. 1554

The enforcement generally begins with a formal order to pay ("commandement de payer") or to abide otherwise by the court's decision. 1555

When the court has ordered the defendant to do something (like recalling infringing products from the sales channel), or to refrain from doing something (like an injunction not to infringe a patent), the judicial officer is usually only permitted to draw up a formal record that the defendant does not do what he has be ordered to do or, conversely, that he is doing what he has be ordered not to do. On the basis of this formal record, the court may order the defendant to pay a recurring penalty ("astreinte") to the plaintiff (e.g. € 10,000 per machine sold or per day of operation of an infringing process). The amount of this penalty can be increased if the defendant does not comply. 1556

To enforce decisions ordering a payment, judicial officers have specific powers: 1557

3 Article 1244–1 of the French Civil Code.
4 Judicial officers are competent within the jurisdiction of the *cour d'appel* where they are established.
5 Article 503 CPC.

1558 investigation: in order to locate the debtor and his assets, they are entitled to obtain information that is not accessible to the public[6], including a direct access to information held by government, tax, financial and social agencies (available in the "Ficoba" database listing all French bank accounts);

1559 action: judicial officers have the power to require the assistance of police officers and may be assisted by removal men and locksmiths if need be.

1560 The enforcement measures carried out by judicial officers for enforcing a judgment in patent matters can be of two kinds:

1561 attachment on a bank account ("saisie-attribution") whereby the creditor can obtain the monies available on the debtor's bank account; and

1562 measures which result eventually in the sale of the debtor's assets: in a preliminary phase, these are used to make the debtor's tangible or intangible assets inalienable; in the final phase the assets are sold to payback the creditor. Such measures are obtained through seizures and sale ("saisie-vente" for movable property, "saisie immobilière" for immovable property). The sale can be forced through public auction.

1563 Although the judicial officers' fees for recovering amounts of money are in principle borne by the creditor, they are by exception charged to the debtors who are found liable for intellectual property right infringement[7].

1564 The enforcement of decisions that are only provisionally enforceable (like an interim injunction) always takes place under the responsibility of the creditor who must restore the debtor's rights in case of damage if the decision is later set aside or modified; cross undertaking is provided by statutory provisions[8].

B. Provisional measures

1565 Before the creditor obtains a final judgment allowing for enforcement, provisional measures can also be sought in order to secure his rights. These can be obtained on the condition that the claim appears to be founded and admissible, and that there is a risk of frustration of recovery. They require prior judicial authorisation from the enforcement judge.

1566 When a provisional attachment ("saisie-conservatoire") is granted, it makes the debtor's assets inalienable. When the creditor eventually obtains an enforceable title, provisional attachment is converted into the appropriate enforcement measure.

6 The only freely accessible information essentially concerns the debtor assets: land register ("*cadastre*" and "*publicité foncière*") for real property, vehicle registration services notably for ships and aircrafts, *Institut National de la Propriété Industrielle* register for intellectual property titles…

7 Article R. 444–55 2° of the French *code de commerce*.

8 Article L. 111–10 CEPC.

C. Enforcing a UPC decision in France

The Agreement on a Unified Patent Court ("UPCA") of 19 February 2013 contains several provisions relevant to the enforcement of UPC decisions, in particular Article 82 (3) which states that "Without prejudice to this Agreement and the Statute, enforcement procedures shall be governed by the law of the Contracting Member State where the enforcement takes place. Any decision of the Court shall be enforced under the same conditions as a decision given in the Contracting Member State where the enforcement takes place". 1567

Therefore, pursuant to the Agreement, every time the enforcement of a UPC decision[9] is sought in France, French enforcement law applies: UPC decisions are enforceable in France under the exact same conditions and through the same measures as those applying to decisions of French courts. 1568

Regulation (EU) N° 1215/2012 of the European Parliament and of the Council of 12 December 2012 "on jurisdiction and the recognition and enforcement of judgments in civil and commercial matters (recast)" (known as the "Brussels I (recast) Regulation")[10] was amended by Regulation (EU) N° 542/2014 of the European Parliament and of the Council of 15 May 2014 "amending Regulation (EU) N° 1215/2012 as regards the rules to be applied with respect to the Unified Patent Court and the Benelux Court of Justice" to take into account the provisions of the Agreement. 1569

As a result, Article 71(a) of the thus modified Brussels I (recast) now considers for its purposes the Unified Patent Court as a "court of a Member State", integrating it fully into the European decision recognition system. 1570

And Article 71(d) in fine provides that "However, where recognition and enforcement of a judgment given by a common court [as is now the UPC] is sought in a Member State party to the instrument establishing the common court, any rules of that instrument on recognition and enforcement shall apply instead of the rules of this Regulation". 1571

The rules thus referred to are in particular Article 82 UPCA, Rule 118 and Rule 354. 1572

Rule 118.8 provides that "The orders of the Court referred to in paragraphs 1 and 2(a) shall be enforceable on the defendant only after the claimant has notified the Court which part of the orders he intends to enforce, a certified translation of the orders in accordance with Rule 7.2, where applicable, into the official language of a Contracting Member State in which the enforcement shall take place has been provided by the claimant and the said notice and, where applicable, a certified translation of the orders have been served on the defendant by the Registry". 1573

9 Or a settlement reached through the use of the UPC patent mediation and arbitration centre, see Article 35.

10 Regulation (EU) N° 1215/2012 amends and repeals Regulation (EC) N° 44/2001 of 22 December 2000 (then referred to as the "Brussels I Regulation").

1574 Rule 354.1 makes decisions and orders of the UPC directly enforceable – without the need for an exequatur – from their date of service.

1575 Consequently, to enforce on the French territory a UPC decision that has not been handed down in French[11], the claimant must provide a certified French translation.

1576 Subject to this, final or provisionally enforceable UPC decisions[12] can be enforced like any French judgment, as explained above.

1577 To sum up, three differences are to be noted:

1578 while recurring penalty ("astreinte") in case the defendant does not abide by a court's order to do or not to do something is paid to the defendant under French law, it is paid to the UPC under Article 82(4) UPCA.

1579 While the French court is normally not informed of the steps taken by the claimant for the enforcement of its judgment, a UPC decision is "enforceable on the defendant only after the claimant has notified the Court which part of the orders he intends to enforce";

1580 Furthermore, while the question of translation does not arise for the enforcement of a French judgment in France, a UPC decision given in a language other than French needs to be translated before being enforced in France.

11 This will be the case every time the language of proceedings is not French, see Article 77 (2).
12 See in particular Article 74 on the suspensive effect of appeals.

Chapter 23: Enforcement in Italy

Contents | Para

For the enforcement of a court decision in Italy, notice of the decision itself must be served on the other party together with the related "order"[1] containing the demand for compliance within a time limit, normally not less than 10 days. **1581**

A. Competence of the Court

Which Court will have competence for enforcement will depend on the subject matter of the expropriation order. **1582**

The Court with competence for enforcement in the case of chattels and real estate will be that for the place where the things concerned are located. **1583**

In the case of registered goods (cars, motor-vehicles and haulage vehicles) the competent Court will be that for the place where the debtor has his/her residence, domicile, home or registered office. **1584**

For the enforcement of obligations to do, or refrain from doing something (e.g. restraining injunctions, destruction, etc.) the competent Court will be that for the area where the obligation has to be performed. **1585**

B. Procedure of the enforcement

The enforcement must be initiated no earlier than 10 days and no later than 90 days from the service of notice of the order. **1586**

To obtain the monies due to him/her, the creditor may have the debtor's assets expropriated in accordance with the rules laid down by the Italian Code of Civil Procedure by means of the seizure of assets forming part of the debtor's property. **1587**

The enforcement begins with the seizure, id est with the injunction that the Court Bailiff imposes on the debtor not to dispose of the property forming the subject matter of the seizure or the income or the profits deriving from the same (Article 492 of the Italian Code of Civil Procedure). **1588**

The subject matter of the seizure may be assets belonging to the debtor or belonging to third parties. The third party will be required to ensure the safe-keeping of the seized property from the date on which the seizure notice is served on him. **1589**

If enforcement action is taken against real property or rights for the enjoyment of real property (easements, surface rights, etc.), after the service of the real estate sei- **1590**

1 Called "precetto", as per Articles 479 and 480 of the Italian Code of Civil Procedure.

zure notice on the debtor by the Court Bailiff, it is then necessary to have the order registered onto a registry named "Conservatoria dei registri immobiliari".

1591 Subsequently the Italian procedure provides for a forced sale or assignment of the seized goods for the satisfaction of creditors. The application for sale or assignment may not normally be made prior to 10 days from the date of the seizure.

1592 Forced sale may be by means of an auction (involving a competitive public auction with a number of bidders designed to identify the successful buyer) or without an auction (with the filing of bids in sealed envelopes with the chancellery of the Enforcement Court).

1593 The seizure will cease to have force and effect on the expiry of a period of 45 days from the date of fulfilment (of the seizure) without an application for assignment or sale.[2]

1594 In addition to the enforcement of judgments, orders for the description of assets and seizure will be effected through the actions of the Court Bailiff who will draw up a formal report and may be assisted by one or more experts. The Bailiff may also use technical, photographic or other means of assessment.

1595 Normally, in Italy enforcement procedures will be laid down in the authorising order to be enforced.

C. Possibilities of Third parties to intervene

1596 The debtor, a third party subject to enforcement and third parties not subject to enforcement (claiming a property right over, or other ius in rem over the seized goods) may dispute the legitimacy of the enforcement or of the individual enforcement actions by means of opposition, in this way giving rise to autonomous proceedings designed to determine the legitimacy of the enforcement or individual enforcement actions.

2 Article 497 of the Italian Code of Civil Procedure.

Chapter 24: Enforcement in the Netherlands

Article 82 of the Agreement on the UPC determines that UPC decisions and orders shall be enforceable in any contracting member state. An order for the enforcement of a decision shall be appended to the decision by the Court. Where appropriate, the enforcement of a decision may be subject to the provision of security or an equivalent assurance to ensure compensation for any damage suffered, in particular in the case of injunctions. It is further determined that enforcement procedures shall be governed by the law of the where the enforcement takes place and any decision of the UPC shall be enforced under the same conditions as a decision given in the where the enforcement takes place. If a party does not comply with the terms of an order of the Court, that party may be sanctioned with a recurring penalty payment payable to the Court. The individual penalty shall be proportionate to the importance of the order to be enforced and shall be without prejudice to the party's right to claim damages or security. 1597

In UPC Rule 118 (8), it is stated that the orders of the Court referred to in paragraphs 1 and 2(a) shall be enforceable on the defendant only after the claimant has notified the Court which part of the orders he intends to enforce, a certified translation of the orders in accordance with UPC Rule 7.2, where applicable, into the official language of a Contracting Member State in which the enforcement shall take place has been provided by the claimant and the said notice and, where applicable, a certified translation of the orders have been served on the defendant by the Registry. The Court may subject any order or measure to a security to be given by the successful party to the unsuccessful party as determined by the Court in accordance with UPC Rule 352. 1598

According to UPC Rule 354 (1), subject to UPC Rule 118.8 and 352 decisions and orders of the Court shall be directly enforceable from their date of service in each Contracting Member State. Enforcement shall take place in accordance with the enforcement procedures and conditions governed by the law of the particular Contracting Member State where enforcement takes place. Part 5, chapter 2 of the UPC Rules contains rules for service of decisions or orders by the Court. See, more in particular, UPC Rule 276 in conjunction with UPC Rule 271 and further. According to UPC Rule 354 (3), the Court's decisions and orders may provide for periodic penalty payments payable to the Court in the event that a party fails to comply with the terms of the order or an earlier order. The value of such payments shall be set by the Court having regard to the importance of the order in question. According to UPC Rule 354 (4), if it is alleged that a party has failed to comply with the terms of the order of the Court, the first instance panel of the division in question may decide on penalty payments provided for in the order upon the request of the other party or of its own motion. The procedure foreseen in the UPC Rules shall apply. After having heard both parties the Court may make an appropriate order which may be subject to an appeal pursuant to UPC Rule 220 (2). 1599

If a division of the Court orders a defendant situated in the Netherlands to pay a specific amount (e.g. damages, legal costs and/or an amount of penalties forfeited) and 1600

the respective decision or order has been served by the Court on the defendant, that decision or order can be enforced with assistance of a bailiff, without the intervention of a (Dutch) Court being required. The bailiff can enforce the decision or order e.g. by levying an executory attachment on assets of the defendant in the Netherlands or on amounts kept by the defendant on bank accounts in the Netherlands and obtain payment of the amount that has to be paid on the basis of the decision or order by means of the proceeds resulting from the executory attachment (the proceeds of public sale of the assets attached, or the amounts on bank accounts that have been attached).

1601 Enforcement of decisions or orders will take place in the manner as described above, whether the division of the Court that renders the decision or order is located in the Netherlands or in another contracting member state. See, in this respect, Art. 71d of Regulation (EU) No 1215/2012 on jurisdiction and the recognition and enforcement of judgments in civil and commercial matters.

Chapter 25: Enforcement in Austria

Contents

The Agreement on a Unified Patent Court (UPCA) and the associated Rules of Procedure essentially provide their own body of regulations for enforcement proceedings, particularly when it comes to the injunction claims which are so important in practice. Thus, the UPCA provides a self-contained regulatory system for the imposition of penalty payments for actions that may not be taken by others (*unvertretbare Handlungen*), for example, as well as for omissions.[1] This leaves little room for the subsidiary application of national laws governing enforcement.[2] Indeed, the national laws are only relevant when it comes to defining the specific details of how the enforcement process is to be implemented. In Austria, these details are governed by the Enforcement Code (*Exekutionsordnung*, EO) and are handled by the respectively competent District Court (*Bezirksgericht*). Since none of this falls within the exclusive competence of the Unified Patent Court, it follows that the international competence of Austrian courts for the way in which compulsory enforcement measures are implemented will be determined on the basis of the Brussels Ia Regulation (Article 24 (5) of (EC) Regulation 1215/2012 as well as Article 32 (2) of the UPCA. **1602**

A number of questions will have to be clarified going forward through the legal precedent established by the Court. For example, whether the UPCA's self-contained system for recurring penalty payments precludes the possibility of coercive detention (*Beugehaft*) – a sanction which is expressly provided for under the Austrian Enforcement Code (cf. Section 354 paragraph 1 and Section 55 paragraph 1 of the EO),[3] even if it only comes into play in extreme cases. **1603**

An additional question to be clarified by the UPC – one of importance to the enforcement of writs of injunction – is whether an injunctive claim's protective scope encompasses only fully comparable actions or – in accord with standing Austrian case law – also includes actions which leave the essential core of the infringing action untouched.[4] **1604**

---

1 Cf. Article 82 of the UPCA.

2 *Leistner*, GRUR 2016, p. 217 with additional references.

3 This is essentially the conclusion drawn by *Leistner*, GRUR 2016, p. 217.

4 On Austrian case law, cf. *Klicka* in Angst/Jakusch/Pimmer, "Exekutionsordnung," Section 355.

1605 National laws play an even more important role for the enforcement of monetary receivables than for writs of injunction, given that the UPCA contains relatively limited provisions for the former.[5] According to Article 82 (3) of the UPCA, the laws of the Contracting Member State in which the receivable is to be enforced will apply. To the extent that Austrian law is applicable, the specifics of the enforcement process will thus be in keeping with the Austrian Enforcement Code (EO).

1606 The discussion that follows therefore presents the key jurisdictional regulations and enforcement options which apply in Austria:

A. Determining the Court of Jurisdiction

1607 In principle, the Austrian District Court which is to function as execution court will be determined as follows:[6]

- when the enforcement targets immoveable assets: the District Court in whose district (*Sprengel*) the immoveable assets are located;
- when the enforcement targets monetary receivables which have not been officially registered as liens: the District Court which serves as the debtor's normal legal venue for legal disputes (usually the place of domicile or regular sojourn or, in the case of enterprises, the registered seat);
- in all other cases, the District Court in whose district the items targeted by the enforcement have been located since the start of the enforcement process. So this primarily applies to enforcement which targets moveable physical assets (chattels). But in the absence of such chattels, the competent District Court will be the one in whose district the first concrete enforcement measure is to be taken.

B. Procedural Aspects

1608 The actual steps of the compulsory enforcement process will vary depending on the object of the enforcement:

I. Enforcement Targeting Moveable Chattels and Physical Items

1609 Where moveable chattels and physical items (*Fahrnisse*) are involved, compulsory enforcement will be performed by the bailiff assigned to the enforcement court, who will then seize/attach the relevant goods. The goods seized in this manner may later be liquidated by way of a public foreclosure auction (Sections 249 et seqq. of the EO). It bears noting that items of personal use or household goods, insofar as they permit the debtor and the members of his household to enjoy a modest standard of living, are exempt from seizure/attachment (Section 250 paragraph 1 of the EO).

5 *Leistner*, GRUR 2016, p. 217.

6 Cf. Section 18 of the EO.

II. Enforcement Targeting Legal Rights and Claims Receivable

Where legal rights/claims are the target of the enforcement – particularly including industrial property rights such as patents or trademarks – the creditor will have the option of having a lien recorded in the relevant register (Patent Register, Trademark Register). These rights/claims may likewise be liquidated through a public foreclosure auction, but they may also be placed under receivership or compulsory lease-out. Licensing rights may be attached as well: This is accomplished by imposing a dual block on both the licensor and licensee. If the rightsholder consents, the licensing right may also be liquidated separately. Otherwise, the attached right may only be liquidated as part of the receivership or compulsory lease-out of the enterprise which holds the license (Section 331 of the EO)[7]. 1610

Where monetary receivables are involved, it is customary to issue a "garnishee order" (*Drittverbot*) which compels a third party – e.g. the debtor's employer – to render payments owed to the debtor directly to the petitioning creditor rather than to the debtor.[8] 1611

III. Enforcement Targeting Real Property

In the case of real property, the creditor will have the option to have a lien (mortgage) recorded in the Land Register (*Grundbuch*). The property's eventual liquidation will usually take the form of a public foreclosure auction. But one can also exploit the property by placing it under receivership insofar as this may serve to generate revenues (Sections 87 et seqq. of the EO). 1612

C. Course of the Proceeding

In Austria, the creditor himself must lodge the corresponding applications with the court in order to commence the enforcement process and the execution of enforcement measures; the court will not take such action upon its own motion. 1613

I. Legal Remedies

The Austrian laws governing compulsory enforcement provide for a number of legal remedies, specifically including: 1614

- action by the debtor to contest the claim (*Oppositionsklage*) (Section 35 of the Enforcement Code (EO));
- action by the debtor to contest approval of enforcement (*Impugnationsklage*), particularly on the grounds of insufficient maturity or enforceability of the claim(s) involved (Section 36 of the EO);
- third-party action to nullify enforcement (*Exszindierungsklage*), insofar as the enforcement affects assets belonging to third parties (Section 37 of the EO).

7 See *Oberhammer* in Angst/Jakusch/Pimmer, "Exekutionsordnung," Section 331, Note 61.
8 Cf. in particular Sections 294 et seqq. of the EO.

1615 In addition, the decisions issued by the court in a compulsory execution proceeding may also be contested through an appeal (*Rekurs*), insofar as the law does not expressly provide (Section 65 of the EO)

II. Insolvency

1616 In the event of the debtor's insolvency, an enforcement freeze will be placed on all enforcement measures which are pending as of the opening date of the insolvency proceeding, insofar as such measures pertain to assets belonging to the insolvency estate (Section 6 paragraph 1 of the Austrian Insolvency Ordinance (*Insolvenzordnung*, IO)).

D. Open Issues

1617 There are a number of open questions which, in the absence of clarifying Austrian legislation, will probably have to be resolved by the legal precedent established by the Unified Patent Court in the wake of the UPCA's ratification. One of these is whether enforcement-related decisions of the UPC should also be subject to the other regulations which are directly applicable in Austria when it comes to enforcing decisions from other EU Member States (Article 39 et seqq. of Regulation 1215/2012 (EU) (Brussels Ia Regulation)), not to mention the added prerequisites for enforcement which said regulations stipulate (e.g. the provision of a translation of the enforcement decision).[9]

1618 It also remains unclear how enforcement of the recurring penalty payments imposed by the Unified Patent Court is to be implemented. One way that would make practical sense would be for the Unified Patent Court to lodge an application for enforcement – by analogy to Article 39 et seqq. of the Brussels Ia Regulation – with the respectively competent Austrian District Court (*Bezirksgericht*).

1619 Open questions also remain when it comes to the enforcement of orders issued by the UPC concerning measures which may be taken by others (known in German as *vertretbare Handlungen*), such as the removal or recall of an infringing product from the channels of commerce and/or its destruction. Neither Article 64 of the UPCA nor the Rules of Procedure contain any provision that specifically defines how enforcement is to be implemented. Austrian law stipulates that the petitioning creditor may perform the enforcement as a proxy (Section 353 paragraph 1 of the Enforcement Code (EO)). The creditor may also use a third party for this purpose or, where appropriate, an expert.[10]

1620 Another moot question which will ultimately have to be clarified through case law pertains to orders to communicate information and lay open the books: Will such orders be governed only by Article 67 of the UPCA and will they be enforceable only via the imposition of penalty payments pursuant to Article 82 (4) of the UPCA (in case of insufficient compliance)? Or will Austrian regulations apply as well? Particu-

9 Cf. Article 42 III, 57 of Regulation 864/2007 (EC).
10 *Klicka* in Angst/Jakusch/Pimmer, "Exekutionsordnung," Section 353 Notes 10 and 11.

larly relevant in this context is Section 151 of the Austrian Patent Act (*Patentgesetz* PatG), which stipulates that the infringer is obliged to have the correctness of his books and records audited by an outside expert, and to compensate for any discrepancy insofar as the audit determines that the correct balance sheet amount is higher than the one shown on the books.

As regards the sworn statements (affidavits) which are also envisioned under the UPC 1621
Agreement,[11] their legal effect for Austria will have to be determined in accordance with Austrian law: Section 288 paragraph 2 of the Austrian Criminal Code (StGB) makes it a criminal offense to give a false statement under oath (with possible imprisonment for up to five years). This makes such sworn affidavits a formidable means of applying pressure which should not be underestimated.

11 Cf. in particular Article 53(1) h of the UPCA as read in conjunction with Rule 170(2) h of the Rules of Procedure.

Chapter 26: Enforcement in Finland

1622 In civil matters a judgement given by the Market Court becomes final and enforceable after the end of the appeal period of two months, unless a leave of appeal is filed and allowed by the Supreme Court. In case the judgement is not voluntarily followed, the matter should be taken to the enforcement authority represented by a competent district enforcement officer (bailiff).

1623 In case of injunctions, a preliminary injunction against an alleged infringer is directly enforcable after the applicant of the preliminary injunction has set a required security to the enforcement officer in accordance with the Enforcement Act. The main action must raised within one month from the date of the preliminary injunction decision. A final injunction judgement can be enhanced with a penalty fine.

Chapter 27: Enforcement in Sweden

Contents Para

1624 Orders and decisions by Swedish courts are enforced by the Swedish Enforcement Authority[1] and under the provisions of the Swedish Enforcement Code[2] and Enforcement Regulation[3]. The Enforcement Authority is institutionally separate from the courts and responsible for collection of public and private claims, evictions of tenants, supervision of bankruptcies etc., throughout the country.

A. Institutions and procedure

1625 An application for enforcement, which may be submitted in the English language, shall be accompanied by a certified copy of the enforceable title. Orders and decisions that have become final, wherein an official certification to this effect is preferably to be annexed, are enforceable titles. Enforceability is not suspended by means of redress invoked by the debtor in an exceptional situation, such as rehearing. National orders and decisions having not yet become final are enforceable under special conditions, including:

- if the court decision expressly allows immediate enforcement, or
- in case of a claim for money, if the debtor refuses to provide security, or
- in case of a claim for movable property, if the creditor provides security.

1626 Further, if a decision has been appealed only in part (e.g., an infringer accepts an injunction on infringing activities but challenges the amount of the damages), the remaining part of the decision remains enforceable.

1627 Although the Enforcement Authority accepts applications for enforcement without a time restriction, strong reasons exist for a creditor to avoid delays. First, many types of claims are normally prescribed after ten years.[4] Secondly, if the debtor goes bankrupt, a creditor who has obtained a seizure decision from the Enforcement Authority in the meantime may be prioritized over other creditors.[5]

1628 The Enforcement Authority charges an application fee of about EUR 30 and, if applicable, a fee for compulsory sale in the range EUR 200–6,000 plus 3–4 % of the selling price. These and other fees are eventually to be covered by the debtor's assets.

1 *Kronofogdemyndigheten* or *Kronofogden*.
2 *Utsökningsbalk*, SFS 1981:774.
3 *Utsökningsförordning*, SFS 1981:981.
4 Section 2 Prescription Act (*Preskriptionslag*, SFS 1981:130); see also Gregow, *Utsökningsrätt*, fourth edition (2012), page 77.
5 Section 8 Rights of Priority Act (*Förmånsrättslag*, SFS 1970:979).

1629 In collecting debts, the Enforcement Authority may avail itself of the following measures:
- Seizure and compulsory sale of debtor's movable property
- Seizure and compulsory sale of debtor's real estate, registered vessels, aircraft etc.
- Seizure of debts owed by third parties to the debtor (third party debt order)
- Seizure of preliminary payments to the Tax Authority
- Attachment of future earnings[6], if the debtor is a natural person

1630 The last point may be applicable also when the debtor is a legal person, namely, when its directors have pierced the corporate veil on account of negligent acts on the legal person's behalf[7]. The UPC is not competent to determine that such negligence has occurred; rather the creditor must obtain, or invoke, a ruling to this effect from a district court.

1631 The Enforcement Authority may further enforce preliminary orders by:
- Sequestration[8] of property, in particular freezing of bank accounts
- Preservation of evidence, such as inspection of defendant's premises, making audio and video recordings, photocopies of documents

1632 Directive 2004/48/EC on the Enforcement of Intellectual Property Rights, has long been implemented in Swedish law, making its full range of investigative measures, preliminary and permanent reliefs available and enforceable by the Enforcement Authority. The Enforcement Authority may enforce decisions involving modification or removal of physical objects by its own officials or sub-contractors, by allowing the claimant to perform the modification or removal, or by ordering the defendant to do so subject to a penalty.

1633 To avoid enforcement of a court decision, a debtor may invoke circumstances that either have occurred after the decision or could not be considered in the court proceedings, including:
- the debtor has already paid what is owed;
- the debtor has an outstanding claim on the creditor;
- sufficient reservation[9] for personal items and expenses has not been made (if the debtor is a natural person);
- interests of third parties are violated;
- the court decision has been set aside; and
- other circumstances.

1634 Such grounds may also be invoked in an appeal against a decision by the Enforcement Authority. The appeal must be filed within three weeks and is examined by the competent district court. The appeal does not have suspensive effect.

1635 If after commencement of enforcement proceedings the decision to be enforced is set aside (e.g., in appeal proceedings or a rehearing), then according to Chapter 3,

6 *Löneutmätning.*
7 *Ansvarsgenombrott.*
8 *Kvarstad.*
9 *Beneficium.*

Section 22 Enforcement Code, the proceedings shall be cancelled, and any already transferred assets shall be returned to the debtor. The debtor is entitled to assistance from the Enforcement Authority if the creditor fails to cooperate. Security that the creditor has provided may be used. Moreover, the creditor may be liable for damages that the debtor has suffered as a result of the enforcement; proceedings to determine such damages may be brought before the district court.

B. Enforcing decisions of the Unified Patent Court

Swedish authorities enforce UPC decisions under the same conditions as they enforce decisions by national courts (Art. 82(3) UPCA, implemented by Chapter 19, Section 3 of the Swedish Patents Act[10]). Accordingly, the Enforcement Authority requires neither an exequatur (authorization to enforce) nor a translation of the UPC's decisions and orders. However, a party submitting with his enforcement application a UPC decision without a corresponding Swedish translation should bear in mind that the Enforcement Authority may translate it into Swedish of its own motion (Chapter 2, Section 8 second paragraph Enforcement Code). The equal enforceability laid down in Art. 82(3) UPCA covers both investigative orders and freezing orders (Arts. 59–61 and 67 UPCA) and permanent and preliminary injunctions (Arts. 62–64, 68, 69 and 80 UPCA), including payment of costs and damages, removal of goods from the market, destroying of goods, dissemination etc. **1636**

A decision ordering a payment of money to a party may be efficiently enforced in Sweden if the debtor has assets on Swedish territory. Information regarding a natural or legal person's taxable assets and income can be obtained from the Swedish Tax Authority[11]. The information is free of charge and inquiries can be made anonymously, without stating their underlying purpose; such inquiries may therefore be conducted before the UPC issues an imminent decision. **1637**

The Swedish Enforcement Authority is further competent to enforce decisions ordering a party to remove or destroy goods or to produce evidence, provided the goods or evidence is located on Swedish territory. The investigative measures and the reliefs available under the UPCA are within the scope of Directive 2004/48/EC and should thus be familiar to the Enforcement Authority. The degree of involvement of the patent proprietor, apart from submitting the application for enforcement, depends on the type of relief sought. For instance, the Enforcement Authority may at its discretion grant the proprietor a right to attend an inspection of the defendant's premises. **1638**

A freezing order (see above) pursuant to Art. 62(3) UPCA is enforceable by the Enforcement Authority on the same terms as an account preservation order by a Swedish court. Alternatively, the creditor may turn directly to the debtor's bank, without assistance from the Enforcement Authority. This time-saving route is expressly allowed by Regulation (EU) No 655/2014 establishing a European Account Preservation **1639**

10 *Patentlag*, SFS 2024:945.
11 *Skatteverket.*

Order procedure, which applies in cases where the creditor is domiciled in a different EU member state than where the bank account is maintained.

1640 When the UPC has prohibited specific activities (because they constitute infringement or are likely to constitute infringement) subject to recurring penalties, the UPC is also competent to determine the individual penalty (Art. 82(4) UPCA) regardless of where the activities take place. Penalties are payable to the UPC, and the patent proprietor has no legal means to enforce the penalties. While national court decisions resulting in fines or penalties are forwarded to the Enforcement Authority as a matter of procedure, it appears to be an open question how the UPC will go about to ensure that such penalties are collected.

1641 UPC decisions revoking a patent granted by the EPO or amending other entries in the European Patent Register (Arts. 65 and 66 UPCA) do not contain an obligation to be fulfilled, and are therefore outside the scope of the Enforcement Code.

Section 8: Comparison with National Law

Chapter 28: Comparison with Opposition Proceedings Before the European Patent Office

Contents | Para

The Unified Patent Court is a newly created judicial institution with its own Rules of Procedure. It is the first truly pan-European court, and thus represents an achievement which has not (yet) received the recognition it deserves beyond the field of property-right protection. 1642

On the other hand, the Unified Patent Court is obviously based on principles and regulations derived and/or adopted from other legal systems. Since practitioners in the field of patent law will have to learn how to deal with this new court system, it might prove useful to compare the practices of the Unified Patent Court with those of national and international courts – at least to the degree possible, given that the UPC has yet to create any case law of its own. We will present such a comparative overview for the most important European Member States in the chapters that follow. This chapter will concentrate on the European Patent Office. 1643

Given that it is not possible to conduct infringement proceedings before the European Patent Office, we must limit our comparative analysis to the EPO's opposition proceeding. This can still give us a number of useful insights, however. 1644

A. Similarities

One evident similarity with proceedings before the UPC is that an opposition proceeding before the European Patent Office is mostly conducted in writing. It also includes an oral hearing, which is conducted by a chairman and which usually lasts only lasts one day. 1645

Following the introduction of new regulations, opposition proceedings before the EPO are subject to certain time limits, even if the European Patent Office is not always so strict in this regard as the Unified Patent Court. The key "dividing line" is normally the deadline date for submitting writing pleadings in advance of the oral hearing held before the Opposition Division. Up to that point, the European Patent Office tends to be quite lenient. Afterwards, however, it becomes relatively difficult to introduce any new facts and/or evidence, including documents. As mentioned earlier, Rule 222 of the UPC's Rules of Procedure corresponds to the practice that used to 1646 be followed by the EPO's Boards of Appeal in years past – despite the fact that said practice has changed in the meantime.[1]

1647 Both lawyers and appropriately qualified patent attorneys are entitled to act as representatives before the European Patent Office.

1648 Just like the UPC, the European Patent Office distinguishes between a Statement of Appeal and a Statement of Grounds for Appeal. Just as in an appeal proceeding before the UPC, these must be lodged within a time limit of two months or four months, respectively.

B. Differences

1649 The salient difference, of course, is that no infringement proceedings are possible before the EPO.

1650 There is also no interim procedure at the EPO like the one conducted before UPC, nor is there is such a thing as a judge-rapporteur.

1651 Appeals cannot be lodged with the EPO's Boards of Appeal during an ongoing proceeding; only an order or interim decision issued by the Opposition Division can be appealed during this time.

1652 The European Patent Office recognizes the principle of *ex officio* investigation. This is in contrast to the Unified Patent Court, for which no such principle has been codified.

1653 It is also not usual for the EPO to grant a recovery of costs. Although possible in principle, this is an option only exercised in extreme cases. The fees payable for this purpose are not contingent on the value of the proceeding.

1654 It is not possible to bring a cross-appeal before the European Patent Office, i.e. a party cannot lodge an appeal – even after the corresponding time limit has expired – when the opposite side lodges an appeal.

1655 Another difference is that both sides in an opposition proceeding before the EPO will still be able to submit pleadings if the preliminary opinions of the Opposition Division and (at least to a certain extent) of the Board of Appeal are already known (see Para. 1061 et seqq.)

1 See e.g. *Anetsberger* et al., epi-information 2015, p. 63: for a highly critical view, see e.g. *Wallinger*, VPP-Randbrief 2015, p. 18; a statistical survey of appeal proceedings can be found in *Nollen*, epi information 2015, p. 17.

Chapter 29: Comparison with Belgian Law

Contents Para

A. Substantive Patent Law

1656 All substantive patent law is contained in Book XI, Title I, of the Code of Economic Law,[1] which entered into effect on 22 September 2014. This title contains the provisions of the Patent Act of 1984, with a substantial number of amendments that were enacted in 2011 to update a number of substantive provisions, modernize the patent granting procedure, and ensure compliance with the Patent Law Treaty. As a result, Belgian substantive patent law is now strongly harmonized with the European Patent Convention and with the Patent Law treaty.

1657 The grant procedure is still a "registration procedure", in which a search report and written opinion are prepared by the European Patent Office, the applicant is invited to comment on the report, and a patent is subsequently granted regardless of the contents of the report. The grant proceedings normally take approximately 18 months, such that the first publication of the patent documents and the actual grant of the patent normally coincide.

B. Descriptive Measures – Preliminary Measures

1658 Belgium has implemented Directive 2004/48/EC of 29 April 2004 on the enforcement of intellectual property rights in the Judicial Code.[2] It must be noted that even before that Directive, Belgian law already provided effective ex parte procedures to obtain description or seizure of allegedly infringing goods. These measures for preservation of evidence must be authorized by the President of the commercial court. They are conducted by a court-appointed expert (often a patent attorney) in the presence of a bailiff[3], but without the claimant being present. While the initial proceedings leading to the authorization of evidence preserving measures are typically conducted in a unilateral (ex parte) procedure, the affected party can subsequently have the decision reexamined by means of an opposition procedure. In order for the evidence to be validly used, proceedings on the merits must be initiated within the periods laid down in article 7(3) of Directive 2004/48/EC.

1 Dutch: "Wetboek van Economisch Recht"; French: "Code de droit économique"; German: "Wirtschaftsgesetzbuch".

2 Dutch: "Gerechtelijk Wetboek"; French: "Code judiciaire"; German "Gerichtsgesetzbuch".

3 Dutch: "gerechtsdeurwaarder"; French: "huissier de justice"; German: "Gerichtsvollzieher".

1659 An order for urgent measures can be obtained in summary proceeding before the president of the commercial court of Brussels in accordance with art. 584 of the Judicial Code.

1660 The rather low threshold of "prima facie validity" traditionally employed by Belgian courts when granting urgent provisional measures or evidence preservation measures has been the subject of both praise and criticism. In any case, the more recent case law of the Supreme Court, notably the judgments of 26 June 2014 and 12 September 2014, indicates that the courts should take into account all relevant facts when judging the "prima facie validity" of a patent, including judgments on foreign counterparts of the same European patent and first-instance judgments, even when these are still subject to appeal.

C. Proceedings on the Merits

1661 With a view to increasing the level of specialization of the judges involved in patent cases, the Belgian legislator has made the commercial court of Brussels the sole competent court for patent litigation as of 1 January 2015.

1662 Proceedings on the merits regarding patent infringement and/or validity are carried out in the same way as all other civil or commercial cases, as detailed in Part IV, Book II, of the Judicial Code. The parties agree on a pleading calendar or have it determined by the court, they exchange written briefs and evidence to present their complete case in accordance with the calendar, and then plead the case before the judge on the appointed date. As all the judges in the commercial court are legally qualified – i.e., there are no "technical judges" – one or more court experts may be appointed to assist the court in assessing the technical side of the case, but they are not allowed to make any legal determinations. As the same court is competent to hear infringement claims invalidity claims, there is no need for a bifurcation of the proceedings. The court may stay the national proceedings pending opposition proceedings before the European Patent Office.

1663 A fast-track procedure exists to obtain an injunction in the case of infringement of an intellectual property right.[4] This procedure is conducted before the president of the commercial court in Brussels, according to the rules for summary proceedings. However, unlike summary proceedings, the fast-track procedure on the merits can lead to a final determination on the issues of infringement and validity. For this reason, this type of procedure is less popular for patent infringement cases.

1664 An appeal lies from the decisions of the commercial court and of the president of the commerical court, at the court of appeals of Brussels. The appeal has devolutive effect: the court of appeal will decide all the aspects of the case brought before it, i.e. both points of fact and points of law.

---

4 Art. XVII.14 Of the Code of Economic Law.

The decision of the court of appeal can be appealed to the Supreme Court,[5] only on the grounds of a breach of law or of substantial formalities. By way of exception, the appeal to the Supreme Court has suspensive effect in patent cases. The Supreme Court does not assess the facts of the case; if a judgment of the court of appeal is reversed, the case is sent back to a (different) court of appeal. **1665**

The prevailing party is entitled to recovery of damages and the legal costs of the proceedings. However, the attorney fees are limited to a "legal process compensation" (Dutch: "rechtsplegingsvergoeding"; French: "indemnité de procédure"; German: "Verfahrensentschädigung") on the basis of a fixed schedule, which is not linked to the actual cost of the legal services employed by the party. It is being debated whether this scheme of limited compensation for the prevailing party's attorney fees in cases concerning intellectual property infringement is compatible with article 14 of Directive 2004/48/EC. **1666**

Apart from the issue of civil liability, patent infringement is also a punishable offense if it is done with malicious or fraudulent intent.[6] Criminal infringement proceedings are outside the jurisdiction of the commercial courts, and will be brought before the competent correctional court. **1667**

5 Dutch: "Hof van Cassatie"; French: "Cour de Cassation"; German: "Kassationshof".
6 Art. XV.103 of the Code of Economic Law.

Chapter 30: Comparison with Danish Law

Contents | Para

1668 In Denmark the Maritime and Commercial High Court (Sø- og Handelsretten) is a court specialized in intellectual property. The courts competences are determined by §§ 225 and 227 in The Danish Administrative of Justice Act (Retsplejeloven) which was amended latest in 1.2.2014. The Maritime and Commercial High Court is one of Denmark's common courts, however it is the only court in the country which is a specialized court, and therefore deals with certain types of cases.

1669 The court is competent to hear actions for revocation of a patent, infringement actions and appeals against decisions by the Danish Patent Office (Decisions from the Patent Appeal Board). The court is also competent to hear both cases relating to preliminary injunction actions in relation to patent infringement and permanent injunction. Preliminary injunction cases must be followed up by a confirmatory action.

1670 Decisions by the court can be referred to the High Court (Landsretten) in accordance with § 368 of The Danish Administrative of Justice Act. Only in special cases decisions from The Maritime and Commercial Court can be appealed to the Supreme Court (Højesteret).

1671 The present contribution will discuss revocation and infringement actions before The Maritime Commercial High Court.

A. Similarities

1672 In Denmark, where cases involve both infringement and validity, both aspects are heard by the same court in the same proceedings, thereby ensuring that the arguments used in those aspects are mutually consistent and that the decision on each aspect is delivered at the same time. Under the Unified Patent Court it is expected that it will be normal for those two aspects be heard together, as in Denmark, although bifurcation will be possible.

1673 Patent infringement proceedings before The Maritime and Commercial Court are commenced by the court's receipt of the claimant's writ (stævning). The court will fix a date for defendant's first response, the statement of defence (svarskrift). In the statement of defence, the defendant must submit the defendant's claim (for example, a rejection or dismissal of the claims) and any counterclaims. The parties will normally exchange additional pleadings, such as reply (replik) and a rejoinder (duplik). When the preparatory phase is concluded, no new claims, allegations or documents can be submitted without the opposing party's or the court's consent. The court will fix a date for the oral hearing and judgment will usually be given three months after the conclusion of the oral hearing. In patent cases, the oral hearing will often take several days.

Writ, statement of defence and other pleadings should be presented by a lawyer authorised to practise before the High Court and The Maritime Commercial High Court. These documents may be submitted by use of electronic procedures. However, the use of the normal way of submitting documents is also possible. However, the court recommends to use only one of the above ways of communication. 1674

The parties to proceedings before the court shall pay court fees cf. The Danish Administrative of Justice Act. 1675

After receiving the writ, the court then issues summons. In the ensuing preparatory phase, the defendant is ordered to submit a statement of defence within a certain deadline, usually within six weeks. The judge may request written clarification on specific issues, and may summon the parties to a preparatory conference cf. The Danish Administrative of Justice Act § 353. At the conference, remaining open issues are summarized, such as the request for expert opinions and a timeline for the rest of the preparatory phase, up to the main hearing, is agreed on. Also a date for the main hearing is set and the length and timing of the trial. If the parties are not able to agree on a binding timetable for the proceedings, it will usually be adopted by the court. 1676

The deadlines for additional pleadings (replik and duplik) are set to four weeks. 1677

In the Maritime and Commercial High Court, the cases are decided by a panel consisting of one or three of the court's professional judges, and two or four assessors (technically qualified judges). 1678

The court has around 140 assessors, all who are mostly recommended by business organisations (approximately 20 assessors with apecific insight into different aspects of patent law). There are also assessors who have particular experience in consumer affairs, shipping, and employment related matters. All the assessors have gotten a particular insight into one or more of the areas of law that the court offers, through their work as an assessor. 1679

In Denmark, as in the UPC, the winning party can claim its litigation costs from the unsuccessful party cf. The Danish Administrative of Justice Act § 312. This includes costs of legal representation as well as process costs. However, the costs may be divided between the parties if the parties have agreed to that. 1680

As briefly mentioned above, decisions of The Maritime and Commercial High Court are appealable to the High Court[1] and in special cases only appealable to the Supreme Court. Before the new system was introduced with the amendments in 2014 mentioned above, decisions from The Maritime and Commercial High Court were appealable directly to the Supreme Court. 1681

In Denmark, the courts should actively encourage an amicable settlement through mediation cf. The Danish Administrative of Justice Act § 268. Mediation may take place already at the preparatory conference. The parties may, however, at any time 1682

1 Cf. The Danish Administrative of Justice Act § 368, stk.6.

in the course of proceedings consider a settlement. As the cases before the court are often long and complicated, and consequently resource demanding, the court often actively make use of traditional mediation.

1683 The main hearing is open to the public cf. The Danish Administrative of Justice Act § 28a. All written pleadings, written evidence, decisions and orders are as a main rule available to the public.[2]

1684 In Denmark, proceedings before The Maritime and Commercial High Court can only be carried out by persons admitted to the Bar and with the right to appear before the High Courts.

B. Differences

1685 In Denmark it is typical that the hearing includes cross-examination of the witnesses, including the expert witnesses. They are usually appointed by the parties and their evidence is often highly influential in the decision of the court, especially issues relating to inventive step.

1686 Legal costs in amount approved by the court are borne by the losing party. Costs are dealt with by the court in the final decision. Usually, only a reasonable amount of the lawyers' fees will be awarded whereas other costs are awarded in full. Unlike the situation in the Unified Patent Court, there is no statutory regulation of the legal costs in relation to the value in dispute. There is also no statutory regulation on attorney fees. The average amount of legal costs may be from € 50,000 for simple cases to € 450,000 or more for complex pharmaceutical cases.

1687 The determination of the amount of damages is usually not the subject of separate proceedings, as it may be in the Unified Patent Court. If the parties agree to deal with the amount of damages out of court, the court may drop this part of the original action. If the negotiations between the parties fail, the parties are free to bring a new action regarding the amount of damages specifically.

1688 The depositing of so-called protective letters is accepted by the Unified Patent Court but not by Danish courts. However, this is generally not an issue since in practice the alleged infringer will almost always be notified.

1689 While a local or regional division of the Unified Patent Court has the discretion to refer an action for revocation of a patent to the central division and proceed with an infringement action relating to the same patent (bifurcation, Art. 33(3)(b) UPCA), infringement and revocation actions are always dealt with in joint proceedings before a Danish court.

2 Cf. The Danish Administrative of Justice Act § 41.

Chapter 31: Comparison with German Law

Contents | Para

A. Similarities

An infringement proceeding under German law seems to be the one which exhibits the most similarities to an infringement proceeding before the Unified Patent Court. Since we cannot cover all these similarities, we will focus on the most important ones in this chapter. 1690

Just like the regulations governing the UPC, German law, too, calls for a three-part proceeding consisting of a written procedure, interim procedure and oral hearing, although the interim procedure is performed in a merely cursory manner by the German court's first-instance panel. In addition, the relevant provisions of the German Code of Civil Procedure (*Zivilprozessordnung*, ZPO) are repeated almost verbatim in the Rules of Procedure of the Unified Patent Court. This means that a German proceeding, just like one before the UPC, is essentially conducted in writing and that the parties, particularly the plaintiff, will be well advised to submit their facts and evidence right at the start of the proceedings if they wish to be successful. 1691

In Germany, the first instance panels of the infringement court will likewise comprise a judge-rapporteur, a standing judge and a presiding judge. 1692

There are also technical judges in Germany, but these only sit on the Federal Patent Court (*Bundespatentgericht*, BPatG). 1693

The principle of cost recovery applies before the German courts, i.e. the party which loses the proceeding has to reimburse the attorney's fees, court costs and other litigation expenses incurred by the opposing side in accordance with a fixed schedule. The value of the action serves as the calculatory basis in this context, just as in a proceeding before the UPC. 1694

German law provides for the possibility of a default decision, as well as for the option of contesting such a decision by lodging a complaint (*Einspruch*). 1695

German law makes it possible to lodge a cross-appeal (Section 567 of the Code of Civil Procedure (ZPO)) but this is not subject to time limits, in contrast to a cross-appeal before the UPC. 1696

The additional pretrial proceedings which are possible before the Unified Patent Court may also occur in a German proceeding. Just like the UPC, a German court may order provisional measures without hearing the opposing side, whereby it may also order a freezing of assets or a seizure of the patent-infringing products. 1697

As is the case with the UPC, a proceeding for provisional measures in Germany may also be followed by the launching of an actual main proceeding on the merits, whe- 1698 reby the party which loses the proceeding for provisional measures may also compel the launch of such a main proceeding.

1699 Just like the UPC, German courts also use the *saisie-contrefaçon* proceeding for preserving evidence. Here, the practice followed by the UPC is in large part modeled after the "Düsseldorf Proceeding," i.e. the actual preservation of evidence is carried out by a neutral expert designated by the Court without the presence of the applicant, whereby the Court is also free to refuse the application for preserving evidence.

B. Differences

1700 One key difference worth mentioning is that a strict principle of segregation (*Trennungsprinzip*) applies in Germany, i.e. the examination of infringement and of invalidity are each conducted by separate courts. The Unified Patent Court, for its part, is allowed to draw such a distinction only the basis of a corresponding decision from the bench. And if the infringement action has been brought before the UPC's central division, then even this option is precluded.

1701 German courts follow the principle of *ex-officio* investigation and thus perform examinations upon their own motion, unlike the UPC.

1702 The German infringement courts do not resort to technical judges, and the panels which hear appeals – whether in connection with infringement or invalidity – are composed differently. Before German infringement courts, the interim procedure is conducted – if only in a cursory manner – by the first-instance panel and not by a judge-rapporteur.

1703 German law does recognize default decisions. In contrast to the UPC's practice, however, such a decision is mandatory if the opposing side requests it, and can be revoked through the lodging of a simple complaint (*Einspruch*) which does not have to rely on supporting reasoning.

1704 In addition, the regulations governing the UPC do not define how attorneys are to settle accounts with their own clients (also after losing a case). Under German law, this is regulated by the Attorneys' Compensation Act (*Rechtsanwaltsvergütungsgesetz*, RVG), which calls for minimum remuneration amounts based on the value of the action.

1705 German law makes representation through an attorney mandatory, at least before the infringement courts.

1706 The various types of appeals which can be lodged before the UPC, even during ongoing proceedings, are not available to nearly the same extent before the German courts.

1707 Another difference is that both sides can still submit additional pleadings in a German revocation proceeding so long as the preliminary opinion of the German Federal Patent Court (BPatG), as expressed in a so-called "qualified indication" (*qualifzierter Hinweis*), is known. No comparable provision exists for purposes of the UPC.

Chapter 32: Comparison with French Law

Contents | Para

The Unified Patent Court system inherits many features of the French national patent litigation system. Therefore, French patent judges and litigators feel at ease with the new system with minor adjustments. 1708

A. Structure

In France, since 2009, the "tribunal judiciaire de Paris" (the new name of the "tribunal de grande instance" since 1st January 2020) has been granted an exclusive jurisdiction for patent cases; it deals with hundreds of patent cases each year (the other 163 ordinary courts of first instance in France have no jurisdiction for such matters). Hence a difference with the UPC which has 14 local or regional divisions in addition to the Paris seat and the two sections of the central division: in France, with a single court sitting in Paris having jurisdiction for the whole country, there is no issue of proper venue or forum shopping. 1709

The tribunal judiciaire de Paris has jurisdiction to decide on both validity and infringement in the same proceedings (the alleged infringer may either raise an invalidity defence or lodge a counterclaim for revocation). With a single court for the whole of France having jurisdiction on validity and infringement, the bifurcation issue does not exist. 1710

The appellate jurisdiction of the tribunal judiciaire de Paris is the cour d'appel de Paris. 1711

The only possible recourse against the rulings of the cour d'appel de Paris is the pourvoi en cassation (appeal on a point of law) brought before France's highest court for civil matters, the Cour de cassation. When such appeal is lodged, the Cour de cassation will only assess whether the law has been correctly interpreted and applied and will not question the facts as found by the cour d'appel de Paris. If the Cour de cassation finds that the cour d'appel correctly applied the law, it will reject the appeal on a point of law. If not, the decision of the cour d'appel will be quashed. In patent cases, when the judgment of the cour d'appel de Paris is quashed, the case is remanded to the same cour d'appel which must, however, be composed of different judges. 1712

1713 A major and obvious difference is that the judgments of the UPC's Court of Appeal are final, no recourse before a higher court being possible against them[1].

B. Composition

1714 All the judges of the tribunal judiciaire de Paris are legally qualified (there are no technically qualified judges in the tribunal). The judges belonging to the IP section of the court (known as the 3rd chamber) have an interest in intellectual property law as they have to apply to join this section, and they gain experience in patent law by sitting for several years in that section.

1715 The IP section of the tribunal judiciaire de Paris currently consists of 9 judges sitting in 3 panels of 3 judges (the situation is different in the UPC when the validity of the patent is at issue, with 4 judges sitting in a panel: 3 legally qualified judges and 1 technically qualified judge).

1716 The IP section of the cour d'appel de Paris comprises 6 judges sitting in 2 panels of 3 judges (a further difference with the UPC, as the panels of the UPC's Court of Appeal include 5 judges: 3 legally qualified judges and 2 technically qualified judges).

1717 At the Cour de cassation, two highly experienced IP senior judges (conseillers) and two junior judges (conseillers référendaires) are in charge of patent cases.

C. Representation

1718 The parties to a dispute pending before the tribunal judiciaire de Paris or the cour d'appel de Paris must be represented by an attorney-at-law member of the Paris Bar (Article 751 FR CPC and Article 899 FR CPC). Before the Cour de cassation, representation by an attorney-at-law admitted before this court (avocat au Conseil d'Etat et à la Cour de cassation) is mandatory (Article 973 FR CPC). The Paris Bar and the Cour de cassation Bar are different: an attorney-at-law cannot be a member of both.

1719 This is a difference with the UPC where parties may be represented not only by an attorney-at-law but also by a patent attorney (Article 48 UPCA).

D. Jurisdiction

1720 While the UPC's jurisdiction is strictly limited by Article 32 UPCA to those actions specifically listed under subparagraphs (a) to (i) (infringement, declaration of non-infringement, provisional measures, revocation, counterclaim for revocation, compensation for provisional protection conferred by a published European patent application, prior use, compensation for licence of right, decisions of the European Patent Office about unitary patents), the tribunal judiciaire de Paris, being an ordinary court, has

1 The only recourse against a final decision of the Unified Patent Court is the "rehearing", with the permission of the Court of Appeal, on discovery of a new and decisive fact that was held by a national court to constitute a criminal offence, or in the event of a fundamental procedural defect (Article 81 UPCA and Rule 247).

a wider, unlimited jurisdiction on patent matters; it may also deal with claims related to ownership (notably rei vindicatio), compensation for employees' inventions, joint R&D, transfer and license agreements, etc.; when seized with a patent case, it may also deal with related claims like unfair competition or infringement of other intellectual property rights (trademarks, designs, copyrights).

E. Procedural Principles

The proceedings before the tribunal judiciaire de Paris and before the UPC share many 1721
common procedural principles, with nuances as to their application:

- the adversarial ("accusatoire") system, by which the burden of proof is borne by the litigants who have to convince judges who remain independent (Article 17 UPCA), impartial and will not investigate the case themselves;
- the principle of party disposition ("dispositif" principle), under which the subject-matter of an action is delimited by the parties' claims and judges cannot rule infra or ultra petita (Article 76 (1) UPCA);
- the "contradictoire" principle, according to which the parties have to exchange every element of fact and law (Article 76 (2) UPCA) and must never communicate privately with the Court (Rule 8.3);
- the front-loading principle set out in the Preamble of the UPC's Rules of procedure ("Parties shall... set out their full case as early as possible in the proceedings") and in Rule 9 (2) ("The Court may disregard any step, fact, evidence or argument which a party has not taken or submitted in accordance with a time limit set by the Court or these Rules") is, however, stronger than the French rules of Article 15 FR CPC ("Parties must disclose in due time to one another factual arguments supporting their claims, the means of evidence they produce and the legal arguments they rely upon so that each party may organise his defence") and Article 135 FR CPC ("The court may disregard the documents which have not been adduced in due time"). The only obligation before French courts is to refrain from raising new arguments or producing new evidence at the last minute; there is no direct and explicit obligation to put anything on the table up-front. This is, however, somewhat theoretical as clever patent litigators usually set out their case in details as early as possible;
- an encouragement towards an amicable settlement (Article 52 (2) UPCA and Rule 11; the recently modified Article 56 FR CPC now places any French litigant before commencing legal proceedings under the obligation to provide evidence that he has previously tried to reach an amicable solution to the dispute);
- attorney-client privilege ("secret professionnel") from disclosure (Article 48 and Rule 287);
- legal aid ("aide juridictionnelle") for parties unable to meet the costs of proceedings (Article 71 UPCA and Rule 375) is available for natural persons in France.

The UPC system is also similar to the French national patent litigation system with 1722
regard to what it does not allow litigants to seek or claim, such as:

- pre-trial discovery: Article 59 UPCA and Rule 190 only allow for very limited and content-specific orders to produce evidence, which in no way compares with common-law-style discovery or disclosure; similarly Article 138 FR CPC (also appli-

cable to documents held by the parties) provides that "If, during the proceedings, a party wishes to rely on… a document held by a third party, he may request the judge, to whom the matter is referred to, to order the production… of the document"); however, the current French judicial practice is extremely restrictive; it only allows such production when a party can identify a document and show that it is crucial to the outcome of the case; it is absolutely impossible to compare this to discovery;
- cross-examination: live-testimony of witnesses is theoretically allowed under French law in civil cases (Article 203 FR CPC), but it is never used in practice (usually this is replaced by a written testimony); cross-examination of witnesses by the parties' attorneys is strictly forbidden before French courts where only the judges may ask questions (Article 214 FR CPC); before the UPC, Article 53 (1) (d) and (2) in fine UPCA and Rules 176, 178.5 and 181 make a limited cross-examination possible, but under the control of the court.

F. Similarites and Differences

1723 Similar traits between the UPC and the French patent litigation procedural system are numerous:
- a written procedure (Article 52 UPCA and Rule 12);
- electronic submission of pleadings, which is the rule before the UPC, has been the standard practice in the tribunal judiciaire de Paris for many years (Article 44 UPCA, Rule 170.1 d) and Rule 178.6);
- the burden of proof lying in principle with the claimant, with the possibility of reversal for patents protecting a process to obtain a product (Article 55 UPCA, similar to Article L. 615-5-1 FR IPC);
- order to preserve evidence and to inspect premises (Article 60 UPCA and Rule 192, similar – albeit less easily accessible – to the "saisie-contrefaçon" of Article L. 615-5 FR IPC);
- provisional and protective measures (Article 62 UPCA and Rule 206), similar to the preliminary injunction proceedings of Article L. 615-3 FR IPC;
- an interim case management phase similar to the French "mise en état" (Article 52 UPCA, Rule 104 and Rule 239), during which parties must exchange their submissions in a timely and fair manner (Rule 36), under the supervision of a designated judge-rapporteur (Rule 18);
- the Court's power to appoint independent experts to assist with a technical question in relation to the case (Article 57 UPCA and Rule 185);
- a similar one-day oral hearing (Rule 113), as a hearing in a patent case before the tribunal judiciaire de Paris usually does not last more than two or three hours;
- the determination of the amount of damages ("dommages-intérêts") can be the subject of separate, further, proceedings in France, as it may be in the Unified Patent Court (Rule 125);
- no suspensive effect of the appeal: UPC appeals do not have a suspensive effect unless the Court of Appeal decides otherwise (Article 74 UPCA); in the same way,

in France, since 1st January 2020, an appeal has no suspensive effect unless otherwise ordered by the lower court or by the court of appeal.

The differences between the Unified Patent Court and the French patent litigation procedural system are not that many: 1724

- language of proceedings: the French patent litigation system is 100 % in French, statements of claims, submissions, evidence and oral pleadings must always be made or given in French; all the documents or exhibits must be translated into French (relevant parts only; no sworn translation generally needed); this is the result of the most antique statutory provision of French law, known as Ordinance of Villers-Cotterêts signed into law by King Francis I of France on 25 August 1539; the language regime of the Unified Patent Court is much more complex (the official language of the Contracting Member State hosting the relevant division or the EPO official language designated by this State; at the central division, the language in which the patent concerned was granted);
- duration of proceedings: it is designed to be around one year at the Unified Patent Court (Preamble of the Rules, paragraph 7), whereas in France it usually is between 18 and 24 months;
- protective letters (shields against preliminary measures which could be granted without the alleged infringer being heard); they are accepted at the Unified Patent Court (Rule 207); they cannot be lodged before the tribunal judiciaire de Paris, but this has no practical consequence because this court would generally not order preliminary measures without the alleged infringer being heard;
- freezing orders (Article 61 UPCA): these are not easily ordered by French courts;
- publicity of justice (Rules 115 and 262): before the UPC, "written pleadings, written evidence lodged at the Court shall be available to the public upon reasoned request to the Registry"; however, "a party may request that certain information of written pleadings or evidence be kept confidential and provide specific reasons for such confidentiality"; the hearings are open to the public unless the Court decides to make a hearing confidential in the interest of one of the parties or both parties, or third parties, or in the general interest of justice or public order. By contrast, in France, the written pleadings and written evidence are not available to third parties. The hearings are, as a rule, open to the public, but the court may order to make a hearing confidential. The decisions are available to the public (however, when the decision contains confidential information, a party may request that only a redacted copy where such information is masked be available to the public);
- dissenting opinions: these are allowed by Article 78 (2) UPCA and Rule 350.3, but forbidden by Article 448 FR CPC which provides that "the deliberations of the judges are secret";
- appeal proceedings: the cour d'appel de Paris reviews the case de novo both in fact and in law; new claims are generally not admissible before the cour d'appel, but new legal grounds may be put forward in some cases; new legal arguments and new documents are admissible (the cour d'appel does not decide only on the documents brought before the tribunal); by contrast, new evidence may not be admissible before the UPC Court of Appeal (Rule 222.2).

G. Costs of Proceedings

1725 Article 36 UPCA sets out the principle that the Court should be self-financed ("The budget of the Court shall be financed by the Court's own financial revenues and, at least in the transitional period referred to in Article 83 as necessary, by contributions from the Contracting Member States. The budget shall be balanced"). In France, the principle of free justice as a public service (Article L. 111-2 of the French code de l'organisation judiciaire), means that litigants only pay nominal fees – around € 100 – to cover administrative costs;

I. Decisions on costs

1726 The decisions on costs (be it court costs ("dépens") and attorney's fees and other legal expenses "frais irrépétibles") are given in France at the same time as the judgment on the issue decided; they are never the subject-matter of separate proceedings, unlike before the UPC (Rule 150);

II. Recovery of costs and attorney's fees:

1727 The cap for recoverable costs before the UPC should be as high as € 2,000,000 (for proceedings where the value at stake exceeds € 50,0000,000 that are particularly complex or involved multiple languages, according to the decision of 24 April 2023 of the Administrative Committee of the UPC on the scale of recoverable costs ceilings). In France, legal costs and attorney's fees in the amount set by the court are borne by the losing party. Decisions on costs are less elaborate and there is no theoretical cap on how much attorney fees a party can recover. The largest amount granted in first instance is about € 300,000. The average amount of costs ordered by the cour d'appel de Paris in patent cases is around € 50,000 while the largest amount is € 300,000.

Chapter 33: Comparison with Italian Law

Contents Para

A. Similarities

1728 Like in Italian Tribunals and Italian Appeal Courts, first-degree Unified Patent Court are composed of three judges. (Second-degree Unified Patent Court are however formed by five judges, except in the case referred to in article 32.1, letter i, Unified Patent Court Agreement).

1729 The means of proof for procedures before the Unified Patent Court are not very different from those of Italian procedure; no swearing is required.

1730 Also the burden of proof seems not to be different: proof must be produced by whoever claims the existence of a certain fact. Italian system also has the inversion of the burden of proof in the case of a process patent when there is an identical product (Art. 67 Code of Civil Procedures).

1731 In Italy too, court and attorney's fees are paid by the losing party, except where there are reasons that invoke partial or total compensation.

1732 In Italy there also exists legal aid, even though it has never been applied in an action involving IP rights.

1733 In Italy too, suits for compensation of damages are extinguished after five years.[1] However, the terms for the extinction runs from the day when the actual damage occurred and not from when the injured party became aware of it as with the Unified Patent Court.

1734 In the Italian system, rulings must be in writing and motivated.

1735 Italian Courts can judge on the nullity whether total or partial of the Italian portions of European Patents, and can limit them, and in Italy too these decisions have ex tunc effect, except for some aspects.[2]

1736 As the Unified Patent Court, the Italian system also includes:
- written and spoken defence;
- adopting of measures for the protection of reserved information;
- issuing of exhibiting orders for information and documents available to the counterpart, for determining the dimension of the illegal activity, including for assessment of a compensation for damages;
- issuing of orders, including cautionary measures and also inaudita altera parte, for acquiring evidence, by means of description and/or seizure. Differently to what is

1 Art. 2947 Civil Code.
2 Art. 77 Italian Industrial Property Code (CPI.

set out in art. 60.8 of the Unified Patent Court Agreement, in Italy the acquisition of prior proofs cease by law to have effect if the ordinary judgement has not commenced within the terms set down by the law itself.[3] It is not the Judge who decides.

- issuing of cautionary and provisional measures akin to those of article 62 of the Unified Patent Court agreement;
- issuing of the definitive injunction (i.e. included with the ruling that decides on the merit). The latter may have as addressees only subjects who are part of the procedure;
- the application of penalties for cases of delay or infringement of the injunction order;
- measures such as the destruction of goods and withdrawal from the market;
- the right to information; this right is to be guaranteed by issuing of exhibiting orders as well as communication orders;
- the pronouncement of liability to settlement of damages, with the exclusion of punitive damages. In the Italian system there can be no condemnation to settlement of damages if the subject that committed the illegal act proves that no intentional wrongdoing or gross negligence existed.

1737 Also in Italy decisions in intellectual property matters are open to appeal. In Italy an appeal against the sentence of a first-degree Judge can regard both questions of law and questions of fact and there are very strict limits to the introduction of new evidences.

1738 In Italy, the appeal against a provisional decision can involve the introduction of new evidences. However, in the Italian system, differently to what is set down in art. 74 of the Unified Patent Court Agreement, the appeal does not stay he effects of the decision. As mentioned in the foregoing, only following application by the losing party can the Appeals Court suspend provisional enforcement.

B. Differences

1739 Differently to the Unified Patent Court (art. 8 and following and articles 15.3 and 16 of the Unified Patent Court Agreement), in the Italian system there is no distinction between legally-qualified and technically-qualified judges.

1740 In Italy first and second degree, Courts judging in matters of Industrial and Intellectual Property are always made up of three judges and it is not possible for the parties to agree that one Judge alone can decide a case, as the Agreement sets down in article 8.7.

1741 The division of the competences before the Unified Patent Court[4] is absent in the Italian procedural system.

1742 In Italy, the competence to judge on the nullity of the Italian portion of an European Patent, at the first and second degrees of justice, is given to the judges of the Speci-

3 Art 132 Italian Industrial Property Code (CPI).

4 Arts. 32 and 33.

alised Sections where is located the patent attorney which is appointed as representative for the patent.[5]

For infringement actions, both the Specialized Section in whose jurisdiction the defendant is located and the Specialized Section in whose jurisdiction the infringing acts have taken place[6] are competent. 1743

A nullity action of the Italian portion of an European Patent[7] can be proposed by way of counterclaim to the Judge to whom the action for infringement has been proposed. 1744

In a suit before the Unified Patent Court the third degree of justice is not available. This is a significant difference with respect to Italian process, in which three degrees of justice are envisaged, i.e. Tribunal, Appeal and Supreme Court ("Corte di Cassazione"). 1745

The decisions of the EU Court of Justice are binding for the Unified Patent Court. This is another difference with respect to the Italian system, where there are no binding pronouncements in the strict sense, except in a case where the Supreme Court nullifies a decision citing a principle of law to which the new Judge will have to adhere[8] 1746

The decisions of the Unified Patent Court are valid for the whole territory of the contracting States and constitute an enforcement order in every contracting State. Differently, the decisions of Italian Judges in the matter of the European Patent are binding only for the territory of the State in relation to the Italian portion. The Unified Patent Court therefore has an international scope, whereas Italian judges in the matter of patents have a national scope. The same is true for precautionary measures. 1747

Another difference is, obviously, the language, which in the Italian system is always Italian[9] both for defences and for documents, which must be translated if in a foreign language, while for the Unified Patent Court procedures it is variable among the official languages. 1748

A further important difference is the fact that in the Unified Patent Court procedures the parties must pay legal costs in advance (i.e. the costs relating to the functioning of the adjudicating body). 1749

Another difference is that a defendant may ask for the Unified Patent Court to order the plaintiff to pay a deposit for covering the judiciary costs and the other expenses incurred by the defendant. This is not possible in Italy: art. 98 of the Civil Procedures Code, which used to include a like rule, was declared non-constitutional in 1960. 1750

The settlement of the dispute, which according to the Unified Patent Court must be validated by the Court can in Italy take place without the Judge's intervention; the 1751

5 Art. 120.3.
6 Art. 120.6 Italian Industrial Property Code (CPI).
7 Art. 120.3 Italian Industrial Property Code (CPI).
8 Art. 384 of the Italian Civil Procedures Code.
9 Art. 122 of the Italian Civil Codes Procedures.

parties can reach an agreement before the Judge, but it is not compulsory. In this case, the record containing the settlement is immediately effective.

1752 In procedures before the Unified Patent Court, the first degree decision is enforceable and the appeal therefore has no suspensive effect, except in two cases: i) if the decision relates to revocation of the patent or ii) if the decision relates to an action concerning EPO decisions as in art. 32 paragraph 1, letter i) of the Agreement. It is always possible, when there are grounds expressly provided for, to request and obtain suspension by Court decision.

1753 According to the Italian law, the first-degree decision is always enforceable, apart from when the unsuccessful party requests, during an appeal procedure, suspension of the order. The suspension can be applied only in the presence of strong and well-founded motives[10].

1754 Differently to the provisions of the Unified Patent Court, in Italy the non-exclusive licensee is in theory empowered to act against the infringer of an Italian European Patent portion, on condition that this is not excluded from the agreement between the parties and that there is an interest in the action.[11]

1755 In procedures before the Unified Patent Court, the parties can be represented not only by lawyers but also by European Patent Attorneys authorised to act in their capacity as professional representatives before the EPO and who are in possession of qualifications such as the European certificate for patent disputes. This is another difference with respect to the Italian procedure: in Italy, the parties can be represented only by a lawyer.[12]

10 Art. 283 Civil Procedures Code.
11 Art. 100 Civil Code Procedure.
12 Art. 82, Civil Procedures Code.

Chapter 34: Comparison with Dutch Law

Contents | Para

A. Introduction

This chapter provides an overview of the main similarities and main differences between patent litigation in the Netherlands and litigation before the Unified Patent Court (UPC). The comparison is based on the "Rules of Procedure of the Unified Patent Court" which entered into force on 1 September 2022. **1756**

For ease of reading the Dutch Rules of Civil Procedure will be referred to as the "Dutch Rules" while the Rules of Procedure of the UPC will be referred to as the "UPC Rules". **1757**

In the Netherlands patent infringement and validity cases are exclusively dealt with by the courts in the Hague, both in first instance and in appeal. The cases are handled by judges specialized in intellectual property matters. The exclusive jurisdiction relates to revocation actions and infringement actions and also to infringement actions in summary proceedings. In proceedings on the merits in first instance, most patent cases are litigated within the so-called accelerated regime. Under this regime the court provides beforehand a litigation schedule with deadlines for filing written submissions and the date of the oral hearing. All in all accelerated regime cases can take about 15–18 months from writ of summons until judgment. Contrary to normal procedures there is only one round of filing of written submissions. It is the plaintiff who decides whether or not he wishes to litigate within the accelerated regime. The District Court no longer allows that FRAND-cases are litigated within the accelerated regime. Normal procedures (as used for other civil litigation) can also be used for patent litigation, but most plaintiffs opt for accelerated regime proceedings. Normal proceedings drag on for longer than accelerated regime proceedings and more extensions of deadlines are possible. Generally, two rounds of written submissions are allowed. **1758**

After a decision has been rendered in first instance either party can lodge an appeal. No leave for appeal is required. Appeals are de novo in the Netherlands. This means that the entire case will be argued from scratch. Parties can submit additional facts and evidence. After a final decision has been rendered by the Court of Appeal, par- **1759** ties may appeal to the Supreme Court only with respect to questions of law and with respect to decisions which are insufficiently (comprehensibly) motivated. No leave for appeal to the Supreme Court is required.

B. Procedure of the Court of 1st Instance

1760 UPC Rule 10 lists the stages of proceedings in first instance:
- Written procedure
- Interim procedure
- Oral procedure
- Procedure for the award of damages
- Procedure for costs decisions

1761 These stages are slightly different in the Netherlands. Proceedings in the Netherlands start with a written part, followed by an oral hearing. There is in principle no interim procedure in patent infringement or revocation proceedings in the Netherlands. A procedure for the award of damages (quantum proceedings) can follow either first instance or appeal proceedings. Cost decisions form part of the decision on the merits, so no separate procedure for cost decisions exists.

1762 Although the Court can propose to the parties to try to settle their dispute by means of arbitration or mediation, this rarely happens in patent infringement cases (cf. 11 UPC Rules).

I. Written Procedure

1763 In the Netherlands, all types of actions in patent matters, i.e. infringement actions, revocation actions and actions for declarations of non-infringement, are handled in the same manner. Also, infringement/declaration of non-infringement actions and revocation actions are handled by the same court, a bifurcated system is alien to Dutch Rules.

1764 In Dutch proceedings the written statements contain similar information as required under UPC Rules, be it that the instructions as to which information should be included are less detailed.

1765 An important difference is that under Dutch Rules no judge-rapporteur is appointed, while this is standard under UPC Rules.

1766 Like under UPC Rules, preliminary objections can be raised. Under the accelerated regime those will generally be dealt with as part of the main proceedings, under the normal regime, preliminary objections are dealt with prior to moving forward with the merits of the case.

1767 Court fees in the Netherlands are relatively low and do not depend on the value of the patent action. By definition, all patent related disputes are considered as disputes of an undetermined value, which is why the court fees are set at a low, standard amount. All parties to the proceedings will have to pay this amount. In addition, it is noted that no separate fees will have to be paid if the defendant files a counterclaim.

Patent litigation in the Netherlands is handled by specialized judges. These judges can be technically qualified, but this is not a requirement. Nor can parties apply for allocating a technically qualified judge in the panel. 1768

II. Interim Procedure

As briefly noted above, Dutch Rules do not recognize the concept of interim procedure. Therefore, no judge-rapporteur is appointed, no interim conference is held and no specific steps in preparation of the oral hearing are taken. 1769

Like under UPC Rules (Rule 109), simultaneous interpretation during oral hearings is possible and happens very often. Parties have to file a request with the court which will in principle be honored. 1770

III. Oral hearing

Like under UPC Rules, oral hearings in the Netherlands last less than a day. Witnesses and experts are generally not heard during the oral hearing but can make statements and the Court can ask questions. The oral hearing is not audio recorded but a party can request this (115 UPC Rules). 1771

A decision on the merits may take 8–12 weeks in the Netherlands, this is similar as under UPC Rules. However, a decision on the merits may also take much more time. UPC Rules keep open the possibility for the court to give the decision immediately after closure of the hearing and provide reasons later. This is not something which is done in the Netherlands, except in very urgent circumstances in preliminary injunction hearings. 1772

Interim awards of damages are not part of a decision on the merits, but are possible in preliminary injunction proceedings whereby a strict threshold for urgency applies (reason why such claims are rarely filed and awarded in preliminary injunction proceedings). 1773

IV. Damages and cost procedures

Damages claims are normally handled in separate proceedings, so-called quantum proceedings. Generally quantum proceedings are only started after decisions on validity and/or infringement have become final. 1774

As mentioned above, costs decisions are part of the main decisions, no separate proceedings are required. The winning party is entitled to recover reasonable and proportionate costs. When awarding costs in patent infringement or revocation cases (if the revocation case can be qualified as a defense in advance of a potential infringement case), the Courts will apply so-called indication rates, which contain maximum amounts which can be awarded by the Court to the prevailing party whereby the maximum amount that can be awarded depends on whether the matter is qualified as simple, normal, complex or very complex. Parties can also (and often) agree on the amount of costs that will be awarded to the prevailing party, which amount can be higher than the maximum amount that can be awarded under the indication rates, and the Courts generally accept such agreement. 1775

1776 Securities for costs are possible in the Netherlands, but very rare.

V. Evidence

1777 In the Netherlands both witnesses and experts generally provide their written statements. Witness and expert hearings are possible but very rare. There is no cross-examination in the Netherlands.

1778 Basically, the same goes for court experts. The court can appoint such experts but rarely does so.

1779 Like under the UPC Rules, under Dutch Rules a court can order to produce certain evidence and/or to communicate certain information. Likewise, seizures of evidence in order to preserve evidence are also possible and the party which has been subject to the seizure can request to lift the seizure. In addition, the court can order the performance of certain experiments to prove certain aspects of the case.

C. Provisional measures

1780 UPC Rules and Dutch Rules both provide the possibility for summary proceedings which can be started either before or after initiation of the proceedings on the merits. The proceedings can be inter partes or ex parte.

1781 Ex parte measures are possible in the Netherlands but unlikely in (complex) patent cases. In the Netherlands a party can file a protective letter in order to avoid an ex parte injunction. However, contrary to the UPC Rules (209 UPC Rules), Dutch judges never turn an ex parte request into inter partes proceedings. In practice, it is common that the patentee who files an application for an ex parte injunction requests the judge to be given the opportunity to withdraw the request if the judge is not willing to grant an ex parte injunction.

1782 Inter partes PI proceedings are pretty common and an oral hearing will always be part of such proceedings.

1783 When a PI is rendered in the Netherlands, the plaintiff is generally not ordered to provide security/bond before the PI is enforceable. Under UPC Rules (211 (5)), this seems to be more common and standard in cases where applications for ex parte injunctions are filed.

1784 Following summary proceedings, proceedings on the merits have to be initiated. In the Netherlands it is common that parties request the judge to set a deadline which may be 6 months from the date of the judgment or shorter. Under UPC Rules, the deadline is set at 31 calendar days or 20 working days "from the date specified in the Court's order."

D. Appeal Procedure

1785 Contrary to the UPC Rules, leave for appeal is not required in the Netherlands. The losing party can always appeal a first instance judgment.

Another important difference is that in the Netherlands an appeal is always *de novo*, new facts and new evidence may in principle be submitted. As a judgment in first instance is in practice almost always enforceable notwithstanding an appeal, filing an appeal will in principle not have a suspensive effect. 1786

A further point to note is that if a statement of appeal is withdrawn, unlike under the UPC, a cross-appeal, if any, shall not be deemed to be withdrawn. 1787

Also, a system of lodging an application for rehearing does not exist under Dutch procedural rules. Nor is a referral to the full court possible; appeal cases are always heard by a panel of three judges. 1788

E. General provisions

An important difference to note is that under the UPC Rules, parties submit all of their documents in electronic form (4 UPC Rules). While this is definitely a direction into which the Netherlands are also heading, documents are still submitted in hard copy form (and in addition on USB sticks at the special requests of the Courts of The Hague). In line of this the UPC Rules determine that it is the registry who forwards all documents to the opposing party (UPC Rule 278). This is different in the Netherlands where it is the obligation of the parties to deliver all submissions to (counsel to) the other party. 1789

A further interesting difference is public access to the register (262 UPC Rules). While oral hearings and judgments are public in the Netherlands, the underlying documents submitted by both parties are not. 1790

As already briefly mentioned above, in the Netherlands there is no such thing as case management organized by the judge-rapporteur. The role of the court is more passive than under UPC Rules. 1791

Dutch courts do not have the power to refuse to hear actions which are bound to fail or manifestly inadmissible (360 UPC Rules). 1792

I. Decisions and orders

In the Netherlands there is always unity of the decision. Dissenting opinions, if any, are not made public (350 UPC Rules). 1793

While decisions might be subject to rendering a security this is really rare in the Netherlands (352 UPC Rules). 1794

If compliance with court orders is subject to penalties, such penalties are always to be paid to the benefit of the winning party, not to the court (354 UPC Rules). 1795

II. Settlement

In the Netherlands, settlements reached among the parties without the intervention of the court can but in practice are not confirmed by the court in a written decision. 1796

Chapter 35: Comparison with Austrian Law

Contents Para

A. Fundamentals

1797 A key difference vis-à-vis the Unified Patent Court is that in Austria – as in Germany – patent cases litigated in the first instance are subject to a mandatory *bifurcation*, i.e. the question of invalidity and the question of infringement are each decided by separate judicial bodies. In the first instance, the question of revocation is decided by the Revocation Division of the Austrian Patent Office (Section 60 paragraph 3 number 4 of the Austrian Patent Act (PatG)), whereas infringement-related disputes are adjudicated by the Commercial Court (*Handelsgericht*) of Vienna (Section 162 paragraph 1 of the PatG). But the questions of revocation and infringement will then be examined concomitantly in the second instance, i.e. by the Higher District Court (*Oberlandesgericht*) of Vienna, as well as in the third instance, i.e. by the Austrian Supreme Court of Justice (*Oberster Gerichtshof*). "Forum shopping" hardly ever occurs in Austria, given that the aforementioned courts enjoy exclusive competence for all revocation and infringement proceedings.

1798 In the first instance, decisions are taken with regard to a patent's revocation only in the context of a proceeding for preliminary injunction – and this in a merely preliminary fashion, as a precursor to addressing the issue of infringement.

1799 A special feature of the Austrian system is the mandatory participation of technical judges in the decision-making process as members of the judicial panel. This is in derogation of the Rules of Procedure of the Unified Patent Court, which call for such participation only in specific cases.

1800 The Austrian action proceeding itself is generally less formally structured than an action proceeding before the Unified Patent Court. For example, it is not formally divided into a written procedure, interim procedure and oral hearing.

1801 In contrast to a proceeding before the Unified Patent Court, representation by a lawyer is mandatory in a patent-infringement proceeding before the Austrian courts. Here, it is customary – but not mandatory – for patent attorneys to "assist" the representing lawyers by contributing their technical expertise. it is possible to be represented by patent attorneys without having lawyers on hand in the first and second instance of revocation proceedings. Representation by a lawyer is mandatory in the third instance, however, i.e. before the Supreme Court of Justice.

B. Proceedings for Preliminary Injunction

Apart from a few exceptions, there are no in-court hearings in an Austrian proceeding for the grant of a preliminary injunction. Instead, this proceeding is generally conducted entirely in writing. Although it is customary to allow two rounds of submissions for both parties, particularly in major cases, it is entirely up to the panel of judges to decide whether to allow one or more such rounds. An applicant will not be entitled to lodge a Rejoinder to the defendant's Reply to the applicant's Application for Preliminary injunction and thereby "force" a second round of pleadings to take place. For this, he will have to obtain consent from the panel of judges. 1802

It is also up to the discretion of the judicial panel whether to order the lodging of a security as a precondition for the enforcement of a preliminary injunction. The aim here is to ensure that the defendant can be compensated for damage/financial losses in the event the preliminary injunction subsequently proves to have been unjustified. Such securities are normally lodged in the form of a bank guarantee. 1803

As a general rule, an Application for Preliminary Injunction is lodged with the Austrian courts in combination with a Statement of Claim for a main proceeding on the merits. If this is not done, then the court, assuming it grants the preliminary injunction requested, must concomitantly order the applicant to bring a main proceeding in support of his application (*Rechtfertigungsklage*) within a certain time limit. 1804

But in any case, Austrian procedural law stipulates that the applicant for preliminary injunction must compensate the defendant for any damage suffered due to an injunction if the asserted claim for which the injunction was granted is later deemed legally invalid, or if the application later proves unjustified (e.g. because the injunction is later revoked by a court of higher instance), or if the applicant misses the deadline for bringing a main proceeding in support of his application (Section 394 paragraph 1 EO). This Austrian regulation differs from the Unified Patent Court's Rule 354.2, which merely calls for appropriate compensation to be rendered in such cases. Depending on how the UPC opts to implement this rule in practice, it could well serve to significantly mitigate the risk which an applicant for preliminary injunction faces as compared to the risk he would face under the Austrian legal system. 1805

C. Revocation Proceedings

In contrast to a proceeding for preliminary injunction, a revocation proceeding must mandatorily be conducted before the Revocation Division of the Austrian Patent Office, while a main proceeding on the question of infringement must be conducted before the Commercial Court of Vienna. A main proceeding on the infringement question will frequently be interrupted until a final and conclusive decision has been issued in the revocation proceeding for the patent concerned. There will be no such interruption in a proceeding for preliminary injunction, however, given its urgent nature. 1806

In the past, it was legally mandatory to interrupt main proceedings on the infringement question when a revocation proceeding was already pending. Austrian law has since changed in this regard: The court must now perform its own initial examination of the 1807 revocation question (Section 156 paragraph 3 of the Austrian Patent Act (PatG)). To this end, the court may invite the Patent Office to prepare a written expert report on whether the patent is likely to be revoked based on the writing pleadings submitted in the court proceeding. (In practice, however, the expert report will almost always be obtained from a qualified patent attorney appointed by the court rather than from the Patent Office). If the court concludes that the patent's revocation is likely, then it must interrupt the proceeding until a final and conclusive decision is issued in the revocation proceeding (Section 156 paragraph 3 of the Patent Act (PatG)). The same will apply by analogy when an opposition proceeding is lodged with the European Patent Office (Section 12 of the Law on the Introduction of Patent Treaties (*Patentverträge-Einführungsgesetz*, PatV-EG)).

1808 If the validity or effectiveness of a patent is adjudged differently by the court hearing the revocation proceeding than by the court hearing the infringement dispute, then the Austrian regulations stipulate that this can be adduced as grounds for bringing an action for a rehearing (Section 156 paragraph 6 of the Patent Act (PatG)). What has yet to be decided through case law is whether this is also possible when the patent has been only partially invalidated in a revocation proceeding, but to such an extent that the patent's surviving claims no longer cover the object of infringement. In the author's opinion, the wording of the law suggests that an action for rehearing should be possible in such a situation as well. If the rehearing is successful, then the original decision on the merits will become invalid. This differs from a proceeding before the Unified Patent Court, where the original patent-infringement decision will not be modified or revoked in the event that the disputed patent is later declared invalid to the extent that it no longer covers the object of potential infringement. In such cases, the defendant can however at least petition the Unified Patent Court to declare the infringement no longer enforceable (UPC Rule of Procedure 354.2). But a potential patent infringer will in any case well advised to request the issuance of a conditional decision in the proceeding pursuant to Rule of Procedure 118.2a, particularly since he will otherwise be unable to claim appropriate compensation for past damage insofar as the original infringement decision remains in place.

D. Infringement Proceedings

1809 When the infringement question is adjudicated in a main proceeding before the Commercial Court of Vienna, the court will in most cases appoint a patent attorney as expert and will decide the infringement question on the basis of said expert's report.

1810 Just as before the Unified Patent Court, the principle of cost recovery also applies before the Austrian courts. Thus, the party which loses a case must reimburse the other side for its attorneys' fees, court costs and other litigation expenses on the basis of fixed rates derived from the value of the action. These costs will almost always be markedly lower than the costs of a proceeding before the Unified Patent Court, however. At least one reason for this is that the value of an action will usually be set rather low (between € 35,000 and € 100,000 and only rarely above) in order to avoid excessive court fees, which are also contingent on the value of the action. Thus, the costs to be recovered will be correspondingly lower than in a proceeding before the UPC.

As also holds true for the Unified Patent Court, there is no Austrian regulation to define how the parties' representatives are to settle accounts with their own clients. The Austrian Bar Association (*Rechtsanwaltskammertag*) does publish a recommended schedule of fees,[1] but this is not binding, not even in terms of defining a minimum rate of remuneration. Thus, deviating fee arrangements are permissible. **1811**

E. Proceedings for Preserving Evidence

Just like the regulations governing the Unified Patent Court, Austrian law also provides for a proceeding for preserving evidence (Section 151b of the Patent Act (PatG)). The Austrian court may also grant an order to preserve evidence in unilateral fashion, i.e. without first hearing the opposing side, if a delay is likely to cause irreparable damage to the applicant/party at risk, or if there is the danger that evidence may be destroyed (Section 151b paragraph 4 of the PatG). **1812**

Aside from preliminary injunction intended to preserve evidence, the Austrian courts, just like the Unified Patent Court, also have the option of ordering other preliminary injunctions without hearing the opposing side. This almost never occurs in practice, however. Thus, proceedings for preliminary injunctions in patent disputes are almost always conducted in an adversarial manner. **1813**

It is not possible to lodge a protective letter before an Austrian court. **1814**

F. Legal Remedies/Appeals

A default decision is also possible under Austrian law, where it is referred to as a *Versäumungsurteil.* The issuance of such a default decision is mandatory if the party opposing the defaulting party lodges a corresponding request/application. The default decision may be contested, and potentially revoked, by lodging a simple objection (*Widerspruch*) (Section 397a of the Austrian Code of Civil Procedure (*Zivilprozessordnung*, ZPO)). **1815**

As regards the legal remedies available in an Austrian proceeding, it bears noting that the applicable time limits for lodging an appeal – particularly in an infringement proceeding – are shorter than in a proceeding before the Unified Patent Court (four weeks in a main proceeding and two weeks in a proceeding for preliminary injunction). In a revocation proceeding, appeals are subject to a two-month deadline. But if an infringement proceeding which is pending alongside the revocation proceeding has been suspended until closure of the revocation proceeding, then the deadline for an appeal in the revocation proceeding is reduced to just one month (Section 157 paragraph 1 number 5 of the Patent Act (PatG)). Both a revocation proceeding and **1816**

1 It is known as the "Autonomous Criteria for Fees" (*Autonome Honorar-Kriterien*, AHK)).

an infringement proceeding can be pursued across a total of three instances (whereby the ability to seise the court of third instance is subject to certain restrictions).

1817 No distinction is drawn between the process of applying for the appeal and the process of carrying out the appeal. The key criterion is that the appeal must be lodged within the specified time limits; a prior application for the appeal is not required.

1818 An appeal lodged in the course of a proceeding for preliminary injunction will not exert suspensive effect except in extreme cases, where suspensive effect may be granted upon application. On the other hand, appeals lodged in a revocation proceeding or in a main proceeding on infringement (i.e. appeals to the court of second instance) will indeed exert suspensive effect. Appeals to the court of third instance (judicial reviews) will have suspensive effect only if this involves an "ordinary judicial review of points of law" (*ordentliche Revision*), i.e. one that has been approved by the respective lower court. An "extraordinary judicial review" (*ausserordentliche Revision)*, on the other hand, will only serve to suspend the legal force of a lower court's decision, but not the decision's enforceability.

1819 The option to lodge a cross-appeal does not exist under Austrian law.

1820 Under Austrian procedural law, orders issued during an ongoing proceeding (*verfahrensleitende Beschlüsse*) are generally contestable only in conjunction with an appeal against a decision on the merits.

1821 Decisions issued in an Austrian revocation proceeding are effective *ex tunc*, i.e. in the event the patent is revoked, the patent becomes retroactively invalid as of the date on which the patent application was lodged (Section 48 paragraph 3 of the Patent Act (PatG)).

1822 While the principle of *ex officio* investigation by the court applies in an Austrian revocation proceeding – in contrast to the practice of the Unified Patent Court – this does not hold true in an Austrian infringement proceeding. Here, the principle of "party disposition" (*Parteiendisposition*) applies, i.e. the court may ultimately adjudicate only those facts and items of evidence which the parties have themselves submitted or offered to submit.

1823 Austrian appeal proceedings are subject to a ban on new submissions (*Neuerungsverbot*). This means, in principle, that only the facts and evidence submitted and/or offered in the first instance can be considered during the appeal proceeding. All Austrian courts of instance are permitted to decide on the merits, i.e. they are able to not only refer a case back to a lower instance but to also modify the decision of a lower instance in whatever direction they deem fit.

Chapter 36: Comparison with Finnish Law

Contents

Intellectual property related matters have been centralized to the Market Court in Finland since September 2013. The Market Court is a specialized court with exclusive jurisdiction in civil IP disputes and administrative IP appeals. The Market also hears competition law, unfair business practice law, consumer law, public procurement law and electricity market law cases. The precise jurisdiction is governed by the Market Court Act and rules of procedure are set forth in the Market Court Procedure Act. The language of the proceedings is either Finnish or Swedish. 1824

In case of civil patent matters the Market Court is competent to hear actions for revocation of a patent, infringement action, as well as cases relating to preliminary injunctions and permanent injunctions. Preliminary injunctions must be followed up by a confirmatory action within a month. The Market Court also decides on matters concerning securing evidence that fall under the scope of the Law on the Protection of Evidence in Intellectual Property Disputes as a form of preliminary action. Further, the Market Court is competent to decide on and order compensation of damages and legal cost compensation. 1825

The Market Court is also the first appeal instance for decisions of the Finnish Patent and Registration Office in IP matters. Decisions of the Market Court in civil intellectual property matters can be appealed to the Supreme Court by leave to appeal. Cases involving both infringement and validity matters can be and are usually heard by the Market Court in the same proceedings. Decisions of the Market Court in appeals against decisions of the Finnish Patent and Registration Office can be appealed to the Supreme Administrative Court by leave to appeal. 1826

In Finland, however, if parties of a particular case agree, an interlocutory judgment can be given in the validity matter before hearing the infringement matter. Further, a decision regarding compensation of damages can be taken with a separate interlocutory judgment after the infringement matter has been decided. The purpose is procedural efficiency. 1827

The present text concentrates on procedure and practices in infringement and revocation matters. 1828

A. Similarities

Patent infringement and revocation proceedings before the Market Court are commenced when the court receives the claimant's writ. The court informs the defendant of the claimant's writ with a fixed date for the defendant's response set by the court. 1829

The time limit for the response is usually two months and with the response the defendant must submit a rejection or dismissal of the claims and any counterclaims. The Market Court may allow extension of the time limit for the defendant's response, if the request is well reasoned and presented in timely manner.

1830 The Market Court has published detailed instructions to attorneys in intellectual property matters including also a recommended structure both for the claimant's writ and for the defendant's response. All documents can be submitted to the Market Court in electronic format, but using paper copies is also allowed.

1831 The Market Court may allow further written statements by the parties with fixed deadlines (preclusion) during the preparatory phase of the proceedings before fixing dates for a preparatory hearing and a main hearing. Any new claims, arguments or documents must be submitted and any witnesses named during the preparatory phase. Any later submission can be done only under exceptional circumstances and by the consent of the adverse party and the court. During the preparatory phase a detailed plan and schedule for the main hearing and a summary of undisputed facts, disputed facts and all evidence to be received at the main hearing as well as schedule for hearing the witnesses is prepared by the judge responsible for the preparations together with the parties to ensure that the main hearing can be carried out efficiently. If needed, the court may allow written submissions after the preparatory hearing with a fixed deadline before closing the preparatory phase and transferring the matter to the main hearing.

1832 The judgement can be given at the end of the main hearing, but in practice the Market Court only provides an estimated deadline when the judgement will be given in writing at the end of the main hearing. The main hearing is open to the public as well as all written submissions, decisions and orders unless some parts of them have been requested to be confidential by either party and confirmed as such by the court.

1833 In the Market Court, patent cases are most commonly decided by three legally qualified judges, one of the judges being responsible for preparatory phase, and 1 to 3 technical judges or court experts. In patent matters a technically qualified judge is a so-called Market Court Engineer bound by the judge's oath.

1834 The Finnish courts should as a main rule actively encourage an amicable settlement of a dispute and during the preparatory phase of the proceedings the responsible judge is required to discuss possibilities of an amicable settlement with the parties. The parties can at any time in the course of the proceedings choose to settle the matter.

B. Differences

I. General

1835 Proceedings before the Market Court in Finland may also include a procedural hearing. The procedural hearing is more informal by nature and is intended for discussion of matters such as the submission of further pleadings and their deadlines or dates for a preliminary hearing and a main hearing. The purpose of the procedural hearing is also to get the parties into discussion with each other and to promote a fluent processing of the matter.

Hearing and cross-examining witnesses is common in infringement and revocation proceedings in Finland. However, expert witnesses are required to provide a written statement when proceedings are initiated and can be further heard in the main hearing if either of the parties, the court or the circumstances at hand otherwise require. The witnesses are named by the parties as a main rule. 1836

The Market Court may ask the Finnish Patent and Registration Office to provide their opinion in revocation matters, e.g. if limitation of patent claims is requested by the defendant as a preliminary action before the revocation proceedings. The Finnish Patent and Registration Office will then issue a statement regarding the proposed claims and their allowability. 1837

Depositing protective letters is not possible in the Market Court in Finland. 1838

II. Representation

A party can represent him or herself before the Market Court. If a party uses a representative, the representative must be a legal practitioner authorized to practice before the courts in Finland, either a registered Licensed Attorney or an Attorney-at-Law admitted to the Bar. The representative can be assisted by a patent attorney and when requested, patent attorneys are typically allowed to speak and present the matter on necessary parts at the court during the proceedings. 1839

III. Costs

A claimant is required to pay a fixed court fee of EUR 2 000 to the Market Court. For a private person the fixed court fee is EUR 500. These fees are based on the Act on Court Fees, an amendment of which entered into force in January 2016. 1840

As a main rule, legal costs are borne by the losing party. However, this is at the discretion of the Market Court, whereby the court can consider all the circumstances of a particular case and take into account the reasonability of the costs in awarding costs. Parties are required to present their costs at the end of the main hearing and are allowed to present opinions on the other party's cost and whether or not they consider them acceptable. In large cases it can be agreed during the preparatory phase that the parties will have some fixed time after the main hearing to provide their comments on the other party's costs. The Market Court deals with the costs in their decision. In Finland, unlike with the UPC, there is no statutory regulation of the legal costs in relation to the value in dispute. There is also no statutory regulation on attorney fees in dispute matters, but the Finnish Bar Association gives certain guidance on the attorney fees for Attorneys at Law. 1841

Chapter 37: Comparison with Swedish Law

Contents Para

1842 A system of courts specialized in intellectual property, market and competition law operates since 1.9.2016. The courts are competent to hear actions for revocation of a patent, infringement actions and appeals against decisions by the Swedish Patent Office. The first instance is named Patent- och Marknadsdomstolen (PMD) and the second instance Patent- och Marknadsöverdomstolen (PMÖD). PMÖD has the dual responsibility of granting leave to appeal a PMD decision before PMÖD and also of granting, in exceptional circumstances, leave to appeal one of PMÖD's own decisions to the Swedish Supreme Court (*Högsta domstolen*), outside the specialized system.

1843 The present contribution will discuss revocation and infringement actions in PMD and PMÖD.

A. Similarities

1844 After receiving a statement of claim complying with formal requirements, PMD examines of its own motion whether it is competent to hear the action,[1] and then issues summons. In the ensuing preparatory phase, the defendant is ordered to submit a statement of defence. The judge may request written clarification on specific issues, and may summon the parties to a preparatory conference. At the conference, remaining open issues are summarized and a timeline for the rest of the preparatory phase, up to the main hearing, is agreed on. The court may disregard new facts and evidence that are submitted at the main hearing in an attempt to delay the proceedings or surprise the other party.[2] Swedish courts further have an option of blocking a party from submitting further facts and evidence after a set date[3] but rarely make use thereof.

1845 Throughout the proceedings, the court shall actively encourage an amicable settlement.[4]

1846 The proceedings in patent cases are purely adversarial, without a faculty for the court to examine facts of its own motion.

1847 A party is not required to state his complete case orally at the main hearing, but may refer to previously filed written documents, audio and video recordings, evidence taken on an earlier occasion as well as written statements by witnesses. In patent cases, it has even been common practice for some years to allow the parties to refer to written arguments that are already on file.

---

1 Chapter 42, Section 4 of the Swedish Code of Judicial Procedure (*Rättegångsbalk*, SFS 1942:740); cf. Rule 260.1 ROP.
2 Chapter 43, Section 10 Code of Judicial Procedure; cf. Rule 9.2 ROP.
3 Chapter 42, Section 15 Code of Judicial Procedure.
4 Chapter 42, Sections 6 and 17 Code of Judicial Procedure; cf. Rule 11.1 ROP.

The main hearing is open to the public.[5] All written pleadings, written evidence, decisions and orders are as a main rule available to the public.[6] 1848

If the defendant fails to submit a statement of defence as requested, the court may issue a default judgement against him.[7] A default judgement may also be given if any of the parties fails to be present at a main hearing.[8] Proceedings are reopened if the party against whom the default judgement has been issued files a request to this effect within one month.[9] 1849

If an alleged infringer pleads that the patent in suit is invalid, he must lodge an action for revocation and notify the Swedish Patent Office of the action.[10] The infringement and revocation actions are dealt with in joint proceedings. 1850

The pre-trial measures available under the Unified Patent CourtA are within the scope of Directive 2004/48/EC on the Enforcement of Intellectual Property Rights. The directive has been implemented in national law of all EU member states, including Sweden. In particular, an order for preservation of evidence can be issued before the claimant has brought the main action and is carried out by the Swedish Enforcement Authority (Kronofogdemyndigheten), sometimes assisted by an expert that the Enforcement Authority appoints. The alleged infringer is entitled to a legal representative unless this would delay the proceedings excessively, and the Enforcement Authority may allow the claimant or his representative a right to attend.[11] 1851

Preliminary injunctions *ex parte* are available in Sweden. There is a rebuttable presumtion that a granted patent is valid, and an alleged infringer has no absolute right to be heard before a preliminary injunction is ordered.[12] Hearing the alleged infringer is the main rule, from which the courts have oftentimes deviated when the statement of claim shows with a high likelihood that the patent is infringed and that the ongoing infringement is causing irreparable harm (e.g., introduction of a competing generic drug). Both parties may put questions to witnesses. The questioning is under the supervision and control of the presiding judge.[13] 1852

A Swedish court may at its discretion allow separate appeal of an order or a decision not terminating the proceedings.[14] The court may exercise such discretion both in respect of procedural orders, e.g., to admit certain evidence, and in respect of decisi- 1853

5 Chapter 5, Section 1 Code of Judicial Procedure; cf. Rule 115 ROP.
6 Rule 262.1 ROP.
7 *Tredskodom*, Chapter 42, Section 11 Code of Judicial Procedure.
8 Chapter 42, Section 12 Code of Judicial Procedure.
9 Chapter 44, Section 9 Code of Judicial Procedure; cf. Art. 37 Unified Patent CourtA.
10 Chapter 17, Section 8 of the Swedish Patents Act (*Patentlag*, SFS 2024:945).
11 Chapter 16, Section 15 Patents Act; cf. Rule 196.3 ROP.
12 Chapter 16, Section 8 Patents Act; cf. Rule 209 ROP.
13 Chapter 36, Section 17 Code of Judiial Procedure; cf. Rule 178(5) ROP.
14 Chapter 17, Section 13 and Chapter 49, Section 1 Code of Judicial Procedure.; cf. Rule 220 ROP.

ons on only a part of the action brought.[15] In patent cases, it is not uncommon for such separate decision to be given on the question of infringement, before the court moves on, if necessary, to the determination of the amount of damages. If the court has agreed to allow a separate appeal and finds that a patent has been infringed, then the defendant has the options of appealing the decision on infringement, lodging an action for revocation of the patent, or accepting the decision.

B. Differences

1854 Normal patent actions in PMD are heard by a panel of two legally and two technically qualified judges.[16] Technically qualified judges are either patent judges (*patentråd*) employed full time by the Court, or engaged on a case-by-case basis after an official pre-qualification. The pre-qualified judges have expertise in their respective technical areas but are not required to be proficient in patent law. The common practice is to appoint one of the patent judges at an early stage of the proceedings, and one further technically qualified judge when the main hearing has been summoned.

1855 Unless the court orders otherwise, the preparatory conference is public.[17]

1856 The determination of the amount of damages is usually not deferred to separate proceedings, as it usually is in the Unified Patent Court.[18] If the parties agree to deal with the amount of damages out of court, the court may drop this part of the original action. If the negotiations between the parties fail, the parties are free to bring a new action regarding the amount of damages specifically.

1857 The Unified Patent Court is required to consider any pre-depositedprotective letters before granting provisional measures.[19] There is no comparable mechanism in Swedish courts, including PMD. A potential defendant wanting to avoid a preliminary injunction *ex parte* therefore has no other option but to inquire frequently with PMD whether it has received a request for such an injunction. As mentioned above, with few exceptions, the court's docket is open to public inspection.

1858 While a local or regional division of the Unified Patent Court has the discretion to refer an action for revocation of a patent to the central division and proceed with an infringement action relating to the same patent (bifurcation, Art. 33(3)(b) Unified Patent Court Agreement), a Swedish court always deals with infringement and revocation actions in joint proceedings.

1859 A party to proceedings in a Swedish court is not obliged to appoint a representative. He is free, however, to appoint basically any natural person with legal capacity as

---

15 *Särskild dom*, Chapter 17, Section 5 Code of Judicial Procedure.

16 Chapter 4, Section 1 of the Swedish Intellectual Property, Market and Competition Law Courts Act (*Lag om patent- och marknadsdomstolar*, SFS 2016:188).

17 Chapter 5, Section 1 Code of Judicial Procedure.

18 Rules 125–126 ROP.

19 Rule 207 ROP.

his representative.[20] In particular, there is no requirement for a legal qualification or membership of the Swedish Bar Association.

The time to final judgment in patent actions has improved significantly with the establishment of PMD and PMÖD. According to official statistics[21], 75 % of the actions before the Intellectual Property Chamber of the Stockholm District Court in the period 2011–2015 were finally disposed of within two years. Nowadays 75 % of the actions are disposed of within 10–12 months, that is, PMD performs in accordance with the one-year timeline of the UPC. 1860

Legal costs in the amount approved by the court are borne by the losing party. Unlike the situation in the Unified Patent Court, there is no statutory cap on the legal costs in relation to the value in dispute. Nor are attorney fees regulated. The average amounts of legal costs approved by the Stockholm District Court in the period 2000–2008 were EUR 100,000 in infringement actions and EUR 180,000 in revocation actions.[22] 1861

The application fee, which is due when filing the statement of claim, is the only fee payable to PMD. Regardless of the value in dispute, the application fee is approximately EUR 300. 1862

20 Chapter 12, Section 2 Code of Judicial Procedure.

21 Presentation 16.2.2016 by A. Dereborg, President of the Chamber.

22 P.-O. Bjuggren, B. Domeij and A. Horn, "Swedish Patent Litigation in Comparison to European", Nordiskt Immateriellt Rättsskydd, issue 5/2015, page 504–522.

Chapter 38: Comparison with US Law

Contents Para

A. Introduction

The European Unified Patent Court (UPC) will ultimately be the sole forum for deciding on matters of patent infringement in those members of the European Union that have joined the Unified Patent Court Agreement and, with the exception of the possibility of opposition proceedings before the European Patent Office commenced within the first nine months after grant of a European Patent the sole forum for litigating the validity of a European Patent. In contrast in the United States, a variety of fora exist: 1863

- Federal district courts, with or without juries;
- The Court of Claims;
- The International Trade Commission; and for validity, but not infringement issues
- The Patent Trial and Appeal Board.

Appeals on patent matters from all of these lie to the Court of Appeals for the Federal Circuit, with the possibility that the United States Supreme Court will issue a writ of *certiorari* to review a decision of the court of Appeals for the Federal Circuit. 1864

This chapter will consider how these for a deal with various aspects of patent litigation and compare them with what will happen before the UPC. 1865

B. Tribunals and their Subject Matter Jurisdiction

The European Unified Patent Court will comprise two separate types of first instance divisions a central division and local/regional divisions. 1866

These types of divisions have different roles. Appeal from all first instance divisions lies to a single court of appeal sitting in Luxemburg. The Court of Justice of the European Union is not directly involved in the new structure, but as with all courts in the EU, the Unified Patent Court can refer any question unsettled question of EU law (which does not generally include issues of substantive patent law) to the Court of Justice of the European Union. 1867

Under Article 33, the local/regional divisions will have jurisdiction over patent infringement issues and the ability to decide counterclaims in infringement actions challenging the validity of the patents in suit.[1] Other challenges to validity of patents or supplementary protection certificates and applications for declarations of non-infringement will have to be brought before the central division.[2] 1868

1 Agreement on a Unified Patent Court Article 33(1).

2 Agreement on a Unified Patent Court Article 33(4).

1869 Whereas the European Unified Patent Court has jurisdiction only over certain specified patent-related issues as set out in Articles 3 and 32 UPCA, of the U.S. tribunals noted above, only the Patent Trial and Appeal Board's jurisdiction is limited to patent-related issues, which unlike the jurisdiction of the UPC.

I. Federal Disctrict Courts

1870 The federal district courts are courts of general jurisdiction having jurisdiction over *inter alia* cases in which the subject matter of the suit is based on federal law such as most issues relating to patents, although it should be noted that issues relating to ownership of patents as items of personal property can still be the subject of actions in state courts. There are 94 federal judicial districts, some of which have more than one division. Each district may have its own rules of procedure as long as they comply with the Federal Rules of Civil Procedure as promulgated by the Supreme Court and approved by Congress.

1871 Patent-related actions typically include actions for infringement of a patent often involving a counterclaim that claims are invalid or unenforceable, and, where a "case or controversy" exists between the parties. actions for a declaratory judgment that one or more claims of a patent is invalid or unenforceable.

1872 The Seventh Amendment to the United States Constitution "preserved" the right to a jury trial in suits "at common law". For the most part, the practical effect of this is that either party is entitled to require that factual issues (including what is an infringement and the amount of damages to be awarded) are decided by a jury in any case where a "legal" as opposed to an "equitable" remedy is sought. Because many cases relating to pharmaceuticals are instituted on the basis if a generic drug manufacturer having received marketing approval for a drug rather than as a result of its actually selling the generic drug, the remedy sought is an injunction, which is an equitable remedy and so such cases are tried without a jury in what is referred to as a bench trial. Today most cases where damages are in issue, the case will be tried before a jury. Cases are handled by a single judge who has no need to have any technical qualification.

II. Court of Claims

1873 The Court of Claims handles claims against the federal government, *inter alia* claims for compensation for the federal government's use of patented inventions.

III. International Trade Comission (ITC)

1874 The International Trade Commission has the power to grant general and specific orders to prevent import into the United States of articles that –
(i) infringe a valid and enforceable United States patent …; or
(ii) are made, produced, processed, or mined under, or by means of, a process covered by the claims of a valid and enforceable United States patent.

Proceedings are normally handled by an Adninstrative Law judge, but decisions are taken by the Commission itself, a six-membered bipartisan group appointed by the President and conformed by the Senate, for nine year terms and subject to a requirement that no more than three may be from the same political party. 1875

All of the above can deal with issues of both validity and infringement, although the remedies that they can grant differ. 1876

IV. Patent Trial and Appeal Board (PTAB)

The Patent Trial and Appeal Board was created in 2012 and has jurisdiction over two types of post grant challenges to the validity of patents: post grant review and *inter partes* review. The first of these can be requested for the first nine months after grant of a patent granted under the "first inventor to file" definition of novelty that was adopted in 2013. *Inter partes* review on the other hand can be requested for any patent as long as it is not currently undergoing post grant review or in the period within which post grant review may be requested. 1877

It has no jurisdiction over issues relating to infringement. It normally sits in panels of three Administrative Paten Judges, who normally have technical qualifications. 1878

V. Appeals/CAFC

As noted above, appeals on patent matters from all of these tribunals lie to the Court of Appeals for the Federal Circuit, which normally sits in panels of three judges.[3] Further appeal to the United States Supreme Court may be possible if the Supreme Court issues a writ of *certiorari* to hear the appeal, which will only occur if four of the nine justices on the Court view the issues raised as justifying review of the lower court's decision by the Supreme Court. 1879

Because in the United States protection for new designs is primarily by application of the patent law, all of the above mentioned tribunals handle not only patents for inventions, but unlike the UPC, also patents for designs. One further point to note is that prior to the creation of the Patent Trial and Appeal Board, most patent cases coming before the courts involved issues of both validity and infringement. The creation of the Patent Trial and Appeal Board has meant that in many cases there is now effective bifurcation of infringement and validity issues with validity being decided by the PTAB and infringement by the district courts. 1880

Because most patent-related disputes are initially heard by either the by a district court or the Patent Trial and Appeal Board, the rest of this chapter will focus on these two fora. 1881

3 Appeals on most other matters will lie of a regional Court of Appeals.

C. Personal Jurisdiction

I. Situation before the Unified Patent Court

1882 Under Article 33 of the UPCA, infringement actions will be able to be brought in the local or regional division where the infringement occurs or in the local or regional division where the defendant resides. If the defendant does not reside in a country party to the agreement, an action for infringement will be able to be brought in the central division as an alternative to the national/regional division where infringement occurs.[4]

1883 Article 33 of the UPC Agreement also provides that for actions to be brought to the central division, parties will have the choice to bring an infringement action before the central division if the defendant is domiciled outside the European Union. Furthermore, if a revocation action is already pending before the central division, the patent holder will have the possibility to bring an infringement action to the central division. There will be no possibility for the defendant to request a transfer of an infringement case from a local division to the central division if the defendant is domiciled within the European Union.

1884 Local/regional divisions will have the option of transferring any issues relating to validity to the central division.[5] Actions for provisional relief and protective measures as well as actions for compensation for pre-grant use of an invention disclosed in a published European patent application must also be brought before a local/regional division.

1885 Article 31 of the UPCA provides the court with limited long arm jurisdiction by reference to Regulation (EU) No 1215/2012 as amended by Regulation 542/2015 and the Lugano Convention. The effect is to provide "long-arm" jurisdiction for assessment of damages where the jurisdiction of the Court is founded on infringements occurring within the UPC contracting member states. Additionally, Article 35 of the Brussels Regulation permits actions for provisional measures to be obtained from any EU Court even if another Court has exclusive jurisdiction as to the substance of the matter. Unified Patent Court has the power to grant provisional measures for infringement of European patents even where proprietors opt-out of the jurisdiction of the Court or in respect of infringement occurring outside of UPC member states.

II. Situation in the US

1886 In the United States, for district court proceedings, two considerations arise as to where an action may be brought: whether the court has personal jurisdiction over the defendant and whether the court is a proper venue for the action

1887 Rule 4 of the Federal Rules of Civil Procedure provides that a party may be served, and so is subject to the personal jurisdiction of the court, anywhere within the state where the federal district court sits and outside these limits if a statute so provides.

4 Agreement on a Unified Patent Court Articles 33(1)(a) and (b).
5 Agreement on a Unified Patent Court Article 33(3).

Most states have enacted so-called "long arm" statutes to provide a basis for bringing parties that are physically located outside their states under the jurisdiction of their courts when the action complained of has caused harm within the state.[6] The due process clause of the Fifth Amendment of the United States Constitution imposes some limitation on the extent of such statutes. In 1945 in International Shoe Co. v. State of Washington[7] the Supreme Court held that

> "due process requires only that in order to subject a defendant to a judgment *in personam*, if he be not present within the territory of the forum, he have certain minimum contacts with it such that maintenance of the suit does not offend traditional notions of fair play and substantial justice."

What constitutes such minimum contacts when there is no systematic and continuous activity in the forum state was considered in Burger King Corporation v. Rudzewicz[8] where it was held that a franchisee who was resident in Michigan was subject to personal jurisdiction in Florida (Burger King's headquarters state) not simply because of the franchisee's contract but because as a franchisee it had substantial contacts with the franchisor and so had 1888

> "purposely directed activities at residents of the forum state and the litigation results form injuries that arise out of or relate to those activities"

Personal jurisdiction over persons outside the state in which the court sits is therefore dependent upon two factors: 1) whether the party is subject to that state's long arm statute (they are not all of the same scope) and (2) if it does whether the minimum contacts requirements of due process noted above exist.[9] 1889

Except where a party has[10], or is deemed to have consented to jurisdiction, the courts have recognized two types of personal jurisdiction over parties who are outside the forum: general and specific.[11] 1890

General personal jurisdiction arises if the defendant has systematic and continuous dealings with the forum state.[12]. Specific personal jurisdiction on the other hand is tied more closely to the dispute in issue. For example, in Ford Motor Co. v. Montana 1891

6 FRCivP Rule 4(k)(1)(A) provides the basis for the federal courts to apply state long-arm statutes. Rule 4(k)(2) provides basis for jurisdiction in cases that arise under federal law and a party has sufficient contacts with the United States as a whole but not with any given state to be brought within the personal jurisdiction of the federal courts. In many states, the long-arm statute extends to the limits of the Supreme Court's requirements for minimal contacts. An example of a state long arm statute that does not is New York's CPLR 302.

7 326 US 310 (1945).

8 471 US 462 (1985).

9 Akro Corp. v. Luker 45 F.3d 1541 33 USPQ2d 1505 (Fed. Cir. 1995).

10 For example in a contract agreeing to submit to the jurisdiction of a particular court.

11 LSI Industries Inc. v. Hubbell Lighting Inc. 232 F.3d 1369 56 USPQ2d 1965 (Fed. Cir. 2000).

12 Perkins v. Benguet Mining Co 342 US 437 (1952).

Eighth Judicial District Court[13] the Supreme Court held that specific jurisdiction exists when a company cultivates a market for a product in the forum State and the product malfunctions there and that there is no need to show a causal link locating jurisdiction only in the State where the product was sold, made or designed. The Court noted that to be subject to specific jurisdiction the defendant must take "some act by which [it] purposefully avails itself of the privilege of conducting activities within the forum State." ...and the plaintiff's claims "must arise out of or relate to the defendant's contacts" with the forum.

1892 In patent cases, emphasizing the need for some purposeful act by the defendant to give rise to personal jurisdiction the Federal Circuit has held that deliberate shipment of goods through an established distribution network can satisfy the minimum contact requirement and give rise to personal liability.[14]

1893 The question of when a patent owner may be subject to personal jurisdiction when a plaintiff seeks a declaratory judgment that a patent claim is invalid raises similar issues. The grant of an exclusive license including the right to litigate can render the licensor subject to personal jurisdiction in the licensee's state or a state in which the licensee does business.[15] On the other hand, the Federal Circuit has held that the mere sending of a cease and desist letter to a suspected infringer or one of its customers in a state does not of itself render the sender liable to personal jurisdiction in that state.[16] Most recently in Apple Inc. v. Zipit Wireless, Inc.[17] the Federal Circuit found that sending "multiple letters and claim charts accusing Apple of patent infringement" and "visiting Apple's offices in California to discuss these accusations" was sufficient contact with California to provide the California district court with personal jurisdiction over the defendant in a declaratory judgment action.

1894 The patent statute itself provides that patentees who are not resident in the United States can appoint someone within the country as an address for service of papers relating to the patent, for example, the institution of a declaratory judgment action, and that if this is not done then the district court for the Eastern District of Virginia (the district within which the Patent Office has its headquarters) shall have jurisdiction and a summons shall be served by publication or otherwise as the court directs.

1895 What is probably more important in patent cases, however, is whether the court chosen is a proper venue for hearing the action. Although in practice the general law on

---

13 141 S.Ct. 1017 (2021).

14 Beverly Hills Fan Co. v. Royal Sovereign Co. 21 F.3d 1558 30 USPQ2d 1001 (Fed. Cir. 1994) which found there was personal jurisdiction where the defendant shipped the allegedly infringing goods into the forum state. A similar conclusion was reached in Polar Electro Oy v. Suunto Oy 110 USPQ2d 1422 (Fed. Cir. 2016).

15 Breckenridge Pharmaceutical Inc. v. Metabolite Laboratories. Inc 78 USPQ2d 1581 (Fed. Cir. 2006).

16 Akro Corp. v. Luker 45 F.3d 1541 33 USPQ2d 1505 (Fed. Cir. 1995).

17 Case 2021–1760 (Fed. Cir. April 18, 2022).

venue provides a plaintiff with a wide choice of where to bring an action, there is a special provision for patent infringement cases:

> Any civil action for patent infringement may be brought in the judicial district where the defendant resides, or where the defendant has committed acts of infringement and has a regular and established place of business.[18]

We deal first with the question of where the defendant "resides". 1896

In TC Heartland, LLC v. Kraft Foods Group Brands LLC[19]., the Supreme Court held 1897 that "residency" under the patent venue statute for persons resident in the United States meant actual residency and that the "deemed residency" that case law had developed for the general venue statute did not apply to patent infringement cases. Consequently, domestic corporations are subject to suit for patent infringement in their states of incorporation or where they commit acts of infringement. Foreign corporations on the other hand can be sued wherever the court has personal jurisdiction over them.

We now turn to the second alternative for establishing venue, namely a district where 1898 the defendant has committed acts of infringement and has a regular and established place of business.

Normally there is not too much difficulty in determining where a defendant has 1899 committed acts of infringement. However, a special situation arises in cases where the act of infringement is one that arises under the Hatch-Waxman Act as a result of a generic drug manufacturer filing an Abbreviated New Drug Application (ANDA) with the Food and Drug Administration for marketing approval for a generic version of a patented drug. The issue was considered in Valeant Pharmaceuticals North America LLC v. Mylan Pharmaceuticals Inc.[20] where the Federal Circuit concluded that for such cases, infringement occurs for venue purposes only in districts where actions related to the submission of an Abbreviated New Drug Application ("ANDA") occur, not in all locations where future distribution of the generic products specified in the ANDA is contemplated.

> 28 U.S.C. § 1404(a). gives district courts discretion to transfer civil actions to other courts "[f]or the convenience of parties and witnesses, [and] in the interest of justice." An appellate court can order *mandamus* where that discretion has been abused.[21]

The plaintiff bears the burden of showing that venue is proper.[22] 1900

18 28 USC 1400(b).
19 137 S.Ct. 1514 (2017).
20 978 F.3d 1374 (Fed. Cir. 2020).
21 In re Samsung Elecs. Co., 2 F.4th 1371 (Fed. Cir. 2021).
22 In re ZTE (USA) Inc. 126 USPQ2d 1626 (Fed. Cir. 2018). In Westech Aerosol Corporation v. 3M Company GTA-NHT Inc, [2019] USPQ2d (Fed. Cir. 2019) it was pointed out that this includes a requirement to set out specific facts in the pleading, which if shown to be true, would support the claim that venue exists in the chosen court.

D. Substantive Law to be Applied by the for a

I. Situation before the Unified Patent Court

1901 Under the UPC, the law to be applied by the court, will, be the same in all divisions and will be: EU law, the UPC agreement itself, the European Patent Convention other international agreements applicable to patents and binding on all contracting states and finally, national law. In most situations, this means that questions of infringement will be decided under the specific provisions of the UPC relating to direct and indirect infringement, limitations on the rights granted by a patent, prior user rights and exhaustion and that questions of validity will be decided under the European Patent Convention.

II. Situation in the US

1902 In the United States in district court proceedings, questions of both infringement and validity are under the provisions of Title 35 of the United States Code which codifies the Patent Act. Review proceedings before the Patent Trial and Appeal Board are confined to issues of validity and the scope of the proceedings depends on the type of review being undertaken. While the PTAB may apply all provisions of the Code applicable to validity when deciding on post grant review petitions, in *inter partes* review proceedings, it is limited to deciding questions of novelty and obviousness over prior patents and publications. (35 USC 311(b)).

1903 A detailed comparison of European and United States substantive patent law would be out of place here, but some differences that affect litigation should be noted.

1904 The traditional concepts of infringement were changed by the Hatch-Waxman amendments (codified in 35 USC 271(e)(2)) which makes it an act of infringement to submit an application for marketing approval for a generic drug if the purpose of such submission is to obtain approval to engage in the commercial manufacture, use, or sale of a drug claimed in a patent or the use of which is claimed in a patent before the expiration of such patent. The effect of this is that there can be infringement before any infringing product has been sold so that normally the only available remedy is the equitable one of an injunction with the consequence that for the reasons noted above, such cases will be decided by a judge in a bench trial without a jury.

1905 A further difference may arise with respect to the remedies available when infringement is found of a patent that has not been found to be invalid as discussed in the next section.

E. Remedies for Infringement

I. Situation before the Unified Patent Court

1906 The European Unified Patent Court will have the power to grant permanent injunction prohibiting a continuation of infringement not only against a direct infringer but also "an intermediary whose services are being used by a third party to infringe a patent."[23] Breach of an injunction may result in "a recurring penalty payment payable to the Court."[24] The powers of the court also include the possibility of making orders not only with respect to infringing products but also Amaterials and implements principally used in the creation or manufacture of those products. Possible orders include recall of products from the channels of commerce.[25]

Damages may be awarded against an "infringer who knowingly or with reasonable grounds to know, engaged in a patent infringing activity". Three principles with respect to damages are stated: 1907
1) the injured party should to the extent possible be placed in the position it would have been in if no infringement had taken place;
2) the infringer should not benefit from the infringement[26]; but
3) damages shall not be punitive.[27]

Article 69 provides that unless special circumstances apply: 1908

Reasonable and proportionate legal costs and other expenses incurred by the successful party shall, as a general rule, be borne by the unsuccessful party unless equity requires otherwise up to a ceiling set by the rules of procedure.[28]

II. Situation in the United States

In the United States, in district court proceedings, the following may be available 1909
- Injunctions;
- Damages based on Lost Profits;
- Damages not less than a reasonable royalty; and
- Attorney fees;

---

23 Whether grant of an injunction will be almost automatic is currently a matter of debate. The EU's Enforcement Directive (2004/48/EC) stipulates the application of a proportionality test before granting injunctions. As noted above, the UPCA provides that where applicable, EU law takes precedence over other law sources. It is to be noted that Article 139(1) of the German law has recently been amended to add a provision that "under the special circumstances of a singular case and considering the principle of good faith, ...enforcement [of an injunction] would result in disproportionate hardship on the infringer or third parties beyond what is justified by the exclusionary right." Thereby effectively placing the burden on the infringer to show why an injunction would be a disproportionate remedy.

24 Unified Patent Court Agreement Article 63. Note: unlike common law systems, the Agreement on the Unified Court does not give the court any power to hold a party who breaches an injunction in contempt of court, only the right to impose such recurring penalties.

25 Unified Patent Court Agreement Article 64.

26 Thereby opening the door to assessment of damages on a theory of unjust enrichment which can be determined by assessment of the profits made by the infringer as a result of the infringement.

27 Unified Patent Court Agreement Article 68.

28 Rules of the Unified Patent Court Rule 152 provides that the Administrative Committee shall adopt a scale of recoverable costs which shall set ceilings for such costs by reference to the value of the dispute.

1910 In the ITC:

An exclusion order preventing importation of infringing goods into the United States, but no award of damages; and

1911 In the Court of Claims:

Reasonable compensation for federal government use. Note there is no remedy for use by state governments unless the state waives sovereign immunity.

1. Injunctions

1912 35 USC 283 states:

> "The several courts having jurisdiction of cases under this title may grant injunctions in accordance with the principles of equity to prevent the violation of any right secured by patent, on such terms as the court deems reasonable."

1913 In 2006 in eBay Inc. v. MercExchange LLC[29], the Supreme Court rejected the traditional view that an injunction was almost invariable available after proof of infringement of a claim that had not been found to be invalid and referred to the language of the statute to assert that the principles of equity need to be applied before granting a permanent injunction, a four factor rule of equity had to be complied with and the court had to be satisfied that the plaintiff had demonstrated:

1) that it has suffered an irreparable injury;
2) that remedies available at law such as monetary damages are inadequate to compensate for that injury;
3) that considering the balance of hardships between the plaintiff and the defendant a remedy in equity is warranted; and
4) that the public interest would not be disserved by a permanent injunction.

1914 The effect of the e-Bay decision was to make it more difficult to obtain an injunction against a defendant who was not a direct competitor against the patent owner or an exclusive licensee because it became more difficult to show that there was irreparable harm or than monetary damages would not suffice. If no injunction is granted, the court will normally require the infringer to pay a continuing royalty which may be set at a higher amount than that which is awarded for damage caused by the infringement prior to the trial and finding of infringement.

1915 Injunctions can be enforced by actions for contempt of court but if the product has been modified after the initial determination of infringement, modified elements of the newly accused product must be evaluated against the asserted claim, on a limitation by limitation basis, to ensure that each limitation continues to be met. If it does not, it will be necessary to bring a new action for infringement.

29 547 U.S. 388 (2006).

2. Damages

35 USC 284 provides that 1916

> Upon finding for the claimant the court shall award the claimant damages adequate to compensate for the infringement but in no event less than a reasonable royalty for the use made of the invention by the infringer, together with interest and costs fixed by the court.
>
> When the damages are not found by a jury, the court shall assess them. In either event the court may increase the damages up to three times the amount found or assessed. ….
>
> The court may receive expert testimony as an aid to the determination of damages or of what royalty would be reasonable under the circumstances

In Aro Mfg. Co v. Convertible Top Replacement Co.[30] the Supreme Court set out the 1917 basic standard by which damages were to be determined by how much had the Patent Holder and Licensee suffered by the infringement. And that question is primarily: had the Infringer not infringed, what would the Patent Holder-Licensee have made?

The determination of the amount of damages is a matter for the jury in a jury trial 1918 and for the judge in the case of a bench trial without a jury.

In principle, the loss my extend to losses not only of lost sales of the patented pro- 1919 duct, but also profit erosion due to competition and loss of sales of products normally sold with the patented article (so called "convoyed sales") and even loss of sales of an alternative to the patented product sold by the patent owner if there are no non-infringing alternatives for the same purpose.

Determining how much the patent holder and license lost, however, may not be easy. 1920 In Panduit v. Stahlin[31] it was held,

> To obtain as damages the profits on sales he would have made absent infringement, i.e. the sales made by the infringer, a patent owner must prove: (1) demand for the patented product, (2) absence of acceptable non-infringing substitutes, (3) his manufacturing and marketing capability to exploit the demand, and (4) the amount of profit he would have made.

If lost profits cannot be determined, it is necessary to resort to determining an appro- 1921 priate royalty that must be not less than what is reasonable. Although determination of what such a royalty should be is to be based on a hypothetical negotiation, as the Panduit case points out, this moght not be the same as would have been reached in a genuine commercial negotiation because if the infringer knew it was never going to have to pay more than it would have done for a commercial license, it has no incen-

30 377 U.S. 476 141 USPQ 681 (1964).

31 575 F.2d 1152 197 USPQ 726 (6th Cir 1978), The opinion was by Judge Markey, later to be the first chief judge of the Federal Circuit.

tive to respect the patent. In Georgia-Pacific Corp. v. United States Plywood Corp.[32] the court set out a non-exclusive list of factors it thought could be relevant as follows:

1. The royalties received by the patentee for the licensing of the patent in suit, proving or tending to prove an established royalty.
2. The rates paid by the licensee for the use of other patents comparable to the patent in suit.
3. The nature and scope of the license, as exclusive or non-exclusive; or as restricted or non-restricted in terms of territory or with respect to whom the manufactured product may be sold.
4. The licensor's established policy and marketing program to maintain his patent monopoly by not licensing others to use the invention or by granting licenses under special conditions designed to preserve that monopoly.
5. The commercial relationship between the licensor and licensee, such as, whether they are competitors in the same territory in the same line of business; or whether they are inventor and promoter.
6. The effect of selling the patented specialty in promoting sales of other products of the licensee; the existing value of the invention to the licensor as a generator of sales of his non-patented items; and the extent of such derivative or convoyed sales.
7. The duration of the patent and the term of the license.
8. The established profitability of the product made under the patent; its commercial success; and its current popularity.
9. The utility and advantages of the patent property over the old modes or devices, if any, that had been used for working out similar results.
10. The nature of the patented invention; the character of the commercial embodiment of it as owned and produced by the licensor; and the benefits to those who have used the invention.
11. The extent to which the infringer has made use of the invention; and any evidence probative of the value of that use.
12. The portion of the profit or of the selling price that may be customary in the particular business or in comparable businesses to allow for the use of the invention or analogous inventions.
13. The portion of the realizable profit that should be credited to the invention as distinguished from non-patented elements, the manufacturing process, business risks, or significant features or improvements added by the infringer.
14. The opinion testimony of qualified experts.
15. The amount that a licensor (such as the patentee) and a licensee (such as the infringer) would have agreed upon (at the time the infringement began) if both had been reasonably and voluntarily trying to reach an agreement; that is, the amount which a prudent licensee-who desired, as a business proposition, to obtain a license to manufacture and sell a particular article embodying the patented invention-would have been willing to pay as a royalty and yet be able to make a reasonable profit

32 318 F. Supp 1116 166 USPQ 235 (S.D.N.Y. 1970). This list was affirmed on appeal 446 F2d. 295 170 USPQ 369 (2d. Cir 1971).

and which amount would have been acceptable by a prudent patentee who was willing to grant a license.

Factor 13 has attracted considerable attention on the question of when it is appropriate to base a royalty on the entire market value of an infringing product if other factors affect actual sales of it. In Lucent Technologies v. Gateway[33] the Federal Circuit stated: 1922

> For the entire market value rule to apply, the patentee must prove that the patent-related feature is the 'basis for customer demand.'

and

> The entire market value rule allows for the recovery of damages based on the value of an entire apparatus containing several features, when the feature patented constitutes the basis for customer demand.

Subsequently in Versata Software Inc, v SAP America Inc[34] the court took the view that 1923

> The entire market value rule is a narrow exception to the general rule that royalties are awarded based on the "smallest saleable patent practising unit"

and

> A patentee may assess damages based on the entire market value of the accused product only where the patented feature creates the basis for consumer demand or substantially creates the value of the component parts.

Another of the Georgia-Pacific factors that has attracted attention is factor 14. For many years experts would testify that there was a "rule of thumb" that the licensor would obtain 25 % of the profit attributable to the use of the invention and then use this as a starting point to calculate what they asserted was an appropriate royalty in a particular case. This approach was rejected in Uniloc USA Inc. v. Microsoft Corp[35] and experts are now required to provide a more sophisticated explanation as to the basis for their proposed damages determinations. This can lead to Daubert hearings to determine the credibility of the expert's hypotheses before the case goes to a jury. 1924

Where an act of infringement occurs in the United States, the 2018 Supreme Court decision in in WesternGeco LLC v. Ion Geophysical Corporation[36] held that loss of sales outside the United States deriving from an act of infringement within the United States could possibly be recompensable. The full significance of this decision, however, is still to be determined. 1925

"Innocent infringers" may escape an award of damages for acts occurring before they became aware of the patent that they are infringing unless the patent owner marks products embodying the invention with the patent number or with advise about a 1926

33 580 F.3d 1301, 92 USPQ2d 1555 (Fed. Cir. 2009).
34 717 F.3d 1255 (Fed. Cir. 2013).
35 632 F.3d 1292 (Fed. Cir. 2011).
36 138 S. Ct. 2129 (S. Ct. 2018).

free, publicly-available web-site on which details of patents relating to its products are set out.

1927 There is a six year statute of limitations for claims for damages for patent infringement.

3. Enhanced damages

1928 As noted above, the statute permits the court to increase damages up to three times the actual damage suffered by the infringer. For many years, the Federal circuit took the view that such increases should occur only when there was willful infringement. In 2016, in its decision in Halo Electronics Inc. v. Pulse Electronics Inc.,[37], the Supreme Court held that willfulness was not the only situation in which increased damages might be awarded. Speaking for the Court, Chief Justice Roberts stated that although there is "no precise rule or formula" for awarding damages under § 284, a district court's discretion should be exercised in light of general considerations to be taken into account when exercising discretion.

1929 The Federal Circuit has now reverted to a test set out in an earlier case, The Read Corp v. Portec Inc.[38] looking more broadly at the egregiousness of the defendant's conduct based on all the facts and circumstances. Where it had noted nine factors to be considered: 1) whether there was deliberate copying; 2) whether, if the infringer when he knew of the other party's patent protection, investigated the sc ope of the patent and formed a good faith belief that it was invalid or not infringed; 3) the defendant's behavior during litigation; 4) the defendant's size and financial condition; 5) the closeness of the case; 6) the duration of the defendant's misconduct; 7) any remedial action undertaken by the defendant; 8) the defendant's motivation for harm; and 9) whether the defendant attempted to conceal its misconduct.

4. Award of Attorney fees

1930 35 USC 285 provides:

> The court in exceptional cases may award reasonable attorney fees to the prevailing party.

1931 For many years, the Federal Circuit construed this to limit awards of attorney fees to the prevailing party to very limited situations. In 2014 in Octane Fitness LLC v. Icon Health & Fitness Inc.[39] the Supreme Court rejected the Federal Circuit's approach to hold that the word "exceptional" had its ordinary meaning and that awards of attorney fees to the prevailing party were to be determined on a totality of the circumstances basis.

1932 The old equitable remedy of an account of the infringer's profits, which is a possible remedy under the UPCA, was omitted for utility patents in the United States by

37 136 S. Ct. 1923 (2016).
38 970 F2d 816 (Fed Cir, 1992).
39 134 S. Ct. 1749 (2014).

the 1946 Patents Act,[40] although it remains a possible remedy for infringement of a design patent. The reason seems to have been that it had become too difficult to determine how much of an infringer's profit was attributable to the fact of infringement and how much to other factors, such as other non-infringing features of the claimed infringement.

F. Provisional and Protective Measures

I. Preliminary Injunctions

Article 62 of the UPCA gives the Unified Court the power to grant preliminary 1933
injunctions to prevent any imminent infringement, or the continuation of the alleged infringement or to make such continuation subject to the lodging of guarantees intended to ensure the compensation of the right holder using its discretion to weigh up the interests of the parties and in particular to take into account the potential harm for either of the parties resulting from the granting or the refusal of the injunction. The Court may also order delivery up of suspected infringing articles and possible freezing of the movement of such articles and even freezing of assets to ensure that an infringer will be able to pay any damages award made against it.

II. Situation in the United States

In the United States, preliminary injunctions are available before trial to enjoin further 1934
infringement while pre-trial proceedings progress. These are granted only on principles of equity discussed above in the context of the grant of permanent injunctions, a key factor being whether it is likely that the plaintiff will succeed at trial. At one time, the defendant needed only to raise a serious question as to validity to resist the grant of a preliminary injunction, but this is no longer the case and a proper evaluation of the plaintiff's likelihood of success is required. Delay on seeking a preliminary injunction is likely to result in rejection of a request for it because the plaintiff's delay may be an indication that the plaintiff is not suffering irreparable harm from the infringement. The Federal rules provide that the plaintiff may be required. to give security in an amount that the court considers proper to pay the costs and damages sustained by any party found to have been wrongfully enjoined.[41]

However, in the United States there are no provisions for pre-trial delivery up or 1935
freezing of assets

III. Production and Preservation of Evidence

Articles 59–61 of the UPCA set out a number of provisions relating to production 1936
and preservation of evidence including provisions similar to French and Belgian *saisie* proceedings and English freezing orders (previously known as Mareva orders). As dis-

40 Act of Aug. 1, 1946, ch. 726, 60 Stat. 778.
41 FRCivP Rule 65(c).

cussed below in considering procedure before the courts and Patent Trial and Appeal Board, such possibilities are largely absent in the United States, where discovery is the primary means for obtaining evidence. Indeed, the United States Supreme Court has specifically held that United States courts lack the inherent power to issue Mareva orders[42], although in some cases equitable relief may be available.

1937 However, this is not to say there are no protections against destruction or hiding of evidence. These include:

1. Subpoenas

1938 Rule 45 of the Federal Rules of Civil Procedure provides that courts can issue *subpoenas* to order any individual to attend a deposition, to produce specified documents, electronically stored information, or tangible things or to permit the inspection of premises, including copying, testing, or sampling of materials that are ordered to be produced. Subpoenas may be issued without the party seeking their issue having to give the court any explanation of why a subpoena is requested. Failure to comply with a *subpoena* unless the recipient is successful in having it quashed, may be a contempt of court.

2. Spoilation

1939 U.S. law recognizes a general duty o preserve evidence after litigation is filed and where it is threatened, or reasonably foreseeable.[43] Once this trigger point has passed, destruction of evidence that a party should have known might be relevant to the litigation, is deemed spoliation of the evidence. Courts have a broad discretion in deciding on appropriate sanctions when spoliation has occurred including issuing adverse jury instructions, preclusion of evidence imposition of fees and costs and even dismissal of the spoliator's case, although the court should "select the least onerous sanction corresponding to the willfulness of the destructive act and the prejudice suffered by the victim".[44] It is common for potential litigants to send "litigation hold" letters to potential adversaries notifying them of the possibility of litigation so as to establish an early "trigger point" after which destruction of possible evidence may be treated as spoliation. The decision to take such action should, however, be balanced against the possibility that it might open the door to the potential adversary commencing a declaratory judgment action that might not otherwise have been open to it.

42 Grupo Mexicano de Desarrollo S.A. v. All. Bond Fund, Inc., 527 U.S. 308 (1999). The Supreme Court referred to the "well-established general rule that a judgment establishing the debt was necessary before a court of equity would interfere with the debtor's use of its property." If this was to be changed, Congress should do so. Congress has not.

43 Micron Tech., Inc. v. Rambus Inc., 645 F.3d 1311 (Fed. Cir. 2011).

44 Schmid v. Milwaukee Elec. Tool Corp., 13 F.3d 76, (3d Cir. 1994).

G. Who can bring Suit for Patent Infringement

I. Situation before the Unified Patent Court

Under Article 47 UPCA, an action for infringement of a European Patent that is subject to the jurisdiction of the court may be brought by the patent proprietor or, unless the licensing agreement provides otherwise, the holder of an exclusive license, provided that the patent proprietor is given prior notice. A non-exclusive licensee may be able to bring suit if this is authorized by the license agreement. It should, however, be noted that the patent proprietor is a required party to the proceedings if there is a counterclaim for invalidity of the patent. If this is not the case, a separate revocation action before the central division will be necessary to challenge the validity of the patent. 1940

UPCA Rules 8.5 and 8.6 address the question of who is the "proprietor" by stating that in relation to the proprietor of a European patent, the person entitled to be registered as proprietor under the law of each Contracting Member State in which such European patent has been validated shall be treated as the proprietor whether or not such person is in fact recorded in the register of patents maintained in such Contracting Member or in the European Patent Register kept by the European Patent Office. 1941

II. Situation in the US

In the United States, two issues have to be considered when considering whether e arty has the right to sue for patent infringement: 1) whether the plaintiff is the "patentee" and 2) whether the plaintiff or co-plaintiff has a "case or controversy" against the defendant. 1942

The statute (35 USC 271) gives a "patentee" the right to sue to enforce a patent. In 1875, the Supreme Court extended this right to certain exclusive licensees[45] Such rights do not extend to non-exclusive licensees[46] or beneficial owners of a patent.[47] However, subject to a six years statute of limitations, the fact that the patent has already expired does not prevent the patentee from suing for damages that occurred before the patent expired.[48] 1943

In the case where a patent is jointly owned, all co-owners must join as plaintiffs.[49] 1944

45 Littlefield v. Perry 88 U.S. 205 (1875).

46 Sicom Systems Ltd. v. Agilent Technologies Inc. 76 USPQ2d 1933 (Fed. Cir. 2005).

47 Crown Die and Tool Company v Nye Tool & Machinery Works 261 U.S. 23 (1923). It was concluded that since a patent is creature of statute only the legal owner had a right to enforce it.

48 Keranos LLC v. Silicon Storage Technology Inc. 116 USPQ2d 1312 (Fed. Cir. 2015).

49 Waterman v. Mackenzie 138 U.S. 252 (1891), where it was held that one who had been assigned an undivided part of a patent could only sue for infringement jointly with the assignor. This decision was interpreted in Switzer Brothers Inc. v. Byrne 242 F.2d 909 113 USPQ 168 (6th Cir., 1957) as meaning that all co-owners of a patent must join in an infringement suit.

1945 Article III of the Constitution of the United States limits the role of the federal courts to resolving "cases" and "controversies". The Supreme Court has held that for a party to have "constitutional standing" to bring such a case or controversy to the federal courts, a plaintiff must be able to show injury in fact that is actual or imminent "which is traceable to the unlawful conduct of the defendant that "a favorable judgment" will redress by the relief sought.

1946 Consequently, if the "patentee" brings an infringement action, others having Article III standing who have been injured by the infringement may join in the action as co-plaintiffs, as is usually the case.

1947 For an exclusive licensee to have the right to bring suit without joining the patent owner either voluntarily or involuntarily, the exclusivity should effectively include all rights in the patent and should specifically include the right to sue infringers if the licensee is to be entitled to sue on its own behalf and not simply as a co-plaintiff with the patent owner.[50] The policy reason behind this is to avoid the risk that a single infringer may find itself as the defendant in suits under the same patent from two different plaintiffs. If this is a risk, the Federal Circuit has held "a patentee should be joined either voluntarily or involuntarily in any infringement action brought by a licensee".[51]

1948 The Federal Circuit reviewed much of its prior case law on this topic in University of South Florida Research Foundation Inc. v. Fujifilm Medical Systems[52], pointing out that the statutory requirement that the action be brought by a party qualifying as a "patentee" under 35 USC 281 and the question of Constitutional standing Article III of the Constitution were separate issues and both had to be considered. On the first, the court noted:

> we examine the 'totality' of the agreement to determine whether a party other than the original patentee has established that it obtained all substantial rights in the patent." *Lone Star*, 925 F.3d at 1229 (quoting *AsymmetRx, Inc. v. Biocare Med., LLC*, 582 F.3d 1314, 1321 (Fed. Cir. 2009)). Among the factors that we consider, the exclusive right to make, use, and sell, as well as the nature and scope of the patentee's retained right to sue accused infringers are the most important considerations in determining whether a license agreement transfers sufficient rights to render the licensee the owner of the patent.

1949 On the question of Constitutional standing, the court noted that it had previously held that constitutional standing is satisfied when a party holds at least one exclusionary right.

---

50 Fieldturf Inc. v. Southwest Recreational Industries Inc. 69 USPQ2d 1795 (Fed. Cir. 2004). In Keranos LLC v. Silicon Storage Technology Inc. 116 USPQ2d 1312 (Fed. Cir. 2015) it was held that where there had been a transfer of substantially all rights, the exclusive licensee was entitled to sue for back damages resulting from infringement of expired patents even if they expired prior to the grant of the license.

51 Prima Tek II LLC v. A-Roo Co. 222 F.3d 1372 55 USPQ2d 1742 (Fed. Cir. 2000).

52 Case 2020–1872 (Fed. Cir. unsealed November 23, 2021).

H. Who Can Seek to Have Patent Declared Invalid or Revoked

I. Situation before the Unified Patent Court

The European Unified Patent Court Agreement contains is no overt requirement for standing in order to bring an action for revocation of a patent before the Central Division. However, after setting out the requirements for a party to bring an infringement action, in its final clause, Article 47 states: 1950

Any other natural or legal person, or any body entitled to bring actions in accordance with its national law, who is concerned by a patent, may bring actions in accordance with the Rules of Procedure.

It remains to be seen whether the words "who is concerned by a patent" will be construed to impose any limitation on parties who can challenge a patent's validity. At present, the Rules of Procedure place no limits on parties who can make such a challenge. 1951

II. Situation in the US

In the United States, the parties entitled to challenge a patent depend upon the type of procedure chosen to bring the challenge, either by seeking a declaratory judgment in a district court pr by challenging validity of onr ormore patent claims in review proceedings before the Patent Trial and Appeal Board. 1952

If the challenger seeks a declaratory judgment that claims are invalid or not infringed before a district court, that party bears the burden of showing that it is involved in a "case" or "controversy" with the patent court that will meet the Constitutional requirement that must be met to justify involvement of the federal courts as noted above. 1953

The United States Supreme Court considered the question of what constitutes a controversy in MedImmune Inc. v. Genentech Inc[53] and held, that a controversy not only existed if there was a real threat of litigation, but also in other cases such as where a licensee wished to contest the validity, enforceability or scope of a claim included in a licensed patent, said patent having been granted after the execution of the agreement so that its scope was not known at the time the agreement was made. The Court held that such a dispute over the terms of a contract was sufficient of a controversy to give the courts the power to render a declaratory judgement. The Supreme Court noted that 1954

> Basically, the question in each case is whether the facts alleged, under all the circumstances, show that there is a substantial controversy, between the parties having adverse legal interests, of sufficient immediacy and reality to warrant the issuance of a declaratory judgment.

The Supreme Court did, however, emphasize that the dispute must be 1955

> definite and concrete, touching the legal relations of the parties having adverse legal interests and that it ... admit of specific relief through a decree of a conclusive character, as

53 549 U.S. 118 (2007).

distinguished from an opinion advising what the law would be on such a hypothetical state of facts.

1956 Since then a number of cases have addressed these requirements, most commonly in the context of "warning letters" sent by a patent owner to a putative infringer. While each case is decided on its own facts and the Federal Circuit has held that a simple letter drawing the existence if a patent to another party does not create a "controversy", more elaborate letters, especially if sent repeatedly, may do.

1957 On the other hand, anyone other than the patent owner may seek to challenge the validity of one or more patent claims in proceedings before the Patent Trial and Appeal Board in post grant review or *inter partes* review proceedings. However, if the challenge fails, because the appeal lies to a federal court (the Court of Appeals for the Federal Circuit), the Constitutional requirement for the need for there to be a case or controversy is applicable. Federal Circuit case law has read this requirement as meaning that a losing challenger must show that it will suffer or be likely to suffer actual harm, for example the likelihood of being sued for infringement, if it was not allowed to appeal. A patent owner who loses in one of these proceedings before the PTAB always has the right to appeal.

1958 Finally for completeness it should be noted that anyone raising a "substantial new ground of patentability" relating to novelty or obviousness over a patent or printed publication or relating to double patenting may request the USPTO to re-examine any patent that it has granted.

I. Procedure in General

I. The Situation before the Unified Patent Court

1959 Article 52 UPCA specifically provides that all proceedings before the Court will be divided into three stages: written, interim and oral. The procedures are specifically designed to be front-loaded with heavy emphasis on the first stage. The stages are

1960 Stage 1: Written procedure requiring fully developed arguments and evidence, likely two rounds from each side. This written procedure will require inter alia for a claim for patent infringement an indication of the facts relied on, in particular:

(i) an indication of the facts relied on including one or more instances of alleged infringements or threatened infringements specifying the date and place of each;
(ii) the identification of the patent claims alleged to be infringed;
(iii) the evidence relied on, where available, and an indication of any further evidence which will be offered in support;
(iv) the reasons why the facts relied on constitute an infringement of the patent claims, including arguments of law and where appropriate an explanation of the proposed claim interpretation.

1961 Stage 2: Interim procedure is to be handled by a single legally qualified judge rapporteur who can give orders to summon witnesses, order production of more evidence and possibly appoint a court expert. However, it is doubted that this will be common and should only be appointed if after reading the papers submitted in stage 1 the judges still cannot understand the case – one exception might be if a *saisie* is ordered where an expert would participate in the "raid" and report findings to the court)

Stage 3: Oral procedure normally to be completed in one day. The exact format may differ on the traditions of the location of the division of the court before which the proceedings are brought. In civil law countries these proceedings might open with the court giving its current assessment of the case; in common law countries by traditional opening statements by counsel; experts who had given opinions to be cross-examined in civil law jurisdictions first by the judges and then by counsel, in common law jurisdictions the other way round. 1962

The rules have been drafted with the objective of ensuring that except in complex cases, the first instance proceedings will be completed within a year from service of the complaint.

Court fees will be a combination of fixed fees and for actions relating to infringement or assessment of damages and the value of the case exceeds € 500,000, fees based on the value of the case.

The Rules provide that the determination of the amount of damages ordered for the successful party may be the subject of separate proceedings. Similarly a separate proceeding may be ordered for a determination of the costs to be paid by the losing party to the winning party.

In the United States, different procedures apply depending on whether the proceedings are before a district court or the Patent Trial and Appeal Board, with the latter showing greater similarity with UPC practice. In both types of proceedings, the onus is heavily on the parties to make their case and the role of the district court judge or administrative patent judges of the Patent Trial and Appeal Board is to decide the issues presented by the parties, not to investigate matters themselves.

II. U.S. District Court Procedure

We deal first with practice in federal district courts. 1963

Although there is no formal breakdown into different stages, in practice different phases can be identified:

- Pleadings;
- Case management conference;
- Claim construction;
- Discovery (that is gathering evidence in support of one's case);
- Final preparation for trial and the trial itself.

1. Pleadings

If a party fails to set out the minimum requirements required by the Federal Rules of Civil Procedure, its claim may be dismissed. However, as compared with the requirements set out above for the UPC, these rules are much less demanding. 1964

1965 In cases where patent infringement is alleged, the complaint should set out the patent or patents involved, a statement of the ownership of the patent or patents and the basis of the plaintiff's right to enforce the patent, the identity of the alleged infringer and a general description of the acts which are alleged to constitute infringement (specifics are not required at this stage) and a statement as to whether the plaintiff's products are marked with a relevant patent number, whether the defendant has been given any prior notice of the impending suit and the relief requested.

1966 The general rules of pleading in federal court are set out in FRCivP Rule 8. The requirements are simple and commonly referred to as employing a "notice pleading standard". Indeed Rule 8(d) specifically states that pleadings shall be simple concise and direct and that no technical forms of pleadings or motions are required. It is specifically provided that pleading in the alternative or of several different types is permitted. It is necessary to provide sufficient factual information to "state a claim to relief that is plausible on its face" this requires sufficient factual content that if assumed to be true would allow "the court to draw the reasonable inference that the defendant is liable for the misconduct alleged".

1967 In this context it should be noted that each district court may have its own rules as to how specific the pleading must be, but in all cases it must at least identify the product that is alleged to infringe and most courts require identification of at least one claim that is alleged to have been infringed. Some courts go further and, at least where the technology is complicated have required an explanation of why the accused product is believed to infringe.

1968 In response to a complaint alleging infringement, the defendant will typically file an answer denying the plaintiff's allegations and will frequently file a counterclaim alleging that the patents under which it is being sued or certain of the claims of such patents are invalid. If this happens, the plaintiff can file an answer to the counterclaim. An important difference from proceedings under the UPC is that there is no provision for the patent owner to amend its claims in response to a counter claim for invalidity. If the patent owner believes that amendment is appropriate, it can seek to do this through re-examination or reissue proceedings in the Patent Office and ask the district court to stay the infringement action until re-examination is complete. However, the decision on whether to stay the infringement action is totally within the discretion of the district court judge handling the case.

1969 As an alternative to filing an answer to the complaint, the defendant may file a motion for dismissal of the case, for example on the ground that the court has no personal jurisdiction over it or that the complaint lacks sufficient facts to make a plausible claim of infringement or that the patent is clearly invalid, for example because on its face it claims something that is unpatentable such as an abstract idea.

The current requirement for the amount of detail required in initial pleadings is governed by the Supreme Court rulings in Bell Atlantic Corporation v. Twombly[54] and Ashcroft v. Iqbal[55] where the Supreme Court explained that 1970

> only a complaint that states a plausible claim for relief survives a motion to dismiss. Determining whether a complaint states a plausible claim for relief will, be a context-specific task that requires the reviewing court to draw on its judicial experience and common sense.... When there are well-pleaded factual allegations, a court should assume their veracity and then determine whether they plausibly give rise to an entitlement to relief.

2. Case Management Conference

After the pleadings are complete, the judge will call a conference with the parties' attorneys to schedule future events, such as the period within which both fact discovery and submission of experts reports has to be completed and a trial date. 1971

The conference will further set out the extent of discovery, and to determine how to deal with confidential information that may emerge during discovery (for example limiting the persons who have access to it by a protective order). The judge may also suggest that the parties should try to settle the case or seek mediation. 1972

Depending on the local rules, the judge may also require the parties to submit their detailed contentions on infringement and validity and to identify any terms in the patent claim that will need to be construed. 1973

3. Claim Construction

Claim construction is a matter for the judge and is often referred to as a Markman determination after the name of the case in which the Supreme Court held this was a job for the judge and not the jury. 1974

The parties will meet prior to the determination to try to agree on a meaning of the claim terms. If they cannot, they will submit briefs to the judge explaining why they believe their understanding of the meaning of the term is correct. Frequently the judge makes his or her ruling on the meaning of the claim terms under consideration after hearing the parties in a "Markman hearing". 1975

In making a determination of the meaning of a disputed term, the judge may take both intrinsic evidence (the language of the claims and specification and the history of examination of the application giving rise to the patent) and extrinsic evidence (dictionary definitions, evidence as to whether a term has any special meaning in a particular technical field) into account. The timing of the determination will vary depending on the nature of the case but will always be before jury selection. Commonly it occurs after discovery has been completed. 1976

---

54 550 US 544 (2007).
55 556 U.S. 662, 129 S.Ct. 1937 (2009).

4. Discovery

1977 Discovery in a patent case normally incudes both fact discovery and expert discovery.

1978 Fact discovery includes a number of different routes for obtaining information including requests for production of documents and objects, interrogatories, requests for admissions, depositions, *sub poenas* of third party witnesses and exchanges of infringement and validity contentions.

1979 There have been many complaints over the years that the scope of discovery in the United States was too broad and permitted "fishing expeditions" The federal rules were, however, amended with effect from December 1, 2015 to try to make the scope of discovery

> "proportional to the needs of the case, considering the importance of the issues at stake in the action, the amount in controversy, the parties' resources, the importance of discovery in resolving the issues and whether the burden or expense of the proposed discovery outweighs its likely benefit."[56]

1980 Under the Federal Rules, certain information such as persons likely to have discoverable information and the location of documents under the control of a party should be disclosed automatically.[57] Where the testimony of experts is to be used, there should also be automatic disclosure to the other side of the expert's report.[58] 35 USC 282(c) provides that a party asserting invalidity or noninfringement shall give notice in the pleadings or otherwise in writing to the adverse party at least thirty days before the trial of certain facts about the prior art on which it may wish to rely. In the absence of such notice proof of the said matters may not be made at the trial except on such terms as the court requires.

1981 With these limited exceptions, however, discovery results from requests made by the parties. There is no equivalent to the ***saisie*** procedures available under the Unified Patent Court procedure.

1982 The scope of discovery is broad. Rule 26(b) of the Federal Rules of Civil Procedure as amended in December 2015 provides that unless otherwise limited by the court, parties may obtain discovery regarding:

any nonprivileged matter that is relevant to any party's claim or defense and is proportional to the needs of the case … Information within this scope of discovery need not be admissible in evidence to be discoverable.[59]

---

56 FRCivP 26(b)(1).

57 FRCivP Rule 26(a)(1). These disclosures are referred to in the rules as "initial disclosure".

58 FRCivP Rule 26(a)(2).

59 Prior to December 1, 2015, the rule stated that for good cause, the court could order discovery of any matter relevant to the subject matter involved in the action. Relevant information need not be admissible at the trial if the discovery appears reasonably calculated to lead to the discovery of admissible evidence. The removal of this reference to

This general statement is, however, subject to a limitation that a court must limit the extent or frequency of discovery if it determines that: 1983

(i) the discovery sought is unreasonably cumulative or duplicative, or can be obtained from some other source that is more convenient, less burdensome, or less expensive;
(ii) the party seeking discovery has had ample opportunity to obtain the information by discovery in the action; or
(iii) the proposed discovery is outside the scope permitted [bearing in mind the requirement for proportionality].[60]

Certain communications are privileged and therefore need not be disclosed. The most important of these are communications between a party and her or his lawyer relating to legal advice given by the lawyer. For the privilege to apply, the communications in question must not have been disseminated outside the lawyer-client relationship. All of such communications must, however, be listed in a "privilege log". 1984

Courts can also limit the extent to which information obtained during discovery may be disseminated by issuing protective orders, for example limiting the disclosure to counsel and named personnel in a party. 1985

Subject to certain safeguards, discovery can also be obtained from third parties having relevant information. This is normally accomplished by the issue of a subpoena.[61] The subpoena can require that the party also produce documents or things in his or her possession or control. 1986

Depositions are carried out under oath and penalty of perjury.[62] Today in patent cases, most depositions are video taped so that any changes in testimony between what a witness says in his or her deposition and what is said at trial can be demonstrated to a jury by playing back the video tape. Parties to the suit are entitled to be present at a deposition. 1987

5. Expert Discovery

Typically experts will include a technical expert, a patent expert and a damages expert. The technical expert will explain the technology and the way in which the invention fits into it and possibly on any tests carried out to demonstrate that an accused pro- 1988

what is "reasonably calculated to lead" to admissible evidence could have a real life impact on the scope of discovery.

60 FRCivP Rule 26(b)(2)(c).

61 FRCivP Rule 45.

62 Under FRCivP Rule 28, when taken in the United States, a deposition is conducted before an officer authorized to administer oaths (typically a notary public) or by a person appointed for this purpose by the court before which the case is pending. Depositions, may also be conducted abroad, for example before a U.S. consular official or under the provisions of a treaty such as the Hague Convention on Taking Evidence Abroad in Civil or Commercial Matters or by use of letters rogatory.

duct does or does not fall within the scope of the patent claims.[63] The patent expert can testify on patenting procedures, but may be stopped from trying to explain patent law to the jury. That is a function for the judge.

1989 The damages expert will testify on issues related to issues such as market demand, comparable licenses, how to calculate lost profits, and what royalty rates could be considered reasonable, in the latter case possibly complemented by a licensing expert.

1990 Special rules apply to discovery of experts.[64] These require that a person who has been identified as an expert who may give evidence at trial shall be subject to deposition before trial. Such experts are normally required to prepare a report on the issues on which they are asked to opine. If such a report is required, a deposition will follow completion of the report and its supply to the other party.[65]

1991 In cases where the scientific basis of the expert's report is questioned, or the relevance of the expert's qualifications are doubted, the court may order a hearing in the absence of a jury to decide whether the expert's report is admissible as evidence.[66]

1992 The expert's testimony at trial should not go beyond what is covered by his or her expert report unless substantially justified or harmless.

1993 However, the reason for excluding expert testimony is not confined to its lack of scientific basis. In Parallel Networks Licensing LLC v. Microsoft Corporation,[67] expert testimony as to the meaning of a survey was excluded on the basis that the survey had not asked the correct questions to enable the expert report to reach the conclusions that it did.

---

63 The importance of using experts to testify on the question of infringement in cases of complex technology was underlined in Centricut LLC v. Esab Group Inc. 73 USPQ2d 1135 (Fed. Cir. 2004) where the Federal Circuit pointed out that the plaintiff bore the burden of proof on questions of infringement and that although in cases where the technology was easy to understand an expert might not be necessary, in cases where the technology is complex "typically expert testimony will be necessary."

64 FRCivP Rule 26.

65 FRCivP Rule 26 (b)(4)(A)).

66 Such hearings are referred to as "Daubert Hearings" named after the case of Daubert v. Merrell Dow Pharmaceuticals, Inc., 509 U.S. 579 (1993) in which the Supreme Court held that the trial judge has the task of ensuring that an expert's testimony both rests on a reliable foundation and is relevant to the task at hand. In doing this, the trial judge must make a preliminary assessment of whether the testimony's underlying reasoning or methodology is scientifically valid and properly can be applied to the facts at issue. The inquiry is a flexible one, and its focus must be solely on principles and methodology used by the expert, not on the conclusions that they generate. Although in patent cases, such issues typically arise with the testimony of the technical expert, it is increasingly common for the thories underlying a dmages expert's report to be attacked and subject to a Daubert hearing.

67 [2019] USPQ2d 240641 (Fed. Cir 2019 – nonprecedential).

6. Trial

Prior to the trial, the judge will normally convene a further conference with the parties' trial lawyers to ensure the smooth running of the trial. 1994

As noted previously, it is now common for patent cases to be tried before a judge and jury.[68] When this occurs, the jury is responsible for making factual determinations on validity, infringement and damages. The judge is responsible for explaining the law to the jury as to what tests to apply in making their factual determinations and also for determining the scope of the claims. 1995

In order to succeed, the party asserting a fact bears the burden of proof. Issues of infringement, damages and, following the Supreme Court's decision in e-Bay Inc. v. MercExchange L.L.C.[69] entitlement to an injunction rather than an on-going damages award, have to be proved such that on the balance of probabilities the act or article complained of was an infringement and that the damage sustained was that which is claimed. Because of the statutory presumption of validity of a patent, challenges to the validity of a patent must be proved by clear and convincing evidence.[70] 1996

Trials open by each side making an opening statement setting out its case. 1997

The plaintiff will then put forward its witnesses in support of its case who will give direct evidence. Such evidence will be given in the form of responses to questions put by counsel for the plaintiff. In doing this, counsel is not permitted to "lead" the witness or frame the questions so as to suggest the answer desired. Following such direct examination, the witness is then cross-examined by counsel for the opposing party. Leading questions (for example of the type "is it not true that ...") are permitted during cross-examination. Following this, the plaintiff's counsel has the opportunity for "redirect" examination to try to clarify matters that may have been addressed during cross-examination. 1998

In addition to witnesses as to factual matters, expert witnesses will also be called.[71] Such experts may give background information and also express their opinions on the issues raised. It is, however, impermissible for a lay witness to give evidence on such issues. 1999

---

68 If there is to be a jury, it should be "selected at random from a fair cross section of the community in the district or division wherein the court convenes." 28 USC 1861. Each party has the right to make up to three peremptory challenges to proposed members of the jury. 28 USC 1870. Juries must have no fewer than six and no more than twelve members. FRCivP Rule 48.

69 547 U.S. 388 (2006).

70 The "clear and convincing evidence" standard establishes a burden of proof intermediate that of "balance of probabilities" or "preponderance of the evidence" that is the normal test for civil cases and "beyond a reasonable doubt" which is required in criminal cases. Use of this test when assessing evidence in trials of patent invalidity was upheld by the Supreme Court in i4i LP v. Microsoft Corp 131 S.Ct 2238 (2011).

71 Under FRE 706, a court can on its own motion or on the motion of any party appoint its own expert witness. This is, however, rare. The rules make it clear that this option should

2000 Once the plaintiff has presented its case, the defendant may make a motion for the case to be dismissed on the ground that the evidence put forward by the plaintiff is so insufficient that no trier of fact could possibly find that there was infringement. Normally, however, the trial continues with the defendant making its case. In a patent infringement case this normally has two main elements: (1) that there was no infringement and/or (2) that the patent is invalid or unenforceable. The defendant's witnesses will then be questioned by counsel for both sides in a similar manner to the plaintiff's witnesses.

2001 The judge also has discretion to allow the plaintiff to call rebuttal witnesses if the case presented by the defendant raises issues that could not reasonably have been foreseen.

2002 If the trial is being carried out before a jury, the judge bears the responsibility of ensuring that the evidence heard by or mentioned to the jury shall, as far as practicable, be confined to that which is admissible under the Rules of Evidence.[72]

2003 During a jury trial if, after a party has been fully heard on an issue, it becomes clear that there is no legally sufficient evidentiary basis for a reasonable jury to find for that party on an issue, the other party may seek a judgment as a matter of law (commonly referred to as a JMOL) on the point in question.[73]

2004 In the case of a jury trial, however, the judge has to instruct the jury as to the relevant law. It is typical for counsel for the parties to submit proposed jury instructions to the judge, sometimes if the court so requests, even as early as the start of the trial. In any case, the judge must inform the parties of his or her proposed jury instructions and give the parties the opportunity to object before they are given to the jury.[74]

2005 The judge may take advantage of a rule[75] that permits him or her to require that the jury returns a special verdict answering particular factual questions to aid it in coming to a conclusion as to whether there was infringement and whether the patent is valid and enforceable and any other issues that may need to be decided. When this is done, the jury instructions may include a questionnaire to lead the jury through the relevant questions.

2006 Once the jury has made its decision, if a party believes that the answers given to the questions are inconsistent with the jury's final determination or that there was no

---

be used only when the issues are complicated. FRCivP Rule 53. When such experts are appointed they provide an expert report, are subject to deposition and give evidence in open court and are subject to cross examination like any other expert witness.

72 FRE Rule 103(c).

73 FRCivP Rule 50 provides that "if a party has been fully heard on an issue during a jury trial and the court finds that a reasonable jury would not have legally sufficient evidentiary basis to find for the party on that issue" the court may grant a motion for judgment on the issue as a matter of law. In making such determination, the court should bear in mind the fact that the jury is free to attach its own weight to the credibility of a witness.

74 FRCivP Rule 51.

75 FRCivP Rule 49.

credible evidence to support one of the jury's factual determinations, it can again seek a judgment as a matter of law, notwithstanding the jury's verdict.[76] Other post-trial motions may also be filed.[77] Thereafter the court will give its final decision.[78]

In the case where there is no jury, the judge will normally take time to issue his or her decision. In doing so, the judge must make findings of the facts necessary to reach a judgment.[79] When the case is tried without a jury, it is normal for the parties to submit post-trial briefs setting out the arguments used at trial and pointing to the parts of the evidence which support such arguments. 2007

Typical trials take from one to two weeks, but can be longer in complex cases or where multiple patents are involved. 2008

In principle the court's decision has immediate effect. The losing party may, however seek a stay of execution from the trial court[80] or if this is impracticable or refused from the appropriate Court of Appeals.[81] 2009

7. Motions

Motions may be made before, during or after trial. 2010

District courts are required to set aside time at which motions requiring notice and a hearing may be dealt with. One specific type of motion, discussed in the next section, is for summary judgment. Other types of pretrial motions include motions to dismiss the suit, motions for judgment on the pleadings, motions to transfer the action to a different court, motions to remove a party form the action, motions to strike part of a party's case on the basis that the claim asserted is not cognizable by the law, motions to exclude certain evidence from the trial, motions to compel provision of certain evidence or to answer particular questions during discovery and motions to seal parts of the evidence filed so as to keep certain information secret. 2011

Possible post trial motions include motions for a judgment as a matter of law where it is claimed that there is no evidence to support a verdict given by a jury, motions for a new trial, motions for an award of costs and motions for relief from a judgment or order. 2012

---

76 FRCivP Rule 50 provides for judgments as a matter of law where "the court finds that a reasonable jury would not have a legally sufficient evidentiary basis to find for the party on that issue."

77 For example for a new trial (FRCivP Rule 59(a)), to alter or amend a judgment (FRCivP Rule 59(e)) or for relief form judgment or an order for example where there was a mistake, new evidence was found or there was evidence of fraud (FRCivP Rule 60).

78 As with the situation in a non-jury trial, if the law changes after the jury gives its verdict before the final decision is rendered, the court should be advised of this.

79 FRCivP Rule 52(a).

80 FRCivP Rule 62.

81 FRAppP Rule 8.

2013 Typically motions must be filed at least five days prior to the date on which they are to be heard and the opposing party must file its affidavits contesting the motion at least one day prior to the hearing of the motion, although different local or judge's rules may apply.

a) Motion for Summary Judgment

2014 One way in which to expedite disposition of a case or of particular issues in it is by a motion for summary judgment. Such motions are decided by a judge without the assistance of a jury assuming that all disputed factual issues will be decided against the party seeking summary judgment. Motions for summary judgment are typically decided upon affidavit evidence. If the court concludes that there is no "genuine issue as to any material fact and the moving party is entitled to a judgment as a matter of law", the court should grant the motion "forthwith". In patent cases, summary judgment motions are more commonly used in seeking to resolve infringement than validity issues. As noted above, motions for summary judgment of the question of patent infringement represent a convenient way to produce a final judgment that can be appealed to the Federal Circuit Court of Appeals after the District Court has made its Markman determination.

2015 Although FRCivP Rule 52(a)(3) states that a court is not required to state findings or conclusions when ruling on a summary judgment motion, the Federal Circuit has made it clear that the court must at least provide an analysis and grounds for entering judgment somewhere in the record.

8. Determination of Damage awards and award of costs

2016 Under the rules of the Unified Patent Court there will typically be separate proceedings to determine the magnitude of an award of damages and also the costs that the losing party must recompense the winning party.

2017 In the United States, such separation of proceedings is rare. As noted above, most cases in which damages may be awarded are tried before a jury and the jury is responsible for determining the amount of compensatory damages to be paid. The jury will therefore heat evidence on this issue as part of the trial and will include a damages award as part of its verdict. As noted above, the judge has only a limited power to overturn such a jury award.

2018 As discussed above in the context of remedies that are available where patent infringement has been found, United States law provides for the possibility that the amount determined to be the appropriate compensation for the damage that the patent owner has suffered from the infringement may be increased up to three times that amount. Any such increase is a matter to be decided by the judge.

2019 The American legal system does not normally provide for the winning party in litigation to be able to recover its costs in the litigation from the losing party (the so-called "American Rule"). The Patent Act does, however, provide that "in exceptional cases" the judge "may" award "reasonable" attorney fees to the prevailing party. This is not common, but when it occurs, the determination will be made by the judge at the end of the trial.

III. PTAB Procedure

2020 The Second type of procedure to be considered is a challenge to the validity of a patent before the Patent Trial and Appeal Board

2021 Since the relevant provisions of the America Invents Act came into effect on, two new proceedings, *inter partes* review and post grant review, have been available to challenge the validity of patents in "mini-litigation" before the Patent Trial and Appeal Board (PTAB).

1. Differences and Similarities of Inter Partes Review and Post Grant Review

2022 For both types of review, the challenger must challenge specific claims. The Director of the USPTO must first make a determination that certain threshold criteria have been met with respect to those challenges and that it is appropriated for the PTAB to carry out the review. Prior to October 20, 2025 this a task was ~~that is~~ in practice delegated to the PTAB itself. Since that date the decision on whether the threshold criteria have been met and whether there are reasons for exercising discretion to deny review have been made by the Director himself after consultation with PTAB judges. This has resulted in a drop in the number of reviews that are instituted. If the Director decides to institute a review, it must be carried out on all of the claims that were challenged and be confined to the grounds set out by the challenger. The rules provide that in normal cases this should be completed within twelve months from the date on which a review is instituted.

2023 For *inter partes* review the threshold question is "does the request show that there is a reasonable likelihood that the requester would prevail" in showing invalidity of at least one claim, based on a prior patent or publication. Such a challenge may be brought at any time on any patent except during a period in which post grant review is proceeding or during which post grant review may be requested, but if the challenger, its real party in interest or one of its privies has been sued for infringement of the patent in question, must be requested within one year of the service of the complaint alleging patent infringement.

2024 Post grant review allows more broadly-based challenges to a patent on any ground that can be used as a defense to an infringement action, but only for patents granted under the new "first inventor to file" provisions of the AIA and only during the period of nine months after grant or reissue of the patent. In this case, the threshold question is whether it is more likely than not that at least one claim will be found to be invalid.

2025 The objective of the changes to create *inter partes* review and post grant review was to permit the challenger greater participation in the proceedings than had been possible previously, while reaching a decision relatively quickly.

2026 Notwithstanding government fees that are high by European standards, *inter partes* review is popular with defendants to infringement actions. Determinations are made on a claim-by-claim basis and this makes statistical analysis complicated. However, for the first two years of Inter partes review it seems that a review was instituted for about two-thirds of the claims challenged and once a review has been instituted in cases that went to a final decision all claims were found invalid in about 75 % of the decisions and some claims found invalid in a further 15 % of the decisions. In about 2/3 of the cases where inter partes review has been requested, the district court has granted a stay or partial stay of the proceedings before it pending determinations in the *inter partes* review procedure. A number of factors may account for the popularity of *inter partes* review and the success of the challengers:

1. The lower burden of proof applying to the party challenging validity in the review proceedings (balance of the probabilities) is lower than that as compared to court proceedings (clear and convincing evidence).
2. The speed with which the review proceedings must be carried out which for most cases is set by the statute as being no more than one year from the institution of proceedings.

2027 On the other hand, if one fails in a Patent Office review, one is estopped from later challenging validity in any district court or ITC proceedings on any ground that was or could reasonable have been raised in the Patent Office review proceeding, which may be one reason why inter partes reviews have proved to be more popular than post grant reviews. If the challenger loses an inter partes review and is then sued for infringement, other possible grounds of invalidity apart from those based on prior patents and publications may be asserted. This is not the case for post grant review.

2028 The two types of review have the following features in common:

No presumption of validity – in both types of review a decision is made on the balance of probabilities rather than on whether there is clear and convincing evidence that a challenged claim is invalid.

Limitations on Institution of Review because of prior proceedings – review may not be instituted if petitioner or its real party in interest has previously filed a civil action challenging the validity of the patent

Possibility of Settlement – Proceedings can be settled by agreement between the parties up to the time at which a decision has been made by the Board. If this is done, the agreement has to be in writing and a copy filed with the USPTO.[82] At the request of "a party" to the proceeding such agreements will be kept "business confidential" and disclosed only to government agencies or others on a showing of good cause. The proceedings may be terminated on a joint request by the parties unless the office has decided on the merits of the proceeding before the request for termination is filed.

82 In its precedential decision in DTN LLC v. Farms Technology LLCCase IPR2018–01412, Paper 21 (June 14, 2019), the PTAB held that collateral agreements referred to in a settlement agreement also had to be supplied to the PTAB.

Estoppel Effect – Challengers or a real party in interest or privy of the challenger in *inter partes* review or post grant review proceedings are estopped from raising any issue that they raised or reasonably could have raised in such proceedings in any subsequent proceedings in the USPTO, a district court or the ITC.

Intervening Rights – Amendment of claims is possible in both inter partes review and post grant review. The issue arises of how to deal with third party use of the invention claimed, for example uses that may not have infringed a valid claim before amendment but do infringe after the claim has been amended. The law provides for absolute rights of use etc. in respect of "specific things". The second sentence of the same section provides for additional equitable rights by which a court can provided for continued manufacture, use or sale of a thing for which substantial preparation was made before the grant of the reissue, and the court may also provide for the continued practice of any process patented by the reissue that is practiced, or for the practice of which substantial preparation was made, before the grant of the reissue, to the extent and under such terms as the court deems equitable.

Apart from a difference in the scope of permitted discovery, procedures to be followed in the two types of review are the same and more similar to proceedings under the UPCA than district court proceedings described above in that they are much more reliant on written materials, the challenger must make out a detailed case in its initial challenge and the patent owner has the possibility of making amendments as part of the proceedings. 2029

2. Sequence of Events

The normal sequence of events is as follows: 2030

1. Petition filed asserting that specific claims of the challenged patent are invalid – The Federal Circuit has repeatedly emphasized that the challenger's full case needs to set out in the petition and that the PTAB may refuse to consider late-filed arguments. If appropriate the petition may supported by expert testimony.
2. Patent owner may file a preliminary response which may be accompanied by testimonial evidence and disclaimer of one or more claims to remove them from the proceedings but no amendment of claims is permitted at this stage.
3. Decision by PTAB on whether to institute review – this requires a determination of whether the threshold requirement for instituting the relevant proceedings has been met and whether to exercise its discretion to institute proceedings which may be exercised to deny review based on factors such as the number of petitions a challenger has filed against the patent, and the existence and status of parallel district court proceedings. No appeal is permitted against the PTAB's decision on whether to institute a review.
4. Issue of a scheduling order.
5. Conference call to discuss possible motions and whether changes needed to scheduling order.
6. Patent owner conducts discovery including providing affidavit evidence affirming any data set out in the patent, possible evidence on the meaning of the claims,

deposing anyone who has filed evidence in support of the challenger (in effect a form of cross examination), and relevant information that is inconsistent with a position advanced during the proceeding and, in the case of post grant review, production of other evidence directly related to factual assertions advanced by either party in the proceeding and, if the PTAB agrees other evidence "necessary in the interests of justice";

7. Patent owner files response and possibly files a motion to make claim amendments – such a motion must be approved by the PTAB before it is admitted into the proceedings and may be contingent on the PTAB finding that a claim that it is sought to replace is found to be invalid. Amendments are permitted only to cancel a challenged claim or to replace a challenged claim with a reasonable number of substitute claims. and only after conferring with the Board.
8. Petitioner conducts discovery similar to that carried out by the patent owner (including depositions of anyone who has filed evidence in support of the patent owner);
9. Petitioner files response confined to addressing "arguments raised in the corresponding patent owner response" and possible opposition to any proposed claim amendments;
10. Patent owner conducts rebuttal discovery;
11. Patent owner responds to petitioner's response by sur-reply and response to any opposition to amendments;
12. Petitioner may file sur-reply to patent owner's response to opposition to proposed amendments
13. Period for observations and motions to exclude evidence;
14. Hearing – normally limited to one hour for each side. Typically the challenger opens, the patent owner responds. Arguments must be strictly confined to what is in the record.
15. Final Written Decision.

2031 As noted below, a losing patent owner can appeal to the Court of Appeals for the Federal Circuit. A losing petitioner can only appeal if it has standing to do so.

IV. Appeal

2032 Under the European Unified Court procedures, appeals may be made against decisions of law and fact made by the first instance court and new evidence may be admitted if "submission thereof by the party concerned during proceedings could not reasonably have been expected before the Court of First instance".

2033 In the United States, the Federal Circuit Court of Appeals reviews decisions of a judge in a bench trial for errors of law and clearly erroneous findings of fact.[83] In reviewing whether the lower court has properly applied the law, the Federal Circuit Court of Appeals is not confined to considering the arguments put forward before the district court, particularly if the issue involved is one of great public concern.[84]

83 Manville Sales Corp. v. Paramount Sys Inc. 917 F.2d 914 16 USPQ2d 1587 Fed. Cir. 1990).
84 Broadcast Innovation LLC v. Charter Communications Inc. 76 USPQ2d 1220.

Where there has been a jury trial, the appeal court reviews issues of law *de novo*. Factual determinations made by the jury, however, are reviewed to determine whether the appealing party can show that the jury's factual findings were not supported by substantial evidence or that the facts were not sufficient to support the conclusions necessarily drawn by the jury on its way to its verdict. As noted in Intellectual Ventures I LLC v. Motorola Mobility LLC[85], where each side presents substantial evidence, the jury is entitled to choose which side's evidence it believes. 2034

In *inter partes* and post grant review cases brought before the PTAB, the statute forbids any appeal against the Board's initial determination on whether to institute a review. Appeals are however, possible from final written decisions of the PTAB. Final decisions of the Board are appealable to the Court of Appeals for the Federal Circuit by either party as long as it can show that it has been injured by the decision of the PTAB.[86] This requirement is not an issue for the patent owner who loses, but can be for a challenger who loses and wishes to appeal who may have to explain why its activities give rise to an apprehension that it may be sued for patent infringement if it wishes to pursue an appeal. 2035

85 124 USPQ2d 1129 (Fed. Cir. 2017).

86 35 USC 319 for *inter partes* review and 35 USC 329 for post grant review. Case law as summarized by the Federal Circuit in General Electric Company v. Raytheon Technologies Corporation has held that when seeking review of a decision by an agency such as the PTAB, an appellant must meet 'the irreducible constitutional minimum of standing.' *Amerigen Pharm. Ltd. v. UCB Pharma GmBH*, 913 F.3d 1076, 1082 (Fed. Cir. 2019). … That "irreducible constitutional minimum" requires the appellant to "have (1) suffered an injury in fact, (2) that is fairly traceable to the challenged conduct of the [appellee], and (3) that is likely to be redressed by a favorable judicial decision." *Spokeo, Inc. v. Robins*, 136 S. Ct. 1540, 1547 (2016), as revised (May 24, 2016). "[W]here Congress has accorded a procedural right to a litigant, such as the right to appeal an administrative decision" some requirements of standing – but not the requirement of injury in fact – "may be relaxed." *Consumer Watchdog v. Wis. Alumni Research Found.*, 753 F.3d 1258, 1261 (Fed. Cir. 2014).

Chapter 39: Comparison with Chinese Law

Contents Para

2036 With the development of the times and changes in the society, China's protection of intellectual property rights has been gradually strengthened, the scope of protection has also been gradually improved and developed, and China's laws and regulations regarding patent and related intellectual property rights are also constantly improving and developing accordingly.

2037 The newly revised *"Patent Law of the People's Republic of China (2020 Amendment)"* (hereinafter referred to as the "***New Patent Law***") came into effect on June 1, 2021. The amendments include (but not limited to): strengthening the protection of the legitimate rights and interests of patentees, promoting the exploitation and utilization of patents, improving the patent granting system, etc. Among these amendments, the newly introduced system of punitive damages against patent infringement is an important update that comes with the *New Patent Law*, which is aimed to impose a heavy price for the infringer(s) to pay.

2038 Between 2022 and 2025, China, based on the actual circumstances of socio-economic development, continued to make refined adjustments to patent infringement litigation procedures, striving to make the entire patent infringement litigation system more efficient and orderly, and to adapt to the general trend of further strengthening intellectual property protection under the conditions of the new era.

2039 In the following sections, we will introduce the litigation proceedings in China regarding patent infringement, discuss the relevant issues involved in judicial practice, and compare the Chinese system to the European Unitary Patent System.

A. Court System and Jurisdiction of Litigations regarding Patent Infringement

I. Situation before the Unified Patent Court

For the European Unified Patent System, pursuant to the "Agreement on a Unified Patent Court" (UPCA), the Unified Patent Court (UPC) consists of the **Court of First Instance**, the **Court of Appeal**, and the **Registry**. While the Court of First Instance shall comprise a central division (seated in Paris, with sections in London and Munich) as well as local and regional divisions, there shall be only one Court of Appeal, which shall have its seat in Luxembourg, and one Registry, which shall be set up at the seat of the Court of Appeal (i.e., in Luxembourg as well). 2040

The Courts of First Instance includes two kinds of courts ("divisions"): a central division as well as local and regional divisions. The local/regional divisions have jurisdiction over patent infringement and possess the power to decide on counterclaims during infringement litigations where the validity of the patent involved is challenged. Other applications challenging the validity of a patent or a Supplementary Protection Certificate ("SPC"), and applications for declaration of non-infringement, shall be submitted to the central division. 2041

The Unified Patent Court has exclusive jurisdiction over the following actions: actions for actual or threatened infringements of patents and SPCs and related defenses, including counterclaims concerning licenses; actions for declarations of non-infringement of patents and SPCs; actions for provisional and protective measures and injunctions; actions for revocation of patents and for declaration of invalidity of SPCs; counterclaims for revocation of patents and for declaration of invalidity of SPCs; actions for damages or compensation derived from the provisional protection conferred by a published European patent application; actions relating to the use of the invention prior to the granting of the patent or to the right based on prior use of the invention; actions for compensation for licenses on the basis of Article 8 of Regulation (EU) No 1257/2012; and actions concerning decisions of the European Patent Office in carrying out the tasks referred to in Article 9 of Regulation (EU) No 1257/2012. 2042

II. Situation in China

In contrast, the court system of China has four levels: the Supreme People's Court, the Higher People's Courts, the Intermediate People's Courts, and the Primary People's Court. The Supreme People's Court is located in Beijing (the national capital), and the Higher People's Courts are located in the capitals of respective provinces, autonomous regions, and municipalities directly under the central government; meanwhile, the two special administrative regions (SARs), Hong Kong and Macau, have their own independent legal systems. 2043

In recent years, cases related intellectual property right have been increasing rapidly but with an overall uneven distribution; at the meantime, for most of such cases, the amount of compensation remained low, and the durations of trial were long. In 2044 such situation, in order to strengthen the public awareness of intellectual property right protection, strengthen judicial protection of intellectual property right, and unify judicial practices and standards in IPR-related cases, China has established **Intellectual Property Courts** and **Intellectual Property Tribunals** in various places throughout the country, mainly for handling highly specialized IPR-related cases (especially patent-related cases).

2045 The Intellectual Property Tribunal of the Supreme People's Court mainly handle appeal cases related to highly specialized IPR-related matters (especially patents) nationwide. The Intellectual Property Tribunal is a permanent judicial institution dispatched by the Supreme People's Court and is located in Beijing (Article 1 of the *"Regulations of the Supreme People's Court on Several Issues Concerning the Intellectual Property Court"*).

2046 Four Intellectual Property Courts (respectively located in the city of Beijing, Shanghai, Guangzhou, and Hainan Province) and the Intermediate People's Courts specially determined by the Supreme People's Court (currently still refers to the 30 Intermediate People's Courts which have their own subordinate intellectual property tribunals) mainly handle first instance cases related to highly specialized IPR-related issues (such as patents).

2047 The jurisdiction of patent infringement cases shall comply with the Civil Procedure Law and relevant laws and regulations regarding "hierarchical jurisdiction" and "territorial jurisdiction". The "hierarchical jurisdiction" refers to which level of the courts to handle the trial of a case, and the "territorial jurisdiction" refers to the location of the court to handle it.

2048 Pursuant to the Civil Procedure Law, the first-instance cases shall be under the jurisdiction of the Primary People's Courts; however, for patent cases, special regulations for the jurisdiction issue are stipulated in judicial interpretation: the first-instance of civil and administrative cases concerning monopoly and the ownership or infringement of patent of invention or utility model shall be under the jurisdiction of Intellectual Property Courts, the Intermediate People's Courts (where the people's governments of provinces, autonomous regions and municipalities directly under the Central Government are located) specially determined by the Supreme People's Court; the jurisdiction over first-instance civil and administrative cases involving disputes over ownership and infringement of design patents largely follows the same mechanism, but with the approval of the Supreme People's Court, specific Primary People's Courts may also exercise jurisdiction on such cases (excluding administrative cases involving design patents) (Article 2 of *"Several Provisions of the Supreme People's Court on Jurisdiction of First Instance Intellectual Property Civil and Administrative Cases"*); cases concerning the authorization and confirmation of patent of invention or utility model shall be under the jurisdiction of the Beijing Intellectual Property Court.

2049 In terms of territorial jurisdiction, the general principle for civil litigation is "the plaintiff to facilitate the defendant". That is, a lawsuit brought for patent infringement shall be under the jurisdiction of the people's court at the place where the infringement is committed or where the defendant is domiciled (Article 2 of *"Several*

Provisions of the Supreme People's Court on Issues concerning the Application of Law in the Trial of Patent Dispute Cases").

2050 For civil and administrative appeal cases involving the ownership or infringement of invention patents, or major and complex civil and administrative appeal cases involving the ownership or infringement of utility model patents, or first-instance civil and administrative cases of the aforementioned types that are major and complex on a nationwide scale, as well as second-instance cases concerning the granting and affirmation of patent rights for designs, inventions, and utility models, all shall be heard by the Intellectual Property Tribunal of the Supreme People's Court; meanwhile, ordinary (non-major or complex) civil and administrative appeal cases involving the ownership or infringement of utility model patents shall instead be heard by the High People's Court in the location of the firs-instance court. ("*Decision of the Standing Committee of the National People's Congress on Several Issues Concerning Litigation Procedures in Patent and Other Intellectual Property Cases*"; Article 2 of the "*Regulations of the Supreme People's Court on Several Issues Concerning the Intellectual Property Court*", revised in 2023).

2051 As for second-instance administrative and civil cases involving disputes over the ownership or infringement of design patent rights, there are certain special provisions. With reference to the aforementioned introduction regarding the jurisdiction of first-instance courts for such cases, generally speaking, the first instance of such cases is heard by an Intermediate People's Court (or an Intellectual Property Court within the jurisdiction), and its second instance is heard by the local High People's Court. If the first instance of such a case is heard by a Primary People's Court approved by the Supreme People's Court, its second instance shall be heard by the local Intermediate People's Court.

B. Eligible Plaintiffs for Patent Infringement Actions

2052 Pursuant to relevant provisions of UPCA, the patentee shall be entitled to bring a patent infringement lawsuit before the court; also, unless the licensing agreement provides otherwise, the licensee of an exclusive licensing agreement has the right bring a patent infringement lawsuit before the court, provided that the patentee is given prior notice; the licensee of the non-exclusive licensing agreement may also be entitled to bring a patent infringement lawsuit before the court, if it is expressly permitted in the licensing agreement and the patentee is given prior notice.

2053 In contrast, according to Chinese law, both the patentee and the interested party (or parties) have the right to bring a patent infringement lawsuit before the court (Article 65 of the *New Patent Law*). The patentee refers to the natural or legal person stated on the patent certificate; "interested party (or parties)" include the licensee(s) in the patent licensing contract (agreement). The licensee of an exclusive licensing contract may file a patent infringement lawsuit before the people's court alone; the licensee of an sole licensing contract may file a patent infringement lawsuit before the people's court alone, if the patentee does not file the same lawsuit; the licensee of an ordinary (non-exclusive) licensing contract may file a patent infringement lawsuit before the people's court in its own name with the express authorization of the patentee. (*"Provisions of the Supreme People's Court on Several Issues Concerning the Application of Law in Review of Intellectual Property Dispute Behavior Preservation Cases"* and relevant regional judicial regulations).

C. Litigation Procedures (2023 Amendment)

2054 According to UPCA, in a patent infringement lawsuit, a counterclaim for patent invalidation can be filed against the patent involved at the same time. In contrast, in a patent infringement lawsuit in China, whether it is in the proceeding of first-instance, second-instance or retrial, the court has no right to examine the validity of the patent right but can only judge on whether the alleged infringement falls within the protection scope of the patent. referee. If a party wants to initiate a patent invalidation action, the party needs to file a request for patent invalidation with the State Intellectual Property Office and submit relevant evidences and other related materials. We will elaborate on the patent invalidation procedures in Section 5.

I. Procedures of First Instance of a Civil Lawsuit

2055 "*Civil Procedure Law of the People's Republic of China* (2021 Amendment):"

2056 (1) Filing of Lawsuit and Acceptance:

The plaintiff submits necessary materials to a competent People's Court, including a written complaint, materials regarding the identity and qualification of the plaintiff, and the relevant evidences. In practice, most courts allow electronic filing through their online systems and/or paper filing through specific postal services.

2057 The People's Court will examine the materials filed by the plaintiff, and, if the case is suitable for mediation, order that a mediation shall be conducted first. If the case meets the criteria and requirements for case establishment, the case shall be officially established, and the parties will be formally notified by the court.

2058 (2) Preparation before Trial:

The People's Court shall send a copy of the complaint to the defendant within five days from the date of case establishment, and the defendant shall file a statement of defense within 15 days from the date of receipt.

If a party has any objection to the court's jurisdiction, it shall be raised during the submission of the statement of defense.

2059 (3) Court Hearing:

The trial of civil cases by the People's Courts shall be open to the public, except for the cases that involve state secrets, personal privacy or other special circumstances stipulated by law. Trial activities are mainly divided into stages of court investigation, court debate, and mediation in court. During the stage of court investigation, both parties would present evidences, expert opinions (if available), and read out the inquest records (if any). The parties may present new evidences in court. During the stage of court debate, debates will occur mainly focusing on the disputed issues discovered during the court investigation. During the stage of court mediation, under supervision monitoring by the judge, the parties are shall express their willingness (or unwillingness) towards mediation and/or other conditions for such mediation.

(4) Judgment Announcement: 2060

The People's Courts shall publicly announce judgments for cases no matter tried publicly or not. The People's Courts may announce judgments in court directly or decide to announce it at another specific time. If the judgment is announced in court, the People's Court shall issue a written judgment to the parties within ten days; if the judgment is to be announced at another specific time, the People's Court shall issue a written judgment immediately after the announcement.

II. Procedures of Second Instance of a Civil Lawsuit:

If a party (or the parties) disagrees with the judgment of the first instance rendered 2061 by the People's Court, the party (parties) is entitled to file an appeal with the People's Court of the next higher level within the prescribed time frame. For a second-instance case regarding patent of invention or utility model, the relevant party (parties) shall file the appeal to the Supreme People's Court or the High People's Court in the location of the firs-instance court (see the previous introduction regarding the court system and jurisdiction). Appeals should be filed through the court of the first instance, where the court of the first instance shall submit all the case files and evidences to the People's Court of second instance within a specific time frame after receiving the appeal and the answer from the other party (parties). (*"Civil Procedure Law of the People's Republic of China* (2021 Amendment)" and "*Decision of the Standing Committee of the National People's Congress on Several Issues concerning Litigation Procedures in Patent and Other Intellectual Property Cases*").

The trial procedures of the second instance is similar to that of the first instance. The 2062 People's Court of second instance shall review the relevant facts concerning the appeal and the applying of legal provisions during the first instance of the case.

III. Retrial of a Civil Lawsuit

If a party (or the parties) considers a legally effective judgment or ruling to be erro- 2063 neous, it may apply to the People's Court of the next higher level (compared to the court of the second instance) for retrial. For retrial of a case regarding patent invention or utility model, the retrial request shall be filed to the Supreme People's Court. The Supreme People's Court may also order a lower-level People's Court to handle the retrial in accordance with the law. ("*Civil Procedure Law of the People's Republic of China* (2023 Amendment)" and *"Decision of the Standing Committee of the National People's Congress on Several Issues concerning Litigation Procedures in Patent and Other Intellectual Property Cases"*).

D. Provisional Protective Measures

2064 Provional protective measures refer to measures taken to protect the interests of the party (parties) before the court makes a final judgment. Such measures are essential to stop ongoing or imminent infringement, preserve important evidences, and prevent further damage to the party's rights and interests.

2065 Under the UPCA, the United Patent Court (UPC) has the power to grant preliminary injunctions, order the transfer of allegedly infringing items, freeze the movement of such items, and freeze assets, in order to ensure that the infringer can pay the compensation imposed on it by the court for any damages caused by its infringement.

2066 All of China's major IPR-related laws, namely the *Copyright Law*, the *Patent Law*, and the *Trademark Law*, have stipulated three types of provisional protective measures: pre-litigation order to stop infringement, pre-litigation evidence preservation and pre-litigation property preservation. At the same time, the Civil Procedure Law not only stipulates that an interested party can apply for provisional protective measures before filing a lawsuit or applying for arbitration, but also stipulates that the party can apply for preservation measures after the filing of lawsuit and before the judgment or arbitration takes effect.

2067 According to the *Patent Law*, if the patentee or an interested party has evidence to prove that others are committing or about to commit an act that infringes upon the patent right or hinders the realization of its rights, and that such act of infringement will cause irreparable damage to its legitimate rights and interests if not being stopped in time, it may, before filing a lawsuit, apply to the People's Court to take measures for property preservation, or to issue order about certain actions to be done or to be prohibited. In order to prevent patent infringement, in the case that the evidences may become lost, destroyed or difficult to obtain in the future, the patentee or interested party may apply to the People's Court for preservation of evidence before filing a lawsuit (Articles 72 and 73 of the *New Patent Law*).

2068 When applying to the court for preservation of act, a written application, relevant evidences and corresponding guarantee (which is often financial) shall be submitted. The evidences shall include proof of existence and ownership of the involved intellectual property rights (such as patent certificates) as well as evidences that the respondent/defendant is carrying out or about to carry out acts that would infringe the said intellectual property rights. Guarantee must be provided at the same time as the application is made; if the guarantee is not provided, the court will reject the application.

2069 For pre-litigation evidence preservation, the applicant shall explain to the court the reasons to apply for such evidence preservation, including specific explanations that the evidence may become lost, destroyed or difficult to obtain in the future, and that the party (parties) and agents ad litem cannot collect them by themselves due to objective reasons. If the applicant's application for pre-litigation evidence preservation may cause the respondent/defendant to suffer property damage, the court may order the applicant to provide corresponding guarantee.

E. Procedures of Patent Invalidation

In China, patent infringement litigation and patent invalidation are two separate proceedings. According to the relevant provisions of the *Patent Law* and the *"Regulations for the Implementation of the Patent Law"*, from the date when the patent administration department under the State Council announces granting of the patent, if any entity or individual believes that the granting of such patent does not comply with the relevant provisions of the *Patent Law*, such entity or individual may apply to the Patent Reexamination Board for declaring that the patent is invalid. 2070

The general procedures of such patent invalidation are as follows 2071

I. Review of Invalidation Requests

After the Patent Reexamination Board has accepted the invalidation request, the Board will conduct formal examination on the request; if the request passed the formal examination and deemed qualified, the invalidation procedures will be officially initiated. Then a collegial panel will be established to conduct a collegial review on the invalidation request as a specific case. The vast majority of such cases are reviewed by a collegial panel composed of three people (comprising one group leader, one chief examiner, and one associate examiner). Only a very small number of cases (which are significant in circumstances and with relatively high difficulty to work on) are reviewed by a 5-member collegial panel (one group leader, one chief examiner, and three associate examiners). 2072

II. Making of the Invalidation Decision

There are three types of decisions of the invalidation request examination: declaring that the patent is totally invalid; declaring that part of the patent is invalid; maintaining the validity of the patent as a whole. 2073

III. Judicial Remedies after Invalidation

If any party is not satisfied with the decision rendered by the Patent Reexamination Board, it may file a lawsuit before the competent People's Court (currently the Beijing Intellectual Property Court), with the Patent Reexamination Board as the defendant, within 3 months from the date of receipt of the notification on the invalidation decision. 2074

IV. Request for a stay of Proceedings

During a patent infringement lawsuit, if the defendant files a request for invalidation before the State Intellectual Property Office, the court handling the patent infringement lawsuit may apply the regulations to suspend the lawsuit—that is, for an infringement lawsuit involving a patent of invention, if the defendant requests within its answering period to declare that the patent is invalid, the court may continue the lawsuit. 2075

2076 If the case involves a utility model patent, the people's court will suspend the case in principle, however, the court may still continue the lawsuit if the following circumstances occur:

- the patent evaluation report or search report submitted by the plaintiff provides a positive result in terms of the stability of the patent claimed by the plaintiff;
- the defendant has provided evidence of publicly known technology, which is sufficient to prove that the defendant has not committed infringement;
- the evidences or reasons for the defendant's request to declare that the patent is invalid is obviously insufficient;
- other circumstances in which the court may deem that the proceedings should not be suspended.

F. Determination of the Amount of Compensation and Undertaking of Reasonable Expenses

2077 In China, the amount of compensation for patent infringement shall be determined according to the actual losses suffered by the right holder (patentee and/or interested party/-ies) due to the infringement, or according to the benefits obtained by the infringer due to its infringement; if it is difficult to determine the losses of the right holder or the benefits obtained by the infringer, a multiple of the patent license fee shall be referred to when determining a reasonable amount of compensation.

2078 In the case of intentional patent infringement, if the circumstances are serious, the amount of compensation may be determined at more than one time but not more than five times the amount determined according to the above method. If it is difficult to determine the loss of the right holder, the benefits obtained by the infringer, and the patent license fee, the People's Court may, based on the type of the patent, the nature and circumstances of the infringement, and other related factors, determine to impose a compensation of no less than 30,000 (thirty thousand) yuan but not more than 5,000,000 (five million) yuan. The amount of compensation shall also include the reasonable expenses paid by the right holder to stop the infringement. (Article 71 of the *New Patent Law*).

2079 In practice, it is usually difficult to provide accurate evidences to determine the actual losses suffered by the right holder due to the infringement, or the benefits obtained by the infringer. In most cases, the amount of compensation is determined by the court through statutory compensation (the last method mentioned above). When determining the final compensation amount, the People's Court will take into account factors such as the type of the patent, the nature and circumstances of the infringement, and the scale, time span and amount of the infringer's sales (of infringing products, etc.).

2080 The amount of reasonable expenses is generally easier to determine, usually including attorney fees, notary fees, evidence collection expenses, travel expenses, etc., which can be proved by providing relevant entrustment contracts, bills and invoices. In practice, on the premise that the court finds that infringement is constituted, the reasonable expenses claimed by the right holder should be supported, and the determination of the amount of support adheres to the requirements of reasonability and relevance. In order to get the support of the court on claims of reasonable expenses, the right holder should provide sufficient evidences for the reasonability and relevance of such expenses.

G. Administrative Protection of Patent

China adopts a "dual-track system" to protect patent rights, i.e. judicial protection and administrative protection. In addition to filing a lawsuit in before the court, the patentee and/or interested party/-ies can also seek administrative protection and request the patent administrative authority to handle patent infringement disputes. 2081

According to the *Patent Law* and the *"Measures for Patent Administrative Law Enforcement"*, the patent administrative authority (currently the patent departments under central and local agencies of administration for market regulation, "AMR") conducts patent administrative law enforcement, including handling patent infringement disputes, mediating patent disputes, and investigation and raids against patent counterfeiting. 2082

The structures of China's judicial and administrative system have determined that the decision of the patent administrative protection agency is less effective than that of the People's Court. If any entity or individual is dissatisfied with the decision of the administrative agency, it can file an administrative lawsuit before the court, and the judgment/ruling of the court will have a final effect. Besides, administrative agencies cannot provide the right holder with any compensation for the infringement, but can only impose fines on the infringer(s) and order it to cease infringement. 2083

The better part is that the evidences collected during administrative investigation and raids against the infringer(s) have the effect of notarization certified by the government and can be used in court proceedings (i.e. no further notarization or certification is needed). Therefore, administrative protection measures are usually used as an effective way to collect evidences before initiating patent infringement lawsuits. 2084

H. Institutional Innovation: Cracking Down on Abuse of Rights

In 2023, in order to strengthen litigation integrity and curb the abuse of rights, the Supreme People's Court added a special provision for its subordinate Intellectual Property Tribunal: the Intellectual Property Tribunal may require parties to disclose information regarding related cases involving the ownership, infringement, or granting and affirmation of the intellectual property rights in question. 2085

If a party refuses to disclose such information truthfully, it may be considered a factor in determining whether they have adhered to the principle of good faith and whether they have committed an abuse of rights. (Article 4 of the "Regulations of the Supreme People's Court on Several Issues Concerning the Intellectual Property Court", revised in 2023). 2086

2087 This new provision helps the Intellectual Property Tribunal gain a comprehensive understanding of the overall dispute landscape regarding the intellectual property rights involved, effectively identify and crack down on behaviors such as malicious repetitive litigation and abuse of the right of action, improve trial efficiency, and safeguard judicial justice.

Chapter 40: Comparison with Japanese Law

Contents

A. Jurisdiction and Framework for Patent Infringement Litigation

In Japan, the Tokyo District Court and Osaka District Court have exclusive jurisdiction over patent infringement lawsuits (Article 6 of Code of Civil Procedure). The Intellectual Property High Court has jurisdiction over these appeal cases. The IP High Court is a special branch of the Tokyo High Court, which was established in 2005 under the Act for Establishment of the Intellectual Property High Court. **2088**

In patent infringement lawsuits, the defendant may assert the defense of invalidity of a patent. If a patent is determined invalid by an infringement court, the patentee may not exercise its rights against the opponent (Article 104-*ter* of the Patent Act). In other words, the decision of invalidity of the patent by the infringement court only works within the parties. **2089**

If the defendant would like to invalidate the patent publicly, it is necessary to file an invalidation trial at the Patent Office (Article 123 of the Patent Act). Thus, in Japan, when a patent infringement lawsuit is filed, in many cases[1], invalidation trial is filed by the defendant. In such cases, the infringement court and the JPO will then decide on the validity over the same patent. In many cases[2], the court and the JPO reach the same result with regard to the validity of the patent. **2090**

An appeal against the decision of the invalidation trial by the JPO is possible by filing a lawsuit for revocation of the trial decision (Article 178 of the Patent Act). The Intellectual Property High Court has exclusive jurisdiction over the lawsuit for revocation of the trial decisions. If an infringement lawsuit is appealed and a lawsuit for revocation of trial decision is filed over the same patent, in many cases, the both cases will be examined almost at the same time by the same panel of the IP High Court. **2091**

1 According to the statistics of the IP High Court in 2021, it is about 74 %.

2 According to statistics published by the Patent Office in 2019, the concordance rate of decisions is 74 %.

2092 Appeal against the ruling of the IP High Court is also possible. The Supreme Court handles the appeal cases. Only legal issues are heard by the Supreme Court and very few cases are substantially examined by the Supreme Court.

B. Courts

2093 The Tokyo District Court has four divisions specialized in intellectual property. The Osaka District Court has two divisions dedicated to intellectual property.

2094 Patent infringement lawsuits are heard by a panel of three judges. The judges are jurists and basically have no technical background. In the patent specialized division, judicial research officials (Article 57 of the Court Act) provide necessary technical support for patent-related cases to judges. The judicial research officials are full-time employees of the court, and their term of office is about three years. Most of the officials are experienced examiner seconded from the JPO, but patent attorneys are also included.

2095 The IP High Court consists of four divisions with 15 judges (as of January 2022). 10 judicial research officials support judges. Cases involving appeals of infringement lawsuits and cases involving revocation of trial decisions are heard by a three-judge panel. In cases involving important legal issues and where the court's decision has a significant impact on the economic activities of a company and the industrial economy[3], the case is heard by a grand panel of five judges (Article 310-*bis* of the Code of Civil Procedure, Article 182-*bis* of the Patent Act).[4] A grand panel consist of one main judge and 4 presiding judges of the four divisions.

C. Counsel

2096 The Counsel for patent infringement lawsuits must be an attorney-at-law as in other lawsuits (Article 54(1) of the Code of Civil Procedure). A patent attorney may pursue litigation as an assistant (Article 5 of the Patent Attorneys Act). If a patent attorney has passed the examination for representation in specific infringement litigation, he/she may pursue litigation as a counsel (Article 6-*bis* (1) of the Patent Attorneys Act). When a patent attorney appears at the court hearing, he/she must appear together with an attorney-at-law (Article 6-*bis* (2) of the Patent Attorneys Act).

2097 With regard to actions for revocation of trial decisions by the JPO, a patent attorney may act as a counsel (Article 6 of the Patent Attorneys Act,) and may pursue the action independently.

---

3 https://www.ip.courts.go.jp/eng/aboutus/current/index.html.

4 Since the establishment of the IP High Court, there have been 13 cases that have been assigned to the Grand Chamber and ruled on (as of January 2022).

D. Characteristics of Patent Infringement Litigation

I. Outline of Procedure

Japanese patent infringement lawsuits are proceeded mainly on written documents basis. The procedural language is Japanese only (Article 74 of the Court Act,). All court documents must be submitted in paper form, but electronic data may also be submitted at the request of the court (Article 3–2 of the Rules of Civil Procedure). 2098

In a patent infringement lawsuit, the court first examines infringement of the patent (including invalidity argument). If the court is of the opinion that the patent is infringing and valid, the case proceeds to the damages calculation stage. 2099

The flow of the hearing is as follows. After the filing of the complaint and answer (which are often relatively short), the first trial hearing is held. The hearing is held in open court. On the hearing date, normally submitted briefs and documents are confirmed and the issues are determined (the hearing is short). Thereafter, preparatory hearings are held approximately every two months (closed to the public), and the parties are required to submit their briefs by a set deadline prior to the hearing date. Substantive arguments on infringement and invalidity are exchanged in these briefs. The plaintiff in a patent infringement lawsuit has the burden of proof for infringement, while the defendant has the burden of proof for invalidity of the patent. Preparatory dates are often attended only by the presiding judge and the chief judge. Since February 2020, preparatory hearing may also be held via a web conference system, but still at trial stages. 2100

When the parties submitted almost all arguments on the infringement and invalidity, a technical presentation hearing is often held. At the technical presentation hearing, both parties give a 30-minute presentation, followed by questions. In addition to the judges and the judicial research official, the technical presentation is sometimes attended by a court-appointed experts (see (4) below). 2101

The subsequent proceedings vary from case to case. If the court is of the mind of non-infringement or the patent is invalid, it may close the argument and render a judgment. The date for closing arguments will also be in open court. In cases where there is room for settlement between the parties, a settlement date may be set and an attempt made to resolve the case through settlement. In Japan, the court involves settlement, if a preparatory hearing for the settlement. Many patent infringement lawsuits in Japan are concluded by settlement. Of the cases closed during the period from 2005 to 2010, approximately 68 % were closed by settlement.[5] 2102

If the court is of the mind that the case is one of infringement or patent validity, it disclose its opinion to the parties and then the case will move on to the damages calculation proceedings. Once in the damages calculation proceeding, the parties are limited to making arguments regarding infringement and patent validity. In some 2103

5 https://www.ip.courts.go.jp/eng/documents/statistics/index.html.

cases, experts are used in the calculation of damages, although this is rare. When a court orders an expert opinion on damages calculation caused by the act of infringement, parties shall explain matters to be needed for the expert opinion (Article 105-*bis* (11) of the Patent Act). When the necessary arguments for the damages calculation are submitted, the court renders a judgment.

2104 Arguments must be in a timely manner, and argument submitted by parties at a later date intentionally or through gross negligence will be dismissed by the court (Article 157 of the Code of Civil Procedure).

2105 If a party appeals against the judgment of the first instance, the finality of the original judgment is suspended (Article 116, paragraph 2 of the Code of Civil Procedure). In the appellate court, new proof of claim can be made based on the newly collected materials, in addition to the evidence filed in the first instance. The trial period for a patent infringement lawsuit of the first instance is approximately 18 months. The duration of an appeal trial is about 9 months.

II. Preliminary injunction

2106 In patent litigations, preliminary injunction procedures are also used to seek an injunction against manufacturing, sales, or other enforcement actions. This is an effective means when the patentee wishes to obtain an early injunction. Stamp fees to be paid to the court are also inexpensive.[6]

2107 Preliminary injunction cases are usually heard by a single judge. In the case of a preliminary injunction in a patent lawsuit, it takes several months before a decision is issued, because the court also hears the invalidity argument. The hearing is closed to the public and is conducted in a bilateral hearing (it is never conducted in a unilateral hearing). Therefore, there is no system for the alleged infringer to submit a protective letter to the court in advance.

III. Evidence

2108 In Japan, there is no discovery system, and the collection of evidence necessary to prove infringement is basically done by the patentee itself. In contrast, when the defendant denies the specific mode of the allegedly infringing product, the defendant must clarify the specific mode (Article 104-*bis* of the Patent Act). In addition, the patentee may file a motion with the court for an order to submit documents necessary to prove the alleged infringement (Article 105(1) of the Patent Act). However, if the owner of the documents has justification for refusing to submit the documents, an order to submit the documents will not be issued (Article 105 (1) of the Patent Act). The court may decide in an in camera proceeding whether or not the document falls under such necessary documents or whether or not there are such justification (Article 105(2) of the Patent Act). On the other hand, if trade secrets are included

6 As of January 2022, the cost is 2,000 JPY.

in the briefs or in the evidence to be examined, a confidentiality order may be issued (Article 105-*quater* of the Patent Act).

According to the amendment of the Patent Act in 2020, Japanese type of inspection system as a procedure for collecting evidence in infringement lawsuits was introduced (105-*bis* of the Patent Act, Article). Under the Japanese inspection system, a petition for the inspection can be filed only in a lawsuit that has already been filed. The inspection is conducted by an inspector designated by the court, such as an attorney, patent attorney, engineer, etc. The inspector prepares a report on the results of the inspection and submits it to the court (Article 105-*bis* (4) of the Patent Act). After the court processes the non-disclosure of statements regarding trade secrets in the report, the patentee can use the report as evidence. 2109

Furthermore, due to the 2021 amendment of the law, a third-party opinion submission system (Article 105-*bis* (11) of the Patent Act) as a special procedure of the evidence collection system available for the parties was introduced. This is a Japanese type of amicus curiae system. In patent infringement litigations, the court broadly invite opinions from the public on matters needed by the court, and if a party submits a copy of those opinions to the court, they can be used as evidence. 2110

IV. Use of Experts

Various experts involve in patent infringement litigation. The above-mentioned judicial research official (Article 57 of the Court Act,) is an expert as a full-time employee of the court. 2111

Experts (Article 92-*bis* of the Code of Civil Procedure), who explain technical points at issue in the case to judges during the proceedings play important roles in patent litigations. The court has a list of about 200 expert members consisting of university professors, patent attorneys, researchers, etc. and depending on the content of the case and technical area, 2–3 appropriate experts are appointed for a case. Those experts are not appointed in every case, but when a technical presentation is held, they are normally appointed. 2112

The court may also appoint an expert witness (Article 212 of the Code of Civil Procedure), but this is rarely used in patent infringement lawsuits. Parties also often utilize experts as written expert opinions. Interrogatories to experts are rarely conducted. 2113

V. Inspection of judgment and case record

Any person may inspect case records and judgments (Article 91 of the Code of Civil Procedure). However, the court may restrict access by decision, for example, when a party's trade secrets are involved (Article 92-*bis* of the Code of Civil Procedure). Judgments in patent litigations including revocation of trial decisions are made public on the court's website. 2114

E. Recovery of litigation costs

2115 Litigation costs shall be borne by the losing party (Article 61 of the Code of Civil Procedure). Litigation costs here mainly consist of filing fees. A plaintiff may claim attorney's fees as part of the damages. The court sometimes orders to pay damages including certain amount of attorney's fees of the plaintiff, when patent infringement is determined. In recent years, there have been cases in which high attorney's fees (for example, approximately 100 million yen in an appeals court) have been awarded.

Chapter 41: Comparison with Korean Law

Contents | Para

In Korea, a civil action and a criminal sanction against one who infringes a patent are the main form of exercise of intellectual property rights. **2116**

Further, the Intellectual Property Trial and Appeal Board ("IPTAB"), which is an administrative tribunal within the Korea Intellectual Property Office("KIPO"), is a forum for disputes regarding the validity and the confirmation scope of a patent. The IPTAB has exclusive subject matter jurisdiction regarding the validity issue of a patent. An interested party such as an infringer may file such patent-related actions-(trials) with the IPTAB. **2117**

The Korean Patent Court, which is an intermediate appeals court which is similar to the U.S. Federal Circuit Court of Appeals, has jurisdiction to review trial decisions rendered in the IPTAB and civil decision of main actions of infringement in a district court. **2118**

A. Korean Court System

In Korea, infringement and invalidity proceedings are generally divided under the patent litigation system. Infringement issues are primarily dealt with by a district court as the forum for first instance, but the validity proceedings are handled initially by the IPTAB. An infringement action and an invalidation action in connection with the same patent can be pending simultaneously at these two tribunals which are the civil court and the IPTAB respectively. The following is an outline of the court system for patent litigation in Korea. **2119**

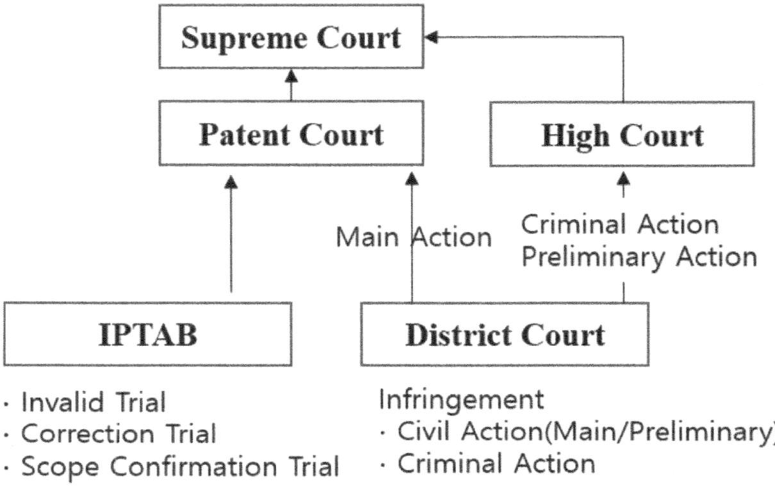

Fig. 41.1 Diagram: The Korean IP System

2120 However, in practice, the IPTAB has the subject matter jurisdiction over patent validity, but a district court dealing with infringement cases usually hear invalid arguments based on lack of novelty or inventiveness regarding the patents in litigation. Despite the bifurcated system, a district court has discretion to reject an infringement claim if it finds that the asserted patent clearly would be held invalid in a separate invalidation action, based on the theory that an attempt to enforce such a defective patent right falls under an abuse of the right.

2121 It usually takes approximately 12 to 18 months for a district court of first instance to render a decision in an infringement proceeding. This time period can vary by a lot in accordance with the number of patents and asserted claims thereof, the complexity of the technology at issue, and whether a damage claim is made or not which would require more time to review. A preliminary injunction action that seeks only an injunction typically takes about 3 to 8 months to reach a final conclusion.

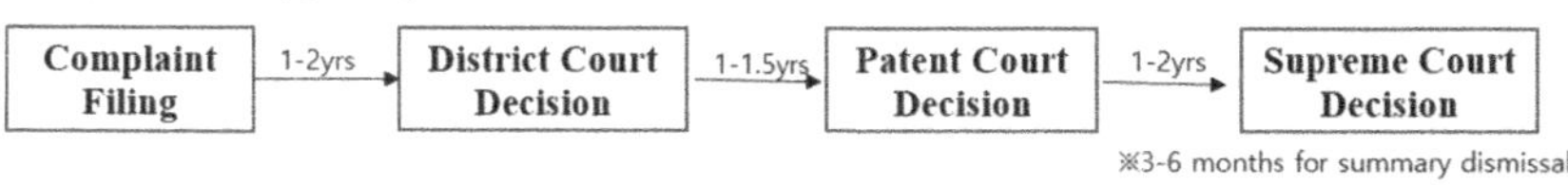

Fig. 41.2 Timeline for an infringement proceeding

2122 At the present pace of IPTAB proceedings, IPTAB decisions typically take approximately 6–12 months to be made in invalidation proceedings. If an infringement action is pending at the same time, the IPTAB will usually conduct a highly expedited review, which takes about 4–6 months.

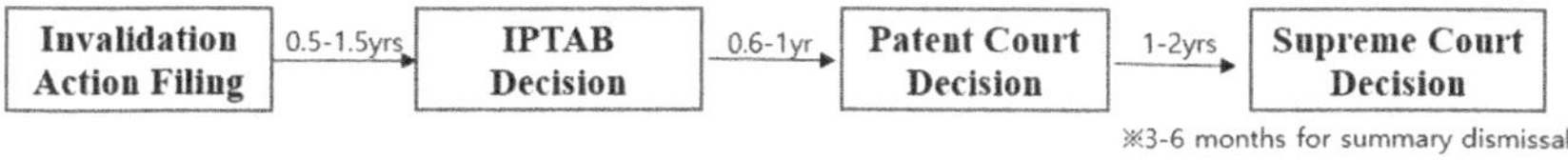

Fig. 41.3 Timeline for an invalidation proceeding

B. Types of Legal Actions

I. Civil Action

There are two kinds of civil suits for patent infringement, a main action and a preliminary injunction action. In a main action, all civil remedies like permanent injunction and monetary compensation are available. A preliminary injunction action may be intuiated when there exists an present or immediate risk of irreparable harm to the plaintiff that is the patent owner, but no remedies other than injunction is usable. A civil action is generally proceeded through a chain of oral hearings in front of three judges. There is no jury trial for patent lawsuits in Korea. 2123

1. Main Action

When a complaint is filed with a court, a first hearing date is set within about two to three weeks for a preliminary injunction action, or within about three to five months for a main action. Subsequent hearings will be usually held in about two to three-week intervals in a preliminary injunction action, or in about four to five-week intervals in a main action. After a court finishes the hearing process, it starts deliberations and then the decision is usually rendered within a few months. If a foreign defendant is involved and the service of process must be made through the Hague Convention or other diplomatic channels, then the whole proceedings may be delayed by several months. 2124

Oral hearings mainly focus on procedural matters such as entry of briefs, introduction of evidence, presentation of motions, requests for inspection of documents and testimony of witnesses. Written briefs should be submitted to the court before each hearing and each party must serve the other copies of each filed brief. The briefs are used to transfer legal arguments on each issue and rebut the other party's arguments. The briefs can be accompanied by exhibits and supporting evidence. Each brief filed in a Korean court must be thorough as substantive issues and judges rely heavily on the submitted briefs for making a decision on the case. After some exchanges of briefs, the court may ask for a technical presentation. 2125

a) Petition for preservation of evidence

There is no extensive pre-trial discovery such as depositions of the U.S. legal system, in Korean legal practice. However, patentees in Korea can resort to the evidence preservation procedure. 2126

Specifically, a patentee can file a petition for preservation of evidence with the district court of proper jurisdiction. The petition must include: 1) indication of the other 2127 party; 2) facts to be proven; 3) evidence to be preserved; and 4) grounds for evidence preservation. According to Article 375 of the Korean Civil Procedure Act ("KCPA"), the petition for evidence preservation may be accepted when it is apparent that access to the relevant evidence would be difficult unless the evidence is preserved in advance (e.g., lack of infringing products in the market, possibility of alteration or export of infringing products and so on).

2128 If the court finds sufficient grounds for evidence preservation, the court may issue an order to force collection of evidence. For example, the court can issue inspection of premises such as manufacturing facilities or collection of documents or a sample. Although the preserved evidence may be utilized by the patentee during the litigation, the evidence will remain in the court's possession, not the patentee's possession. In addition to a request for evidence preservation, a party of a patent infringement action may file a petition requesting the court to issue an order to a holder of documentary evidence to produce documents to the court if the documents fall within certain categories (e.g., a document cited by a party).

2129 Under the Korean Patent Act("KPA") (applicable to patent infringement actions filed on or after June 30, 2016), relevant materials may no longer be withheld from the court simply because the accused infringer claims that they contain trade secrets if the requested materials are necessary to prove infringement or damages. Alternatively, if the party submitting materials worries about the revelation of its trade secrets, it may request the court to restrict the range of materials to be submitted or the persons allowed to access the materials after explaining to the court that the materials include trade secrets.

2130 Further, the KPA specifies that a court may presume that "the facts that the requesting party intended to prove based on the requested materials" are true if the requested materials are not produced and the requesting party would otherwise have substantial difficulty in proving these facts.

2131 Further, the KPA (applicable to patent infringement actions filed on or after July 9, 2019) requires the accused infringer to submit details regarding the product or process which the infringer is actually utilizing, when the plaintiff has shown it is plausible that the infringer is using the patent. If a defendant refuses to submit such details without justifiable reasons, the court may presume that the defendant has actually committed the infringing activity claimed by the plaintiff.

b) Claims

2132 A patentee prevailing on the merits under a main suit for patent infringement may claim permanent injunctive relief (allowed as a matter of right) and/or monetary damages. Other remedies available to the patentee in a main suit include, for example, a court order to destroy and remove infringing articles and equipment used in manufacturing the infringing articles, and restoration of damaged business reputation and trustworthiness.

In order to lessen the burden of proof for the amount of damages, Article 128 of the KPA provides the methods for calculating damages, as follows: (i) Plaintiff's lost profits (which generally may be calculated by multiplying the number of infringing products sold by the per unit profit patentee would have earned but for infringement); (ii) Defendant's profits from infringing act (rebuttably presumed as patentee's damages); or (iii) Ordinary royalties. **2133**

Although a patentee may select any of the above theories of damages, typically, patentees seek to prove either their lost profits or the infringer's profits as damages. If such damages cannot be properly proven, then a reasonable royalty will be calculated. The court has wide discretion to determine the amount of damages. Even in case of a reasonable royalty, the court can exert broad discretionary power in calculating the royalty by considering the type of the industry, case specific facts, etc. Specifically, under the Article 128(7) of the KPA, where the fact of damage is established by the court but evidence of the amount of damage is difficult to establish due to the nature of the case, the court can determine a reasonable damages amount based on the overall tenor of the proceedings and an examination of the collected evidence. **2134**

Under the KPA effective on or after July 9, 2019, courts are now authorized to award damages as a punitive damage of up to three times the amount of actual damages for intentional or willful acts of infringement. When the amount of such punitive damages is calculated, the following factors can be considered: **2135**

(i) whether the infringer has a dominant position,
(ii) (whether the infringer knew the act of infringement would cause harm to a patent owner, or intended such harm,
(iii) the significance of any such damages,
(iv) the economic benefits to the infringer from the infringement,
(v) how frequently and how long the infringing activity was committed,
(vi) the criminal penalty for the infringing activity,
(vii) the infringer's financial status, and
(viii) what efforts the infringer has made to reduce the harm to the patent owner.

2. Preliminary Injunction Action

A plaintiff has to prove (i) likelihood of success on the merits (infringement), and (ii) the necessity of provisional relief (balance of hardships) to get a preliminary injunction. In determining the need for provisional relief, courts balance the irreparable harm to the plaintiff arising from ongoing infringement with the economic harm to the defendant in granting the injunction. Courts also consider the appropriateness of damages to redress the injury which the plaintiff has suffered from the infringement and the likelihood of invalidation of the subject patent right. **2136**

In addition, execution of a preliminary injunctive order that is later found to have been improperly issued may constitute a form of tort under the Korean law. The right holder to execute the order will be held liable for ordinary damages suffered by the defendant due to such execution, as well as any extraordinary damages that were reasonably foreseeable to the right holder at the time of execution. If a preliminary **2137** injunction executed by a right holder is determined to have been improperly issued, the right holder is rebuttably presumed to have been negligent in enforcing the injunction.

2138 Absent exceptional circumstances, courts generally review a petition for a preliminary injunction by an *inter partes* proceedings. In principle, court reviews only readily examinable evidence (only affidavits, no witnesses, no expert-testing, no on-site inspection). Witnesses generally are limited to written testimony by way of affidavits and are not permitted to take the stand during hearings. Courts generally require the plaintiff to post a security deposit or bond for preliminary injunctive relief to issue, for the purpose of compensating for possible damages resulting from the injunction in the event the injunction is later overturned or revoked.

3. Invalidation Action

2139 An interested person can file an invalidation action (trial) with the IPTAB of KIPO at any time, even after a expire of a patent. In particular, an interested party is any person who is or who is likely to be in the business using a patented invention. A petitioner of an invalidation trial should specify that the petitioner has an interesting with the validity of the patent in question.

2140 While a decision of an invalid trial filed with the IPTAB is rendered within 12 months, an invalid trial relating with an infringement action pending in a court is granted as an expedited trial in which the parties are usually to take a decision within three months. An invalidation trial where a patent owner sent a warning letter with respect to the patent can be categorized as a priority trial. The parties of the priority trial can generally receive a decision within six months.

2141 The Korean Patent Court has exclusive jurisdiction to review decision of the invalidation trials. At this appeal stage, the parties can submit new prior arts which were not submitted at the trial stage.

4. Confirmation of Scope Action

2142 An action (trial) for confirming the scope of a patent may be filed with the IPTAB. A petitioner of the trial shall seek a decision on whether a certain article or process falls within the scope of claims of the patent. Therefore, such actions are normally filed by an interested party who seeks a decision that his article or process does not fall within the scope of a patent right (referred to as a "negative confirmation of scope action") to defend the patent owner's offense. However, a patentee may also bring such action (referred to as a "positive confirmation of scope action"). In order for the patentee to file such a trial, it must be verified that the article or process presented in the trial is, or at least is likely to be used by others.

2143 A civil court of the infringement action is not bound by the decision of the IPTAB. However, the court may consider the decision only as an advisory opinion. Further, such a decision is not in the nature of an enforceable judgment, and if an accused infringer refuses to acknowledge the IPTAB decision, the patentee must seek an infringement action to have the district court accept the IPTAB findings.

Filing of a confirmation of scope action generally does not stay the corresponding district court action. However, it may complicate the issues and may sometimes have the effect of somewhat delaying the court action. 2144

II. Criminal Action

An infringement of another's patent may lead to criminal prosecution, with possible imprisonment or fines imposed on the infringer. In most cases, a formal criminal accusation is necessary to indict infringers of IP rights. In 2015, the Daejeon District Prosecutor's Office established a special patent investigation department to conduct investigations against patent infringement professionally. 2145

III. Other Actions

1. Warning Letter

Intellectual property owners often send a warning letter to the infringer before taking a legal action in a court. Such a warning letter generally gives notice to the infringer of the infringing nature of his/her activity and demands that the infringing activity stops immediately. The warning letter is generally used a way to initiate a conversation with the infringer by bringing the infringer to the negotiation table. 2146

However, warning letters must be carefully prepared and must be based on supportable allegations. If not, a civil action against the sender may be commenced for tortious obstruction with business. In some cases, sending warning letters to a third party believed to be infringing upon the patent right, or the customers or vendors thereof, may be considered a violation of the relevant laws or regulations. 2147

In practice, it appears highly unlikely that simply sending a warning letter to a potential infringer would be subject to criminal or civil liability as long as the person sending the letter is the legitimate owner of the patent. In order to avoid any potential liability, however, it is desirable that the sender makes sure that (i) he/she is the rightful owner of the patent right, and (ii) there is a reasonable ground (or a good faith basis) for asserting an infringement of the patent right. In this regard, if possible, the sender should first make efforts to secure supporting evidence such as samples of the infringing goods, test results and expert opinion, etc. 2148

If a letter claiming infringement of a patent is sent to a customer or vendor of the possible infringer despite the absence of an actual infringement, the sender of the letter may be subject to criminal and/or civil liabilities. Specifically, the sender may be liable for obstruction of business, injury of credibility, or defamation. Therefore, when sending a letter to a third party, the letter must be based on clear and accurate facts to the extent possible, and special care must be taken when sending letters to a third party who is not directly related to the possible infringer. In particular, the relevant facts and wording of the letter need to be thoroughly examined. 2149

2. Trade Sanction

2150 The Korea Trade Commission("KTC"), a government agency, is responsible for overseeing the import-related relief system in Korea and serves to prevent and remedy unfair trade practices that harm domestic industry. The KTC is empowered to initiate investigation of and to impose sanctions for unfair trade practices (analogous to ITC in the U.S.). The KTC has the power to initiate and impose sanctions on unfair trade practices, especially the import, export, and manufacture of goods infringing IP rights of Korea.

2151 Several remedies are available to the petitioner under a KTC action:
(i) provisional measures (e.g., injunction),
(ii) corrective measures (e.g., suspension of the import and sale, destruction of infringing goods),
(iii) penalties, and
(iv) criminal sanctions.

2152 In particular, corrective measures include
(i) exclusion order barring importation of infringing articles; and/or
(ii) order the violator to:
(1) stop import, export, sale or manufacture for export of the infringing articles,
(2) have the infringing articles destroyed, and/or
(3) publicly announce that it has received a corrective order from the KTC.

Part 4: Strategic Options

Chapter 42: Summary Overview of the Strategic Options

Contents

The following chapter will present a summary overview – necessarily abbreviated and thus not entirely comprehensive – of the various strategic options which have been presented in this book. For more detailed explanations, the reader is invited to refer to the respective discussions in the previous chapters. **2153**

A. The Unitary Patent

The Unitary Patent is a supplemental option which can serve to replace national validation in those states which are signatory to the UPC Agreement at the time the patent in question is granted, provided that the publication of grant is after 1 June 2023. **2154**

The Unitary Patent will allow one to avoid the costs otherwise incurred in these states, namely for national validation fees, for correspondence with national attorneys, and for translations of the patent description. Effective during a certain transitional period, however, it will still be necessary to translate a patent not originally formulated in English into that language (English), and to translate a patent not originally formulated in English into a language of the EU. A disadvantage of the Unitary Patent is that the patent proprietor will no longer be able to exploit the "dilution" approach, i.e. to allow his patent to gradually expire by and by in selected individual states. **2155**

The larger the number of states in which a patent proprietor has customarily validated his patents thus far, the more it will make sense for him to select the Unitary Patent in lieu of national validation. The critical threshold will be crossed once about four or five states have ratified the UPC. **2156**

Seeking a Unitary Patent will look particularly attractive if Italy is at least potentially relevant. For one thing, this will eliminate the need for translations into Italian. For another, it will make it possible to prosecute patent infringements occurring in Italy before the Unified Patent Court, so that one can then dispense with national proceedings in Italy. **2157**

B. The Unified Patent Court

The Unified Patent Court is far more important than the Unitary Patent, since it will be competent over the long term for all existing and future European patents and Unitary Patents. Many observers and stakeholders even see the Unified Patent Court **2158** as the forum of choice for many of the worldwide patent disputes likely to arise in the future – a forum which will be able to compete with the courts of the United States.[1]

2159 On the negative side, the costs of proceedings before the UPC will probably be higher than they currently are for patent litigation before the German courts. But this added expense will often be offset by the larger territorial reach of a decision handed down by the UPC.

I. Opting Out of the Jurisdiction of the Unified Patent Court

2160 In principle, the Unified Patent Court will also be competent for existing European patents and patent registrations. During a transitional period of almost seven years after the UPC's coming into force, a patent proprietor will be permitted to lodge a declaration of intent to "opt-out" of the UPC's jurisdiction for purposes of a given patent. This will cause the national courts to retain jurisdiction over the patent. The opt-out declaration will be free of charge. It will not be available for Unitary Patents, however, but only for conventionally validated European patents.

2161 Unless an opt-out declaration is lodged, bringing legal action on the national level on the basis of a European patent will no longer be possible once the transitional period expires. An opt-out will be precluded if no legal action concerning the patent in question has been brought before the Unified Patent Court by the end of the transitional period.

2162 During the aforementioned transitional period, declaring an opt-out will make sense only if a revocation action before the UPC's central division is feared. But this will apply only in the rarest cases, unless the patent proprietor himself takes action in this regard, e.g. by contacting the patent infringer in writing. Thus, there would seem to be no need to declare an opt-out across the board for all one's European patents. On the other hand, an opt-out should definitely be considered before making contact with a potential patent infringer or before bringing legal action.

2163 Since the opt-out will be available only temporarily, one should try to gain insights into the actual practice of the Unified Patent Court in a timely manner. This would also include conducting proceedings of one's own before the Unified Patent Court.

2164 As the end of the transitional period approaches, however, it will become necessary to take a general decision as to whether an opt-out declaration should be lodged for all those patents which are eligible for such a declaration.

II. National Patents as an Alternative

2165 Over the long term, circumventing the Unified Patent Court will also mean circumventing the European Patent Office, given that all European patents will in future fall under the jurisdiction of the Unified Patent Court.

---

1 See the survey conducted by the Allen Overy law firm, published on their website on 2 June 2014.

National patents will mostly likely qualify as a viable alternative only if they appear attractive without any regard to the Unified Patent Court, e.g. due to the costs charged by the European Patent Office. 2166

The option of deviating off a German utility model is certainly worth mentioning in this context. This would make it possible to bring national legal action at least in Germany, the most important European country for patent litigation, even if the patent in question has been registered with the European Patent Office. 2167

III. General Considerations

A proceeding before the Unified Patent Court is a highly streamlined process which provides only limited options for submitting information. Based on how the UPC's Rules of Procedure are structured, the proceeding will be subject to strict time limits. One must also presume that the individual divisions of the UPC will adhere to these scheduling rules, at least during the initial years of the Court's operations. 2168

This makes it essential to be well organized. It is a safe bet that, more often than not, the party which prevails will not necessarily be the one in an objectively stronger position but the one which is better organized! 2169

The Unified Patent Court and its underlying legal regulations constitute a *sui generis* system. One should by no means assume that the Court will simply adopt this or that national regulation. Instead, one should be prepared to adapt one's in-house practices accordingly and, in case of doubt, adhere closely to the UPC Agreement and to the UPC's Rules of Procedure, while also using these as a basis for interpretation. 2170

1. Considerations for Patent Proprietors

When it comes to evaluating the legal validity of their patents, patent proprietors should essentially look to the legal precedent established by the European Patent Office, at least so long as the Unified Patent Court has not yet created its own case law. 2171

The streamlined character of proceedings before the UPC works to the advantage of patent proprietors, given that they are able to prepare in advance. But if the defendant lodges a revocation counterclaim, the patent proprietor will have to lodge a Defense along with all his auxiliary requests within two months' time. 2172

The local divisions in Germany will continue to be available as legal venues. It bears noting that this is where the most experienced judges sit. These judges will also be the ones who will find it easiest to adjust to the workings of the UPC, given its similarities to the German legal system and given their own familiarity with expedited proceedings. So in order to ensure that an experienced patent judge will handle the submitted legal action as judge-rapporteur, German should be selected as the language of the action. 2173

The central division should not be seised, however, not least because this will automatically preclude the option of splitting off a revocation counterclaim without suspending the infringement proceeding. 2174

2175 The Unified Patent Court will make it possible for petitioners to obtain the first truly transnational preliminary injunctions in Europe. Thus, the option of applying to the Court for a preliminary injunction should most definitely be considered, or at least not dismissed out of hand.

2176 German-speaking or French-speaking patent proprietors should use their respective languages when registering their patents with the European Patent Office. This is because a revocation action brought before the UPC's central division must be formulated in the same language in which the patent was registered with the EPO. This will pose something of an additional hurdle for potential plaintiffs from outside the European Union.

2177 Under certain preconditions, licensees, too, will have legal capacity to bring action before the Unified Patent Court. But if a counterclaim for revocation is lodged, the patent proprietor will automatically become a party to the proceeding. This means that the patent proprietor will have to coordinate with his licensees and, if needed, adapt his licensing agreements in advance in order to deal with this eventuality.

2. Considerations for Potential Patent Infringers

2178 When it comes to the topic of equivalent patent infringement, there is no UPC case law to rely on and the individual Member States' legal tradition differs widely. Thus, one should proceed carefully when addressing the question of whether a given product is covered by a patent, since it cannot be ruled out that the Court may opt for a broad interpretation.

2179 Given that the streamlined nature of proceedings before the UPC offers definite advantages for patent proprietors, one should give increased consideration to the option of lodging opposition proceedings before the European Patent Office in order to avoid legal actions and/or obtain suspensions. In the alternative, a nullity suit before the Unified Patent Court can be considered, this has the drawback, however, that non-UPC-Countries such as Great Britain or Spain would be unaffected.

2180 Obtaining the grant of a provisional measure will become a far more dangerous weapon than before, given that this was previously a viable option in only a few countries. And since protective letters will henceforth become expressly codified and easily available, they should be used as a matter of course, e.g. before important trade fairs or when rolling out a new product.

2181 If one receives service of legal action, one should adhere to the relevant time limits rather than taking a chance by "seeking refuge in default." The latter would seem to be a viable option more in theory than in actual practice.

2182 Lodging a counterclaim for revocation in an infringement proceeding should be regarded as the general rule. But timely action will be required here: A revocation counterclaim must be lodged together with the first Statement of Defense to a Statement of Claim. One should make every effort to also include the state of the technical art which one wishes to adduce, since it will be very difficult to bring this information into the ongoing proceeding later on. Finally, if one becomes the target of legal action before the Unified Patent Court, one should make mounting an effective defense a top priority.

Annexes

Annex 1 Regulation (EU) No 1257/2012

of 17 December 2012

implementing enhanced cooperation in the area of
the creation of unitary patent protection

THE EUROPEAN PARLIAMENT AND THE COUNCIL OF THE EUROPEAN UNION,

Having regard to the Treaty on the Functioning of the European Union and in particular the first paragraph of Article 118 thereof,

Having regard to Council Decision 2011/167/EU of 10 March 2011 authorising enhanced cooperation in the area of the creation of unitary patent protection (1),

Having regard to the proposal from the European Commission,

After transmission of the draft legislative act to the national parliaments,

Acting in accordance with the ordinary legislative procedure (2),

Whereas:

(1) The creation of the legal conditions enabling undertakings to adapt their activities in manufacturing and distributing products across national borders and providing them with greater choice and more opportunities contributes to the attainment of the objectives of the Union set out in Article 3(3) of the Treaty on European Union. Uniform patent protection within the internal market, or at least a significant part thereof, should feature amongst the legal instruments which undertakings have at their disposal.

(2) Pursuant to the first paragraph of Article 118 of the Treaty on the Functioning of the European Union (TFEU), measures to be taken in the context of the establishment and functioning of the internal market include the creation of uniform patent protection throughout the Union and the establishment of centralised Union-wide authorisation, coordination and supervision arrangements.

(3) On 10 March 2011, the Council adopted Decision 2011/167/EU authorising enhanced cooperation between Belgium, Bulgaria, the Czech Republic, Denmark, Germany, Estonia, Ireland, Greece, France, Cyprus, Latvia, Lithuania, Luxembourg, Hungary, Malta, the Netherlands, Austria, Poland, Portugal, Romania, Slovenia, Slovakia, Finland, Sweden and the United Kingdom (hereinafter 'participating Member States') in the area of the creation of unitary patent protection.

---

1 OJ L 76, 22.3.2011, p. 53.

2 Position of the European Parliament of 11 December 2012 (not yet published in the Official Journal) and decision of the Council of 17 December 2012.

(4) Unitary patent protection will foster scientific and technological advances and the functioning of the internal market by making access to the patent system easier, less costly and legally secure. It will also improve the level of patent protection by making it possible to obtain uniform patent protection in the participating Member States and eliminate costs and complexity for undertakings throughout the Union. It should be available to proprietors of a European patent from both the participating Member States and from other States, regardless of their nationality, residence or place of establishment.

(5) The Convention on the Grant of European Patents of 5 October 1973, as revised on 17 December 1991 and on 29 November 2000 (hereinafter 'EPC'), established the European Patent Organisation and entrusted it with the task of granting European patents. This task is carried out by the European Patent Office (hereinafter 'EPO'). A European patent granted by the EPO should, at the request of the patent proprietor, benefit from unitary effect by virtue of this Regulation in the participating Member States. Such a patent is hereinafter referred to as a 'European patent with unitary effect'.

(6) In accordance with Part IX of the EPC a group of Contracting States to the EPC may provide that European patents granted for those States have a unitary character. This Regulation constitutes a special agreement within the meaning of Article 142 of the EPC, a regional patent treaty within the meaning of Article 45(1) of the Patent Cooperation Treaty of 19 June 1970 as last modified on 3 February 2001 and a special agreement within the meaning of Article 19 of the Convention for the Protection of Industrial Property, signed in Paris on 20 March 1883 and last amended on 28 September 1979.

(7) Unitary patent protection should be achieved by attributing unitary effect to European patents in the post-grant phase by virtue of this Regulation and in respect of all the participating Member States. The main feature of a European patent with unitary effect should be its unitary character, i.e. providing uniform protection and having equal effect in all the participating Member States. Consequently, a European patent with unitary effect should only be limited, transferred or revoked, or lapse, in respect of all the participating Member States. It should be possible for a European patent with unitary effect to be licensed in respect of the whole or part of the territories of the participating Member States. To ensure the uniform substantive scope of protection conferred by unitary patent protection, only European patents that have been granted for all the participating Member States with the same set of claims should benefit from unitary effect. Finally, the unitary effect attributed to a European patent should have an accessory nature and should be deemed not to have arisen to the extent that the basic European patent has been revoked or limited.

(8) In accordance with the general principles of patent law and Article 64(1) of the EPC, unitary patent protection should take effect retroactively in the participating Member States as from the date of publication of the mention of the grant of the European patent in the European Patent Bulletin. Where unitary patent protection takes effect, the participating Member States should ensure that the

European patent is deemed not to have taken effect on their territory as a national patent, so as to avoid any duplication of patent protection.

(9) The European patent with unitary effect should confer on its proprietor the right to prevent any third party from committing acts against which the patent provides protection. This should be ensured through the establishment of a Unified Patent Court. In matters not covered by this Regulation or by Council Regulation (EU) No 1260/2012 of 17 December 2012 implementing enhanced cooperation in the area of unitary patent protection with regard to the applicable translation arrangements [3], the provisions of the EPC, the Agreement on a Unified Patent Court, including its provisions defining the scope of that right and its limitations, and national law, including rules of private international law, should apply.

(10) Compulsory licences for European patents with unitary effect should be governed by the laws of the participating Member States as regards their respective territories.

(11) In its report on the operation of this Regulation, the Commission should evaluate the functioning of the applicable limitations and, where necessary, make appropriate proposals, taking account of the contribution of the patent system to innovation and technological progress, the legitimate interests of third parties and overriding interests of society. The Agreement on a Unified Patent Court does not preclude the European Union from exercising its powers in this field.

(12) In accordance with the case-law of the Court of Justice of the European Union, the principle of the exhaustion of rights should also be applied to European patents with unitary effect. Therefore, rights conferred by a European patent with unitary effect should not extend to acts concerning the product covered by that patent which are carried out within the participating Member States after that product has been placed on the market in the Union by the patent proprietor.

(13) The regime applicable to damages should be governed by the laws of the participating Member States, in particular the provisions implementing Article 13 of Directive 2004/48/EC of the European Parliament and of the Council of 29 April 2004 on the enforcement of intellectual property rights [4].

(14) As an object of property, a European patent with unitary effect should be dealt with in its entirety, and in all the participating Member States, as a national patent of the participating Member State determined in accordance with specific criteria such as the applicant's residence, principal place of business or place of business.

(15) In order to promote and facilitate the economic exploitation of an invention protected by a European patent with unitary effect, the proprietor of that patent should be able to offer it to be licensed in return for appropriate consideration. To that end, the patent proprietor should be able to file a statement with the

3 See page 89 of this Official Journal.

4 OJ L 157, 30.4.2004, p. 45.

EPO that he is prepared to grant a license in return for appropriate consideration. In that case, the patent proprietor should benefit from a reduction of the renewal fees as from the EPO's receipt of such statement.

(16) The group of Member States making use of the provisions of Part IX of the EPC may give tasks to the EPO and set up a select committee of the Administrative Council of the European Patent Organisation (hereinafter 'Select Committee').

(17) The participating Member States should give certain administrative tasks relating to European patents with unitary effect to the EPO, in particular as regards the administration of requests for unitary effect, the registration of unitary effect and of any limitation, licence, transfer, revocation or lapse of European patents with unitary effect, the collection and distribution of renewal fees, the publication of translations for information purposes during a transitional period and the administration of a compensation scheme for the reimbursement of translation costs incurred by applicants filing European patent applications in a language other than one of the official languages of the EPO.

(18) In the framework of the Select Committee, the participating Member States should ensure the governance and supervision of the activities related to the tasks entrusted to the EPO by the participating Member States, ensure that requests for unitary effect are filed with the EPO within one month of the date of publication of the mention of the grant in the European Patent Bulletin and ensure that such requests are submitted in the language of the proceedings before the EPO together with the translation prescribed, during a transitional period, by Regulation (EU) No 1260/2012. The participating Member States should also ensure the setting, in accordance with the voting rules laid down in Article 35(2) of the EPC, of the level of the renewal fees and the share of the distribution of the renewal fees in accordance with the criteria set out in this Regulation.

(19) Patent proprietors should pay a single annual renewal fee for a European patent with unitary effect. Renewal fees should be progressive throughout the term of the patent protection and, together with the fees to be paid to the European Patent Organisation during the pre-grant stage, should cover all costs associated with the grant of the European patent and the administration of the unitary patent protection. The level of the renewal fees should be set with the aim of facilitating innovation and fostering the competitiveness of European businesses, taking into account the situation of specific entities such as small and medium-sized enterprises, for example in the form of lower fees. It should also reflect the size of the market covered by the patent and be similar to the level of the national renewal fees for an average European patent taking effect in the participating Member States at the time when the level of the renewal fees is first set.

(20) The appropriate level and distribution of renewal fees should be determined in order to ensure that, in relation to the unitary patent protection, all costs of the tasks entrusted to the EPO are fully covered by the resources generated by the European patents with unitary effect and that, together with the fees to be paid to the European Patent Organisation during the pre-grant stage, the revenues

from the renewal fees ensure a balanced budget of the European Patent Organisation.

(21) Renewal fees should be paid to the European Patent Organisation. The EPO should retain an amount to cover the expenses generated at the EPO in carrying out tasks in relation to the unitary patent protection in accordance with Article 146 of the EPC. The remaining amount should be distributed among the participating Member States and should be used for patent-related purposes. The share of distribution should be set on the basis of fair, equitable and relevant criteria, namely the level of patent activity and the size of the market, and should guarantee a minimum amount to be distributed to each participating Member State in order to maintain a balanced and sustainable functioning of the system. The distribution should provide compensation for having an official language other than one of the official languages of the EPO, having a disproportionately low level of patenting activity established on the basis of the European Innovation Scoreboard, and/or having acquired membership of the European Patent Organisation relatively recently.

(22) An enhanced partnership between the EPO and central industrial property offices of the Member States should enable the EPO to make regular use, where appropriate, of the result of any search carried out by central industrial property offices on a national patent application the priority of which is claimed in a subsequent European patent application. All central industrial property offices, including those which do not perform searches in the course of a national patent-granting procedure, can play an essential role under the enhanced partnership, inter alia, by giving advice and support to potential patent applicants, in particular small and medium-sized enterprises, by receiving applications, by forwarding applications to the EPO and by disseminating patent information.

(23) This Regulation is complemented by Regulation (EU) No 1260/2012, adopted by the Council in accordance with the second paragraph of Article 118 of the TFEU.

(24) Jurisdiction in respect of European patents with unitary effect should be established and governed by an instrument setting up a unified patent litigation system for European patents and European patents with unitary effect.

(25) Establishing a Unified Patent Court to hear cases concerning the European patent with unitary effect is essential in order to ensure the proper functioning of that patent, consistency of case-law and hence legal certainty, and cost-effectiveness for patent proprietors. It is therefore of paramount importance that the participating Member States ratify the Agreement on a Unified Patent Court in accordance with their national constitutional and parliamentary procedures and take the necessary steps for that Court to become operational as soon as possible.

(26) This Regulation should be without prejudice to the right of the participating Member States to grant national patents and should not replace the participating Member States' laws on patents. Patent applicants should remain free to obtain either a national patent, a European patent with unitary effect, a European patent taking effect in one or more of the Contracting States to the EPC or a European

patent with unitary effect validated in addition in one or more other Contracting States to the EPC which are not among the participating Member States.

(27) Since the objective of this Regulation, namely the creation of unitary patent protection, cannot be sufficiently achieved by the Member States and can therefore, by reason of the scale and effects of this Regulation, be better achieved at Union level, the Union may adopt measures, where appropriate by means of enhanced cooperation, in accordance with the principle of subsidiarity as set out in Article 5 of the Treaty on European Union. In accordance with the principle of proportionality, as set out in that Article, this Regulation does not go beyond what is necessary in order to achieve that objective,

HAVE ADOPTED THIS REGULATION:

Article 1
Subject matter

1. This Regulation implements enhanced cooperation in the area of the creation of unitary patent protection, authorised by Decision 2011/167/EU.

2. This Regulation constitutes a special agreement within the meaning of Article 142 of the Convention on the Grant of European Patents of 5 October 1973, as revised on 17 December 1991 and on 29 November 2000 (hereinafter 'EPC').

Article 2
Definitions

For the purposes of this Regulation, the following definitions shall apply:

(a) 'Participating Member State' means a Member State which participates in enhanced cooperation in the area of the creation of unitary patent protection by virtue of Decision 2011/167/EU, or by virtue of a decision adopted in accordance with the second or third subparagraph of Article 331(1) of the TFEU, at the time the request for unitary effect as referred to in Article 9 is made;

(b) 'European patent' means a patent granted by the European Patent Office (hereinafter 'EPO') under the rules and procedures laid down in the EPC;

(c) 'European patent with unitary effect' means a European patent which benefits from unitary effect in the participating Member States by virtue of this Regulation;

(d) 'European Patent Register' means the register kept by the EPO under Article 127 of the EPC;

(e) 'Register for unitary patent protection' means the register constituting part of the European Patent Register in which the unitary effect and any limitation, licence, transfer, revocation or lapse of a European patent with unitary effect are registered;

(f) 'European Patent Bulletin' means the periodical publication provided for in Article 129 of the EPC.

Article 3
European patent with unitary effect

1. A European patent granted with the same set of claims in respect of all the participating Member States shall benefit from unitary effect in the participating Member States provided that its unitary effect has been registered in the Register for unitary patent protection.

A European patent granted with different sets of claims for different participating Member States shall not benefit from unitary effect.

2. A European patent with unitary effect shall have a unitary character. It shall provide uniform protection and shall have equal effect in all the participating Member States.

It may only be limited, transferred or revoked, or lapse, in respect of all the participating Member States.

It may be licensed in respect of the whole or part of the territories of the participating Member States.

3. The unitary effect of a European patent shall be deemed not to have arisen to the extent that the European patent has been revoked or limited.

Article 4
Date of effect

1. A European patent with unitary effect shall take effect in the participating Member States on the date of publication by the EPO of the mention of the grant of the European patent in the European Patent Bulletin.

2. The participating Member States shall take the necessary measures to ensure that, where the unitary effect of a European patent has been registered and extends to their territory, that European patent is deemed not to have taken effect as a national patent in their territory on the date of publication of the mention of the grant in the European Patent Bulletin.

Article 5
Uniform protection

1. The European patent with unitary effect shall confer on its proprietor the right to prevent any third party from committing acts against which that patent provides protection throughout the territories of the participating Member States in which it has unitary effect, subject to applicable limitations.

2. The scope of that right and its limitations shall be uniform in all participating Member States in which the patent has unitary effect.

3. The acts against which the patent provides protection referred to in paragraph 1 and the applicable limitations shall be those defined by the law applied to European patents with unitary effect in the participating Member State whose national law

is applicable to the European patent with unitary effect as an object of property in accordance with Article 7.

4. In its report referred to in Article 16(1), the Commission shall evaluate the functioning of the applicable limitations and shall, where necessary, make appropriate proposals.

Article 6
Exhaustion of the rights conferred by a European patent with unitary effect

The rights conferred by a European patent with unitary effect shall not extend to acts concerning a product covered by that patent which are carried out within the participating Member States in which that patent has unitary effect after that product has been placed on the market in the Union by, or with the consent of, the patent proprietor, unless there are legitimate grounds for the patent proprietor to oppose further commercialisation of the product.

Article 7
Treating a European patent with unitary effect as a national patent

1. A European patent with unitary effect as an object of property shall be treated in its entirety and in all the participating Member States as a national patent of the participating Member State in which that patent has unitary effect and in which, according to the European Patent Register:
(a) the applicant had his residence or principal place of business on the date of filing of the application for the European patent; or
(b) where point (a) does not apply, the applicant had a place of business on the date of filing of the application for the European patent.

2. Where two or more persons are entered in the European Patent Register as joint applicants, point (a) of paragraph 1 shall apply to the joint applicant indicated first. Where this is not possible, point (a) of paragraph 1 shall apply to the next joint applicant indicated in the order of entry. Where point (a) of paragraph 1 does not apply to any of the joint applicants, point (b) of paragraph 1 shall apply accordingly.

3. Where no applicant had his residence, principal place of business or place of business in a participating Member State in which that patent has unitary effect for the purposes of paragraphs 1 or 2, the European patent with unitary effect as an object of property shall be treated in its entirety and in all the participating Member States as a national patent of the State where the European Patent Organisation has its headquarters in accordance with Article 6(1) of the EPC.

4. The acquisition of a right may not be dependent on any entry in a national patent register.

Article 8
Licences of right

1. The proprietor of a European patent with unitary effect may file a statement with the EPO to the effect that the proprietor is prepared to allow any person to use the invention as a licensee in return for appropriate consideration.

2. A licence obtained under this Regulation shall be treated as a contractual licence.

Article 9
Administrative tasks in the framework of the European Patent Organisation

1. The participating Member States shall, within the meaning of Article 143 of the EPC, give the EPO the following tasks, to be carried out in accordance with the internal rules of the EPO:
(a) to administer requests for unitary effect by proprietors of European patents;
(b) to include the Register for unitary patent protection within the European Patent Register and to administer the Register for unitary patent protection;
(c) to receive and register statements on licensing referred to in Article 8, their withdrawal and licensing commitments undertaken by the proprietor of the European patent with unitary effect in international standardisation bodies;
(d) to publish the translations referred to in Article 6 of Regulation (EU) No 1260/2012 during the transitional period referred to in that Article;
(e) to collect and administer renewal fees for European patents with unitary effect, in respect of the years following the year in which the mention of the grant is published in the European Patent Bulletin; to collect and administer additional fees for late payment of renewal fees where such late payment is made within six months of the due date, as well as to distribute part of the collected renewal fees to the participating Member States;
(f) to administer the compensation scheme for the reimbursement of translation costs referred to in Article 5 of Regulation (EU) No 1260/2012;
(g) to ensure that a request for unitary effect by a proprietor of a European patent is submitted in the language of the proceedings as defined in Article 14(3) of the EPC no later than one month after the mention of the grant is published in the European Patent Bulletin; and
(h) to ensure that the unitary effect is indicated in the Register for unitary patent protection, where a request for unitary effect has been filed and, during the transitional period provided for in Article 6 of Regulation (EU) No 1260/2012, has been submitted together with the translations referred to in that Article, and that the EPO is informed of any limitations, licences, transfers or revocations of European patents with unitary effect.

2. The participating Member States shall ensure compliance with this Regulation in fulfilling their international obligations undertaken in the EPC and shall cooperate to that end. In their capacity as Contracting States to the EPC, the participating Member States shall ensure the governance and supervision of the activities related

to the tasks referred to in paragraph 1 of this Article and shall ensure the setting of the level of renewal fees in accordance with Article 12 of this Regulation and the setting of the share of distribution of the renewal fees in accordance with Article 13 of this Regulation.

To that end they shall set up a select committee of the Administrative Council of the European Patent Organisation (hereinafter 'Select Committee') within the meaning of Article 145 of the EPC.

The Select Committee shall consist of the representatives of the participating Member States and a representative of the Commission as an observer, as well as alternates who will represent them in their absence. The members of the Select Committee may be assisted by advisers or experts.

Decisions of the Select Committee shall be taken with due regard for the position of the Commission and in accordance with the rules laid down in Article 35(2) of the EPC.

3. The participating Member States shall ensure effective legal protection before a competent court of one or several participating Member States against the decisions of the EPO in carrying out the tasks referred to in paragraph 1.

Article 10
Principle on expenses

The expenses incurred by the EPO in carrying out the additional tasks given to it, within the meaning of Article 143 of the EPC, by the participating Member States shall be covered by the fees generated by the European patents with unitary effect.

Article 11
Renewal fees

1. Renewal fees for European patents with unitary effect and additional fees for their late payment shall be paid to the European Patent Organisation by the patent proprietor. Those fees shall be due in respect of the years following the year in which the mention of the grant of the European patent which benefits from unitary effect is published in the European Patent Bulletin.

2. A European patent with unitary effect shall lapse if a renewal fee and, where applicable, any additional fee have not been paid in due time.

3. Renewal fees which fall due after receipt of the statement referred to in Article 8(1) shall be reduced.

Article 12
Level of renewal fees

1. Renewal fees for European patents with unitary effect shall be:
(a) progressive throughout the term of the unitary patent protection;
(b) sufficient to cover all costs associated with the grant of the European patent and the administration of the unitary patent protection; and

(c) sufficient, together with the fees to be paid to the European Patent Organisation during the pre-grant stage, to ensure a balanced budget of the European Patent Organisation.

2. The level of the renewal fees shall be set, taking into account, among others, the situation of specific entities such as small and medium-sized enterprises, with the aim of:
(a) facilitating innovation and fostering the competitiveness of European businesses;
(b) reflecting the size of the market covered by the patent; and
(c) being similar to the level of the national renewal fees for an average European patent taking effect in the participating Member States at the time the level of the renewal fees is first set.

3. In order to attain the objectives set out in this Chapter, the level of renewal fees shall be set at a level that:
(a) is equivalent to the level of the renewal fee to be paid for the average geographical coverage of current European patents;
(b) reflects the renewal rate of current European patents; and
(c) reflects the number of requests for unitary effect.

Article 13
Distribution

1. The EPO shall retain 50 per cent of the renewal fees referred to in Article 11 paid for European patents with unitary effect. The remaining amount shall be distributed to the participating Member States in accordance with the share of distribution of the renewal fees set pursuant to Article 9(2).

2. In order to attain the objectives set out in this Chapter, the share of distribution of renewal fees among the participating Member States shall be based on the following fair, equitable and relevant criteria:
(a) the number of patent applications;
(b) the size of the market, while ensuring a minimum amount to be distributed to each participating Member State;
(c) compensation to the participating Member States which have:
  (i) an official language other than one of the official languages of the EPO;
  (ii) a disproportionately low level of patenting activity; and/or
  (iii) acquired membership of the European Patent Organisation relatively recently.

Article 14
Cooperation between the Commission and the EPO

The Commission shall establish a close cooperation through a working agreement with the EPO in the fields covered by this Regulation. This cooperation shall include regular exchanges of views on the functioning of the working agreement and, in particular, on the issue of renewal fees and their impact on the budget of the European Patent Organisation.

Article 15
Application of competition law and the law relating to unfair competition

This Regulation shall be without prejudice to the application of competition law and the law relating to unfair competition.

Article 16
Report on the operation of this Regulation

1. Not later than three years from the date on which the first European patent with unitary effect takes effect, and every five years thereafter, the Commission shall present to the European Parliament and the Council a report on the operation of this Regulation and, where necessary, make appropriate proposals for amending it.

2. The Commission shall regularly submit to the European Parliament and the Council reports on the functioning of the renewal fees referred to in Article 11, with particular emphasis on compliance with Article 12.

Article 17
Notification by the participating Member States

1. The participating Member States shall notify the Commission of the measures adopted in accordance with Article 9 by the date of application of this Regulation.

2. Each participating Member State shall notify the Commission of the measures adopted in accordance with Article 4(2) by the date of application of this Regulation or, in the case of a participating Member State in which the Unified Patent Court does not have exclusive jurisdiction with regard to European patents with unitary effect on the date of application of this Regulation, by the date from which the Unified Patent Court has such exclusive jurisdiction in that participating Member State.

Article 18
Entry into force and application

1. This Regulation shall enter into force on the twentieth day following that of its publication in the *Official Journal of the European Union.*

2. It shall apply from 1 January 2014 or the date of entry into force of the Agreement on a Unified Patent Court (the 'Agreement'), whichever is the later.

By way of derogation from Articles 3(1), 3(2) and 4(1), a European patent for which unitary effect is registered in the Register for unitary patent protection shall have unitary effect only in those participating Member States in which the Unified Patent Court has exclusive jurisdiction with regard to European patents with unitary effect at the date of registration.

3. Each participating Member State shall notify the Commission of its ratification of the Agreement at the time of deposit of its ratification instrument. The Commission shall publish in the *Official Journal of the European Union* the date of entry into force of the Agreement and a list of the Member States who have ratified the Agreement

at the date of entry into force. The Commission shall thereafter regularly update the list of the participating Member States which have ratified the Agreement and shall publish such updated list in the *Official Journal of the European Union*.

4. The participating Member States shall ensure that the measures referred to in Article 9 are in place by the date of application of this Regulation.

5. Each participating Member State shall ensure that the measures referred to in Article 4(2) are in place by the date of application of this Regulation or, in the case of a participating Member State in which the Unified Patent Court does not have exclusive jurisdiction with regard to European patents with unitary effect on the date of application of this Regulation, by the date from which the Unified Patent Court has such exclusive jurisdiction in that participating Member State.

6. Unitary patent protection may be requested for any European patent granted on or after the date of application of this Regulation.

This Regulation shall be binding in its entirety and directly applicable in the participating Member States in accordance with the Treaties.

Done at Brussels, 17 December 2012.

For the European Parliament The President

M. SCHULZ

For the Council

The President

A. D. MAVROYIANNIS

Annex 2 Regulation (EU) No 1260/2012

of 17 December 2012

implementing enhanced cooperation in the area of the creation of unitary patent protection with regard to the applicable translation arrangements

THE COUNCIL OF THE EUROPEAN UNION,

Having regard to the Treaty on the Functioning of the European Union, and in particular the second paragraph of Article 118 thereof,

Having regard to Council Decision 2011/167/EU of 10 March 2011 authorising enhanced cooperation in the area of the creation of unitary patent protection [1],

Having regard to the proposal from the European Commission,

After transmission of the draft legislative act to the national parliaments,

Having regard to the opinion of the European Parliament,

Acting in accordance with a special legislative procedure,

Whereas:

(1) Pursuant to Decision 2011/167/EU, Belgium, Bulgaria, the Czech Republic, Denmark, Germany, Estonia, Ireland, Greece, France, Cyprus, Latvia, Lithuania, Luxembourg, Hungary, Malta, the Netherlands, Austria, Poland, Portugal, Romania, Slovenia, Slovakia, Finland, Sweden and the United Kingdom (hereinafter "participating Member States") were authorised to establish enhanced cooperation between themselves in the area of the creation of unitary patent protection.

(2) Under Regulation (EU) No 1257/2012 of the European Parliament and of the Council of 17 December 2012 implementing enhanced cooperation in the area of the creation of unitary patent protection [2], certain European patents granted by the European Patent Office (hereinafter 'EPO') under the rules and procedures of the Convention on the Grant of European Patents of 5 October 1973, as revised on 17 December 1991 and on 29 November 2000 (hereinafter 'EPC') should, at the request of the patent proprietor, benefit from unitary effect in the participating Member States.

(3) Translation arrangements for European patents benefiting from unitary effect in the participating Member States (hereinafter 'European patent with unitary effect') should be established by means of a separate Regulation, in accordance with the second paragraph of Article 118 of the Treaty on the Functioning of the European Union (TFEU).

1 OJ L 76, 22.3.2011, p. 53.

2 See page 1 of this Official Journal.

(4) In accordance with Decision 2011/167/EU the translation arrangements for European patents with unitary effect should be simple and cost-effective. They should correspond to those provided for in the proposal for a Council Regulation on the translation arrangements for the European Union patent, presented by the Commission on 30 June 2010, combined with the elements of compromise proposed by the Presidency in November 2010 that had wide support in the Council.

(5) Such translation arrangements should ensure legal certainty and stimulate innovation and should, in particular, benefit small and medium-sized enterprises (SMEs). They should make access to the European patent with unitary effect and to the patent system as a whole easier, less costly and legally secure.

(6) Since the EPO is responsible for the grant of European patents, the translation arrangements for the European patent with unitary effect should be built on the current procedure in the EPO. Those arrangements should aim to achieve the necessary balance between the interests of economic operators and the public interest, in terms of the cost of proceedings and the availability of technical information.

(7) Without prejudice to the transitional arrangements, where the specification of a European patent with unitary effect has been published in accordance with Article 14(6) of the EPC, no further translations should be required. Article 14(6) of the EPC provides that the specification of a European patent is published in the language of the proceedings before the EPO and includes a translation of the claims into the other two official languages of the EPO.

(8) In the event of a dispute concerning a European patent with unitary effect, it is a legitimate requirement that the patent proprietor at the request of the alleged infringer should provide a full translation of the patent into an official language of either the participating Member State in which the alleged infringement took place or the Member State in which the alleged infringer is domiciled. The patent proprietor should also be required to provide, at the request of a court competent in the participating Member States for disputes concerning the European patent with unitary effect, a full translation of the patent into the language used in the proceedings of that court. Such translations should not be carried out by automated means and should be provided at the expense of the patent proprietor.

(9) In the event of a dispute concerning a claim for damages, the court hearing the dispute should take into consideration the fact that, before having been provided with a translation in his own language, the alleged infringer may have acted in good faith and may have not known or had reasonable grounds to know that he was infringing the patent. The competent court should assess the circumstances of the individual case and, inter alia, should take into account whether the alleged infringer is a SME operating only at local level, the language of the proceedings before the EPO and, during the transitional period, the translation submitted together with the request for unitary effect.

(10) In order to facilitate access to European patents with unitary effect, in particular for SMEs, applicants should be able to file their patent applications at the EPO in any official language of the Union. As a complementary measure, certain applicants obtaining European patents with unitary effect, having filed a European patent application in one of the official languages of the Union, which is not an official language of the EPO, and having their residence or principal place of business within a Member State, should receive additional reimbursements of the costs of translating from the language of the patent application into the language of the proceedings of the EPO, beyond what is currently in place at the EPO. Such reimbursements should be administered by the EPO in accordance with Article 9 of Regulation (EU) No 1257/2012.

(11) In order to promote the availability of patent information and the dissemination of technological knowledge, machine translations of patent applications and specifications into all official languages of the Union should be available as soon as possible. Machine translations are being developed by the EPO and are a very important tool in seeking to improve access to patent information and to widely disseminate technological knowledge. The timely availability of high quality machine translations of European patent applications and specifications into all official languages of the Union would benefit all users of the European patent system. Machine translations are a key feature of European Union policy. Such machine translations should serve for information purposes only and should not have any legal effect.

(12) During the transitional period, before a system of high quality machine translations into all official languages of the Union becomes available, a request for unitary effect as referred to in Article 9 of Regulation (EU) No 1257/2012 should be accompanied by a full translation of the specification of the patent into English where the language of the proceedings before the EPO is French or German, or into any official language of the Member States that is an official language of the Union where the language of the proceedings before the EPO is English. Those arrangements would ensure that during a transitional period all European patents with unitary effect are made available in English which is the language customarily used in the field of international technological research and publications. Furthermore, such arrangements would ensure that with respect to European patents with unitary effect, translations would be published in other official languages of the participating Member States. Such translations should not be carried out by automated means and their high quality should contribute to the training of translation engines by the EPO. They would also enhance the dissemination of patent information.

(13) The transitional period should terminate as soon as high quality machine translations into all official languages of the Union are available, subject to a regular and objective evaluation of the quality by an independent expert committee established by the participating Member States in the framework of the European Patent Organisation and composed of the representatives of the EPO and the users of the European patent system. Given the state of technological develop-

ment, the maximum period for the development of high quality machine translations cannot be considered to exceed 12 years. Consequently, the transitional period should lapse 12 years from the date of application of this Regulation, unless it has been decided to terminate that period earlier.

(14) Since the substantive provisions applicable to a European patent with unitary effect are governed by Regulation (EU) No 1257/2012 and are completed by the translation arrangements provided for in this Regulation, this Regulation should apply from the same date as Regulation (EU) No 1257/2012.

(15) This Regulation is without prejudice to the rules governing the languages of the Institutions of the Union established in accordance with Article 342 of the TFEU and to Council Regulation No 1 of 15 April 1958 determining the languages to be used by the European Economic Community ([3]). This Regulation is based on the linguistic regime of the EPO and should not be considered as creating a specific linguistic regime for the Union, or as creating a precedent for a limited language regime in any future legal instrument of the Union.

(16) Since the objective of this Regulation, namely the creation of a uniform and simple translation regime for European patents with unitary effect, cannot be sufficiently achieved by the Member States and can therefore, by reasons of the scale and effects of this Regulation, be better achieved at Union level, the Union may adopt measures, where appropriate by means of enhanced cooperation, in accordance with the principle of subsidiarity as set out in Article 5 of the Treaty on European Union. In accordance with the principle of proportionality, as set out in that Article, this Regulation does not go beyond what is necessary in order to achieve that objective,

HAS ADOPTED THIS REGULATION:

Article 1
Subject matter

This Regulation implements enhanced cooperation in the area of the creation of unitary patent protection authorised by Decision No 2011/167/EU with regard to the applicable translation arrangements.

Article 2
Definitions

For the purposes of this Regulation, the following definitions shall apply:

(a) 'European patent with unitary effect' means a European patent which benefits from unitary effect in the participating Member States by virtue of Regulation (EU) No 1257/2012;

(b) 'Language of the proceedings' means the language used in the proceedings before the EPO as defined in Article 14(3) of the Convention on the Grant of European

3 OJ 17, 6.10.1958, p. 385/58.

Patents of 5 October 1973, as revised on 17 December 1991 and on 29 November 2000 (hereinafter 'EPC').

Article 3
Translation arrangements for the European patent with unitary effect

1. Without prejudice to Articles 4 and 6 of this Regulation, where the specification of a European patent, which benefits from unitary effect has been published in accordance with Article 14(6) of the EPC, no further translations shall be required.

2. A request for unitary effect as referred to in Article 9 of Regulation (EU) No 1257/2012 shall be submitted in the language of the proceedings.

Article 4
Translation in the event of a dispute

1. In the event of a dispute relating to an alleged infringement of a European patent with unitary effect, the patent proprietor shall provide at the request and the choice of an alleged infringer, a full translation of the European patent with unitary effect into an official language of either the participating Member State in which the alleged infringement took place or the Member State in which the alleged infringer is domiciled.

2. In the event of a dispute relating to a European patent with unitary effect, the patent proprietor shall provide in the course of legal proceedings, at the request of a court competent in the participating Member States for disputes concerning European patents with unitary effect, a full translation of the patent into the language used in the proceedings of that court.

3. The cost of the translations referred to in paragraphs 1 and 2 shall be borne by the patent proprietor.

4. In the event of a dispute concerning a claim for damages, the court hearing the dispute shall assess and take into consideration, in particular where the alleged infringer is a SME, a natural person or a non-profit organisation, a university or a public research organisation, whether the alleged infringer acted without knowing or without reasonable grounds for knowing, that he was infringing the European patent with unitary effect before having been provided with the translation referred to in paragraph 1.

Article 5
Administration of a compensation scheme

1. Given the fact that European patent applications may be filed in any language under Article 14(2) of the EPC, the participating Member States shall in accordance with Article 9 of Regulation (EU) No 1257/2012, give, within the meaning of Article 143 of the EPC, the EPO the task of administering a compensation scheme for the reimbursement of all translation costs up to a ceiling, for applicants filing patent applications at the EPO in one of the official languages of the Union that is not an official language of the EPO.

2. The compensation scheme referred to in paragraph 1 shall be funded through the fees referred to in Article 11 of Regulation (EU) No 1257/2012 and shall be available only for SMEs, natural persons, non-profit organisations, universities and public research organisations having their residence or principal place of business within a Member State.

Article 6
Transitional measures

1. During a transitional period starting on the date of application of this Regulation a request for unitary effect as referred to in Article 9 of Regulation (EU) No 1257/2012 shall be submitted together with the following:
(a) where the language of the proceedings is French or German, a full translation of the specification of the European patent into English; or
(b) where the language of the proceedings is English, a full translation of the specification of the European patent into any other official language of the Union.

2. In accordance with Article 9 of Regulation (EU) No 1257/2012, the participating Member States shall give, within the meaning of Article 143 of the EPC, the EPO the task of publishing the translations referred to in paragraph 1 of this Article as soon as possible after the date of the submission of a request for unitary effect as referred to in Article 9 of Regulation (EU) No 1257/2012. The text of such translations shall have no legal effect and shall be for information purposes only.

3. Six years after the date of application of this Regulation and every two years thereafter, an independent expert committee shall carry out an objective evaluation of the availability of high quality machine translations of patent applications and specifications into all the official languages of the Union as developed by the EPO. This expert committee shall be established by the participating Member States in the framework of the European Patent Organisation and shall be composed of representatives of the EPO and of the non-governmental organisations representing users of the European patent system invited by the Administrative Council of the European Patent Organisation as observers in accordance with Article 30(3) of the EPC.

4. On the basis of the first of the evaluations referred to in paragraph 3 of this Article and every two years thereafter on the basis of the subsequent evaluations, the Commission shall present a report to the Council and, if appropriate, make proposals for terminating the transitional period.

5. If the transitional period is not terminated on the basis of a proposal of the Commission, it shall lapse 12 years from the date of application of this Regulation.

Article 7
Entry into force

1. This Regulation shall enter into force on the twentieth day following that of its publication in the *Official Journal of the European Union*.

2. It shall apply from 1 January 2014 or the date of entry into force of the Agreement on a Unified Patent Court, whichever is the later.

This Regulation shall be binding in its entirety and directly applicable in the participating Member States in accordance with the Treaties.

Done at Brussels, 17 December 2012.

For the Council

The President

S. ALETRARIS

Annex 3 Agreement on a Unified Patent Court (2013/C 175/01)

Agreement

on a Unified Patent Court

(2013/C 175/01)

THE CONTRACTING MEMBER STATES,

CONSIDERING that cooperation amongst the Member States of the European Union in the field of patents contributes significantly to the integration process in Europe, in particular to the establishment of an internal market within the European Union characterised by the free movement of goods and services and the creation of a system ensuring that competition in the internal market is not distorted;

CONSIDERING that the fragmented market for patents and the significant variations between national court systems are detrimental for innovation, in particular for small and medium-sized enterprises which have difficulties to enforce their patents and to defend themselves against unfounded claims and claims relating to patents which should be revoked;

CONSIDERING that the European Patent Convention ('EPC') which has been ratified by all Member States of the European Union provides for a single procedure for granting European patents by the European Patent Office;

CONSIDERING that by virtue of Regulation (EU) No 1257/2012 ([1]), patent proprietors can request unitary effect of their European patents so as to obtain unitary patent protection in the Member States of the European Union participating in the enhanced cooperation;

WISHING to improve the enforcement of patents and the defence against unfounded claims and patents which should be revoked and to enhance legal certainty by setting up a Unified Patent Court for litigation relating to the infringement and validity of patents;

CONSIDERING that the Unified Patent Court should be devised to ensure expeditious and high quality decisions, striking a fair balance between the interests of right holders and other parties and taking into account the need for proportionality and flexibility;

CONSIDERING that the Unified Patent Court should be a court common to the Contracting Member States and thus part of their judicial system, with exclusive

1 Regulation (EU) No 1257/2012 of the European Parliament and of the Council of 17 December 2012 implementing enhanced cooperation in the area of the creation of unitary patent protection (OJ L 361, 31.12.2012, p. 1) including any subsequent amendments.

competence in respect of European patents with unitary effect and European patents granted under the provisions of the EPC;

CONSIDERING that the Court of Justice of the European Union is to ensure the uniformity of the Union legal order and the primacy of European Union law;

RECALLING the obligations of the Contracting Member States under the Treaty on European Union (TEU) and the Treaty on the Functioning of the European Union (TFEU), including the obligation of sincere cooperation as set out in Article 4(3) TEU and the obligation to ensure through the Unified Patent Court the full application of, and respect for, Union law in their respective territories and the judicial protection of an individual's rights under that law;

CONSIDERING that, as any national court, the Unified Patent Court must respect and apply Union law and, in collaboration with the Court of Justice of the European Union as guardian of Union law, ensure its correct application and uniform interpretation; the Unified Patent Court must in particular cooperate with the Court of Justice of the European Union in properly interpreting Union law by relying on the latter's case law and by requesting preliminary rulings in accordance with Article 267 TFEU;

CONSIDERING that the Contracting Member States should, in line with the case law of the Court of Justice of the European Union on non-contractual liability, be liable for damages caused by infringements of Union law by the Unified Patent Court, including the failure to request preliminary rulings from the Court of Justice of the European Union;

CONSIDERING that infringements of Union law by the Unified Patent Court, including the failure to request preliminary rulings from the Court of Justice of the European Union, are directly attributable to the Contracting Member States and infringement proceedings can therefore be brought under Article 258, 259 and 260 TFEU against any Contracting Member State to ensure the respect of the primacy and proper application of Union law;

RECALLING the primacy of Union law, which includes the TEU, the TFEU, the Charter of Fundamental Rights of the European Union, the general principles of Union law as developed by the Court of Justice of the European Union, and in particular the right to an effective remedy before a tribunal and a fair and public hearing within a reasonable time by an independent and impartial tribunal, the case law of the Court of Justice of the European Union and secondary Union law;

CONSIDERING that this Agreement should be open to accession by any Member State of the European Union; Member States which have decided not to participate in the enhanced cooperation in the area of the creation of unitary patent protection may participate in this Agreement in respect of European patents granted for their respective territory;

CONSIDERING that this Agreement should enter into force on 1 January 2014 or on the first day of the fourth month after the 13th deposit, provided that the Contracting Member States that will have deposited their instruments of ratification or accession include the three States in which the highest number of European patents was in force in the year preceding the year in which the signature of the Agreement takes place, or on the first day of the fourth month after the date of entry into force of the amendments to Regulation (EU) No 1215/2012 [2] concerning its relationship with this Agreement, whichever is the latest,

HAVE AGREED AS FOLLOWS:

Article 1
Unified Patent Court

A Unified Patent Court for the settlement of disputes relating to European patents and European patents with unitary effect is hereby established.

The Unified Patent Court shall be a court common to the Contracting Member States and thus subject to the same obligations under Union law as any national court of the Contracting Member States.

Article 2
Definitions

For the purposes of this Agreement:
(a) 'Court' means the Unified Patent Court created by this Agreement.
(b) 'Member State' means a Member State of the European Union.
(c) 'Contracting Member State' means a Member State party to this Agreement.
(d) 'EPC' means the Convention on the Grant of European Patents of 5 October 1973, including any subsequent amendments.
(e) 'European patent' means a patent granted under the provisions of the EPC, which does not benefit from unitary effect by virtue of Regulation (EU) No 1257/2012.
(f) 'European patent with unitary effect' means a patent granted under the provisions of the EPC which benefits from unitary effect by virtue of Regulation (EU) No 1257/2012.
(g) 'Patent' means a European patent and/or a European patent with unitary effect.
(h) 'Supplementary protection certificate' means a supplementary protection certificate granted under Regulation (EC) No 469/2009 [3] or under Regulation (EC) No 1610/96 [4].

2 Regulation (EU) No 1215/2012 of the European Parliament and of the Council of 12 December 2012 on jurisdiction and the recognition and enforcement of judgments in civil and commercial matters (OJ L 351, 20.12.2012, p. 1) including any subsequent amendments.

3 Regulation (EC) No 469/2009 of the European Parliament and of the Council of 6 May 2009 concerning the supplementary protection certificate for medicinal products (OJ L 152, 16.6.2009, p. 1) including any subsequent amendments.

4 Regulation (EC) No 1610/96 of the European Parliament and of the Council of 23 July 1996 concerning the creation of a supplementary certificate for plant protection products (OJ L 198, 8.8.1996, p. 30) including any subsequent amendments.

(i) 'Statute' means the Statute of the Court as set out in Annex I, which shall be an integral part of this Agreement.
(j) Rules of Procedure' means the Rules of Procedure of the Court, as established in accordance with Article 41.

Article 3
Scope of application

This Agreement shall apply to any:
(a) European patent with unitary effect;
(b) supplementary protection certificate issued for a product protected by a patent;
(c) European patent which has not yet lapsed at the date of entry into force of this Agreement or was granted after that date, without prejudice to Article 83; and
(d) European patent application which is pending at the date of entry into force of this Agreement or which is filed after that date, without prejudice to Article 83.

Article 4
Legal status

1. The Court shall have legal personality in each Contracting Member State and shall enjoy the most extensive legal capacity accorded to legal persons under the national law of that State.

2. The Court shall be represented by the President of the Court of Appeal who shall be elected in accordance with the Statute.

Article 5
Liability

1. The contractual liability of the Court shall be governed by the law applicable to the contract in question in accordance with Regulation (EC) No 593/2008 ([5]) (Rome I), where applicable, or failing that in accordance with the law of the Member State of the court seized.

2. The non-contractual liability of the Court in respect of any damage caused by it or its staff in the performance of their duties, to the extent that it is not a civil and commercial matter within the meaning of Regulation (EC) No 864/2007 ([6]) (Rome II), shall be governed by the law of the Contracting Member State in which the damage occurred. This provision is without prejudice to the application of Article 22.

---

5 Regulation (EC) No 593/2008 of the European Parliament and of the Council of 17 June 2008 on the law applicable to contractual obligations (Rome I) (OJ L 177, 4.7.2008, p. 6) including any subsequent amendments.

6 Regulation (EC) No 864/2007 of the European Parliament and of the Council of 11 July 2007 on the law applicable to non-contractual obligations (Rome II) (OJ L 199, 31.7.2007, p. 40) including any subsequent amendments.

3. The court with jurisdiction to settle disputes under paragraph 2 shall be a court of the Contracting Member State in which the damage occurred.

Article 6
The Court

1. The Court shall comprise a Court of First Instance, a Court of Appeal and a Registry.

2. The Court shall perform the functions assigned to it by this Agreement.

Article 7
The Court of First Instance

1. The Court of First Instance shall comprise a central division as well as local and regional divisions.

2. The central division shall have its seat in Paris, with sections in London and Munich. The cases before the central division shall be distributed in accordance with Annex II, which shall form an integral part of this Agreement.

3. A local division shall be set up in a Contracting Member State upon its request in accordance with the Statute. A Contracting Member State hosting a local division shall designate its seat.

4. An additional local division shall be set up in a Contracting Member State upon its request for every one hundred patent cases per calendar year that have been commenced in that Contracting Member State during three successive years prior to or subsequent to the date of entry into force of this Agreement. The number of local divisions in one Contracting Member State shall not exceed four.

5. A regional division shall be set up for two or more Contracting Member States, upon their request in accordance with the Statute. Such Contracting Member States shall designate the seat of the division concerned. The regional division may hear cases in multiple locations.

Article 8
Composition of the panels of the Court of First Instance

1. Any panel of the Court of First Instance shall have a multinational composition. Without prejudice to paragraph 5 of this Article and to Article 33(3)(a), it shall sit in a composition of three judges.

2. Any panel of a local division in a Contracting Member State where, during a period of three successive years prior or subsequent to the entry into force of this Agreement, less than fifty patent cases per calendar year on average have been commenced shall sit in a composition of one legally qualified judge who is a national of the Contracting Member State hosting the local division concerned and two legally qualified judges who are not nationals of the Contracting Member State concerned and are allocated from the Pool of Judges in accordance with Article 18(3) on a case by case basis.

3. Notwithstanding paragraph 2, any panel of a local division in a Contracting Member State where, during a period of three successive years prior or subsequent to the entry into force of this Agreement, fifty or more patent cases per calendar year on average have been commenced, shall sit in a composition of two legally qualified judges who are nationals of the Contracting Member State hosting the local division concerned and one legally qualified judge who is not a national of the Contracting Member State concerned and is allocated from the Pool of Judges in accordance with Article 18(3). Such third judge shall serve at the local division on a long term basis, where this is necessary for the efficient functioning of divisions with a high work load.

4. Any panel of a regional division shall sit in a composition of two legally qualified judges chosen from a regional list of judges, who shall be nationals of the Contracting Member States concerned, and one legally qualified judge who shall not be a national of the Contracting Member States concerned and who shall be allocated from the Pool of Judges in accordance with Article 18(3).

5. Upon request by one of the parties, any panel of a local or regional division shall request the President of the Court of First Instance to allocate from the Pool of Judges in accordance with Article 18(3) an additional technically qualified judge with qualifications and experience in the field of technology concerned. Moreover, any panel of a local or regional division may, after having heard the parties, submit such request on its own initiative, where it deems this appropriate. In cases where such a technically qualified judge is allocated, no further technically qualified judge may be allocated under Article 33(3)(a).

6. Any panel of the central division shall sit in a composition of two legally qualified judges who are nationals of different Contracting Member States and one technically qualified judge allocated from the Pool of Judges in accordance with Article 18(3) with qualifications and experience in the field of technology concerned. However, any panel of the central division dealing with actions under Article 32(1)(i) shall sit in a composition of three legally qualified judges who are nationals of different Contracting Member States.

7. Notwithstanding paragraphs 1 to 6 and in accordance with the Rules of Procedure, parties may agree to have their case heard by a single legally qualified judge.

8. Any panel of the Court of First Instance shall be chaired by a legally qualified judge.

Article 9
The Court of Appeal

1. Any panel of the Court of Appeal shall sit in a multinational composition of five judges. It shall sit in a composition of three legally qualified judges who are nationals of different Contracting Member States and two technically qualified judges with qualifications and experience in the field of technology concerned. Those technically qualified judges shall be assigned to the panel by the President of the Court of Appeal from the pool of judges in accordance with Article 18.

2. Notwithstanding paragraph 1, a panel dealing with actions under Article 32(1) (i) shall sit in a composition of three legally qualified judges who are nationals of different Contracting Member States.

3. Any panel of the Court of Appeal shall be chaired by a legally qualified judge.

4. The panels of the Court of Appeal shall be set up in accordance with the Statute.

5. The Court of Appeal shall have its seat in Luxembourg.

Article 10
The Registry

1. A Registry shall be set up at the seat of the Court of Appeal. It shall be managed by the Registrar and perform the functions assigned to it in accordance with the Statute. Subject to conditions set out in this Agreement and the Rules of Procedure, the register kept by the Registry shall be public.

2. Sub-registries shall be set up at all divisions of the Court of First Instance.

3. The Registry shall keep records of all cases before the Court. Upon filing, the sub-registry concerned shall notify every case to the Registry.

4. The Court shall appoint the Registrar in accordance with Article 22 of the Statute and lay down the rules governing the Registrar's service.

Article 11
Committees

An Administrative Committee, a Budget Committee and an Advisory Committee shall be set up in order to ensure the effective implementation and operation of this Agreement. They shall in particular exercise the duties foreseen by this Agreement and the Statute.

Article 12
The Administrative Committee

1. The Administrative Committee shall be composed of one representative of each Contracting Member State. The European Commission shall be represented at the meetings of the Administrative Committee as observer.

2. Each Contracting Member State shall have one vote.

3. The Administrative Committee shall adopt its decisions by a majority of three quarters of the Contracting Member States represented and voting, except where this Agreement or the Statute provides otherwise.

4. The Administrative Committee shall adopt its rules of procedure.

5. The Administrative Committee shall elect a chairperson from among its members for a term of three years. That term shall be renewable.

Article 13
The Budget Committee

1. The Budget Committee shall be composed of one representative of each Contracting Member State.

2. Each Contracting Member State shall have one vote.

3. The Budget Committee shall take its decisions by a simple majority of the representatives of the Contracting Member States. However, a majority of three-quarters of the representatives of Contracting Member States shall be required for the adoption of the budget.

4. The Budget Committee shall adopt its rules of procedure.

5. The Budget Committee shall elect a chairperson from among its members for a term of three years. That term shall be renewable.

Article 14
The Advisory Committee

1. The Advisory Committee shall:
(a) assist the Administrative Committee in the preparation of the appointment of judges of the Court;
(b) make proposals to the Presidium referred to in Article 15 of the Statute on the guidelines for the training framework for judges referred to in Article 19; and
(c) deliver opinions to the Administrative Committee concerning the requirements for qualifications referred to in Article 48(2).

2. The Advisory Committee shall comprise patent judges and practitioners in patent law and patent litigation with the highest recognised competence. They shall be appointed, in accordance with the procedure laid down in the Statute, for a term of six years. That term shall be renewable.

3. The composition of the Advisory Committee shall ensure a broad range of relevant expertise and the representation of each of the Contracting Member States. The members of the Advisory Committee shall be completely independent in the performance of their duties and shall not be bound by any instructions.

4. The Advisory Committee shall adopt its rules of procedure.

5. The Advisory Committee shall elect a chairperson from among its members for a term of three years. That term shall be renewable.

Article 15
Eligibility criteria for the appointment of judges

1. The Court shall comprise both legally qualified judges and technically qualified judges. Judges shall ensure the highest standards of competence and shall have proven experience in the field of patent litigation.

2. Legally qualified judges shall possess the qualifications required for appointment to judicial offices in a Contracting Member State.

3. Technically qualified judges shall have a university degree and proven expertise in a field of technology. They shall also have proven knowledge of civil law and procedure relevant in patent litigation.

Article 16
Appointment procedure

1. The Advisory Committee shall establish a list of the most suitable candidates to be appointed as judges of the Court, in accordance with the Statute.

2. On the basis of that list, the Administrative Committee shall appoint the judges of the Court acting by common accord.

3. The implementing provisions for the appointment of judges are set out in the Statute.

Article 17
Judicial independence and impartiality

1. The Court, its judges and the Registrar shall enjoy judicial independence. In the performance of their duties, the judges shall not be bound by any instructions.

2. Legally qualified judges, as well as technically qualified judges who are full-time judges of the Court, may not engage in any other occupation, whether gainful or not, unless an exception is granted by the Administrative Committee.

3. Notwithstanding paragraph 2, the exercise of the office of judges shall not exclude the exercise of other judicial functions at national level.

4. The exercise of the office of technically qualified judges who are part-time judges of the Court shall not exclude the exercise of other functions provided there is no conflict of interest.

5. In case of a conflict of interest, the judge concerned shall not take part in proceedings. Rules governing conflicts of interest are set out in the Statute.

Article 18
Pool of Judges

1. A Pool of Judges shall be established in accordance with the Statute.

2. The Pool of Judges shall be composed of all legally qualified judges and technically qualified judges from the Court of First Instance who are full-time or part-time judges of the Court. The Pool of Judges shall include at least one technically qualified judge per field of technology with the relevant qualifications and experience. The technically qualified judges from the Pool of Judges shall also be available to the Court of Appeal.

3. Where so provided by this Agreement or the Statute, the judges from the Pool of Judges shall be allocated to the division concerned by the President of the Court

of First Instance. The allocation of judges shall be based on their legal or technical expertise, linguistic skills and relevant experience. The allocation of judges shall guarantee the same high quality of work and the same high level of legal and technical expertise in all panels of the Court of First Instance.

Article 19
Training framework

1. A training framework for judges, the details of which are set out in the Statute, shall be set up in order to improve and increase available patent litigation expertise and to ensure a broad geographic distribution of such specific knowledge and experience. The facilities for that framework shall be situated in Budapest.

2. The training framework shall in particular focus on:
(a) internships in national patent courts or divisions of the Court of First Instance hearing a substantial number of patent litigation cases;
(b) improvement of linguistic skills;
(c) technical aspects of patent law;
(d) the dissemination of knowledge and experience in civil procedure for technically qualified judges;
(e) the preparation of candidate-judges.

3. The training framework shall provide for continuous training. Regular meetings shall be organised between all judges of the Court in order to discuss developments in patent law and to ensure the consistency of the Court's case law.

Article 20
Primacy of and respect for Union law

The Court shall apply Union law in its entirety and shall respect its primacy.

Article 21
Requests for preliminary rulings

As a court common to the Contracting Member States and as part of their judicial system, the Court shall cooperate with the Court of Justice of the European Union to ensure the correct application and uniform interpretation of Union law, as any national court, in accordance with Article 267 TFEU in particular. Decisions of the Court of Justice of the European Union shall be binding on the Court.

Article 22
Liability for damage caused by infringements of Union law

1. The Contracting Member States are jointly and severally liable for damage resulting from an infringement of Union law by the Court of Appeal, in accordance with Union law concerning non-contractual liability of Member States for damage caused by their national courts breaching Union law.

2. An action for such damages shall be brought against the Contracting Member State where the claimant has its residence or principal place of business or, in the absence of residence or principal place of business, place of business, before the competent authority of that Contracting Member State. Where the claimant does not have its residence, or principal place of business or, in the absence of residence or principal place of business, place of business in a Contracting Member State, the claimant may bring such an action against the Contracting Member State where the Court of Appeal has its seat, before the competent authority of that Contracting Member State.

The competent authority shall apply the *lex fori*, with the exception of its private international law, to all questions not regulated by Union law or by this Agreement. The claimant shall be entitled to obtain the entire amount of damages awarded by the competent authority from the Contracting Member State against which the action was brought.

3. The Contracting Member State that has paid damages is entitled to obtain proportional contribution, established in accordance with the method laid down in Article 37(3) and (4), from the other Contracting Member States. The detailed rules governing the Contracting Member States' contribution under this paragraph shall be determined by the Administrative Committee.

Article 23
Responsibility of the Contracting Member States

Actions of the Court are directly attributable to each Contracting Member State individually, including for the purposes of Articles 258, 259 and 260 TFEU, and to all Contracting Member States collectively.

Article 24
Sources of law

1. In full compliance with Article 20, when hearing a case brought before it under this Agreement, the Court shall base its decisions on:
(a) Union law, including Regulation (EU) No 1257/2012 and Regulation (EU) No 1260/2012 [7];
(b) this Agreement;
(c) the EPC;
(d) other international agreements applicable to patents and binding on all the Contracting Member States; and
(e) national law.

7 Council Regulation (EU) No 1260/2012 of 17 December 2012 implementing enhanced cooperation in the area of the creation of unitary patent protection with regard to the applicable translation arrangements (OJ L 361, 31.12.2012, p. 89) including any subsequent amendments.

2. To the extent that the Court shall base its decisions on national law, including where relevant the law of non-contracting States, the applicable law shall be determined:
(a) by directly applicable provisions of Union law containing private international law rules, or
(b) in the absence of directly applicable provisions of Union law or where the latter do not apply, by international instruments containing private international law rules; or
(c) in the absence of provisions referred to in points (a) and (b), by national provisions on private international law as determined by the Court.

3. The law of non-contracting States shall apply when designated by application of the rules referred to in paragraph 2, in particular in relation to Articles 25 to 28, 54, 55, 64, 68 and 72.

Article 25
Right to prevent the direct use of the invention

A patent shall confer on its proprietor the right to prevent any third party not having the proprietor's consent from the following:
(a) making, offering, placing on the market or using a product which is the subject-matter of the patent, or importing or storing the product for those purposes;
(b) using a process which is the subject-matter of the patent or, where the third party knows, or should have known, that the use of the process is prohibited without the consent of the patent proprietor, offering the process for use within the territory of the Contracting Member States in which that patent has effect;
(c) offering, placing on the market, using, or importing or storing for those purposes a product obtained directly by a process which is the subject-matter of the patent.

Article 26
Right to prevent the indirect use of the invention

1. A patent shall confer on its proprietor the right to prevent any third party not having the proprietor's consent from supplying or offering to supply, within the territory of the Contracting Member States in which that patent has effect, any person other than a party entitled to exploit the patented invention, with means, relating to an essential element of that invention, for putting it into effect therein, when the third party knows, or should have known, that those means are suitable and intended for putting that invention into effect.

2. Paragraph 1 shall not apply when the means are staple commercial products, except where the third party induces the person supplied to perform any of the acts prohibited by Article 25.

3. Persons performing the acts referred to in Article 27(a) to (e) shall not be considered to be parties entitled to exploit the invention within the meaning of paragraph 1.

Article 27
Limitations of the effects of a patent

The rights conferred by a patent shall not extend to any of the following:

(a) acts done privately and for non-commercial purposes;

(b) acts done for experimental purposes relating to the subject-matter of the patented invention;

(c) the use of biological material for the purpose of breeding, or discovering and developing other plant varieties;

(d) the acts allowed pursuant to Article 13(6) of Directive 2001/82/EC ([8]) or Article 10(6) of Directive 2001/83/EC ([9]) in respect of any patent covering the product within the meaning of either of those Directives;

(e) the extemporaneous preparation by a pharmacy, for individual cases, of a medicine in accordance with a medical prescription or acts concerning the medicine so prepared;

(f) the use of the patented invention on board vessels of countries of the International Union for the Protection of Industrial Property (Paris Union) or members of the World Trade Organisation, other than those Contracting Member States in which that patent has effect, in the body of such vessel, in the machinery, tackle, gear and other accessories, when such vessels temporarily or accidentally enter the waters of a Contracting Member State in which that patent has effect, provided that the invention is used there exclusively for the needs of the vessel;

(g) the use of the patented invention in the construction or operation of aircraft or land vehicles or other means of transport of countries of the International Union for the Protection of Industrial Property (Paris Union) or members of the World Trade Organisation, other than those Contracting Member States in which that patent has effect, or of accessories to such aircraft or land vehicles, when these temporarily or accidentally enter the territory of a Contracting Member State in which that patent has effect;

(h) the acts specified in Article 27 of the Convention on International Civil Aviation of 7 December 1944 ([10]), where these acts concern the aircraft of a country party to that Convention other than a Contracting Member State in which that patent has effect;

(i) the use by a farmer of the product of his harvest for propagation or multiplication by him on his own holding, provided that the plant propagating material was sold or otherwise commercialised to the farmer by or with the consent of the patent

---

8 Directive 2001/82/EC of the European Parliament and of the Council of 6 November 2001 on the Community code relating to veterinary medicinal products (OJ L 311, 28.11.2001, p. 1) including any subsequent amendments.

9 Directive 2001/83/EC of the European Parliament and of the Council of 6 November 2001 on the Community code relating to medicinal products for human use (OJ L 311, 28.11.2001, p. 67) including any subsequent amendments.

10 International Civil Aviation Organization (ICAO), 'Chicago Convention', Document 7300/9 (9th edition, 2006).

proprietor for agricultural use. The extent and the conditions for this use correspond to those under Article 14 of Regulation (EC) No 2100/94 ([11]);
(j) the use by a farmer of protected livestock for an agricultural purpose, provided that the breeding stock or other animal reproductive material were sold or otherwise commercialised to the farmer by or with the consent of the patent proprietor. Such use includes making the animal or other animal reproductive material available for the purposes of pursuing the farmer's agricultural activity, but not the sale thereof within the framework of, or for the purpose of, a commercial reproductive activity;
(k) the acts and the use of the obtained information as allowed under Articles 5 and 6 of Directive 2009/24/EC ([12]), in particular, by its provisions on decompilation and interoperability; and
(l) the acts allowed pursuant to Article 10 of Directive 98/44/EC ([13]).

Article 28
Right based on prior use of the invention

Any person, who, if a national patent had been granted in respect of an invention, would have had, in a Contracting Member State, a right based on prior use of that invention or a right of personal possession of that invention, shall enjoy, in that Contracting Member State, the same rights in respect of a patent for the same invention.

Article 29
Exhaustion of the rights conferred by a European patent

The rights conferred by a European patent shall not extend to acts concerning a product covered by that patent after that product has been placed on the market in the European Union by, or with the consent of, the patent proprietor, unless there are legitimate grounds for the patent proprietor to oppose further commercialisation of the product.

Article 30
Effects of supplementary protection certificates

A supplementary protection certificate shall confer the same rights as conferred by the patent and shall be subject to the same limitations and the same obligations.

---

11 Council Regulation (EC) No 2100/94 of 27 July 1994 on Community plant variety rights (OJ L 227, 1.9.1994, p. 1) including any subsequent amendments.
12 Directive 2009/24/EC of the European Parliament and of the Council of 23 April 2009 on the legal protection of computer programs (OJ L 111, 5.5.2009, p. 16) including any subsequent amendments.
13 Directive 98/44/EC of the European Parliament and of the Council of 6 July 1998 on the legal protection of biotechnological inventions (OJ L 213, 30.7.1998, p. 13) including any subsequent amendments.

Article 31
International jurisdiction

The international jurisdiction of the Court shall be established in accordance with Regulation (EU) No 1215/2012 or, where applicable, on the basis of the Convention on jurisdiction and the recognition and enforcement of judgments in civil and commercial matters (Lugano Convention) ([14]).

Article 32
Competence of the Court

1. The Court shall have exclusive competence in respect of:
(a) actions for actual or threatened infringements of patents and supplementary protection certificates and related defences, including counterclaims concerning licences;
(b) actions for declarations of non-infringement of patents and supplementary protection certificates;
(c) actions for provisional and protective measures and injunctions;
(d) actions for revocation of patents and for declaration of invalidity of supplementary protection certificates;
(e) counterclaims for revocation of patents and for declaration of invalidity of supplementary protection certificates;
(f) actions for damages or compensation derived from the provisional protection conferred by a published European patent application;
(g) actions relating to the use of the invention prior to the granting of the patent or to the right based on prior use of the invention;
(h) actions for compensation for licences on the basis of Article 8 of Regulation (EU) No 1257/2012; and
(i) actions concerning decisions of the European Patent Office in carrying out the tasks referred to in Article 9 of Regulation (EU) No 1257/2012.

2. The national courts of the Contracting Member States shall remain competent for actions relating to patents and supplementary protection certificates which do not come within the exclusive competence of the Court.

Article 33
Competence of the divisions of the Court of First Instance

1. Without prejudice to paragraph 7 of this Article, actions referred to in Article 32(1) (a), (c), (f) and (g) shall be brought before:
(a) the local division hosted by the Contracting Member State where the actual or threatened infringement has occurred or may occur, or the regional division in which that Contracting Member State participates; or

14 Convention on jurisdiction and the recognition and enforcement of judgments in civil and commercial matters, done at Lugano on 30 October 2007, including any subsequent amendments.

(b) the local division hosted by the Contracting Member State where the defendant or, in the case of multiple defendants, one of the defendants has its residence, or principal place of business, or in the absence of residence or principal place of business, its place of business, or the regional division in which that Contracting Member State participates. An action may be brought against multiple defendants only where the defendants have a commercial relationship and where the action relates to the same alleged infringement.

Actions referred to in Article 32(1)(h) shall be brought before the local or regional division in accordance with point (b) of the first subparagraph.

Actions against defendants having their residence, or principal place of business or, in the absence of residence or principal place of business, their place of business, outside the territory of the Contracting Member States shall be brought before the local or regional division in accordance with point (a) of the first subparagraph or before the central division.

If the Contracting Member State concerned does not host a local division and does not participate in a regional division, actions shall be brought before the central division.

2. If an action referred to in Article 32(1)(a), (c), (f), (g) or (h) is pending before a division of the Court of First Instance, any action referred to in Article 32(1)(a), (c), (f), (g) or (h) between the same parties on the same patent may not be brought before any other division.

If an action referred to in Article 32(1)(a) is pending before a regional division and the infringement has occurred in the territories of three or more regional divisions, the regional division concerned shall, at the request of the defendant, refer the case to the central division.

In case an action between the same parties on the same patent is brought before several different divisions, the division first seized shall be competent for the whole case and any division seized later shall declare the action inadmissible in accordance with the Rules of Procedure.

3. A counterclaim for revocation as referred to in Article 32(1)(e) may be brought in the case of an action for infringement as referred to in Article 32(1)(a). The local or regional division concerned shall, after having heard the parties, have the discretion either to:

(a) proceed with both the action for infringement and with the counterclaim for revocation and request the President of the Court of First Instance to allocate from the Pool of Judges in accordance with Article 18(3) a technically qualified judge with qualifications and experience in the field of technology concerned.
(b) refer the counterclaim for revocation for decision to the central division and suspend or proceed with the action for infringement; or
(c) with the agreement of the parties, refer the case for decision to the central division.

4. Actions referred to in Article 32(1)(b) and (d) shall be brought before the central division. If, however, an action for infringement as referred to in Article 32(1)

(a) between the same parties relating to the same patent has been brought before a local or a regional division, these actions may only be brought before the same local or regional division.

5. If an action for revocation as referred to in Article 32(1)(d) is pending before the central division, an action for infringement as referred to in Article 32(1)(a) between the same parties relating to the same patent may be brought before any division in accordance with paragraph 1 of this Article or before the central division. The local or regional division concerned shall have the discretion to proceed in accordance with paragraph 3 of this Article.

6. An action for declaration of non-infringement as referred to in Article 32(1)(b) pending before the central division shall be stayed once an infringement action as referred to in Article 32(1)(a) between the same parties or between the holder of an exclusive licence and the party requesting a declaration of non-infringement relating to the same patent is brought before a local or regional division within three months of the date on which the action was initiated before the central division.

7. Parties may agree to bring actions referred to in Article 32(1)(a) to (h) before the division of their choice, including the central division.

8. Actions referred to in Article 32(1)(d) and (e) can be brought without the applicant having to file notice of opposition with the European Patent Office.

9. Actions referred to in Article 32(1)(i) shall be brought before the central division.

10. A party shall inform the Court of any pending revocation, limitation or opposition proceedings before the European Patent Office, and of any request for accelerated processing before the European Patent Office. The Court may stay its proceedings when a rapid decision may be expected from the European Patent Office.

Article 34
Territorial scope of decisions

Decisions of the Court shall cover, in the case of a European patent, the territory of those Contracting Member States for which the European patent has effect.

Article 35
Patent mediation and arbitration centre

1. A patent mediation and arbitration centre ('the Centre') is hereby established. It shall have its seats in Ljubljana and Lisbon.

2. The Centre shall provide facilities for mediation and arbitration of patent disputes falling within the scope of this Agreement. Article 82 shall apply mutatis mutandis to any settlement reached through the use of the facilities of the Centre, including through mediation. However, a patent may not be revoked or limited in mediation or arbitration proceedings.

3. The Centre shall establish Mediation and Arbitration Rules.

4. The Centre shall draw up a list of mediators and arbitrators to assist the parties in the settlement of their dispute.

Article 36
Budget of the Court

1. The budget of the Court shall be financed by the Court's own financial revenues and, at least in the transitional period referred to in Article 83 as necessary, by contributions from the Contracting Member States. The budget shall be balanced.

2. The Court's own financial revenues shall comprise court fees and other revenues.

3. Court fees shall be fixed by the Administrative Committee. They shall consist of a fixed fee, combined with a value-based fee above a pre-defined ceiling. The Court fees shall be fixed at such a level as to ensure a right balance between the principle of fair access to justice, in particular for small and medium-sized enterprises, micro-entities, natural persons, non-profit organisations, universities and public research organisations and an adequate contribution of the parties for the costs incurred by the Court, recognising the economic benefits to the parties involved, and the objective of a self-financing Court with balanced finances. The level of the Court fees shall be reviewed periodically by the Administrative Committee. Targeted support measures for small and medium-sized enterprises and micro entities may be considered.

4. If the Court is unable to balance its budget out of its own resources, the Contracting Member States shall remit to it special financial contributions.

Article 37
Financing of the Court

1. The operating costs of the Court shall be covered by the budget of the Court, in accordance with the Statute.

Contracting Member States setting up a local division shall provide the facilities necessary for that purpose. Contracting Member States sharing a regional division shall provide jointly the facilities necessary for that purpose. Contracting Member States hosting the central division, its sections or the Court of Appeal shall provide the facilities necessary for that purpose. During an initial transitional period of seven years starting from the date of the entry into force of this Agreement, the Contracting Member States concerned shall also provide administrative support staff, without prejudice to the Statute of that staff.

2. On the date of entry into force of this Agreement, the Contracting Member States shall provide the initial financial contributions necessary for the setting up of the Court.

3. During the initial transitional period of seven years, starting from the date of the entry into force of this Agreement, the contribution by each Contracting Member State having ratified or acceded to the Agreement before the entry into force thereof shall be calculated on the basis of the number of European patents having effect in the territory of that State on the date of entry into force of this Agreement and the

number of European patents with respect to which actions for infringement or for revocation have been brought before the national courts of that State in the three years preceding entry into force of this Agreement.

During the same initial transitional period of seven years, for Member States which ratify, or accede to, this Agreement after the entry into force thereof, the contributions shall be calculated on the basis of the number of European patents having effect in the territory of the ratifying or acceding Member State on the date of the ratification or accession and the number of European patents with respect to which actions for infringement or for revocation have been brought before the national courts of the ratifying or acceding Member State in the three years preceding the ratification or accession.

4. After the end of the initial transitional period of seven years, by which the Court is expected to have become self-financing, should contributions by the Contracting Member States become necessary, they shall be determined in accordance with the scale for the distribution of annual renewal fees for European patents with unitary effect applicable at the time the contribution becomes necessary.

Article 38
Financing of the training framework for judges

The training framework for judges shall be financed by the budget of the Court.

Article 39
Financing of the Centre

The operating costs of the Centre shall be financed by the budget of the Court.

Article 40
Statute

1. The Statute shall lay down the details of the organisation and functioning of the Court.

2. The Statute is annexed to this Agreement. The Statute may be amended by decision of the Administrative Committee, on the basis of a proposal of the Court or a proposal of a Contracting Member State after consultation with the Court. However, such amendments shall not contradict or alter this Agreement.

3. The Statute shall guarantee that the functioning of the Court is organised in the most efficient and cost-effective manner and shall ensure equitable access to justice.

Article 41
Rules of Procedure

1. The Rules of Procedure shall lay down the details of the proceedings before the Court. They shall comply with this Agreement and the Statute.

2. The Rules of Procedure shall be adopted by the Administrative Committee on the basis of broad consultations with stakeholders. The prior opinion of the European Commission on the compatibility of the Rules of Procedure with Union law shall be requested.

The Rules of Procedure may be amended by a decision of the Administrative Committee, on the basis of a proposal from the Court and after consultation with the European Commission. However, such amendments shall not contradict or alter this Agreement or the Statute.

3. The Rules of Procedure shall guarantee that the decisions of the Court are of the highest quality and that proceedings are organised in the most efficient and cost effective manner. They shall ensure a fair balance between the legitimate interests of all parties. They shall provide for the required level of discretion of judges without impairing the predictability of proceedings for the parties.

Article 42
Proportionality and fairness

1. The Court shall deal with litigation in ways which are proportionate to the importance and complexity thereof.

2. The Court shall ensure that the rules, procedures and remedies provided for in this Agreement and in the Statute are used in a fair and equitable manner and do not distort competition.

Article 43
Case management

The Court shall actively manage the cases before it in accordance with the Rules of Procedure without impairing the freedom of the parties to determine the subject-matter of, and the supporting evidence for, their case.

Article 44
Electronic procedures

The Court shall make best use of electronic procedures, such as the electronic filing of submissions of the parties and stating of evidence in electronic form, as well as video conferencing, in accordance with the Rules of Procedure.

Article 45
Public proceedings

The proceedings shall be open to the public unless the Court decides to make them confidential, to the extent necessary, in the interest of one of the parties or other affected persons, or in the general interest of justice or public order.

Article 46
Legal capacity

Any natural or legal person, or any body equivalent to a legal person entitled to initiate proceedings in accordance with its national law, shall have the capacity to be a party to the proceedings before the Court.

Article 47
Parties

1. The patent proprietor shall be entitled to bring actions before the Court.

2. Unless the licensing agreement provides otherwise, the holder of an exclusive licence in respect of a patent shall be entitled to bring actions before the Court under the same circumstances as the patent proprietor, provided that the patent proprietor is given prior notice.

3. The holder of a non-exclusive licence shall not be entitled to bring actions before the Court, unless the patent proprietor is given prior notice and in so far as expressly permitted by the licence agreement.

4. In actions brought by a licence holder, the patent proprietor shall be entitled to join the action before the Court.

5. The validity of a patent cannot be contested in an action for infringement brought by the holder of a licence where the patent proprietor does not take part in the proceedings. The party in an action for infringement wanting to contest the validity of a patent shall have to bring actions against the patent proprietor.

6. Any other natural or legal person, or any body entitled to bring actions in accordance with its national law, who is concerned by a patent, may bring actions in accordance with the Rules of Procedure.

7. Any natural or legal person, or any body entitled to bring actions in accordance with its national law and who is affected by a decision of the European Patent Office in carrying out the tasks referred to in Article 9 of Regulation (EU) No 1257/2012 is entitled to bring actions under Article 32(1)(i).

Article 48
Representation

1. Parties shall be represented by lawyers authorised to practise before a court of a Contracting Member State.

2. Parties may alternatively be represented by European Patent Attorneys who are entitled to act as professional representatives before the European Patent Office pursuant to Article 134 of the EPC and who have appropriate qualifications such as a European Patent Litigation Certificate.

3. The requirements for qualifications pursuant to paragraph 2 shall be established by the Administrative Committee. A list of European Patent Attorneys entitled to represent parties before the Court shall be kept by the Registrar.

4. Representatives of the parties may be assisted by patent attorneys, who shall be allowed to speak at hearings of the Court in accordance with the Rules of Procedure.

5. Representatives of the parties shall enjoy the rights and immunities necessary for the independent exercise of their duties, including the privilege from disclosure in proceedings before the Court in respect of communications between a representative and the party or any other person, under the conditions laid down in the Rules of Procedure, unless such privilege is expressly waived by the party concerned.

6. Representatives of the parties shall be obliged not to misrepresent cases or facts before the Court either knowingly or with good reasons to know.

7. Representation in accordance with paragraphs 1 and 2 of this Article shall not be required in proceedings under Article 32(1)(i).

Article 49
Language of proceedings at the Court of First Instance

1. The language of proceedings before any local or regional division shall be an official European Union language which is the official language or one of the official languages of the Contracting Member State hosting the relevant division, or the official language(s) designated by Contracting Member States sharing a regional division.

2. Notwithstanding paragraph 1, Contracting Member States may designate one or more of the official languages of the European Patent Office as the language of proceedings of their local or regional division.

3. The parties may agree on the use of the language in which the patent was granted as the language of proceedings, subject to approval by the competent panel. If the panel does not approve their choice, the parties may request that the case be referred to the central division.

4. With the agreement of the parties the competent panel may, on grounds of convenience and fairness, decide on the use of the language in which the patent was granted as the language of proceedings.

5. At the request of one of the parties and after having heard the other parties and the competent panel, the President of the Court of First Instance may, on grounds of fairness and taking into account all relevant circumstances, including the position of parties, in particular the position of the defendant, decide on the use of the language in which the patent was granted as language of proceedings. In this case the President of the Court of First Instance shall assess the need for specific translation and interpretation arrangements.

6. The language of proceedings at the central division shall be the language in which the patent concerned was granted.

Article 50
Language of proceedings at the Court of Appeal

1. The language of proceedings before the Court of Appeal shall be the language of proceedings before the Court of First Instance.

2. Notwithstanding paragraph 1 the parties may agree on the use of the language in which the patent was granted as the language of proceedings.

3. In exceptional cases and to the extent deemed appropriate, the Court of Appeal may decide on another official language of a Contracting Member State as the language of proceedings for the whole or part of the proceedings, subject to agreement by the parties.

Article 51
Other language arrangements

1. Any panel of the Court of First Instance and the Court of Appeal may, to the extent deemed appropriate, dispense with translation requirements.

2. At the request of one of the parties, and to the extent deemed appropriate, any division of the Court of First Instance and the Court of Appeal shall provide interpretation facilities to assist the parties concerned at oral proceedings.

3. Notwithstanding Article 49(6), in cases where an action for infringement is brought before the central division, a defendant having its residence, principal place of business or place of business in a Member State shall have the right to obtain, upon request, translations of relevant documents in the language of the Member State of residence, principal place of business or, in the absence of residence or principal place of business, place of business, in the following circumstances:
(a) jurisdiction is entrusted to the central division in accordance with Article 33(1) third or fourth subparagraph, and
(b) the language of proceedings at the central division is a language which is not an official language of the Member State where the defendant has its residence, principal place of business or, in the absence of residence or principal place of business, place of business, and
(c) the defendant does not have proper knowledge of the language of the proceedings.

Article 52
Written, interim and oral procedures

1. The proceedings before the Court shall consist of a written, an interim and an oral procedure, in accordance with the Rules of Procedure. All procedures shall be organized in a flexible and balanced manner.

2. In the interim procedure, after the written procedure and if appropriate, the judge acting as Rapporteur, subject to a mandate of the full panel, shall be responsible for convening an interim hearing. That judge shall in particular explore with the parties

the possibility for a settlement, including through mediation, and/or arbitration, by using the facilities of the Centre referred to in Article 35.

3. The oral procedure shall give parties the opportunity to explain properly their arguments. The Court may, with the agreement of the parties, dispense with the oral hearing.

Article 53
Means of evidence

1. In proceedings before the Court, the means of giving or obtaining evidence shall include in particular the following:
(a) hearing the parties;
(b) requests for information;
(c) production of documents;
(d) hearing witnesses;
(e) opinions by experts;
(f) inspection;
(g) comparative tests or experiments;
(h) sworn statements in writing (affidavits).

2. The Rules of Procedure shall govern the procedure for taking such evidence. Questioning of witnesses and experts shall be under the control of the Court and be limited to what is necessary.

Article 54
Burden of proof

Without prejudice to Article 24(2) and (3), the burden of the proof of facts shall be on the party relying on those facts.

Article 55
Reversal of burden of proof

1. Without prejudice to Article 24(2) and (3), if the subject-matter of a patent is a process for obtaining a new product, the identical product when produced without the consent of the patent proprietor shall, in the absence of proof to the contrary, be deemed to have been obtained by the patented process.

2. The principle set out in paragraph 1 shall also apply where there is a substantial likelihood that the identical product was made by the patented process and the patent proprietor has been unable, despite reasonable efforts, to determine the process actually used for such identical product.

3. In the adduction of proof to the contrary, the legitimate interests of the defendant in protecting its manufacturing and trade secrets shall be taken into account.

Article 56
The general powers of the Court

1. The Court may impose such measures, procedures and remedies as are laid down in this Agreement and may make its orders subject to conditions, in accordance with the Rules of Procedure.

2. The Court shall take due account of the interest of the parties and shall, before making an order, give any party the opportunity to be heard, unless this is incompatible with the effective enforcement of such order.

Article 57
Court experts

1. Without prejudice to the possibility for the parties to produce expert evidence, the Court may at any time appoint court experts in order to provide expertise for specific aspects of the case. The Court shall provide such expert with all information necessary for the provision of the expert advice.

2. To this end, an indicative list of experts shall be drawn up by the Court in accordance with the Rules of Procedure. That list shall be kept by the Registrar.

3. The court experts shall guarantee independence and impartiality. Rules governing conflicts of interest applicable to judges set out in Article 7 of the Statute shall by analogy apply to court experts.

4. Expert advice given to the Court by court experts shall be made available to the parties which shall have the possibility to comment on it.

Article 58
Protection of confidential information

To protect the trade secrets, personal data or other confidential information of a party to the proceedings or of a third party, or to prevent an abuse of evidence, the Court may order that the collection and use of evidence in proceedings before it be restricted or prohibited or that access to such evidence be restricted to specific persons.

Article 59
Order to produce evidence

1. At the request of a party which has presented reasonably available evidence sufficient to support its claims and has, in substantiating those claims, specified evidence which lies in the control of the opposing party or a third party, the Court may order the opposing party or a third party to present such evidence, subject to the protection of confidential information. Such order shall not result in an obligation of self-incrimination.

2. At the request of a party the Court may order, under the same conditions as specified in paragraph 1, the communication of banking, financial or commercial

documents under the control of the opposing party, subject to the protection of confidential information.

Article 60
Order to preserve evidence and to inspect premises

1. At the request of the applicant which has presented reasonably available evidence to support the claim that the patent has been infringed or is about to be infringed the Court may, even before the commencement of proceedings on the merits of the case, order prompt and effective provisional measures to preserve relevant evidence in respect of the alleged infringement, subject to the protection of confidential information.

2. Such measures may include the detailed description, with or without the taking of samples, or the physical seizure of the infringing products, and, in appropriate cases, the materials and implements used in the production and/or distribution of those products and the documents relating thereto.

3. The Court may, even before the commencement of proceedings on the merits of the case, at the request of the applicant who has presented evidence to support the claim that the patent has been infringed or is about to be infringed, order the inspection of premises. Such inspection of premises shall be conducted by a person appointed by the Court in accordance with the Rules of Procedure.

4. At the inspection of the premises the applicant shall not be present itself but may be represented by an independent professional practitioner whose name has to be specified in the Court's order.

5. Measures shall be ordered, if necessary without the other party having been heard, in particular where any delay is likely to cause irreparable harm to the proprietor of the patent, or where there is a demonstrable risk of evidence being destroyed.

6. Where measures to preserve evidence or inspect premises are ordered without the other party in the case having been heard, the parties affected shall be given notice, without delay and at the latest immediately after the execution of the measures. A review, including a right to be heard, shall take place upon request of the parties affected with a view to deciding, within a reasonable period after the notification of the measures, whether the measures are to be modified, revoked or confirmed.

7. The measures to preserve evidence may be subject to the lodging by the applicant of adequate security or an equivalent assurance intended to ensure compensation for any prejudice suffered by the defendant as provided for in paragraph 9.

8. The Court shall ensure that the measures to preserve evidence are revoked or otherwise cease to have effect, at the defendant's request, without prejudice to the damages which may be claimed, if the applicant does not bring, within a period not exceeding 31 calendar days or 20 working days, whichever is the longer, action leading to a decision on the merits of the case before the Court.

9. Where the measures to preserve evidence are revoked, or where they lapse due to any act or omission by the applicant, or where it is subsequently found that there has been no infringement or threat of infringement of the patent, the Court may order the applicant, at the defendant's request, to provide the defendant with appropriate compensation for any damage suffered as a result of those measures.

Article 61
Freezing orders

1. At the request of the applicant which has presented reasonably available evidence to support the claim that the patent has been infringed or is about to be infringed the Court may, even before the commencement of proceedings on the merits of the case, order a party not to remove from its jurisdiction any assets located therein, or not to deal in any assets, whether located within its jurisdiction or not.

2. Article 60(5) to (9) shall apply by analogy to the measures referred to in this Article.

Article 62
Provisional and protective measures

1. The Court may, by way of order, grant injunctions against an alleged infringer or against an intermediary whose services are used by the alleged infringer, intended to prevent any imminent infringement, to prohibit, on a provisional basis and subject, where appropriate, to a recurring penalty payment, the continuation of the alleged infringement or to make such continuation subject to the lodging of guarantees intended to ensure the compensation of the right holder.

2. The Court shall have the discretion to weigh up the interests of the parties and in particular to take into account the potential harm for either of the parties resulting from the granting or the refusal of the injunction.

3. The Court may also order the seizure or delivery up of the products suspected of infringing a patent so as to prevent their entry into, or movement, within the channels of commerce. If the applicant demonstrates circumstances likely to endanger the recovery of damages, the Court may order the precautionary seizure of the movable and immovable property of the alleged infringer, including the blocking of the bank accounts and of other assets of the alleged infringer.

4. The Court may, in respect of the measures referred to in paragraphs 1 and 3, require the applicant to provide any reasonable evidence in order to satisfy itself with a sufficient degree of certainty that the applicant is the right holder and that the applicant's right is being infringed, or that such infringement is imminent.

5. Article 60(5) to (9) shall apply by analogy to the measures referred to in this Article.

Article 63
Permanent injunctions

1. Where a decision is taken finding an infringement of a patent, the Court may grant an injunction against the infringer aimed at prohibiting the continuation of the infringement. The Court may also grant such injunction against an intermediary whose services are being used by a third party to infringe a patent.

2. Where appropriate, non-compliance with the injunction referred to in paragraph 1 shall be subject to a recurring penalty payment payable to the Court.

Article 64
Corrective measures in infringement proceedings

1. Without prejudice to any damages due to the injured party by reason of the infringement, and without compensation of any sort, the Court may order, at the request of the applicant, that appropriate measures be taken with regard to products found to be infringing a patent and, in appropriate cases, with regard to materials and implements principally used in the creation or manufacture of those products.

2. Such measures shall include:
(a) a declaration of infringement;
(b) recalling the products from the channels of commerce;
(c) depriving the product of its infringing property;
(d) definitively removing the products from the channels of commerce; or
(e) the destruction of the products and/or of the materials and implements concerned.

3. The Court shall order that those measures be carried out at the expense of the infringer, unless particular reasons are invoked for not doing so.

4. In considering a request for corrective measures pursuant to this Article, the Court shall take into account the need for proportionality between the seriousness of the infringement and the remedies to be ordered, the willingness of the infringer to convert the materials into a non-infringing state, as well as the interests of third parties.

Article 65
Decision on the validity of a patent

1. The Court shall decide on the validity of a patent on the basis of an action for revocation or a counterclaim for revocation.

2. The Court may revoke a patent, either entirely or partly, only on the grounds referred to in Articles 138(1) and 139(2) of the EPC.

3. Without prejudice to Article 138(3) of the EPC, if the grounds for revocation affect the patent only in part, the patent shall be limited by a corresponding amendment of the claims and revoked in part.

4. To the extent that a patent has been revoked it shall be deemed not to have had, from the outset, the effects specified in Articles 64 and 67 of the EPC.

5. Where the Court, in a final decision, revokes a patent, either entirely or partly, it shall send a copy of the decision to the European Patent Office and, with respect to a European patent, to the national patent office of any Contracting Member State concerned.

Article 66
Powers of the Court concerning decisions of the European Patent Office

1. In actions brought under Article 32(1)(i), the Court may exercise any power entrusted on the European Patent Office in accordance with Article 9 of Regulation (EU) No 1257/2012, including the rectification of the Register for unitary patent protection.

2. In actions brought under Article 32(1)(i) the parties shall, by way of derogation from Article 69, bear their own costs.

Article 67
Power to order the communication of information

1. The Court may, in response to a justified and proportionate request of the applicant and in accordance with the Rules of Procedure, order an infringer to inform the applicant of:
(a) the origin and distribution channels of the infringing products or processes;
(b) the quantities produced, manufactured, delivered, received or ordered, as well as the price obtained for the infringing products; and
(c) the identity of any third person involved in the production or distribution of the infringing products or in the use of the infringing process.

2. The Court may, in accordance with the Rules of Procedure, also order any third party who:
(a) was found in the possession of the infringing products on a commercial scale or to be using an infringing process on a commercial scale;
(b) was found to be providing on a commercial scale services used in infringing activities; or
(c) was indicated by the person referred to in points (a) or (b) as being involved in the production, manufacture or distribution of the infringing products or processes or in the provision of the services,

to provide the applicant with the information referred to in paragraph 1.

Article 68
Award of damages

1. The Court shall, at the request of the injured party, order the infringer who knowingly, or with reasonable grounds to know, engaged in a patent infringing activity, to pay the injured party damages appropriate to the harm actually suffered by that party as a result of the infringement.

2. The injured party shall, to the extent possible, be placed in the position it would have been in if no infringement had taken place. The infringer shall not benefit from the infringement. However, damages shall not be punitive.

3. When the Court sets the damages:

(a) it shall take into account all appropriate aspects, such as the negative economic consequences, including lost profits, which the injured party has suffered, any unfair profits made by the infringer and, in appropriate cases, elements other than economic factors, such as the moral prejudice caused to the injured party by the infringement; or

(b) as an alternative to point (a), it may, in appropriate cases, set the damages as a lump sum on the basis of elements such as at least the amount of the royalties or fees which would have been due if the infringer had requested authorisation to use the patent in question.

4. Where the infringer did not knowingly, or with reasonable grounds to know, engage in the infringing activity, the Court may order the recovery of profits or the payment of compensation.

Article 69
Legal costs

1. Reasonable and proportionate legal costs and other expenses incurred by the successful party shall, as a general rule, be borne by the unsuccessful party, unless equity requires otherwise, up to a ceiling set in accordance with the Rules of Procedure.

2. Where a party succeeds only in part or in exceptional circumstances, the Court may order that costs be apportioned equitably or that the parties bear their own costs.

3. A party should bear any unnecessary costs it has caused the Court or another party.

4. At the request of the defendant, the Court may order the applicant to provide adequate security for the legal costs and other expenses incurred by the defendant which the applicant may be liable to bear, in particular in the cases referred to in Articles 59 to 62.

Article 70
Court fees

1. Parties to proceedings before the Court shall pay court fees.

2. Court fees shall be paid in advance, unless the Rules of Procedure provide otherwise. Any party which has not paid a prescribed court fee may be excluded from further participation in the proceedings.

Article 71
Legal aid

1. A party who is a natural person and who is unable to meet the costs of the proceedings, either wholly or in part, may at any time apply for legal aid. The conditions for granting of legal aid shall be laid down in the Rules of Procedure.

2. The Court shall decide whether legal aid should be granted in full or in part, or whether it should be refused, in accordance with the Rules of Procedure.

3. On a proposal from the Court, the Administrative Committee shall set the level of legal aid and the rules on bearing the costs thereof.

Article 72
Period of limitation

Without prejudice to Article 24(2) and (3), actions relating to all forms of financial compensation may not be brought more than five years after the date on which the applicant became aware, or had reasonable grounds to become aware, of the last fact justifying the action.

Article 73
Appeal

1. An appeal against a decision of the Court of First Instance may be brought before the Court of Appeal by any party which has been unsuccessful, in whole or in part, in its submissions, within two months of the date of the notification of the decision.

2. An appeal against an order of the Court of First Instance may be brought before the Court of Appeal by any party which has been unsuccessful, in whole or in part, in its submissions:
(a) for the orders referred to in Articles 49(5), 59 to 62 and 67 within 15 calendar days of the notification of the order to the applicant;
(b) for other orders than the orders referred to in point (a):
   (i) together with the appeal against the decision, or
   (ii) where the Court grants leave to appeal, within 15 days of the notification of the Court's decision to that effect.

3. The appeal against a decision or an order of the Court of First Instance may be based on points of law and matters of fact.

4. New facts and new evidence may only be introduced in accordance with the Rules of Procedure and where the submission thereof by the party concerned could not reasonably have been expected during proceedings before the Court of First Instance.

Article 74
Effects of an appeal

1. An appeal shall not have suspensive effect unless the Court of Appeal decides otherwise at the motivated request of one of the parties. The Rules of Procedure shall guarantee that such a decision is taken without delay.

2. Notwithstanding paragraph 1, an appeal against a decision on actions or counterclaims for revocation and on actions based on Article 32(1)(i) shall always have suspensive effect.

3. An appeal against an order referred to in Articles 49(5), 59 to 62 or 67 shall not prevent the continuation of the main proceedings. However, the Court of First Instance shall not give a decision in the main proceedings before the decision of the Court of Appeal concerning an appealed order has been given.

Article 75
Decision on appeal and referral back

1. If an appeal pursuant to Article 73 is well-founded, the Court of Appeal shall revoke the decision of the Court of First Instance and give a final decision. The Court of Appeal may in exceptional cases and in accordance with the Rules of Procedure refer the case back to the Court of First Instance for decision.

2. Where a case is referred back to the Court of First Instance pursuant to paragraph 1, the Court of First Instance shall be bound by the decision of the Court of Appeal on points of law.

Article 76
Basis for decisions and right to be heard

1. The Court shall decide in accordance with the requests submitted by the parties and shall not award more than is requested.

2. Decisions on the merits may only be based on grounds, facts and evidence, which were submitted by the parties or introduced into the procedure by an order of the Court and on which the parties have had an opportunity to present their comments.

3. The Court shall evaluate evidence freely and independently.

Article 77
Formal requirements

1. Decisions and orders of the Court shall be reasoned and shall be given in writing in accordance with the Rules of Procedure.

2. Decisions and orders of the Court shall be delivered in the language of proceedings.

Article 78
Decisions of the Court and dissenting opinions

1. Decisions and orders of the Court shall be taken by a majority of the panel, in accordance with the Statute. In case of equal votes, the vote of the presiding judge shall prevail.

2. In exceptional circumstances, any judge of the panel may express a dissenting opinion separately from the decision of the Court.

Article 79
Settlement

The parties may, at any time in the course of proceedings, conclude their case by way of settlement, which shall be confirmed by a decision of the Court. A patent may not be revoked or limited by way of settlement.

Article 80
Publication of decisions

The Court may order, at the request of the applicant and at the expense of the infringer, appropriate measures for the dissemination of information concerning the Court's decision, including displaying the decision and publishing it in full or in part in public media.

Article 81
Rehearing

1. A request for rehearing after a final decision of the Court may exceptionally be granted by the Court of Appeal in the following circumstances:
(a) on discovery of a fact by the party requesting the rehearing, which is of such a nature as to be a decisive factor and which, when the decision was given, was unknown to the party requesting the rehearing; such request may only be granted on the basis of an act which was held, by a final decision of a national court, to constitute a criminal offence; or
(b) in the event of a fundamental procedural defect, in particular when a defendant who did not appear before the Court was not served with the document initiating the proceedings or an equivalent document in sufficient time and in such a way as to enable him to arrange for the defence.

2. A request for a rehearing shall be filed within 10 years of the date of the decision but not later than two months from the date of the discovery of the new fact or of the procedural defect. Such request shall not have suspensive effect unless the Court of Appeal decides otherwise.

3. If the request for a rehearing is well-founded, the Court of Appeal shall set aside, in whole or in part, the decision under review and re-open the proceedings for a new trial and decision, in accordance with the Rules of Procedure.

4. Persons using patents which are the subject-matter of a decision under review and who act in good faith should be allowed to continue using such patents.

Article 82
Enforcement of decisions and orders

1. Decisions and orders of the Court shall be enforceable in any Contracting Member State. An order for the enforcement of a decision shall be appended to the decision by the Court.

2. Where appropriate, the enforcement of a decision may be subject to the provision of security or an equivalent assurance to ensure compensation for any damage suffered, in particular in the case of injunctions.

3. Without prejudice to this Agreement and the Statute, enforcement procedures shall be governed by the law of the Contracting Member State where the enforcement takes place. Any decision of the Court shall be enforced under the same conditions as a decision given in the Contracting Member State where the enforcement takes place.

4. If a party does not comply with the terms of an order of the Court, that party may be sanctioned with a recurring penalty payment payable to the Court. The individual penalty shall be proportionate to the importance of the order to be enforced and shall be without prejudice to the party's right to claim damages or security.

Article 83
Transitional regime

1. During a transitional period of seven years after the date of entry into force of this Agreement, an action for infringement or for revocation of a European patent or an action for infringement or for declaration of invalidity of a supplementary protection certificate issued for a product protected by a European patent may still be brought before national courts or other competent national authorities.

2. An action pending before a national court at the end of the transitional period shall not be affected by the expiry of this period.

3. Unless an action has already been brought before the Court, a proprietor of or an applicant for a European patent granted or applied for prior to the end of the transitional period under paragraph 1 and, where applicable, paragraph 5, as well as a holder of a supplementary protection certificate issued for a product protected by a European patent, shall have the possibility to opt out from the exclusive competence of the Court. To this end they shall notify their opt-out to the Registry by the latest one month before expiry of the transitional period. The opt-out shall take effect upon its entry into the register.

4. Unless an action has already been brought before a national court, proprietors of or applicants for European patents or holders of supplementary protection certificates issued for a product protected by a European patent who made use of the opt-out in accordance with paragraph 3 shall be entitled to withdraw their opt-out at any

moment. In this event they shall notify the Registry accordingly. The withdrawal of the opt-out shall take effect upon its entry into the register.

5. Five years after the entry into force of this Agreement, the Administrative Committee shall carry out a broad consultation with the users of the patent system and a survey on the number of European patents and supplementary protection certificates issued for products protected by European patents with respect to which actions for infringement or for revocation or declaration of invalidity are still brought before the national courts pursuant to paragraph 1, the reasons for this and the implications thereof. On the basis of this consultation and an opinion of the Court, the Administrative Committee may decide to prolong the transitional period by up to seven years.

Article 84
Signature, ratification and accession

1. This Agreement shall be open for signature by any Member State on 19 February 2013.

2. This Agreement shall be subject to ratification in accordance with the respective constitutional requirements of the Member States. Instruments of ratification shall be deposited with the General Secretariat of the Council of the European Union (hereinafter referred to as 'the depositary').

3. Each Member State having signed this Agreement shall notify the European Commission of its ratification of the Agreement at the time of the deposit of its ratification instrument pursuant to Article 18(3) of Regulation (EU) No 1257/2012.

4. This Agreement shall be open to accession by any Member State. Instruments of accession shall be deposited with the depositary.

Article 85
Functions of the depositary

1. The depositary shall draw up certified true copies of this Agreement and shall transmit them to the governments of all signatory or acceding Member States.

2. The depositary shall notify the governments of the signatory or acceding Member States of:
(a) any signature;
(b) the deposit of any instrument of ratification or accession;
(c) the date of entry into force of this Agreement.

3. The depositary shall register this Agreement with the Secretariat of the United Nations.

Article 86
Duration of the Agreement

This Agreement shall be of unlimited duration.

Article 87
Revision

1. Either seven years after the entry into force of this Agreement or once 2 000 infringement cases have been decided by the Court, whichever is the later point in time, and if necessary at regular intervals thereafter, a broad consultation with the users of the patent system shall be carried out by the Administrative Committee on the functioning, efficiency and cost-effectiveness of the Court and on the trust and confidence of users of the patent system in the quality of the Court's decisions. On the basis of this consultation and an opinion of the Court, the Administrative Committee may decide to revise this Agreement with a view to improving the functioning of the Court.

2. The Administrative Committee may amend this Agreement to bring it into line with an international treaty relating to patents or Union law.

3. A decision of the Administrative Committee taken on the basis of paragraphs 1 and 2 shall not take effect if a Contracting Member State declares within twelve months of the date of the decision, on the basis of its relevant internal decision-making procedures, that it does not wish to be bound by the decision. In this case, a Review Conference of the Contracting Member States shall be convened.

Article 88
Languages of the Agreement

1. This Agreement is drawn up in a single original in the English, French and German languages, each text being equally authentic.

2. The texts of this Agreement drawn up in official languages of Contracting Member States other than those specified in paragraph 1 shall, if they have been approved by the Administrative Committee, be considered as official texts. In the event of divergences between the various texts, the texts referred to in paragraph 1 shall prevail.

Article 89
Entry into force

1. This Agreement shall enter into force on 1 January 2014 or on the first day of the fourth month after the deposit of the thirteenth instrument of ratification or accession in accordance with Article 84, including the three Member States in which the highest number of European patents had effect in the year preceding the year in which the signature of the Agreement takes place or on the first day of the fourth month after the date of entry into force of the amendments to Regulation (EU) No 1215/2012 concerning its relationship with this Agreement, whichever is the latest.

2. Any ratification or accession after the entry into force of this Agreement shall take effect on the first day of the fourth month after the deposit of the instrument of ratification or accession.

Annex 4 Rules of Procedure of the Unified Patent Court

as adopted by decision of the Administrative Committee on 8 July 2022
entry into force: 1 September 2022;

amended by decision of the Administrative Committee on 4 November 2025
entry into force: 1 January 2026

Abbreviations

Agreement: Agreement on a Unified Patent Court of 19 February 2013 (OJ C 175, 20.6.2013, p. 1) including any subsequent amendments

Directive 98/5/EC: Directive 98/5/EC of the European Parliament and of the Council of 16 February 1998 to facilitate practice of the profession of lawyer on a permanent basis in a Member State other than that in which the qualification was obtained (OJ L 77, 14.3.1998, p. 36) including any subsequent amendments

EPC: Convention on the Grant of European Patents of 5 October 1973 (European Patent Convention) including any subsequent amendments

The Hague Convention: Convention on the Service Abroad of Judicial and Extrajudicial Documents in Civil or Commercial Matters of 15 November 1965 including any subsequent amendments

Lugano Convention: Convention on Jurisdiction and the Recognition and Enforcement of Judgments in Civil and Commercial Matters of 30 October 2007 (OJ L 147, 10.6.2009, p. 5) including any subsequent amendments

Regulation (EU) 2020/1783: Regulation (EU) 2020/1783 of the European Parliament and of the Council of 25 November 2020 on cooperation between the courts of the Member States in the taking of evidence in civil or commercial matters (taking of evidence) (recast), OJ L 405, 2.12.2020, p. 1 including any subsequent amendments

Regulation (EU) No 1215/2012: Regulation (EU) No 1215/2012 of the European Parliament and of the Council of 12 December 2012 on jurisdiction and the recognition and enforcement of judgments in civil and commercial matters (OJ L 351, 20.12.2012, p. 1) including any subsequent amendments

Regulation (EU) No 1257/2012: Regulation (EU) No 1257/2012 of the European Parliament and of the Council of 17 December 2012 implementing enhanced cooperation in the area of the creation of unitary patent protection (OJ L 361, 31.12.2012, p. 1) including any subsequent amendments

Regulation (EU) No 1260/2012: Regulation (EU) No 1260/2012 of the Council of 17 December 2012 implementing enhanced cooperation in the area of the creation of unitary patent protection with regard to the applicable translation arrangements

(OJ L 361, 31.12.2012, p. 89) including any subsequent amendments including any subsequent amendments

Regulation (EU) 2020/1784: Regulation (EU) 2020/1784 1783 of the European Parliament and of the Council of 25 November 2020 on the service in the Member States of judicial and extrajudicial documents in civil or commercial matters (service of documents) (recast), OJ L 405, 2.12.2020; p. 40

Statute: Statute of the Unified Patent Court (OJ C 175, 20.6.2013, p. 29) including any subsequent amendments

PREAMBLE

1. The Court shall conduct proceedings in accordance with the Agreement, the Statute and these Rules. In the event of a conflict between the provisions of the Agreement and/or the Statute on the one hand and of the Rules on the other hand, the provisions of the Agreement and/or the Statute shall prevail.

2. The Rules shall be applied and interpreted in accordance with Articles 41(3), 42 and 52(1) of the Agreement on the basis of the principles of proportionality, flexibility, fairness and equity.

3. Proportionality shall be ensured by giving due consideration to the nature and complexity of each action and its importance.

4. Flexibility shall be ensured by applying all procedural rules in a flexible and balanced manner with the required level of discretion for the judges to organise the proceedings in the most efficient and cost effective manner.

5. Fairness and equity shall be ensured by having regard to the legitimate interests of all parties.

6. In accordance with these principles, the Court shall apply and interpret the Rules in a way which shall ensure decisions of the highest quality.

7. In accordance with these principles, proceedings shall be conducted in a way which will normally allow the final oral hearing on the issues of infringement and validity at first instance to take place within one year whilst recognising that complex actions may require more time and procedural steps and simple actions less time and fewer procedural steps. Decisions on costs and/or damages may take place at the same time or as soon as practicable thereafter. Case management shall be organised in accordance with these objectives. Parties shall cooperate with the Court and set out their full case as early as possible in the proceedings.

8. The Court shall endeavour to ensure consistent application and interpretation of these Rules by all first instance divisions and the Court of Appeal. Due consideration shall also be given to this objective in any decision concerning leave to appeal against procedural orders.

APPLICATION AND INTERPRETATION OF THE RULES

Rule 1 – Application of the Rules and general principles of interpretation

1. The Court shall conduct proceedings in accordance with the Agreement, the Statute and these Rules, which include the Preamble to these Rules and the principles set out therein. In the event of a conflict between the provisions of the Agreement and/or the Statute on the one hand and of the Rules on the other hand, the provisions of the Agreement and/or the Statute shall prevail.

2. Where these Rules provide for the Court to perform any act other than an act exclusively reserved for a panel of the Court, the President of the Court of First Instance or the President of the Court of Appeal, that act may be performed by:

(a) the presiding judge or the judge-rapporteur of the panel to which the action has been assigned;

(b) a single legally qualified judge where the action has been assigned to a single judge;

(c) the standing judge designated pursuant to Rule 345.5.

3. References to persons in these Rules may apply to legal persons as well as natural persons. Words importing the masculine gender shall include the feminine and vice versa. Unless the contrary intention appears, words in the singular include the plural and vice versa.

Relation with Agreement: Article 8(7)

Relation with Statute: Article 19(3) and (4)

Rule 2 – Supplementary protection certificate

1. Subject to paragraph 2, in these Rules with the exception of Rule 5 the expression "patent" and "proprietor" shall whenever appropriate include, respectively, a supplementary protection certificate as defined in Article 2(h) of the Agreement and granted in respect of the patent and the holder of such certificate.

2. References in these Rules to the language in which the patent was granted shall mean that language and not the language in which a supplementary protection certificate in respect of the patent was granted.

Rule 3 – Power of staff of the Registry and a sub-registry to perform functions of the Registry

Where these Rules refer to the Registry or Registrar and provide to perform any act that reference shall include – where applicable – the Deputy-Registrar and the relevant sub-registry and that act may be performed by the Registrar, the Deputy-Registrar or by a member of staff of the Registry or sub-registry of the relevant division.

Rule 4 – Lodging of documents

1. Written pleadings and other documents shall be signed and lodged at the Registry or relevant sub-registry in electronic form. Parties shall make use of the official forms available online. The receipt of documents shall be confirmed by the automatic issue of an electronic receipt, which shall indicate the date and local time of receipt.

2. Where it is not possible to lodge a document electronically for the reason that the electronic case management system of the Court has ceased to function a party may lodge a document in hard-copy form at the Registry or a sub-registry. An electronic copy of the document shall be lodged as soon as practicable thereafter.

Relation with Agreement: Article 44

Rule 5 – Lodging of an Application to opt out and withdrawal of an opt-out

1. The proprietor of a European patent (including a European patent that has expired) or the applicant for a published application for a European patent (hereinafter in this Rule 5 an "application") who wishes to opt out that patent or application from the exclusive competence of the Court in accordance with Article 83(3) of the Agreement shall lodge an Application (hereinafter in this Rule 5 an "Application to opt out") with the Registry.

(a) Where the patent or application is owned by two or more proprietors or applicants, all proprietors or applicants shall lodge the Application to opt out. Where the person lodging an Application to opt out is not recorded as the proprietor or applicant in the registers referred to in Rule 8.5(a) and (b), respectively, the person shall lodge a declaration pursuant to paragraph 3(e).

(b) The Application to opt out shall be made in respect of all of the states for which the European patent has been granted or which have been designated in the application.

2. An Application to opt out or an Application to withdraw an opt-out pursuant to paragraph 7 (hereinafter in this Rule 5 an "Application to withdraw") shall extend to any supplementary protection certificate based on the European patent.

(a) Where any such supplementary protection certificate has been granted at the date of lodging the Application to opt out or the Application to withdraw, the holder of the supplementary protection certificate shall, if different from the proprietor of the patent, lodge the Application to opt out or the Application to withdraw together with the proprietor.

(b) Where any such supplementary protection certificate is granted subsequent to lodging the Application to opt out, the opt-out shall take effect automatically on grant of said supplementary protection certificate.

(c) Paragraphs 6 and 8 shall apply *mutatis mutandis*. For the purposes of paragraphs 6 and 8, reference to actions
(i) in respect of a European patent shall apply to all supplementary protection certificates based on that European patent, and
(ii) in respect of a supplementary protection certificate shall apply to the European patent on which such supplementary protection certificate is based and
(iii) in respect of a supplementary protection certificate shall apply to all other supplementary protection certificates based on the same European patent.

(d) For the avoidance of doubt, it is not possible to opt out supplementary protection certificates, whether granted by the authorities of a Contracting Member State or otherwise, based on a European patent with unitary effect.

3. The Application to opt out shall contain:

(a) the name of each proprietor or applicant for the European patent or application and of the holder of any supplementary protection certificate based on the European patent in question, and all relevant postal and, where applicable, electronic addresses;

(b) the name and postal address and electronic address of
(i) the representative appointed by the applicant or the proprietor in accordance with Article 48 of the Agreement or
(ii) any other person lodging the Application to opt out on behalf of the proprietor or the applicant and the mandate for lodging the Application to opt out;

(c) details of the patent and/or application including the EP publication number;

(d) details of any supplementary protection certificate granted based on the patent concerned, including the number; and

(e) for the purposes of paragraph 1(a), a declaration by or on behalf of each proprietor or applicant pursuant to Rule 8.5 that he is entitled to be registered in the national patent register.

4. Rule 8 shall not apply to Applications to opt out and to Applications to withdraw made pursuant to this Rule 5.

5. The Registrar shall as soon as practicable enter the Application to opt out in the register. Subject to paragraph 6, the opt-out which meets the requirements laid down in this Rule shall be regarded as effective from the date of entry in the register. If the requirements recorded in the register are missing or incorrect, a correction may be lodged with the Registry. The date of entry of the correction shall be noted in the register. The opt-out shall be effective from the date of correction.

6. In the event that an action has been commenced before the Court in respect of a patent and/or an application contained in an Application to opt out prior to the date of entry of the Application to opt out in the register or prior to the date of correction pursuant to paragraph 5, the Application to opt out shall be ineffective in respect of the patent and/or application in question, irrespective of whether the action is pending or has been concluded.

7. A proprietor of a patent or an application the subject of an opt-out pursuant to this Rule may lodge an Application to withdraw in respect of the patent or application, but not in respect of different states for which the European patent has been granted or which have been designated in the application. The Application to withdraw shall contain the particulars in accordance with paragraph 3. The Registrar shall as soon as practicable enter the Application to withdraw in the register and the withdrawal shall be regarded as effective from the date of entry in the register. Paragraphs 1(a) and 5 shall apply *mutatis mutandis.*

8. In the event that an action has been commenced before a court of a Contracting Member State in a matter over which the Court also has jurisdiction pursuant to Article 32 of the Agreement in respect of a patent or application contained in an Application to withdraw, prior to the entry of the Application to withdraw in the register or any time before the date pursuant to paragraph 5, the Application to withdraw shall be ineffective in respect of the patent or application in question, irrespective of whether the action is pending or has been concluded.

9. Where an application for a European patent subject to an opt-out pursuant to this Rule proceeds to grant as a European patent with unitary effect the opt-out shall be deemed to have been withdrawn and the Registrar shall as soon as practicable enter the withdrawal in the register.

10. A patent or application the subject of an Application to withdraw which has been entered on the register may not thereafter be the subject of a further Application to opt out.

11. The Registrar shall as soon as practicable notify the European Patent Office and the national patent office of any Contracting Member States concerned of the entries in the register pursuant to paragraphs 5 and 7.

12. Applications accepted by the Registry before the entry into force of the Agreement shall be treated as entered on the register on the date of entry into force of the Agreement.

Relation with Agreement: Article 83(3) and (4)

Rule 5A – Application to remove an unauthorised application to opt out or unauthorised withdrawal of an opt-out

1. Without prejudice to the lodging of an Application to opt out or withdraw an opt-out in accordance with Rule 5, the proprietor of a European patent or the applicant for a published application for a European patent or holder of a supplementary protection certificate in relation to which an Application to opt out or withdraw the opt-out is entered in the register may lodge an Application to remove the entry of an unauthorised Application to opt out or withdrawal of the opt-out from the Registry setting out the reasons.

2. The Registrar shall mark the status of the Application to opt out or withdraw the opt-out entered in the register as subject to an Application for removal. The Registrar

shall decide on the Application for removal as soon as practicable. If the final decision is to remove the Application to opt out or withdrawal of an opt-out the Registrar shall delete it in the register.

3. The decision on the Application for removal may be subject to an Application for review to the President of the Court of Appeal. The Application for review shall be lodged with the Registrar in one of the official languages of the European Patent Office, within one month of the notification of the challenged decision setting out the request, facts, evidence and arguments. If the Application for review is allowable, the President of the Court of Appeal shall order the Registrar to remove the opt-out or the withdrawal of the opt-out.

Rule 6 – Service and supply of orders, decisions, written pleadings and other documents

1. The Registry shall as soon as practicable serve, in accordance with Part 5, Chapter 2:

(a) orders and decisions of the Court on the parties;

(b) written pleadings and other documents of a party on the other party.

Where applicable, the Registry shall inform the parties of the opportunity to reply or to take any other appropriate step in the proceedings and of any time period for so doing.

2. The Registry shall also as soon as practicable supply to the parties copies of documents referred to in these Rules and lodged with pleadings and written evidence.

3. Where the postal or electronic address for service provided by a party pursuant to these Rules has changed that party shall give notice to the Registry and to every other party as soon as such change has taken place.

Rule 7 – Language of written pleadings and written evidence

1. Written pleadings and other documents, including written evidence, shall be lodged in the language of the proceedings unless the Court or these Rules otherwise provide.

2. Where these Rules or the Court require a pleading or other document to be translated it shall not be necessary to provide a formal certification by the translator as to the accuracy of such translation unless the accuracy is challenged by a party or such certification is ordered by the Court or required by these Rules.

Rule 8 – Party and party's representative

1. A party shall be represented in accordance with Article 48 of the Agreement unless otherwise provided by these Rules [Rules 5, 88.4 and 378.5].

2. For the purpose of all proceedings in relation to a patent, where these Rules provide that a party performs any act or that any act be performed upon a party that act shall be performed by or upon the representative for the time being of the party.

3. Except where these Rules provide otherwise, a party shall not communicate with the Court without informing the other party. Where such communication is in writing, the communication should be copied to the other party unless these Rules provide that the Court will supply a copy to the other party.

4. For the purposes of proceedings under these Rules in relation to the proprietor of a European patent with unitary effect, the person shown in the Register for unitary patent protection [Regulation (EU) No 1257/2012, Article 2(e)] as the proprietor shall be treated as such. If during proceedings before the Court a new proprietor is recorded in the Register for unitary patent protection, the former registered proprietor may apply to the Court pursuant to Rule 305.1(c) for the substitution of the new proprietor.

5. Subject to paragraph 6, for the purposes of proceedings under these Rules:

(a) in relation to the proprietor of a European patent, the person entitled to be registered as proprietor under the law of each Contracting Member State in which such European patent has been validated shall be treated as the proprietor whether or not such person is in fact recorded in the register of patents maintained in such Contracting Member State (hereinafter "national patent register"); and

(b) in relation to the applicant for a European patent, the person entitled to be registered as applicant whether or not such person is in fact recorded as such in the European Patent Register kept by the European Patent Office.

(c) For the purposes of paragraph 5, there shall be a rebuttable presumption that the person shown in each national patent register and the European Patent Register kept by the European Patent Office is the person entitled to be registered as proprietor or applicant as the case may be.

6. For the purposes of proceedings pursuant to Rules 42 and 61 in relation to a European patent, the person shown in the national patent register [Rule 8.5(a)] as the proprietor shall be treated as such for each Contracting Member State or, as far as no such person is registered in a national patent register, the last person shown recorded as proprietor in the European Patent Register kept by the European Patent Office.

Relation with Agreement: Article 48

Rule 9 – Powers of the Court

1. The Court may, at any stage of the proceedings, of its own motion or on a reasoned request by a party, make a procedural order such as to order a party to take any step, answer any question or provide any clarification or evidence, within time periods to be specified.

2. The Court may disregard any step, fact, evidence or argument which a party has not taken or submitted in accordance with a time limit set by the Court or these Rules.

3. Subject to paragraph 4, on a reasoned request by a party, the Court may:

(a) extend, even retrospectively, a time period referred to in these Rules or imposed by the Court; and

(b) shorten any such time period.

4. The Court shall not extend the time periods referred to in Rules 198.1, 213.1 and 224.1.

PART 1 – PROCEDURES BEFORE THE COURT OF FIRST INSTANCE

Rule 10 – Stages of the proceedings (inter partes proceedings)

Proceedings before the Court of First Instance shall consist of the following stages:

(a) a written procedure;

(b) an interim procedure, which may include an interim conference with the parties;

(c) an oral procedure which, subject to Rules 116.1 and 117, shall include an oral hearing of the parties unless the Court dispenses with the oral hearing with the agreement of the parties;

(d) a procedure for the award of damages, which may include a procedure to lay open books;

(e) a procedure for cost decisions.

Relation with Agreement: Articles 52, 68 and 69

Rule 11 – Settlement

1. At any stage of the proceedings, if the Court is of the opinion that the dispute is suitable for a settlement, it may propose that the parties make use of the facilities of the Patent Mediation and Arbitration Centre ("the Centre") in order to settle or to explore a settlement of the dispute. In particular, the judge-rapporteur shall during the interim procedure, especially at an interim conference in accordance with Rule 104(d), explore with the parties the possibility of a settlement, including through mediation and/or arbitration, using the facilities of the Centre. Parties who choose mediation in an attempt to settle a dispute are subsequently not prevented from initiating judicial proceedings before the Court in relation to that dispute by the expiry of limitation or prescription periods during the mediation process, which will stay the limitation or prescription periods until the end of the mediation process. If mediation proceedings are terminated without a dispute settlement agreement, the period shall continue to run from that moment.

2. Pursuant to Rule 365 the Court shall, if requested by the parties, by decision confirm the terms of any settlement or arbitral award by consent (irrespective of whether it was reached using the facilities of the Centre or otherwise), including a term which obliges the patent owner to limit, surrender or agree to the revocation of a patent or not to assert it against the other party and/or third parties. The parties may agree on

costs to be awarded or may request the Court to decide on costs to be awarded in accordance with Rules 150 to 156 *mutatis mutandis*.

3. Save for the purpose of enforcing the terms of any such settlement agreement by any person no opinion expressed, suggestion made, proposal put forward, concession made or document drawn up for the purposes of settlement may be relied on as evidence by the Court or the parties in proceedings before the Court or any other court unless such matter was expressed to be made on an open basis and freely disclosable to the Court or any other court.

Relation with Agreement: Articles 35, 52(2) and 79

CHAPTER 1 – WRITTEN PROCEDURE

SECTION 1 – INFRINGEMENT ACTION

Rule 12 – Exchange of written pleadings (infringement action)

1. The written procedure shall consist of:

(a) the lodging of a Statement of claim (by the claimant) [Rule 13];

(b) the lodging of a Statement of defence (by the defendant) [Rules 23 and 24]; and, optionally

(c) the lodging of a Reply to the Statement of defence (by the claimant) [Rule 29(b)]; and

(d) the lodging of a Rejoinder to the Reply (by the defendant) [Rule 29(c)].

2. The Statement of defence may include a Counterclaim for revocation [Rule 25.1].

3. If a Counterclaim for revocation is lodged:

(a) the claimant and any proprietor who becomes a party pursuant to Rule 25.2 (hereinafter in this Rule 12 and Rules 29 to 32, "the proprietor") shall lodge a Defence to the Counterclaim for revocation [Rule 29(a)], which may include an Application to amend the patent by the proprietor [Rule 30];

(b) the defendant may lodge a Reply to the Defence to the Counterclaim [Rule 29(d)]; and

(c) the claimant and the proprietor may lodge a Rejoinder to the Reply to the Defence to the Counterclaim [Rule 29(e)].

4. If an Application to amend the patent is lodged by the proprietor, the defendant shall lodge a Defence to the Application to amend the patent in the Reply to the Defence to the Counterclaim, the proprietor may lodge a Reply to the Defence to the Application to amend and the defendant may lodge a Rejoinder to such Reply [Rule 32].

5. The judge-rapporteur may allow the exchange of further written pleadings, within time periods to be specified [Rule 36].

STATEMENT OF CLAIM

Rule 13 – Contents of the Statement of claim

1. The claimant shall lodge a Statement of claim with the division chosen by him [Article 33 of the Agreement] which shall contain:

(a) the name of the claimant, and, where the claimant is a corporate entity, the location of its registered office, and of the claimant's representative;

(b) the name of the party against whom the Statement is made (the defendant), and, where the defendant is a corporate entity, the location of its registered office;

(c) postal and electronic addresses for service on the claimant and the names of the persons authorised to accept service;

(d) postal and, where available, electronic addresses for service on the defendant and the names of the persons authorised to accept service, if known;

(e) where the claimant is not the proprietor or not the only proprietor of the patent concerned, postal and where available, electronic addresses for service on the proprietor and the names and addresses of the persons authorised to accept service, if known;

(f) where the claimant is not the proprietor of the patent concerned, or not the only proprietor, evidence to show the claimant is entitled to commence proceedings [Article 47(2) and (3) of the Agreement];

(g) details of the patent concerned, including the number;

(h) where applicable, information about any prior or pending proceedings relating to the patent concerned before the Court including any action for revocation or a declaration of non-infringement pending before the central division and the date of any such action, the European Patent Office or any other court or authority;

(i) an indication of the division which shall hear the action [Article 33(1) to (6) of the Agreement] with an explanation of why that division has competence; where the parties have agreed in accordance with Article 33(7) of the Agreement, the indication of the division which shall hear the action shall be accompanied by evidence of the defendant's agreement;

(j) where applicable, an indication that the action shall be heard by a single judge [Article 8(7) of the Agreement], accompanied by evidence of the defendant's agreement;

(k) the nature of the claim, the order or the remedy sought by the claimant;

(l) an indication of the facts relied on, in particular:
(i) one or more instances of alleged infringements or threatened infringements specifying the date and place of each;
(ii) the identification of the patent claims alleged to be infringed;

(m) the evidence relied on [Rule 170.1], where available, and an indication of any further evidence which will be offered in support;

(n) the reasons why the facts relied on constitute an infringement of the patent claims, including arguments of law and where appropriate an explanation of the proposed claim interpretation;

(o) an indication of any order the claimant will seek during the interim procedure [Rule 104(e)];

(p) where the claimant assesses that the value of the infringement action exceeds EUR500.000, an indication of the value; and

(q) a list of the documents, including any witness statements, referred to in the Statement of claim, together with any request that all or part of any such document need not be translated and/or any request pursuant to Rule 262.2 or Rule 262A.

2. The claimant shall at the same time supply a copy of each of the documents referred to in the Statement of claim.

3. The judge-rapporteur shall decide on any request made pursuant to paragraph 1(q) as soon as practicable after his designation pursuant to Rule 18.

Rule 14 – Use of languages under Article 49(1) and (2) of the Agreement

1. Without prejudice to Articles 49(3) to (6) of the Agreement and subject to paragraph 2 and Rules 271.7, 321 to 323, proceedings shall be conducted:

(a) in the official language or one of the official languages designated as language(s) of proceedings pursuant to Article 49(1) of the Agreement; or

(b) in a language designated as language of proceedings by a Contracting Member State pursuant to Article 49(2) of the Agreement.

2. Where a Contracting Member State hosts a local division or participates in a regional division for which several languages have been designated pursuant to Article 49(1) and/or Article 49(2) of the Agreement:

(a) subject to paragraphs 2(b) and (c), the claimant may choose as the language of proceedings any of the language(s) designated pursuant to Article 49(1) and/or Article 49(2) of the Agreement;

(b) in proceedings before a local or regional division in a Contracting Member State against a defendant who has his domicile or principal place of business in that Contracting Member State where the action could not be brought pursuant to Article 33(1)(a) of the Agreement before any other local or regional division, proceedings shall be conducted in the official language of the Contracting Member State (paragraph 1(a)). Where a designation by a Contracting Member State having several official regional languages so indicates, proceedings shall be conducted in the official language of the region in which the defendant has his domicile or principal place of business. Where there are two or more such defendants whose domicile or principle place of business has different regional languages, the claimant may choose the language from the regional languages in question. Where a designation by a Contracting Member

State having several official languages so indicates, proceedings shall be conducted in the official language of the defendant. Where there are two or more such defendants with different official languages, the claimant may choose the language from the official languages in question.

(c) Where a designation of a language under Article 49(2) of the Agreement for a regional division or for one or more local division(s) hosted in a Member State so indicates, the judge-rapporteur may order in the interest of the panel to provide that judges may use in the oral proceedings the language according to paragraph 1(a) and/or to provide that the Court may make any order and deliver any decision in the language according to paragraph 1(a) together with a certified translation for the purpose of Rule 118.8 into the language according to paragraph 1(b).

3. The Registrar shall maintain a list of languages communicated by Contracting Member States pursuant to Article 49(1) and Article 49(2) of the Agreement as well as designations by Contracting Member States made pursuant to paragraph 2(b) and (c). The list shall be made publically available online.

4. The Registrar shall return any pleading lodged in a language other than the language of proceedings.

Rule 15 – Fee for the infringement action

1. The claimant shall pay the fixed fee and, where applicable, the value-based fee for the infringement action in accordance with Part 6.

2. The Statement of claim shall not be deemed to have been lodged until the fixed fee and, where applicable, the value-based fee for the infringement action has been paid, unless otherwise provided.

3. Paragraphs 1. and 2. apply *mutatis mutandis* to counterclaims concerning licenses.

Relation with Agreement: Articles 36(3), 70 and 71

Rule 16 – Examination as to formal requirements of the Statement of claim

1. The Registry shall as soon as practicable check whether the patent concerned is the subject of an opt-out pursuant to Article 83(3) of the Agreement and Rule 5. In the event of an opt-out the Registry shall as soon as practicable inform the claimant who may withdraw or amend the Statement of claim as appropriate.

2. The Registry shall, as soon as practicable after the lodging of the Statement of claim, examine whether the requirements of Rules 13.1 (a) to (j),.2, 14 and 15.1 have been complied with.

3. If the claimant has not complied with the requirements referred to in paragraph 2, the Registry shall as soon as practicable invite the claimant to:

(a) correct the deficiencies within 14 days of service of such notification; and

(b) where applicable, pay the fee for the infringement action within said 14 days.

4. The Registry shall at the same time inform the claimant that if the claimant fails to correct the deficiencies or pay the fee within the time stated, a decision by default may be given, in accordance with Rule 355.

5. If the claimant fails to correct the deficiencies or pay the fee, the Registry shall inform a judge of the division who may reject the action as inadmissible by a decision by default. The judge may give the claimant an opportunity to be heard beforehand.

Rule 17 – Recording in the register and assignment (Court of First Instance, infringement action)

1. If the requirements referred to in Rule 16.2 or 16.3 have been complied with, the Registry shall as soon as practicable:

(a) record the date of receipt of the Statement of claim and attribute an action number to the file;

(b) record the file in the register; and

(c) inform the claimant of the action number of the file and the date of receipt.

2. The action shall be assigned to a panel of a division according to Rule 345.3. Where requested by the parties the action shall be assigned to a single judge in accordance with Rule 345.6.

3. The following shall determine the distribution of actions between the seat of the central division and its sections.

(a) Where an action involves a single patent having a single classification, the Registry shall allocate the action to the seat or the section of the central division appropriate to the classification of the patent according to Annex II of the Agreement. The Registry shall assign the action to a panel in accordance with Rule 345.3.

(b) Where an action involves more than one patent and a majority of the patents have a single classification appropriate to the seat or a single section of the central division according to Annex II of the Agreement, the Registry shall allocate the action to the seat or that section of the central division. The Registry shall assign the action to a panel in accordance with Rule 345.3.

(c) Where neither paragraph (a) nor (b) applies, especially where
(i) the action involves a single patent having more than one classification or
(ii) where the action involves more than one patent and no majority of the patents have a single classification corresponding to the seat or to one of the sections of the central division,

the Registry shall assign the action in accordance with Rule 345.3 to the panel at the seat or the section appropriate to the first classification of either the single patent or, where the action involves more than one patent, the patent first listed in the Statement of claim, according to Annex II of the Agreement. If the presiding judge of the respective panel considers that the reference of the action is appropriate, he shall accept it. If he considers otherwise, he shall instruct the Registry to refer the action in accordance with Rule 345.3 to the presiding judge of a panel of either the seat or the other section of the central division he considers appropriate, who shall likewise consider whether the re-allocation of the action is appropriate. If that presiding judge considers otherwise, he shall inform the President of the Court of First Instance, who shall allocate the action to the seat or the section of the central division he considers appropriate. The Registry shall assign the action to a panel in accordance with Rule 345.3.

4. The action shall be regarded as having commenced before the Court as from the date of receipt attributed to the Statement of claim.

Relation with Agreement: Article 7(2), Article 10

Rule 18 – Designation of the judge-rapporteur

The presiding judge of the panel to which the action has been assigned [Rule 17.2] shall designate one legally qualified judge of the panel as judge-rapporteur. The presiding judge may designate himself as judge-rapporteur. The Registry shall as soon as practicable notify the claimant and defendant of the identity of the judge-rapporteur.

PROCEDURE WHEN THE DEFENDANT RAISES A PRELIMINARY OBJECTION

Rule 19 – Preliminary objection

1. Within one month of service of the Statement of claim, the defendant may lodge a Preliminary objection concerning:

(a) the jurisdiction and competence of the Court, including any objection that an opt-out pursuant to Rule 5 applies to the patent that is the subject of the proceedings;

(b) the competence of the division indicated by the claimant [Rule 13.1(i)];

(c) the language of the Statement of claim [Rule 14].

2. A Preliminary objection shall contain:

(a) particulars in accordance with Rule 24(a) to (c);

(b) the decision or order sought by the defendant;

(c) the grounds upon which the Preliminary objection is based; and

(d) where appropriate the facts and evidence relied on.

3. The Preliminary objection shall be drawn up in the language pursuant to Rule 14.

4. If the action has been commenced before a regional division the defendant may by a Preliminary objection request a transfer of the action to the central division pursuant to Article 33(2) of the Agreement. The Preliminary objection shall in such a

case contain all facts and evidence supporting the existence of the same infringement in the territories of three or more regional divisions.

5. The Registry shall as soon as practicable invite the claimant to comment on the Preliminary objection. Where applicable, the claimant may of his own motion correct any deficiency [paragraph 1(b) or (c)], within 14 days of service of notification of the Preliminary objection. Alternatively the claimant may submit written comments within the same period. The judge-rapporteur shall be informed of any correction made or written comments submitted by the claimant. If the deficiency referred to in paragraph 1(b) is corrected and the claimant has indicated another division, which is competent, the judge-rapporteur shall refer the action to the division indicated by the claimant.

6. The period for lodging the Statement of defence [Rule 23] shall not be affected by the lodging of a Preliminary objection, unless the judge-rapporteur decides otherwise.

7. The defendant's failure to lodge a Preliminary objection within the time period referred to in paragraph 1 shall be treated as a submission to the jurisdiction and competence of the Court and the competence of the division chosen by the claimant.

Rule 20 – Decision or order on a Preliminary objection

1. As soon as practicable after the expiry of the period referred to in Rule 19.5, the judge-rapporteur shall decide the Preliminary objection. The judge-rapporteur shall give the parties an opportunity to be heard. The decision shall include instructions to the parties and to the Registry concerning the next step in the proceedings.

2. Where the Preliminary objection is to be dealt with in the main proceedings, the judge-rapporteur shall inform the parties.

Rule 21 – Appeal against decision or order on a Preliminary objection

1. A decision of the judge-rapporteur allowing the Preliminary objection may be appealed pursuant to Rule 220.1(a). An order of the judge-rapporteur rejecting the Preliminary objection may only be appealed pursuant to Rule 220.2.

2. If an appeal is lodged, proceedings at first instance may be stayed by the judge-rapporteur or the Court of Appeal on a reasoned request by a party.

VALUE-BASED FEE FOR THE INFRINGEMENT ACTION

Rule 22 – Determination of value-based fee for the infringement action

1. The value of the infringement action including an action for compensation derived from the provisional protection conferred by a published European patent application shall be determined by the judge-rapporteur under Rule 370.6, taking into account the value as assessed by the parties, by way of an order during the interim procedure.

2. Where the value of the infringement action exceeds EUR 500.000, the claimant shall pay a value-based fee for the infringement action, in accordance with Part 6. Rule 16.3 to .5 shall apply *mutatis mutandis*.

STATEMENT OF DEFENCE

Rule 23 – Lodging of the Statement of defence

The defendant shall lodge a Statement of defence within three months of service of the Statement of claim.

Rule 24 – Contents of the Statement of defence

The Statement of defence shall contain:

(a) the names of the defendant and of the defendant's representative;

(b) postal and electronic addresses for service on the defendant and the names and addresses of the persons authorised to accept service;

(c) the action number of the file;

(d) an indication whether the defendant has lodged a Preliminary objection [Rule 19];

(e) an indication of the facts relied on, including any challenge to the facts relied on by the claimant;

(f) the evidence relied on [Rule 170.1], where available, and an indication of any further evidence which will be offered in support;

(g) the reasons why the action shall fail, arguments of law and any argument arising from the provisions of Article 28 of the Agreement and where appropriate any challenge to the claimant's proposed claim interpretation;

(h) an indication of any order the defendant will seek in respect of the infringement action during the interim procedure [Rule 104(e)];

(i) a statement whether the defendant disputes the claimant's assessment of the value of the infringement action and the grounds for such dispute; and

(j) a list of the documents, including any witness statements, referred to in the Statement of defence together with any request that all or part of any such document need not be translated

and/or any request pursuant to Rule 262.2 or Rule 262A. Rule 13.2 and .3 shall apply *mutatis mutandis*.

Rule 25 – Counterclaim for revocation

1. If the Statement of defence includes an assertion that the patent alleged to be infringed is invalid the Statement of defence shall include a Counterclaim against the proprietor of the patent for revocation of said patent in accordance with Rule 42. The Counterclaim for revocation shall contain:

(a) an indication of the extent to which revocation of the patent is requested;

(b) one or more grounds for revocation, which shall as far as possible be supported by arguments of law, and where appropriate an explanation of the defendant's proposed claim construction;

(c) an indication of the facts relied on;

(d) the evidence relied on, where available, and an indication of any further evidence which will be offered in support;

(e) an indication of any order the defendant will seek during the interim procedure [Rule 104(e)];

(f) a statement of his position, if any, on the options provided for in Article 33(3) of the Agreement and Rule 37.4;

(g) a list of the documents, including any witness statements, referred to in the Counterclaim for revocation together with any request that all or part of any such documents need not be translated and/or any request pursuant to Rule 262.2 or Rule 262A. Rule 13.2 and .3 shall apply *mutatis mutandis*; and

(h) insofar as the proprietor of the patent is not claimant in the infringement proceedings, the information required by Rule 13.1(b) and (d) in respect of said proprietor.

2. Where the claimant is not the proprietor or not the only proprietor of the patent concerned, the Registry shall as soon as practicable serve a copy of the Counterclaim for revocation on the relevant proprietor in accordance with Rule 13.1(e) and shall supply a copy of each document referred to in paragraph 1(h). Rule 271 shall apply *mutatis mutandis*. The proprietor in question shall become a party to the revocation proceedings and shall be treated as defendant in all subsequent proceedings. The proprietor shall provide details pursuant to Rule 13.1(e) if not already provided by the claimant.

Rule 26 – Fee for the Counterclaim for revocation

The defendant shall pay the fee for the Counterclaim for revocation in accordance with Part 6. Rule 15.2 shall apply *mutatis mutandis*.

Rule 27 – Examination as to formal requirements of the Statement of defence and Counterclaim for revocation

1. The Registry shall, as soon as practicable after the lodging of the Statement of defence:

(a) examine whether the requirements of Rule 24(a) to (d) have been complied with; and

(b) if the Statement of defence includes a Counterclaim for revocation, examine whether the requirements of Rule 25.1(g) and (h), and the obligation to pay the fee pursuant to Rule 26 has been complied with.

2. If the Registry considers that the Statement of defence or the Counterclaim for revocation does not comply with any of the requirements referred to in paragraph 1, it shall as soon as practicable invite the defendant to:

(a) correct the deficiencies noted, within 14 days of service of such notification; and

(b) where applicable, pay the fee for the Counterclaim for revocation, within said 14 days.

3. The Registry shall at the same time inform the defendant that if the defendant fails to correct the deficiencies or pay the fee within the time stated, a decision by default may be given, in accordance with Rule 355.

4. If the defendant fails to correct the deficiencies or to pay the fee for the Counterclaim for revocation, as appropriate, within said 14 days, the Registry shall inform the judge-rapporteur who may give a decision by default. He may give the defendant an opportunity to be heard beforehand.

Rule 28 – Further schedule

As soon as practicable after service of the Statement of defence, the judge-rapporteur shall, after consulting the parties, set a date and time for an interim conference (where necessary [Rule 101.1]) and set a date for the oral hearing. The judge-rapporteur may set one alternative date.

DEFENCE TO THE COUNTERCLAIM FOR REVOCATION, REPLY TO THE STATEMENT OF THE DEFENCE AND APPLICATION TO AMEND THE PATENT AND REJOINDER TO THE REPLY

Rule 29 – Lodging of Defence to the Counterclaim for revocation, Reply to the Statement of defence and Rejoinder to the Reply

(a) Within two months of service of a Statement of defence which includes a Counterclaim for revocation, the claimant shall lodge a Defence to the Counterclaim for revocation together with any Reply to the Statement of defence and any Application to amend the patent pursuant to Rule 30, if applicable.

(b) Within two months of service of a Statement of defence which does not include a Counterclaim for revocation, the claimant may lodge a Reply to the Statement of defence.

(c) Within one month of service of a Reply to the Statement of defence which does not include a Counterclaim for revocation the defendant may lodge a Rejoinder to the Reply to the Statement of defence. The Rejoinder to the Reply to the Statement of defence shall be limited to a response to the matters raised in the Reply to the Statement of defence.

(d) Within two months of service of the Defence to Counterclaim the defendant may lodge a Reply to the Defence to the Counterclaim together with any Rejoinder to the Reply to the Statement of defence and any Defence to an Application to amend the patent pursuant to Rule 32, if applicable.

(e) Within one month of the service of the Reply to the Defence to the Counterclaim, the claimant may lodge a Rejoinder to the Reply together with any Reply to the Defence to an Application to amend the patent pursuant to Rule 32, if applicable. The Rejoinder to the Reply to the Statement of defence shall be limited to a response to the matters raised in the Reply to the Statement of defence.

(f) Where the claimant is not the proprietor of the patent, all references to the claimant in this Rule 29 regarding an Application to amend the patent shall be read as including the proprietor.

Rule 29A – Contents of the Defence to the Counterclaim

The Defence to the Counterclaim for revocation shall contain:

(a) an indication of the facts relied on, including any challenge to the facts relied on by the defendant;

(b) the evidence relied on [Rule 170.1], where available, and an indication of any further evidence which will be offered in support;

(c) the reasons why the Counterclaim for revocation shall fail, including arguments of law and any argument as to why any dependent claim of the patent is independently valid;

(d) an indication of any order the claimant and the proprietor will seek in respect of the revocation action at the interim conference [Rule 104(e)];

(e) the claimant's and the proprietor's response to the defendant's choice of option, if any, provided for in Article 33(3) of the Agreement and Rule 37.4; and

(f) a list of the documents, including any witness statements, referred to in the Defence to the Counterclaim together with any request that all or part of any such document shall not be translated and/or any request pursuant to Rule 262.2 or Rule 262A. Rule 13.2 and .3 shall apply *mutatis mutandis.*

Rule 30 – Application to amend the patent

1. The Defence to the Counterclaim for revocation may include an Application by the proprietor of the patent to amend the patent which shall contain:

(a) the proposed amendments of the claims of the patent concerned and/or specification, including where applicable and appropriate one or more alternative sets of claims (auxiliary requests), in the language in which the patent was granted; where the language of the proceedings [Rule 14.3] is not the language in which the patent was granted, the proprietor shall lodge a translation of the proposed amendments in the language of the proceedings, and where the patent is a European patent with unitary effect in the language of the defendant's domicile in a Member State of the

EU or of the place of the alleged infringement or threatened infringement in a Contracting Member State if so requested by the defendant;

(b) an explanation as to why the amendments satisfy the requirements of Articles 84 and 123(2), (3) EPC and why the proposed amended claims are valid and, if applicable, why they are infringed; and

(c) an indication whether the proposals are conditional or unconditional; the proposed amendments, if conditional, must be reasonable in number in the circumstances of the case.

2. Any subsequent request to amend the patent may only be admitted into the proceedings with the permission of the Court.

3. Where other proceedings involving the patent subject to an Application to amend the patent are pending, the claimant shall notify the Court or the authority in question that such an Application has been made and provide the information required in paragraph 1(a).

DEFENCE TO THE APPLICATION TO AMEND THE PATENT

Rule 32 – Lodging of the Defence to the Application to amend the patent, the Reply to the Defence and the Rejoinder to the Reply

1. Within two months of service of an Application to amend the patent, the defendant shall lodge a Defence to the Application to amend the patent setting out whether he opposes the Application to amend the patent and, if so, why:

(a) the proposed amendments are not allowable; and

(b) the patent cannot be maintained as requested.

2. Where appropriate in view of the proposed amendments, the Defence to the Application to amend the patent may contain submissions in accordance with Rule 44(d) to (h) and alternative non-infringement submissions.

3. The proprietor may lodge a Reply to the Defence to the Application to amend the patent within one month of service of the Defence and the defendant may within one month of the service of the Reply lodge a Rejoinder to the Reply. The Rejoinder shall be limited to the matters raised in the Reply.

APPLICATION FOR ALLOCATING A TECHNICALLY QUALIFIED JUDGE TO THE PANEL

Rule 33 – Application by a party for allocating a technically qualified judge

1. Any party to the proceedings may lodge an Application for allocating a technically qualified judge to the panel which shall contain an indication of the relevant field of technology.

2. The Application shall be lodged as early as possible in the written procedure. An Application lodged after the closure of the written procedure [Rule 35] shall only be granted if justified in view of changed circumstances, such as new submissions presented by the other party, and allowed by the Court.

3. If the requirements of paragraphs 1 and 2 have been complied with, the President of the Court of First Instance shall allocate a technically qualified judge to the panel, after consulting the judge-rapporteur.

Rule 34 – Request by the judge-rapporteur for allocating a technically qualified judge

1. The judge-rapporteur may at any time during the written procedure, after consulting the presiding judge and the parties, request the President of the Court of First Instance to allocate a technically qualified judge to the panel.

2. Where a technically qualified judge is allocated to the panel, the judge-rapporteur may at any time consult the technically qualified judge.

LAST STEPS IN THE WRITTEN PROCEDURE

Rule 35 – Closure of the written procedure

Following the exchange of written pleadings in accordance with Rule 12.1 and, where applicable, in accordance with Rule 12.2 to .4, the judge-rapporteur shall:

(a) inform the parties of the date on which he intends to close the written procedure, without prejudice to Rule 36; and

(b) where an interim conference is necessary [Rules 28 and 101.1], confirm the date and the time set for the interim conference [Rule 28] or inform the parties that an interim conference will not be held.

Rule 36 – Further exchanges of written pleadings

Without prejudice to the powers of the judge-rapporteur pursuant to Rule 110.1, on a reasoned request by a party lodged before the date on which the judge-rapporteur intends to close the written procedure [Rule 35(a)], the judge-rapporteur may allow the exchange of further written pleadings, within a period to be specified. Where the exchange of further written pleadings is allowed, the written procedure shall be deemed closed upon expiry of the specified period.

Rule 37 – Application of Article 33(3) of the Agreement

1. As soon as practicable after the closure of the written procedure the panel shall decide by way of order how to proceed with respect to the application of Article 33(3) of the Agreement. The parties shall be given an opportunity to be heard [Rule 264]. The panel shall set out in its order brief reasons for its decision.

2. The Panel may by order take an earlier decision if appropriate having considered the parties' pleadings and having given the parties an opportunity to be heard [Rule 264].

3. Where the panel decides to proceed in accordance with Article 33(3)(a) of the Agreement, the judge-rapporteur shall request the President of the Court of First Instance to allocate to the panel a technically qualified judge if not already allocated pursuant to Rules 33 and 34.

4. Where the panel decides to proceed in accordance with Article 33(3)(b) of the Agreement, the panel may stay the infringement proceedings pending a final decision in the revocation proceedings and shall stay the infringement proceedings where there is a high likelihood that the relevant claims of the patent will be held to be invalid on any ground by the final decision in the revocation proceedings.

5. Where the panel decides to proceed in accordance with Article 33(3)(b) of the Agreement and not to stay the proceedings, the judge-rapporteur of the regional or local division shall communicate to the central division the dates set for the interim conference and for the oral hearing according to Rule 28.

COUNTERCLAIM FOR REVOCATION REFERRED TO THE CENTRAL DIVISION UNDER ARTICLE 33(3)(B) OF THE AGREEMENT

Rule 38 – Written procedure when the central division deals with a Counterclaim for revocation under Article 33(3)(b) of the Agreement

When a Counterclaim for revocation is referred to the central division, it shall be dealt with as follows:

(a) Rule 17.2 and .3 shall apply *mutatis mutandis*;

(b) Rule 18 shall apply *mutatis mutandis*: the presiding judge of the panel to which the Counterclaim for revocation has been assigned shall designate one legally qualified judge of the panel as judge-rapporteur;

(c) The judge-rapporteur shall give any further directions necessary for the future conduct of the written procedure before the central division;

(d) Rule 28 shall apply *mutatis mutandis*: the judge-rapporteur shall after consulting the parties set a date and a time for the interim conference (where necessary [Rules 28 and 101]) and set a date, and one alternative date, for the oral hearing.

Rule 39 – Language of the proceedings before the central division

1. Where the language of the proceedings before the local division or the regional division which referred the Counterclaim for revocation to the central division is not the language in which the patent was granted, the judge-rapporteur may order that the parties lodge, within a period of one month, a translation in the language in which the patent was granted of any written pleadings and such other documents lodged during the written procedure as the judge-rapporteur may direct.

2. Where appropriate, the judge-rapporteur may specify in his order that only excerpts of parties' written pleadings and other documents shall be translated.

3. Where the language of the proceedings before the local division or the regional division is the language in which the patent was granted the pleadings served in accordance with Rules 24, 25, 29, 29a, 30 and 32 shall stand.

Rule 40 – Accelerated proceedings before the central division

The judge-rapporteur shall accelerate proceedings before the central division where

(a) an Application for provisional measures has been lodged [Rule 206]; or

(b) the regional or local division has referred the Counterclaim for revocation to the central division and where the infringement action has not been stayed.

In the latter case, the judge-rapporteur of the panel of the central division shall endeavour to set a date for the oral hearing on the revocation action prior to the date of the oral hearing of the infringement action.

ACTION REFERRED TO THE CENTRAL DIVISION UNDER ARTICLE 33(3)(C) OF THE AGREEMENT

Rule 41 – Written procedure when the central division deals with the action under Article 33(3)(c) of the Agreement

When an action is referred to the central division under Article 33(3)(c) of the Agreement, it shall be dealt with as follows:

(a) Rule 17.2 and .3 shall apply *mutatis mutandis*. The parties may request that the action be heard by a single judge;

(b) Rule 18 shall apply *mutatis mutandis*: the presiding judge of the panel to which the action has been assigned shall designate one judge of the panel as judge-rapporteur;

(c) dates already set under Rule 28 shall be confirmed wherever possible;

(d) Rule 39 shall apply *mutatis mutandis*: the judge-rapporteur may order that the parties lodge a translation in the language in which the patent was granted of any written pleadings lodged during the written procedure; where appropriate, the judge-rapporteur may specify in his order that only excerpts of parties' written pleadings and other documents shall be translated. Otherwise the pleadings lodged during the written procedure shall stand;

(e) The judge-rapporteur shall give any further directions necessary for the future conduct of the written procedure before the central division.

SECTION 2 – REVOCATION ACTION

Rule 42 – Action to be directed against the patent proprietor

1. Any action for the revocation of a patent shall be directed against the proprietor of the patent.

2. If the action for revocation is directed against the proprietor in accordance with Rule 8.6 ("the registered proprietor") but the registered proprietor is not a proprietor within the meaning of Rule 8.5(a) or (b) ("the Rule 8.5 proprietor") each such registered proprietor shall as soon as practicable after service of the Statement for revocation apply to the Court pursuant to Rule 305.1(c) for the substitution of the registered proprietor by the Rule 8.5 proprietor.

Relation with Agreement: Articles 47(5) and 65(1)

Rule 43 – Exchange of written pleadings (revocation action)

1. The written procedure shall consist of:

(a) the lodging of a Statement for revocation (by the claimant) [Rule 44]; and

(b) the lodging of a Defence to revocation (by the defendant) [Rule 49]; and optionally

(c) the lodging of a Reply to the Defence to revocation (by the claimant) [Rule 51];

(d) the lodging of a Rejoinder to the Reply (by the defendant) [Rule 52].

2. The Defence to revocation may include:

(a) an Application to amend the patent; and

(b) a Counterclaim for infringement by the proprietor of the patent.

3. If an Application to amend the patent is lodged, the claimant shall lodge a Defence to the Application to amend the patent. The defendant may lodge a Reply to the Defence to the Application. The claimant may lodge a Rejoinder to the Reply. The Rejoinder shall be limited to a response to the matters raised in the Reply.

4. If a Counterclaim for infringement is lodged, the claimant shall lodge a Defence to the Counterclaim for infringement [Rule 56], the defendant may lodge a Reply to the Defence to the Counterclaim [Rule 56.3] and the claimant may lodge a Rejoinder to the Reply [Rule 56.4].

5. Rule 12.5 shall apply.

STATEMENT FOR REVOCATION

Rule 44 – Contents of the Statement for revocation

The claimant shall, subject to point (b), lodge a Statement for revocation at the Registry in accordance with Article 7(2) of the Agreement and Annex II thereto. The Statement for revocation shall contain:

(a) particulars in accordance with Rule 13.1(a) to (d) and (g), (h);

(b) where the parties have agreed to bring the action before a local division or a regional division in accordance with Article 33(7) of the Agreement, an indication of the division which shall hear the action, accompanied by evidence of the defendant's agreement;

(c) where applicable, an indication that the action shall be heard by a single judge [Article 8(7) of the Agreement], accompanied by evidence of the defendant's agreement;

(d) an indication of the extent to which revocation of the patent is requested;

(e) one or more grounds for revocation, which shall as far as possible be supported by arguments of law, and where appropriate an explanation of the claimant's proposed claim construction;

(f) an indication of the facts relied on;

(g) the evidence relied on, where available, and an indication of any further evidence which will be offered in support;

(h) an indication of any order the claimant will seek during the interim procedure [Rule 104(e)]; and

(i) a list of the documents, including any witness statements, referred to in the Statement for revocation together with any request that all or part of any such document need not be translated and/or any request pursuant to Rule 262.2 and Rule 262A. Rule 13.2 and .3 shall apply *mutatis mutandis*.

Rule 45 – Language of the Statement for revocation

1. Subject to paragraph 2, the Statement for revocation shall be drawn up in the language in which the patent was granted.

2. Where the parties have agreed to bring the action before a local or a regional division in accordance with Article 33(7) of the Agreement, the Statement for revocation shall be drawn up in one of the languages referred to in Rule 14.1(a) and (b).

Relation with Agreement: Article 49

Rule 46 – Fee for the revocation action

The claimant shall pay the fee for the revocation action in accordance with Part 6. Rule 15.2 shall apply *mutatis mutandis*.

Relation with Agreement: Articles 70 and 71

Rule 47 – Examination as to formal requirements, recording in the register, assignment (Court of First Instance, revocation action) and designation of the judge-rapporteur

1. Rules 16 to 18 shall apply *mutatis mutandis*.

2. The Registrar shall notify the European Patent Office that the patent in question is subject to an action for revocation.

Relation with Agreement: Articles 10 and 33

Rule 48 – Preliminary objection

Rule 19.1 to .3 and .5 to .7 as well as Rules 20 and 21 shall apply *mutatis mutandis*.

DEFENCE TO REVOCATION

Rule 49 – Lodging of the Defence to revocation

1. The defendant shall lodge a Defence to revocation within two months of service of the Statement for revocation.

2. The Defence to revocation may include:

(a) an Application to amend the patent;

(b) a Counterclaim for infringement.

Rule 50 – Contents of the Defence to revocation and Counterclaim for infringement

1. The Defence to revocation shall contain the matters referred to in Rule 24(a) to (c). Rule 29A(a) to (d) and (f) shall apply *mutatis mutandis*.

2. Any Application to amend the patent shall contain the matters referred to in Rule 30.1(a), (c) and an explanation as to why the amendments satisfy the requirements of Articles 84 and 123(2), (3) EPC and why the proposed amended claims are valid. Rule 30.2 shall apply.

3. Any Counterclaim for infringement shall contain the matters referred to in Rule 13.1(k) to (q). Rule 13.2 and .3 shall apply.

Rule 51 – Reply to Defence to revocation

Within two months of service of the Defence to revocation the claimant may lodge a Reply to the Defence to revocation together with any Defence to an Application to amend the patent pursuant to Rule 43.3 and 55 as well as any Defence to the Counterclaim for infringement pursuant to Rule 56.1, if applicable.

Rule 52 – Rejoinder to the Reply

Within one month of the service of the Reply the defendant may lodge a Rejoinder to the Reply to the Defence to revocation together with any Reply to the Defence to an Application to amend the patent pursuant to Rule 43.3 and 55 as well as any Reply to the Defence to the Counterclaim for infringement pursuant to Rule 56.3, if applicable. The Rejoinder shall be limited to a response to the matters raised in the Reply.

Rule 53 – Fee for the Counterclaim for infringement

The defendant shall pay the fixed fee and, where applicable, the value based fee for the Counterclaim for infringement in accordance with Part 6. Rule 15 and Rule 16.3 to 5 shall apply *mutatis mutandis.*

Rule 54 – Examination as to formal requirements and further schedule

Rules 27 and 28 shall apply *mutatis mutandis.*

DEFENCE TO THE APPLICATION TO AMEND THE PATENT AND DEFENCE TO THE COUNTERCLAIM FOR INFRINGEMENT

Rule 55 – Lodging of the Defence to the Application to amend the patent, the Reply to the Defence and the Rejoinder to the Reply

Rule 32 shall apply *mutatis mutandis.*

Rule 56 – Lodging of the Defence to the Counterclaim for infringement

1. Within two months of service of a Counterclaim for infringement, the claimant shall lodge a Defence to the Counterclaim for infringement.

2. The Defence to the Counterclaim for infringement shall contain the matters referred to in Rule 24.1(e) to (h) and (j) and a statement whether the claimant disputes the defendant's assessment of the value of the Counterclaim pursuant to Rule 50.3 and the reasons for such dispute.

3. The defendant may lodge a Reply to the Defence to the Counterclaim for infringement within one month.

4. Within one month of the service of the Reply to the Defence to the Counterclaim for infringement the claimant may lodge a Rejoinder to the Reply together with any Rejoinder to the Reply to the Defence to the Application to amend the patent pursuant to Rule 43.3 and 55. The Rejoinder shall be limited to matters raised in the Reply.

Rule 57 – Request for allocating a technically qualified judge

Rules 33 and 34 shall apply *mutatis mutandis.*

Rule 58 – Closure of the written procedure subject to the possible exchange of further pleadings

Rules 35 and 36 shall apply *mutatis mutandis.*

Rule 60 – Determination of the value-based fee for the Counterclaim for infringement

1. The value of the Counterclaim for infringement shall be determined by the judge-rapporteur under Rule 370.6, taking into account the value as assessed by the parties, by way of an order during the interim procedure.

2. Where the value of the Counterclaim for infringement exceeds EUR 500.000, the defendant shall pay a value-based fee in accordance with Part 6. Rule 16.3 to .5 shall apply *mutatis mutandis.*

SECTION 3 – ACTION FOR DECLARATION OF NON-INFRINGEMENT

Rule 61 – Declaration of non-infringement

1. A declaration that the performance of a specific act does not, or a proposed act would not, constitute an infringement of a patent may be made by the Court in proceedings between the person doing or proposing to do the act and the patent proprietor or licensee entitled to commence infringement proceedings pursuant to Article 47 of the Agreement, if the patent proprietor or such licensee has asserted that the act is an infringement, or, if no such assertion has been made by the patent proprietor or licensee, if:

(a) that person has applied in writing to the proprietor or licensee for a written acknowledgment to the effect of the declaration claimed, and has provided him with full particulars in writing of the act in question; and

(b) the proprietor or licensee has refused or failed to give any such acknowledgment within one month.

2. The action for a declaration shall be directed against the proprietor of the patent or the licensee who has asserted an infringement or refused or failed to give an acknowledgement pursuant to paragraph 1(b).

3. If the action for a declaration of non-infringement is directed against the proprietor of the patent in accordance with Rule 8.6 ("the registered proprietor") but the registered proprietor is not a proprietor within the meaning of Rule 8.5(a) or (b) ("the Rule 8.5 proprietor") each such registered proprietor shall as soon as possible after service of the Statement for a declaration of non-infringement apply to the Court pursuant to Rule 305.1(c) for the substitution of the registered proprietor by the Rule 8.5 proprietor.

Rule 62 – Exchange of written pleadings (action for declaration of non-infringement)

1. The written procedure shall consist of:

(a) the lodging of a Statement for a declaration of non-infringement (by the claimant) [Rule 63];

(b) the lodging of a Defence to the Statement for a declaration of non-infringement (by the defendant) [Rules 67 and 68]; and, optionally

(c) the lodging of a Reply to the Defence to the Statement for a declaration of non-infringement [Rule 69];

(d) the lodging of a Rejoinder to the Reply [Rule 69].

2. Rule 12.5 shall apply.

Rule 63 – Contents of the Statement for a declaration of non-infringement

The claimant shall, subject to point (b), lodge at the Registry in accordance with Article 33(4), Article 7(2) of the Agreement and Annex II thereto, a Statement for a declaration of non-infringement which shall contain:

(a) particulars in accordance with Rule 13.1(a) to (h) and particulars confirming that the requirements of Rule 61 are met;

(b) where the parties have agreed to bring the action before a local division or a regional division in accordance with Article 33(7) of the Agreement, an indication of the division which shall hear the action, accompanied by evidence of the defendant's agreement;

(c) where applicable, an indication that the action shall be heard by a single judge [Article 8(7) of the Agreement], accompanied by evidence of the defendant's agreement;

(d) the declaration sought by the claimant;

(e) the reasons why the performance of a specific act does not, or a proposed act would not, constitute an infringement of the patent concerned, including arguments of law and where appropriate an explanation of the claimant's proposed claim construction;

(f) an indication of the facts relied on;

(g) the evidence relied on, where available, and an indication of any further evidence which will be offered in support;

(h) an indication of any order the claimant will seek at the interim conference [Rule 104(e)];

(i) where the claimant assesses that the value of the declaratory action exceeds EUR 500.000, an indication of the value; and

(j) a list of the documents, including any witness statements, referred to in the Statement for a declaration together with any request that all or part of any such document need not be translated and/or any request pursuant to Rule 262.2 or Rule 262A. Rule 13.2 and .3 shall apply *mutatis mutandis*.

Rule 64 – Language of the Statement for a declaration of non-infringement

Rule 45 shall apply *mutatis mutandis*.

Rule 65 – Examination as to formal requirements, recording in the register, assignment and designation of the judge-rapporteur

Rules 16 to 18 shall apply *mutatis mutandis*.

Rule 66 – Preliminary objection

Rule 19.1 to .3 and .5 to .7 as well as Rules 20 and 21 shall apply *mutatis mutandis*.

Rule 67 – Lodging of the Defence to the Statement for a declaration of non-infringement

The defendant shall lodge a Defence to the Statement for a declaration of non-infringement within two months of service of the Statement for a declaration of non-infringement.

Rule 68 – Contents of the Defence to the Statement for a declaration of non-infringement

The Defence to the Statement for a declaration of non-infringement shall contain the matters referred to in Rule 24(a) to (j). Rule 13.2 and .3 shall apply *mutatis mutandis*.

Rule 69 – Reply to Defence to the Statement for a declaration of non-infringement and Rejoinder to the Reply

1. The claimant may lodge a Reply to the Defence to the Statement for a declaration of non-infringement within one month.

2. The defendant may lodge a Rejoinder to the Reply within one month of service of the Reply. The Rejoinder shall be limited to the matters raised in the Reply.

Rule 70 – Fee for the action for a declaration of non-infringement

The claimant shall pay the fixed fee and, where applicable, the value-based fee for the action for a declaration of non-infringement including the action relating to the use of the invention prior to the granting of the patent or to the right based on prior use of the invention in accordance with Part 6. Rule 15.2 and Rule 16.3 to .5 shall apply *mutatis mutandis*.

Rule 71 – Examination as to formal requirements and further schedule

Rules 27 and 28 shall apply *mutatis mutandis*.

Rule 72 – Request for allocating a technically qualified judge

Rules 33 and 34 shall apply *mutatis mutandis*.

Rule 73 – Closure of the written procedure subject to the possible exchange of further pleadings

Rules 35 and 36 shall apply *mutatis mutandis.*

Rule 74 – Value-based fee for the action for a declaration of non-infringement

1. The value of the action for a declaration of non-infringement shall be determined by the judge-rapporteur under Rule 370.6, taking into account the value as assessed by the parties, by way of an order during the interim procedure.

2. Where the value exceeds EUR500.000 the claimant shall pay a value-based fee for the action for a declaration of non-infringement in accordance with Part 6. Rule 16.3 to .5 shall apply *mutatis mutandis.*

SECTION 4 – ACTIONS WITHIN ARTICLE 33(5) AND (6) OF THE AGREEMENT

Rule 75 – Revocation action and subsequent infringement action in a local or regional division (Article 33(5) of the Agreement)

1. Where a claimant has lodged a Statement for revocation [Rule 44] before the central division and the defendant or a licensee entitled to commence proceedings pursuant to Article 47 of the Agreement subsequently initiates an infringement action in a local or regional division against the claimant in respect of the same patent the following procedures shall apply.

2. The Registry at the local or regional division shall proceed in accordance with Rules 16 and 17. The Registry shall as soon as practicable notify the President of the Court of First Instance of the revocation action in the central division, the infringement action in the local or regional division and any Counterclaim for revocation in the infringement action. The presiding judges of the panels seized shall be informed likewise about actions in the other divisions.

3. Where a Counterclaim for revocation is brought in the infringement action and there is identity of parties as between the two actions, unless otherwise agreed by the parties, the panel appointed in the central division to hear the revocation action shall stay all further proceedings in the revocation action pending a decision of the panel hearing the action for infringement pursuant to Article 33(3) of the Agreement and Rule 37.

4. The panel hearing the action for infringement shall when exercising its discretion under Article 33(3) of the Agreement take into consideration how far the revocation action in the central division was advanced prior to the stay referred to in paragraph 3.

5. Where the panel hearing the action for infringement decides to proceed in accordance with Article 33(3)(a) of the Agreement, Rules 33 and 34 shall apply *mutatis mutandis* to the action for infringement.

6. Where the panel hearing the action for infringement decides to proceed in accordance with Article 33(3)(b) or (c) of the Agreement, Rules 37.4 and 39 to 41 shall apply *mutatis mutandis.*

Rule 76 – Actions for declaration of non-infringement within Article 33(6) of the Agreement

1. Where a claimant has lodged an action for declaration of non-infringement (Rule 61) before the central division against the patent proprietor or a licensee entitled to commence infringement proceedings pursuant to Article 47 of the Agreement and the defendant proprietor or licensee subsequently initiates an action for infringement in a local or regional division against the claimant in respect of the same patent and with respect to the same alleged infringement the following procedure shall apply.

2. The Registry shall proceed in accordance with Rule 16 and 17. The Registry shall as soon as practicable notify the President of the Court of First Instance of the co-pending actions and the dates attributed to them. The presiding judges of the panels seized shall be informed likewise about the action in the other division.

3. If the date attributed by the Registry to the action for infringement pursuant to Rule 17.1(a) is within three months of the date attributed to the action for declaration of non-infringement the panel of the central division shall stay all further proceedings in the action for a declaration. If the date attributed to the action for infringement is outside the said three month period there shall be no stay but the presiding judges of the central division and the local or regional division concerned shall consult to agree on the future progress of proceedings including the possibility of a stay of one action pursuant to Rule 295(f).

Rule 77 – Action for declaration of non-infringement and action for revocation

An action for declaration of non-infringement may be lodged together with an action for revocation of the patent in question. Fees shall be paid in accordance with both Rules 46 and Rules 70 and 74.

SECTION 5 – ACTION FOR COMPENSATION FOR LICENCES ON THE BASIS OF ARTICLE 8 OF REGULATION (EU) No 1257/2012

Rule 80 – Compensation for a licence of right

1. The Application for appropriate compensation [Article 32(1)(h) of the Agreement] shall contain:

(a) particulars in accordance with Rule 13.1(a) to (d);

(b) information on the filing of the statement as referred to in Article 8(1) of Regulation (EU) No 1257/2012;

(c) the licence agreement referred to in Article 8(2) of Regulation (EU) No 1257/2012.

2. Rules 132, 133, 134, 135 and 137 to 140 apply *mutatis mutandis* to the procedure for appropriate compensation.

Relation with Agreement: Article 32(1)(h)

SECTION 6 – ACTION AGAINST DECISIONS OF THE EUROPEAN PATENT OFFICE IN CARRYING OUT THE TASKS REFERRED TO IN ARTICLE 9 OF REGULATION (EU) No 1257/2012

Relation with Agreement: Articles 32(1)(i), 47(7) and 66

Rule 85 – Stages of the proceedings (ex parte proceedings)

1. Subject to paragraph 2, where an action is brought against a decision of the European Patent Office in carrying out the tasks referred to in Article 9 of Regulation (EU) No 1257/2012 (hereinafter "decision of the Office"), proceedings before the Court of First Instance shall consist of:

(a) a written procedure, which shall include a possibility for interlocutory review by the European Patent Office;

(b) an interim procedure, which may include an interim conference; and

(c) an oral procedure which, at the request of the claimant or at the instance of the Court, may include an oral hearing.

2. This Rule and Rules 88 (save as expressly provided for in Rule 97.2), 89 and 91 to 96 shall not apply to an expedited action against a decision of the Office pursuant to Rule 97.

Rule 86 – Suspensive effect

An action against a decision of the Office shall have suspensive effect.

Rule 87 – Grounds for annulling or altering a decision of the Office

An action against a decision of the Office may be brought on grounds of:

(a) infringement of Regulation (EU) No 1257/2012 or of Regulation (EU) No 1260/2012 or of any rule of law relating to their application;

(b) infringement of any of the implementing rules of the European Patent Office for carrying out the tasks referred to in Article 9(1) of Regulation (EU) No 1257/2012;

(c) infringement of an essential procedural requirement;

(d) misuse of power.

Rule 88 – Application to annul or alter a decision of the Office

1. The claimant shall lodge an Application at the Registry, in accordance with Article 7(2) of the Agreement and Annex II thereto, to annul or alter a decision of

the Office in the language in which the patent was granted, within two months of service of the decision of the Office.

2. The Application to annul or alter a decision of the Office shall contain:

(a) the names of the claimant and, where applicable, of the claimant's representative;

(b) where the claimant is not the proprietor of or applicant for the European patent with unitary effect, an explanation and evidence that he is adversely affected by the decision of the Office and entitled to start proceedings [Article 47(7) of the Agreement];

(c) postal and electronic addresses for service on the claimant and the names and addresses of the persons authorised to accept service;

(d) a reference to the contested decision of the Office;

(e) where applicable, information about any prior or pending proceedings relating to the patent concerned before the Court, the European Patent Office or any other court or authority;

(f) an indication whether the action shall be heard by a single judge;

(g) the order or the remedy sought by the claimant;

(h) one or more grounds for annulling or altering the contested decision, in accordance with Rule 87;

(i) the facts, evidence and arguments relied on; and

(j) a list of the documents, including any witness statements, referred to in the Application

together with any request that all or part of any such document need not be translated and/or any request pursuant to Rule 262.2 or Rule 262A. Rule 13.2 and 3 shall apply *mutatis mutandis.*

3. The claimant shall pay the fee for the action against a decision of the Office, in accordance with Part 6. Rule 15.2 shall apply *mutatis mutandis.*

4. Rule 8 shall not apply.

Relation with Agreement: Articles 32(1)(i), 33(9), 47(7), 48(7) and 49(6)

Rule 89 – Examination as to formal requirements (ex parte proceedings)

1. The Registry shall, as soon as practicable after an Application to annul or alter a decision of the Office has been lodged, examine whether the requirements of Articles 47(7) and 49(6) of the Agreement and Rule 88.1,.2(a) to (d) and .3 have been complied with.

2. If the Registry considers that any of the requirements referred to in paragraph 1 has not been complied with, it shall invite the claimant to:

(a) correct the deficiencies noted, within 14 days from the date of service of such notification; and

(b) where applicable, pay the fee for the action against a decision of the Office, within said 14 days.

3. The Registry shall at the same time inform the claimant that if the claimant fails to correct the deficiencies or pay the fee within the time stated, a decision by default may be given in accordance with Rule 355.

4. If the claimant fails to correct the deficiencies noted or to pay the fee for the action against a decision of the Office, the Registry shall inform the President of the Court of First Instance who may reject the action as inadmissible by a decision by default. He may give the claimant an opportunity to be heard beforehand.

Rule 90 – Recording in the register (ex parte proceedings)

If the requirements referred to in Rule 89.1 have been complied with, the Registry shall as soon as practicable:

(a) record the date of receipt of the Application to annul or alter a decision of the Office and attribute an action number to the file;

(b) record the file in the register;

(c) inform the claimant of the action number of the file and the date of receipt; and

(d) forward the Application to the European Patent Office, with an indication that the Application is admissible.

Rule 91 – Interlocutory revision by the European Patent Office

1. If the European Patent Office considers that the Application to annul or alter a decision of the Office is well founded, it shall within two months of the date of receipt of the Application:

(a) rectify the contested decision in accordance with the order or remedy sought by the claimant [Rule 88.2(g)]; and

(b) inform the Court that the decision has been rectified.

2. Where the Court is informed by the European Patent Office that the contested decision has been rectified, it shall inform the claimant that the action is closed. It may order full or partial reimbursement of the fee for the action against a decision of the Office, in accordance with Part 6.

Rule 92 – Assignment to panel or to single judge, designation of judge-rapporteur

Where the action is not closed in accordance with Rule 91.2, the action shall, as soon as practicable after the expiry of the period referred to in Rule 91.1, be assigned to a panel of the central division or to a single judge if requested by the claimant [Rule 88.2(f)] in accordance with Rule 345.3. Rule 18 shall apply.

Rule 93 – Examination of the Application to annul or alter a decision of the Office

1. In the examination of the Application to annul or alter a decision of the Office, the judge-rapporteur may invite the claimant to lodge further written pleadings, within a time period to be specified.

2. Where appropriate, the judge-rapporteur may, after consulting the claimant, set a date and time for an interim conference.

3. Rule 35 shall apply *mutatis mutandis.*

Rule 94 – Invitation to the President of the European Patent Office to comment

The judge-rapporteur may, on his own initiative or on request by the President of the European Patent Office, invite the President of the European Patent Office to comment in writing on any question arising in the course of proceedings under this Section including any appeal by the claimant pursuant to Rule 220. The claimant shall be entitled to submit his observations on the President's comments.

Rule 95 – Lex specialis for the interim procedure (ex parte procedure)

During the interim procedure, the judge-rapporteur shall invite the claimant to indicate whether he wishes that an oral hearing be convened. The judge-rapporteur may convene an oral hearing at his own instance.

Rule 96 – Lex specialis for the oral procedure (ex parte procedure)

1. Rules 110.3, 111, 115 and 118.6 shall apply to the oral hearing and to the decision of the Court.

2. If an oral hearing is not convened, the panel shall decide in accordance with Rule 117.

Rule 97 – Application to annul a decision of the Office to reject a request for unitary effect

1. The proprietor of a patent whose request for unitary effect has been rejected by the Office shall lodge an Application at the Registry in accordance with Article 7(2) of the Agreement and Annex II thereto, to reverse the decision of the Office, in the language in which the patent was granted, within three weeks of service of the decision of the European Patent Office.

2. The Application shall contain particulars in accordance with Rule 88.2(a), (c), (d) and (g) to (j) and the proprietor shall pay the fee for the action against the decision of the Office in accordance with Part 6. Rule 15.2 and Rule 89 shall apply *mutatis mutandis.*

3. If the requirements referred to in paragraph 2 have been complied with, Rule 90 shall apply *mutatis mutandis.*

4. The Registry shall as soon as practicable forward the Application to the standing judge who may invite the President of the European Patent Office to comment on the Application, but shall in any event decide the Application within three weeks of the date of receipt of the Application.

5. A Statement of appeal by the proprietor of the patent or the President of the European Patent Office against the decisions of the standing judge pursuant to paragraph 4 may be lodged within three weeks of service of the said decision. The Statement of appeal shall contain the particulars previously lodged pursuant to paragraph 2 and also the reasons for setting aside the contested decision. The appellant shall pay the fee for the appeal in accordance with Part 6. Rule 15.2 shall apply *mutatis mutandis.* If the requirements of this paragraph 5 have been complied with, the Registry shall record the appeal in accordance with Rule 230.1 and shall as soon as practicable assign the appeal to the standing judge of the Court of Appeal [Rule 345.5 and 345.8] who may invite the other party to comment on the appeal but shall in any event decide the appeal within three weeks of receipt by the Registry of the Statement of appeal.

6. The Registry shall as soon as practicable notify the Office of the decision on the Application or on the appeal as the case may be.

Rule 98 – Costs

The parties shall bear their own costs in any action pursuant to Rule 85 or 97.

CHAPTER 2 – INTERIM PROCEDURE

Rule 101 – Role of the judge-rapporteur (Case management)

1. During the interim procedure, the judge-rapporteur shall make all necessary preparations for the oral hearing. He may in particular, where appropriate, and subject to the mandate of the panel, hold an interim conference with the parties which may be held on more than one occasion and may exercise the powers provided for in Rule 334.

2. The judge-rapporteur shall have the obligation to ensure a fair, orderly and efficient interim procedure.

3. Without prejudice to the principle of proportionality, the judge-rapporteur shall complete the interim procedure within three months of the closure of the written procedure.

Relation with Agreement: Articles 43 and 52(2)

Rule 102 – Referral to the panel

1. The judge-rapporteur may refer any matter to the panel for decision and the panel may of its own motion review any decision or order of the judge-rapporteur or the conduct of the interim procedure.

2. Any party may request that a decision or order of the judge-rapporteur be referred to the panel for a review pursuant to Rule 333. Pending review, the decision or order of the judge-rapporteur shall be effective.

Rule 103 – Preparation for the interim conference

1. Whether or not the judge-rapporteur decides to hold an interim conference, he may order the parties, within time periods to be specified, in particular to:

(a) provide further clarification on specific points;

(b) answer specific questions;

(c) produce evidence;

(d) lodge specific documents including each party's summary of the orders to be sought at the interim conference.

The judge-rapporteur shall at the same time inform the party concerned that if the party fails to comply with the order within the time period specified, a decision by default may be given in accordance with Rule 355.

2. If a party fails to comply with an order of the judge-rapporteur within the time period specified, the judge-rapporteur may give a decision by default pursuant to Rule 355.

INTERIM CONFERENCE

Rule 104 – Aim of the interim conference

The interim conference shall enable the judge-rapporteur to:

(a) identify main issues and determine which relevant facts are in dispute;

(b) where appropriate, clarify the position of the parties as regards those issues and facts;

(c) establish a schedule for the further progress of the proceedings;

(d) explore with the parties the possibilities to settle the dispute or to make use of the facilities of the Centre;

(e) where appropriate, issue orders regarding production of further pleadings, documents, experts (including court experts), experiments, inspections, further written evidence, the matters to be the subject of oral evidence and the scope of questions to be put to the witnesses;

(f) where appropriate, but only in the presence of the parties, hold preparatory discussions with witnesses and experts with a view to properly preparing for the oral hearing;

(g) make any other decision or order as he deems necessary for the preparation of the oral hearing including, after consultation with the presiding judge, an order for a separate hearing of witnesses and experts before the panel;

(h) set a date for any separate hearing pursuant to point (g) of this Rule, confirm the date for the oral hearing and order, where appropriate, after consultation with the presiding judge and the parties that the oral hearing or a separate hearing of witnesses and experts be wholly or partly by video conference in accordance with Rule 112.3;

(i) decide the value of the action in accordance with Rule 370.6.;

(j) decide the value of the proceeding for the purpose of applying the scale of ceilings for recoverable costs (Rule 152.3);

(k) order the parties to submit, in advance of the decision at the oral hearing, a preliminary estimate of the legal costs that they will seek to recover.

Relation with Agreement: Article 52(2)

Rule 105 – Holding the interim conference

1. The interim conference should, where practicable, be held by telephone conference or by video conference.

2. On request by a party, subject to paragraph 1 and the approval of the judge-rapporteur, the interim conference may be held in Court. If the interim conference is held in Court, it shall be open to the public unless the Court decides to make it, to the extent necessary, confidential in the interests of one or both parties or third parties or in the general interests of justice or public order.

3. The judge-rapporteur may hold the interim conference in any language agreed by the parties' representatives.

4. Rule 103 shall apply *mutatis mutandis.*

5. Following the interim conference, the judge-rapporteur shall issue an order setting out the decisions taken.

Rule 106 – Recording of the interim conference

The interim conference shall be audio recorded. The recording shall be made available at the premises of the Court to the parties or their representatives after the hearing.

Relation with Agreement: Articles 44 and 45

PREPARATION FOR THE ORAL HEARING

Rule 108 – Summons to the oral hearing

The judge-rapporteur shall summon the parties to the oral hearing which shall take place before the panel on the date(s) set under Rules 28 and/or 41(c) and 104(h). If no date(s) have been set the judge-rapporteur shall set a date for the oral hearing. At least two months' notice shall be given, unless the parties agree to a shorter time period.

Rule 109 – Simultaneous interpretation during oral hearings

1. At the latest one month before the oral hearing including any separate hearing of witnesses and experts a party may lodge a Request for simultaneous interpretation which shall contain:

(a) an indication of the language to or from which the party requests simultaneous interpretation during the oral hearing;

(b) the reasons for the Request;

(c) the field of technology concerned;

(d) any other information of relevance for the Request.

2. The judge-rapporteur shall decide whether and to what extent simultaneous interpretation is appropriate and shall instruct the Registry to make all necessary arrangements for simultaneous interpretation. In the event that the judge-rapporteur refuses to order simultaneous interpretation the parties may request arrangements to be made, so far as practically possible, for simultaneous interpretation at their cost.

3. The judge-rapporteur may decide of his own motion to order simultaneous interpretation and shall instruct the Registry and inform the parties accordingly.

4. A party wishing to engage an interpreter at its own expense shall inform the Registry at the latest two weeks before the oral hearing.

5. Costs for simultaneous interpretation are costs of the proceedings to be decided upon under Rule 150 except where a party engages an interpreter at its own expense under paragraph 4; these costs are borne solely by that party.

Relation with Agreement: Article 51(2)

Rule 110 – Closure of the interim procedure

1. As soon as the judge-rapporteur considers that the state of preparation of the file is adequate, he shall inform the presiding judge and the parties that the interim procedure is closed in view of the oral hearing.

2. Where final dates have been set pursuant to Rules 103 and 104 the interim procedure shall be deemed closed on the last date set.

3. The oral procedure shall start immediately after the interim procedure is closed. The presiding judge shall, in consultation with the judge-rapporteur, take over the management of the action.

CHAPTER 3 – ORAL PROCEDURE

Rule 111 – Role of the presiding judge (Case management)

The presiding judge shall:

(a) have all authority to ensure a fair, orderly and efficient oral procedure; and

(b) ensure that the action is ready for decision on the merits at the end of the oral hearing.

Rule 112 – Conduct of the oral hearing

1. The oral hearing shall be held before the panel and shall be under the control of the presiding judge.

2. The oral hearing shall consist of:

(a) the hearing of the parties' oral submissions;

(b) the hearing of witnesses and experts under the control of the presiding judge.

3. The Court may decide to:

(a) allow a party, representative or accompanying person, to attend the oral hearing by videoconference,

(b) hear a party, witnesses or expert through electronic means, such as video conference or

(c) hold the oral hearing by videoconference if all parties agree or the Court considers it appropriate to do so due to exceptional circumstances.

In all cases, the oral hearing shall be transmitted simultaneously in picture and sound to the court room.

4. The presiding judge and the judges of the panel may provide a preliminary introduction to the action and put questions to the parties, to the parties' representatives and to any witness or expert.

5. Under the control of the presiding judge, the parties may put questions to the witness or expert. The presiding judge may prohibit any question which is not designed to adduce admissible evidence.

6. With the consent of the Court a witness may give evidence in a language other than the language of proceedings.

Relation with Agreement: Articles 52(3) and 53(1)

Rule 113 – Duration of the oral hearing

1. Without prejudice to the application of the principle of proportionality, the presiding judge shall endeavour to complete the oral hearing within one day. The presiding judge may set time limits for parties' oral submissions in advance of the oral hearing.

2. Oral testimony at the oral hearing or at any separate hearing shall be limited to issues identified by the judge-rapporteur or the presiding judge as having to be decided on the basis of oral evidence.

3. The presiding judge may, after consulting the panel, limit a party's oral submissions if the panel is sufficiently informed.

Rule 114 – Adjournment where the Court considers that further evidence is required

In exceptional cases, the Court may, after hearing the parties' oral submissions, decide to adjourn proceedings and call for further evidence.

Rule 115 – The oral hearing

The oral hearing and any separate hearing of witnesses shall be open to the public unless the Court decides to make a hearing, to the extent necessary, confidential in the interests of one or both parties or third parties or in the general interests of justice or public order. The hearing shall be audio recorded. The recording shall be made available to the parties or their representatives at the premises of the Court after the hearing. Rule 103 shall apply *mutatis mutandis.*

Relation with Agreement: Article 45

Rule 116 – Absence of a party from the oral hearing

1. A party which does not wish to be represented at the oral hearing shall inform the Registry in good time. Where both parties have informed the Registry that they do not wish to be represented at the oral hearing, the Court may decide the action in accordance with Rule 117.

2. The Court shall not be obliged to delay any step in the procedure, including the decision on the merits, by reason only of the absence of a party from the oral hearing.

3. A party that is not represented at the oral hearing shall be treated as relying only on its written case.

4. If due to an exceptional occurrence a party is prevented from being represented at the oral hearing, the Court shall on a reasoned request of that party, adjourn the oral hearing.

5. The provisions of this Rule are without prejudice to the power of the Court to give a decision by default pursuant to Rule 355.

Rule 117 – Absence of both parties from the oral hearing

Where both parties have informed the Registry that they do not wish to be represented at the oral hearing the Court shall take a decision on the merits on the basis of the pleadings and evidence submitted by the parties and the court expert, if applicable, and otherwise in accordance with Rules 118 and 350 to 354.

Rule 118 – Decision on the merits

1. In addition to the orders and measures and without prejudice to the discretion of the Court referred to in Articles 63, 64, 67 and 80 of the Agreement the Court may, if requested, order the payment of damages or compensation according to Articles 68 and 32(1)(f) of the Agreement. The amount of the damages or the compensation may be stated in the order or determined in separate proceedings [Rules 125–144].

2. If, while there are infringement proceedings before a local or regional division, a revocation action is pending between the same parties before the central division or an opposition is pending before the European Patent Office, the local or regional division:

(a) may render its decision on the merits of the infringement claim, including its orders, under the condition subsequent pursuant to Article 56(1) of the Agreement that the patent is not held to be wholly or partially invalid by the final decision in the revocation proceedings or a final decision of the European Patent Office or under any other term or condition; or

(b) may stay the infringement proceedings pending a decision in the revocation procedure or a decision of the European Patent Office and shall stay the infringement proceedings if it is of the view that there is a high likelihood that the relevant claims of the patent will be held to be invalid on any ground by the final decision in the revocation proceedings or of the European Patent Office where such decision of the European Patent Office may be expected to be given rapidly.

3. Where, in the decision on the merits of a revocation action, the patent is found to be entirely or partially invalid, the Court shall revoke the patent entirely or partially according to Article 65 of the Agreement.

4. Where the Court has made orders in accordance with paragraph 2(a) any party may apply to the local or regional division within two months following a final decision of the central division or the Court of Appeal or the European Patent Office as the case may be on the validity of the patent for orders consequential on such final decision [Rule 354.2].

5. The Court shall decide in principle on the obligation to bear legal costs in accordance with Article 69 of the Agreement. The Court may order in advance of the decision that the parties submit a preliminary estimate of the legal costs that they will seek to recover.

6. The Court shall give the decision on the merits as soon as possible after the closure of the oral hearing. The Court shall endeavour to issue the decision on the merits in writing within six weeks of the oral hearing. The Court shall give reasons for its decision.

7. The Court may give its decision immediately after the closure of the oral hearing and provide its reasons on a subsequent date.

8. The orders of the Court referred to in paragraphs 1 and 2(a) shall be enforceable on the defendant only after the claimant has notified the Court which part of the orders he intends to enforce, a certified translation of the orders in accordance with Rule 7.2, where applicable, into the official language of a Contracting Member State in which the enforcement shall take place has been provided by the claimant and the said notice and, where applicable, a certified translation of the orders have been served on the defendant by the Registry. The Court may subject any order or measure to a security to be given by the successful party to the unsuccessful party as determined by the Court in accordance with Rule 352.

Relation with Agreement: Article 77

Rule 119 – Interim award of damages

The Court may order an interim award of damages to the successful party in the decision on the merits, subject to any conditions that the Court may order. Such award shall at least cover the expected costs of the procedure for the award of damages and compensation on the part of the successful party.

CHAPTER 4 – PROCEDURE FOR THE DETERMINATION OF DAMAGES AND COMPENSATION

Rule 125 – Separate proceedings for determining the amount of damages ordered

The determination of the amount of damages ordered for the successful party may be the subject of separate proceedings. The determination shall include the determination of the amount of compensation, if any, to be awarded as a result of the provisional protection conferred by a published European patent application [Article 32(1)(f) of the Agreement, Article 67 EPC] and compensation to be paid pursuant to Rules 118.1, 198.2, 213.2 and 354.2. The expression "damages" used in Chapter 4 shall be deemed to include such compensation and interest at the rate and for the period that the Court shall decide.

Rule 126 – Start of proceedings for the determination of damages

Where the successful party wishes to have the amount of damages determined, it shall no later than one year from service of the final decision on the merits (including any final decision on appeal) on both infringement and validity (or in the case of an award under Rules 118.1, 198.2, 213.2 or 354.2 from the date of the order for such award) lodge an Application for the determination of damages, which may include a request for an order to lay open books.

Relation with Agreement: Article 68

SECTION 1 – APPLICATION FOR THE DETERMINATION OF DAMAGES

Rule 131 – Contents of the Application for the determination of damages

1. The Application for the determination of damages shall contain:

(a) particulars in accordance with Rule 13.1(a) to (d);

(b) the date of the decision on the merits and the action number of the file;

(c) if required a request for an order to lay open books (Rules 141 to 144) in which case the applicant shall provide the matters set out in Rule 141(b) to (e).

2. After any procedure for the laying open of books is complete, or, if that has not been requested in the Application referred to in paragraph 1 the applicant shall indicate:

(a) the redress (damages, licence fees, profits) and the interest thereon requested by him;

(b) an indication of the facts relied on, in particular calculations concerning lost profits or profits made by the unsuccessful party;

(c) the evidence relied on;

(d) a statement as to whether the decision on the merits is the subject of an appeal;

(e) his assessment of the amount of damages due to him.

Rule 132 – Fee for the Application for the determination of damages

The applicant shall pay the fixed fee and, where applicable, the value based fee for the determination of damages in accordance with Part 6. Rule 15.2 shall apply *mutatis mutandis*.

Rule 133 – Determination of the value-based fee for the determination of damages

Where the value of the action exceeds EUR500.000 the applicant shall pay a value based fee for the determination of damages in accordance with Part 6.

Rule 134 – Examination as to formal requirements of the Application for the determination of damages

1. The Registry shall, as soon as practicable after the lodging of the Application for the determination of damages, examine whether the requirements of Rules 126, 131.1 and .2(d) and (e) and 132 have been complied with.

2. If the Application for the determination of damages does not comply with the requirements referred to in paragraph 1, the Registry shall invite the applicant to correct the deficiencies noted within a time period to be specified.

3. Rule 16.4 to .5 shall apply *mutatis mutandis*.

Rule 135 – Recording in the register (Application for the determination of damages) and service

1. If the requirements referred to in Rule 131.1 and .2(d) and (e) have been complied with, the Registry shall as soon as practicable:

(a) record the date of receipt of the Application for the determination of damages;

(b) record the Application in the register;

(c) inform the applicant of the date of receipt;

(d) inform the panel which has given the decision on the merits on infringement that an Application for the determination of damages has been lodged;

(e) serve the Application upon the unsuccessful party.

2. The panel which has given the decision on the merits on infringement shall be the panel for the determination of damages unless for any reason this is not possible or practical in which case the presiding judge of the division concerned shall appoint a fresh panel. Rules 17.2 and 18 shall apply *mutatis mutandis*.

Rule 136 – Stay of the Application for a determination of damages

The Court may stay the Application for a determination of damages pending any appeal on the merits pursuant to Rule 295(h) on a reasoned request by the unsuccessful party. The applicant shall be given the opportunity to be heard. If the Court continues the proceedings on the Application, it may order the applicant to render a security according to Rule 352.

Rule 137 – Reply of the unsuccessful party

1. If the unsuccessful party accepts the claim made in the Application for the determination of damages, it shall within two months inform the Registry. The judge-rapporteur shall make the order for the determination of damages in accordance with the Application for the determination of damages.

2. If the unsuccessful party contests the claim made in the Application for the determination of damages, it shall within two months of service of the Application for the determination of damages or, where there was a procedure for the laying open of books, within two months of service of the indication pursuant to Rule 131.2, lodge a Defence to the Application for the determination of damages.

Rule 138 – Contents of the Defence to the Application for the determination of damages

The Defence to the Application for the determination of damages shall contain:

(a) the names of the unsuccessful party and of that party's representative;

(b) postal and electronic addresses for service on the unsuccessful party and the names and addresses of the persons authorised to accept service;

(c) the action number attributed to the file;

(d) the reasons why the Application for the award of damages is contested;

(e) an indication of the facts relied on; and

(f) the evidence relied on.

Rule 139 – Reply to the Defence to the Application for the determination of damages and Rejoinder to the Reply

The applicant may within one month lodge a Reply to the Defence to the Application for the determination of damages, limited to the matters raised in the Defence. The unsuccessful party may lodge a Rejoinder to the Reply within one month of service of the Reply, limited to the matters raised in the Reply.

Rule 140 – Further procedure (Application for the determination of damages)

1. The judge-rapporteur may order further exchange of written pleadings, within time periods to be specified.

2. The provisions of Part 1, Chapters 2 (Interim procedure) and 3 (Oral procedure) shall apply *mutatis mutandis* but with such reduced timetable as the judge-rapporteur may order. He shall decide on the obligation to bear the legal costs of the proceedings for the determination of damages in accordance with Article 69 of the Agreement.

SECTION 2 – REQUEST TO LAY OPEN BOOKS

Rule 141 – Contents of the Request to lay open books

If the applicant has made a request pursuant to Rule 131.1(c), Rules 134 to 136 shall apply *mutatis mutandis*. The Request shall contain:

(a) particulars in accordance with Rule 131.1(a) and (b);

(b) details of any information ordered by the Court and given by the other party pursuant to Rule 191;

(c) a description of the information held by the unsuccessful party to which the applicant requests access, in particular documents relating to turnover and profits generated by the infringing products or regarding the extent of use of the infringing process as well as accounts and bank documents, and any related document concerning the infringement;

(d) the reasons why the applicant needs access to this information;

(e) the facts relied on; and

(f) the evidence offered in support.

Rule 142 – Defence of the unsuccessful party, Reply to the Defence and Rejoinder to the Reply

1. If the unsuccessful party accepts the Request to lay open books, it shall within two months of service of the Request to lay open books inform the Registry. The judge-rapporteur shall make the order to lay open books in accordance with the Request to lay open books.

2. If the unsuccessful party contests the Request to lay open books, it shall within two months of service of the Request to lay open books lodge a Defence to the Request to lay open books.

3. The applicant may within 14 days of service of the Defence to the Request lodge a Reply to the Defence to the Request to lay open books, limited to the matters raised

in the Defence. The unsuccessful party may within 14 days of service of the Reply lodge a Rejoinder, limited to the matters raised in the Reply.

Rule 143 – Further procedure

Rule 140 shall apply *mutatis mutandis.*

Rule 144 – Decision on the Request to lay open books

1. The Court may:

(a) order the unsuccessful party to open its books to the applicant within a time period to be specified and subject to such terms as the Court may deem appropriate having regard inter alia to Article 58 of the Agreement and Rule 190.1 and .4;

(b) inform the applicant and specify a time period within which the procedure for the award of damages shall be continued.

2. Where the Request to lay open books is not allowable, the Court shall inform the applicant and specify a time period within which the procedure for the award of damages shall be continued [Rule 131.2].

CHAPTER 5 – PROCEDURE FOR COST DECISION

Rule 150 – Separate proceedings for cost decision

1. A cost decision may be the subject of separate proceedings following a decision on the merits and, if applicable, a decision for the determination of damages. The cost decision shall cover costs incurred in the proceedings by the Court such as costs for simultaneous interpretation and costs incurred pursuant to Rules 173, 180.1, 185.7, 188 and 201 and, subject to the Rules 152 to 156, the costs of the successful party including Court fees paid by that party [Rule 151(d)]. Costs for interpretation and translation which is necessary for the judges of the Court in order to conduct the case in the language of proceedings are borne solely by the Court.

2. The Court may order an interim award of costs to the successful party in the decision on the merits [Rule 119] or in a decision for the determination of damages, subject to any conditions that the Court may decide.

Rule 151 – Start of proceedings for cost decision

Where the successful party (hereinafter "the applicant") wishes to seek a cost decision, it shall within one month of service of the decision lodge an Application for a cost decision which shall contain:

(a) particulars in accordance with Rule 13.1(a) to (d);

(b) the date of the decision and the action number of the file;

(c) a statement as to whether the decision on the merits is the subject of an appeal, if known at the date of the Application;

(d) an indication of the costs for which compensation is requested, which may include recovery of court fees and costs of representation, of witnesses, of experts, and other expenses; and

(e) the preliminary estimate of the legal costs that the party submitted pursuant to Rule 118.5.

Rule 152 – Compensation for representation costs

1. The applicant shall be entitled to recover reasonable and proportionate costs for representation.

2. The Administrative Committee shall adopt a scale of ceilings for recoverable costs by reference to the value of the proceedings. The scale may be adjusted from time to time.

3. Where a claim, counterclaim, application, request or appeal subject to only a fixed fee is made, the party concerned shall, in the first submission, assess its respective value for the purpose of calculating the applicable ceiling. The other party shall be heard. Rule 370.6 shall apply *mutatis mutandis.*

Rule 153 – Compensation for costs of experts

The compensation for costs of experts of the parties [Rule 181] exceeding the expenses referred to in Rule 180.1 shall be based on the rates that are customary in the respective sector, with due regard to the required expertise, the complexity of the issue and the time spent by the expert for the services rendered.

Rule 154 – Compensation for costs of witnesses

Where the Court has ordered the deposit of a sum sufficient to cover the expenses of a witness in accordance with Rule 180.2 or of a party's expert in accordance with Rule 181, compensation may be requested for payments made by the Registry towards the expenses incurred by a witness or an expert.

Rule 155 – Compensation for costs of interpreters and translators

1. The compensation for costs of interpreters shall be the rates that are customary in the country of the division in question, depending on the interpreter's training and professional experience.

2. The compensation for costs of translators shall be the rates that are customary in the country of the division in question, depending on the translator's training and professional experience.

Rule 156 – Further procedure

1. The judge-rapporteur may request the applicant to provide written evidence of all costs requested in Rule 151(d). The judge-rapporteur shall allow the unsuccessful party an opportunity to comment in writing on the costs requested including any

item of costs that should be apportioned or borne by each party in accordance with Article 69(1) to (3) of the Agreement.

2. The judge-rapporteur shall decide in writing on the costs to be awarded or apportioned in accordance with Article 69(1) to (3) of the Agreement.

3. The costs shall be paid within the period ordered by the judge-rapporteur.

Rule 157 – Appeal against the cost decision

The decision of the judge-rapporteur as to costs only may be appealed to the Court of Appeal in accordance with Rule 221.

Relation with Agreement: Article 69

CHAPTER 6 – SECURITY FOR COSTS

Rule 158 – Security for costs of a party

1. At any time during proceedings, following a reasoned request by one party, the Court may order the other party to provide, within a specified time period, adequate security for the legal costs and other expenses incurred and/or to be incurred by the requesting party, which the other party may be liable to bear. Where the Court decides to order such security, it shall decide whether it is appropriate to order the security by deposit or bank guarantee.

2. The Court shall give the parties an opportunity to be heard before making an order for security. Rule 354 shall apply to the enforcement of the order.

3. The order for security shall indicate that an appeal may be lodged in accordance with Article 73 of the Agreement and Rule 220.2.

4. The Court shall, when specifying the time period in paragraph 1, inform the party concerned that if the party fails to provide adequate security within the time stated, a decision by default may be given, in accordance with Rule 355.

5. If a party fails to provide adequate security within the time stated, the Court may give a decision by default pursuant to Rule 355.

Relation with the Agreement: Article 69(4)

Rule 159 – Security for costs of the Court

Except where deposits are rendered pursuant to Rule 180.2, the Court may order that either or both parties provide adequate security (either by deposit or bank guarantee) to cover costs incurred and/or to be incurred in the proceedings by the Court, pending a cost decision pursuant to Rule 150.1. Rule 158.2 and .3 shall apply.

PART 2 – EVIDENCE

Rule 170 – Means of evidence and means of obtaining evidence

1. In proceedings before the Court, the means of evidence shall include in particular the following:

(a) written evidence, whether printed, hand-written or drawn, in particular documents, written witness statements, plans, drawings, photographs;

(b) expert reports and reports on experiments carried out for the purpose of the proceedings;

(c) physical objects, in particular devices, products, embodiments, exhibits, models;

(d) electronic files and audio/video recordings.

2. Means of obtaining evidence shall include in particular the following:

(a) hearing of the parties;

(b) requests for information;

(c) production of documents;

(d) summoning, hearing and questioning of witnesses;

(e) appointing, receiving opinions from, summoning and hearing and questioning of experts;

(f) ordering inspection of a place or a physical object;

(g) conducting comparative tests and experiments;

(h) sworn statements in writing (written witness statements).

3. Means of obtaining evidence shall further include [Article 59 and 60 of the Agreement]:

(a) ordering a party or a third party to produce evidence;

(b) ordering measures to preserve evidence.

Rule 171 – Offering of evidence

1. A party making a statement of fact that is contested or likely to be contested by the other party shall indicate the means of evidence to prove it. In case of failure to indicate the means of evidence regarding a contested fact, the Court shall take such failure into account when deciding the issue in question.

2. A statement of fact that is not specifically contested by any party shall be held to be true as between the parties.

Rule 172 – Duty to produce evidence

1. Evidence available to a party regarding a statement of fact that is contested or likely to be contested by the other party must be produced by the party making that statement of fact.

2. The Court may at any time during the proceedings order a party making a statement of fact to produce evidence that lies in the control of that party. If the party fails to produce the evidence, the Court shall take such failure into account when deciding on the issue in question.

Relation with Agreement: Article 53

Rule 173 – Judicial Cooperation in the taking of evidence

For the judicial cooperation in the taking of evidence, the Court shall apply any method provided by:

1. The Regulation (EU) No 2020/1783, where it applies;

2. The Hague Convention of 18 March 1970 on the Taking of Evidence Abroad in Civil or Commercial Matters, where it applies, or any other applicable convention or agreement; or

3. to the extent that there is no such convention or agreement in force, national law on the procedures to be followed for the judicial cooperation in the taking of evidence.

CHAPTER 1 – WITNESSES AND EXPERTS OF THE PARTIES

Rule 175 – Written witness statement

1. A party seeking to offer witness evidence shall lodge a written witness statement or a written summary of the evidence to be given.

2. A written witness statement shall be signed by the witness and shall include a statement of the witness that he is aware of his obligation to tell the truth and of his liability under applicable national law in the event of any breach of this obligation. The statement shall set out the language in which the witness shall give oral evidence, if necessary.

3. The written witness statement or written summary of the evidence to be given shall set out:

(a) any current or past relationship between the witness and the party offering the evidence; and

(b) any actual or potential conflict of interest that may affect the impartiality of the witness.

Rule 176 – Application for the hearing of a witness in person

Subject to the orders of the Court referred to in Rules 104(e) and 112.2(b) a party seeking to offer oral witness evidence shall make an Application for the hearing of a witness in person which shall set out:

(a) the reasons why the witness should be heard in person;

(b) the facts which the party expects the witness to confirm; and

(c) the language in which the witness shall give evidence.

Rule 177 – Summoning of witnesses to the oral hearing

1. The Court may order that a witness be heard in person:

(a) of its own motion;

(b) where a written witness statement is challenged by the other party; or

(c) on an Application for the hearing of a witness in person [Rule 176].

2. An order of the Court summoning a witness to the oral hearing shall in particular indicate:

(a) the name, address and description of the witness;

(b) the date and place of the oral hearing;

(c) an indication of the facts of the action about which the witness is to be examined;

(d) information about the reimbursement of expenses incurred by the witness;

(e) a statement that the witness will be questioned by the Court and the parties; and

(f) the language of the proceedings and the possibility of arranging simultaneous interpretation between that language and the language of the witness, if necessary [Rule 109].

3. In its order summoning the witness, the Court shall also inform the witness of his duties and rights as a witness under Rules 178 and 179, including the sanctions which may be imposed on a defaulting witness.

Rule 178 – Hearing of witnesses

1. After the identity of the witness has been established and before hearing his evidence, the presiding judge shall ask the witness to make the following declaration:

"I solemnly, sincerely and truly declare and affirm that the evidence I shall give shall be the truth, the whole truth and nothing but the truth."

2. The witness shall give his evidence to the Court.

3. The hearing of a witness who has signed a written witness statement shall begin with the confirmation of the evidence given therein. The witness may elaborate on the evidence contained in his written witness statement.

4. The presiding judge and the judges of the panel may put questions to the witness.

5. Under the control of the presiding judge, the parties may put questions to the witness. The presiding judge may prohibit any question which is not designed to adduce admissible evidence.

6. With the consent of the Court a witness may give evidence in a language other than the language of proceedings.

Rule 179 – Duties of witnesses

1. Witnesses who have been duly summoned shall obey the summons and attend the oral hearing.

2. Without prejudice to paragraph 3, if a witness who has been duly summoned fails to appear before the Court or refuses to give evidence or to make the declaration referred to in Rule 178.1, the Court may impose upon him a pecuniary sanction not exceeding EUR50.000 and may order that a further summons be served at the witness's own expense.

3. Nobody shall be obliged to sign a written witness statement or to give evidence at an oral hearing if he is a spouse, partner equal to a spouse under applicable national law, descendant, sibling or parent of a party. A witness may also refuse to answer questions if answering them would violate a professional privilege or other duty of confidentiality imposed by the national law applicable to the witness or expose him or his spouse, partner equal to a spouse under applicable national law, descendant, sibling or parent to criminal prosecution under applicable national law.

4. The Court may decide to report to the competent authorities of the Contracting Member States whose courts have criminal jurisdiction in case of the giving of false evidence on the part of a witness.

Rule 180 – Reimbursement of expenses of witnesses

1. A witness shall be entitled to reimbursement of:

(a) expenses for travelling and stay; and

(b) loss of income caused by his hearing in person.

After the witness has carried out his duties and upon his request, the Registry shall make a payment to the witness towards the expenses incurred.

2. The Court shall make the summoning of a witness conditional upon the deposit by the party relying on the witness of a sum sufficient to cover the expenses referred to in paragraph 1.

Rule 181 – Experts of the parties

1. Subject to the orders of the Court referred to in Rules 104(e) and 112.2(b) a party may provide any expert evidence that it considers necessary. Rules 175 to 180 shall apply mutatis mutandis to experts of the parties.

2. An order of the Court under Rule 177 summoning the expert shall additionally set out that:

(a) an expert has a duty to assist the Court impartially on matters relevant to his area of expertise which overrides any duty to the party retaining him; and

(b) an expert is to be independent and objective, and shall not act as an advocate for any party to the proceedings.

CHAPTER 2 – COURT EXPERTS

Rule 185 – Appointment of a court expert

1. Where the Court must resolve a specific technical or other question in relation to the action, it may of its own motion, and after hearing the parties, appoint a court expert.

2. The parties may make suggestions regarding the identity of the court expert, his technical or other relevant background and the questions to be put to him.

3. The court expert shall be responsible to the Court and shall possess the expertise, independence and impartiality required for being appointed as court expert. The parties shall be entitled to be heard on the expertise, independence and impartiality of the court expert.

4. The Court shall appoint a court expert by way of order which shall in particular specify:

(a) the name and address of the expert appointed;

(b) a short description of the facts of the action;

(c) the evidence submitted by the parties in respect of the technical or other question;

(d) the questions put to the expert, with the appropriate level of detail, including where appropriate suggestions relating to any experiments to be carried out;

(e) when and under what conditions the expert may receive other relevant information;

(f) the time period for the presentation of the expert report;

(g) information about the reimbursement of expenses incurred by the expert;

(h) information about the sanctions which may be imposed on a defaulting expert; and

(i) his duties under Rule 186.

5. The expert shall receive a copy of the order, together with the documents and other evidence that the Court considers to be necessary for carrying out his task.

6. The expert shall be required upon receipt of the order to confirm in writing that he will present the expert report within the time period specified by the Court.

7. The Court shall agree with the expert on a fee covering his written expert report and his participation in the oral hearing. The Court may reduce this fee by an equitable amount if the expert does not deliver his report within the time period specified by the Court or if the report did not have the quality to be expected of the expert.

8. If an appointed court expert does not present his report within the time period specified or, if extended at the expert's request, the extended period, the Court may appoint another expert in his place. The Court may hold the expert liable for all or part of the costs of appointing and reimbursing another expert.

9. The Registry shall maintain an indicative list of technical experts.

Rule 186 – Duties of a court expert

1. The court expert shall present an expert report in writing within the time period specified by the Court [Rule 185.4(f)].

2. The court expert shall be under the supervision of the Court and shall inform the Court of his progress in carrying out his task.

3. The court expert shall give expert advice only on questions which have been put to him.

4. The court expert shall not communicate with one party without the other party being present or without the consent of the other party. He shall document all communications with the parties in his report.

5. The court expert shall not communicate the contents of his report to third parties.

6. The court expert shall attend the oral hearing if requested to do so by the Court and shall answer questions from the Court and the parties.

7. The court expert has an overriding duty to assist the Court impartially on matters relevant to his area of expertise. He is to be independent and objective, and shall not act as an advocate for any party to the proceedings.

Rule 187 – Expert report

Once the report of the court expert has been presented to the Court, the Court shall invite the parties to comment on it either in writing or during the oral hearing.

Rule 188 – Hearing of a court expert

Rules 178 to 180 shall apply *mutatis mutandis* to a court expert.

Relation with Agreement: Article 57

CHAPTER 3 – ORDER TO PRODUCE EVIDENCE AND TO COMMUNICATE INFORMATION

ORDER TO PRODUCE EVIDENCE

Rule 190 – Order to produce evidence

1. Where a party has presented reasonably available and plausible evidence in support of its claims and has, in substantiating those claims, specified evidence which lies in the control of the other party or a third party, the Court may on a reasoned request by the party specifying such evidence, order that other party or third party to produce such evidence. For the protection of confidential information the Court may order that the evidence be disclosed to certain named persons only and be subject to appropriate terms of non-disclosure.

2. During the written and interim procedures, a party may request such an order to produce evidence.

3. The judge-rapporteur may make such order in the written procedure or in the interim procedure having given the other/third party an opportunity to be heard.

4. An order to produce evidence shall in particular specify:

(a) under which conditions, in what form and within what time period the evidence shall be produced;

(b) any sanction which may be imposed if the evidence is not produced according to the order.

5. Where the Court orders a third party to produce evidence, the interests of that third party shall be duly taken into account.

6. An order to produce evidence shall be subject to the provisions of Rules 179.3, 287 and 288. The order shall indicate that an appeal may be brought in accordance with Article 73 of the Agreement and Rule 220.1.

7. If a party fails to comply with an order to produce evidence, the Court shall take such failure into account when deciding on the issue in question.

Relation with Agreement: Article 59

ORDER TO COMMUNICATE INFORMATION

Rule 191 – Application for order to communicate information

The Court may in response to a reasoned request by a party order the other party or any third party to communicate such information in the control of that other party or third party as is specified in Article 67 of the Agreement or such other information as is reasonably necessary for the purpose of advancing that party's case. Rule 190.1 second sentence,.5 and .6 shall apply *mutatis mutandis.*

Relation with the Agreement: Article 67

CHAPTER 4 – ORDER TO PRESERVE EVIDENCE (SAISIE) AND ORDER FOR INSPECTION

ORDER TO PRESERVE EVIDENCE (SAISIE)

Rule 192 – Application for preserving evidence

1. An Application for preserving evidence may be lodged by a party (within the meaning of Article 47 of the Agreement) (hereinafter "the applicant") at the division where the applicant has commenced infringement proceedings on the merits. If the application is lodged before proceedings on the merits have been started it shall be lodged at the division where the applicant intends to start proceedings on the merits.

2. The Application for preserving evidence shall contain:

(a) particulars in accordance with Rule 13.1(a) to (i);

(b) a clear indication of the measures requested [Rule 196.1], including the exact location of the evidence to be preserved where it is known or suspected with good reason;

(c) the reasons why the proposed measures are needed to preserve relevant evidence; and

(d) the facts and evidence relied on in support of the Application.

Where main proceedings on the merits of the case have not yet been started before the Court, the Application shall in addition contain a concise description of the action which will be started before the Court, including an indication of the facts and evidence which may be relied on in support.

3. Where the applicant requests that measures to preserve evidence be ordered without hearing the other party (hereinafter "the defendant"), the Application for preserving evidence shall in addition set out the reasons for not hearing the defendant having regard in particular to Rule 197. The applicant shall be under a duty to disclose any material fact known to it which might influence the Court in deciding whether to make an order without hearing the defendant. The application shall not be entered on the register until notice has been given to the defendant pursuant to Rule 197.2.

4. Where the Application for preserving evidence is lodged after main proceedings on the merits of the case have been started before the Court, the Application shall be drawn up in the language of the proceedings. Where the Application is lodged before main proceedings on the merits of the case have been started before the Court, Rule 14 shall apply *mutatis mutandis.*

5. The applicant shall pay the fee for the Application for preserving evidence, in accordance with Part 6. Rule 15.2 shall apply *mutatis mutandis.*

Relation with Agreement: Article 60

Rule 193 – Examination as to formal requirements, recording in the register, assignment to panel, designation of judge-rapporteur, single judge

1. Where main proceedings on the merits of the case have not yet been started before the Court, the Application for preserving evidence shall be dealt with in accordance with Rule 16 (formalities examination by Registry), Rule 17.1(a) to (c) and .2 (date of receipt, recording in the register, action number, assignment to panel) and Rule 18 (designation only of judge-rapporteur by presiding judge).

2. Where main proceedings on the merits of the case have already been started before the Court, an Application for preserving evidence shall immediately be examined by the Registry in accordance with Rule 16 and forwarded to the panel to which the action has been assigned or to the judge to whom the action has been assigned [Rules 17.2, 194.3 and .4].

3. The judge deciding on an Application for preserving evidence shall have all necessary powers of the Court.

Rule 194 – Examination of the Application for preserving evidence

1. The Court shall have the discretion – including where the Application is made pursuant to Rule 192.3

- to:

(a) inform the defendant about the Application and invite him to lodge, within a time period to be specified, an Objection to the Application for preserving evidence which shall contain:
(i) the reasons why the Application shall fail;
(ii) the facts and evidence relied on, in particular any challenge to the facts and evidence relied on by the applicant;
(iii) where main proceedings on the merits of the case have not yet been started before the Court, the reasons why the action which will be started before the Court shall fail and an indication of the facts and evidence relied on in support;

(b) summon the parties to an oral hearing;

(c) summon the applicant to an oral hearing without the presence of the defendant;

(d) decide the Application without having heard the defendant.

2. In exercising its discretion, the Court shall take into account:

(a) the urgency of the action;

(b) whether the reasons for not hearing the defendant [Rules 192.3 and 197] appear well-founded;

(c) the probability that evidence may be destroyed or otherwise cease to be available [Rule 197].

3. The presiding judge may decide that he or the judge-rapporteur or other single judge or the standing judge may decide on the Application.

4. In cases of extreme urgency the standing judge appointed in accordance with Rule 345.5 may decide immediately on an Application to preserve evidence and the procedure to be followed on the Application.

5. If the Court decides to inform the defendant about the Application the Court will first give the applicant the possibility to withdraw the Application. In the event of such withdrawal the applicant may request that the Court shall order that the Application and its contents shall remain confidential.

6. If the patent the subject of the Application is also the subject of a Protective letter pursuant to Rule 207 the applicant may withdraw the Application pursuant to paragraph 5.

Rule 195 – Oral hearing

1. Where the Court decides to summon the parties to an oral hearing, the date for the oral hearing shall be set as soon as possible after the date of receipt of the Application for preserving evidence.

2. Rules 111 to 116 shall apply *mutatis mutandis*. Where the applicant is absent from the oral hearing without a reasonable excuse, the Court shall reject the Application for preserving evidence.

3. The decision of the Court on the Application for preserving evidence shall be given in writing as soon as possible after the closure of the oral hearing. If the Court deems appropriate, the decision may be given orally to the parties at the end of the oral hearing but shall as soon as practicable thereafter be given in writing.

Relation with Agreement: Article 60

Rule 196 – Order on the Application for preserving evidence

1. The Court may order, in particular, the following:

(a) preserving evidence by detailed description, with or without the taking of samples;

(b) physical seizure of allegedly infringing goods;

(c) physical seizure of the materials and implements used in the production and/or distribution of these goods and any related document;

(d) the preservation and disclosure of digital media and data and the disclosure of any passwords necessary to access them.

For the protection of confidential information the Court may order that any of the above be disclosed only to certain named persons and subject to appropriate terms of non-disclosure.

2. An order to preserve evidence shall specify that, unless otherwise ordered by the Court, the outcome of the measures to preserve evidence may only be used in the proceedings on the merits of the case.

3. The order to preserve evidence shall be enforceable immediately, unless the Court decides otherwise. The Court may set conditions to the enforceability of the order, specifying in particular:

(a) who may represent the applicant when the measures to preserve evidence are being carried out and under what conditions;

(b) any security which shall be provided by the applicant.

If necessary, the Court may set penalties applicable to the applicant if these conditions are not observed.

4. The order to preserve evidence shall specify a person who shall carry out the measures referred to in paragraph 1 and present a written Report on the measures to preserve evidence, all in accordance with the national law of the place where the measures are executed, to the Court within a time period to be specified.

5. The person referred to in paragraph 4 shall be a professional person or expert, who guarantees expertise, independence and impartiality. Where appropriate and allowed under applicable national law, the person may be a bailiff or assisted by a bailiff. In no circumstances may an employee or director of the applicant be present at the execution of the measures.

6. The Court may order the applicant to provide adequate security for the legal costs and other expenses and compensation for any injury incurred or likely to be incurred by the defendant which the applicant may be liable to bear. The Court shall do so where the order to preserve evidence was made without the defendant having been heard, unless there are special circumstances not to do so. The Court shall decide whether it is appropriate to order the security by deposit or bank guarantee.

7. The order to preserve evidence shall indicate that an appeal may be lodged in accordance with Article 73 of the Agreement and Rule 220.1.

Relation with Agreement: Article 60(1)-(4)

Rule 197 – Order to preserve evidence without hearing the defendant

1. The Court may order measures to preserve evidence [Rule 196.1] without the defendant having been heard, in particular where any delay is likely to cause irreparable harm to the applicant or where there is a demonstrable risk of evidence being destroyed or otherwise ceasing to be available.

2. Where measures to preserve evidence are ordered without the defendant having been heard, Rule 195 shall apply *mutatis mutandis* to the oral hearing without the presence of the defendant. In such cases, the defendant shall be given notice, immediately at the time of the execution of the measures.

3. Within 30 days after the execution of the measures, the defendant may request a review of the order to preserve evidence. The Request for review shall set out:

(a) the reasons why the order to preserve evidence shall be revoked or modified; and

(b) the facts and evidence relied on.

4. The Court shall order an oral hearing to review the order without delay. Rule 195 shall apply. The Court may modify, revoke or confirm the order. In case the order is modified or revoked the Court shall oblige the persons to whom confidential information has been disclosed to keep this information confidential [Rule 196.1].

Relation with Agreement: Article 60(6)

Rule 198 – Revocation of an order to preserve evidence

1. The Court shall ensure that an order to preserve evidence is revoked or otherwise ceases to have effect, upon request of the defendant, without prejudice to the damages which may be claimed, if, within a time period not exceeding 31 calendar days or 20 working days, whichever is the longer, from the date specified in the Court's order with due account to the date where the Report referred to in Rule 196.4 shall be presented, the applicant does not start proceedings on the merits of the case before the Court.

2. Where the measures to preserve evidence are revoked, or where they lapse due to any act or omission by the applicant, or where it is subsequently found that there has been no infringement or threat of infringement of the patent, the Court may order the applicant, upon request of the defendant, to provide the defendant appropriate compensation for any injury caused by those measures [Rule 354.2].

3. The applicant shall pay a fee for the request under paragraph 1 in accordance with Part 6.

Relation with Agreement: Article 60(8) and (9)

ORDER FOR INSPECTION

Rule 199 – Order for inspection

1. The Court may, on a reasoned request by a party, order an inspection of products, devices, methods, premises or local situations *in situ*. For the protection of confidential information the Court may order that any of the above be disclosed only to certain named persons and subject to appropriate terms of non-disclosure in accordance with Article 58 of the Agreement.

2. Rules 192 to 198 shall apply *mutatis mutandis*.

Relation with Agreement: Article 60

CHAPTER 5 – OTHER EVIDENCE

Rule 200 – Order to freeze assets

1. Where a party has presented reasonably available and plausible evidence in support of its claim that a patent has been or is about to be infringed the Court may, whether before or after proceedings have been commenced, order a party not to remove from its jurisdiction any assets or particular assets located therein nor to deal in any assets, whether located within its jurisdiction or not.

2. Rules 192 to 198 shall apply *mutatis mutandis*.

Relation with Agreement: Article 61

Rule 201 – Experiments ordered by the Court

1. Without prejudice to the possibility for parties or parties' experts to carry out experiments, the Court may, on a reasoned request by a party, order an experiment to prove a statement of fact for the purpose of proceedings before the Court.

2. A party requesting to be allowed to prove a statement of fact by means of experiments shall lodge a request as soon as practicable in the written procedure or the interim procedure to carry out experiments which shall:

(a) identify the facts intended to be established by the experiments, describe the proposed experiments in detail and the reasons for carrying out the proposed experiments;

(b) propose an expert to carry out such experiments; and

(c) disclose any previous attempts to carry out similar experiments.

3. Other parties to the proceedings shall be invited to state whether they dispute the facts intended to be established by the experiments. They shall also be invited to comment on the request, including the identity of the expert proposed and the description of the experiments.

4. Unless otherwise ordered by the Court the party requesting experiments shall initially bear the costs of the experiment.

5. The order of the Court allowing the experiments shall specify the detailed experiments and:

(a) the name and address of the expert who is to carry out the experiments as Court's expert and draw up the report on the experiments;

(b) the time period for carrying out the experiments and, where appropriate, the exact time and place where they are to be carried out;

(c) if necessary, other conditions for carrying out the experiments; and

(d) the time period for presenting the report on the experiments and, where appropriate, directions relating to the contents of the report.

6. Where appropriate, the Court may order that the experiments be carried out in the presence of the parties and their experts.

7. Once the report on the experiments is presented to the Court, it shall invite the parties to comment on it either in writing or during the oral hearing. The expert may be summoned to the oral hearing.

PART 3 – PROVISIONAL MEASURES

Rule 205 – Stages of the proceedings (summary proceedings)

Provisional measures are treated by way of summary proceedings which shall consist of the following stages:

(a) a written procedure; and

(b) an oral procedure, which may include an oral hearing of the parties or of one of the parties.

Rule 206 – Application for provisional measures

1. An Application for provisional measures may be lodged by a party (hereinafter "the applicant") before or after main proceedings on the merits of the case have been started before the Court.

2. An Application for provisional measures shall contain:

(a) particulars in accordance with Rule 13.1(a) to (i);

(b) a indication of the provisional measures which are being requested [Rule 211.1];

(c) the reasons why provisional measures are necessary to prevent a threatened infringement, to forbid the continuation of an alleged infringement or to make such continuation subject to the lodging of guarantees;

(d) the facts and evidence relied on in support of the Application, including evidence to support the claim that provisional measures are necessary including the matters referred to in Rule 211.2 and .3; and

(e) a concise description of the action which will be started before the Court, including an indication of the facts and evidence which will be relied on in support of the main proceedings on the merits of the case.

3. Where the applicant requests that provisional measures be ordered without hearing the other party (hereinafter "the defendant"), the Application for provisional measures shall in addition contain:

(a) the reasons for not hearing the defendant having regard in particular to Rule 197; and

(b) information about any prior correspondence between the parties concerning the alleged infringement.

4. The applicant shall be under a duty to disclose any material fact known to it which might influence the Court in deciding whether to make an order without hearing the defendant including any pending proceedings and/or any unsuccessful attempt in the past to obtain provisional measures in respect of the patent.

5. Rule 14 shall apply *mutatis mutandis*. The applicant shall pay the fee for the Application for provisional measures, in accordance with Part 6. Rule 15.2 shall apply *mutatis mutandis*.

Relation with Agreement: Articles 32(1)(c) and 62

Rule 207 – Protective letter

1. If a person entitled to start proceedings under Article 47 of the Agreement considers it likely that an Application for provisional measures against him as a defendant may be lodged before the Court in the near future, he may file a Protective letter.

2. The Protective letter shall be filed with the Registry in the language of the patent and shall contain:

(a) the name of the defendant or defendants filing the Protective letter and of the defendant's representative;

(b) the name of the presumed applicant for provisional measures;

(c) postal and electronic addresses for service on the defendant filing the Protective letter and the names of the persons authorised to accept service;

(d) postal and, where available, electronic addresses for service on the presumed applicant for provisional measures and the names of the persons authorised to accept service if known;

(e) where available, the number of the patent concerned and, where applicable, information about any prior or pending proceedings referred to in Rule 13.1(h); and

(f) the statement that the letter is a Protective letter.

3. The Protective letter may contain:

(a) an indication of the facts relied on, which may include a challenge to the facts expected to be relied on by the presumed applicant and/or, where applicable, any assertion that the patent is invalid and the grounds for such assertion;

(b) any available written evidence relied on;

(c) the arguments of law, including the reasons why any Application for provisional measures should be rejected.

4. The defendant or defendants filing the Protective letter shall pay the fee for filing a Protective letter, in accordance with Part 6. Rule 15.2 shall apply *mutatis mutandis*.

5. The Registry shall as soon as practicable examine whether the requirements of paragraphs 2(a) to (f) and 4 have been complied with. If these requirements have been complied with, the Registry shall as soon as practicable:

(a) record the date of receipt and assign a number to the Protective letter;

(b) subject to paragraph 7, record the Protective letter in the register;

(c) provide details of the Protective letter to all divisions; and

(d) where an Application for provisional measures has already been lodged, inform the panel or the single judge dealing with the Application about the filing of the Protective letter.

6. If the defendant has not complied with the requirements of paragraph 2 the Registry shall as soon as practicable invite the defendant to:

(a) correct the deficiencies within 14 days of service of such notification; and

(b) where applicable, pay the fee referred to in paragraph 4.

7. The protective letter shall not be publicly available on the register until it has been forwarded to the applicant pursuant to paragraph 8.

8. Where an Application for provisional measures is subsequently lodged the Registrar shall forward a copy of the protective letter to the panel or judge appointed under Rule 208 together with the Application for provisional measures and shall forward a copy to the applicant as soon as practicable.

9. If no Application for provisional measures has been lodged within six months from the date of receipt of the Protective letter, the Protective letter shall be removed from the register unless the person who has lodged the Protective letter has prior to the expiry of such period applied for an extension of six months and paid a fee for the extension in accordance with Part 6. Further extensions may be obtained on further payments of the fee.

10. Rule 15.2 shall apply *mutatis mutandis*.

Rule 208 – Examination as to formal requirements, recording in the register, assignment to panel, designation of judge-rapporteur, single judge

1. The Application for provisional measures shall be examined by the Registry in accordance with Rule 16. The Registry shall in addition examine whether any Protective letter relevant for the Application is recorded in the register.

2. Where main proceedings on the merits of the case have not yet been started before the Court, Rule 17 (date of receipt, recording in the register, action number, assignment to panel) and Rule 18 (designation of judge-rapporteur by presiding judge) shall apply *mutatis mutandis*. In urgent cases, the presiding judge may decide that he or an

experienced judge of the panel, acting as single judge, may decide on the Application in accordance with Rules 209 to 213 with a reduced time-table.

3. Where main proceedings on the merits of the case have already been started before the Court, the Application for provisional measures shall immediately be forwarded to the panel to which the action has been assigned or to the single judge. In urgent cases (where the action has not been assigned to a single judge), the presiding judge may decide that he or the judge-rapporteur, acting as single judge, may decide on the Application in accordance with Rules 209 to 213 with a reduced time-table.

4. The single judge deciding on the Application for provisional measures shall have all necessary powers of the Court.

Relation with Statute: Article 19

Rule 209 – Examination of the Application for provisional measures

1. Without prejudice to the Court's decision on the Application for provisional measures, the Court shall have the discretion – including where the Application is made pursuant to Rule 206.3 – to:

(a) inform the defendant about the Application and invite him to lodge, within a time period to be specified, an Objection to the Application for provisional measures which shall contain:
(i) the reasons why the Application shall fail;
(ii) the facts and evidence relied on, in particular any challenge to the facts and evidence relied on by the applicant; and
(iii) where main proceedings on the merits of the case have not yet been started before the Court, the reasons why the action which will be started before the Court shall fail and the facts and evidence relied on in support;

(b) summon the parties to an oral hearing;

(c) summon the applicant to an oral hearing without the presence of the defendant.

2. In exercising its discretion pursuant to paragraph 1, the Court shall in particular take into account:

(a) whether the patent has been upheld in an opposition procedure before the European Patent Office or has been the subject of proceedings in any other court;

(b) the urgency of the action;

(c) whether the applicant has requested provisional measures without hearing the defendant and whether the reasons for not hearing the defendant appear well-founded; and

(d) any Protective letter filed by the defendant; the Court shall in particular consider summoning parties to an oral hearing if a relevant Protective letter has been filed by the defendant.

3. In cases of extreme urgency the standing judge appointed in accordance with Rule 345.5 may decide immediately on the Application for provisional measures and the procedure to be followed on the Application.

4. If the applicant has applied for provisional measures without hearing the defendant and the Court decides not to grant provisional measures without hearing the defendant the applicant may withdraw the Application and may request that the Court order that the Application and the contents of the Application remain confidential.

5. If the patent the subject of the Application is also the subject of a protective letter pursuant to Rule 207 the applicant may withdraw the Application pursuant to paragraph 4.

Rule 210 – Oral hearing

1. Where the Court decides to summon the parties to an oral hearing, the date for the oral hearing shall be set as soon as possible after the date of receipt of the Application for provisional measures.

2. The Court may order the parties to provide further information, documents and other evidence before or during the oral hearing, including evidence to enable the Court to make its decision in accordance with Rule 211. Part 2 of these Rules on Evidence shall be applicable only to the extent determined by the Court.

3. Rules 111 to 116 shall apply *mutatis mutandis*. Where the applicant is absent from the oral hearing without a reasonable excuse, the Court shall reject the Application for provisional measures.

4. The decision of the Court on the Application for provisional measures shall be given in writing as soon as possible after the closure of the oral hearing. If the Court deems appropriate, its decision may be given orally to the parties at the end of the oral hearing, prior to providing its decision in writing.

Rule 211 – Order on the Application for provisional measures

1. The Court may in particular order the following provisional measures:

(a) injunctions against a defendant;

(b) the seizure or delivery up of the goods suspected of infringing a patent right so as to prevent their entry into or movement within the channels of commerce;

(c) if an applicant demonstrates circumstances likely to endanger the recovery of damages, a precautionary seizure of the movable and immovable property of the defendant, including the blocking of his bank accounts and other assets;

(d) an interim award of costs.

2. In taking its decision the Court may require the applicant to provide reasonable evidence to satisfy the Court with a sufficient degree of certainty that the applicant is

entitled to commence proceedings pursuant to Article 47, that the patent in question is valid and that his right is being infringed, or that such infringement is imminent.

3. In taking its decision the Court shall in the exercise of its discretion weigh up the interests of the parties and, in particular, take into account the potential harm for either of the parties resulting from the granting or the refusal of the injunction.

4. The Court shall have regard to any unreasonable delay in seeking provisional measures.

5. The Court may order the applicant to provide adequate security for appropriate compensation for any injury likely to be caused to the defendant which the applicant may be liable to bear in the event that the Court revokes the order for provisional measures. The Court shall do so where interim measures are ordered without the defendant having been heard unless there are special circumstances not to do so. The Court shall decide whether it is appropriate to order the security by deposit or bank guarantee. The order shall be effective only after the security has been given to the defendant in accordance with the Court's decision.

6. The order on provisional measures shall indicate that an appeal may be brought in accordance with Article 73 of the Agreement and Rule 220.1.

Relation with Agreement: Article 62(2) and (4)

Rule 212 – Order on provisional measures without hearing the defendant

1. The Court may order provisional measures without the defendant having been heard, in particular where any delay is likely to cause irreparable harm to the applicant or where there is a demonstrable risk of evidence being destroyed. Rule 197 shall apply *mutatis mutandis.*

2. Where provisional measures are ordered without the defendant having been heard, Rule 210 shall apply *mutatis mutandis* to the oral hearing without the presence of the defendant. In such cases, the defendant shall be given notice of the provisional measures without delay and at the latest immediately at the time of execution of the measures.

3. The defendant may request a review. Rule 197.3 and .4 shall apply *mutatis mutandis.*

Relation with Agreement: Article 60(5) and (6)

Rule 213 – Revocation of provisional measures

1. The Court shall ensure that provisional measures are revoked or otherwise cease to have effect, upon request of the defendant, without prejudice to the damages which may be claimed, if, within a time period not exceeding 31 calendar days or 20 working days, whichever is the longer, from the date specified in the Court's order, the applicant does not start proceedings on the merits of the case before the Court. When specifying the date, the Court shall take due account, where applicable, of the date on which the Report referred to in Rule 196.4 shall be presented.

2. Where provisional measures are revoked, or where they lapse due to any act or omission by the applicant, or where it is subsequently found that there has been no infringement or threat of infringement of the patent, the Court may order the applicant, upon request of the defendant, to provide the defendant with appropriate compensation for any injury caused by those measures [Rule 354.2].

3. The applicant shall pay a fee for the request under paragraph 1 in accordance with Part 6.

Relation with Agreement: Article 60(9)

PART 4 – PROCEDURES BEFORE THE COURT OF APPEAL

Rule 220 – Appealable decisions

1. An appeal by a party adversely affected may be brought against:

(a) final decisions of the Court of First Instance;

(b) decisions terminating proceedings as regards one of the parties;

(c) orders referred to in Articles 49(5), 59, 60, 61, 62 or 67 of the Agreement.

2. Orders other than those referred to in paragraph 1 and Rule 97.5, may be either the subject of an appeal together with the appeal against the decision or may be appealed with the leave of the Court of First Instance within 15 days of service of the Court's decision to that effect.

3. In the event of a refusal of the Court of First Instance to grant leave within 15 days of the order of one of its panels a request for a discretionary review to the Court of Appeal may be made within 15 calendar days from the end of that period. Rule 333.3 shall apply *mutatis mutandis*. The request shall set out the matters referred to in Rule 221.2.

4. The Registrar shall assign the request for a discretionary review to the standing judge (Rule 345.5 and .8). The standing judge may deny the request without giving reasons. If the standing judge allows the request after having heard the other party, he shall order what further steps, if any, the parties shall take and within what time limits and the President of the Court of Appeal shall assign the review to a panel of the Court of Appeal for a decision. The Court of Appeal may consult the presiding judge or the judge-rapporteur of the panel of the Court of First Instance which has refused the leave order.

5. The Court of Appeal may hear appeals against separate decisions on the merits in infringement proceedings and in validity proceedings together.

Relation with Agreement: Article 73

Rule 221 – Application for leave to appeal against cost decisions

1. A party adversely affected by a decision referred to in Rule 157 may lodge an Application for leave to appeal to the Court of Appeal within 15 days of service of the decision of the Court.

2. The Application for leave to appeal shall set out:

(a) the reasons why the appeal should be heard;

(b) where necessary, the facts, evidence and arguments relied on.

3. The Application for leave to appeal shall be assigned to the standing judge (Rule 345.5 and .8) who shall decide on granting leave to appeal.

4. If leave to appeal a cost decision is granted the standing judge shall decide the appeal.

Rule 222 – Subject-matter of the proceedings before the Court of Appeal

1. Requests, facts, evidence and arguments submitted by the parties under Rules 221, 225, 226, 236 and 238 shall, subject to paragraph 2, constitute the subject-matter of the proceedings before the Court of Appeal. The Court of Appeal shall consult the file of the proceedings before the Court of First Instance.

2. Requests, facts and evidence which have not been submitted by a party during proceedings before the Court of First Instance may be disregarded by the Court of Appeal. When exercising discretion, the Court shall in particular take into account:

(a) whether a party seeking to lodge new submissions is able to justify that the new submissions could not reasonably have been made during proceedings before the Court of First Instance;

(b) the relevance of the new submissions for the decision on the appeal;

(c) the position of the other party regarding the lodging of the new submissions.

Relation with Agreement: Article 73(4)

Rule 223 – Application for suspensive effect

1. A party may lodge an Application for suspensive effect, in accordance with Article 74 of the Agreement. The applicant shall pay a fee for the Application in accordance with Part 6.

2. The Application for suspensive effect shall set out:

(a) the reasons why the lodging of the appeal shall have suspensive effect;

(b) the facts, evidence and arguments relied on.

3. The Court of Appeal shall decide the Application without delay.

4. In cases of extreme urgency the applicant may apply at any time without formality for an order for suspensive effect to the standing judge [Rule 345.5 and .8]. The standing judge shall have all the powers of the Court of Appeal and shall decide the procedure to be followed on the application, which may include a subsequent written Application.

5. There shall be no suspensive effect for an appeal of an order pursuant to Rule 220.2, Rule 220.3 or 221.3.

Relation with Agreement: Article 74

CHAPTER 1 – WRITTEN PROCEDURE

SECTION 1 – STATEMENT OF APPEAL, STATEMENT OF GROUNDS OF APPEAL

Rule 224 – Time periods for lodging the Statement of appeal and the Statement of grounds of appeal

1. A Statement of appeal shall be lodged by the appellant:

(a) within two months of service of a decision referred to in Rule 220.1(a) and (b); or

(b) within 15 days of service of an order referred to in Rule 220.1(c) or a decision referred to in Rule 220.2 or 221.3.

2. The Statement of grounds of appeal shall be lodged by the appellant:

(a) within four months of service of a decision referred to in Rule 220.1(a) and (b); or

(b) within 15 days of service of an order referred to in Rule 220.1(c) or a decision referred to in Rule 220.2 or 221.3.

Relation with Agreement: Article 73(1) and (2)

Rule 225 – Contents of the Statement of appeal

The Statement of appeal shall contain:

(a) the names of the appellant and of the appellant's representative;

(b) the names of the respondent and of the respondent's representative;

(c) postal and electronic addresses for service on the appellant and on the respondent, as well as the names of the persons authorised to accept service;

(d) the date of the decision or order appealed against and the action number attributed to the file in proceedings before the Court of First Instance; and

(e) the order or remedy sought by the appellant, including any order for expedition of the appeal pursuant to Rule 9.3(b) and the reasons justifying such order for expedition.

Rule 226 – Contents of the Statement of grounds of appeal

The Statement of grounds of appeal shall contain:

(a) an indication of which parts of the decision or order are contested;

(b) the reasons for setting aside the contested decision or order; and

(c) an indication of the facts and evidence on which the appeal is based in accordance with Rule 222.1 and .2.

Rule 227 – Language of the Statement of appeal and of the Statement of grounds of appeal

The Statement of appeal and the Statement of grounds of appeal shall be drawn up:

(a) without prejudice to Article 50(3) of the Agreement, in the language of the proceedings before the Court of First Instance; or

(b) where the parties have agreed in accordance with Article 50(2) of the Agreement, in the language in which the patent was granted. Where the parties have agreed in accordance with Article 50(2) of the Agreement, evidence of the respondent's agreement shall be lodged by the appellant together with the Statement of appeal.

Relationship with Agreement: Article 50

Rule 228 – Fee for the appeal

The appellant shall pay the fixed fee and, where applicable, the value based fee for the appeal, in accordance with Part 6. Rule 15.2 shall apply *mutatis mutandis.*

Rule 229 – Examination as to formal requirements of the Statement of appeal

1. The Registry shall, as soon as practicable after the lodging of the Statement of appeal, examine whether the requirements of Rules 224.1, 225, 227 and 228 have been complied with.

2. If the appellant has not complied with the requirements referred to in Rules 225, 227 or 228, the Registry shall invite the appellant to:

(a) correct the deficiencies within 14 days of service of such notification; and

(b) where applicable, pay the fee for the appeal within said 14 days.

3. The Registry shall at the same time inform the appellant that if the appellant fails to correct the deficiencies or to pay the fee within the time stated, a decision by default may be given in accordance with Rule 357.

4. If the appellant has not met the requirements of Rules 225, 227 and 228 and fails to correct the deficiencies or pay the fee the Registry shall inform the President of the Court of Appeal who shall reject the appeal as inadmissible by a decision by default. He may give the appellant an opportunity to be heard beforehand.

5. If the appellant has not met the requirements of Rule 224.1, the Registry shall inform the President of the Court of Appeal who shall reject the appeal as inadmissible. He may give the appellant an opportunity to be heard beforehand.

Rule 230 – Recording in the register (Court of Appeal)

1. If the Statement of appeal complies with the requirements referred to in Rule 229.1, the Registry shall:

(a) record the date of receipt to the Statement of appeal and an action number to the appeal file;

(b) record the appeal file in the register;

(c) inform the appellant of the action number and the date of receipt; and

(d) serve the Statement of appeal on all parties to the proceedings at first instance.

2. The action shall be assigned to a panel according to Rule 345.3 and .8.

3. The panel shall as soon as practicable decide whether to grant any order for expedition pursuant to Rule 225(e) having given the parties an opportunity to be heard.

Rule 231 – Designation of the judge-rapporteur

The presiding judge of the panel to which the action has been assigned shall designate one legally qualified judge of the panel as judge-rapporteur. The presiding judge may designate himself as the judge-rapporteur. The Registry shall as soon as practicable notify the appellant and respondent of the identity of the judge-rapporteur.

Rule 232 – Translation of file

1. If the language of the proceedings before the Court of Appeal is not the language of the proceedings before the Court of First Instance, the judge-rapporteur may order the appellant to lodge, within a time period to be specified, translations into the language of the proceedings before the Court of Appeal of:

(a) written pleadings and other documents lodged by the parties before the Court of First Instance, as specified by the judge-rapporteur;

(b) decisions or orders of the Court of First Instance.

The judge-rapporteur shall at the same time inform the appellant that if the appellant fails to lodge the translations within the time period specified, a decision by default may be given in accordance with Rule 357.

2. If the appellant fails to lodge the translations under paragraph 1 within the time period specified, the judge-rapporteur shall reject the appeal by a decision by default in accordance with Rule 357. He may give the appellant an opportunity to be heard beforehand.

3. The appellant may request that documented costs of translations be taken into account when the Court fixes the amount of costs in accordance with Part 1, Chapter 5.

Relation with Agreement: Article 50(2) and (3)

Rule 233 – Preliminary examination of the Statement of grounds of appeal

1. The judge-rapporteur shall examine whether the Statement of grounds of appeal satisfies the requirements of Rule 226.

2. If the Statement of grounds of appeal does not comply with the requirements of Rule 226, the judge-rapporteur shall give the appellant leave to amend the Statement of grounds of appeal within such period as he may decide. If the appellant fails to amend the Statement within such period the judge-rapporteur may reject the appeal as inadmissible. He shall give the appellant an opportunity to be heard beforehand.

3. Grounds of appeal which are not raised within the period specified for the Statement of grounds of appeal in Rule 224.2 shall not be admissible.

Rule 234 – Challenge to the decision to reject an appeal as inadmissible

1. The appellant may challenge a decision to reject the appeal as inadmissible under Rules 224.1 or 233.2 within one month of service of the decision, without providing new grounds of appeal.

2. The action shall be assigned to a panel according to Rule 345.3 and .8.

3. If a decision to reject an appeal as inadmissible is set aside, the appeal shall take its normal course.

4. The appellant shall pay a fee for the challenge in accordance with Part 6.

SECTION 2 – STATEMENT OF RESPONSE

Rule 235 – Statement of response

1. Within three months of service of the Statement of grounds of appeal pursuant to Rule 224.2(a), any other party to proceedings before the Court of First Instance (hereinafter "respondent") may lodge a Statement of response, which shall be served on the appellant.

2. Within 15 days of service of grounds of appeal pursuant to Rule 224.2(b), any other party to proceedings before the Court of First Instance (hereinafter "respondent") may lodge a Statement of response, which shall be served on the appellant.

3. If the respondent fails to lodge a Statement of response, the Court of Appeal may give a reasoned decision.

Rule 236 – Contents of the Statement of response

1. The Statement of response shall contain:

(a) the names of the respondent and the respondent's representative;

(b) postal and electronic addresses for service on the respondent and the names and addresses of the persons authorised to accept service;

(c) the action number of the appeal file; and

(d) a response to the grounds of appeal.

2. The respondent may support the decision of the Court of First Instance on grounds other than those given in the decision.

Rule 237 – Statement of cross-appeal

1. A party who has not lodged a Statement of appeal within the period referred to in Rule 224.1 may still bring an appeal by way of cross-appeal within the period referred to in Rule 235 if one of the other parties has lodged a Statement of appeal.

2. A Statement of cross-appeal shall be included in the Statement of response. It shall comply with the requirements of Rules 225 and 226. Rules 229, 233 and 234 shall apply *mutatis mutandis* to the Statement of cross-appeal.

3. A Statement of cross-appeal shall not be admissible in any other way or at any other time.

4. A cross-appeal shall be treated as an appeal as far as the fee for the appeal is concerned. Rule 228 shall apply *mutatis mutandis.*

5. If the Statement of appeal is withdrawn, any Statement of cross-appeal shall be deemed to be withdrawn.

SECTION 3 – REPLY TO A STATEMENT OF CROSS-APPEAL

Rule 238 – Reply to a Statement of cross-appeal and further schedule

1. The appellant may, within two months of service of any Statement of cross-appeal under Rules 237, 235.1, lodge a Reply to the Statement of cross-appeal which shall contain a response to the grounds of appeal raised in the Statement of cross-appeal.

2. The appellant may, within 15 days of service of the Statement of cross-appeal under Rules 237 and 235.2, lodge a Reply to the Statement of cross-appeal which shall contain a response to the grounds of appeal raised in the Statement of cross-appeal.

3. Rule 28 shall apply *mutatis mutandis.*

SECTION 4 – REFERRAL TO THE FULL COURT

Rule 238A – Decision to refer

1. The panel to which the action has been assigned may refer it to the full Court of Appeal if the panel considers, on a proposal from the presiding judge, the case to be of exceptional importance and, in particular, where the decision in the action may affect the consistency and unity of the case law of the Court.

2. The presiding judge of the panel shall request the President of the Court of Appeal and the two judges of the Court of Appeal who are members of the Presidium to appoint the judges of the Court of Appeal to the full Court. The appointees shall be the President of the Court of Appeal and not less than ten (legally and technically qualified) judges of the Court of Appeal to represent the initial two panels of the Court of Appeal. In the event that the Court of Appeal shall have more than two panels the appointees to the full Court shall increase by five judges, (legally and technically qualified), for each additional panel.

3. Decisions of the full Court shall be by no less than a three-quarters majority of the judges of the full Court.

CHAPTER 2 – INTERIM PROCEDURE

Rule 239 – Role of the judge-rapporteur

1. Upon the expiry of the periods specified in Rules 224 to 238 the judge-rapporteur shall make all necessary preparations for the oral hearing. Subject always to the provisions of Rule 222, the judge-rapporteur shall, to the extent appropriate, have the powers and exercise the duties set out in Rules 101 to 110 *mutatis mutandis*.

2. As soon as the judge-rapporteur considers that the appeal is ready for oral hearing he shall summon the parties to the oral hearing. Except for appeals against the orders referred to in Rule 220.1(c) and 220.2, and subject to any order for expedition pursuant to Rule 230.3, at least two months' notice shall be given unless the parties agree to a shorter time period. The interim procedure shall be deemed closed and oral procedure shall start immediately on the giving of such summons. The presiding judge shall, in consultation with the judge-rapporteur take over the management of the action.

CHAPTER 3 – ORAL PROCEDURE

Rule 240 – Conduct of the oral hearing

Subject to Rule 241 the oral hearing shall be held before the panel and shall be directed by the presiding judge. Subject always to Rule 222, Rules 111, 112, 115, 116 and 117 shall apply *mutatis mutandis*.

Rule 241 – Conduct of the oral hearing for an appeal of a cost decision

The oral hearing for an appeal of a cost decision pursuant to Rule 157 shall be heard by the standing judge [Rule 345.5 and .8] who shall have all the powers of the Court of Appeal.

CHAPTER 4 – DECISIONS AND EFFECT OF DECISIONS

Rule 242 – Decision of the Court of Appeal

1. The Court of Appeal shall either reject the appeal or set the decision or order aside totally or in part substituting its own decision or order, including an order for costs both in respect of the proceedings at first instance and on appeal.

2. The Court of Appeal may:

(a) exercise any power within the competence of the Court of First Instance;

(b) in exceptional circumstances refer the action back to the Court of First Instance for decision or for retrial [Rule 243]. It shall not normally be an exceptional circumstance justifying a referral back that the Court of First Instance failed to decide an issue which it is necessary for the Court of Appeal to decide on appeal.

Relation with Agreement: Article 75

Rule 243 – Referral back

1. The decision referring an action back to the Court of First Instance shall specify whether the same panel whose earlier decision or order is revoked shall deal further with the action or whether another panel shall be appointed by the presiding judge of the division concerned.

2. Where an action is referred back to the Court of First Instance, the Court shall be bound by the decision of the Court of Appeal and its *ratio decidendi.*

Relation with Agreement: Article 75

CHAPTER 5 – PROCEDURE FOR APPLICATION FOR REHEARING

Rule 245 – Lodging of an Application for rehearing

1. An Application for rehearing may be lodged by any party adversely affected by a final decision (hereinafter "the final decision") of the Court of First Instance for which the time for lodging an appeal has expired or of the Court of Appeal (hereinafter "the petitioner").

2. The Application for rehearing shall be lodged at the Court of Appeal within the following periods:

(a) where the Application for rehearing is based on the ground of a fundamental procedural defect, within two months of the discovery of the fundamental defect or of service of the final decision, whichever is the later;

(b) where the Application for rehearing is based on an act which has been held, by a final court decision, to constitute a criminal offence, within two months of the date on which the criminal offence has been so held or service of the final decision, whichever is the later;

(c) but in any event no later than ten years of service of the final decision.

Relation with Agreement: Article 81

Rule 246 – Contents of the Application for rehearing

1. The Application for rehearing shall contain:

(a) the names of the petitioner and of the petitioner's representative;

(b) postal and electronic addresses for service on the petitioner and the names and addresses of the persons authorised to accept service; and

(c) an indication of the decision to be reviewed.

2. The Application for rehearing shall indicate the reasons for setting aside the final decision, as well as the facts and evidence on which the Application is based.

Rule 247 – Fundamental procedural defects

A fundamental procedural defect under Article 81(1) of the Agreement may have occurred, for example, where:

(a) a judge of the Court took part in the decision in breach of Article 17 of the Agreement or Article 7 of the Statute;

(b) a person not appointed as a judge of the Court sat on the panel which took the final decision;

(c) a fundamental violation of Article 76 of the Agreement occurred in the proceedings which have led to the final decision;

(d) the decision was made without deciding on a request relevant to that decision; or

(e) a breach of Article 6 of the Convention for the Protection of Human Rights and Fundamental Freedoms has occurred.

Rule 248 – Obligation to raise objections

1. An Application for rehearing based on the ground of a fundamental procedural defect is only admissible where an objection in respect of the procedural defect was raised during the proceedings before the Court of First Instance or the Court of Appeal and dismissed by the Court, except where such objection could not have been raised during the proceedings before the Court of First Instance or the Court of Appeal.

2. An application for rehearing based upon the ground of a fundamental procedural defect is not admissible where the party could have brought an appeal in respect of the defect but failed to do so.

Rule 249 – Definition of criminal offence

A criminal offence shall only be considered to have occurred if it is finally held to be such an offence by a competent court or authority. A conviction is not necessary.

Rule 250 – Fee for the rehearing

The petitioner shall pay the fee for the rehearing, in accordance with Part 6. Rule 15.2 shall apply *mutatis mutandis*. The Court may waive payment of the fee in the circumstances contemplated by Rule 245.2(a) or (b).

Rule 251 – Recording in the register

Rule 230.1 shall apply *mutatis mutandis*.

Rule 252 – Suspensive effect

The lodging of an Application for rehearing shall not have suspensive effect unless the Court of Appeal decides otherwise.

Relation with Agreement: Article 81(2)

Rule 253 – Examination as to formal requirements of the Application for rehearing

1. The Registry shall, as soon as practicable after the lodging of the Application for rehearing, examine whether the requirements of Rules 245, 246 and 250 have been complied with.

2. If the petitioner has not complied with the requirements referred to in paragraph 1, the Registry shall invite the petitioner to:

(a) correct the deficiencies within 14 days; and

(b) where applicable, pay the fee for the rehearing within 14 days.

If the petitioner fails to correct the deficiencies or pay the fee the case shall be assigned to the standing judge by the Registrar (Rule 345.5 and .8) who may reject the Application for rehearing as inadmissible. He shall give the petitioner an opportunity to be heard beforehand.

Rule 254 – Assignment of Application for rehearing to a panel

1. Immediately after the Application for rehearing has been recorded in the register, the Registry shall serve a copy of the Application for rehearing on all other parties and shall inform the President of the Court of Appeal that a Request for rehearing has been lodged.

2. The action shall be assigned to a panel consisting of three legally qualified judges. The President of the Court of Appeal may order that judges of the Court who participated in taking the decision to be reviewed shall not sit on the panel.

Rule 255 – Examination of the Application for rehearing

After hearing the parties the panel may make:

(a) a decision to reject the Application for rehearing as not allowable; such a decision shall be by a majority vote of the judges on the panel.

(b) a decision to allow the Application for rehearing; such a decision shall set aside or suspend the decision under review, in whole or in part, and re-open the proceedings for a new hearing and decisions. Where proceedings are re-opened, the panel shall give directions for the future proceedings.

Relation with Agreement: Article 81(3)

PART 5 – GENERAL PROVISIONS

CHAPTER 1 – GENERAL PROCEDURAL PROVISIONS

Rule 260 – Examination by the Registry of its own motion

1. In any proceedings before the Court, the Registry shall, as soon as practicable in the proceedings, of its own motion, examine whether an opt-out has effect for the patent concerned.

2. Where the Registry notes that two or more actions concerning the same patent are initiated before several divisions (whether or not between the same parties), it shall as soon as practicable inform the divisions concerned.

Relation with Agreement: Article 83(3) and (4)

Relation with Statute: Articles 23 and 24

Rule 261 – Date of pleadings

All pleadings and documents lodged with pleadings shall bear a time and a date which shall be the time and date of receipt of pleadings at the Registry. The time shall be the local time of the Registry. The Registrar shall be responsible for time and date marking.

Rule 262 – Public access to the register

1. Without prejudice to Articles 58 and 60(1) of the Agreement and subject to Rules 190.1, 194.5, 196.1, 197.4, 199.1, 207.7, 209.4, 315.2 and 365.2, and following, where applicable, redaction of personal data within the meaning of Regulation (EU) 2016/679 and confidential information according to paragraph 2

(a) decisions and orders made by the Court shall be published,

(b) written pleadings and evidence, lodged at the Court and recorded by the Registry shall be available to the public upon reasoned request to the Registry; the decision is taken by the judge-rapporteur after consulting the parties.

2. A party may request that certain information of written pleadings or evidence be kept confidential and provide specific reasons for such confidentiality. To this end content of the register is made publicly available according to paragraph 1 (b) only 14 days after it has been available to all recipients. The Registrar shall ensure that beyond this time period information subject of a request for confidentiality shall not be made available pending an Application pursuant to paragraph 3 or an appeal pursuant to Rule 220.2. When a party lodges a request that parts of written pleadings or evidence shall be kept confidential, he shall also provide copies of the said documents with the relevant parts redacted when making the request.

3. A member of the public may lodge an Application with the Court for an order that any information excluded from public access pursuant to paragraph 2 may be made available to the applicant.

4. The Application shall contain:

(a) details of the information alleged to be confidential, so far as possible;

(b) the grounds upon which the applicant believes the reasons for confidentiality should not be accepted; and

(c) the purpose for which the information is needed.

5. The Court shall invite written comments from the parties prior to making any order.

6. The Court shall allow the Application unless legitimate reasons given by the party concerned for the confidentiality of the information outweigh the interest of the applicant to access such information.

7. The Registrar shall as soon as practicable take all such steps with regard to access to the register as may be necessary to give effect to an order of the Court under this Rule.

Relation with Agreement: Articles 10, 45, 58 and 60(1)

Relation with Statute: Article 24(2)

Rule 262A – Protection of Confidential Information

1. Without prejudice to Article 60(1) of the Agreement and Rules 190.1, 194.5, 196.1, 197.4, 199.1, 207.7, 209.4, 315.2 and 365.2 a party may make an Application to the Court for an order that certain information contained in its pleadings or the collection and use of evidence in proceedings may be restricted or prohibited or that access to such information or evidence be restricted to specific persons.

2. The Application shall contain the grounds upon which the applicant believes the information or evidence in question should be restricted in accordance with Article 58 of the Agreement.

3. The Application shall be made at the same time as lodging a document containing the information or evidence and shall provide a copy of the unredacted relevant document and, if applicable, a copy of the redacted document.

4. The Court shall invite written comments from the representatives of the other parties prior to making any order.

5. The Court may allow the Application considering in particular whether the grounds relied upon by the applicant for the order significantly outweigh the interest of the other party to have full access to the information and evidence in question.

6. The number of persons referred to in paragraph 1 shall be no greater than necessary in order to ensure compliance with the right of the parties to the legal proceedings to an effective remedy and to a fair trial, and shall include, at least, one natural person from each party and the respective lawyers or other representatives of those parties to the legal proceedings.

7. The Registrar shall as soon as practicable take all such steps with regard to access to the evidence as may be necessary to give effect to the order of the Court under this Rule.

Relation with Agreement: Article 58

Rule 263 – Leave to change claim or amend case

1. A party may at any stage of the proceedings apply to the Court for leave to change its claim or to amend its case, including adding a counterclaim. Any such application shall explain why such change or amendment was not included in the original pleading.

2. Subject to paragraph 3, leave shall not be granted if, all circumstances considered, the party seeking the amendment cannot satisfy the Court that:

(a) the amendment in question could not have been made with reasonable diligence at an earlier stage; and

(b) the amendment will not unreasonably hinder the other party in the conduct of its action.

3. Leave to limit a claim in an action unconditionally shall always be granted.

4. The Court may re-consider fees already paid in the light of an amendment.

Rule 264 – An opportunity to be heard

Where these Rules provide that a party shall or may be given an opportunity to be heard before the Court makes an order or takes some action, the Court shall or may (as the case may be) request the parties to provide written submissions within a specified period and/or shall or may invite the parties to an oral hearing on a fixed date by the Court. The Court may also order that a hearing takes place by telephone or video conference. Rules 105 and 106 shall apply *mutatis mutandis*.

Rule 265 – Withdrawal

1. As long as there is no final decision in an action, a claimant may apply to withdraw his action. The Court shall decide the application after hearing the other party.

The application to withdraw shall not be permitted if the other party has a legitimate interest in the action being decided by the Court.

2. If withdrawal is permitted, the Court shall:

(a) give a decision declaring the proceedings closed;

(b) order the decision to be entered on the register; and

(c) issue a cost decision in accordance with Part 1, Chapter 5.

The withdrawal of an action by the claimant shall have no effect on any counterclaim in the action. The Court may however refer any counterclaim for revocation to the Central Division.

Rule 266 – Preliminary references to the Court of Justice of the European Union

1. At any stage of the proceedings where a question is raised before the Court and the Court considers that a decision on the question by the Court of Justice of the European Union ("CJEU") is necessary before the Court can give judgment, the Court of First Instance may and the Court of Appeal shall request the CJEU to give a ruling thereon.

2. The Court shall in requesting a ruling follow the procedure set out in the Rules of the CJEU.

3. If the Court requests the CJEU to apply its expedited procedure the request shall in addition set out:

(a) the matters of fact and law which establish its urgency; and

(b) the reasons why an expedited ruling is appropriate.

4. The Registrar shall as soon as practicable forward the request and any request to apply the expedited procedure to the Registrar of the CJEU.

5. The Court may stay the proceedings. Where it does not stay proceedings, it shall not give judgement until the CJEU has given a ruling on the question.

Rule 267 – Actions pursuant to Article 22 of the Agreement

Where an action for damages has been brought against a Contracting Member State pursuant to Article 22 of the Agreement, the President of the Court of Appeal shall, as soon as practicable following a request from the competent authority in the Contracting Member State, provide the competent authority with copies of all pleadings, evidence, decisions and orders available to the Court in its proceedings that are relevant to the action for damages. The President of the Court of Appeal shall have an opportunity to comment.

CHAPTER 2 – SERVICE

SECTION 1 – SERVICE WITHIN THE CONTRACTING MEMBER STATES

Rule 270 – Scope of this Section

1. For service of the Statement of claim within the Contracting Member States the law of the European Union on the service of documents in civil and commercial matters [Regulation (EU) 2020/1784] and the rules set out in this Section, in particular Rule 271.2 shall apply.

2. For the purpose of Rules 270 to 275 the term Statement of claim shall, where appropriate, mean all originating pleadings in actions referred to in Article 32(1) of the Agreement.

Rule 271 – Service of the Statement of claim

1. The Registry shall serve the Statement of claim by electronic means if the conditions referred to in Article 19 of the Regulation (EU) 2020/1784 are met

(a) on the defendant at an electronic address which the defendant has provided for the purpose of service in the proceedings; or

(b) on a representative of the defendant if the defendant has provided the electronic address of a representative pursuant to Rule 8.1 as an address at which the defendant may be served with the Statement of claim; or

(c) on a representative of the defendant pursuant to Rule 8.1 if the representative has notified the Registry or the claimant that he accepts service of the Statement of claim on behalf of the defendant at an electronic address.

2. Where a representative pursuant to Rule 8.1 accepts service on behalf of a party service may be effected within the closed electronic system of the UPC Case Management System (CMS).

3. For the purpose of serving a Statement for revocation [Rule 44] or of serving a Statement for declaration of non-infringement [Rule 63], reference to representative under paragraph 2(b) or (c) shall additionally include professional representatives and legal practitioners as defined in Article 134 EPC who are recorded as the appointed representative for the patent, the subject of the proceedings, in the Register for unitary patent protection [Regulation (EU) No 1257/2012, Article 2(e)] or in the national patent register [Rule 8.5(a)].

4. Where service by electronic means cannot be effected, the Registry shall serve the Statement of claim on the defendant by:

(a) any other method foreseen by the law of the European Union on the service of documents in civil and commercial matters [Regulation (EU) 2020/1784], in particular by registered letter with acknowledgement of receipt or equivalent [Article 18 Regulation (EU) 2020/1784]; or

(b) where service in accordance with paragraph 4(a) could not be effected any method permitted by the law of the Member State of the European Union where service is to be effected or authorised by the Court under Rule 275.

5. Service under this Section shall be effected at the following place:

(a) where the defendant is a company or other legal person, at its statutory seat, central administration or principal place of business within the Contracting Member States or at any place within the Contracting Member States where the company or other legal person has a permanent or temporary place of business;

(b) where the defendant is an individual, at his usual or last known residence within the Contracting Member States; or

(c) for the purpose of serving a Statement for revocation [Rule 44] or of serving a Statement for a declaration of non-infringement [Rule 63], at the place of business of a professional representative or legal practitioner as defined in Article 134 EPC who is recorded as the appointed representative for the patent, the subject of the proceedings, in the Register for unitary patent protection [Regulation (EU) No 1257/2012, Article 2(e)] or of the patent office of a Contracting Member State.

6. Subject to Rule 272.2 and .3, a Statement of claim served in accordance with paragraphs 1 to 5 is deemed to be served on the defendant:

(a) where service takes place by means of electronic communication, on the day when the relevant electronic message was sent (GMT+1);

(b) where service takes place by registered letter with acknowledgement of receipt or equivalent such letter shall be deemed to be served on the addressee on the tenth day following posting unless it has failed to reach the addressee, has in fact reached him on a later date or the acknowledgement of receipt or equivalent has not been returned. Such service shall, except where paragraph 8 applies, be deemed effective even if acceptance of the letter has been refused.

7. The Registry shall advise the defendant that he may refuse to accept a Statement of Claim if it is not written or not accompanied by a translation into a language that he understands or that is an official language of the place where service is to be effected, by enclosing with the document to be served form L in Annex I of Regulation (EU) 2020/1784.

8. Where the defendant is entitled to refuse service and where he has notified the refusal to the Registry within two weeks of the attempted service together with an indication of the language(s) he understands, the Registry shall inform the claimant. The claimant shall provide to the Registry translations of at least the Statement of claim and the information required in Rule 13.1(a) to (p) in a language provided for by paragraph 7.

Rule 272 – Notice of service and non-service of the Statement of claim

1. The Registry shall inform the claimant of the date on which the Statement of claim is deemed served under Rule 271.6.

2. Where the Registry has served the Statement of claim by registered letter with acknowledgement of receipt or equivalent and the Statement of claim is returned to the Registry for any reason, the Registry shall inform the claimant.

3. Paragraph 2 shall apply *mutatis mutandis* where the Registry has served the Statement of claim by means of electronic communication and the relevant electronic message appears not to have been received.

SECTION 2 – SERVICE OUTSIDE THE CONTRACTING MEMBER STATES

Rule 273 – Scope of this Section

This Section applies to service of a Statement of claim outside the Contracting Member States.

Rule 274 – Service outside the Contracting Member States

1. Where a Statement of claim is to be served outside the Contracting Member States, it shall be so served by the Registry

(a) by any method provided by:
(i) The law of the European Union on the service of documents in civil and commercial matters [Regulation (EU) 2020/1784] where it applies;
(ii) The Hague Service Convention or any other applicable convention or agreement where it applies; or
(iii) to the extent that there is no such convention or agreement in force, either by service through diplomatic or consular channels from the Contracting Member State in which the sub-registry of the relevant division is established;

(b) where service in accordance with paragraph 1(a) could not be effected by any method permitted by the law of the state where service is to be effected or as authorised by the Court under Rule 275.

2. No Statement of claim may be served under this Rule 274 in a manner which is contrary to the law of the state where service is effected.

3. The Registry shall inform the claimant of the date on which the Statement of claim is deemed served under paragraph 1.

4. The Registry shall inform the claimant if for any reason service pursuant to paragraph 1 cannot be effected.

SECTION 3 – SERVICE BY AN ALTERNATIVE METHOD

Rule 275 – Service of the Statement of claim by an alternative method or at an alternative place

1. Where service in accordance with Section 1 or 2 could not be effected the Court on an application by the claimant that there is a good reason to authorise service by a method or at a place not otherwise permitted by this Chapter, the Court may by way of order permit service by an alternative method or at an alternative place.

2. On a reasoned request by the claimant, the Court may order that steps already taken to bring the Statement of claim to the attention of the defendant by an alternative method or at an alternative place is good service.

3. An order under this rule shall specify:

(a) the method or place of service;

(b) the date on which the Statement of claim is deemed served; and

(c) the period for filing the Statement of defence.

4. No order for alternative service under this Rule shall be made permitting service in a manner that is contrary to the law of the state where service is to be effected.

SECTION 4 – SERVICE OF ORDERS, DECISIONS AND WRITTEN PLEADINGS

Rule 276 – Service of orders and decisions

1. Any order or decision of the Court shall be served on each of the parties in accordance with the provisions of Sections 1, 2 or 3 of this Chapter 2, as the case may be.

2. Decisions by default pursuant to Rule 355 resulting from failure of the defendant to lodge a Defence to revocation [Rule 50] or failure to lodge a Defence to the Statement for a declaration of non-infringement [Rule 67] within the time limit set by these Rules or by the Court, may be served on the defendant at the place of business of a professional representative or legal practitioner as defined in Article 134 EPC who is recorded as the appointed representative for the subject European patent with unitary effect, the subject of the proceedings, in the Register for unitary patent protection [Regulation (EU) No 1257/2012, Article 2(e)] or in the national patent register [Rule 8.5(a)].

Rule 277 – Decisions by default under Part 5, Chapter 11

No decision by default shall be entered under Part 5, Chapter 11 unless the Court is satisfied that either:

(a) the Statement of claim was served by a method prescribed by the internal law of the state addressed for the service of documents in domestic actions upon persons who are within its territory; or

(b) the Statement of claim was actually served on the defendant under this Chapter 2.

Rule 278 – Service of written pleadings and other documents

1. As soon as practicable after written pleadings have been received at the Registry, the Registry shall serve the pleadings and any other document lodged with the pleadings on the other party by means of electronic communication except if the pleading contains a request for an ex parte proceeding.

2. Where service by means of electronic communication cannot be effected, the Registry shall serve the written pleadings on the party by:

(a) registered letter with acknowledgement of receipt or equivalent; or

(b) any method authorised by the Court under Rule 275.

3. Service under paragraph 2(a) shall be effected at the following place:

(a) where the party is a company or other legal person: at its statutory seat, central administration, principal place of business or at any place within the Contracting Member States where the company or other legal person has a place of business;

(b) where the party is an individual: at his usual or last known residence within the Contracting Member States.

4. Rule 271.6 and 272 shall apply *mutatis mutandis.*

5. Where a party is represented pursuant to Rule 8.1, the pleadings and other documents referred to in paragraph 1 shall be served on that representative. Paragraph 2 shall apply *mutatis mutandis.*

Rule 279 – Change of electronic address for service

Where the electronic address for service of a party changes, that party must give notice in writing of the change as soon as it has taken place to the Registry and every other party [Rule 6.3].

CHAPTER 3 – RIGHTS AND OBLIGATIONS OF REPRESENTATIVES

Rule 284 – Duty of representatives not to misrepresent facts or cases

A representative of a party shall not misrepresent cases or facts before the Court either knowingly or with good reasons to know.

Relation to Agreement: Article 48(6)

Rule 285 – Powers of attorney

1. A representative who claims to be representing a party shall be accepted as such provided however the Court may order a representative to produce a written authority if his representative powers are challenged.

2. In the event of a successful challenge to a representative's authority pursuant to paragraph 1 the Court may make an order pursuant to Rule 291.

Rule 286 – Certificate that a representative is authorised to practice before the Court

1. A representative pursuant to Article 48(1) of the Agreement shall lodge at the Registry a certificate that he is a lawyer authorised to practise before a court of a Member State of the European Union. A lawyer within the meaning of Article 48(1) of the Agreement is a person who is authorised to pursue professional activities under a title referred to in Article 1 of Directive 98/5/EC and by way of exception a person with equivalent legal professional qualifications who, owing to national rules, is permitted to practice in patent infringement and invalidity litigation but not under such title. In subsequent actions the representative may refer to the certificate previously lodged.

2. A representative pursuant to Article 48(2) of the Agreement shall lodge at the Registry the European Patent Litigation Certificate as defined by the Administrative Committee or otherwise justify that he has appropriate qualifications to represent a party before the Court. In subsequent actions such representative may refer to the certificate or other evidence of appropriate qualification previously lodged.

Rule 287 – Attorney-client privilege

1. Where a client seeks advice from a lawyer or a patent attorney he has instructed in a professional capacity, whether in connection with proceedings before the Court or otherwise, then any confidential communication (whether written or oral) between them relating to the seeking or the provision of that advice is privileged from disclosure, whilst it remains confidential, in any proceedings before the Court or in arbitration or mediation proceedings before the Centre.

2. This privilege applies also to communications between a client and a lawyer or patent attorney employed by the client and instructed to act in a professional capacity, whether in connection with proceedings before the Court or otherwise.

3. This privilege extends to the work product of the lawyer or patent attorney (including communications between lawyers and/or patent attorneys employed in the same firm or entity or between lawyers and/or patent attorneys employed by the same client) and to any record of a privileged communication.

4. This privilege prevents the lawyer or patent attorney and his client from being questioned or examined about the contents or nature of their communications.

5. This privilege may be expressly waived by the client.

6. For the purpose of Rules 287 and 288:

(a) the expression "lawyer" shall mean a person as defined in Rule 286.1 and any other person who is qualified to practise as a lawyer and to give legal advice under the law of the state where he practises and who is professionally instructed to give such advice.

(b) the expression "patent attorney" shall include a person who is recognised as eligible to give advice under the law of the state where he practises in relation to the protection of any invention or to the prosecution or litigation of any patent or patent application and is professionally consulted to give such advice.

7. The expression "patent attorney" shall also include a professional representative before the European Patent Office pursuant to Article 134 (1) EPC.

Relation to Agreement: Article 48(4)

Rule 288 – Litigation privilege

Where a client, or a lawyer or patent attorney as specified in Rule 287.1, .2, .6 and .7 instructed by a client in a professional capacity, communicates confidentially with a third party for the purposes of obtaining information or evidence of any nature for the purpose of or for use in any proceedings, including proceedings before the European Patent Office, such communications shall be privileged from disclosure in the same way and to the same extent as provided for in Rule 287.

Relation to Agreement: Article 48(5)

Rule 289 – Privileges, immunities and facilities

1. Representatives appearing before the Court shall enjoy immunity in respect of words spoken or written by them concerning the action or the parties.

2. Representatives shall enjoy the following further privileges and facilities:

(a) papers and documents relating to the proceedings shall be exempt from both search and seizure;

(b) any allegedly infringing product or device relating to the proceedings shall be exempt from both search and seizure when brought to the Court for the purposes of the proceedings.

In the event of a dispute, customs officials or police may seal those papers, documents or allegedly infringing products or devices. They shall then be immediately forwarded to the Court for inspection in the presence of the Registrar and of the person concerned.

3. Representatives shall be entitled to travel in the course of duty without hindrance.

4. The privileges, immunities and facilities specified in paragraphs 1 to 3 are granted exclusively in the interests of the proper conduct of proceedings.

5. The Court may waive the immunity where it considers that a representative is guilty of conduct which is contrary to the proper conduct of proceedings.

Relation with Agreement: Article 48

Rule 290 – Powers of the Court as regards representatives

1. As regards representatives who appear before it, the Court shall have the powers normally accorded to courts of law, under the conditions laid down in Rule 291.

2. Representatives who appear before the Court shall strictly comply with any code of conduct adopted for such representatives by the Administrative Committee.

Rule 291 – Exclusion from the proceedings

1. If the Court considers that the conduct of a party's representative towards the Court, towards any judge of the Court or towards any member of the staff of the Registry is incompatible with the dignity of the Court or with the requirements of the proper administration of justice, or that such representative uses his rights for purposes other than those for which they were granted, or that such representative is otherwise in breach of any code of conduct adopted pursuant to Rule 290.2 it shall so inform the person concerned. On the same grounds, the Court may at any time, after having given the person concerned an opportunity to be heard, exclude that person from the proceedings by way of order. That order shall have immediate effect.

2. Where a party's representative is excluded from the proceedings, the proceedings shall be stayed for a period fixed by the presiding judge in order to enable the party concerned to appoint another representative.

Rule 292 – Patent attorneys' right of audience

1. For the purposes of Article 48(4) of the Agreement, the term "patent attorneys" assisting a representative referred to in Article 48(1) and/or (2) of the Agreement shall mean persons meeting the requirements of Rule 287.6(b) or.7 and practising in a Contracting Member State.

2. Such patent attorneys shall be allowed to speak at hearings of the Court at the discretion of the Court and subject to the representative's responsibility to coordinate the presentation of a party's case.

3. Rules 285 and 287 to 291 shall apply *mutatis mutandis*.

Relation with Agreement: Article 48(4)

Rule 293 – Change of a representative

Any change of representative shall take effect from the receipt by the Registry of notification that a new representative shall in future be representing the party concerned. Until the moment where such statement is received, the former representative remains responsible for the conduct of the proceedings and for communications between the Court and the party concerned.

Rule 294 – Removal from the register of representatives

An Application to remove a representative's name, being a representative qualified pursuant to Article 48(1) of the Agreement, from the register of representatives may be made:

(a) by the representative himself in the event he retires or for any other reason ceases to satisfy the requirements of Rule 286;

(b) by a representative on behalf of a listed representative who has died.

CHAPTER 4 – STAY OF PROCEEDINGS

Rule 295 – Stay of proceedings

The Court may stay proceedings:

(a) where it is seized of an action relating to a patent which is also the subject of opposition proceedings or limitation proceedings (including subsequent appeal proceedings) before the European Patent Office or a national authority where a decision in such proceedings may be expected to be given rapidly;

(b) where it is seized of an action relating to a supplementary protection certificate which is also the subject of proceedings before a national court or authority;

(c) where an appeal is brought before the Court of Appeal against a decision or order of the Court of First Instance:
(i) disposing of the substantive issues in part only;
(ii) disposing of an admissibility issue or a Preliminary objection;

(d) at the joint request of the parties;

(e) pursuant to Rule 37;

(f) pursuant to Rules 75 and 76;

(g) pursuant to Rule 118;

(h) pursuant to Rule 136;

(i) pursuant to Rule 266;

(j) pursuant to Rules 310 and 311;

(k) pursuant to Rule 346;

(l) to give effect to Union law, in particular the provisions of Regulation (EU) No 1215/2012 and the Lugano Convention;

(m) in any other case where the proper administration of justice so requires.

Rule 296 – Duration and effects of a stay of proceedings

1. The stay of proceedings shall take effect on the date indicated in the order to stay or, in the absence of such an indication, on the date of that order. The Court shall stipulate what effect the stay shall have on any existing orders.

2. Where the order to stay does not fix the length of the stay, it shall end on the date indicated in the order to resume proceedings or, in the absence of such indication, on the date of the order to resume.

3. While proceedings are stayed, time shall cease to run for the purposes of procedural periods. Time shall begin to run afresh for the purposes of procedural periods from the date on which the stay of proceedings comes to an end.

Rule 297 – Resumption of proceedings

Any decision referred to in Rule 296.2 ordering the resumption of proceedings before the end of the stay shall be made by order of the judge-rapporteur after hearing the parties. The judge-rapporteur may refer the matter to the panel.

Rule 298 – Accelerated proceedings before the European Patent Office

The Court may of its own motion or at the request of a party request that opposition proceedings or limitation proceedings (including any subsequent appeal proceedings) before the European Patent Office be accelerated in accordance with the proceedings of the European Patent Office. The Court may stay its proceedings in accordance with Rule 295(a) pending the outcome of such request and any subsequent accelerated proceedings.

CHAPTER 5 – TIME PERIODS

Rule 300 – Calculation of periods

Any period of time prescribed by the Agreement, the Statute, these Rules or any order of the Court for the taking of any procedural step shall be laid down in terms of full days, weeks, months or years and shall be reckoned as follows:

(a) computation shall start on the day following the day on which the relevant event occurred; in the case of service of a document, the relevant event shall be the receipt of that document in accordance with Part 5, Chapter 2;

(b) when a period is expressed as one year or a certain number of years, it shall expire in the relevant subsequent year in the month having the same name and on the day having the same number as the month and the day on which the said event occurred. If the relevant subsequent month has no day with the same number, the period shall expire on the last day of that month;

(c) when a period is expressed as one month or a certain number of months, it shall expire in the relevant subsequent month on the day which has the same number as the day on which the said event occurred. If the relevant subsequent month has no day with the same number, the period shall expire on the last day of that month;

(d) when a period is expressed as one week or a certain number of weeks, it shall expire in the relevant subsequent week on the day having the same name as the day on which the said event occurred;

(e) day shall mean a calendar day unless expressed as a working day;

(f) calendar days shall include official holidays of the Contracting Member State in which the division or the seat of the central division or its section concerned or the Court of Appeal is located, Saturdays and Sundays;

(g) working days shall not include official holidays of the Contracting Member State in which the division or the seat of the central division or its section concerned or the Court of Appeal is located, Saturdays and Sundays;

(h) periods shall not be suspended during the judicial vacations.

Rule 301 – Automatic extension of periods

1. If a period expires on a Saturday, Sunday or official holiday of the Contracting Member State in which the division or the seat of the central division or its section concerned or the Court of Appeal is located, it shall be extended until the end of the first following working day.

2. Paragraph 1 shall apply *mutatis mutandis* if documents filed in electronic form cannot be received by the Court.

CHAPTER 6 – PARTIES TO PROCEEDINGS

SECTION 1 – PLURALITY OF PARTIES

Rule 302 – Plurality of claimants or patents

1. The Court may order that proceedings commenced by a plurality of claimants or in respect of a plurality of patents be heard in separate proceedings.

2. Where the Court orders a separation of proceedings the Court shall decide on the payment of a new court fee or court fees in accordance with Part 6.

3. The Court may order that parallel infringement or revocation proceedings relating to the same patent or patents and before the same local or regional division or the central division or the Court of Appeal be heard together where it is in the interests of justice to do so.

Rule 303 – Plurality of defendants

1. Proceedings may be started against a plurality of defendants if the Court has competence in respect of all of them.

2. The Court may separate the proceedings into two or more separate proceedings against different defendants.

3. Where the Court orders a separation of proceedings under paragraph 2, the claimants in the new proceedings shall pay a new court fee in accordance with Part 6, unless the Court decides otherwise.

SECTION 2 – CHANGE IN PARTIES

Rule 305 – Change in parties

1. The Court may, on application by a party, order a person to:

(a) be added as a party;

(b) cease to be a party;

(c) be substituted for a party.

2. The Court shall invite other parties to the proceedings to comment on the application, as soon as practicable after service of the application.

3. When ordering that a person shall become a party or shall cease to be a party, the Court may make appropriate orders as to payment of court fees and costs as regards such party.

Rule 306 – Consequences for the proceedings

1. Where the Court orders that a party be added, removed or substituted under Rule 305.1, it shall give directions to regulate the consequences as to case management.

2. The Court shall also determine the extent to which a new party is bound by the proceedings as then constituted.

SECTION 3 – DEATH, DEMISE OR INSOLVENCY OF A PARTY

Rule 310 – Death or demise of a party

1. If a party dies or ceases to exist during proceedings, the proceedings shall be stayed until such party is replaced by his successor. The Court may specify a period in this respect.

2. If there are more than two parties to the proceedings, the Court may decide that:

(a) proceedings between the remaining parties be continued separately; and

(b) the stay shall only concern the proceedings regarding the party that no longer exists.

3. If the successor of the party that died or ceased to exist does not continue the proceedings of his own motion, within a period specified by the Court, any other party may apply to have the successor added to or substituted for a party.

4. The Court shall decide who shall be added or substituted as a party pursuant to Rule 305 and 306 shall apply *mutatis mutandis*.

Rule 311 – Insolvency of a party

1. If a party is declared insolvent under the law applicable to the insolvency proceedings the Court shall stay the proceedings up to three months. They may be stayed until the competent national authority or person dealing with the insolvency has decided whether to continue the proceedings or not. Where the competent national authority or person dealing with the insolvency decides not to continue the proceedings, the Court may decide, upon a reasoned request by the other party, that the proceedings should be continued in accordance with the applicable national insolvency law.

2. Proceedings may also be stayed at the request of a temporary administrator who has been appointed before a party is declared insolvent.

3. The claimant may withdraw the action against an insolvent defendant in accordance with Rule 265 and a defendant may withdraw a Counterclaim against an insolvent claimant. Such withdrawal shall not prejudice the action against other parties.

4. If proceedings are continued, the effect of a decision of the Court as regards the insolvent party in the action shall be determined by the law applicable to the insolvency proceedings.

SECTION 4 – TRANSFER OF PATENT

Rule 312 – Transfer of the patent or patent application during proceedings

1. If a patent or patent application is transferred, for one or more Contracting Member States, to another proprietor after proceedings have been started before the Court, the Court may authorise the new proprietor to be added as a party or substituted for a party pursuant to Rule 305 to the extent that the patent and the claims in the proceedings have been assigned to the new proprietor. Rule 306 shall apply *mutatis mutandis*.

2. If the new proprietor takes over the proceedings, no new court fee shall be payable, even if the new proprietor is represented by a new representative.

3. If the new proprietor chooses not to take over the proceedings, any decision in proceedings that have been recorded in the register shall be binding upon him.

SECTION 5 – INTERVENTION

Rule 313 – Application to intervene

1. An Application to intervene may be lodged at any stage of the proceedings before the Court of First Instance or the Court of Appeal by any person establishing a legal interest in the result of an action submitted to the Court (hereinafter "the intervener").

2. An Application to intervene shall be admissible only if it is made in support, in whole or in part, of a claim, order or remedy sought by one of the parties and is made before the closure of the written procedure unless the Court of First Instance or Court of Appeal orders otherwise.

3. The intervener shall be represented in accordance with Article 48 of the Agreement.

4. The Application to intervene shall contain:

(a) a reference to the action number of the file;

(b) the names of the intervener and of the intervener's representative, as well as postal and electronic addresses for service and the names of the persons authorised to accept service;

(c) the claim, order or remedy in support of which intervention is sought by the intervener; and

(d) a statement of the facts establishing the right to intervene under paragraphs 1 and 2.

Rule 314 – Order on Application to intervene

The judge-rapporteur shall decide on the admissibility of the Application to intervene by way of order. The other parties shall be given an opportunity to be heard beforehand.

Rule 315 – Statement in intervention

1. If an Application to intervene is admissible, the judge-rapporteur or the presiding judge shall:

(a) inform the parties to proceedings; and

(b) specify a period within which the intervener may lodge a Statement in intervention.

2. The Registry shall as soon as practicable serve on the intervener any written pleading served by the parties. On a reasoned request by a party the Court may for the protection of confidential information order that a pleading or part of a pleading be disclosed only to certain named persons and subject to appropriate terms of non-disclosure.

3. The Statement in intervention shall contain:

(a) a statement as to the issues involving the intervener and one or more of the parties, and their connection to the matters in dispute;

(b) the arguments of law; and

(c) the facts and evidence relied on.

4. The intervener shall be treated as a party, unless otherwise ordered by the Court.

Rule 316 – Invitation to intervene

1. The judge-rapporteur or the presiding judge may, of his own motion after hearing the parties, or on a reasoned request from a party, invite any person concerned by the

outcome of the dispute to inform the Court, within a period to be specified, whether he wishes to intervene in the proceedings.

2. If the person wishes to intervene, he shall present his Application to intervene within one month of service of the invitation and his Statement in intervention within such further period to be specified by the judge-rapporteur or the presiding judge. Rules 313.3,.4, 314 and 315 shall apply *mutatis mutandis*.

3. An intervener shall be bound by the decision in the action.

Rule 316A – Forced intervention

1. A party who contends that the person should be bound by the decision in the action even if he refuses to intervene shall give reasons for this contention in its reasoned request. In such a case the invitation must include these reasons and must state that the party making the request contends that the person should be bound by the decision in the action even if that person refuses to intervene.

2. If the person invited to intervene pursuant to Rule 316.1 does not intervene but wishes to contend that he should not be bound by the decision in the action, he shall lodge a statement to that effect within the one month period referred to in Rule 316.2. If no such statement is lodged within the time specified he shall be bound by the decision in the action as between himself and any other party to the action and shall not be entitled to argue that the decision in the action was wrong or that the inviting party did not conduct the proceedings leading to the decision in the action properly. If a statement is lodged within the time specified then the Court shall decide whether the person invited to intervene shall be bound having heard the parties and the person invited to intervene. If the Court so decides, the person invited to intervene may present an Application to intervene within one month of service of the Court's decision. Rule 316.2 shall apply. If the person invited to intervene fails to present such an application, he shall be bound by the decision in the action.

Rule 317 – No appeal against an order on the Application to intervene

There shall be no appeal against an order refusing an Application to intervene.

SECTION 6 – RE-ESTABLISHMENT OF RIGHTS

Rule 320 – Re-establishment of rights

1. Where a party has failed to observe a time-limit set by these Rules or the Court for a cause which, despite all due care having been taken by the party, was outside his control and the non-observance of this time limit has had the direct consequence of causing the party to lose a right or means of redress, the relevant panel of the Court may upon the request of that party re-establish the right or means of redress.

2. The Application for Re-establishment of rights shall be lodged with the Registry within one month of the removal of the cause for non-observance of the time-limit but in any event within six months of the non-observed time-limit. Within that

time-limit a fee shall be paid for a Request for Re-establishment of rights, in accordance with Part 6.

3. The Application shall:

(a) state the grounds on which it is based and shall set out the facts on which it relies; and

(b) contain the evidence relied on in the form of affidavits from all persons involved in the non-observance of the time-limit and the persons involved in establishing the precautionary measures of due care taken in order to avoid such cases of non-compliance.

4. The omitted act shall be performed or completed together with Application for Re-establishment within the time-limit mentioned in paragraph 2.

5. There shall be no grant of Re-establishment of rights in respect of the non-observance of the time limit mentioned in paragraphs 2 and 4 of this Rule.

6. The panel shall decide on the Application for Re-establishment of rights by way of order. The other parties shall be given an opportunity to be heard beforehand.

7. There shall be no right to appeal from an order rejecting an Application for Re-establishment of rights or from an order granting Re-establishment of rights.

CHAPTER 7 – MISCELLANEOUS PROVISIONS ON LANGUAGES

Rule 321 – Application by both parties to use of the language in which the patent was granted as language of the proceedings

1. At any time during the written procedure, any party may lodge an Application by both parties to use the language in which the patent was granted as language of the proceedings, in accordance with Article 49(3) of the Agreement. The Application shall state that both parties agree to use the language in which the patent was granted as the language of the proceedings.

2. As soon as practicable, the Registry shall forward the Application to the panel.

3. The panel shall, as soon as practicable, decide whether it approves the Application by both parties to use the language in which the patent was granted as the language of the proceedings. Where the panel does not approve the Application, the Registry shall as soon as practicable inform the parties who may request, within 10 days, that the action be referred to the central division and the action shall be transferred accordingly.

4. Where the action is transferred to the central division Rule 41 shall apply *mutatis mutandis*.

Relation with Agreement: Article 49(3)

Rule 322 – Proposal from the judge-rapporteur to use of the language in which the patent was granted as language of the proceedings

At any time during the written procedure and the interim procedure, the judge-rapporteur may, of his own motion or on a request by a party, after consulting the panel, propose to the parties that the language of the proceedings be changed to the language in which the patent was granted, in accordance with Article 49(4) of the Agreement. If the parties and panel agree the language of the proceedings shall be changed.

Relation with Agreement: Article 49(4)

Rule 323 – Application by one party to use the language in which the patent was granted as language of the proceedings

1. If a party wishes to use the language in which the patent was granted as language of the proceedings, in accordance with Article 49(5) of the Agreement, the party shall include such Application in the Statement of Claim, in the case of a claimant, or in the Statement of Defence, in the case of a defendant. The judge-rapporteur shall forward the Application to the President of the Court of First Instance.

2. The President shall invite the other party to indicate, within 10 days, its position on the use of the language in which the patent was granted as language of the proceedings.

3. The President, having consulted the panel of the division, may order that the language in which the patent was granted shall be the language of the proceedings and may make the order conditional on specific translation or interpretation arrangements.

Relation with Agreement: Article 49(5)

Rule 324 – Consequences where the language of the proceedings is changed in the course of the proceedings

An Application under Rule 321.1 or 323.1 shall specify whether existing pleadings and other documents should be translated and at whose cost. If the parties cannot agree the judge-rapporteur or the President of the Court of First Instance, as the case may be, shall decide in accordance with Rule 323.3.

CHAPTER 8 – CASE MANAGEMENT

Relation with Agreement: Article 43

Rule 331 – Responsibility for case management

1. During the written procedure and the interim procedure, case management shall be the responsibility of the judge-rapporteur subject to Rules 102 and 333.

2. The judge-rapporteur may refer a proposed order to the panel.

3. After the closure of the interim conference, case management shall be the responsibility of the presiding judge in consultation with the judge-rapporteur.

4. The Registry shall serve any case management orders on the parties as soon as practicable after the decision of the judge-rapporteur, presiding judge or panel.

Rule 332 – General principles of case management

Active case management includes:

(a) encouraging the parties to co-operate with each other during the proceedings;

(b) identifying the issues at an early stage;

(c) deciding promptly which issues need full investigation and disposing summarily of other issues;

(d) deciding the order in which issues are to be resolved;

(e) encouraging the parties to make use of the Centre and facilitating the use of the Centre;

(f) helping the parties to settle the whole or part of the action;

(g) fixing timetables or otherwise controlling the progress of the action;

(h) considering whether the likely benefits of taking a particular step justify the cost of taking it;

(i) dealing with as many aspects of the action as the Court can on the same occasion;

(j) dealing with the action without the parties needing to attend in person;

(k) making use of available technical means; and

(l) giving directions to ensure that the hearing of the action proceeds quickly and efficiently.

Rule 333 – Review of case management orders

1. Case management decisions or orders made by the judge-rapporteur or the presiding judge shall be reviewed by the panel, on a reasoned Application by a party.

2. An Application for the review of a case management order shall be lodged within 15 days of service of the order. The Application shall set out the grounds for review and the evidence, if any, in support of the grounds. The other party shall be given an opportunity to be heard.

3. The party seeking a review shall pay the fee for the review of a case management order, in accordance with Part 6. Rule 15.2 shall apply *mutatis mutandis*.

4. The panel shall as soon as practicable decide the Application for review and make any necessary revised case management order.

5. A decision of the panel on an Application for review is a procedural decision for the purposes of Rule 220.2.

Rule 334 – Case management powers

Except where the Agreement, the Statute or these Rules provide otherwise, the judge-rapporteur, the presiding judge or the panel may:

(a) extend or shorten the period for compliance with any rule or order [Rule 9.3];

(b) adjourn or bring forward the interim conference or the oral hearing;

(c) communicate with the parties to instruct them about wishes or requirements of the Court;

(d) direct a separate hearing of any issue;

(e) decide the order in which issues are to be decided;

(f) exclude an issue from consideration;

(g) dismiss or decide on a claim after a decision on a preliminary issue makes a decision on further issues irrelevant to the outcome of the action;

(h) dismiss a claim summarily if it has no prospect of succeeding;

(i) consolidate any matter or issue or order them to be heard together;

(j) make any order pursuant to Rules 103 to 109.

Rule 335 – Varying or revoking orders

The power of the Court to make a case management order includes a power to vary or revoke such order.

Rule 336 – Exercise of case management powers

The Court may exercise its case management powers on the application by a party or of its own motion, unless otherwise provided.

Rule 337 – Orders of the Court's own motion

Where the Court proposes to make an order of its own motion, it may do so but only after hearing the parties.

Rule 340 – Connection Joinder

1. In the interests of the proper administration of justice and of avoiding inconsistent decisions, where more than one action concerning the same patent (whether or not between the same parties) is pending before:

(a) different panels (whether in the same or different divisions); or

(b) different panels of the Court of Appeal,

the panels may by agreement, at any time, after hearing the parties, order that two or more actions shall, on account of the connection between them, be heard together. Article 33 of the Agreement shall be respected.

2. The actions may subsequently be disjoined.

CHAPTER 9 – RULES RELATING TO THE ORGANISATION OF THE COURT

Rule 341 – Precedence

1. With the exception of the President of the Court of Appeal and the President of the Court of First Instance, the judges shall rank in precedence according to their seniority in office.

2. Where there is equal seniority in office, precedence shall be determined by age.

3. Retiring judges who are reappointed shall retain their former precedence.

4. The Presidium may determine the presiding judge of a panel. In the absence of such a determination by the Presidium and unless otherwise agreed by the panel the most senior judge shall be the presiding judge.

Rule 342 – Dates, times and place of the sittings of the Court

1. The duration of judicial vacations shall be fixed by the President of the Court of Appeal, on a proposal from the Presidium. The dates and times of the sittings of the Court shall be decided by the presiding judge of the panel in question.

2. The Court may choose to hold one or more particular sittings in a place other than that in which it has its seat. Subject to any rules agreed by the relevant Contracting Member States pursuant to Article 7(5) of the Agreement where an action is pending before a regional division the judge-rapporteur or the presiding judge shall designate the place within the region for each hearing having regard to the residence or place of business of the defendant and all other relevant circumstances such as the facilities available, the financial means of the parties and the place of actual or threatened infringement.

Relation with Statute: Article 17

Rule 343 – Order in which actions are to be dealt with

1. The Court shall deal with the actions before it in the order in which they become ready for hearing in accordance with Rule 108.

2. The presiding judge of a panel may, after hearing the parties [Rule 264]:

(a) direct that a particular action be given priority and that time limits provided for in these Rules be shortened;

(b) defer an action to be dealt with later, in particular with a view to facilitating an amicable settlement of the dispute.

Rule 344 – Deliberations

1. The Court shall deliberate in closed session.

2. The presiding judge shall preside over the deliberations. Only those judges who were present at the oral hearing may take part in the deliberations on the decision.

3. The deliberation of the Court shall take place as soon as possible after the closure of the oral hearing.

Rule 345 – Composition of panels and assignment of actions

1. The President of the Court of First Instance or a judge to whom he has delegated this task in a division, the seat of the central division or one of its sections shall allocate the judges to the panels of the local and regional divisions, the seat of the central division and its sections.

2. The allocation shall be in conformity with Article 8 of the Agreement.

3. The actions pending in the division, the seat of the central division or one of its sections shall be assigned to the panels by the Registrar following an action-distribution-scheme established by the presiding judge of each local or regional division, the seat of the central division and its sections (being the judge appointed by the Presidium as the presiding judge) for the duration of one calendar year, preferably distributing the actions according to the date of receipt of the actions at the division or section.

4. Each panel may delegate to one or more judges of the panel:

(a) the function of acting as a single judge; or

(b) the function of acting for the panel in the procedures of Part 1 Chapter 4 (Procedure for the Determination of Damages and Compensation, including the procedure for the laying open of books) and Chapter 5 (Procedure for Cost Decisions). These functions may be delegated to the judge-rapporteur who has prepared the action for the oral hearing.

5. The President of the Court of First Instance or a judge to whom he has delegated this task in a division, the seat of the central division or one of its sections shall designate the judges assigned to each division, the seat of the central division and each of its sections as standing judges for urgent actions. The assignment may be limited to certain periods of time.

6. If all parties agree to having the action heard by a single judge, the presiding judge of the panel to which the action is allocated shall assign the action to a legally qualified judge of the panel.

7. Where paragraphs 1 to 6 apply to decisions by the presiding judge of the seat of the central division or one of its sections, the President of the Court of First Instance may of his own motion review that decision.

8. Paragraphs 1 to 6 shall apply *mutatis mutandis* to the Court of Appeal; the President of the Court of Appeal exercising the respective functions.

Relation with Statute: Article 19

Rule 346 – Application of Article 7 of the Statute

1. A party who believes to have reason to object to a judge taking part in proceedings pursuant to Article 7(4) of the Statute shall as soon as is reasonably practicable in the circumstances notify the President of the Court of First Instance or the President of the Court of Appeal wherever the case is pending that it objects to the judge taking part in the proceedings.

2. Any failure to notify an objection as soon as is reasonably practicable shall amount to a waiver of such objection.

3. The President concerned shall, after hearing the judge involved, decide whether the objection is valid pursuant to Article 7(2) and (4) of the Statute and considering the circumstances.

4. In case of any difficulty within the meaning of Article 7(5) of the Statute the President concerned shall refer the matter to the Presidium.

5. If it is decided that the objection is valid the judge concerned shall be replaced on the panel of judges allocated to the case concerned.

6. The panel assigned to the proceedings may decide to continue with the proceedings or to stay the proceedings pending the final decision of the President concerned or the Presidium. The President concerned or the Presidium may give instructions in the final decision as to the future conduct of the proceedings.

Relation with Statute: Article 7

CHAPTER 10 – DECISIONS AND ORDERS

Rule 350 – Decisions

1. Any decision shall contain:

(a) the statement that it is a decision of the Court;

(b) the date of its delivery;

(c) the names of the presiding judge, the judge-rapporteur and other judges taking part in it;

(d) the names of the parties and of the parties' representatives;

(e) an indication of the claim, order or remedy sought by the parties;

(f) a summary of the facts; and

(g) the grounds for the decision.

2. The order of the Court consequential upon the decision (other than costs) including any order giving immediate effect to an injunction, shall be appended to the decision. The order shall comply with Rule 351.

3. Any dissenting opinion shall be attached to the Court's decision.

4. The decision of the Court of First Instance shall contain a summary of the requests and facts submitted by the parties and a statement of the facts and arguments on which the Court bases its decision.

5. All decisions shall be recorded in the register.

Relation with Statute: Article 35(4)

Rule 351 – Orders

1. Every order shall contain:

(a) the statement that it is an order of the judge-rapporteur, of the standing judge, of the single judge, of the presiding judge, of a President of the Court or of the Court;

(b) the date of its adoption;

(c) the names of any judge taking part in its adoption;

(d) the names of the parties and of the parties' representatives; and

(e) the operative part of the order.

2. Where, in accordance with these Rules the Court grants leave to appeal an order the order shall in addition contain:

(a) a statement of the forms of order sought by the parties;

(b) a summary of the facts; and

(c) the grounds for the order.

3. All orders shall be recorded in the register.

Rule 352 – Binding effect of decisions or orders subject to security

1. Decisions and orders may be subject to the rendering of a security (whether by deposit or bank guarantee or otherwise) by a party to the other party for legal costs and other expenses and compensation for any damage incurred or likely to be incurred by the other party if the decisions and orders are enforced and subsequently revoked.

2. The Court may upon the application of a party release a security by order.

Rule 353 – Rectification of decisions and orders

The Court may, by way of order, of its own motion or on application by a party made within one month of service of the decision or order to be rectified, after hearing the parties, rectify clerical mistakes, errors in calculation and obvious slips in the decision or order.

Rule 354 – Enforcement

1. Subject to Rule 118.8 and 352 decisions and orders of the Court shall be directly enforceable from their date of service in each Contracting Member State. Enforce-

ment shall take place in accordance with the enforcement procedures and conditions governed by the law of the particular Contracting Member State where enforcement takes place.

2. Where during an action an enforceable decision or order of the Court is subsequently varied or revoked, the Court may order the party which has enforced such decision or order, upon the request of the party against whom the decision or order has been enforced, to provide appropriate compensation for any injury caused by the enforcement. Rule 125 shall apply *mutatis mutandis*. Where an enforceable decision or order has been made pursuant to a finding of infringement of a patent and, following the conclusion of the action, the patent is amended or revoked, the Court may order, upon the request of the party against whom the decision or order would be enforceable, that the decision or order ceases to be enforceable.

3. The Court's decisions and orders may provide for periodic penalty payments payable to the Court in the event that a party fails to comply with the terms of the order or an earlier order. The value of such payments shall be set by the Court having regard to the importance of the order in question.

4. If it is alleged that a party has failed to comply with the terms of the order of the Court, the first instance panel of the division in question may decide on penalty payments provided for in the order upon the request of the other party or of its own motion. The applicant shall pay a fee for the request in accordance with Part 6. The procedure foreseen in Rule 264 shall apply. After having heard both parties the Court may make an appropriate order which may be subject to an appeal pursuant to Rule 220.2.

Relation with Agreement: Article 82

CHAPTER 11 – DECISION BY DEFAULT

Rule 355 – Decision by default (Court of First Instance)

1. Upon request a decision by default may be given against a party where:

(a) the Rules of Procedure so provide if a party fails to take a step within the time limit foreseen in these Rules or set by the Court; or

(b) without prejudice to Rules 116 and 117, the party which was duly summoned fails to appear at an oral hearing.

2. A decision by default against the defendant of the claim or counterclaim may only be given where the facts put forward by the claimant justify the remedy sought and the procedural conduct of the defendant does not preclude to give such decision.

3. A decision by default against the defendant of the claim or counterclaim may only be given where the time limits for the defence to the claim or counterclaim have expired and thus, it is established that the service of the claim or counterclaim was effected in sufficient time to enable the defendant to enter a defence.

4. A decision by default shall be enforceable. The Court may, however:

(a) grant a stay of enforcement until it has given its decision on any Application under Rule 356; or

(b) make enforcement subject to the provision of security; this security shall be released if no Application is made or if the Application fails.

Rule 356 – Application to set aside a decision by default

1. A party against whom a decision by default has been given may lodge an Application to set aside that decision within one month of service of the decision.

2. The Application to set aside a decision by default shall contain the party's explanation for the default. It shall mention the date and number of the decision by default. The party shall pay a fee for the Application to set aside the decision by default, in accordance with Part 6. In the case of Rule 355.1(a) the Application shall be accompanied by the step the party has failed to take.

3. If the provisions of paragraph 2 are met the Application shall be allowed unless a party has been put on notice in an earlier decision that a further decision by default shall be final. If the Application is allowed, a note of allowance shall be included in any publication of the decision by default.

Relation with Statute: Article 37

Rule 357 – Decision by default (Court of Appeal)

1. Rules 355 and 356 shall apply *mutatis mutandis*, in particular where a respondent on whom a Statement of appeal and a Statement of the grounds of appeal have been duly served fails to lodge a Statement of response or where a party fails to file a Reply to a Statement of Cross-Appeal or translations ordered by the judge-rapporteur.

2. When considering whether to give a decision by default, the Court of Appeal may consider the merits of the appeal.

3. Rules 355 and 356 shall apply *mutatis mutandis* where the appellant fails to correct the deficiencies or to pay the fee pursuant to Rule 229.4 or to lodge the translations pursuant to Rule 232.1 within the period specified.

CHAPTER 12 – ACTIONS BOUND TO FAIL OR MANIFESTLY INADMISSIBLE

Rule 360 – No need to adjudicate

If the Court finds that an action has become devoid of purpose and that there is no longer any need to adjudicate on it, it may at any time, on the application of a party or of its own motion, after giving the parties an opportunity to be heard, dispose of the action by way of order.

Rule 361 – Action manifestly bound to fail

Where it is clear that the Court has no jurisdiction to take cognisance of an action or of certain of the claims therein or where the action or defence is, in whole or in part, manifestly inadmissible or manifestly lacking any foundation in law, the Court may, after giving the parties an opportunity to be heard, give a decision by way of order.

Rule 362 – Absolute bar to proceeding with an action

The Court may at any time, on the application of a party or of its own motion, after giving the parties an opportunity to be heard, decide that there exists an absolute bar to proceeding with an action, for example because of the application of the principle of *res judicata.*

Rule 363 – Orders dismissing manifestly inadmissible claims

1. Orders under Rules 360, 361 and 362 shall be taken by the panel upon the recommendation of the judge-rapporteur.

2. Where the decision is taken by the Court of First Instance pursuant to Rules 360, 361 and 362 it is a final decision within the meaning of Rule 220.1(a).

CHAPTER 13 – SETTLEMENT

Rule 365 – Confirmation by the Court of a settlement

1. Where the parties have concluded their action by way of settlement, they shall inform the judge-rapporteur. The Court shall confirm the settlement by decision of the Court [Rule 11.2], if requested by the parties, and the decision may be enforced as a final decision of the Court.

2. At the request of the parties the Court may order that details of the settlement are confidential.

3. Subject to paragraph 2 the decision of the Court under paragraph 1 shall be entered on the register.

4. The judge-rapporteur shall give a decision as to costs in accordance with the terms of the settlement or, failing that, at his discretion.

Relation with Agreement: Article 79

PART 6 – FEES AND LEGAL AID

COURT FEES

Rule 370 – Court fees

1. Court fees provided for in these Rules shall be paid in accordance with the provisions contained in this Part and the table of fees adopted by the Administrative Committee pursuant to Article 36 (3) of the Agreement (hereinafter: table of fees).

The level of the Court fees with respect to inflation shall be reviewed by the Administrative Committee every two years.

2. A fixed fee shall be paid in accordance with Section I (fixed fees) of the table of fees for the following actions at the Court of First Instance:

(a) Infringement action or counterclaims concerning licenses [Rule 15, Art. 32 (1) (a) UPCA],

(b) Counterclaim for infringement [Rule 53],

(c) Action for declaration of non-infringement [Rule 70],

(d) Action for compensation for licence of right [Rule 80.3],

(e) Application to determine damages [Rule 132],

(f) Application for provisional measures [Rule 206.5],

(g) Application to preserve evidence [Rule 192.5],

(h) Application for an order for inspection [Rule 199.2],

(i) Application for an order to freeze assets [Rule 200.2].

3. In addition to the fixed fee a value-based fee shall be paid in accordance with Section II (value-based fees) of the table of fees for those actions at the Court of First Instance set out in paragraph 2, which exceed a value of 500,000 EUR. In the case of applications under Rule 370.2(g), (h) and (i), the value-based fee shall not apply if an infringement action is pending at the Court between the same parties and based on the same patent.

4. For the following procedures and actions at the Court of First Instance a fee shall be paid in accordance with Section III (other procedures and actions) of the table of fees adopted by the Administrative Committee:

(a) Revocation action [Rule 46],

(b) Counterclaim for revocation [Rule 26],

(c) (unused item)

(d) Action against a decision of the European Patent Office [Rule 88.3, 97.2],

(e) (unused item)

(f) (unused item)

(g) (unused item)

(h) Filing a protective letter [Rule 207.3],

(i) Application to prolong the period of a protective letter to be kept on the register [Rule 207.9],

(j) Application for rehearing [Rule 250],

(k) Application for re-establishment of rights [Rule 320.2],

(l) Application to review a case management order [Rule 333.3],

(m) Application to set aside decision by default [Rule 356 2],

(o) Application to enforce a decision [Rule 354.4],

(p) Requests under Rule 198.1,

(q) Requests under Rule 213.1.

5. For the following procedures at the Court of Appeal a fixed fee and, where applicable, a value-based fee shall be paid in accordance with Section V. of the table of fees:

(a) Appeal pursuant to Rule 220.1 (a) and (b) [Rule 228],

(b) Interlocutory appeal pursuant to Rule 220.1(c), appeal with leave of the Court of First Instance pursuant to Rule 220.2 or allowance by the Court of Appeal pursuant to Rule 220.4 or appeal of a cost decision with leave of the Court of Appeal pursuant to Rule 221.4 [Rule 228],

(c) Application for leave to appeal against cost decision pursuant to Rule 221 [Rule 228],

(d) Request for discretionary review pursuant to Rule 220.3, [Rule 228],

(e) Application for re-establishment of rights [Rule 320.2],

(f) Application to review a case management order pursuant to Rule 220.2 [Rule 333.3],

(g) Application to set aside decision by default pursuant to Rule 357 [Rule 356.2],

(h) Application for rehearing pursuant to Rule 245.2 [Rule 250],

(i) Challenge a decision to reject an appeal as inadmissible [Rule 234.1],

(j) Application for suspensive effect [Rule 223],

(k) Appeal against a decision on enforceability [Rules 354.4 and 220.2].

5a. In the case of appeals against decisions under Rule 370.2(g), (h) and (i), the value-based fee shall not apply if an infringement action is pending at the Court between the same parties and based on the same patent.

6. The assessment of the value of the relevant action in paragraphs 3 and 5 shall reflect the objective interest pursued by the filing party at the time of filing the action. In deciding on the value, the Court may in particular take into account the guidelines laid down in a decision of the Administrative Committee for this purpose.

7. If an action has more than one claimant and/or more than one defendant or if an action concerns a plurality of patents only one fixed fee and, if applicable, one value-based fee shall apply.

8. Small enterprises and micro-enterprises are required to pay only 50% of the fees provided for in paragraphs 2 to 5 above (hereinafter: regular fees) subject to the following:

(a) In the Statement of claim or Counterclaim or in the application for a procedure or an appeal the party shall lodge with the Registry a notification in an electronic form in the language of the proceedings. In this notification the party shall provide an affirmation that he fulfils either the criteria of a "small enterprise" or a "micro-enterprise" as defined in Title I of the Annex to the Recommendation of the European Commission n° 2003/361 of 6 May 2003.

(b) If the requirements referred to above have not been met Rule 16.3 to .5 shall apply mutatis mutandis.

(c) The Court may, of its own motion, order the party to supply further documentation including any document relating to that party's financial resources. The application shall be dealt with by the Court as soon as practicable.

(d) The Court may, at any time, of its own motion, and after having heard the party order payment of
(i) the remainder of the regular fee, in the event that payment of 50% of the regular fees is manifestly disproportionate and unreasonable having regard to the financial capacity of the party;
(ii) the remainder of the regular fee plus an additional 50% of that regular fee, if the affirmation provided by the party is found to be wholly or partially incorrect. An order for the payment of an additional fee pursuant to (i) and (ii) above shall state the reasons for such order.

(e) If the additional fee is not paid within the time limit set by the Court, a decision by default against the party shall be given by the Court pursuant to Rule 355.

9. Fixed and value-based fees may be reimbursed as follows:

(a) (unused item)

(b) In case of the withdrawal of an action [Rule 265] the party liable for the Court fees will be reimbursed by 50% if the action is withdrawn before the closure of the written procedure.

(c) If the parties have concluded their action
(i) by way of settlement at the Centre or
(ii) by an arbitral award of the Centre

before the closure of the interim procedure or before the date specified by the judge rapporteur in the interim conference the party liable for the Court fees will be reimbursed by 65%.

(d) Only one of the reimbursements referred to in paragraph 9 (b) and (c) will apply per action and party. Where more than one reimbursement is applicable, the larger will be applied for each party.

(e) In exceptional cases, having regard, in particular, to the stage of the proceedings and the procedural behaviour of the party, the Court may deny or decrease the reimbursement payable according to paragraph 9 (b) and (c) of the aforementioned provisions.

10. If the amount of Court fees threatens the economic existence of a party who is not a natural person, and has presented reasonably available and plausible evidence to support that the amount of Court fees threatens its economic existence, the Court may upon request by that party, wholly or partially reimburse the fixed and value-based fee. In reaching a decision the Court shall reflect on all circumstances of the case including the procedural behaviour of the party. Before making such a decision the Court may give the other party an opportunity to be heard.

11. The party seeking reimbursement under paragraphs 9 and 10 shall lodge a reasoned Application for reimbursement to the Court. The Court shall deal with the application without delay and if satisfied that the reimbursement is appropriate shall direct the Registrar to make the payment as soon as practicable.

Rule 371 – Time periods for paying court fees

1. The fixed fees provided for in Section I and Section IV of the table of fees and fees for other procedures and actions provided for in Section III of the table of fees shall be paid at the time of lodging the relevant pleading or application. The payment shall be made to one of the bank accounts indicated by the Court and it shall indicate the paying party or its representative together with the number of the patent involved and the number of the case.

2. Proof of payment shall be provided together with the relevant pleading or application.

3. In cases of urgency, where a payment in advance is not possible, the representative of the party in question shall pay the fixed fee within the period set by the Court and the Court may order that the relevant pleading or application shall be deemed lodged and effective when received by the Registry if payment of the fixed fee is made within such period.

4. The value-based fee provided for in Section II of the table of fees shall be paid according to the claimant's assessment of the value at the time of lodging the relevant pleading or application. In the event that a higher value is determined by the judge-rapporteur the remaining fees due shall be paid within 10 days of service of the order determining the value of the action in accordance with the Rules 22, 60, 74, and 133. Where the value is lower, the Court will reimburse overpaid fees.

5. Where an Application for legal aid has been lodged in accordance with Rule 377, the rules on the obligation as to the time when to pay the fees under paragraph 1 shall not apply.

Relation with Agreement: Article 70

LEGAL AID

Rule 375 – Aim and scope

1. In order to ensure effective access to justice, the Court may grant legal aid to a party (hereinafter "the applicant").

2. Legal aid may be granted in respect of any proceedings before the Court.

Rule 376 – Costs eligible for legal aid

1. Subject to Article 71(3) of the Agreement, legal aid may cover, in whole or in part, the following costs:

(a) court fees;

(b) costs of legal assistance and representation regarding:
(i) pre-litigation advice with a view to reaching a settlement prior to commencing legal proceedings;
(ii) commencing and maintaining proceedings before the Court;
(iii) all costs relating to proceedings including the application for legal aid;
(iv) enforcement of decisions;

(c) other necessary costs related to the proceedings to be borne by a party, including costs of witnesses, experts, interpreters and translators and necessary travel, accommodation and subsistence costs of the applicant and his representative.

2. Subject to Article 71(3) of the Agreement, legal aid may also cover the costs awarded to the successful party, in the event that the applicant loses the action.

Rule 376A – Maximum amount to be paid for representation

1. For the costs of representation pursuant to Rule 376.1(b) the maximum level of legal aid that may be granted by the Court shall be the maximum amount of recoverable costs laid down in the decision of the Administrative Committee pursuant to Article 69(1) of the Agreement and Rule 152.2.

2. The Administrative Committee may define thresholds below the level set in paragraph 1 for the maximum level of legal aid for representation pursuant to Rule 376.1(b), taking into account necessary costs for legal representation in the Contracting Member States and the need to guarantee adequate access to justice.

Rule 377 – Conditions for granting legal aid

1. The applicant shall be entitled to apply for legal aid where:

(a) owing to his economic situation, he is wholly or partly unable to meet the costs referred to in Rule 376; and

(b) the action in respect of which the application for legal aid is made has a reasonable prospect of success, considering the applicant's procedural position; and

(c) the claimant applying for legal aid is entitled to bring actions under Article 47 of the Agreement.

2. The Administrative Committee may define thresholds above which legal aid applicants are deemed wholly or partly able to bear the costs of proceedings set out in Rule 376. These thresholds may not prevent applicants whose economic situation

is above the thresholds from being granted legal aid if they prove that they are in fact unable to pay the costs of the proceedings referred to in Rule 376 as a result of the high level of the cost of living in the Contracting Member State of domicile or habitual residence.

3. When deciding on the grant of legal aid the Court shall, without prejudice to paragraph 1(a), consider all relevant circumstances including the importance of the action to the applicant and also the nature of the action when the application concerns a claim arising directly out of the applicant's trade or self-employed profession.

Rule 377A – Conditions regarding the financial situation of the applicant

1. When assessing a party's financial situation, his income and assets must be taken into account.

2. Income shall include all earnings in money or equivalent value after deducting all costs required by the applicant and dependent persons in order to cover their reasonable living expenses (disposable income).

3. The Administrative Committee shall define the deductions from income and assets to be taken into account when assessing the applicant's financial situation. It shall also define levels of monthly instalments to be paid by the applicant. All thresholds set by the Administrative Committee shall be adapted regularly to price and income indices.

Rule 378 – Application for legal aid

1. An application for legal aid may be lodged before or after proceedings have been started before the Court.

2. The Application for legal aid shall contain in a language of a Contracting Member State:

(a) the name of the applicant;

(b) postal and electronic addresses for service on the applicant and the names of the persons authorised to accept service;

(c) the name of the other party as well as postal and electronic addresses for service on the other party where available and the names of the persons authorised to accept service, if known;

(d) the action number of the action in respect of which the application is made or, where the application is lodged before the action has been brought, a brief description of the action;

(e) an indication of the value of the action and the costs to be covered by legal aid;

(f) where legal aid is requested for costs of legal assistance and representation, the name of the proposed representative;

(g) an indication of the applicant's financial resources, such as income, assets and capital, and of the applicant's family situation including an assessment of the resources of persons who are financially dependent on the applicant;

(h) where appropriate, a reasoned request for suspension of a time limit which would otherwise need to be observed until the date of notification of the order deciding on legal aid.

3. The application for legal aid must be supported by:

(a) evidence of the applicant's need for assistance, such as certificates attesting his income, assets and capital and family situation; and

(b) where the application is lodged before the action has been brought, an indication of the evidence in support of the action.

4. In the event of an appeal, a new application shall be lodged.

5. Rule 8 shall not apply.

Rule 378A – Type of proof

1. To be admissible, the application must contain a statement of the facts and legal situation, with specific mention of the evidence to be presented. The application must also contain a statement regarding the economic and financial situation of the applicant. The following documents shall be attached to the application:

(a) latest property and income declarations of the applicant;

(b) a document showing the personal monthly income for the previous year, or a declaration of unemployment delivered by the competent authorities, or a certificate proving that the applicant is receiving aid or financial support under a social welfare scheme;

(c) a certificate of composition of household;

(d) any other official document that can provide proof of the financial situation of the applicant.

2. Where appropriate, a certificate relating to the income of other members of the household of the applicant should also be attached to the application. The official documents shall not be older than 3 months. At the request of the Court, the applicant shall produce further documentation and, if so requested, an affidavit of the truthfulness of his statements, otherwise the application will not be admissible.

Rule 379 – Examination and decision

1. The Registry shall examine the formal admissibility of the application for legal aid and the conditions regarding the financial situation of the applicant pursuant to Rules 377.1(a),.2 and 377A.

2. If the requirements referred to in Rules 377.1(a),.2, 377A, 378 and 378A have not been met, the applicant shall, as soon as practicable, be invited to correct the deficiencies within 14 days.

3. If the requirements referred to in Rules 377.1(a),.2, 377A, 378 and 378A have been met or the applicant fails to correct a deficiency, the decision on such application shall be taken, by way of order, by the judge-rapporteur or, where the application is lodged before the action has been brought, by the standing judge.

4. Before making a decision on an application for legal aid, the Court shall invite the other party to submit written observations unless it is already apparent from the information submitted that the conditions referred to in Rule 377.1(b) have not been met. Documents regarding the economic and financial situation of the applicant shall be made accessible to the other party only where the applicant has consented or the applicant's refusal of consent is unreasonable or in the view of the Court the other party has a right to information on the economic or financial situation of the applicant.

5. An order refusing legal aid shall state the reasons on which it is based.

6. An order granting legal aid may provide for:

(a) an exemption, wholly or partly, from Court fees;

(b) an interim amount to be paid to enable the applicant and/or the representative of the applicant to meet any request of the judge-rapporteur or standing judge prior to making a final order;

(c) an amount to be paid to the representative of the applicant or a limit which the representative's disbursements and fees may not exceed;

(d) a contribution to be made by the applicant to the costs referred to in Rule 376.1(c).

7. Legal aid may be granted only for the period from receipt of the application with the Court.

8. Where the legal aid covers, in whole or in part, the costs of legal assistance and representation the order granting legal aid shall designate the representative of the applicant.

9. On a request by the designated representative, the Court may order that an amount shall be paid by way of advance.

10. Where requested by the applicant in accordance with Rule 378.2(h), the Court shall decide on the suspension of any time limit.

Rule 379A – Alteration of economic situation

The applicant shall inform the Court promptly of any alteration in his economic situation.

Rule 380 – Withdrawal of legal aid

1. If the economic situation of the applicant which has led to the grant of legal aid according to Rule 377.1(a) alters during the proceedings, the Court may at any time, of his own motion or on a reasoned request by the other party, withdraw wholly or partly legal aid but only after having heard the applicant.

2. The Court may withdraw wholly or partly legal aid if the applicant:

(a) by inaccurately representing the circumstances of the case, has misrepresented its prospects of success, which are determinative for the approval of assistance with Court costs; or

(b) has grossly negligently made false statements as to his personal or economic circumstances; or

(c) has not immediately informed the Court of a considerable improvement to his financial circumstances;

(d) has been in arrears for longer than three months with the payment of a monthly instalment or with the payment of any other amount.

3. An order withdrawing legal aid shall state the reasons on which it is based.

Rule 381 – Appeal

1. An order wholly or partly refusing or withdrawing legal aid may be appealed to the Court of Appeal. The appeal shall be filed with the Court of Appeal within a period of one month after receiving the order and satisfy the provisions of Rules 377 to 379. The President of the Court of Appeal shall appoint a panel which shall decide on the appeal having heard the applicant.

2. An application for legal aid to appeal a decision of the Court of First Instance shall be filed with the Court of Appeals and shall satisfy the provisions of Rules 377 to 379. The Application for legal aid to bring an appeal against a decision of the Court of First Instance shall be filed within the time limit provided for the appeal as specified in Rule 224 and should, where possible, be accompanied by the appeal itself. The Application shall be assigned according to Rule 345.8.

Rule 382 – Recovery

1. Where the Court has ordered another party to pay the costs of the applicant for legal aid, that other party shall be required to refund to the Court any sums advanced by way of legal aid. In the event of a shortfall between the costs so ordered and the sums advanced by way of legal aid the applicant may be required to meet such shortfall from any damages or compensation awarded by the Court or from any sum received by way of settlement.

2. In the event of withdrawal of legal aid under Rule 380, the applicant may be required to refund to the Court any sums advanced by way of legal aid.

Annex 5 Annex I to the UPCA: Statute of the Unified Patent Court

Article 1
Scope of the Statute

This Statute contains institutional and financial arrangements for the Unified Patent Court as established under Article 1 of the Agreement.

Article 2
Eligibility of judges

1. Any person who is a national of a Contracting Member State and fulfils the conditions set out in Article 15 of the Agreement and in this Statute may be appointed as a judge.

2. Judges shall have a good command of at least one official language of the European Patent Office.

3. Experience with patent litigation which has to be proven for the appointment pursuant to Article 15(1) of the Agreement may be acquired by training under Article 11(4)(a) of this Statute.

Article 3
Appointment of judges

1. Judges shall be appointed pursuant to the procedure set out in Article 16 of the Agreement.

2. Vacancies shall be publicly advertised and shall indicate the relevant eligibility criteria as set out in Article 2. The Advisory Committee shall give an opinion on candidates' suitability to perform the duties of a judge of the Court. The opinion shall comprise a list of most suitable candidates. The list shall contain at least twice as many candidates as there are vacancies. Where necessary, the Advisory Committee may recommend that, prior to the decision on the appointment, a candidate judge receive training in patent litigation pursuant to Article 11(4)(a).

3. When appointing judges, the Administrative Committee shall ensure the best legal and technical expertise and a balanced composition of the Court on as broad a geographical basis as possible among nationals of the Contracting Member States.

4. The Administrative Committee shall appoint as many judges as are needed for the proper functioning of the Court. The Administrative Committee shall initially appoint the necessary number of judges for setting up at least one panel in each of the divisions of the Court of First Instance and at least two panels in the Court of Appeal.

5. The decision of the Administrative Committee appointing full-time or part-time legally qualified judges and full-time technically qualified judges shall state the instance

of the Court and/or the division of the Court of First Instance for which each judge is appointed and the field(s) of technology for which a technically qualified judge is appointed.

6. Part-time technically qualified judges shall be appointed as judges of the Court and shall be included in the Pool of Judges on the basis of their specific qualifications and experience. The appointment of these judges to the Court shall ensure that all fields of technology are covered.

Article 4
Judges' term of office

1. Judges shall be appointed for a term of six years, beginning on the date laid down in the instrument of appointment. They may be re-appointed.

2. In the absence of any provision regarding the date, the term shall begin on the date of the instrument of appointment.

Article 5
Appointment of the members of the Advisory Committee

1. Each Contracting Member State shall propose a member of the Advisory Committee who fulfils the requirements set out in Article 14(2) of the Agreement.

2. The members of the Advisory Committee shall be appointed by the Administrative Committee acting by common accord.

Article 6
Oath

Before taking up their duties judges shall, in open court, take an oath to perform their duties impartially and conscientiously and to preserve the secrecy of the deliberations of the Court.

Article 7
Impartiality

1. Immediately after taking their oath, judges shall sign a declaration by which they solemnly undertake that, both during and after their term of office, they shall respect the obligations arising therefrom, in particular the duty to behave with integrity and discretion as regards the acceptance, after they have ceased to hold office, of certain appointments or benefits.

2. Judges may not take part in the proceedings of a case in which they:
(a) have taken part as adviser;
(b) have been a party or have acted for one of the parties;
(c) have been called upon to pronounce as a member of a court, tribunal, board of appeal, arbitration or mediation panel, a commission of inquiry or in any other capacity;

(d) have a personal or financial interest in the case or in relation to one of the parties; or

(e) are related to one of the parties or the representatives of the parties by family ties.

3. If, for some special reason, a judge considers that he or she should not take part in the judgement or examination of a particular case, that judge shall so inform the President of the Court of Appeal accordingly or, in the case of judges of the Court of First Instance, the President of the Court of First Instance. If, for some special reason, the President of the Court of Appeal or, in the case of judges of the Court of First Instance, the President of the Court of First Instance considers that a judge should not sit or make submissions in a particular case, the President of the Court of Appeal or the President of the Court of First Instance shall justify this in writing and notify the judge concerned accordingly.

4. Any party to an action may object to a judge taking part in the proceedings on any of the grounds listed in paragraph 2 or where the judge is suspected, with good reason, of partiality.

5. Any difficulty arising as to the application of this Article shall be settled by decision of the Presidium, in accordance with the Rules of Procedure. The judge concerned shall be heard but shall not take part in the deliberations.

Article 8
Immunity of judges

1. The judges shall be immune from legal proceedings. After they have ceased to hold office, they shall continue to enjoy immunity in respect of acts performed by them in relation to their official capacity.

2. The Presidium may waive the immunity.

3. Where immunity has been waived and criminal proceedings are instituted against a judge, that judge shall be tried, in any of the Contracting Member States, only by the court competent to judge the members of the highest national judiciary.

4. The Protocol on the privileges and immunities of the European Union shall apply to the judges of the Court, without prejudice to the provisions relating to immunity from legal proceedings of judges which are set out in this Statute.

Article 9
End of duties

1. Apart from replacement after expiry of a judge's term pursuant to Article 4, or death, the duties of a judge shall end when that judge resigns.

2. Where a judge resigns, the letter of resignation shall be addressed to the President of the Court of Appeal or, in the case of judges of the Court of First Instance, the President of the Court of First Instance for transmission to the Chairman of the Administrative Committee.

3. Save where Article 10 applies, a judge shall continue to hold office until that judge's successor takes up his or her duties.

4. Any vacancy shall by filled by the appointment of a new judge for the remainder of his or her predecessor's term.

Article 10
Removal from office

1. A judge may be deprived of his or her office or of other benefits only if the Presidium decides that that judge no longer fulfils the requisite conditions or meets the obligations arising from his or her office. The judge concerned shall be heard but shall not take part in the deliberations.

2. The Registrar of the Court shall communicate this decision to the Chairman of the Administrative Committee.

3. In the case of a decision depriving a judge of his or her office, a vacancy shall arise upon that notification.

Article 11
Training

1. Appropriate and regular training of judges shall be provided for within the training framework set up under Article 19 of the Agreement. The Presidium shall adopt Training Regulations ensuring the implementation and overall coherence of the training framework.

2. The training framework shall provide a platform for the exchange of expertise and a forum for discussion, in particular by:
(a) organising courses, conferences, seminars, workshops and symposia;
(b) cooperating with international organisations and education institutes in the field of intellectual property; and
(c) promoting and supporting further vocational training.

3. An annual work programme and training guidelines shall be drawn up, which shall include for each judge an annual training plan identifying that judge's main training needs in accordance with the Training Regulations.

4. The training framework shall in addition:
(a) ensure appropriate training for candidate-judges and newly appointed judges of the Court;
(b) support projects aimed at facilitating cooperation between representatives, patent attorneys and the Court.

Article 12
Remuneration

The Administrative Committee shall set the remuneration of the President of the Court of Appeal, the President of the Court of First Instance, the judges, the Registrar, the Deputy-Registrar and the staff.

Article 13
President of the Court of Appeal

1. The President of the Court of Appeal shall be elected by all judges of the Court of Appeal for a term of three years, from among their number. The President of the Court of Appeal may be re-elected twice.

2. The elections of the President of the Court of Appeal shall be by secret ballot. A judge obtaining an absolute majority shall be elected. If no judge obtains an absolute majority, a second ballot shall be held and the judge obtaining the most votes shall be elected.

3. The President of the Court of Appeal shall direct the judicial activities and the administration of the Court of Appeal and chair the Court of Appeal sitting as a full Court.

4. If the office of the President of the Court of Appeal falls vacant before the date of expiry of his or her term, a successor shall be elected for the remainder thereof.

Article 14
President of the Court of First Instance

1. The President of the Court of First Instance shall be elected by all judges of the Court of First Instance who are full-time judges, for a term of three years, from among their number. The President of the Court of First Instance may be re-elected twice.

2. The first President of the Court of First Instance shall be a national of the Contracting Member State hosting the seat of the central division.

3. The President of the Court of First Instance shall direct the judicial activities and the administration of the Court of First Instance.

4. Article 13(2) and (4), shall by analogy apply to the President of the Court of First Instance.

Article 15
Presidium

1. The Presidium shall be composed of the President of the Court of Appeal, who shall act as chairperson, the President of the Court of First Instance, two judges of the Court of Appeal elected from among their number, three judges of the Court of First Instance who are full-time judges of the Court elected from among their number, and the Registrar as a non-voting member.

2. The Presidium shall exercise its duties in accordance with this Statute. It may, without prejudice to its own responsibility, delegate certain tasks to one of its members.

3. The Presidium shall be responsible for the management of the Court and shall in particular:
(a) draw up proposals for the amendment of the Rules of Procedure in accordance with Article 41 of the Agreement and proposals regarding the Financial Regulations of the Court;
(b) prepare the annual budget, the annual accounts and the annual report of the Court and submit them to the Budget Committee;
(c) establish the guidelines for the training programme for judges and supervise the implementation thereof;
(d) take decisions on the appointment and removal of the Registrar and the Deputy-Registrar;
(e) lay down the rules governing the Registry including the sub-registries;
(f) give an opinion in accordance with Article 83(5) of the Agreement.

4. Decisions of the Presidium referred to in Articles 7, 8, 10 and 22 shall be taken without the participation of the Registrar.

5. The Presidium can take valid decisions only when all members are present or duly represented.

Decisions shall be taken by a majority of the votes.

Article 16
Staff

1. The officials and other servants of the Court shall have the task of assisting the President of the Court of Appeal, the President of the Court of First Instance, the judges and the Registrar. They shall be responsible to the Registrar, under the authority of the President of the Court of Appeal and the President of the Court of First Instance.

2. The Administrative Committee shall establish the Staff Regulations of officials and other servants of the Court.

Article 17
Judicial vacations

1. After consulting the Presidium, the President of the Court of Appeal shall establish the duration of judicial vacations and the rules on observing official holidays.

2. During the period of judicial vacations, the functions of the President of the Court of Appeal and of the President of the Court of First Instance may be exercised by any judge invited by the respective President to that effect. In cases of urgency, the President of the Court of Appeal may convene the judges.

3. The President of the Court of Appeal or the President of the Court of First Instance may, in proper circumstances, grant leave of absence to respectively judges of the Court of Appeal or judges of the Court of First Instance.

Article 18
Setting up and discontinuance of a local or regional division

1. A request from one or more Contracting Member States for the setting up of a local or regional division shall be addressed to the Chairman of the Administrative Committee. It shall indicate the seat of the local or regional division.

2. The decision of the Administrative Committee setting up a local or regional division shall indicate the number of judges for the division concerned and shall be public.

3. The Administrative Committee shall decide to discontinue a local or regional division at the request of the Contracting Member State hosting the local division or the Contracting Member States participating in the regional division. The decision to discontinue a local or regional division shall state the date after which no new cases may be brought before the division and the date on which the division will cease to exist.

4. As from the date on which a local or regional division ceases to exist, the judges assigned to that local or regional division shall be assigned to the central division, and cases still pending before that local or regional division together with the sub-registry and all of its documentation shall be transferred to the central division.

Article 19
Panels

1. The allocation of judges and the assignment of cases within a division to its panels shall be governed by the Rules of Procedure. One judge of the panel shall be designated as the presiding judge, in accordance with the Rules of Procedure.

2. The panel may delegate, in accordance with the Rules of Procedure, certain functions to one or more of its judges.

3. A standing judge for each division to hear urgent cases may be designated in accordance with the Rules of Procedure.

4. In cases where a single judge in accordance with Article 8(7) of the Agreement, or a standing judge, in accordance with paragraph 3 of this Article, hears a case that judge shall carry out all functions of a panel.

5. One judge of the panel shall act as Rapporteur, in accordance with the Rules of Procedure.

Article 20
Pool of Judges

1. A list with the names of the judges included in the Pool of Judges shall be drawn up by the Registrar. In relation to each judge, the list shall at least indicate the linguistic skills, the field of technology and experience of, as well as the cases previously handled by, that judge.

2. A request addressed to the President of the Court of First Instance to assign a judge from the Pool of Judges shall indicate, in particular, the subject-matter of the case,

the official language of the European Patent Office used by the judges of the panel, the language of the proceedings and the field of technology required.

Article 21
Panels

1. The allocation of judges and the assignment of cases to panels shall be governed by the Rules of Procedure. One judge of the panel shall be appointed as the presiding judge, in accordance with the Rules of Procedure.

2. When a case is of exceptional importance, and in particular when the decision may affect the unity and consistency of the case law of the Court, the Court of Appeal may decide, on the basis of a proposal from the presiding judge, to refer the case to the full Court.

3. The panel may delegate, in accordance with the Rules of Procedure, certain functions to one or more of its judges.

4. One judge of the panel shall act as Rapporteur, in accordance with the Rules of Procedure.

Article 22
Appointment and removal from office of the Registrar

1. The Presidium shall appoint the Registrar of the Court for a term of six years. The Registrar may be re-appointed.

2. Two weeks before the date fixed for appointing the Registrar, the President of the Court of Appeal shall inform the Presidium of the applications which have been submitted for the post.

3. Before taking up his or her duties, the Registrar shall take oath before the Presidium to perform the duties of the Registrar impartially and conscientiously.

4. The Registrar may be removed from office only if the Registrar no longer meets the obligations arising from his or her office. The Presidium shall take its decision after having heard the Registrar.

5. If the office of the Registrar falls vacant before the date of expiry of the term thereof, the Presidium shall appoint a new Registrar for a term of six years.

6. If the Registrar is absent or prevented from attending or where such post is vacant, the President of the Court of Appeal after having consulted the Presidium shall designate a member of the staff of the Court to carry out the duties of the Registrar.

Article 23
Duties of the Registrar

1. The Registrar shall assist the Court, the President of the Court of Appeal, the President of the Court of First Instance and the judges in the performance of their

functions. The Registrar shall be responsible for the organisation and activities of the Registry under the authority of the President of the Court of Appeal.

2. The Registrar shall in particular be responsible for:
(a) keeping the register which shall include records of all cases before the Court;
(b) keeping and administering lists drawn up in accordance with Articles 18, 48(3) and 57(2) of the Agreement;
(c) keeping and publishing a list of notifications and withdrawals of opt-outs in accordance with Article 83 of the Agreement;
(d) publishing the decisions of the Court, subject to the protection of confidential information;
(e) publishing annual reports with statistical data; and
(f) ensuring that the information on opt-outs in accordance with Article 83 of the Agreement is notified to the European Patent Office.

Article 24
Keeping of the register

1. Detailed rules for keeping the register of the Court shall be prescribed in the Rules governing the Registry, adopted by the Presidium.

2. The rules on access to documents of the Registry shall be provided for in the Rules of Procedure.

Article 25
Sub-registries and Deputy-Registrar

1. A Deputy-Registrar shall be appointed for a term of six years by the Presidium. The Deputy-Registrar may be re-appointed.

2. Article 22(2) to (6) shall apply by analogy.

3. The Deputy-Registrar shall be responsible for the organisation and activities of sub-registries under the authority of the Registrar and the President of the Court of First Instance. The duties of the Deputy-Registrar shall in particular include:
(a) keeping records of all cases before the Court of First Instance;
(b) notifying every case before the Court of First Instance to the Registry.

4. The Deputy-Registrar shall also provide administrative and secretarial assistance to the divisions of the Court of First Instance.

Article 26
Budget

1. The budget shall be adopted by the Budget Committee on a proposal from the Presidium. It shall be drawn up in accordance with the generally accepted accounting principles laid down in the Financial Regulations, established in accordance with Article 33.

2. Within the budget, the Presidium may, in accordance with the Financial Regulations, transfer funds between the various headings or subheadings.

3. The Registrar shall be responsible for the implementation of the budget in accordance with the Financial Regulations.

4. The Registrar shall annually make a statement on the accounts of the preceding financial year relating to the implementation of the budget which shall be approved by the Presidium.

Article 27
Authorisation for expenditure

1. The expenditure entered in the budget shall be authorised for the duration of one accounting period unless the Financial Regulations provide otherwise.

2. In accordance with the Financial Regulations, any appropriations, other than those relating to staff costs, which are unexpended at the end of the accounting period may be carried forward, but not beyond the end of the following accounting period.

3. Appropriations shall be set out under different headings according to type and purpose of the expenditure, and subdivided, to the extent necessary, in accordance with the Financial Regulations.

Article 28
Appropriations for unforeseeable expenditure

1. The budget of the Court may include appropriations for unforeseeable expenditure.

2. The employment of these appropriations by the Court shall be subject to the prior approval of the Budget Committee.

Article 29
Accounting period

The accounting period shall commence on 1 January and end on 31 December.

Article 30
Preparation of the budget

The Presidium shall submit the draft budget of the Court to the Budget Committee no later than the date prescribed in the Financial Regulations.

Article 31
Provisional budget

1. If, at the beginning of the accounting period, the budget has not been adopted by the Budget Committee, expenditure may be effected on a monthly basis per heading or other division of the budget, in accordance with the Financial Regulations, up to one-twelfth of the budget appropriations for the preceding accounting period,

provided that the appropriations thus made available to the Presidium do not exceed one-twelfth of those provided for in the draft budget.

2. The Budget Committee may, subject to the observance of the other provisions laid down in paragraph 1, authorise expenditure in excess of one-twelfth of the budget appropriations for the preceding accounting period.

Article 32
Auditing of accounts

1. The annual financial statements of the Court shall be examined by independent auditors. The auditors shall be appointed and if necessary dismissed by the Budget Committee.

2. The audit, which shall be based on professional auditing standards and shall take place, if necessary, in situ, shall ascertain that the budget has been implemented in a lawful and proper manner and that the financial administration of the Court has been conducted in accordance with the principles of economy and sound financial management. The auditors shall draw up a report after the end of each accounting period containing a signed audit opinion.

3. The Presidium shall submit to the Budget Committee the annual financial statements of the Court and the annual budget implementation statement for the preceding accounting period, together with the auditors' report.

4. The Budget Committee shall approve the annual accounts together with the auditors' report and shall discharge the Presidium in respect of the implementation of the budget.

Article 33
Financial Regulations

1. The Financial Regulations shall be adopted by the Administrative Committee. They shall be amended by the Administrative Committee on a proposal from the Court.

2. The Financial Regulations shall lay down in particular:
(a) arrangements relating to the establishment and implementation of the budget and for the rendering and auditing of accounts;
(b) the method and procedure whereby the payments and contributions, including the initial financial contributions provided for in Article 37 of the Agreement are to be made available to the Court;
(c) the rules concerning the responsibilities of authorising and accounting officers and the arrangements for their supervision; and
(d) the generally accepted accounting principles on which the budget and the annual financial statements are to be based.

Article 34
Secrecy of deliberations

The deliberations of the Court shall be and shall remain secret.

Article 35
Decisions

1. When a panel sits in composition of an even number of judges, decisions of the Court shall be taken by a majority of the panel. In case of equal vote, the vote of the presiding judge shall prevail.

2. In the event of one of the judges of a panel being prevented from attending, a judge from another panel may be called upon to sit in accordance with the Rules of Procedure.

3. In cases where this Statute provides that the Court of Appeal shall take a decision sitting as a full court, such decision shall be valid only if it is taken by at least 3/4 of the judges comprising the full court.

4. Decisions of the Court shall contain the names of the judges deciding the case.

5. Decisions shall be signed by the judges deciding the case, by the Registrar for decisions of the Court of Appeal, and by the Deputy-Registrar for decisions of the Court of First Instance. They shall be read in open court.

Article 36
Dissenting opinions

A dissenting opinion expressed separately by a judge of a panel in accordance with Article 78 of the Agreement shall be reasoned, given in writing and shall be signed by the judge expressing this opinion.

Article 37
Decision by default

1. At the request of a party to an action, a decision by default may be given in accordance with the Rules of Procedure, where the other party, after having been served with a document instituting proceedings or with an equivalent document, fails to file written submissions in defence or fails to appear at the oral hearing. An objection may be lodged against that decision within one month of it being notified to the party against which the default decision has been given.

2. The objection shall not have the effect of staying enforcement of the decision by default unless the Court decides otherwise.

Article 38
Questions referred to the Court of Justice of the European Union

1. The procedures established by the Court of Justice of the European Union for referrals for preliminary rulings within the European Union shall apply.

2. Whenever the Court of First Instance or the Court of Appeal has decided to refer to the Court of Justice of the European Union a question of interpretation of the Treaty on European Union or of the Treaty on the Functioning of the European Union or a question on the validity or interpretation of acts of the institutions of the European Union, it shall stay its proceedings.

Annex 6 Decision of the Administrative Committee under Article 87 (2) UPCA amending the Agreement

DECISION OF THE ADMINISTRATIVE COMMITTEE OF 26 JUNE 2023 AMENDING THE AGREEMENT ON A UNIFIED PATENT COURT

THE ADMINISTRATIVE COMMITTEE

CONSIDERING that the Agreement on a Unified Patent Court has entered into force on 1 June 2023;

CONSIDERING that the Unified Patent Court is a common Court of Contracting States of the European Union for the settlements of disputes relating to European patents, supplementary protection certificates and European patents with unitary effect under regulation (EU) No 1257/2012 implementing enhanced cooperation in the area of the creation of unitary patent protection;

HAVING REGARD to Article 50 of the Treaty on the European Union and to the Agreement on the withdrawal of the United Kingdom of Great Britain and Northern Ireland (hereinafter, the United Kingdom) from the European Union, entered into force on 1 February 2020, as well as to the notification by the Government of the United Kingdom on the withdrawal from the Agreement on a Unified Patent Court on 20 July 2020;

HAVING REGARD to the Agreement on a Unified Patent Court and in particular Articles 1, 7 paragraph 2, 87 paragraphs 2 and 3 and Annex II thereof;

HAVING REGARD to the decision by the Presidium of the UPC dated 8 May 2023, on the provisional distribution of actions related to patents in IPC sections (A) and (C) pending before the Central Division.

HAS ADOPTED THE FOLLOWING DECISION:

Article 1

The Agreement on a Unified Patent Court is amended as follows:

1. Paragraph 2 of Article 7 is amended as follows:

> "2. The central division shall have its seat in Paris, with sections in London and Milan and Munich. The cases before the central division shall be distributed in accordance with Annex II, which shall form an integral part of this Agreement."

2. The following amendments (in bold) in the distribution of cases within the Central Division ([1]) are made in Annex II:

1 (The classification into 8 sections (A to H) is based on the International Patent Classification of the World Intellectual Property Organisation (http://www.wipo.int/classifications/ipc/en).

~~London~~ *Milan Section*	Paris Seat	Munich Section
	President's Office	
(A) **Human necessities,** ***without Supplementary protection certificates***	(B) Performing operations, transporting	***(C) Chemistry, metallurgy, without Supplementary protection certificates***
	(D) Textiles, paper	(F) Mechanical engineering, lighting, heating, weapons, blasting
	(E) Fixed constructions	
	(G) Physics	
	(H) Electricity	
	Supplementary protection certificates	

Article 2

In advance of the general review of the Agreement foreseen in Article 87 paragraph 1 of the Agreement on a Unified Patent Court, the Administrative Committee shall launch a specific review of the implementation of this decision three years after its adoption.

Article 3

Preparatory work will be launched, under the supervision of the Administrative Committee, to ensure that the Milan section will be fully and immediately operational when this decision takes effect, without prejudice to Article 87 paragraph 3 of the Agreement on a Unified Patent Court.

Article 4

This decision shall enter into force on the date of its adoption and will take effect twelve months after the date of its adoption, provided that no declaration is made according to Article 87 paragraph 3 of the Agreement on a Unified Patent Court.

Index